Forming American Politics

Forming American Politics

Ideals, Interests, and Institutions in Colonial New York and Pennsylvania

Alan Tully

The Johns Hopkins University Press
BALTIMORE AND LONDON

This book has been brought to publication with the generous
assistance of the National Endowment for the Humanities

03 02 01 00 99 98 97 96 95 94   5 4 3 2 1

The Johns Hopkins University Press
2715 North Charles Street
Baltimore, Maryland 21218-4319
The Johns Hopkins Press Ltd., London

ISBN 0-8018-4831-8

Endpapers: Map of the Province of Pennsylvania (William Scull,
1770); Chronological Map of the Province of New York
(Claude Southier, 1779). Courtesy of The Historical Society
of Pennsylvania.

Contents

vi / *Contents*

Maps

Preface

THE ORGANIZATION of comparative history is always problematic because of the need to reconcile chronology with analysis in depth and to maintain respect for the individual entities under examination while simultaneously finding meaningful points of comparison. In Part I of this book, I offer readings at two levels. The first and simplest is a descriptive narrative, with sparing analysis, of the main contours of provincial politics in New York and Pennsylvania. It is possible to read the first or second section of each of the first five chapters and come away with a reasonable sense of political events in New York and Pennsylvania from the late seventeenth century until the eve of the Revolution. At the same time, I have organized these chronological episodes around particular problems—the establishment of the English colonial regimes, the development of popular power, the concern for popular rights, the organization of popular politics, and the role of the electorate in popular politics—that are fundamental to an understanding of the roots of American political culture. Comparing New York and Pennsylvania on these grounds, which I do specifically in the concluding sections of each chapter, highlights the structural similarities in the political experience of each colony, yet at the same time indicates important differences in their development. Simultaneous readings on both these two levels provide a reasonably self-contained view of politics in eighteenth-century New York and Pennsylvania, as well as constituting the indispens-able background to Part II.

Part II comprises five chapters attempting to understand the various layers of colonial thought and behavior most expressive of early American political culture in New York and Pennsylvania. Chapters 6 and 7 make explicit what is increasingly obvious from the repeated juxtapositions of the two colonies in Part I—that residents of each colony had their own ways of ordering and comprehending their provincial politics. After making the point that we must fully acknowledge the distinctive features of the two provincial political cultures, Part II then brings the colonies back together again for close comparison in chapters 8, 9, and 10. Chapter 8 compares the ways in which New Yorkers and Pennsylvanians structured political life around their provincial institutions and examines some of the connections they established between politics and social behavior. Chapter 9 addresses the question of how we characterize the power relationships and the politi-cal systems that these power relationships spawned in the two colonies. And Chapter 10 closes out Part II with observations about the ways in which the cumulative political experiences of the two colonies prompted New Yorkers and Pennsylvanians to initiate new ways of thinking about the character of politics in the New World.

Finally, the Conclusion to both books has three objectives. First, to recapitulate my understanding of what political behavior in New York and Pennsylvania adds to our knowledge of the British-American political expe-rience. Second, to offer a few observations about the wider comparative dimensions of colonial politics. And third, to suggest some of the implica-tions this study has for the articulation of late eighteenth- and early nineteenth-century American political culture.

In trying to come to terms with the pre-Revolutionary political experi-ence of New York and Pennsylvania, and thereby appreciate something of the rich political heritage those colonies bequeathed, I have treated the ten chapters of this monograph as ten distinct vantage points from which to view the colonial tale. Despite their different concerns and different organ-izing principles, Part I and Part II comprise a series of complementary perspectives, constituting what might best be called "layered" history. The inevitable result of this approach has been some repetition, but I hope that rather than being bothersome, this will not only encourage familiarity with the political character of colonial New York and Pennsylvania, which are too frequently slighted, but also convey a greater sense of appreciation than might otherwise be achieved of the manner in which provincial particular-ism, tradition, and innovation came together to define the political culture of early America.

Acknowledgments

I HAVE INCURRED a great number of debts during the decade and a half in which this book has matured from a possibility to a project to a manuscript. Foremost is the support that the Social Sciences and Research Council of Canada has extended to me. I have benefited from several research grants from that agency, the most important of which included a released time grant during the late 1980s. Without the latter I doubt this book would yet be finished. The American Philosophical Society and the Philadelphia Center for Early American Studies also provided money for research that ultimately has informed this book. I owe some thanks, too, to the Small Grants Committee of the University of British Columbia for its occasional support.

I am, of course, deeply indebted to a large number of archives and libraries for giving me access to manuscripts and providing copies of relevant published work. These include the Pennsylvania Historical Society; the New York Historical Society; the New York Public Library; the New York State Library; New York State Archives; the Presbyterian Historical Society; the American Philosophical Society; the Museum of the City of New York; the Albany Institute of History and Art; Pennsylvania State Archives; the Library of Congress; Chester County Historical Society; Haverford College Library–Quaker Collection; Friends Historical Library, Swarthmore College; Beinecke and Sterling Memorial Libraries, Yale University; the New York Genealogical Society; Van Pelt Library, University of Pennsylvania; Columbia University Library; First Presbyterian Church, New York City; and the University of British Columbia Library. In particular, I would like to thank the staff members of the Interlibrary Loan Departments at Sterling Memorial Library and the University of British Columbia Library for their good humor and considerable efforts on my behalf.

Above all, I owe personal thanks to many. The historian who has encouraged me most in my pursuit of this enterprise has been Mike Zuckerman. His enthusiasm in response to some initial hypotheses I floated back in 1982 at a Philadelphia Center Conference on the founding of Pennsylvania prompted me to broaden the project. In April 1990, he provided me with the opportunity to run through my argument with his "Transformation Project" seminar, in Philadelphia. That evening's discussion was of particular importance in helping me rethink some issues at a crucial moment, and I wish to thank all the members of that group for their suggestions. Finally, Mike read the manuscript and provided me with an incredibly thorough running commentary. Although I have been able to answer only a few of his questions, the book is the better because of his intellectual acuity and extreme generosity.

Others have contributed in different ways. In the course of our long friendship, Eric Nellis has been a constant source of encouragement, imagination, and telling humor. Ian Steele gave me a sympathetic ear and some good ideas early in this project. Dave Flaherty gave me the opportunity to talk about it at the University of Western Ontario. Richard Beeman lent me support in his capacity as Director of the Philadelphia Center in the early 1980s. My colleague, Ed Hundert has read chapters of this book and has always been most generous with his critical abilities. Both Jocelyn Smith and Bob Stoddard have read the manuscript closely and have offered many helpful suggestions. Members of my graduate readings courses in Early American History during 1991–92 and 1992–93 have also tangled with various drafts of this book and have improved its qualities through their attention to argument and editorial detail. Sarina Pearson contributed to the book's content with her work as a research assistant. I have profited, too, from the encouragement, enthusiasm, and suggestions of Wayne Bodle, Mike Harris, Tina Loo, Elizabeth Manke, Bob McDonald, Louise Robert, Steve Rosswurm, Dick Ryerson, and Marianne Wokeck. John Murrin has been helpful in the course of several conversations. I wish to extend special gratitude to my present and former colleagues in European and British History. Their searching criticisms at department colloquia, at examinations, and in more casual conversation have taught me a great deal. Last, my continuing thanks to Jack Greene for his valuable advice and his sustained interest over the years.

Two of my colleagues have been of assistance in more practical ways. Peter Ward gave me important encouragement at a critical time in the genesis of this book, and Dick Unger facilitated an association with the History Department at Yale University. My thanks to Harry Miskimin of Yale for helping to make that association a rewarding one. Thanks, too, to those people who extended their friendship to Deborah and me while we were in New Haven in the late 1980s. Ed and Marie Morgan included us in their lives in warm and memorable ways; Barbara Oberg was generous with her precious time; Donka Farkas shared her delightful mind and practical resources; and Elizabeth and Carrie Griffith, and Peter Vicinanza were helpful in countless ways.

Others who have been supportive over the years are my family members. Andre Arpin has been kind with his computing skills and his time. Margaret Arpin has shouldered burdens on behalf of us both. Rosanne Edmondson has never flagged in her encouragement of my work. And Jean Lantz has always been deeply sympathetic. Knowing it is but poor recompense, I also thank Caitlin, Alexandra, Kate, and Joanne for time forgone.

The individual who has contributed most to this project is my long-time friend and companion, Deborah Bennett. She encouraged me to cast the book in broad terms despite knowing the commitment of years that was involved. She tolerated and indulged me, when for weeks at a time, my head was immersed in the eighteenth century. She lent me freely her superb critical skills, her literary talents, and her inventive technical mind. Most important, she remained her affectionate and forgiving self through both the high and the low points of this book's writing. The results, insofar as they are worthwhile, are as much hers as mine.

I want to extend a final word of appreciation to those who have played a direct part in the appearance of this book. Thanks to Bob Brugger, History Editor at the Johns Hopkins University Press for his interest and assistance from the time he first asked, "What have you been doing lately?" Also to Peter Dreyer for his sensitive editorial touch. Finally, most historians know how important archivists are to our craft. Without them we simply could not do the work we value. A special thanks to two former manuscript curators, Linda Stanley and Margaret Heilbrun, whose professionalism, generosity, and warmth not only made this book possible but also made the research for it enjoyable times.

Forming American Politics

Introduction

I Heard that you ask'd for something to prove this puzzle
the New World,
And to define America, her athletic Democracy . . .

WALT WHITMAN wrote these lines in introducing his exultant *Leaves of Grass.*[1] Like Whitman, if less lyrical, many Americans in both earlier and later times have been outspoken in celebrating the character of their country's political culture.[2] In America, more than in many other societies, the search for an encompassing public self-definition has centered on concepts, such as "republicanism," "liberalism," and "democracy," that are fundamental components of political thought. Of course, many Americans have remained outside such discourse—alienated from it, critical of it, marginalized by circumstances like gender, ethnicity, and religion, excluded by race or socioeconomic environment, or perhaps, personally attuned to other nonpolitical expressions of public identity. Indeed, one of the enduring conundrums of American society has been that indifference to and active estrangement from various political processes exist *simultaneously* with a vigorously articulated popular political culture. Periodic noninvolvement or resigned acceptance notwithstanding, politicized Americans have shaped compelling versions of an inclusive public ethos through the cultivation of civic consciousness, the creation of political practices, and the construction of political discourses.

The long-standing question of how this vital American political culture evolved has repeatedly led historians back to the eighteenth-century roots of

American society, and in particular to the last quarter of the century, when the Revolutionary experience, the establishment of new constitutions, and the first decades of American political autonomy had considerable impact on the developing political culture. In so doing, they have inevitably neglected to give the colonial years of the mainland colonies of British North America their proper due.

Recent writing is a case in point. During the past quarter century, the most influential work on early American political culture has emphasized the "republican" temper of the late eighteenth century.[3] The Revolutionary generation, so the argument runs, distinguished itself by its ardent embrace of "classical republicanism," a political ideology that looked to the past, cherished communalism, emphasized leadership by the few who were capable of subordinating self-interest to the public good, focused on the necessity and means of keeping power in check, and stressed adherence to the standards of public or civic virtue—a commitment that alone could keep the excesses of commerce and the deleterious forces of corruption at bay.[4] The advocates of a republican interpretation have not, of course, had it all their own way. The most direct questioning of their work has come from "liberal" critics. These are commentators who have argued that the emergence of early American political society was intimately connected with such precepts as individualism, rationalism, natural law, contractualism, and the pursuit of private interest—notions that cumulatively give a very different turn to public thought than follows from republican assumptions.[5] While liberal writers have raised important questions about the limits of republicanism, they have nevertheless reinforced the republican historians' focus on the late eighteenth and early nineteenth centuries.[6] The political culture of early America and the origins and character of American democracy, it has come to seem, are best understood through scholarly attentiveness to the Revolutionary and Early National eras.

One major consequence of this emphasis has been to continue to obscure the colonial past with the long, late-afternoon shadows of Revolutionary ideologies. The significance of the colonial political experience has frequently been reduced to one or two mimetic strands, emanating from early modern England, that seem to anticipate late eighteenth-century concerns.[7] There have been few recent efforts to search for greater complexity in the colonial past,[8] a minimal willingness to grant the courtesy of integrity to a century or so of colonial political experience,[9] and little interest in strengthening our appreciation of the breadth of colonial political experience in ways that might, in turn, enhance our understanding of late eighteenth- and early nineteenth-century American politics.[10]

That we might profit from undertaking such study is clear from the findings of a recent generation of social historians of the seventeenth and eighteenth centuries. During the past two decades, these writers have clearly demonstrated that the thirteen colonies comprised a wide variety of resilient regional societies, which had ample opportunity to develop their own provincial ways during a century and a half of loose British oversight.[11] Conditioned by locale, the character of immigration, differing and changing demographic profiles, economic opportunities and constraints, the elaboration of structured and more-or-less stratified societies, racial, ethnic, and religious group membership, the development of peculiar provincial habits and social practices, and other such factors, the mainland colonies displayed an extensive range of cultural variation. The challenge these findings offer to observers interested in political concerns is an obvious one—in what ways were the integrity and diversity of these societies reflected in the articulation of American political culture?

I have made three important assumptions in attempting to meet this challenge. The first is that the complex character of the richly differentiated colonies calls for a specific, rather than general, focus in the investigation of large questions. One of the circumstances that the diversity of the colonies has frequently encouraged in purportedly all-encompassing studies is a kind of historical high-grading that eschews the rigor of consistent contextualization. Only within a specific colonial society is it possible simultaneously (1) to examine such issues as power, rights, and political organization and mobilization; (2) to explore the subtleties of political ideologies, the relationship between provincial and local institutions, the nature of extra-institutional politics, the impingement of social and legal forces on politics, and the interaction of factors like deference, equality, consensus, hierarchy, anglicization, and authority; and (3) to develop an overall sense of the character of the political culture that was gradually forming. Second, I believe one colony alone is not enough. Preoccupation with one society can too easily lead to a loss of perspective. A comparative study of provincial political cultures—one *both* specific enough *and* structured enough to force juxtapositions and spark insights that might otherwise not easily come to mind—seems preferable. Finally, given the lavish attention colonial historians have already paid Massachusetts and Virginia, and the overwhelming emphasis frequently placed on these societies in general accounts of early American history, it seems worthwhile to broaden our perspective by making use of the vantage points other major colonies offer.

When eighteenth-century Europeans looked to North America to take the measure of the new society unfolding there, their eyes frequently came to rest, not on Massachusetts or Virginia, but on the newer colonies of New York and Pennsylvania. After traveling through parts of New France, sections of the Ohio country, and a few communities in Pennsylvania, Michel

St. John de Crèvecoeur (1735–1813) settled in New York; his well-known rhetorical question, "What then is the American, this new man?" articulated a perspective developed in the cultural milieu of the Hudson Valley.[12] Like Crèvecoeur, Voltaire found little of interest in either the ice and snow of New France or the early English coastal colonies in New England and the South. Rather, he turned his attention to Pennsylvania, which he perceived to be the most important experiment in colonization taking place in the New World. To the French philosophes, William Penn's Quaker colony was what was new about the New World, the one facet of European expansion into the Americas that might rescue colonization from being no more than a foolish distraction. Led by Voltaire, the philosophes "made Pennsylvania the best known, most studied, and certainly the most appreciated of all the North American colonies."[13]

European intellectuals were not the only ones to turn their attention to the four colonies surrounding the Hudson and Delaware waterways. Contemporaries frequently distinguished these settlements from those of New England and the South by referring to them as the "middle colonies" or "Middle Provinces."[14] In hindsight, such commentators might better have called them the "lower north" or "north-central" British-American colonies, but the point is that they recognized a family of colonies clustered along the mid-Atlantic coast (see map 1). Some contemporary observers included Maryland among the "Midland Provinces," some historians have argued that because of cultural similarities much of the southern backcountry was really "greater Pennsylvania," and both contemporaries and later chroniclers have recognized that New Englanders successfully invaded both New York and New Jersey with their well-organized town governments.[15] Despite this shading from one area into another, however, the broad boundaries of the region are pretty clear. New Yorkers recognized that their society was very different from those of the Yankee easterners.[16] And Pennsylvanians drew a sharp distinction between themselves and their "hominy" neighbors in the Chesapeake colonies.[17]

Although New York, New Jersey, Pennsylvania, and the three Lower Counties (Delaware) were separate societies, they shared a political comity that was unique among the mainland British provinces. A number of the politically prominent found it easy to move from an appointed or elected office in one colony to a new place of influence in a neighboring province.[18] Such political interchanges most commonly took place along New York/ East Jersey and Delaware/Pennsylvania/West Jersey lines, but there was sufficient overlap to create a mutual political awareness between New York City and Philadelphia. Historic circumstances linked middle colony governments together,[19] common legal and business interests and market ties spanned political boundaries, and in time familial and community connec-

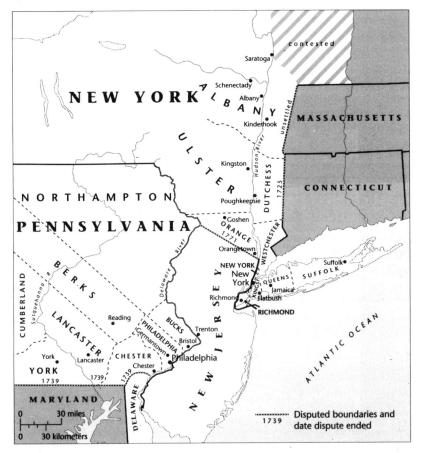

MAP 1. The Middle Colonies. Drawn by Eric Leinberger based on maps in *Atlas of Early American History: The Revolutionary Era, 1760–1790*, Lester J. Cappon, ed. (Princeton, 1976).

tions expanded over two or three colonies as easily as they spread from one county to another.

The north-central or middle colonies were an important aggregation, not only because of the interest their social experimentation generated, the crucial geographical linkage they provided between the northeastern and southern colonies, and the interlocking character of their political relationships, but also because of their demographic and economic dynamism and their exceptional diversity. Although New York, New Jersey, Pennsylvania, and the Lower Counties accounted for only 16.6 percent of the estimated white and black population of the thirteen colonies in 1690, by 1730 that proportion had grown to 23.3 percent, and by 1770 to 25.9 percent (see map 2). Whereas in 1690 the enumerated populations of New York and Pennsylvania were in the former case slightly more and in the latter slightly less than one quarter the population of the Bay Colony, by 1770 New York was 69 percent as populous as Massachusetts, and Pennsylvania had surpassed it.[20] Economically, middle colony communities prospered as they grew. Farmers exploited the rich agricultural land, tradesmen multiplied in response to opportunity and demand, and laborers, entrepreneurs, shopkeepers, merchants, and professionals proliferated in the increasingly complex societies. Fueled by the export market in lumber and foodstuffs, standards of living in the middle colonies grew at a rapid pace, lending credibility to claims of competence and prosperity.[21]

A considerable part of the population increase that caused the north-central colonies to grow so quickly stemmed from immigration, and much of that immigration came from the non-English regions of the British Isles and from German-speaking areas in Europe. As a Dutch possession before the English conquest, New York had attracted such a multifarious collection of colonists that one observer reported "men of eighteen different languages . . . scattered here and there."[22] In the process of consolidating themselves as the province's largest population group and forming distinctive "Batavianized" communities in such areas as New York City, Albany, Schenectady, Kingston, and Kings County, the New Netherlanders absorbed, overwhelmed, or marginalized many of these European fragments.[23] But when eighteenth-century Scotch Irish, German, and New England immigrants were added, along with black slaves and the offspring of the earlier English, New England, and French settlers, and then intermingled in varying degrees with native Americans, the result was a motley social fabric indeed.[24] Pennsylvania did not initially project quite the same sense of social segmentation, notwithstanding substantial blocs of Welsh, Irish, and English, and a sprinkling of Scandinavians, Dutch, French, blacks, and Indians, but by the mid eighteenth century, great inpourings of Scotch Irish and German settlers had transformed it into a society of minorities.[25]

With the ethnic diversity that distinguished these waves of British and European immigration came the religious complexity that so often gained the attention of observers. In the late seventeenth century, New York Governor Thomas Dongan was appalled by what he saw: in addition to representatives of the "Church of England" were "Dutch Calvinist[s] . . . French Calvinist[s] . . . Dutch Lutheran[s] . . . [a] few Roman Catholicks . . . [an] abundance of Quakers preachers men and Women especially; Singing Quakers; Ranting Quakers; Sabbatarians; Antisabbatarians; Some Anabaptists some Independents; some Jews, in short all sorts of opinions there

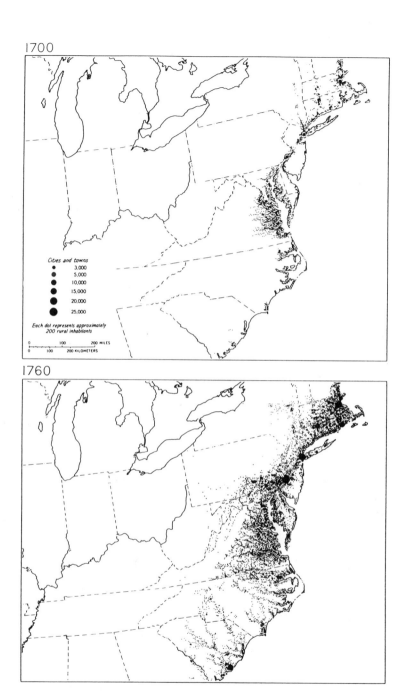

MAP 2. Growth and Dispersal of Enumerated Population in the Mainland British Colonies, 1700–1760. Reproduced, with permission of the American Geographical Society, from Herman R. Friis, "A Series of Population Maps of the Colonies and the United States," *Geographical Review* 30 (1940): 464–465.

are some and most part none at all."[26] Once the mainline churches became stronger in New York, the scene there was not unlike the one the Maryland physician Dr. Alexander Hamilton observed in Philadelphia in 1744: "I dined at a tavern with a very mixed company. . . . There were Scots, English, Dutch, Germans, and Irish; there were Roman Catholics, Churchmen, Presbyterians, Quakers, Newlightmen, Methodists, Seventhdaymen, Moravians, Anabaptists, and one Jew. The whole company consisted of twenty-five, planted round an oblong table, in a great hall well stocked with flies."[27]

While the characteristics that the family of north-central colonies shared are sufficient to invite comparison among them, it is important to recognize at the outset that large differences set New York apart from Pennsylvania. For that reason, scholars have always debated whether or not the middle colonies' varied natural and social geography, their separate and contrasting institutional and political histories, and their complex of cultural idiosyncrasies precluded their forming a distinctive and coherent region.[28] But the fault lines among the four colonies fortuitously facilitate comparison. There were two metropolises, New York City and Philadelphia, with two major hinterlands surrounding the Hudson and Delaware rivers. New Jersey was divided, socially, economically, and to some degree politically, into New York-oriented East Jersey and Pennsylvania-influenced West Jersey, and the Lower Counties were largely an adjunct to Pennsylvania. Massachusetts and Connecticut influenced the eastern Hudson Valley and eastern Long Island, and Maryland occasionally contested Pennsylvania's suzerainty over the Lower Counties. But conflict over cultural and political boundaries merely confirmed the powerful presence of New York and Pennsylvania, not only among the four middle colonies but also in their relationships with their long-established New England and Chesapeake neighbors. There were two major focal points of regional political culture on the mid-Atlantic coast, and either could match any of their New England or southern counterparts in prominence. In juxtaposition, then, New York and Pennsylvania have the potential to tell us a good deal about the ways in which the middle colonies shaped the early American political experience.

Part I

The Contours of Provincial Politics

Chapter One

Seventeenth-Century Beginnings

WHEN THE ENGLISH took New York by conquest and allowed Pennsylvania to be settled under Quaker auspices, it was not at all clear how these experiments in colonization would fare. Comparable North American ventures had all faced years of uncertainty, as colonists learned to survive in their new environment, to deal with the demands of various English courtiers, proprietors, and investors, to ride out dissent among themselves, and to establish a workable political order. Early colonial years were frequently filled with conflict and distinguished by rapid change; although the established character of a few New York communities and Pennsylvania's quick growth reduced economic pressures in both societies, there is no reason to expect either New Yorkers or Pennsylvanians to have avoided the instabilities that other first settlers experienced.

The unsettled nature of early New York and Pennsylvania affairs began with their respective forms of governance. First as proprietor and then as monarch, James Stuart exercised considerable power in New York. As for Pennsylvania, although the charter privileges of the proprietor, William Penn, were certainly not monarchical, he, too, enjoyed great latitude within which to exercise his rights. And both king and Quaker recognized the importance of using their power to create strong political institutions, which they in turn expected would encourage the rapid development of an ordered polity. But James paid only limited attention to New York, and when he did, his colonial policies oscillated between extreme intransigence and grudging conciliation. In Pennsylvania, William Penn vacillated wildly between close personal supervision of colonial issues and a remoteness born of his periodic preoccupation with English affairs. The inconsistent guidance of monarchical and proprietary hands bred confusion in both colonies.

If James Stuart's and William Penn's actions appeared contradictory or disruptive, their changing policies resulted less from personal predilection, or from the convolutions that tangled their British affairs, than from their reactions and need to respond to the varied and dearly held concerns of their colonists. In New York, for example, the Dutch expected the promise of substantial liberties, which they had extracted from the English on surrender in 1664, to be honored. But they were by no means unanimous in their perception of what those promises implied in the way of governance. Of course, many Britons in New York expected to enjoy traditional English rights, notwithstanding the Stuart family's reputation for tyrannous rule. In addition, New York was riven by deep social discord. Conflicts fed by sectional, class, ethnic, and religious divisions were so much a part of Leisler's Rebellion (the New York counterpart of the Glorious Revolution ending James II's kingship) that factional hostility, in the form of cutthroat rivalry between Leislerians and anti-Leislerians, lived on into the eighteenth century. In Pennsylvania, circumstances were different, but they led in the same direction as those in New York. Quakers arrived in the New World with a strong group identity, an anti-authoritarian attitude, and a strong commitment to autonomy. Although such characteristics could, and in a variety of situations did, produce cohesiveness, they also occasioned conflict. Quakers quarreled with William Penn and ignored him when they could; they were in a constant state of political disagreement with the earlier non-Quaker settlers from the three Lower Counties; they were so wracked with internal strife at one point that several groups of colonists broke away from the Society of Friends; thereafter, the Quakers continued to fight with the Anglicans and Baptists that the schism had produced. And both within and without Quaker society, there were constellations of ethnic and regional groups whose particular concerns complicated public affairs even further.

As if proprietorial inconsistency and colonial complexity were not unsettling enough, imperial developments further disrupted New York and Pennsylvania affairs. The late seventeenth century was one of the most unsettled periods of English colonialism prior to the American Revolution. The Stuart bid to consolidate monarchical power, the Glorious Revolution, and the establishment of a Protestant line of succession to the English throne all affected the North American provinces. New and intensified colonial rivalries emerged out of the circumstances accompanying these changes. Frequently, those conflicts were exacerbated both by James Stuart's and William Penn's direct involvement in the main events of English politics and by the willingness of colonists to establish overseas connections with other important participants. Given the interplay of forces in England and in the two colonies, it is hardly surprising that confusion and conflict typified public affairs in New York and Pennsylvania during much of the late seventeenth century.

Conquest and Conflict on the Hudson

On Monday, August 29, 1664, Dutch soldiers marched out of Fort Amsterdam on Manhattan Island, with "drums beating . . . colours flying, and matches . . . [lit]" to mask their humiliation.[1] As English troops strutted in to replace them, the old fort became Fort James and New Amsterdam became "New Yorke."[2] Given the mere 450 soldiers involved in the ritual, the exchange had the appearance of an inconsequential military pageant. That was deceptive. Before organizing his little foray against New Amsterdam, James, duke of York, had secured from his brother Charles II a hastily drafted charter granting him a huge portion of eastern North America. In addition to eastern Maine, Martha's Vineyard, Nantucket, Long Island, and the Hudson Valley, the new English colony was to extend "from the West side of Connecticut to the East side [of] Delaware Bay."[3] This grant included almost the entire coastline of what were subsequently called the middle colonies.

While it is true that in the face of favorable odds, Lord High Admiral James Stuart was one who preferred to fight rather than quietly patrol the seas, there were other, larger reasons for his attack on New Amsterdam. In the mid 1660s, England's chief commercial rival was Holland, and the New Netherlanders' seductive reach for the Chesapeake tobacco trade and the New England import business was notorious. For English colonists both to the south and to the northeast of the Hudson River, commercial intercourse with the Dutch had been profitable. Given the opportunity, they would choose to continue it, for the restrictive English trade laws, excises, and customs duties of the restored monarchy promised to be onerous. But in the Stuarts' view, not until the Dutch were cleared from the strategic mid-Atlantic coast would England's North American empire begin to pay off as it should.[4]

In addition to the long-term strategic and dynastic advantages to the Crown of reducing New Amsterdam, there were short-term pecuniary ones that appealed directly to James. With a population of some 8,000 to 10,000 whites clustering in Manhattan, Long Island, and the Hudson Valley, New

York appeared to have an economy, built on furs, farms, and fish, that might generate both income and patronage for the strapped English heir apparent.[5] Yet the immense territory granted to satisfy such greed threatened to be its own undoing. Together with the duke of York's European enemies, the Algonquian and Iroquoian Indian nations (who were the major inhabitants of the mid-Atlantic region and who in peacetime sustained the fur trade) posed a hydra-headed threat to New York's security. And there was much to defend.

Far to the south and west, Dutch, Finns, and Swedes were scattered along the west side of the Delaware River and felt constantly jeopardized by both European powers and neighboring Marylanders.[6] Closer to the Hudson lay communities of a somewhat more settled character. On the mainland north of Manhattan Island, and scattered throughout all but the western end of Long Island, several towns were anchored by the land claims of prickly migrants from New England. Their Dutch counterparts, who, once conquered, were less vocal in provincial affairs, were gathered at the western end of Long Island. Smaller Dutch hamlets lay to the southwest of the Hudson River, while the farming villages of New Haarlem and Wiltwyk followed the river valley north. Most substantial in numbers and economy were the towns of Albany and New York. But both were exposed to attack—New York from the sea, and Albany from the surrounding wilds. Moreover, both were of uncertain character. Albany was a bizarre mixture of Dutch traditionalism and fur-trade frontierism surrounded by white hangers-on and native Americans;[7] to outsiders, upriver residents appeared "wild and untamed, reckless, unrestrained [and] haughty."[8] As for New York City, the complimentary modern term is "cosmopolitan." Some contemporaries, however, thought "Babel" best described the confusion produced by eighteen different languages and the variety of social relations among individuals from Europe, the British Isles, Africa, and North America.[9]

The duke of York could do nothing immediately to strengthen his province's numbers and social cohesion. His only hope of control lay in reducing his commitment there. Within months of his victory, James gave New Jersey to a pair of titled English cronies and accepted a New York–Connecticut boundary agreement that overrode his charter-based claim to western Connecticut. There were still problems in the far reaches of the colony: Massachusetts challenged New York's northern boundaries and Maryland the southern. But the former was never a burning issue, and James handed away the problems that defense and conflicting land claims posed in the latter case when he agreed to Charles II's grant of Pennsylvania and the Lower Counties (Delaware) to his friend William Penn.[10]

For twenty-one years, from 1664 until 1685 (with one brief hiatus in 1673–1674 when the Dutch recaptured their old colony), James was sole proprietor of the central areas of New York. He could thus shape New York's central political institutions much as he pleased. His first priority was the establishment of a provincial political structure responsive to himself; that he accomplished by placing supreme governing authority in a governor-in-council. The governor was the duke's man, and the council consisted of a handful of provincial placemen. Executive, legislative, and high judicial authority was located in this one governing institution. A central nervous system of appointed justices and sheriffs carried the governor's orders and proclamations from an annual court of assize to the outlying counties in the body politic.[11] While this highly autocratic form of government may be viewed as an anglicized version of its oligarchic Dutch predecessor, its character owed more to the duke's opinions than to any concern for continuity. Influenced by his cousin Louis XIV's absolutism, James was determined to do without the nettlesome assemblies that periodically nipped at the hamstrings of every colonial governor. Even on a leash they could not be trusted. "I cannot but suspect they would be of dangerous consequence," wrote the duke, "nothing being more knowne then the aptness of such bodyes to assume to themselves many priviledges wch prove destructive to, or very oft disturbe, the peace of ye governmt wherein they are allowed."[12] The lapdoglike council was enough of a concession to local opinion.

For the governors in New York who personally had to deny representative institutions to interested provincials, a serviceable rationale lay at hand. In James Stuart's mind, New York was a colony of conquest; to the victor went the right to establish political ground rules.[13] New Englanders, who had originally settled on Long Island under Connecticut jurisdiction or under town charters that the Dutch had granted, responded angrily to such a dismissal of their rights. In their minds, their lineage tied them to an English colony of settlement, and because of that they believed they had carried all English rights with them to New York. As for the colony's New Netherlanders, they had the cumulative knowledge of a great variety of European traditions of representative and autonomous government, the best-known of which was that of the United Provinces. Although they had been conquered by the English, New Netherlanders had reason to believe that the articles of capitulation to which their leaders had agreed confirmed the principles of representation as well as provided for the continuation of various legal, religious, and cultural traditions established in their colony.[14] As a concession, particularly to the English settlers, the duke of York's first governor, Richard Nicolls, drew up the so-called Duke's Laws, a code designed to draw English, Dutch, and New England precedents together. But the code failed to sanction any of the popular political forums associated with representative government.[15]

The saving grace of the new regime was that it was not as rigid as this law code suggests. The town meetings of Long Island communities continued to take place as often as they had in earlier years. And "all freeholders, not scandalous in their lives & conversations, [were] capable to vote att the election of officers, military and civil, in their severall townshipps."[16] A centralized, unrepresentative provincial government simply did not have the power to control political behavior on the local level. The results of the duke's efforts, then, were the reverse of his intentions. Rather than choking off dissent at the local level, his policies encouraged townsmen, whether English or Dutch, to guard their interests by protecting their local institutions. From these tenaciously defended fortresses, they could mount forays against provincial power when crucial issues arose.

One of those issues was taxation. Provincial taxes were levied by the governor-in-council, and they were large. The cost of maintaining civil officials who felt they were entitled to personal enrichment, and a defense establishment that included garrisons and forts at both New York City and Albany, was a heavy burden.[17] By 1680, the weight of these taxes, coupled with the long-standing English colonial grievance of no elected assembly, prompted New Yorkers to challenge the authority of the governor-in-council with a tax revolt. Momentarily weakened in England by a movement to exclude him from succession to the throne, and influenced by legal opinions that questioned his assumed proprietary powers, James reluctantly agreed to grant the long-sought-for assembly.[18]

On meeting, the first New York Assembly passed the well-known Charter of Liberties, which contemporaries thought traded off some traditional local rights for others of a more general nature, and established a model of government similar to that of other royal colonies of the day.[19] By the time the charter was readied for final approval in the fall of 1684, however, circumstances had changed. Charles II was heeding the advice of those who advocated revocation of colonial charters and the combining of existing colonies into consolidated administrative units. Once James succeeded to the throne in February 1685, he endorsed this new policy. The new monarch reneged on his promise of an assembly and the Charter of Liberties. Three years later he included New York in the Dominion of New England, a bloated royal province run by a governor-in-council seated in Boston, with lieutenants overseeing affairs in New York, New Jersey, and the other New England colonies.[20] Like James's kingship, however, the Dominion of New England was not to last long. Its Boston leaders would be swept away in early 1689 by the Massachusetts counterpart of the English Glorious Revolution, and shortly thereafter, the Dominion's New York regime was overthrown in Leisler's Rebellion, the salient event shaping political relationships in New York during the late seventeenth and early eighteenth centuries.

Jacob Leisler, a rich, well-educated and well-connected New York merchant, pushed himself into prominence in June 1689 by leading a company of militia in taking control of Fort James, accepting military command of the fort (and thus, of the colony), and proclaiming the province's allegiance to William and Mary when the New York officers of the Dominion of New England repeatedly refused to take that step.[21] Subsequently, when William and Mary dispatched a commission from England placing temporary authority in the hands of James II's old appointees, or alternatively in the hands of those who "for the time being take care for Preserving the Peace and administring the Lawes" of New York, Leisler accepted the charge.[22] He called an assembly, commissioned officers of government, raised taxes, and tried to organize a multicolonial military campaign against *les Canadiens* after their sack of Schenectady in February 1690.[23] Yet the regime met with defiance in Albany, considerable, if uneven, opposition on Long Island, and sporadic resistance in New York City.[24] Most important, many prominent citizens, who out of concern for their own hides had balked at proclaiming William and Mary until they were certain the Orangists were in firm control of England (and hence were blackened as traitors by the Leislerian gang) vilified Leisler and resisted his administration at every opportunity. As compliance fell off, and as William and Mary seemed increasingly inclined to back the old administration, Leisler and his supporters tried to consolidate their strength with incarcerations, court proceedings, interference in local government, mobbings, and demonstrations of military force aimed at their opponents.[25]

By January 1690, five months after Leisler had taken charge of New York as commander-in-chief, the Crown had commissioned an administration headed by Governor Henry Sloughter. But Sloughter's representative, Captain Richard Ingoldsby, did not arrive in New York until one year later. When he did, Leisler refused to surrender to Ingoldsby and his accompanying British troops until he had seen the new commission. Ingoldsby, in turn, refused to show it—for the good reason that he did not have it. The commission was with Governor Sloughter, who had set out with Ingoldsby, but whose ship had been delayed in Bermuda. A seven-week standoff ensued between Leisler and Ingoldsby. Under the tension violence flared: in mid March the two sides exchanged gunfire, and several participants and onlookers were wounded or killed. When Governor Sloughter finally arrived two days later, he demanded Leisler's submission and then quickly gave full rein to his anti-Leislerian advisors. Within a week they had convened a special court of oyer and terminer, which between March 31 and April 17 tried the leading Leislerians for treason. Of those brought to trial, eight were condemned. Determined to give full vent to their vindictiveness, and fearful that delay would bring renewed revolt in New York or reprieve from

England, Governor Sloughter's councillors pressed for immediate execution. Unwilling to dispatch all eight, Sloughter struck a compromise, which the anti-Leislerians were quick to accept. On May 16, 1691, Jacob Leisler and his son-in-law Jacob Milborne were hanged and their heads separated from their bodies.[26]

The chief characteristics of the Leislerian interregnum were the almost anarchic conditions that appeared in the colony and the bitterness that divided the two parties. The first of these is, perhaps, the easiest to explain. The officers who represented the Dominion of New England in early 1689 in New York, and who were to become the anti-Leislerians, were discredited by the regime's quick disintegration in Massachusetts. Once the Dominion's central authority collapsed, New York's dependent provincial administration had little legitimacy. On the other hand, Jacob Leisler's de facto government was clearly a revolutionary one without claim to represent any English government until, and if, William and Mary chose to acknowledge it. In the absence of clear provincial authority, the tendency among outlying New York communities was to assert their autonomy. European settlers in New York had been accustomed to a highly differentiated world of independent, or loosely confederated, cities, principalities, states, and regions, and New York's towns gave expression to that impulse. As for the colonists of English ancestry who came to New York from Connecticut, they also brought their own well-developed standards of town autonomy and continuing loyalty to the kind of decentralized government that, through their own experience, they associated with the New England way.

The propensity to assert regional and local autonomy that these traditions involved was strengthened among New York's outlying towns by the animosities that the Stuart monarchs' penchant for monopolies had created, and by geographic circumstances peculiar to New York. Rivalry between Albany and New York City frequently revolved around James's authorization of a fur-trading monopoly for Albany and a monopoly on overseas trade for New York City. It was an unstable mix, because the two functions were interrelated, yet each town had strong historic and cultural claims to autonomy.[27] Other Hudson Valley residents had their own grievances, some against Albany for its fur-trading privileges, but most against New York City.[28] From 1680, the city enjoyed a bolting monopoly on all flour destined for export, and in 1688, Dominion of New England officials tried to enhance New York's flour-milling capacity by prohibiting the export of unbolted grain. Upriver millers and farmers felt their economic interests were being sacrificed to city greed. Of all the New York communities that were anxious to stay clear of central authority, those on eastern Long Island were the most extreme. And they believed they had reason to be so. The boundary commission that had settled the New York / Connecticut border in 1664 had stripped Suffolk County towns away from Connecticut and placed them under New York jurisdiction. Because of geographic and cultural ties, English Long Islanders looked across the Sound to Connecticut and around the Cape to Boston as destinations for the grain and whale oil they produced for market. But New York City was made the province's only port in 1670. That meant that exports from Southampton destined for Boston had to be cleared through New York City. European goods were likewise required to enter the province through the city. This law turned Long Islanders into smugglers and political opportunists ready to exploit any occasion on which they might resist the colony's central authorities.[29]

The impact of these animosities was obvious once the legitimacy of the central authority was called into question in 1689. The strategically important town of Albany refused cooperation with Leisler until after the Schenectady tragedy, and Hudson Valley and eastern Long Island settlements had as little to do with the regime as they possibly could. In New York City itself, in the areas immediately surrounding it, and in Albany, conflict between Leislerians and anti-Leislerians was either too immediate or the issues too important to be ignored. In all of those areas, intense polarization took place between the contending parties, producing the kind of vindictiveness that cost Leisler and Milborne their lives.

The primary reason why the Leislerian revolt was such a traumatic experience for New Yorkers was its analogous relationship to the religion-infused political disputes that, as a continuation of post-Reformation hostilities, tore at late seventeenth-century western Europe and England. The major conflict that New Yorkers perceived in the United Provinces, France, and England was the resurgence of Catholicism under the absolutist policies of Louis XIV and his English cousins Charles and James Stuart. Louis XIV's tacit approval of the persecution of French Huguenots gave way to outright encouragement with the revocation of the Edict of Nantes in 1685. And that same year, James II's succession to the English throne established a ruler openly committed to the re-Catholicizing of his realm. Protestants in England and the United Provinces, who leaned toward Erastianism or episcopacy, or who might benefit from policies of religious toleration primarily intended to benefit Catholics, were frequently willing to work for some accommodation with Catholic rulers. Other Protestants, consisting largely of those Calvinists who emphasized the need for a continuing reformation away from Catholic, and Catholic-influenced church practices, excoriated and resisted the new developments.[30]

In New York, the confrontation was particularly acute. James II's Dominion of New England was an obvious expression of absolutism, while his preferment of various Catholics under both his old proprietary administration and the new royal regime seemed to presage a popish future. The willing collusion of irreligious opportunists, Erastian-minded church members, and sectarians favoring broad toleration of the New York Catholics, along with both the proximity and apparent aggressiveness of Catholic New France, exaggerated the danger. Alarmed by these circumstances, opposition groups composed of strict Calvinists, Reform-influenced Protestants, refugee Huguenots, and any other denominationally indifferent, nominal Protestants who were vigorously anti-Catholic began to appear in various sections of the colony. They castigated those Protestants who openly supported the existing regime as "Popish Trumpets";[31] when James II's New York placemen refused to renounce their allegiance to the Stuart monarch and proclaim William and Mary, who were reputedly strict Calvinists, in the spring of 1689, the insurgents believed that Dominion officials were planning to establish a Catholic tyranny in the colony. As Jacob Leisler testified from the gallows, his purpose in taking control of government in New York was "to maintaine against popery or any Schism or heresy whatever the interest of our Sovereign Lord & Lady that now is & the reformed protestant Churches in these parts." Jacob Milborne eloquently agreed. "It is for the king and queen I die, and the Protestant religion to which I was born and bred."[32]

Although the conflict between Leislerians and anti-Leislerians was primarily a religious one, there were other complicating factors. One of these was an ill-defined, but noticeable class component in some facets of the division. This was not a particularly important dimension of the rivalry between the political *leaders* of each faction.[33] The principal Leislerians were of sufficient wealth and standing, either locally or in the larger transatlantic reformed Protestant network, to vie with their anti-Leislerian opponents, who may have been better known within provincial New York society. What class element there was reflected the fact that strict Calvinism tended to be strongest among the poor-to-moderately-well-off farmers and city residents who made up the bulk of the Dutch Reformed congregations. On the other hand, Erastian notions tended to be widespread among the well-to-do, and particularly among a small number of well-connected and affluent Reformed clergymen.[34] What complicated the character of this division even further was that it also had a cultural dimension. Erastian views were most prevalent in the liberal commercial cities of the United Provinces, and the influence of these centers among New York's merchants and leading clergymen continued to be strong even after the conquest. Yet much of New York's Dutch population had a closer affinity to another European tradition. This was the strict Calvinist and conservative culture that flourished in the outlying villages and small towns of the Low Countries, which frequently defined itself in opposition to the cosmopolitan cities.[35] Finally, there was the issue of the relationship between English and

Dutch. Some of the most successful New York merchants and entrepreneurs, along with the major Dutch Reformed clergy, had led the way in collaborating with the English, particularly since the Dutch reconquest of New York and its subsequent return to England in 1673–1674. There is evidence that some lower-class and middling Dutch resented such leadership because, as a symbol of anglicization, it represented a betrayal of the colony's New Netherlands identity.[36] But again, this issue did not stand on its own. The high-profile Dutch leaders may have been cultural quislings, but they also frequently leaned toward Erastianism, threatened to betray strict Calvinism with their liberal cosmopolitan views, and, above all, appeared to accept the growing strength of Catholicism in New York. The point is that class divisions, cultural antagonisms, and ethnic quarrels tended, in large, to reinforce religious conflict and thus, both deepened and broadened the gulf that separated antagonists during Leisler's Rebellion.

For the better part of two decades following New York's provincial version of the Glorious Revolution, the divisions between so-called Leislerians and anti-Leislerians dominated public life. Yet over this period the dynamics of factional conflict continually evolved in complex ways. The most important change was immediate. With William and Mary's succession to the English throne, the issue of Catholicism was no longer so relevant. Given the war against New France, the specter of Jacobitism and fifth-column Catholicism persisted, but with the anti-Leislerians pledged to support the Protestant House of Orange, it could not serve as a rallying cry for the Leislerian survivors. With the exception of a Leislerian/anti-Leislerian split within the New York City Dutch Reformed church, which apparently gained intensity at the turn of the century, other facets of the religious division were also not as clear as they had once been.[37] True, the differences between Erastian liberals and strict Calvinists continued to exist, both in their emphasis on religious doctrine and in their respective cultural preferences for urban cosmopolitanism and rural conservatism, but without the same clarity. In the face of Anglican assertiveness, for example, the Dutch Reformed dominies began to resist gubernatorial claims to exercise a licensing right over their ministers and schoolmasters.[38] During these years, too, attitudes toward pietism cut across the Leislerian/anti-Leislerian division. Strict Calvinists who shared much in common might differ over the acceptability of radical pietism.[39] And among the ranks of the anti-Leislerians were both radical sectarian pietists and people deeply antagonistic to exaggerated devotionalism.

Given Leisler's execution and the changing nature of religious concerns following the accession of William and Mary, the simplest way to chart the turn-of-the-century Leislerian/anti-Leislerian division is to begin with the factional leaders. Once the two Jacobs (Leisler and Milborne) were hanged, other Leislerians either scattered or adopted a very low profile, while their most prominent allies lobbied in England for exoneration and the appointment of a New York governor sympathetic to their plight. The Leislerians knew as well as their opponents that the only way either group could enjoy political power in New York was through the governor's ear—and that could best be gained through English connections.[40] Whichever faction could gain a governor's confidence and consequent influence in the council could expect to control the government. Although an elected assembly had become a part of New York's provincial constitution in 1691, initially councillors and their friends could usually control its elections through a combination of patronage, cajolery, and blatantly partisan election management. In the early 1690s, anti-Leislerian politicians proved to be far more adept at cultivating Tory contacts at Whitehall than their Leislerian enemies were. Governors Sloughter and Fletcher thus landed in New York prepared to embrace them as councillors and friends.[41] But while the anti-Leislerians enjoyed their preeminence, their Leislerian opponents gained influence with the English Whigs. Fletcher's replacement, Governor Bellomont, consequently arrived in 1698 ready to take a more evenhanded stance. Once in New York, Bellomont soon sided with the Leislerians. But not for long. His death in 1701 coincided with a renewed Tory presence in Queen Anne's government and a related increase in anti-Leislerian influence. Within a year, Lord Cornbury, heir to the earldom of Clarendon, succeeded as governor of New York. To a man with such a pedigree, sorting through the provincial councillors he had inherited was no difficult task.[42] The Tory Cornbury quickly put together a new coalition of anti-Leislerians, which lasted through most of his six years as governor. Finally, with Cornbury's departure and the passage of time, the old alignments began to lose much of their political salience in and around New York City.[43]

The overwhelming political predominance of the anti-Leislerians during the turn-of-the-century decades and the particular characters of the governors with whom they associated explain one of the most important differences between themselves and their Leislerian opponents. The anti-Leislerians were the main recipients of the huge land grants for which New York became notorious.[44] The differences between the anti-Leislerians and Leislerians in this respect began back in the 1680s with Governor Dongan's decision to favor his political friends with large grants of land, some of which carried manorial status. Because they were privileged insiders, all of the recipients either actively or passively opposed Jacob Leisler's revolutionary regime. Had the Leislerian government, rather than its opponents, gained William and Mary's recognition, it is possible that the Leislerians might have eventually prevailed on a friendly governor to grant them gargantuan estates as well. Never having the necessary influence, however, they were not tempted, and some came to see political opportunity in portraying such grants as a betrayal of the public trust. Once the Leislerian interlude had passed, the participation of the anti-Leislerians in the systematic looting of New York lands continued under the venal Governor Fletcher. He created five manorial patents and deeded away, in large tracts, millions of additional acres in the Hudson and Mohawk Valleys. All of this largesse went to council members or to men closely associated with Fletcher's war efforts against the French.[45] In the Anglo-American world of the late seventeenth century, property, once granted, seemed safe, but Fletcher's friends had not counted on his successor. Lord Bellomont arrived in New York with instructions to annul all "exorbitant" land patents, and in 1699, the governor and a Leislerian-dominated assembly passed a law vacating eight Fletcher-granted deeds.[46] Bellomont clearly had hopes of breaking other large land grants and of reforming the province's quitrent system, but his sudden death in March 1701 ended those initiatives. The Tory-appointed Lord Cornbury succeeded Bellomont, and the anti-Leislerians bounded back to Fort Anne, happy to fawn at the governor's knee. Within seven months of the new governor's arrival, the New York Assembly had repealed Bellomont's Vacating Act, and by 1708, Cornbury had granted his favorites a dozen patents so extensive that they rivaled Fletcher's earlier extravagant giveaways.[47]

The most significant feature of New York's early land-grant policies was that the Leislerians were cut off from an important source of wealth and influence that their opponents fully exploited. While Bellomont's view that land grants should be limited in size was an acceptable administrative policy in England, it was an idiosyncratic one in New York. The governor's Leislerian supporters were as filled with greed as their anti-Leislerian opponents, and the former fully expected that they should receive whatever land was expropriated from their old antagonists. What kept the Leislerians away from large land grants was not principle, but simply their failure to gain the blessings of the English in 1690, and the policies of the quixotic governor who presided over their brief ascendancy at the turn of the century. But that circumstance was an important one, for the Leislerians' failure to exploit all the avenues to riches and influence that New York offered political insiders hastened their demise as a coherent political faction.

As Bellomont's Vacating Act of 1699 illustrates, the anti-Leislerians did not always have their way, despite their overall dominance of New York politics during the late seventeenth and early eighteenth centuries. Buoyed by success in the New York City assembly elections of 1694 and 1695, Parliament's reversal of Leisler's and Milbourne's attainders, the queen's pardon of a half dozen of the principal leaders of Leisler's Rebellion, and good relations with English Whigs, the office-hungry Leislerians were prepared to cooperate with whatever governor the Whigs sent to New York in Fletcher's stead.[48] Initially, Governor Bellomont hoped to patch over New Yorkers' factional differences by cooperating with both Leislerians and anti-Leislerians, but that proved impossible. That he was prepared to accept some Leislerians as advisors, coupled with his determination to cleanse New York of the piracy, smuggling, and land giveaways from which Fletcher and his anti-Leislerian freebooters had profited, led to a sharp break between Bellomont and the principal anti-Leislerians.[49] Encouraged by the turnout of a huge Dutch crowd to witness the reinterment of Leisler's and Milborne's remains in New York City's Dutch Reformed Church in October 1698, Bellomont and his confidants decided to use what leverage they had to try to convert the extensive community sympathy for the old Leislerian cause into electoral power.[50] Bellomont replaced anti-Leislerian militia officers and sheriffs throughout the province and, during the eight months preceding the 1699 provincial election, persuaded over three hundred individuals to claim eligibility as New York City voters by taking out freemanship in the city corporation.[51] Aided by such efforts, the Leislerians dominated in the 1699 election and took control of the New York Assembly. They managed to continue their dominance in the succeeding 1701 provincial election, and put up a strong showing in the hotly contested New York municipal elections that same year.[52] But Bellomont's death in early 1701 robbed them of their best asset, and although they managed to keep control of the provincial legislature under the sympathetic lieutenant-governor, John Nanfan, the arrival of Lord Cornbury in 1702 ended the Leislerian resurgence. Cornbury gathered the chief dissidents around him and, with the help of friendly sheriffs and both the votes and intimidating presence of British soldiers stationed in New York City, the anti-Leislerians swept back into political power in the assembly as well.[53]

The turn-of-the-century conflict between Leislerians and anti-Leislerians involved a number of issues. Central, of course, was Governor Bellomont's determination to clean up New York government, befouled by the anti-Leislerians' flagrant collusion with pirates, disregard for the Navigation Acts, and engrossment of Indian land that fell within the province's putative boundaries.[54] The governor's priorities were bound to alienate the anti-Leislerians and draw their opponents to his side. Such polarization was further encouraged by the orientation of Bellomont and the Leislerians toward the English Whigs, and of the anti-Leislerians toward the Tories; relationships between the two New York factions, however, were chiefly envenomed by the vindictiveness that a handful of leading members of each group felt for their counterparts. The anti-Leislerians responded to their humiliation and punishment under Jacob Leisler by hanging him and persecuting his allies. Subsequently, they tried to entrench their power and protect themselves from any Leislerian resurgence by destroying documentation that might aid their opponents' appeals in England.[55] These actions, in turn, fostered deep resentment among a number of the surviving Leislerians. As Governor Fletcher remarked after some experience with the local squalls, "neither Party will be satisfied with less than the necks of their Adversaries."[56] For the anti-Leislerian Nicholas Bayard, that observation came distressingly close to prophecy. In 1702, an increasingly desperate handful of Leislerians used their last months of power before Lord Cornbury's arrival to mete out a measure of ironic punishment to the leading anti-Leislerian. Using a law that the anti-Leislerians themselves had passed in the wake of the rebellion to frighten their opponents from further plots, the Leislerians convicted Bayard of treason and sentenced him to be hanged, drawn, and quartered. Only Bayard's qualified admission of guilt won him a reprieve while he prepared an ultimately successful appeal to the Crown.[57]

Intensely focused on factional leaders as New York's current political conflict was, the divisions were not without broader dimensions. From the earliest days of contact between New Netherlands and English colonists, Dutch-English rivalry occasionally spiced their sociopolitical relationships.[58] The conquest, recapture, and subsequent surrender of the New Netherlands in the 1660s and 1670s undoubtedly exacerbated that conflict. And Dutch-English tensions over differing conceptions of, and priorities for, colonists' rights may have again flared up in the 1680s during the drafting of the province's ill-fated Charter of Liberties.[59] During Leisler's Rebellion, ethnic strife was definitely subordinated to religious conflict, but it again gained salience during the turn-of-the-century squabbles. Although Bellomont pointed out that the "meer Dutch" (that is, those who spoke little English and were clearly a product of a New Netherlands provincialism) were as well-represented among the leaders of the anti-Leislerians as among their opponents, it is clear that the bulk of those who paid homage to Leisler's remains, who inspired Bellomont and his Leislerian friends to recruit voters for the 1699 and 1701 elections, and who ultimately supported the Leislerians at the polls were Dutch.[60]

It was the anti-Leislerians, however, rather than their Leislerian antagonists, who brought the ethnic issue to the forefront of politics. The Bellomont/Leislerian intrusion upon the anti-Leislerians was comparable to a pack of hounds happening on a yard full of cats. As they scrambled for a safe perch, the anti-Leislerians puffed themselves up and spat out that they were "the English party."[61] To the local electorate, and in slightly more restrained tones to Whitehall, they yowled that they had lost their delicacies of favor and office to the "Dutch and . . . the meanest . . . [most] mercenary people."[62] Aside from their perception of where ultimate political power lay, demographics lay behind the anti-Leislerians' attempt to exploit the ethnic issue. The 1680s and 1690s had seen the Dutch of New York City shore up their local composite of New Netherlands culture by absorbing numerous colonials whose European *cum* New York or New Jersey background was more closely in touch with Dutch society than with that of the English. In addition, some provincials of British heritage were either neutralized or absorbed into the Dutch community through marriage to Dutch women who maintained their family and religious traditions. Compared to the consolidating and expanding New York City Dutch, and the relatively cohesive block of Huguenot émigrés, the British were a ragged lot, subject to rapid turnover and divided both religiously and culturally.[63] As a result, leading representatives of the English community sometimes felt beleaguered. To Anglicans huddled in worship in the Fort's small chapel and casting sidelong glances at the well-housed Dutch Reformed congregation, five times as large as their own, New York seemed more like a "conquered Foreign Province held by the terror of a Governor, than an English Colony."[64] As long as the British and their allies kept the ear of the governor, and thereby monopolized high office and those patronage positions crucial to the winning of provincial and local elections, they could ignore their numerical inferiority. When threatened with displacement, however, they reacted in terror. As the "English party," they represented the right to rule born of conquest. And, although such shrill self-identification might raise problems in local electoral politics, those disadvantages were likely to be more than offset by its potential appeal in England. Claims to represent the English cause could not be overlooked at Whitehall, and ultimately it was the English government that, through its gubernatorial appointments, could again put the anti-Leislerians at their ease.

Given the circumstances of politics and the multicultural character of the New York City populace, it is hardly surprising that the electorate did divide heavily along ethnoreligious lines in the 1701 municipal election. In that contest, a large majority of Dutch voters supported the Leislerians, and most identifiable British and French voters supported the anti-Leislerians.[65] But as in many other instances of political conflict in New York, the issue was not merely ethnoreligious conflict. The New York City Dutch among whom sympathy for the Leislerian tradition was the strongest were mostly the lower-class working poor and middling-ranked tradesmen. Along with the ability of the anti-Leislerians to draw significant leadership from very wealthy Dutch and French merchants, some well-off Dutch clergymen, and from both upper- and upper-middle-class British merchants, shopkeepers, placemen, and professionals, this perpetuated some of the sense of class division that had political relevance during the Glorious Revolution.[66] It is also likely that the intra-ethnic cultural and religious differences that had recently been so strong had not faded away.[67]

The ethnoreligious divisions of the 1701 New York City election also need to be considered in the light of subsequent events. By 1703, the predominantly Dutch Leislerian rank and file had begun to fade from view, and they did not, so far as we know, reappear in comparable form. Perhaps Dutch Leislerians had no stomach for further political confrontation once the anti-Leislerians had begun their political counterattack under Governor Cornbury. Perhaps there was a predominantly Dutch accommodationist cultural ethic that predisposed such colonists to quiescent politics.[68] Perhaps the yellow fever epidemic that swept through New York in 1703 was so severe that it rearranged the survivors' sociopolitical perceptions and their worldly priorities.[69] But it is more likely, however, that an ethnic vote in a complicated society such as New York City was only what the historical record shows—a momentary political division largely along ethnoreligious lines. Although New York City's Dutch did have a distinctive cultural identity observable to outsiders, they also had a remarkably varied background, with strong traditions of local loyalty.[70] They might coalesce as an electorate in response to a given set of circumstances, but they could just as easily divide or dissipate politically in response to a larger sense of intragroup variation, cultural parochialness, or indifference.[71] Moreover, the whole texture of turn-of-the century New York society was much more complex than any simple, politically induced ethnocultural profile suggests. Certainly, discrete ethnoreligious communities were gaining strength, but their broader municipal relationships suggests the existence of a pragmatic tolerance, a tolerance that, when combined with cultural segmentation and "ethnicization," enhanced rather than diminished the stability of their political community.[72] Out of this matrix could come transitory political polarization along ethnoreligious lines, but such occurrences did not produce— in fact, could not produce—a similar social polarization. On the one hand, the 1701 election demonstrated the intensity of the Leislerian/anti-Leislerian rivalry. On the other, the short duration of such struggles demonstrated that New York was beginning to develop a multicultural society that limited the very conflicts its diversity tended to encourage.

Utopian Dissonance on the Delaware

Unlike New York, which came into the British empire as a minor bit of wartime booty, Pennsylvania entered in the service of the "lamb's war."[73] The Quaker William Penn founded Pennsylvania as a peaceful haven in a world overbrimming with violence and repression. Situated west of the Delaware River between New York and Maryland, with an abundance of rich land, sparsely populated by Europeans and Amerindians, protected from ocean-borne enemies yet with access to the sea, and flanked by significant Quaker presences in both New Jersey and Maryland, Pennsylvania seemed an ideal location for such an experiment. More to the point, the land was available and Penn could get it.

Although in retrospect, William Penn indicated that he had cherished a long-standing interest in the New World, evidence suggests he was more of an opportunist than he wished to appear.[74] A haphazard assignment in the late 1670s as an arbitrator to resolve disagreements among Quaker proprietors of New Jersey first drew his attention to both the religious and economic advantages of colonization. That soon proved fortuitous. By 1679–1680, Penn realized that his attempts, both through electoral politics and through influence with Charles II, to achieve liberty of conscience in England had failed. Persecution of Quakers was severe, and there seemed little hope of relief. Simultaneously, Penn confronted serious financial problems. He lived far beyond his means and clearly had no inclination to cut less of a figure in British society.[75] A proprietary colony seemed the answer to both Penn's problems. "I desire to extend religious freedom," he wrote, "yet I want some recompense for my trouble."[76]

Mystery surrounds the actual granting of the Pennsylvania charter. What we may surmise is that investor interest and leverage at court coupled with Penn's friendship with King Charles II and his brother James prompted them to override prejudice against such grants and, in exchange for the discharge of an old debt the Crown owed Penn's father, deed the colony to "William Penn, his heires and assignes forever."[77] According to Penn, there was also a nuisance factor. The Stuarts were "glad to be rid of us, at so cheap a rate as a little parchment, . . . [so long as Quakerism was] to be practis'd in a desart, 3000 Miles off."[78]

By the terms of the royal charter that Charles II signed in March 1681, William Penn became "true and absolute . . . [proprietor] of all the Lands and Dominions" encompassed by five longitudinal degrees measured west from the Delaware River, between 40 and 43 degrees latitude.[79] As proprietor, Penn held title to all Pennsylvania land and was responsible for organizing a colonial government. To be sure, there were some restrictions on what the proprietor could do. He was required to legislate as Governor with the "advice, assent and approbacon of the freemen . . . or of their Delegates or Deputies," and Pennsylvania laws were to "bee not repugnant or contrarie, but as neere as conveniently . . . [might] bee agreeable to the Lawes, statutes and rights of . . . [the] Kingdome of England."[80] Pennsylvania laws were to be reviewed in England within five years of their passage, Penn was to maintain an agent to answer for colonial activities, Parliament could impose customs duties on the colony without Pennsylvanians' consent, and Anglicans were guaranteed the right to their own "preachers . . . without any . . . molestacon whatsoever."[81] Given these and other restrictions, Penn had less freedom than the king's brother James possessed in New York, but the charter still gave him immense latitude. Once he had extinguished aboriginal titles, he could sell or rent land on virtually any terms he chose. And in governmental affairs, he could design whatever set of institutions he wished around the few demands the royal charter made.[82]

Even before King Charles had set his seal to the Pennsylvania Charter, Penn had busied himself preparing for the anticipated colonial enterprise. By the late seventeenth century, it was common knowledge that such ventures could never have a surfeit of capital and human resources. The only way Penn could ensure quick success as a colonizer was to generate substantial interest among potential investors and elicit numerous commitments to immigrate. Fortunately for Penn, the role of promoter was not difficult to assume. In his efforts to extend Quakerism and liberty of conscience, Penn had developed all of the promotional tools he would need. He knew intimately the value of favorable publicity, the importance of rich and powerful friends, the advantages of a wide exposure to great numbers of potential settlers, and the seductive appeal of a worthy cause. Serving as his own publicist, Penn wrote numerous pamphlets and broadsides, and recruited influential friends to distribute them in Great Britain, Ireland, and the Continent. According to Penn, there was something in his colony for everyone. He appealed to wealthy investors by promising rapid economic development and sizable bonuses of urban lots to be laid out in the capital city of Philadelphia. He awakened the interest of the industrious by describing a country salubrious and rich, eager to surrender its bounty to the attentive husbandman. To those Welsh and German spokespersons who proposed buying thousands of acres in order to transplant their countrymen to the new world, Penn seemed to offer encouragement. Moreover, all the material advantages Pennsylvania could grant were showcased within a larger framework of benevolence. Immigrants would come to Pennsylvania knowing that religious liberty was guaranteed, and those investors who stayed behind believed that they would enjoy vicarious participation in an important social experiment.[83]

Preoccupied as he was during 1681 and early 1682 with the sale of Pennsylvania land and the recruitment of settlers, Penn nonetheless had time to design a colonial constitution. When it came to affairs of government, William Penn's ideas are an intriguing mixture. Then in his thirties, Penn certainly viewed himself as a visionary reformer with strong republican inclinations. In 1677, he had a hand in drawing up the most radical constitutional document in colonial history, the West Jersey Concessions and Agreements.[84] Under this government, West Jersey residents annually elected both a legislature and a ten-person executive commission. The legislature held a virtual monopoly of power, the executive was shorn of prerogative rights, and the inhabitants were guaranteed trial by jury, freedom from debtors' prison, and a number of other legal and administrative reforms.[85] Four years later, when Penn first committed the draft "Fundamentall Constitutions" for Pennsylvania to paper, he had not strayed far. The governor and council were weak, the annually elected legislature relatively strong, and a good deal of power lay in the hands of the electorate. They had a right systematically to instruct their representatives, who were bound by such orders. The proprietor himself was to retain nothing in the way of extraordinary powers.[86]

At this point, Penn's ideas began to change. It may be that some of the purchasers of large tracts who intended to immigrate pushed Penn on to more conservative ground in return for their support.[87] But it is also clear that Penn was capable of moving in that direction on his own. His religious radicalism was always combined with elements of social conservatism, and he frequently took pragmatic sidesteps in English politics as well as in his business affairs. In any event, Pennsylvania's First Frame of Government went through a number of moderating drafts before Penn published it, along with a calendar of intended laws, in May 1682.[88]

Rather than centering legislative power in a unicameral body or a lower house of assembly, as the West Jersey Concessions and Penn's earlier Fundamentall Constitutions had done, the First Frame of Government empowered a governor and council with the right to prepare all legislation and joint responsibility for "duely and diligently" executing the laws.[89] The council was intended to play a major role in the administration of the colony through four standing committees ("Justice and Safety," "Trade and Treasury," "Plantations," and "Manners, Education and Arts") and through its right to elect judicial and administrative officers.[90] On the other hand, the lower house was restricted to a nine-day meeting yearly, at which it was limited to either affirming or vetoing the legislation prepared by governor and council. Both council and assembly were to be elected, the former consisting of seventy-two representatives, one-third of whom were to be replaced every year, and the latter composed of two hundred or more delegates, to be chosen annually. Compared to West New Jersey, the franchise was somewhat restrictive, requiring most voters to possess a sizable freehold and an improvement thereon.[91]

In light of Penn's earlier efforts at constitution making, it is certainly plausible to see the First Frame as an attempt to give considerable weight in Pennsylvania's government to well-to-do first purchasers. It was reasonable to assume that the propertied would dominate the prestigious provincial council. Conversely, the most democratic house in any bicameral legislature would most likely be the lower house, which Penn had emasculated in his constitution.[92] On the other hand, it is clear that in later decades Pennsylvania's popular leaders did not see the First Frame as particularly restrictive. They emphasized the fact that, council or no, the main governing institution was to be an *elected* body, in which Pennsylvania freemen had a great deal of administrative power, and which, in turn, elected judicial officers.[93] Moreover, the First Frame and the proposed laws that accompanied it established such rights as a secret ballot, rotation of office, religious toleration, trials by jury, and equitable judicial procedures.[94] Like William Penn, the First Frame had an ambiguous character that was capable of being viewed in a variety of ways.

While retrospective criticism historians have leveled at Pennsylvania's first constitution, only a few of the known potential colonists registered their disapproval.[95] Many voted with their feet and their fortunes. The first year of immigration brought twenty-three ships to Pennsylvania; twelve months after Penn disembarked on the shores of the Delaware, in October 1682, he could rhapsodize on the colony's vitality: "3000 soules" had arrived, "the Towne of Philadelphia . . . [was growing] dayly, about 600 people in it, & 100 houses built," and "Many hundred Farmes [were] settled about her."[96] "God had not cast . . . [Penn's] Lott [in Pennsylvania] but for a service to his truth. [Surely God's] hand was . . . in it."[97]

While the successful initiation of Penn's "Holy Experiment" demonstrated the widespread appeal of his vision, it did not signify the end of the proprietor's political experimentation. During the months Penn was negotiating his charter, he realized that the establishment of the fortieth parallel as the common boundary between his colony and Maryland could present serious problems. If the boundary line was too far north, Penn's colony would be cut off from access to the Atlantic Ocean. One possible remedy for this, which Penn was quick to exploit, was to prevail on the duke of York to cede the three Lower Counties (Delaware) to him. While his accession of the eastern Delaware peninsula in August 1682 solved the potential problem of access to the Atlantic, it created another difficulty.[98] How would the Lower Counties be incorporated into Penn's scheme of government?

Confident that the benevolent spirit of Quakerism would prove contagious, Penn opted to govern Pennsylvania and the Lower Counties as one unit.[99] That, of course, required a revision of the First Frame. Gaining support for a constitutional change was not difficult, for the realities of colonial life pointed to the need for modifications to the First Frame of Government from its introduction in late 1682. Realizing that provision for the election of seventy-two councillors and two hundred assemblymen was absurd in a colony of a few thousand, most of whom were preoccupied with a multitude of mundane tasks, electors in the three Lower Counties and in the three comparable counties of Pennsylvania provided for only seventy-two legislators to fill the council and assembly.[100] Three from each county were to serve on the council, and nine in the assembly. The council did not speak for everyone, but it certainly reflected a general sentiment when it voted "unanimously" to adopt a new frame of government.[101] Adopted on April 5, 1683, the Second Frame provided for the unification of Pennsylvania and the three Lower Counties and accepted a new eighteen-person council and thirty-six-person assembly. In the debate that accompanied the constitutional revisions, a few important issues were clarified. The power William Penn had assumed to appoint all administrative and judicial officers was to continue during the proprietor's lifetime.[102] The council, although not the assembly, seems to have recognized Penn's right to veto any legislation, and the power of initiating tax bills lay uncontested with the governor-in-council.[103] For its part, the assembly gained the right to highlight problems that the council might then address in legislation and seemed to enjoy a reasonable access to the governor-in-council.[104] Although there were contradictory currents in these changes, the alterations did have a cumulative tendency—to concentrate power in the hands of the proprietor and a dozen or so councillors who shared his confidence.[105]

Although Penn's title to the eastern Delaware peninsula and his subsequent absorption of the Lower Counties strengthened his hold on the Delaware valley, it did not set to rest the larger issue of the Pennsylvania/Maryland boundary. Lord Baltimore's Maryland charter specified the 40th parallel as his colony's northern boundary; both proprietors realized shortly after Penn acquired his grant that this line lay north of Philadelphia. Baltimore hoped to use this as a bargaining point to gain as much of southeastern Pennsylvania as possible; Penn, on the other hand, fixed covetous eyes on the mouth of the Susquehanna River and hoped to use an old, recently discredited yardstick for measuring the distance between latitudes to force the Maryland boundary below the head of Chesapeake Bay. Both proprietors became intransigent once they bumped heads in North America. Baltimore countered Penn's incorporation of the Lower Counties into his government with a claim of his own to the eastern Delaware peninsula. When Penn shared some success in winning the support of leading Delaware planters, Baltimore promised more favorable landholding terms than Penn had offered. When Baltimore sent an appeal to the Lords of Trade, Penn countered by dispatching his trusted cousin, William Markham, to press his case. Eventually, no doubt influenced by the fact that his opponent was a Quaker, Baltimore decided to use force. In the spring of 1684, he sent "Musqueters" to intimidate recalcitrant residents of the Lower Counties, and by early summer, Penn concluded that he had a revolt on his hands.[106] Threatened both in the New World and in the Old, Penn felt he had no choice but to return to England to defend his colony before the Lords of Trade.[107]

When William Penn departed Pennsylvania in August 1684, his intention may well have been to defend his proprietary title, collect his wife and children, and return promptly to North America. In fact, it was fifteen years before he again walked Philadelphia's waterfront. On his arrival in England, Penn was startled by the discovery that he had left behind the copious documentation he had gathered to prove his territorial claims before the Lords of Trade. Ruefully, he admitted there was little he could do save stand "with . . . [his] finger in . . . [his] mouth."[108] A year later, after the forgotten brief had made its way across the ocean, the Lords of Trade upheld the proprietor's claim to the Lower Counties. But by that time, Penn had been willingly sucked into the whirlpool of English politics.[109] The succession to the throne in February 1685 of Penn's longtime patron James II brought the Quaker leader impressive influence as an advocate of religious toleration. Unwilling in such heady times to retreat to colonial isolation, before long Penn was unable to do so. The Glorious Revolution left him under deep suspicion as a Jacobite and drove him into seclusion. Thereafter, a number of circumstances—his first wife's death, his remarriage, his desire to reassert public leadership among British Friends, his determination to rebuild an effective network of political influence, his need to reclaim his proprietorship in Pennsylvania after the Crown had placed it under the administration of New York's Governor Fletcher between 1691 and 1694, and his disinclination to deal with the problems residence in Pennsylvania would thrust upon him—prevented him from returning to the Delaware Valley. For the last years of the seventeenth century, then, Pennsylvanians had the opportunity to go their own way.[110]

When Penn took ship for England in 1684, he left behind an experiment in collective leadership. Rather than appointing a deputy-governor to act on his behalf, Penn authorized the council, under its president, Thomas Lloyd, to perform all the executive functions of government, and placed authority over proprietary land in the hands of two boards well-stocked with trusted Quaker acquaintances. Together these groups demonstrated that Penn had been right—collective leadership was possible. Unfortunately for Penn, they proved it at the proprietor's expense. For the next four years, they cut the ground out from under their benefactor, refusing to implement his land policies, sabotaging his efforts to secure a proprietary income, making their own administrative and judicial appointments, and eventually even claiming the right to proclaim their laws valid "by the authority of the President and Council."[111] In 1688, Penn tried to bring them to heel with an unlikely innovation. He appointed a Puritan, John Blackwell, as governor and instructed him to defend proprietary rights.[112] Within a year, however, Blackwell had resigned, driven from his office by the pestiferous Quakers. As Blackwell rode out of Philadelphia, many of his opponents cobbled together a new coalition of Quaker leaders and presented themselves to Penn as the only viable alternative.[113]

The most formidable obstacle Pennsylvania's Quaker leaders had to face in the early 1690s was not Penn, who quietly acquiesced to their demands, but the Crown. The Lords of Trade, concerned about coordinating an effective colonial defense in the recently initiated King William's War with France, and nervous over reports of Philadelphia merchants trading with the enemy, recommended (with Penn under suspicion of treason) that Pennsylvania be placed under royal administration. In April 1693, New York's Governor Benjamin Fletcher descended on Philadelphia. Although Fletcher met with stiff Quaker resistance, he demonstrated that a royal governor with a fixed agenda (in this case a demand for military appropriations) was no mean antagonist. Ultimately, William Penn turned out to be the Pennsylvanians' best ally, for his unsurpassed talent at the politics of court ingratiation led William and Mary to restore Penn's proprietorial governing rights in August 1694. Although he appointed William Markham as governor, and from time to time exerted himself against renewed attacks on his proprietorship, Penn left Pennsylvania affairs largely to local Quakers for the rest of the decade.[114]

If Pennsylvania's political leaders learned one thing from their experiences with Governors Blackwell and Fletcher, it was that the provincial council was not always an effective bastion against executive authority. The House of Assembly could be made far more secure. Consequently, they demanded that Governor Markham accept a new constitution specifying two council members and six assembly members per county, and granting powers of initiating legislation and sitting on their own adjournments to the lower house. This so-called Markham's Frame of Government was adopted in 1696 without any consultation with the proprietor. Sheltered by their new frame of government and bolstered by changes in suffrage that strengthened Quaker electoral power, a rejuvenated Quaker elite was determined to resist outside authority. Neither royal customs officials, the newly formed Board of Trade, nor William Penn had much success in curbing Quaker autonomy during the last years of the century.[115]

During the fifteen years prior to William Penn's brief return to his colony in late 1699, the most distinctive feature of Pennsylvania politics was the antiproprietary stance of most local Quaker leaders. During the short period in which Penn was a Pennsylvania resident in the early 1680s, his enthusiasm, charm, high social status, and utopian vision elicited considerable goodwill. But when he left his colony, his patriarchal aura faded as quickly as that autumn's hardwood hues. In the flat light of the succeeding winter, more and more residents came to see the proprietor primarily as an absentee landlord, one made more dangerous than most they had known by the extent of his baronial claims. Disillusionment had begun to set in even before Penn's departure, when the proprietor arbitrarily changed the conditions of landholding in Philadelphia. His substantial reduction of the size of urban lots promised to first purchasers, his favoritism in allocating these lands, and his determination to levy quitrents on them evoked feelings of betrayal, particularly among the well-heeled Quakers whose resources had underwritten the colonial enterprise. Antiproprietary sentiment quickly spread to rural areas in 1685. No sooner had the calendar changed to the new year than Penn began to push for quitrent payments. Having promised a tax abatement only through 1684, technically Penn committed no breach of trust, but his haste bespoke a lawyerlike literal-mindedness and the greed of the rich, rather than Quaker benevolence.[116]

As time passed, popular intransigence and proprietary disillusionment fed on each other. Why should settlers pay quitrents and high land purchase prices to an absentee landlord? Their circumstances were meager and his affluent. And after all, Penn did have his perquisites of government, his manor lands, and an immense quantity of unallocated land. Why, too, should settlers pay purchase money for land that might actually belong to Lord Baltimore? Why pay quitrents to a man who might sell the province to the Crown? Why cooperate at all with someone who acted as high-handedly as Penn? And the proprietor did act in an arbitrary manner. Angered by what he perceived as ungratefulness, Penn ordered the repossession of large land tracts locals held for speculation. He commanded his collectors to distrain for back rents. In order to facilitate these legal actions, he encouraged his Board of Property to constitute itself as a prerogative court, fully competent to try property-related issues without a jury.[117] Yet jury trial was a right Penn had unequivocally guaranteed to his colonists. Then there was Governor Blackwell. How could Penn possibly have selected a Puritan to govern his people? Especially one who had been "ripen[ed] . . . in Cruelty [toward Quakers]" in that benighted, Quaker-hanging land of New England?[118] That was unanswerable. For Penn's part, the appointment was more than just another example of ill-considered proprietary judgment. The deeper he fell into debt, the more he simultaneously blamed Pennsylvanians for his financial dilemma and saw the colony as his one opportunity to recoup his fortune. Blackwell's appointment was Penn's effort both to punish his colonists and to profit from their successes.

There is no question that Penn's policies would have created problems for anyone in his position, but their effect in Pennsylvania was exaggerated by the close relationship between the proprietor and a number of his leading colonists. "When I was among you," recalled Penn a decade after leaving Pennsylvania, "we were a People."[119] In the early days of colonial planning and first settlement, the emphasis Friends put upon unity encouraged close feelings between Penn and his colonists. Occasionally, these sentiments found expression in patriarchal language. Pennsylvania was "a birth of thy owne [Penn's] begeting."[120] Consequently, Penn had an obligation to extend to his settlers the same nurturing "fatherly care" he bestowed upon his natural children in England.[121] Far more frequent than paternal metaphors, moreover, were fraternal and contractual sentiments. Leading Pennsylvania Quakers felt that they were full partners with Penn in a shared venture. "Wee the Settlers of thy Cuntry are not such as have beene Reprived from gaoles or executions nor fled our Cuntry for misdemeanors."[122] In England "wee . . . [were] but fellow Subjects."[123] Once embarked on Penn's venture, colonists owed "fidellity" to the proprietor because their "interest and habitation" was in Pennsylvania. But loyalty was dependent upon his recognition of "recipro[c]all Obligations."[124] Settlers' "privelidges. . . . Shall not be weakened or Lessened, but Corroberated and Enlarged."[125] For their part, Pennsylvanians had "laboured & spent . . . [themselves, their] Estates & some theire lives to get for themselves & familyes a meane livelyhood & to Raise thee [William Penn] & thyne [an] estate."[126] Ultimately, many felt, it was Penn who owed them.

The sense of fraternal betrayal that leading Quakers felt when confronted with proprietary policies was matched by Penn's disenchantment. "Considering how little I am in fault & how ill I am rewarded by some in that Province," complained the proprietor, "The lord forgive them for their unspeakable Injury to me & myne."[127] High expectations led to severe disillusionment and even vengefulness. "I shall keep the power & priviledges I have left," muttered Penn, "& recover the rest as their misbehavours shall forfitt them back into my hands."[128]

Although both Penn's policies and the nature of relations between settlers and proprietor contributed to the antiproprietary caste of early Pennsylvania politics, neither was more important than the peculiar antiauthoritarian attitudes Quakers imported with their families. Despite his concern for order, Penn himself frequently personified such values. Coupled with his uncompromising instructions to Governor Blackwell to enforce proprietary prerogatives went equally sincere assurances to provincial political leaders that Blackwell would be "layd aside" if they found the governor too much to stomach.[129] When Governor Fletcher of New York took over the administration of Pennsylvania in the early 1690s, Penn urged his leading colonists to stand on their "Patent" and challenge the royal governor's right to rule.[130]

Pennsylvania Quakers required little urging from their proprietor, for collectively they were "steeped in a tradition of opposing prescriptive authority."[131] By the 1670s and 1680s, Quakerism had become synonymous with resistance to civil authority. Determined to uphold God's truth in their social relations and religious practices, Friends refused to conform to laws inconsistent with or intruding upon the "spiritualized intimite relations" central to Quaker self-definition.[132] They believed their primary duty was to rediscover the righteous paths of primitive Christianity, and that obligation was not to be compromised for the sake of any worldly authority. Their unbending attitudes led to "sporadic and capricious" prosecution under the British legal system, which, while frequently inefficient and open to challenge, gave a good deal of latitude to Quaker-haters and informers.[133] For their part, Friends celebrated the suffering they experienced through fines, jailings, beatings, and harassment as an opportunity to bear witness to the truth and to expose the corruption of the persecuting authority. Over half Pennsylvania's early land purchasers had experienced persecution in England.[134] Among Welsh immigrants, the rate of persecution exceeded that of their Quaker countrymen who remained in Great Britain.[135] The scars of their experiences determined Pennsylvania Quakers to prevent similar suffering in their part of the New World. Conditioned by their past, Pennsylvania Friends tended to see traditional political authority as confining, oppressive, and ultimately tyrannous. Their remedy for such abuse was a simple one—circumscribe prescriptive authority. That could be done by extending considerable political power to the people's [i.e., Quakers'] representatives and by giving the government few excuses and little ability to coerce private citizens. The former could be accomplished by ignoring William Penn's demands, the latter by adopting liberal laws and espousing pacifism. Anti-authoritarian predilections were so pervasive among Pennsylvania Quakers that Penn had little prospect of developing any sustained support for his proprietary privileges.[136]

Initially, of course, Penn was able to exploit the sense of unity that informed Quakerism. As "children of the light," "a people among people," and "seekers after truth," the Friends were a unique association of men and women, who had established a strong sectarian identity in the seventeenth century. In attacking hireling ministers, in denying the sacramental nature of baptism, in deemphasizing the historic Christ, and in opening their souls to direct inspiration from God, the Quakers demonstrated that they had the will to reject established orthodoxies they felt to be confining rather than liberating. At the same time, Friends had the imagination to come up with alternative ways of defining themselves as a coherent group. Their pyramidal meeting organizations, their adoption of a plain style of speech, dress, and demeanor, and their adoption of testimonies offering guidance on such issues as oath taking and war, gradually transformed a prophetically inspired counterculture into a new religious orthodoxy.[137] When the first Quakers came to Pennsylvania, they recognized that they had an obligation to develop a political order compatible with their sense of religious identity. Initially that obligation encompassed their proprietor. But when he seemed to demonstrate a primary preoccupation with private interests and separated himself physically from Pennsylvania, Penn lost whatever ability he had once had to shape the innovative efforts provincial leaders would make to give political expression to their community enterprise. From afar Penn recognized that the Pennsylvania Quakers were "a people Called and In measure saved by the Lord."[138] As such they would strive to order Pennsylvania's political affairs in ways that would best express their sense of community autonomy. Most frequently, those innovations took an antiproprietary turn; about that Penn could not be so philosophic. "For the love of God, me and the poor country," he anguished, "be not so governmentish, so noisy and open in your dissatisfactions."[139] But the prevailing winds were westerlies and blew his pleadings back in his face.

While the strength of Pennsylvania's antiproprietary political leaders owed a good deal to their religiously inspired, self-confident assertion of a right to redesign their peaceable kingdom, it is important to keep in mind that William Penn was not the force his admirers have sometimes made him out to be. Throughout the 1680s and 1690s, he repeatedly cast some discredit on himself among British Friends with his political activities, his rapid second marriage, and his un-Quakerlike financial failings.[140] Under such circumstances, Pennsylvania's elite found it easier to claim a moral right to lead their community into political water high enough to keep afloat their Quaker aspirations. To many Pennsylvanians, Penn may have played a crucial part in launching the "Holy Experiment," but he had threatened to run it aground on the shoals of proprietary privilege. Temperamentally and historically predisposed to seize the initiative in such a danger, Pennsylvania Quakers tacked away on antiproprietary winds. Once in control, they were determined to remain so in order to guide Pennsylvania to safe political destinations.

Despite the pervasiveness and intensity of antiproprietary attitudes among early Pennsylvanians, colonists were rarely of one mind in expressing their dissatisfactions. The results were repeated bouts of political factionalism, which resounded through the colony. The most severe and longest-lasting political split arose from the Maryland boundary dispute. By taking control of the three Lower Counties, Penn had solved the problem of assured ocean access for Pennsylvania, but only at tremendous cost. His annexation of the eastern side of the Delaware peninsula led to the abandonment of the 1682 constitution and to a provision in the 1683 Frame of Government that guaranteed the three Lower Counties parity of representation in both council and assembly with Pennsylvania's three original counties. Although representatives of the older Delaware society and their recently immigrated counterparts from Pennsylvania accepted unification, they could agree on little else. Accustomed to the loose hand of administrators in New York and the duke of York's low quitrents, residents of the Lower Counties resented Penn's close oversight and the prospect of paying higher rates for lands. They chafed at the settlement to the north with its sense of purpose, its assumed superiority, its veneer of corporate enterprise, and its galloping growth. Philadelphia promised to outstrip the chief Delaware port, New Castle, in a few months and leave town and hinterland a languid backwater. Animosity of old immigrants toward new, and of the excluded toward the preferred, was intensified by ethnic and religious differences. The settlers on the lower Delaware were a potpourri of Swedes, Finns, Dutch, and English, who looked askance at the way Penn's predominantly English settlers overrode old Swedish land rights in and around Philadelphia. Although the spiritual predilections of the peninsula residents were ill defined, there was one issue on which most agreed: pacifism was absurd. As colonists in an exposed location, during an era of European expansion and warfare, they could ill afford the luxury of defenselessness. Although Quakers in both Pennsylvania and Maryland gained some quiet influence in the Lower Counties, the majority of settlers reacted strongly against the unctuous Quakerism that hid upriver away from the dangers of naval raids and privateers. Much better to support a religion, like Anglicanism, that clearly accepted the right of self-defense.[141]

Ill feelings between the two parts of Penn's colony were not confined to one side. Initially, Quakers feared that unification would prevent them from controlling the government and proceeding with their colonial experiment. They argued that Penn's appetite for empire had sabotaged the 1682 Frame of Government, undermined rights the proprietor had promised in his engagement with the first purchasers, and created the possibility of Quakers being outmanned in what they regarded as their own colony. Once Pennsylvania's population outstripped that of the Lower Counties, Quaker political leaders tended to dismiss Delaware affairs in an offhanded manner and set their sights on increasing Pennsylvania representation to reflect the suzerainty they felt Quakers should enjoy.[142]

The best that could have emerged from this strained marriage was bickering cohabitation. While that did typify relations for sizable stretches of time, there were also periods of bitter separation. From mid 1683 through the following summer, Lower County residents were prepared to run off with paramour Lord Baltimore. Flattered by Baltimore's attentions and his lenient land terms, several Lower County politicians withdrew from the council in the spring of 1684. This rejection, lasting only a month or so, was but a harbinger. When King William's War broke out in 1689 between France and Great Britain, Lower County residents were determined to make some effort to defend themselves. Consequently, their representatives refused to participate in joint government under the Quaker-controlled council that succeeded Governor Blackwell. For approximately four years, through March 1695, the Lower Counties took it upon themselves to keep their own house as a separate legislative unit. Although they agreed to join with Pennsylvania again under Markham's Frame of Government, the relationship had failed to improve by the time Penn returned to America in late 1699.[143]

While conflict between Pennsylvanians and Lower County residents contributed substantially to political factionalism in William Penn's colony, there were other causes. The Quakers who settled in the three original Pennsylvania counties came from different areas, and the peculiar local mix that appeared gave each county a distinct character and power structure of its own. Their reaction to each other and to proprietary policies frequently varied.[144] Tensions developed at different times between leading proprietary officials and Welsh, German, and Swedish settlers, as well as among various groups of Quaker leaders, whose attitudes toward Penn, Governor Blackwell, and President of the Council Thomas Lloyd varied over time.[145] Important as these factional differences were in calling into question the political effectiveness of Quaker professions of unity, none of these low-level conflicts of the 1680s shook the roots of the "Holy Experiment." That only occurred in the following decade with the Keithian schism.

In 1689, the Quaker minister, or "public Friend," George Keith came to Philadelphia as head of the Friends' Latin School.[146] A Scotsman with a college education and impressive intellectual attainments, Keith belonged to the second generation of British Friends and was concerned about supplementing prophetic Quakerism with a systematic sectarian theology.[147] Along with William Penn and Robert Barclay, Keith was determined to force Congregational, Presbyterian, and Baptist critics (who frequently asserted that Quakers were not Christians) up against the walls of logic until they were forced to admit their error. As Keith struggled to pin his theological foes, he became increasingly aware that some Quaker practices in Pennsylvania left him dangerously exposed to counterattack. The secret of success in theological tournaments abroad was thus reform at home.[148]

At the heart of Quakerism was the concept of the "Inner Light." Friends believed that God's truth was born into each individual, and that all might open themselves to the word through communal meetings and "tender" dealings.[149] If they were successful in doing so, individuals' lives would attest a "holy conversation"—that is, a behavior and demeanor that reflected Christian values.[150] Charity, truthfulness, honesty, and faithfulness would permeate their "speech . . . gesture, conduct, and presence" and be expressed in the behavior that set Friends apart from other religious groups.[151] While such regeneration ultimately came from Christ's Resurrection, the vast majority of leading Friends were not overly interested in theological exactitude. Their most important concern was to extend the influence of the Inner Light among their families and close friends. "Holy conversation" could best be promoted by paying heed to the Christ within oneself, not to the historical Jesus and scriptural exegesis.[152]

Calvinist critics condemned Quakers as antinomians whose disregard for scriptural authority cut them off from their Christian roots. In the Puritans' view, knowledge of the historical Christ was essential for salvation. The indwelling Holy Spirit only had Christian meaning through epistemological connections to the "Christ without." Coming from a Scottish background strong in systematic theology, Keith found his enemies more persuasive than they found him. While continuing to defend Quakerism, he undertook its revision. "Holy conversation" was not sufficient for salvation. What Quakers needed to do was to provide for their own and their children's education in Christian doctrine.[153]

Believing that the place to start was with youth, Keith suggested that the Philadelphia Meeting adopt "A Plain Short Catechism for Children and Youth" that he drew up in 1690.[154] Dedicated to explaining such doctrines as the Incarnation, Crucifixion, and Resurrection of Christ, the catechism was designed to move Quakers away from what he had identified as a tendency to rear their children as "virtuous heathens" and to encourage them to inculcate Christian principles in their offspring.[155] An appropriate catechism would school a new generation of Friends in Christian doctrine, and that would facilitate the drawing up of an explicit creed and confession of faith. It would also stop the gradual and easy transition of Quaker youth brought up in "holy conversation," but without Keith's version of respect for Christian doctrine or ritual, into full-fledged Quaker members. Keith envisioned a religious system in which all prospective Friends would have to demonstrate a knowledge of doctrine and relate some satisfactory evidence of their receptiveness to God's grace.[156]

It did not take long for other Pennsylvania leaders to conclude that Keith proposed "diverse things new and strange to us."[157] By the fall of 1691, two public Friends had charged Keith with heresy, notably that he "deny[ed] . . . the sufficiency of the Light within."[158] Keith countercharged that his opponents ignored the crucial mediating role Christ had played between man and God. The fundamental question at issue, as one commentator put it, was "whether . . . faith ['in Christ without, as He died for our sins, and rose again'] was indispensably necessary to all mankind, and that none could be saved without it, [not infants, young children, the mentally incapacitated, or heathens] though they had not the means, opportunity, or capacity to know or not."[159] Keith believed it was. Thus Quakers should recognize that "holy conversation" was not enough to ensure salvation for those who died as children. Only a new emphasis on ritual and doctrine would prompt Friends to educate their children in Christian principles at the earliest stages of comprehension and save them from the perils of damnation.

Once the issue was openly joined between Keith and his critics, factionalism ran rampant. Commandeering the sympathetic ear of Philadelphia's only printer, Keith and his supporters papered the City of Brotherly Love with polemical writings attacking prominent public Friends. They were "fools, ignorant heathens, infidels, silly souls, lyars, hereticks, rotten ranters, [and] miggletonians."[160] They charged these ministers with harboring heretical views, illegitimately exercising magisterial authority, and sanctioning privateering, slavery, and the slave trade.[161] Acting in their capacity as magistrates, his opponents responded by jailing the printer, William Bradford, confiscating part of his press, and fining Keith for slander.[162] As ministers, they mobilized the Philadelphia Yearly Meeting and disowned the dissident Quaker leader. An unpenitent Keith led his followers in separate worship, and in 1693, the Keithians challenged their adversaries by building their own gallery in the Philadelphia meetinghouse opposite the magistrate ministers' gallery.[163] During the meetings that followed, competitive harangues gave way to destruction. In frustration, champions of the two factions set on their opponents' galleries with sharpened axes, tearing down "posts, seats, railing, and stairs."[164] Shortly after this frenzied finale, Keith left to plead his case before Friends in England. There, too, he was soon disowned.[165]

The Keithian disputes cut deeply into the fabric of Pennsylvania Quakerism. By 1690, a tight group of minister magistrates dominated Pennsylvania society through their preeminence in Friends' ministerial and business meetings and their control of the major political and judicial offices of state. They were quietly supported by most of Pennsylvania's solid Friends, Quakers who were self-satisfied with their agricultural and business success and with their family commitment to the ways of "holy conversation." But because Keith's assault was a fraternal one that raised serious questions about the godliness of the "holy experiment," it forced Pennsylvania Quakers to confront the challenge rather than shrug it off. Keith's characterization of Quaker minister magistrates as false prophets who had concentrated too much power in their own hands and led Pennsylvania's honest folk on a heathen path was close enough to the mark to arouse dissidents. The remnants of a "contrary faction" from Governor Blackwell's days were encouraged to capitalize on the disenchantment Keith precipitated.[166] The invigorated political opposition first opposed a provincial tax that the provincial council wanted to levy and then welcomed the royal governor Benjamin Fletcher when he arrived in 1694.[167]

Most solid Quakers in both city and country repudiated Keith, but there were others, frequently Friends with limited financial resources, who formed the political and religious rank and file in the Keithian protests. In early Pennsylvania, the less well-to-do were doubly cursed. Not only did they feel the frustration that ordinarily accompanies relative economic failure in a fast-growing society, they also felt relegated to marginal status in the Quaker meetinghouse. Because they did not have the financial resources to insulate themselves and their children in a protected web of "holy conversation," they were most at risk for disciplinary action. The more they were cited for debt, for intoxication, or for letting their children marry outside the meeting, the more remote any possibility of gaining status within the Quaker community became. Many economically disadvantaged Friends felt shut out by a nascent sociopolitical oligarchy, and they responded by striking out against the sanctimonious.[168]

The Keithian explosion was no short-lived controversy, but a schism that perpetuated factional politics into the later 1690s. By pointing out what he perceived as the contradiction in Quaker ministers' monopolizing magisterial offices, and by arguing that Friends' pacifism rendered them unfit for public service in wartime, Keith established a persuasive rationale for political dissent. Moreover, in drawing numerous Quakers away from their meetings, and encouraging them to found alternative gatherings, Keith seeded Pennsylvania with Anglican and Baptist congregations. Various members of these churches were prepared to keep political opposition alive. In 1697, for example, a coalition of Anglicans, Baptists, Quakers, and others declared their disapproval of the new Markham Frame of Government by selecting their own slate of candidates under the old 1683 constitution.[169] Although the Pennsylvania insurgents had little local success, they were encouraged by events in England. The establishment of the Board of Trade in 1696 and two Anglican missionary organizations, the Society for the Propagation of Christian Knowledge in 1698 and the Society for the Propagation of the Gospel in 1702, promised support for Pennsylvania dissidents. Anglican placemen whom the Board of Trade sent to enforce the Navigation Acts, and teachers and clergymen whom the two benevolent societies dispatched to the Delaware valley, frequently encouraged factional political behavior. Political turmoil, they reasoned, might bring Friends into such disrepute that the Crown would step in and wrench political power from Quaker hands.[170]

It was in the context of factionalized politics and continued antiproprietary sentiment that Penn returned to his colony in 1699. With proprietary government under unrelenting attack, the proprietor felt the only way he could save title to his colony was to travel to Pennsylvania and ensure its compliance with the Navigation Acts. Momentarily reinvigorated on his arrival in December 1699, Penn set out to take more effective control of government, reorganize his proprietary affairs, and force local merchants to respect restrictions on trade. After a brief six-month honeymoon, in which colonists seemed to accept his paternal embrace, public opinion began to turn. In response, the proprietor sequestered himself on his country estate, managed his affairs at arm's length through agents and friends, and prepared to outwait his critics. In the spring of 1701, however, a new crisis arose. A bill reuniting all proprietary governments to the Crown had been introduced in the House of Lords. Although Parliament's dissolution had killed the bill, a second effort was sure to follow. Penn's only option was to return to England to defend his property.[171]

The threat of royal expropriation galvanized Penn into action. His intermittent confrontations with royal customs and admiralty officials over the previous year had already predisposed him to work out a new accommodation with his fellow Quakers. Encouraging them to draw up documents protecting their rights against possible royal encroachment, Penn settled a new constitution on his province in 1701. This was his last, and in some ways most important, colonial innovation, for it established a provincial constitutional framework that was to endure until the Revolution. Under the 1701 Charter of Privileges, Pennsylvanians were to develop the provincial political culture that they had only begun to establish during the prior two decades.[172]

"There is not after all a single kind of strife . . . "

The conflict and confusion that characterized New York and Pennsylvania during the late seventeenth century indicate that both societies faced similar problems in adjusting to proprietary and royal policies, in establishing viable provincial constitutions, and in creating a sociopolitical order acceptable to the communities' most powerful and vocal interests. Those similarities should not, however, obscure the fact that in their adjustment to conflict, change, and growth, each society underwent unique tempering processes. New York became part of the English colonial empire by force, while Pennsylvanians came to North America by inducement. Conquest, the personal predilections of James Stuart, and the institutionalization of royal government, established a degree of governmental centralization in New York that, in turn, frequently aroused opposition from traditions of localism with deep roots in the towns and mentality of many settlers of that colony. In contrast, Pennsylvanians felt that their provincial experiment was a major group enterprise and that, in its proprietary form, provincial authority should accommodate itself to the consensual processes they perceived to be an essential feature of their community. The fact that the latter did not work particularly well in society at large during the early years of settlement did not at all change Pennsylvanians' minds about proprietary obligations. In New York, of course, the authority of the governors, and the willingness of leading colonists to work closely with them, frequently focused opposition on the chief executive, his advisors, and the policies they tried to pursue. In Pennsylvania, proprietary governors were perceived as ciphers, and the result was that popular opposition to provincial authority centered on the proprietor despite his long absence from the New World. Because of the comparative strength of their governors, New Yorkers never experienced the kind of provincial autonomy that Pennsylvanians enjoyed during the late 1680s and 1690s. The only comparable period in the New York experience was during Jacob Leisler's months of leadership. But the coercion that accompanied that experiment, and Leisler's death on the gallows, simply magnified the difference in public temperament between the two colonies. Left to their own devices, New Yorkers evinced a streak of vindictiveness in contrast to Pennsylvanians' more moderate political disposition.

Conflicting views about the proper course public policy should follow and intense rivalry among colonial leaders were at the root of much of the divisiveness that characterized early New York and Pennsylvania. Political conflict in each colony thus developed its own peculiar logic. And in each case, conflict produced a shifting factionalism that is difficult to follow. Although it is certainly possible to stress the orderliness of the confrontation between Leislerians and anti-Leislerians by pointing out continuities in leadership, political attitudes, and electoral support, the overriding feature of New York politics between 1690 and 1710 was fluidity. Issues changed, and so did the stances of various factional leaders. When continued loyalty seemed to threaten wealth, power, or eminence, there were always some prepared to slip under the political fence that snaked through Manhattan, nominally dividing Leislerian from anti-Leislerian turf. Similarly, in Pennsylvania, the antiproprietary leanings of popular factions imparted some order to political affairs. But at the same time, the various expressions of antiproprietary sentiment changed significantly over time, operated from several distinct geographical bases, and premised their criticism on differing visions of what Pennsylvania might become.

The idiosyncrasies of early New York and Pennsylvania politics owed much, too, to the different mix of religious and ethnic diversity that distinguished each colony. In New York, religious conflict between Catholics and Protestants, and both inter- and intradenominational rivalries among Protestants, proved their relevance by their integral relationship to Leisler's Rebellion. Similarly, in Pennsylvania, rifts within the Society of Friends developed into fault lines that eventually expressed themselves through the Keithian schism. At the same time, the respective religious configuration of each colony had ramifications beyond the Leislerian and Keithian crises.

The "churchly" orientation of Catholics, Reformed Dutch, and Anglicans in New York, an orientation that assumed a privileged relationship between one church and the state, not only fostered uncompromising attitudes among some political opponents (witness the feuds between Leislerians and anti-Leislerians), but also reinforced various efforts to strengthen a provincially centered, top-down authority structure in the colony. That in turn encouraged resistance on the part of those New Yorkers who understood the church-state relationship more in terms of local establishments than as part of a centralizing process of institutionalization. In Pennsylvania, however, the religious environment was sectarian rather than churchly. As such, the colony was bound to attract religious radicals, whose penchant for argument is well known, but whose views on church-state relations ran in an anti-institutional, laissez-faire direction, and whose politics, while susceptible to angry outbursts, ultimately had to be reconciled with a live-and-let-live principle of community organization and some commitment to liberty of conscience. In both colonies, then, religious affairs were volatile and could have important effects on political behavior, but they did so during these early decades in ways that started New York and Pennsylvania along two different, if related, paths of sociopolitical development.

As for ethnicity and religiously reinforced ethnic distinctions, they were important also—but, again, in different ways for each colony. The subjugation of New York, the continuing existence of vital New Netherlands' communities, and the relatively slow expansion of the English-speaking population, meant that both ethnic divisions *and* interethnic cooperation would be an ongoing feature of provincial society in New York. In Pennsylvania, however, because most non-English European settlers were scattered along the western bank of the Delaware, or in large numbers in the three Lower Counties, they were either swamped by incoming migrants or excluded from Pennsylvania by the creation of a separate colony at the turn of the century. The results were that very different patterns of ethnic and ethnoreligious relationships, and expressions of those relationships in public affairs, developed in the two major mid-Atlantic colonies. In New York, both inter- and intragroup conflict among representatives of different ethnic and ethnoreligious groups was commonplace in public affairs. Because of the substantial numbers of New Netherlanders, French, and British, the considerable subdivisions even among these groups, and their interspersal with enclaves of various other minorities to form a kaleidoscope of fractured ethnic identities, political conflict of any dimension always involved some degree of ethnoreligious division. But that was not the whole story. Simultaneously, representatives of different ethnic or ethnoreligious groups were learning to extend mutual recognition to one another; frequently, they continued to subsume ethnic uniqueness beneath local and regional identi-

ties; and at the many interstices among them, they developed social processes of interpenetration that mediated their differences. In Pennsylvania,
on the other hand, much of the ethnoreligious conflict of the 1680s and
1690s was encompassed within the differences between Pennsylvania and
the three Lower Counties. In Pennsylvania proper, Quakerism tended to
soften the ethnic differences among various British immigrants and a handful of Europeans. Although at times volatile, Quakerism proved to be much
more a unifying than divisive force. The heavy concentration of British
Friends in the eastern counties allowed Quakers to dominate Pennsylvania's
public forum in the early colonial years. Later on, in the eighteenth century,
when large numbers of Germans and Scotch-Irish Presbyterians began to
immigrate, the potential for ethnoreligious conflict much like what New
York had experienced in its early years increased. To some extent, that took
place. But serious segmentation was also offset, not only by the same incidence of intra-ethnoreligious group conflict and of mutual recognition and
interdependence that occurred in New York, but also by the powerful and
seductive cultural ethos of Pennsylvania Quakerism.

The differences that set New York and Pennsylvania apart during their
early years were certainly marked, and in later decades these fundamental
differences continued both to perpetuate the uniqueness of each colony *and*
to shape the various ways in which their political cultures converged. In the
light of these initial differences, the most significant harbinger of the processes of convergence was the tectonic drift of each colony's political affairs.
On one level, of course, New Yorkers were much more accepting of traditional political authority than Pennsylvanians—a circumstance that had
important implications for the future. But beneath that difference there was
a discernable common drift. During the later seventeenth century, both
colonies moved to a point at which it was possible for them to begin to
develop popular political traditions. In the case of New York, that evolution
was a protracted one. Beginning as a fiefdom of James Stuart, New York had
a long distance to travel before an elected assembly became part of the
provincial constitution under William and Mary. The direction of New
York's political evolution was also as much dependent on external forces as
on internal ones. The commitment of numerous New Netherlanders, and
particularly of English Long Island townsfolk, to some form of representative government was clear, but considerable impetus came, too, from the
examples of neighboring New England and New Jersey. And ultimately it
was the Whiggery of England's Glorious Revolution that brought elected
assemblymen to New York. Yet there was a tentative aspect to this change
even when it took place, for the continuing habits of authoritarian central-
ism and of political opportunism kept the governor's council at the center of
public affairs during many of the late seventeenth-century political contests.

In comparison with New Yorkers, Pennsylvanians guided their colony in a direction that led to popular government with much more vigor and conviction. Granted, their predilections were informed by English republicanism and the New Jersey initiative in liberal government, but Pennsylvanians quickly built up a powerful momentum of their own as they pressed William Penn for considerable provincial autonomy. Throughout the various constitutional experiments that Pennsylvanians tried, they repeatedly demonstrated their overriding interest in one feature: a representative body that could adequately protect their provincial concerns. Their handicap, of course, was that by the late seventeenth century, they were still in the process of constitutional negotiations with William Penn, and in a proprietary colony there could be no certainty of outcome. Overall, while Pennsylvania was considerably in advance of New York in shifting the focus of colonial politics toward provincial representative institutions, both colonies entered the eighteenth century well positioned to establish powerful traditions of popular government.

Chapter Two

The Proving of Popular Power

IN THE PERIOD during which the English were integrating New York into their North American empire and establishing colonial Pennsylvania, arbitrary governmental power seemed to enjoy a renaissance. In France, Louis XIV became the model of monarchical absolutism; in England, Charles II and James II seemed intent on gaining the power that James I and Charles I had hoped to consolidate; and in the New World, proprietors took control over vast new colonies.[1] Although there would appear to be some contradiction between England's overall policy of reorganizing and centralizing its colonies under royal control and that of giving away North American proprietaries, from the colonial perspective there was often little to choose between them. Both types of administration raised the specter of adventitious and perfidious power. In 1664, James Stuart promised New Yorkers the same standard of "freedomes and immunityes" New England enjoyed, and then proceeded to support a succession of autocratic administrations, to renege on promises of greater popular participation in government and to promote that well-known religion of oppression, Catholicism.[2] As for Pennsylvanians, many Quaker immigrants had felt the lash of persecution in the British Isles and, although willing to acknowledge the beneficence of William Penn's religious policies, were acutely aware of the wide sweep of proprietary privilege.

In the thick of this threatening environment, politically articulate New Yorkers and Pennsylvanians tried to check arbitrary power by drawing on the English libertarian tradition, to which all English colonies could lay some claim. The most useful and most easily understood part of that tradition was the notion of popular sovereignty. Developed in the English Civil War from much earlier roots, the ideology of popular sovereignty posited that a representative body—in the English case, Parliament—should ultimately limit monarchical behavior and retain considerable governmental power in its corporate hands.[3] In transferring this concept west across the Atlantic, colonists demonstrated the innovative cast of mind that they brought along with old-world ideologies. On the one hand, they virtually ignored the "sovereign" aspect of popular sovereignty. After all, the colonies were dependent societies and seemingly happy to be so until the last quarter of the eighteenth century. On the other, they placed a great deal of emphasis on developing elective institutions, which were viewed as the essence of "popular" government, no matter how narrow the clientele they served. That tendency began with experiments in participatory government in some of the early colonizing ventures and was reinforced by the needs of colonial officials for both information and cooperation from immigrants.[4]

By the time New York and Pennsylvania were being woven into the network of English colonies, strong traditions of representative government emanated from the West Indies, the Chesapeake, and New England.[5] And a number of circumstances conspired to encourage the establishment of popular political institutions in the mid-Atlantic colonies. Paradoxical though it may seem, a number of new-world proprietors had been influenced by English republican thought, and that intellectual predisposition, along with the practical need to attract settlers to their colonies, prompted proprietors to include a place for the peoples' representatives in their various efforts at constitution making.[6] At the same time, the very extent of proprietary power and the Stuart monarchs' efforts to disband provincial assemblies drew attention to the value of representative institutions. Once the English Whig settlement of 1691 finally brought an assembly to provincial New York, a colonial history of central autocracy, along with a sense of past deprivation derived from comparisons with the broadly based New England and New Jersey experiments with representative government, enhanced New Yorkers' appreciation of elective institutions. And in Pennsylvania, the past experiences of Friends and the social imperatives of Quakerism combined to underline the importance of a strong popular government.

Opportunistic New Yorkers

The form of New York's post-1691 government was much like that of other Crown colonies. The functional head was the governor and captain-general, a royal appointee responsible to the Crown. A royal commission granted the governor his power as the monarch's representative, while a set of instructions, subject to both modification and augmentation at any time during the governor's term, directed him on policy matters.[7] Bound by the same instructions was a lieutenant-governor, frequently appointed from among colonial notables, to serve as interim executive in case of the governor's death or personal absence. A council composed of a few prominent citizens, appointed by the Crown on the recommendation of the governor, served both as executive advisors to the governor and as an upper legislative chamber analogous to the British House of Lords. Finally, there was the popular part of government. The governor's commission required that he pass laws "with the advice & consent of the Council and Assembly."[8] The "General Assembly" of the province of New York was expected to assemble on the governor's call "according to the usage of our other Plantations in America," to vote taxes for the support of government and to ensure that the legislative needs of the colony were met.[9] The apportionment of assembly representatives varied slightly during the late seventeenth and early eighteenth centuries, but by 1726 interested parties had agreed on an acceptable formula.[10] All counties save New York would have two representatives, New York City and County would have four, and a small number of towns and manors gained entitlement to a single assembly seat.

Although the outline of New York's provincial government was fairly clear, the allocation of powers between the three component parts was not. The governor's commission and instructions conferred powers that exceeded those of the British Crown in its relationship to Parliament. The power to call assemblies, adjourn, prorogue, and dissolve them, the right to nominate and remove judges, the capacity to create and fill administrative offices, the authority to act as captain-general of provincial military forces, the choice of vetoing legislation, and the authority to grant land were designed to make the governor the cornerstone of colonial government.[11] It could be argued, as some governors did, that the council and assembly owed their existence to the governor's letters patent, that his instructions should bind those two institutions as well as the chief executive, that the governor should be sole interpreter of the instructions, and that colonial rights should consist only of "such [privileges] as the Queen is pleased to allow."[12] Although few New Yorkers agreed with this sweeping interpretation of the royal prerogative, a number of prominent provincials were prepared to honor the turn-of-the-century governors who articulated such views. The colony's recent turbulence and its tradition of administrative centralization under James Stuart predisposed numerous leading colonists to flock around the chief executive if it was politically expedient for them to do so. Tolerance of exaggerated gubernatorial claims was not a prohibitive price to pay for supporting the current sociopolitical order, for the status that attendance at the governor's entertainments conferred, and for the profitable land grants and public contracts that could come their way.

Of the two thoroughly provincial parts of government, the council and the assembly, the former was most tightly bound up with the prerogative. Because the governor could both recommend and suspend councillors, and because there were no separate social orders in the colony from which councillors were recruited, council members were usually either supportive of, or silent on, the royal prerogative. Not so for the assembly, however. No matter how much individual assemblymen might be drawn to the executive, as a body they asserted an institutional legitimacy grounded, not in the governor's letters patent, but in the inherent rights of Englishmen.[13] It was not clear to very early provincial legislators exactly what powers they should possess in the name of the people, but they certainly felt these should be more extensive than royal directives initially appeared to grant. Firsthand knowledge of New England autonomy, Dutch acquaintanceship both with Low Country republicanism and the potential efficacy of English-rights language in protecting local traditions, recollection of the popular Concessions and Agreements that East Jersey proprietors had granted to New England migrants, rumors of the very liberal 1676 West Jersey constitution, and years of experience with highly autonomous units of local government encouraged New Yorkers to believe they should have a greater say in governmental affairs.[14] Despite their parochialism, popular politicians knew enough to liken their assembly to those of other colonies and to claim an autonomous, inviolable heritage that stretched through Parliament back to Magna Charta.[15] But at the same time such ideas were often intermingled with a continuing respect for the prerogative. Elected friends of Lord Cornbury might agree with him thoroughly when he admitted that certain privileges were "the Rights of the House of Commons . . . and of . . . [New York's] Assembly," but they also recognized that the prerogative had its own continuing claims to preeminence.[16]

Given the unsettled and varied interpretations of prerogative claims and popular rights in early New York, the relationship between imperial officials and provincials was bound to have a delicate side. Yet into this situation the British introduced a pair of governors, Fletcher and Cornbury, who were extremely insensitive to New York's needs. It is not that they were uniquely imperious or particularly inept, but that they were disconcertingly venal. In addition to fees, there were three basic ways in which public revenue came into a governor's hands in turn-of-the-century New York. Two of these were related to King William's and Queen Anne's wars (1689–1697 and 1702–1713) with the French, in which the colonies understandably became involved. First, recognizing the crucial role New York played in defending their North American possessions from New France, the British stationed four companies of soldiers in the Hudson River colony after 1695, and sent money to the governor to pay for the wages, outfitting, and partial maintenance of these troops.[17] Second, the governors often demanded from the assembly what was called an extraordinary revenue—that is, money to be raised for singular military campaigns or for garrisoning costs. If the assembly heeded the governor's requests, it would lay taxes, usually on personalty and realty, apportion those taxes among the various counties, and vote the proceeds to the Crown's representative for dispersal. Finally, the assembly was expected to raise a separate category of ordinary revenue to support the regular administrative and executive expenses associated with the normal operation of government.[18]

Cumulatively, the revenue from these sources could be a sizable amount; and both Fletcher and Cornbury did their best to divert as much of it as they possibly could to their own use. Although it was customary at this time for governors, in their capacity as captains-general, to profit from military payrolls, that was little solace to provincials who expected protection from British troops but found that gubernatorial peculation left the companies undermanned, poorly equipped and ill prepared to fight.[19] Even more distressing was the governors' free hand with both extraordinary and ordinary revenues. Of the approximately £30,000 that New Yorkers raised for military purposes, large amounts were siphoned off for the governors' private purposes, while huge public debts were left unpaid.[20] Of the ordinary revenue that the assembly voted at two- to six-year intervals to cover administrative salaries and contingent expenses, some indeterminate fraction went to the appropriate purposes and the rest disappeared. Moreover, avaricious New Yorkers were ever ready to join their governors in fleecing the public. Not only did such placemen as the receiver-general, the attorney-general, the deputy auditor, and the port weighmaster profit from corruption, the provincial councillors also shared in kickbacks, inflated supply and services contracts, and the opportunity to lend money to the government at usurious interest rates.[21]

The problem with excessively corrupt administrations is twofold. First, there is never enough to satisfy all of the powerful suitors all of the time. There were always some influential individuals left out of the last round of pork-barrel politics who were ready to take the lead against those who benefited at the colony's expense. Second, taxpayers tend to get mad. The soft hands of the governors might initially divert attention from their calloused souls, but not for long. Before Fletcher's tenure had run many months, and shortly after Cornbury began his administration, community members began to protest against their maladministration. But public scrutiny soon moved beyond the governors to focus on the realization that the assembly's obligation to the community involved more than simply voting money for the exigencies of government. It required oversight of those funds to ensure they were spent for their intended purposes.

The major problem assemblymen faced was how to accomplish this objective. In the case of the extraordinary grants for defense, the assembly tried two tactics: it pressed the governors for leave to audit their accounts, and it wrote increasingly detailed appropriations into tax bills. The first initiative was bogged down in a quagmire of executive noncooperation. The second failed because there was no means of forcing compliance. The receiver-general, who held the tax money, was a royal appointee under no obligation to compare the terms of any act of appropriation with the warrants for payment that the governor signed and sent to him. The receiver-general's sole responsibility was to pay out whatever amounts the governor, on the advice of council, demanded. By 1704, exasperated assemblymen turned to more direct action. They would only vote extraordinary taxes if the revenue went into the hands of a newly created assembly-appointed official, the provincial treasurer. Because the treasurer was the assembly's appointee, he would make sure governors' warrants complied with the intent of the appropriating act. In quiet acknowledgment of its governors' perfidy, Whitehall agreed to this innovation, and by 1706 the new system was in place.[22]

The one major part of the colonial revenue that was still outside the assembly's reach in 1706 was the ordinary revenue. When Governor Sloughter arrived in New York in 1691, the first of many such royal representatives to be armed with instructions demanding a permanent revenue to support ongoing administrative and executive expenses, New York's assemblymen refused to follow the precedents of Virginia, Barbados, and the Leeward Islands.[23] Distrustful of any taxation measures that might contribute to autocracy, the most the first assembly would offer was to authorize an excise and tariff revenue for two years.[24] But in 1702, an anxious group of anti-Leislerians found some relief in trading a revenue extension, to run through May 1709, for Cornbury's goodwill and his approval of legislation repealing the Vacating Act of 1699.[25] The Revenue Act provided a governmental income from import and export duties that was completely under the control of the receiver-general, the governor, and his closest advisors. In addition to the financial autonomy it bestowed on Cornbury's administration, it legitimized a customs system that the governor's officials could brazenly use to extort money from both overseas and coastal shippers.[26] As one Long

Island critique described it, the customs offices were so filled with "subtil Fellows to inspect into every nice Point in the Law," that no one could safely take a vessel into New York harbor "except he were a Lawyer."[27] Angered by Cornbury's continued mishandling of the revenue monies, and adamant that the customs racketeering should come to an end, by 1707 the governor's opponents were blackening his name with rumors of transvestitism and asserting that the assemblymen had determined never to vote a future revenue that was not minutely appropriated, administered by the provincial treasurer, and renewable only "from year to year."[28]

These turn-of-the-century conflicts between elected politicians and their governors, and the factional fights that accompanied them, were particularly important in shaping New Yorkers' attitudes toward their provincial political institutions. Local experiences with Fletcher and Cornbury demonstrated very clearly that many governors were not to be relied on. They arrived in New York puffed up with their extravagant prerogative claims, symbolic proximity to royalty, and unbridled greed.[29] The most common way colonials responded to the threatening stance of these outsiders was to try to puncture their pretensions by neutralizing some of their prerogative privileges. The one body that was capable of doing so was the assembly. With its ability to draw strength from the House of Commons analogy, and, when that failed or was inappropriate, from the argument that local legislative innovation was justifiable in defense of English rights, the assembly was well equipped to claim a sizable area of political competence for provincials to control.[30]

The various sociopolitical conflicts that New Yorkers experienced reinforced this tendency. Divisions between regional, economic, ethnic, and religious groups, between the Leislerians and anti-Leislerians, and, in the upper reaches of society, between those who at any one time preferred greater popular control of tax revenues and those who supported greater gubernatorial autonomy, encouraged the development of a provincial self-consciousness among the colony's prominent and well-connected residents.[31] But at the same time, two decades of factional conflict revolving around the personalities and preferences of successive provincial governors failed to provide the kind of security many established New Yorkers craved. Life and property remained in jeopardy as long as different groups of local antagonists were determined to wreak vengeance on their opponents the moment they gained the governor's ear. Tired and scared, New Yorkers at last acknowledged that no one group could count on enlisting the support of a succession of capricious governors. Their best option, then, was to limit the cost of internecine squabbling. This they could do by building popular power at the governors' expense and then staging their battles in the less deadly arenas of assembly management and electoral politics. Self-protection was a very early and very powerful motivating force behind the New York Assembly's encroachment on prerogative claims.

Crown land policy is one notable illustration of how self-interest brought provincials together to promote assembly power. In principle, New York landholders were to pay quitrents to the Crown, but few in fact did. Exemptions on old Dutch patents and a succession of large land grants at nominal rates meant that huge areas within the colony produced no quitrent income.[32] In 1708, the Privy Council issued new instructions pertaining to land to Governor Lovelace. Henceforth a quitrent of two shillings and sixpence was to be paid on all newly patented lands, and no individual was to receive more than 2,000 acres in a single grant.[33] Accompanying the instructions was news of a royal veto of the 1702 New York statute that had repealed the 1699 Vacating Act.[34] The royal veto, upholding the Leislerian legislation voiding a number of Governor Fletcher's land grants, sent a nervous shudder through many of New York's large landowners. The reason for the annulment of the patents was that they had been extravagant and paid only nominal quitrents. On such grounds, any number of New York patents would be eligible for similar treatment.

The fact that the greatest threat to existing land titles arose from an act of their own provincial assembly was not lost on New York's political leaders. Rather than try to use the assembly's power to get at each other, they needed to turn it into a bulwark against whatever new threats the Crown might pose. If like-minded locals refused to pass further legislation revoking old patents or calling for strict new surveys of old deeds, they could frustrate any royal attempt to meddle with what locals regarded as their property. The only realistic option Whitehall would have left would be an act of Parliament, which was unlikely, given the reluctance of the British upper classes to call property rights into question. The land issue was also useful to those popular politicians who wanted to generate public support for aggressive assembly actions. Although tensions always existed between large landholders who sat in the assembly and their smaller neighbors who voted for them, it is also true that the questioning of old deeds and the promise of more effective quitrent collection frightened little men as well as big. Many small landholdings had been carved out of large patents, and doubts about the validity of the latter always threatened the integrity of the former.[35] By suggesting that its ministers might alter or enquire into the terms of colonial property rights, the Crown made it easier for local political leaders to claim to speak for a popular antiprerogative consensus that urged a further expansion of assembly power.

New York's early political experiences and the patterns of popular political thought to which they gave rise had the cumulative effect of prompting assemblymen to push their institutional powers with considerable intensity. Drawing on the confidence legislators gained from the frequent meetings that wartime demands necessitated, and building on such powers as the right to specify the qualifications of provincial voters, to determine the conditions under which elections would be held, and to regulate its own membership, the New York General Assembly acted purposefully to augment its role in government.[36] By withholding the salaries and expenses of the assembly clerk and public printer, the provincial representatives made the point that no matter the formers' appointment by the governor, their livelihood depended on loyalty to the assembly.[37] In cooperation with the speaker of the assembly, these two officials took a hand in shaping the political news that traveled to the council chamber and to the province at large. The speaker of the assembly was, of course, a crucial figure; in that position the lawyers William Nicoll and James Graham drew heavily on the analogy between their assembly and the House of Commons.[38] In addition to claiming consistently all the rights and privileges of English legislators, the speakers fostered the development of a strong committee system, which in turn distributed responsibility for protecting parliamentary privileges among assemblymen, built up legislative experience among New Yorkers, and strengthened the institutional basis of representative government.[39]

In their quest for greater institutional power, the assemblymen deliberately struck at the other two branches of government. The council, overweight and content with its status, was an easy opponent. The assembly representatives quickly knocked that body out of serious contention by steadfastly denying it the right to amend money bills.[40] The royal prerogative, however, was a far tougher opponent. The assembly first tried to bruise the chief executive with a flurry of blows, increasing the number of representatives in the legislature, publishing their own schedule of fees for various administrative and legal procedures, and using their power over military appropriations to dictate tactical decisions that had once lain with the governor.[41] When Whitehall disallowed the legislation augmenting assembly representation and setting fees, the assembly pressed on in other areas of executive power where it had enjoyed some past success. During preparations for the 1709 attack against New France, the assembly appointed commissioners to organize the campaign and administer the money the legislature voted for the war effort.[42] This extreme form of encroachment on the prerogative rarely occurred in other colonies before the mid eighteenth century.[43]

Following Lord Cornbury's departure from New York, the assembly continued to press against the prerogative. Its members expanded their list of legislative patronage, tried to replace appointed officials with elected ones, attempted to hand what limited revenues they did raise to the provincial treasurer, fostered local government in manor lands and newly settled townships, and ardently defended its dismissal of the council's claim to amend money bills.[44] When Governor Robert Hunter reasserted the prerogative right to set provincial fees by executive ordinance and reestablished a chancery court that dispensed equity law under the governor's personal direction, the assembly protested loudly, arguing that all fees and courts should be authorized by statute only.[45] In addition, New York legislators tried to establish precedents to adjourn the assembly over extended periods, framed a bill to establish a colonial agent in London answerable only to themselves (rather than to both legislature and executive), and tried to intrude on the governor's unlimited discretion in appointing sheriffs.[46] All of these demands, however, were secondary. The assemblymen's main goal was to force Hunter to accept annual revenue bills minutely detailing appropriations and placing the monies the assembly raised in the hands of the assembly-appointed provincial treasurer rather than in the grasp of the receiver-general.[47] After jousting with the legislature for some time, a flagging Hunter wrote Whitehall that to his mind "ye Assemblye . . . claim[ed] . . . all ye privileges of a House of Commons and stretch[ed] . . . them even beyond what they were ever imagined to be . . . [in Britain]. . . . They will be a Parliament."[48]

Initially, Hunter had as much difficulty as later commentators in trying to understand the intensity of assembly intransigence over the revenue. To outsiders, the issue appeared simple: governors had a compelling interest in gaining a perpetual revenue, assemblies in keeping their executives on as short a leash as possible. What complicated the conflict in New York, however, was that in the minds of many provincials a revenue was synonymous with customs duties. This occurred because for over twenty years legislators had funded the ordinary revenue on imposts. The specter of a long-term revenue thus conjured up memories, not only of uncontrolled executive spending, but also of numerous instances of customs corruption, which many believed to have seriously weakened New York's commercial economy.[49] Moreover, a number of New York City merchants who "tho't it their interest" to avoid such taxes, used their "Arts" to strengthen the association of imposts with the revenue and thereby to discourage debate on the two as separate issues.[50] By 1713, however, Hunter had discerned the problem, and he addressed it in an election screed, pointing out that a revenue need not be funded by duties on trade goods. He would be quite willing to accept a revenue based on a land tax—that is, a tax on real and personal property— despite his personal opinion that taxes on commerce were less injurious to the middling and poorer people.[51] Hunter's appeal was politically astute, because even representatives of rural constituencies in some cases preferred a land tax to the possibility of resumed racketeering under a renewed customs system.[52]

During this period of intense political conflict, antipathy to the royal prerogative became as strong as it ever would in New York prior to the Revolutionary crisis. Even before Cornbury's colonial fling, Fletcher had Westchester freeholders muttering that "if the Kinge of England had don as Ill . . . as our Governor . . . . They would have shortened him by the head."[53] By 1714, the infection was of epidemic proportions. So soured were New Yorkers that when Governor Hunter proclaimed George I's succession to the throne, he met with "some awkward half huzza's . . . but few."[54] Such thoroughgoing alienation was not, however, a comfortable state for most members of New York's political elite. The attractions that had drawn provincials to serve and connive with early governors—status, cupidity, power, and some sense of noblesse oblige—tugged at their sleeves. New York's popular politicians had staked out claims to a huge area of legislative activity, within which they might exercise power if they could but consolidate their position, compose their differences with the governor, and integrate their new roles into the web of patronage, place, and influence that centered on the province's chief executive. Motivated by these large considerations, as well as by the fear of disorder that the 1712 New York City slave rebellion had awakened,[55] apprehensive of unfavorable British intervention in their revenue dispute with the governor, and newly appreciative of Governor Hunter's ability to placate British politicians of both Whig and Tory persuasions, many assemblymen began to look among themselves for guides who might lead them through the deadfall of past factional storms to reach an accommodation with the executive.

Hunter, too, was interested in some kind of rapprochement. Early in his administration, he had convinced New Yorkers that he was "a Man as tenacious of Power" as any.[56] He unequivocally asserted his unilateral right to establish a chancery court and to publish a provincial fee schedule. And once he began to see how intransigent many legislators were on the question of a permanent revenue, the new governor tried to find a way to outflank his adversaries. He urged Whitehall to apply the new quitrent schedule announced under Governor Lovelace retroactively to old land grants, and in the meantime, he hauled a number of quitrent delinquents before his court of chancery to force them to pay up.[57] Under current conditions, efficient quitrent collection would bring in a few hundred pounds per annum, but if all provincial landowners were required to pay two shillings and sixpence per 100 acres annually, the yearly revenue would potentially total thousands of pounds.[58] Such a levy would not only provide a good income for the executive, it would also tend to break up the large land grants in the province, because the owners would be unable to afford the quitrent payments. That, in turn, would facilitate the development of New York and ultimately provide a broader economic base for the support of the provincial government. But by 1714, the British attorney-general had advised that the new schedule of quitrents could not be applied to New York's pre-1708 land grants.[59] That decision dashed whatever hope Hunter had nourished of gaining an independent income for himself and other Crown officers, save in the very unlikely circumstance that Parliament, itself, would provide a revenue for New York governors.[60]

Rather than give up in disgust at this juncture, Hunter proved that "he knew well how to use . . . [the 'power' he did have] as most Men."[61] By skillfully employing patronage, his pen, the pleasing side of his personality, and a streak of pragmatic ruthlessness, Hunter worked to build a following among New York's various interest groups and put together a coterie of prominent provincials who were willing to take the lead in supporting his administration.[62] Led by Lewis Morris, an assemblyman (soon to be both assemblyman and chief justice), and Robert Livingston, a manor lord (soon to be assemblyman in a Hunter-created manorial seat), those political leaders who favored consolidating assembly power through conciliation took control of the assembly. Four provincial acts passed between 1714 and 1717, and a small number of informal understandings between Governor Hunter and the province's leading legislators, formed the basis for legislative-executive accommodation.[63] Two of the relevant provincial statutes, known as Public Debt Acts, provided for the payment of all unsatisfied claims against the government running from the current administration back over twenty-five years through the Leislerian regime. While many of the debts were small-scale, service-related obligations arising from New York's various military enterprises, others were sizable ones that the politically prominent traced back to the days of Leislerian/anti-Leislerian battles.[64] The latter category remained as an irritating reminder of old injustices and of competing claims to legitimacy. By the second decade of the eighteenth century, however, there was enough support from a new generation of politicians and a handful of the old, who were finally willing to profit from the past, if not forget it, to induce most diehard members of the old factions and their heirs to acknowledge each other indirectly by paying these old obligations. Having cleared up the problems left over from the misappropriations of past revenues, the assembly and governor were prepared to deal on the issue of a new revenue law. In return for his signing a sweeping Naturalization Act that granted citizenship to virtually all foreigners residing in New York, Hunter obtained a five-year revenue act.[65] The money generated by its imposts was to be lodged in the hands of the provincial treasurer, not the receiver-general, however, and although the treasurer was to acknowledge Hunter's warrants on the advice of council, the governor had promised to issue these warrants for precisely the amounts the assembly resolved upon as payment for government services.[66] What underlay the agreement was a joint executive-legislative accord on the amounts Crown officers should receive, and an understanding that any future change in the salary schedule of government officers was to take place only after consultation between governor and assembly.[67] Other informal aspects of the settlement were that assemblymen should have considerable input into patronage decisions on justice of the peace and militia appointments in their counties, and that Hunter would cease his efforts to have the British apply the new quitrent schedules to old patents.[68] The assemblymen wanted Crown officials to be low-paid and dependent upon the goodwill of the province's legislators for their income, and Hunter was prepared to agree to that.[69] With the revenue question out of the way and related issues resolved, Hunter and his legislators quickly developed the most amicable relationship that New Yorkers had ever experienced in their provincial government.

Popular criticism of the assembly settlement with Hunter was sparse, and for good reason.[70] Between 1705 and 1715, New York's provincial politicians had gained control of virtually all of the colony's public finances and had turned the General Assembly into a powerful advocate of popular privileges. That contemporaries perceived the conflict between Cornbury and the assembly to be of epic dimensions is clear from the way in which it entered New York's political mythology. In 1765, for example, Peter R. Livingston tried to set in perspective New Yorkers' "most Noble Resolves" against the Stamp Act.[71] He did so by celebrating them as the best "since Lord Cornbury's time," when the General Assembly had outspokenly voiced its determination to protect the populace from prerogative-bred predation.[72] And if Robert Hunter was subsequently perceived to have been one of New York's better governors (despite his willingness to use tax money to buy off anyone of consequence in the Public Debt Acts), it was in no small measure owing to the considerable powers he yielded up to the assembly in order to achieve political accord. Secure in the power base that the Hunter settlement acknowledged to be theirs, New York's provincial politicians recognized how much easier it would henceforth be to guard their perimeters and to strike out on punishing forays against prerogative privileges should occasion arise. With power came the confidence necessary to establish the assembly as the dominant political force in the province. During the fifteen years in which the Hunter settlement structured provincial politics, the bulk of politically conscious New Yorkers came to believe that what made them "in Reality a *free People*" was the power they had through their representatives to be the "Divisors of" their own "Excellent Lawes." Only when the assembly held the upper hand could New Yorkers enjoy the "freedom" on which "Happiness . . . depends."[73]

What undermined the Hunter settlement, after fifteen years of relative peace between executive and legislature, was a bitter factional battle between a vocal band of critics, the best known of whom were Lewis Morris, Sr., and James Alexander, and a determined group of elected and appointed officials who supported Governor William Cosby.[74] The political circumstances of this falling-out went back into the 1720s. In the assembly election of 1726, some of the old gang of Hunter supporters had failed to be returned because of popular dissatisfaction with their friendliness toward Hunter's successor, Governor Burnet. Their assembly replacements, led by Speaker of the House Adolphe Philipse, quietly cozied up to Governors John Montgomerie and William Cosby. Stung by this turn, and by Cosby's subsequent dismissal of Lewis Morris, Sr., as chief justice, a group of Morris's friends attacked the Cosby coterie as tyrannical, capricious, and corrupt—charges that led to the well-known Zenger trial on freedom of the press.[75]

One of the reasons why the public brawls of the mid 1730s were so intense was that they touched a very sensitive nerve in the New York body politic—land titles.[76] The province was a patchwork of large patents, bearing nominal quitrents, that had never been adequately surveyed, and many landowners avoided registering their deeds.[77] One important consequence of this was that those who did owe quitrents would rather "stand a . . . suit" than pay up.[78] They felt their intransigence was justified because so many others were either exempt or kept their titles hidden.[79] At the same time, various New York officials saw provincial land as a potential source of income. Individuals such as Surveyor-General Cadwallader Colden and Receiver-General Archibald Kennedy tried to encourage the efficient collection of quitrents in hopes of sharing in the proceeds.[80] But the real threat was the governor. Governor Burnet had loved to sit in chancery flexing his prerogative muscle, and quitrent income noticeably increased as a result.[81] Governor Cosby was even more menacing. His interest appeared to be less in seizing on quitrent delinquents than in using the chancery court to void uncertain patents.[82] Such rulings would allow him to regrant the land, providing fees for his purse as well as the opportunity to extort a substantial share of the new land grant from the petitioners.[83] Under these circumstances, the chancery court and provincial land policy became explosive political issues, contributing significantly to the political conflict that wracked New York in the early to mid 1730s.

Although Adolphe Philipse, the pro-Cosby Speaker of the House, kept the assembly pretty well out of the specific wrangles between Governor Cosby and the Morris/Alexander faction that led to the Zenger case in 1735, the latter group did include the legislature in its attack on the Cosby administration. They claimed that Cosby's corruption had infected both placemen and assemblymen, and that the only way to counter that influence was to replace the old assembly representatives. The main reason why the New York Assembly had become lethargic, its critics asserted, was that along with his power of prorogation and dissolution, the governor had the option of prolonging an assembly's life as long as he wished. Between 1716 and 1737, New York had two ten-year assemblies; and the Morris/Alexander faction used its intimate acquaintance with the behavior of the first of these to argue that members of the second had been bought off by their high per diem compensation, their influence over militia and judicial appointments, and their ego-stroking association with the high officers of government. The way to cleanse the House of Representatives, then, was to require annual, or at least triennial elections, and vote by ballot. Once that had been accomplished, the representatives could exercise closer supervision over appointive offices by restricting revenue appropriations to yearly grants.[84] The momentum that this clamor for reform generated was considerable, and it carried over into the administration of Cosby's successor, Lieutenant-Governor George Clarke.

For his part, Clarke hoped to restore some political peace to the province. An extremely successful land jobber in his own right, Clarke had no intention of either vigorously collecting quitrents or threatening existing land patents with legal reinterpretation or expropriation.[85] Nor did he have any particular interest in parading prerogative powers in chancery. Politically, he was prepared to use both carrot and stick to achieve his objective of a five-year revenue act. He tried to signal conciliatory intentions by signing a Triennial Act in 1737 (how convincing that action was is unclear, for Clarke undoubtedly expected the Privy Council to disallow the act), but then he reached for a shillelagh.[86] The governor would only put his signature on an excise-continuation bill necessary to prevent New York's outstanding paper currency from plunging in value if, in return, the assembly would provide long-term government revenue.[87] Before the lieutenant-governor's resolve could be tested, however, the British went to war with Spain. Needing legislative cooperation in order to raise wartime funds, Clarke dropped his demands and began to sign yearly appropriation bills that marked a new milestone in assembly power. The annual appropriations listed government officers by name in addition to position, forcing the lieutenant-governor to come to the legislature to approve any replacement.[88] Whitehall's response to these innovations was predictable. The Privy Council disallowed the Triennial Act (although it did accept a Septennial Act in 1743), and when Governor George Clinton left England to take over from Clarke in 1743, he brought renewed royal instructions to insist on a permanent revenue.[89]

By the 1740s, provincial politicians in New York were becoming more adept at dealing with governors who were either malleable or stubbornly confrontational. Clinton, however, proved to be both. Initially, Chief Justice and Councillor James DeLancey found the new governor receptive to DeLancey's pragmatic advice: view the small loss of power involved in the shift from the Hunter settlement to annual appropriations as an acceptable price for peace. Clinton acquiesced, until the outbreak of the French phase of King George's War in 1744 pulled him from his pool table. As befit a career naval officer, Clinton adopted a vigorous military policy that promoted the invasion and reduction of Canada. In doing so, he broke with the popular faction of councillors and assemblymen led by James DeLancey and David Jones and took as his principal advisor the most disliked public official in colonial New York, Surveyor-General and Councillor Cadwallader Colden.[90]

The DeLancey/Jones coalition that controlled the council and assembly during the late 1740s was composed of a group of Albany and New York City delegates who preferred trade to hostilities with New France and a number of Long Island and Hudson Valley representatives who did not want an expensive war that their constituents would have to finance. They were also very suspicious of the motives behind Clinton's martial ardor. They knew that the governor was disappointed with the income his office provided, and that the quickest way for Clinton to add profit to his post was through control and exploitation of a large military budget.[91] Determined to prevent this and to stop the place- and power-hungry Colden from entrenching himself more deeply in the provincial administration, the assembly, advised and assisted by a small group of councillors, went on the offensive. It appointed its own commissioners and paymasters to handle military appropriations; it decided what was needed in the way of fortifications, and its appointees handled the building contracts; it intruded on the governor's management of Indian affairs; it pushed Clinton into signing the legislation it wanted by keeping the annual revenue bill back until he had acquiesced; and it continued the practice of passing annual salary bills and of voting compensation to specific officials rather than to the offices.[92] Knowing Whitehall would condemn these practices, it appointed an agent solely responsible to the assembly through its speaker, David Jones.[93] By 1749, Clinton was complaining that "the Assembly have made such Encroachments on his Majesty's Prerogative by their having the power of the purse that they in effect assume the whole executive powers into their own hands."[94]

Clinton's lament is not to be taken literally, but it is true that during his tenure popular forces seemed to overwhelm the prerogative. Goaded by the governor's insistence that the Crown's representative could "put Bonds &

Limitations upon your Rights & Priviledges, and alter them at Pleasure," the assembly went as far as it ever would to enlarge its effective power.[95] Among the judiciary, supreme court judges pressed for, and secured, appointments for "good behavior" that made them immune to threats of removal. So strong was provincial prejudice against military expressions of gubernatorial authority that New Yorkers denied the chief executive a unilateral right to order militia mobilization. If there was no act of assembly conferring such power, "the people . . . [believed they might] obey or not as they please[d]."[96] And finally there were negotiations with Amerindians to consider. Since the late seventeenth century, a Board of Indian Commissioners had handled relations between the New York and the Iroquois Confederacy. Although all members of this board, with the exception of the secretary, were gubernatorial appointments, the commissioners, who were from the Albany area, were far more sensitive to local opinion than to executive demands.[97] Opposed by assemblymen, councillors, judges, and Indian commissioners, Clinton felt beleaguered, and the prerogative seemed to be pared to the bone.

Governor Clinton was not one to suffer in silence. He spent long hours formulating, composing, and recomposing his complaints.[98] Eventually, the Board of Trade responded to his incessant laments with an inquiry into New York affairs. As a result of this investigation, the Privy Council sent a new governor, Sir Danvers Osborne, to the colony with very strict formal instructions. They expressed the Crown's deep displeasure with New Yorkers, ordered the assembly to retreat from its encroachment on the prerogative, demanded a permanent revenue, required that the appropriation of provincial monies be by executive warrant "and no other wise," and conferred on the Crown's deputy the right to suspend any royal appointee who showed evidence of collusion in restricting executive privilege.[99] Having arrived in New York and recognized in the shocked faces of his councillors the impossibility of fulfilling his mandate, the emotionally unstable Osborne promptly hanged himself.[100]

With Osborne's suicide in 1754, less than forty-eight hours after he assumed office, responsibility for governing New York devolved on Lieutenant-Governor James DeLancey, and until DeLancey's own death in 1760, the administration of the province was largely in his hands.[101] Although the problem of reconciling British prerogative demands with popular provincial prejudices was immense, DeLancey was extraordinarily capable; with the help of his political partner, Speaker of the Assembly David Jones, he fashioned a political settlement as far-ranging and stable as Robert Hunter's had been decades earlier.

The most important precondition of any political agreement is a willingness to compromise, and DeLancey quickly convinced Whitehall of the wisdom of doing just that. Governmental paralysis was not something the British wanted on the eve of war with France. By 1755, the Privy Council refrained from further censure of the New York government and allowed the executive to accept temporary revenue grants in situations of great "exigency or EMERGENCY."[102] In cases in which "a good understanding between the governor and the assembly" was essential, the British would accept yearly revenue laws even if they were tightly appropriated.[103] What Whitehall demanded of the assembly was that it should honor the governor's warrant and cease appropriations by name of royal appointee rather than by office.

The assembly's leaders found it relatively easy to back down from the pugnacity they had directed at Clinton. They allowed themselves one last blast, defending their past actions and maligning their former governor. Thereafter the DeLancey/Jones coalition spoke in restrained tones. They would not yield to British demands for a permanent revenue, because it would "unhinge . . . their interior system of government."[104] DeLancey could successfully urge this type of moderate, rational approach because he was a trusted native of the province, closely associated with the assertion of assembly power during the past decade. His closest allies and advisors were popular politicians, he championed the independence of the courts, and he fully understood the importance of keeping provincial officers on a low salary and tight leash if New Yorkers were to exercise the kind of control over their provincial affairs to which they felt entitled.[105] Under DeLancey's stewardship, the assembly was willing to swallow the British demand that some small discretionary financial power should remain in the governor's hands.

Although the executive-legislative agreement over the power of the purse was an essential feature of the DeLancey settlement, the compromise had other important features, including efforts by contemporaries to address some of the colony's land-related problems. Many of the province's early land patents had been issued to several owners in joint tenancy. The reason for this was twofold: the inclusion of influential individuals in applications for land increased the likelihood that a governor would grant approval; and petitioners preferred to share the often-extreme administrative and legal costs of soliciting and defending a patent.[106] As time passed and joint tenancies passed on to various heirs, ownership of these tracts became increasingly complicated; individuals who owned a share could neither alienate nor improve the land until they had split up the original grant. While they could accomplish this objective by writ of partition, that legal process was expensive, complicated, and time-consuming. Knowing this, the assembly had passed an Act of Partition in 1708 that established an easy method by which a minority of owners, resident in the colony, might swiftly achieve their objective.[107] But the problem with that act, from the point of view of the officials concerned with quitrent income, was that partitioning would validate both property and quitrent exemption claims that were doubtful under any careful enquiry into the circumstances and extent of the original patent. Once a partition had taken place, and land had been rented or sold to numerous farmers, it would be virtually impossible for the Crown to obtain what might still be reclaimed under an original grant. Surveyor-General Cadwallader Colden led the charge against partitioning acts, and by 1720, the Crown began repealing any such statutes the assembly passed.[108]

Landowners' concerns about the difficulties of partitioning their lands subsequently merged with other fears they shared about retroactive quitrents, the potential use of the chancery court to vacate land titles, and the possibility of direct British interference in matters of provincial land policy. The extent to which New York's big landowners wanted a partition act became obvious in the early 1740s, when the assembly offered to legislate some order into quitrent collection (probably in response to haphazard prosecutions by the attorney-general), in return for a simple partitioning procedure.[109] Recognizing that the quitrent collection procedures that the New York legislature outlined, might, in fact, create more, rather than fewer, legal loopholes through which quitrent delinquents might escape, and determined to protect the prerogative in such areas, Whitehall repealed the legislation.[110] The whole cluster of land problems touching on partitioning, quitrent payments and the chancery court thus continued to simmer quietly, if uneasily, into the midcentury years.

Once the lieutenant-governorship of New York passed to James DeLancey, however, circumstances quickly changed. DeLancey immediately made overtures to Surveyor-General Cadwallader Colden and somehow silenced the most vocal New York critic of a partitioning act.[111] By mid 1755, the assembly had passed such legislation; with DeLancey's support and no outspoken New York opposition, the British accepted the new statute.[112] When, in one of his few demanding moments, Governor Charles Hardy suggested the New York Assembly might vacate three old land patents, DeLancey faded into the background and let his creole confidants sink the initiative.[113] What many leading New Yorkers quickly recognized was that DeLancey continued to be one of their own, no matter his royal commission. Although personally more involved in New York City real estate than in speculating in outlying lands, James DeLancey was well aware that his politically indispensable brother, Oliver, was one of the most important land jobbers in New York. And the future well-being of many other DeLancey friends, relatives, and political supporters was tied to the status quo. The lieutenant-governor made it clear that he had no intention of using his chancery court powers either to pursue quitrent evaders or to threaten old land titles. Heaving a collective sigh of relief, New York landowners relaxed somewhat. On the one hand, they continued their quiet resistance to the tax gatherer; on the other, they resorted to the chancery court as never before. In friendly hands, the court was no longer perceived as a danger, and it quickly became a very important dispenser of equity in the face of the peculiarities of colonial society and the rigidities of the common law.[114]

Like the earlier Hunter agreement, the DeLancey settlement was an important achievement, given the intermittent bickering that had divided legislature and executive for two decades. Yet political conflict during these years was never quite as vituperative as it had been during the 1690s and early 1700s. Although acrimony divided contending factions, all celebrated the British connection, shared a common approach to imperial politics, and measured their success in much the same terms. Once James DeLancey headed the government, he personified the belief that a colony with a powerful assembly and a reduced prerogative, led by a competent creole elite, could be consistent with a strong British connection. His settlement, of course, institutionalized that belief, and it became the prevailing orthodoxy in New York politics until well into the Revolutionary crisis.

In functional terms, too, the settlement created a solid foundation on which legislative/executive relationships would rest for some time. The assembly gave up little of its practical control over the purse in the 1750s concessions.[115] During the French and Indian War, it relinquished to the governor and the British military some of the supervisory roles over extraordinary wartime appropriations that it had earlier exercised. Later, in the 1760s, the Crown refused to continue commissioning supreme court judges on good behavior, preferring to reassert the privilege of appointing judges at royal pleasure. And under Lieutenant-Governor Cadwallader Colden's indelicate hand, the security of land titles and of trial by jury seemed to be threatened.[116] But none of these changes or challenges significantly reduced the assembly's dominance in colonial politics.[117] The DeLancey settlement had made explicit and unshakeable (short of revolutionary parliamentary intervention) what the Hunter agreement had made possible—provincials' control of provincial politics.

Aggressive Pennsylvanians

When William Penn heard that Parliament might repossess for the Crown the proprietary powers of government Charles II had granted him, he knew that this was no hollow threat. It is one measure of the man that his thoughts immediately turned to the protection of his colonists. Royal governors would be unlikely to look favorably on a whole range of Quaker-influenced laws and constitutional guarantees. "Think, therefore . . . of some suitable expedient and Provision for your safety, as well in your Privileges as Property, and you will find me ready to Comply," the colonists heard Penn say. "Review again your Laws, propose new ones that may better your Circumstances and . . . do it quickly."[118] This was such surprisingly sweet music that popular political leaders froze for a moment, perhaps doubting their ears. Recovering quickly, however, they drafted a new constitution, entitled the Charter of Privileges, which Penn hastily, and with some reservations, signed on October 28, 1701, a few days before his departure for England.

The Charter of Privileges, which was to survive through 1776, was a remarkably innovative document. By increasing the number of elected officers in the provincial government and concentrating power in a House of Representatives, it gave unprecedented structural recognition to Pennsylvanians' sustained quest for greater provincial autonomy. Henceforth, laws were to be passed by a governor, in concurrence with a unicameral legislature. The assembly possessed an array of powers that included control over all its officers, the right to "be Judges of the Qualifications and Elections of their own members," power "to sitt upon their own adjournments, appoint Committees, prepare bills in or to pass into Laws, [and] Impeach Criminals and Redress Grievances." Beyond that they were to "have all other powers and Privileges of an Assembly, according to the Rights of the free born subjects of England, and as . . . [was] usual in any of the King's Plantacons in America." The charter gave no legislative role whatsoever to the provincial council; laws were to be passed "by the Governor with the Consent and approbation of the freemen in General Asembly mett." No governor could prevent the assembly from meeting at least once a year, because the charter provided for annual elections on October 1, with the new assembly to convene each October 14. The county sheriffs would supervise elections, and to ensure a minimum of executive-inspired electoral manipulation, the charter required that the sheriffs themselves face the electorate every three years. This provision and the election of county coroners sharply departed from the practice in other colonies, as well as in Pennsylvania at the time, of including such offices in the governor's patronage bag.[119] In placing such considerable powers in the hands of the people and the assembly, the 1701 charter reflected the major trend of political development in Pennsylvania during the previous two decades.[120]

Two other major initiatives were part of the 1701 reforms. One was a new Philadelphia charter that reorganized the corporate structure of the city; the other was a judicature act that reorganized the colonial courts.[121] Both measures shared a common purpose with the Charter of Privileges, to insulate Pennsylvanians from capricious executive and proprietary acts, the former by expanding the city's autonomy, the latter by attempting to locate as much judicial power as possible in the colony's regular provincial courts. The Judicature Act was as iconoclastic as the Charter of Privileges, for it took traditional equity jurisdiction, normally administered in juryless prerogative courts established by governors, and gave it to the common law county courts, with appeals in all cases to go, not to the governor-in-council, but to an autonomous supreme court. Penn or his deputy still possessed the right to appoint judges, issue a number of writs, and generally oversee the administration of justice, but the executive could have no direct input into actual court decisions.[122] This legislation made possible what the 6th article of the Charter of Privileges promised, that "no person . . . [should] be obliged to answer any Complaint, matter or thing whatsoever Relating to Property before the Governor and Council, or in any other place but in the ordinary Courts of Justice, unless appeals thereto" were allowed by law.[123]

Although the Charter of Privileges and the Judicature Act gave considerable power and protection to Pennsylvanians, leading provincial politicians thought these changes had not gone far enough. The province's future seemed to involve either a continuing proprietary overlordship or expropriation by the Crown. In the former case, provincials would have to contend with the self-interested demands of self-centered proprietors; in the latter, with the close scrutiny of an unsympathetic royal governor. In either case, locals felt they needed to expand their political power in order to protect their society's provincial concerns.

In the ensuing campaign to achieve that end, Pennsylvanians were led by David Lloyd, a contentious Welshman who had been in the forefront of the opposition to proprietary and royal authority for over a decade. Originally recruited as Penn's attorney-general, Lloyd had teamed up with his kinsman Thomas Lloyd, former president of the council, to oppose Governor John Blackwell during the late 1680s. During the succeeding decade, David Lloyd served as chief prosecutor in the court hearings against George Keith, conspired with other prominent Pennsylvanians to try to protect their political power by adopting Markham's Frame of Government, and defied the royal authority of both Governor Fletcher and Whitehall-appointed customs and admiralty officials. During the brief period of Penn's second Pennsylvania sojourn, Lloyd was prominent among the provincial notables who wanted to seize the opportunity to remedy local grievances and consolidate their power. A rare individual, whose mind was liberated rather than shackled by an exceptional command of the law and English constitutional history, Lloyd was up to the challenge. The new constitution, the Philadelphia municipal charter, a reorganization of the colony's courts and a document designed to protect Pennsylvanians' property rights—all owed either their drafting or inspiration to the Welsh Quaker.[124]

Once the Charter of Privileges was in place in 1701, Lloyd was determined to pursue the goals he had outlined in his burst of creative thinking during Penn's last months in Pennsylvania. As speaker of the assembly through almost the entire first decade of the eighteenth century, Lloyd never tired of pushing the assembly to prominence. Encouraged by his provincial predecessors who had resolved to follow "the orderly Method of Parliaments, and the Demeanor of the Members thereof . . . in *England*," Lloyd took the initiative and strengthened the speaker's ability to manage legislative affairs, laid the groundwork for the future establishment of standing committees, and insisted on the adoption of rules of order and decorum— all of which promoted a sense of institutional integrity.[125] Following the same rationale, that the provincial assembly should be Pennsylvania's House of Commons, subsequent assemblies went on to establish control over their own officers, regulate the fees of all governmental officers, set franchise requirements and election procedures for provincial offices, and exercise close control over the editing and dissemination of their official minutes.[126] When the logic of replication did not suit their purposes, Lloyd and his friends simply turned the argument on its head. Conditions in the colony were different from those in the Old World, and William Penn intended his colonists to have more privileges than Englishmen had.[127] When Governor John Evans refused to sign a bill that explained the assembly's charter right of sitting on its own adjournments as the ability to decide the timing and duration of all its meetings, members simply went ahead and created their own precedents for such action.[128] Innovation, in the ostensible pursuit of Penn's stated ideals, in keeping with the peculiar needs of the province, and in harmony with popular interpretations of the colony's seventeenth-century constitutional traditions, was a laudable goal. Augmentation of the assembly's power was not simply an end in itself, but a means of accomplishing larger goals.

The most significant consequence of expanding the Pennsylvania Assembly's effective power in the early eighteenth century was that it enabled popular political leaders to invade territory that William Penn had marked off as his own turf. One such area was proprietary management of Pennsylvania real estate. Complaints had long accumulated against the shoddy way in which proprietary appointees had run the Pennsylvania land office, and in 1701 Lloyd had pushed Penn hard to sign a charter of property along with other reform measures. The proposed charter was to remedy some of the worst grievances—corruption in the surveyor-general's office, arbitrary re-surveys, high-handed inquiries into titles, dilatory confirmation of patents, preemption of old property rights with new patents, and the Board of Property's assertion of quasi-judicial powers.[129] Penn angrily refused to have anything to do with the document, and on leaving Pennsylvania ordered his officious secretary, James Logan, to investigate all land titles in the province in order to maximize the proprietor's return from both land purchases and quitrents.[130] That response only roused David Lloyd to greater efforts. In the summer of 1704, Lloyd drafted a bill that brought the proprietary land office and the activities of the surveyor-general and proprietary secretary under the regulation of the assembly.[131] Governor Evans, of course, refused to pass the bill, but the point had been made: the assembly saw provincial property affairs as too important to the public interest to be left uncontested in proprietary hands. Popular political leaders would return to this part of Lloyd's agenda numerous times in future decades.

Governor Evans's stubborn defense of proprietary rights was not the only obstacle Lloyd faced at the turn of the century. Legal advisors to the Crown took a dim view of Pennsylvanians' efforts to use statute law to depart too radically from English law, or to ride roughshod over the prerogative. That became obvious in 1705, when Whitehall repealed over one half of the 105 provincial acts William Penn had signed into law.[132] Characteristically, however, Lloyd tried to turn adversity into advantage. By that time he had become convinced that one of the most important of the annulled statutes, the 1701 Judicature Act, had not gone far enough. Referring back to the 1682 Frame of Government and Penn's enthusiastic promises from those heady years, Lloyd argued that Penn had promised to establish courts independent of executive influence.[133] The Charter of Privileges had moved a step toward acknowledging that promise by requiring elected sheriffs, but the recently repealed Judicature Act had failed to advance that objective. This time Lloyd hoped to gain more ground. In the revised version of the act, he added clauses designed to promote court independence. While the power of judicial appointment continued firmly fixed in gubernatorial hands, Lloyd hoped to offset that bias by requiring that the executive remove judges on an address from the assembly: the proprietor might appoint, but the representatives could fire.[134] To encourage further court autonomy, Lloyd drew on English precedents that allowed the courts to choose their own clerks and control the licensing of taverns and public houses. Both of these changes struck directly at proprietary prerogatives. Clerks were patronage appointments that gave the proprietor significant influence in the judicial and administrative system, and licensing of taverns brought him income.[135] There were other innovations that furthered the assembly's ends, but none drew so much opposition as these. Although Penn much preferred to see courts established by legislative act, Governor Evans and Proprietary Secretary James Logan were adamant against such concessions. So heated did the battle over the courts become that the governor eventually provided for the continuance of provincial courts by executive ordinance, and the assembly responded with an unsuccessful attempt to impeach Evans's chief advisor, James Logan.[136]

During the first decade of the eighteenth century, David Lloyd drafted a basic blueprint for Pennsylvanians to follow in order to attain the kind of political power they felt they should have. He identified the importance of the assembly, and in establishing its foundations demonstrated ways in which it might continue to accrete power both in internal affairs and in its relationship with Whitehall. He identified the proprietary land office as a crucial place for popular politicians to watch if they were to protect their fellow colonists' property rights. Finally, he pointed out the importance of keeping equity jurisdiction away from the proprietor and of installing independent court officers throughout the judicial system. Of course, Lloyd's assemblies fell short of reconstructing Pennsylvania's government along the lines the speaker specified. But they did attain a good deal. There were few assembly gains in future years that were not encompassed within Lloyd's original vision.

In a general way the circumstances that prompted Pennsylvanians to push for political power were much like those of New York. The early Quaker elite, however fissured, quickly concluded that strong provincial institutions were the best defense against the vagaries of outside authority; and the colonial institution best suited for the accumulation of provincial political power was the assembly. Like New Yorkers, Pennsylvanians became very adept at ferreting out parliamentary precedents that bolstered the assembly's powers, and at pleading local exceptionalism to promote the same end. So, too, did gubernatorial claims, wrapped in Pennsylvania's peculiar packaging of proprietary prerogatives, seem proportionately larger than the English constitution sanctioned. Transplanted in an overgrown form, they inspired compulsive, if intermittent, trimming to reduce them to a style in keeping with colonial taste.

But the drive for popular power in early Pennsylvania was far more focused than in New York. Friends, toughened by persecution, were determined to build a society in keeping with both Quaker principles and their recollections of what William Penn had promised. Pennsylvania was to be a colony with greater popular privileges than others. It was to be free of religious persecution and any other intrusions of authority that might threaten Quaker standards of behavior. The workings of the Inner Light provided a paradigm for society at large. Pennsylvania's public world should be built from the inside out, its political character shaped by the religious precepts that Friends held dear. Quakers, for example, should stand firm against governors who wanted to encourage martial behavior.[137] So should Friends incorporate their religion into Pennsylvania law: while legal fictions were necessary under English law to carry out ejectment proceedings against squatters or delinquent tenants, Pennsylvania law should be tailored to reflect Quaker values (i.e., that a lie was a lie, notwithstanding its legal status, and that lies were unacceptable), not English precedent.[138] There should be no compromise with fundamental truths.

Concern for the integrity of the "holy experiment" was one sentiment William Penn shared with his colonists, but their respective understandings of what that included differed immensely. And from the gulf that lay between colonists and proprietor came additional impetus for the development of popular power. In respect to the Crown, Penn was both an advocate and a cheerleader for his settlers. He vigorously defended the reputation of Pennsylvania's merchants when customs and vice-admiralty officials arraigned them for illegal trade;[139] he urged Quakers to fight for a universal substitution of affirmations for oaths so that Friends could qualify, if they chose, for all offices in the Pennsylvania government;[140] he counseled Pennsylvanians to resist administrative orders from the Board of Trade or from Crown lawyers that were not explicitly grounded in English or Pennsylvania law;[141] and, of course, when Crown expropriation of Pennsylvania seemed likely in 1701, he invited his colonists to strengthen their position "as well in . . . [their] Privileges as Property."[142] In his encouragement of colonial self-assertion, Penn was oblivious of the close connection between the Crown's relationship to Pennsylvania and his own. His urgings against British administrative authority and oppressive English law were meant as just that and nothing more. His promise to "better . . . [his colonists'] Circumstances" in 1701 meant that he wished to strengthen *both* proprietor *and* Pennsylvanians vis-à-vis the Crown.[143] When Pennsylvania's political leaders came up with new constitutional proposals, they would "find . . . [him] ready to Comply with whatsoever . . . [might] render *us* happy, by a nearer Union of *our* Interest."[144] In Penn's mind the eighteenth century began, not with an explicit endorsement of colonial autonomy, but with a mutual rededication of the Pennsylvania enterprise to proprietary/colonist comity.

It is doubtful whether any Pennsylvania political leader even heard Penn's emphasis on meeting adversity with reaffirmations of unity. What they extrapolated from his words were blessings on their inclinations to enlarge the popular sphere of provincial competence. But what they subsequently saw juxtaposed against such encouragement was an apparent determination to frustrate their ambitions. No sooner had he left Philadelphia in 1701, than Penn tried to claim a proprietary veto over all Pennsylvania legislation. When that idea failed to fly, he appeared to favor both an augmentation of council power and a diminution of assembly privileges. The appointive council should be acknowledged as a primary part of government, while the chief executive should wield a power of dissolution and prorogation over the annual assemblies elected under the Charter of Privileges.[145] With respect to property, the proprietor's actions were even more offensive. Penn established a "Court of Inquiry" with wide powers to examine Pennsylvania land patents.[146] In part intended to remedy grievances relating to bound-aries, location, and quantities, it was also a means by which proprietary officials could repossess "overplus" land, enforce settlement covenants, and calculate delinquent quitrents.[147] Despite a recession in the early 1700s, Penn encouraged Proprietary Secretary James Logan to dun for land debts and collect back taxes that the assembly had levied for proprietary ex-penses.[148] From Penn's perspective, his demands were perfectly acceptable ones. His idea of a proper relationship between colonists and colonizer was a paternal one. Oversight of provincial government was his duty, and collec-tion of proprietary debts was his right.

To Pennsylvania's political leaders, who had enjoyed such a slack propri-etary rein in the 1680s and 1690s, and who had heard only the founder's exhortations to defend themselves, Penn's policies revealed a perfidious proprietor. By the early 1700s, they were detailing William Penn's sad fall from a charitable idealist to a power-hungry, tight-fisted "Tyrant."[149] In view of what the proprietor had once promised his first settlers, they argued that even the Charter of Privileges was "Diminutive of former privi-leges."[150] When word arrived in Pennsylvania in 1704 that the proprietor was trying to sell his governing rights to the Crown in order to pay off his debts, his colonists paid little attention to the fact that Penn was determined to protect as many of their rights as possible.[151] Rather, they arraigned his administration in blackest terms.[152] Approximately a year later, when Penn-sylvanians became aware of Penn's huge debt to his former business agent Philip Ford, and thus had a means of explaining away some of his apparent avariciousness, perhaps a few felt some sympathy for their old benefactor.[153] But charity soon dissolved into anger when they learned that Penn might have deeded Pennsylvania to Ford as long ago as 1696, thereby rendering uncertain all land titles granted during the previous decade.[154] The more Pennsylvanians learned about their proprietor, the more they were con-vinced that the best part of William Penn had been his advice to expand their power and steadfastly resist encroachment.

Relationships between William Penn and Pennsylvania's popular politi-cal leaders were often highly emotional ones, in which Penn alternated between anger and self-pity in the face of successive waves of antiproprietary sentiment.[155] In such circumstances, personalities came to play an impor-tant part in the conflicts of the day. David Lloyd, for example, believed that the way the proprietor treated him was a microcosm of Penn's betrayal of the province. During a second appointment as Pennsylvania's attorney-general in the late 1690s, Lloyd felt he had Penn's tacit approval in frustrating the efforts by customs and vice-admiralty court officials to augment their au-thority. But when the proprietor arrived on the scene in 1699, he quickly acceded to the Privy Council's demands that he sack Lloyd.[156] To someone of Lloyd's character, a man who "knew not what it was to bend," this was unconscionable.[157] Thereafter, Lloyd turned his unrivaled political talents to humiliating Penn and undermining the proprietary system. And as the scars from Lloyd's attacks accumulated, Penn retaliated in kind. Excusing himself with the same rationale Lloyd employed (as Penn put it, Lloyd had "turned" against his benefactor as easily "as a nose of wax"), the proprietor periodically whirled on his tormentor and aimed a vicious blow at Lloyd's exposed political flank.[158]

Although the distance between Philadelphia and London prevented direct confrontation between Lloyd and Penn, it did not prevent battles by proxy. Lloyd provided information to Penn's English opponents, while in Philadelphia, Penn's administration was led by officials anxious to best Lloyd.[159] Governor Evans was one such Philadelphia resident, but he was an inexperienced lightweight, whose impolitic actions did more damage to Penn's interest than he ever inflicted on Lloyd.[160] Although Evans was Penn's titular representative, it was Proprietary Secretary Logan who was Penn's chief surrogate. And in Logan, a man dismissive of "meer Pennsilvanian[s]," Lloyd had a serious opponent. To Lloyd and his friends, the arrogant, intellectually precocious Logan seemed to personify the true character of the proprietary regime.[161] Logan's power derived not from the Pennsylvania community but from England; his chief political goal was to augment the power of appointed officials and diminish that of elected representatives; he ran the land office like a personal fiefdom; and the proprietary policies he strained to implement frequently seemed at odds with the colonists' best interests.[162] From 1706 through 1709, one of David Lloyd's priorities was to impeach James Logan, and Philadelphians' ears echoed with the charges and countercharges that the two exchanged.[163] The cumulative effect of their seemingly interminable spat was to widen the already sizable gulf between proprietor and people.

No matter how much personal rivalry seemed to generate differences between Penn and Pennsylvania's popular leaders, that was not, of course, the fundamental reason for the conflict. Lloyd's antiproprietary movement sprang from deep roots within the Quaker subculture. Friends were predisposed to reject any authority that was not consistent with and did not enhance their family and community life. Contribution to the socioreligious integrity of Quakerism was the only acceptable criterion for remodeling British society in Pennsylvania. And only the community of Quakers in Pennsylvania, not a far-off proprietary landlord, was capable of deciding what governmental policies were consistent with Quaker values. Pennsylvania Friends had experienced some of that freedom in the 1680s and 1690s when they fought off external threats, and when Penn intermittently left them alone. Having tasted the wine of freedom and power just yesterday, they were not about to relinquish the bottle to the proprietor today. Encouraged by their new constitution and provoked by proprietary policies that seemed so out of touch with new-world Quaker attitudes, Pennsylvania's political leaders strove to curtail proprietary influence and consolidate as much political autonomy as they possibly could.

Preoccupied with William Penn's proprietary claims, and viewing their position within the English domain as that of residents of a private colony, provincials in Pennsylvania were less concerned than residents of a royal colony like New York about questions regarding their relationship to the Crown and of what loyalty to their sovereign meant. To most Pennsylvanians, their governor was primarily the proprietor's deputy rather than the Crown's representative. They did not perceive an attack on proprietary/executive power as a challenge to royalty, and neither did the questionable conduct of governors bring any great disrepute on the Crown. There were, however, a small number of Pennsylvanians who saw the fighting between proprietary and antiproprietary factions as an opportunity for themselves to emerge as the chief advocates of royal government. This shrill choir was largely composed of Anglicans, a few leading tenors from the customs and vice-admiralty court services, and a disharmonious chorus of old settlers, recent immigrants, and Keithian refugees from Quakerism.[164] What brought them together to perform was their sense of grievance stemming from Friends "not suffering them to be superior" as befit members of the Church of England.[165] They hoped to exploit the loyalty issue, claiming that neither proprietor nor Quaker populace paid proper respect to Crown policies and English law. Anglicans felt that they might end up with the positions and influence that rightfully belonged to men of their creed if the Pennsylvania experiment could be discredited in England and Penn's proprietorship expropriated.[166]

The Quakers' response was their standard one to any threat of outside authority: they resisted it with intelligence and vigor. When a vice-admiralty court was established for the Delaware region in 1696, the Pennsylvania government, led by David Lloyd, passed an act ostensibly to comply with the Navigation Act that authorized the court. Despite its professed intent, the law actually required that all alleged violations of the Navigation Acts occurring on inland waterways (including the Delaware River) should be tried, not before vice-admiralty courts, but before a jury in the province's common law courts.[167] Of course, the short-run successes of such trickery did not dull Quakers' appreciation of the extreme dangers that royalization might pose. The drafting of parliamentary legislation to repossess proprietary governments, and the possibility of Penn voluntarily selling his governing rights, encouraged Pennsylvania's political leaders to push for as much autonomy as possible. The 1701 Charter of Privileges was an attempt to guard Quaker powers and rights against royal intrusion. Subsequent assembly gains were as much a hedge against future royal government as a rejection of an overbearing proprietor. The cagey David Lloyd was quick to recruit Anglican critics of proprietary government, knowing that whatever popular political gains came through their help could quickly be turned against Anglican placemen should Pennsylvania be royalized.[168] Because the focal point of local politics was proprietary, not royal, power, relatively few local Anglicans concerned themselves with the implications of Lloyd's activities. When they did, they were unsuccessful in effectively raising the issue in the appropriate English court circles.

That left Pennsylvania's political leaders free to use the issue of royal government in whatever way they chose. They might confront royal officials directly and challenge their role in a proprietary government.[169] They might, as David Lloyd occasionally did, exploit the loyalty issue by contrasting the rights the Crown had so generously granted in the Royal Charter with Penn's parsimony in the years that followed.[170] But never did the Quaker leaders suggest that royal government would be preferable to proprietary.[171] They all believed that loyalty to the Crown was perfectly consistent with proprietary government; to demonstrate that, they participated, to the extent that Quaker principles allowed, in the public ceremonies and rituals that citizenship of the British empire required.[172] Pennsylvania's Quaker political leaders were as much loyal Englishmen as any other group of comparable colonials, but their primary objective was to secure as much autonomy as they possibly could within the imperial scheme of things.

By the end of the first decade of the eighteenth century, the animosity that had characterized relations under the Charter of Privileges began to quiet down. More moderate politicians temporarily took assembly leadership out of David Lloyd's hands; Governor Evans was replaced in 1709; James Logan departed on an extended trip to the British Isles in the same year; and William Penn suffered an incapacitating stroke in 1712. Although Penn lived on until 1718, provincial affairs lacked authoritative proprietary direction from the onset of Penn's illness through 1732, when a settlement was finally reached among his heirs. During most of that time, Penn's second wife, Hannah Callowhill Penn, provided administrative leadership from Great Britain, while Governors Charles Gookin, Sir William Keith, and Patrick Gordon served as the proprietary deputies in Pennsylvania.

Different as Gookin, Keith, and Gordon were, all shared one important characteristic—all needed, or felt they needed, a sizable income to build themselves estates and "support the dignity of government."[173] That placed them at the mercy of the assembly, because members of the proprietary family, deeply in debt, unclear of their respective responsibilities, and with little income from Pennsylvania, believed they could no longer afford to support the province's governmental establishment. Long before that time, under Governor Fletcher, David Lloyd had demonstrated to fellow Pennsylvanians how to deal with hungry governors: offer to trade financial support for the legislation provincials wanted.[174] A successful exchange of that sort took place during a brief interlude in the almost constant war between Governor Evans and the assembly. Early in 1706, the representatives agreed to pay Evans over £800 for his assent to fifty acts.[175] There were no subsequent deals, because the two parties soon resumed their paper war. Once the unpredictable and avaricious Governor Gookin arrived in Philadelphia, however, "the trade" became an integral part of legislative-executive dealings. Under Keith and Gordon, the bargaining was far less blatant, but both recognized that passage of popular legislation was the sine qua non of financial support of the governor.[176]

In order to facilitate productive bargaining, the assembly dropped some of its old antiproprietary demands, such as insistence on changing the land office from a private to a public one and on the right of the people to strip judges who misbehaved of their commissions.[177] But in so doing the legislators lost little of their aggressiveness. They simply switched their attention to other, more realizable goals. By the end of the 1720s, they had secured a series of acts that restored much of the court system outlined in David Lloyd's repealed Judicature Act of 1701;[178] they persisted in drafting bills that allowed Quakers to substitute an affirmation for the oaths public officials and citizens were required to swear;[179] they sponsored legislation that increasingly confined the activities of the proprietary land office to the sale of new land and the collection of quitrents;[180] they established a new elective county commission system of government that undercut much of the administrative power of appointed justices of the peace;[181] they provided for a measure of popular input into the running of Philadelphia City by requiring that elected assessors raise all local taxes;[182] they demonstrated that they had the power to create new counties and assign representation to those areas by their creation of Lancaster County in 1729;[183] and they expanded their patronage privileges over a number of administrative appointments.[184] Cumulatively these measures placed substantial power in popular hands.

A second way in which the assembly augmented its power was to exert popular control over provincial finances. Back in the days of David Lloyd's dominance, the groundwork had been well laid. In an early Revenue Act, the assembly had participated in choosing a new provincial treasurer.[185] In a subsequent act, it reconfirmed the choice, required that all tax revenues be lodged with that official, specifically appropriated what was to go to the governor, and provided for other funds to be drawn in accordance with assembly resolve and the speaker's warrant.[186] Although the council briefly challenged the assembly over the nature of the treasurer's obligations, the House of Representatives clearly controlled the disposition of tax monies subsequent to that 1706 Act.[187] Thereafter, as the level and range of taxation grew, so did the assembly's reach, extending its power over the appointment of new tax collectors, putting more proprietary placemen, such as the chief justice and attorney-general, on its payroll, tightening its oversight of the treasurer by auditing his accounts, and confirming its own nominee in that post when the position fell vacant in 1714.[188]

From the point of view of popular politicians, their virtual monopoly on financial power was a fine accomplishment. But there was a problem with it. Constituents now knew exactly whom to blame for the tax load they carried. From one side, the proprietor pressed them for his land-purchase payments, while on the other, the local collectors demanded current provincial levies and arrears from earlier laws.[189] Assemblymen were unperturbed by the discontent proprietary exactions generated, but they worried when complaints came their way. Fortunately, from their perspectives, the representatives found an ingenious solution to their problem.

During the 1720s, economic pressures drove the assembly to adopt a paper currency, a step that other colonies had followed when threatened by large government expenses or by a severe shortage of specie. The Pennsylvania legislation put the bulk of the newly printed currency into circulation through the agency of a provincial loan office. The trustees of this agency loaned out the currency in small amounts, between £12 10s. and £100, to those who could offer land or personalty as security. The recipients were required to make regular yearly remittances, which included equal installments of principal and modest, under-market interest payments. In addition, the assembly spent some of the currency for the support of government and for provincial and county public works. These provincial expenses were to be paid back by future tax levies, the most important of which were excise taxes on alcoholic beverages.[190]

The Pennsylvania loan office was a remarkable success, and in becoming so, significantly increased the power of elected politicians. First, many constituents credited the House of Representatives with saving property and businesses during bad times, and, in better days, with giving capital-poor but ambitious Pennsylvanians the opportunity to improve their lot. The loan office was an institution that in tangible ways really could benefit ordinary people. Second, the assembly noticeably extended its power of patronage. The loan office provided paying jobs for cash-hungry politicians and influence over loan decisions and collection policies. Finally, in the annual income accruing from interest payment on loans, the legislators enjoyed a secure income to be appropriated as they wished. As long as the loan office re-emitted loans and the excise tax was continued, the assembly was financially autonomous, able to avoid levying unpopular land taxes and to maintain complete control of government expenses.[191]

By the end of the 1720s, Pennsylvania's popular politicians had made their assembly the most powerful in the British colonial world. But knowledge of that inspired little complaisance. They continued to cultivate the convictions and habits of mind that had brought them so much, and as old leaders gave way to new, the succeeding generation fell heir to a provincial political tradition that demanded an exceptional degree of autonomy. Thus, in the 1730s and 1740s, the assembly continued to accrete power. Under Andrew Hamilton's leadership, the House of Representatives became more forceful about its rights, clarifying them and elaborating on them when it felt the need.[192] After an argument with Governor Gordon, Hamilton shut down the anemic chancery court that, in a rush of post-rapprochement rapture, representatives had allowed Governor Keith to establish in 1720.[193] Under Hamilton's successor, John Kinsey, the assemblymen became more aggressive. They cut off Governor George Thomas's salary to bring him to heel, ("Starve him into compliance or into silence is the common language . . . here," stormed Thomas) and then lengthened the duration of the excise tax and loan office re-emissions in 1746 to provide the legislature with an assured income through the next decade.[194] In addition, they augmented their patronage list of appointed officials, established a colonial agent in England answerable only to the assembly, and increased the number of elected local officers in Philadelphia.[195]

During the early 1740s, when the assembly was locked in conflict with Governor Thomas over the chief executive's enlistment of indentured servants (to serve with the British in the West Indies) and over the assembly's unwillingness to undertake the preparations for defense that Thomas thought the outbreak of war with Spain warranted, spokespersons for the executive branch of government finally began to realize how thoroughly the assembly dominated Pennsylvania government.[196] "Fatal was the complaisance in . . . Governmt," lamented Provincial Secretary Richard Peters, that in the 1720s allowed the assembly to begin the practice of disposing of "the Publick Money" "independent of the Governor."[197] Fresh from his experiences in the British West Indies, Governor Thomas was equally discerning. "When the Assembly was vested with the sole Power of Disposing of the publick Money & of adjourning to their own time," Thomas concluded, "they were vested with the Powers of Governmt so amply as to render the Governor a cypher or no more than nominal."[198]

What compounded the depression that Peters, Thomas, and a handful of other administrators felt was their recognition that the executive's weakness lay rooted in deep-seated popular hostility to the proprietary. Despite the gains that the Pennsylvania Assembly had made under William Penn and

later under Hannah Penn's custodial eye, politically aware provincials periodically reminded one another of past proprietary pretensions and the
Penns' resistance to popular power. And the recent residence of William
Penn's son Thomas in Pennsylvania had sharpened the edge of the province's
antiproprietary folk memory. Thomas Penn's chief purpose in coming to
Pennsylvania in 1732 was to bring order to the land office and to turn the
family's colonial enterprise into a lucrative business.[199] To that end, he
raised the price of land by 50 percent, doubled the quitrent rate, set about
collecting old debts, demanded public compensation for accepting the province's paper currency in lieu of sterling on old quitrents, and did little to
lessen the cronyism and corruption that attended land office affairs.[200] The
cumulative effect of Thomas Penn's land policies was clear to Governor
George Thomas: "Every disappointment in a bargain of land, or something
else as trifling is a good reason for opposing the Government," wrote
Thomas, "the governor being appointed by the Proprietors, who have dis-
obliged . . . [the people] either by demanding what is due or giving a
preference to one thought more worthy."[201] When the few leading Philadelphians who did support a stronger executive disgraced themselves by
their implication in the well-known election riot of 1742, Governor Thomas
felt he had no option but to placate the assembly, confirming and consolidating the powers that the legislature claimed.[202]

If Pennsylvania's popular leaders had slipped slightly into complaisance
after gaining control of the province's financial system during the 1720s, the
activities of Thomas Penn and initial policies of Governor Thomas bestirred
their successors. "Young fiery men have too much sway," complained Richard Peters. "The members [of the assembly] are . . . stiff & unyielding in
every popular Case."[203] In 1750–1751, for example, the provincial representatives increased the powers of elected officials in Philadelphia and renewed
attempts, for the first time since David Lloyd's day, to regulate the land
office.[204] That merely confirmed Thomas Penn's view that "as often as an
Assembly meets, they . . . desire to throw something onto the peoples
scale."[205] And when the proprietor suggested that a chancery court constituted by gubernatorial ordinance might help the proprietary cause, Governor James Hamilton treated Penn to a dose of reality: "as the road to both
power and wealth passes entirely through the channel of the People in this
province, Our lawyers . . . will not hazard their interest with them, by . . .
[applying to practice in such a] Court."[206] By the early 1750s, the beleaguered Governor Hamilton was sounding the same lament as his counterpart, Clinton, in New York. The colonial bird of state was so "pluckt" of
"the powers of . . . Government," "as scarcely to have a feather left, either
for Ornament or Defence."[207]

Unlike the situation in New York, however, in which a provincially trusted lieutenant-governor and a backpedaling Privy Council created some room for executive-legislative accommodation, Pennsylvania met with an uncompromising proprietor and accentuated conflict. In 1746, Thomas Penn succeeded his elder brother John as chief proprietor and began to implement policies that he pursued virtually until the Revolution. Influenced by his Pennsylvania placemen crying their weakness, encouraged by a personal financial position that could withstand some temporary disruption in his Pennsylvania income, and backed by a rejuvenated Board of Trade, Penn decided that he would try to turn affairs in Pennsylvania around by enhancing executive power at the expense of the assembly.[208] Early in the 1750s, Penn promised to come to Pennsylvania to lead the anticipated battle, but in fact, he had no stomach for the direct confrontation such a journey would entail; throughout his life, Penn preferred to fight through proxies. That was easy enough to do in Pennsylvania. In the decades that followed William Penn's ill-fated attempt to claim a proprietary veto over colonial legislation, the proprietary had always maintained the right to load its governors with specific instructions, just as the Crown freighted its chief executives in royal colonies. The assembly had from time to time fought such pretensions, most notably during Sir William Keith's governorship, when Hannah Penn had demanded that Keith take no action without the consent of his council.[209] Since that time, the assembly had usually been successful in forcing Pennsylvania governors to disregard their instructions when these conflicted with cherished provincial priorities.[210] Knowing this, Thomas Penn chose his ground carefully. In 1756, the excise tax would expire and the loan office's currency would begin to be withdrawn from circulation. That would steadily cut the assembly's income until it became a trickle, and simultaneously focus popular pressure on the legislature to pass a statute authorizing the loan office to re-emit funds for new mortgages. Penn's price for allowing his governor to sign a new excise bill and the re-emitting legislation was to be heavy: joint executive-legislative appropriation of all revenues the new laws produced. In demanding executive participation in the appropriation of provincial monies, the proprietor was aiming to turn the clock back by half a century.[211]

Once cursed by their proprietor, the representatives were again cursed by international events. The French and Indian War broke out in 1755, and in order to defend their province, Pennsylvania's legislators had to finance a large war effort. That meant both renewing the excise duties and, for the first time since Queen Anne's War, levying large land taxes. In the case of the excise, the assembly protestingly bowed to the proprietary yoke by accepting joint executive-legislative appropriation of the revenue.[212] In the case of the land tax, the representatives found themselves in a prolonged stalemate with the proprietor. Knowing that his father had always claimed exemption from land taxes, Thomas Penn demanded the same treatment. The poor freeholder and tenant should ante up for the province's defense, but from the colony's largest landholder, not one shilling. And this was precisely at a time that Penn was orchestrating an unprecedentedly large legal offensive against quitrent and land-purchase debtors.[213] For the next eight years, the assembly kept after Penn as he twisted to avoid taxation. First, he granted a gift of £5,000 in lieu of taxation. But when the time came to collect, the assembly found that Penn had instructed the money to come out of delinquent quitrents, which, of course, put the burden back on the freeholders.[214] Next, he agreed to taxation in principle, but then exempted all his located unimproved land, quitrent income, and purchase money at interest.[215] As Benjamin Franklin put it, that left only "a Ferry-house . . . a Kitchen, and a Dog Kennel," eligible for taxation.[216] Finally, when the Privy Council eventually interceded to hasten a settlement, Penn's agents put an initial construction on the language of the agreement that would have resulted in all Penn's lands paying taxes at the lowest possible provincial rate.[217] Once this last had been fought, the assembly did establish its right to tax the proprietor. But the price was that the House of Representatives had to share powers of appropriation either directly with the governor or with commissioners chosen jointly by executive and legislature.

The long and rancorous dispute between Pennsylvania's local leaders and Thomas Penn led popular provincial politicians to extremes reminiscent of the colony's early decades. Goaded by the inventive duplicity of both Penn and his few Pennsylvania allies, the assembly's masterminds, Isaac Norris, Benjamin Franklin, and Joseph Galloway, became as uncompromising as David Lloyd had been long ago. They argued that the popular powers Pennsylvanians enjoyed were the price William Penn had paid "in order to settle his Province without any charge to himself or to the Crown."[218] By midcentury, these powers were firmly grounded in the province's charters and laws, in the assembly's origins as an "*English* Representative Body," and in the Privy Council's past willingness to accept the province's internal system of government.[219] And when opportunity appeared in 1758–1759, in the form of a governor who could be bought, they sponsored a clutch of laws that harkened back to David Lloyd's agenda.[220] Among the most important of these were acts appointing Pennsylvania judges for good behavior, taking over the administration of the land office, and setting up a new civil appellate court staffed with assembly appointees.[221] Predictably, the Privy Council disallowed much of this legislation at the same time as it oversaw the ultimately binding compromise between the assembly and proprietor over the taxation of his colonial estate.[222]

"Soured" by the loss of their punitive legislation and angered by the subsequent proprietary efforts to avoid fair taxation of Thomas Penn's lands, Pennsylvania's popular politicians then initiated one of the most bizarre episodes in colonial history.[223] Under Benjamin Franklin's leadership, the Quaker Party tried to orchestrate a popular movement in favor of royal government. In order to comprehend how Franklin, Joseph Galloway, and other popular leaders came to embrace this unlikely way of protecting the political autonomy Pennsylvanians had striven to maintain over the previous three quarters of a century, especially when Whitehall's decision to tighten imperial controls was already evident in the early 1760s, it is necessary to appreciate something of Benjamin Franklin's intense loathing of Thomas Penn.[224] But just as important (and more relevant in this context) was the way in which the short-lived campaign for royal government revealed how Franklin and his friends fell victim to the arrogance of power. Put a different way, the policy of petitioning for royal government testified to how completely the assembly had dominated Pennsylvania government: late colonial popular leaders were so certain of their preeminence that they could not imagine even the direct supervision of the Crown reducing their stature.[225] At the same time, years of distant, unreflective obeisance—feeding the British lion, as it were, without feeling its breath—had lulled Pennsylvania legislators into thinking that predation had somehow given way to protectiveness.

Despite the intermittent conflict between assembly and proprietor during the 1750s and 1760s, the Pennsylvania Assembly remained the same powerhouse it had developed into during earlier colonial days. Determined to develop a society with as much internal autonomy as a colony could possess, and imaginatively aggressive in their pursuit of such ends, Pennsylvania's popular politicians established the assembly as the dominant political force in the province in the early eighteenth century. And that tradition continued on through the colonial period. What the assembly lost in the 1750s and 1760s in the way of sole powers of appropriation was, in practice, quite limited. Throughout the French and Indian War, the representatives had an effective veto over commissioners in charge of wartime expenditures and, in fact, many of them were popular political leaders. Moreover, the assembly continued to pick up ancillary powers—considerable control over the Indian trade; recognition from Thomas Penn that the land office should function as a public office; and the right to tax proprietary property in the same way, and with the same personnel, as other owners.[226] By the late colonial years, the Pennsylvania Assembly stood muscular and solid, little touched by the proprietary challenges that had come its way.[227] No colony's record is more illustrative of British North American settlers' taste for popular power than Pennsylvania's.

"We are not striving for Grants of Power but what are essential . . ."

The most striking similarity between early eighteenth-century New York and Pennsylvania was the rapidity with which provincial leaders developed popular political power. Frustrated by unfulfilled promises, fearful of autocratic forces that had frequently swept through Europe, Britain, and the English colonial empire, convinced of their right to political representation, and encouraged by the example of older colonies with well-established assemblies, both New Yorkers and Pennsylvanians pushed early and hard to establish a powerful, popular political presence. Vexed by years of arbitrary taxation and financial mismanagement, at the first opportunity the New York Assembly went straight for the strategic center of prerogative power— the provincial purse. Given great financial leverage by the demands of early eighteenth-century wartime budgets, the House of Representatives quickly took advantage of the executive's dependence and annexed a series of powers New York governors had formerly enjoyed. In Pennsylvania, provincial leaders tended to advance on the proprietor over a broader front, with a general swarming attack. But motivated as they were by an intense Quaker-based desire to establish a colonial society largely on their own terms, and encouraged both by William Penn's intermittent urgings to protect themselves and by his proprietorial weaknesses, they were, if anything, more effective than their New York counterparts. Early in the eighteenth century, much earlier, in fact, than in the more leisurely southern colonies, the provincial representatives of New York and Pennsylvania established their assemblies as the dominant force in colonial government.[228] This early assertion of popular power was of utmost importance in each colony's political development, for it stood out in the collective memory of later generations of political leaders as a standard by which they measured and justified their own activities. In New York, turn-of-the-century victories over Lord Cornbury became the measure of patriotic provincial politics, while in Pennsylvania, the Charter of Privileges was frequently perceived as a reference point provincials could use to judge whether they had gained all that William Penn had promised and that earlier charters (including Penn's Royal Charter) had established in principle.[229]

This built-in provincial dynamic that enabled New Yorkers and Pennsylvanians to continue to emphasize, both consciously and unconsciously, the accretion and consolidation of popular power throughout later decades was reinforced, of course, by other circumstances. Two notable antiauthoritarian strands of English political thought—the first, the language of seventeenth-century English opposition to the Crown, the second, the radi-

cal Whig description of post–Glorious Revolution politics as an unrelenting battle between liberty and the forces of ministerial corruption—
influenced public opinion in the colonies to support assembly initiatives
circumscribing prerogative and proprietary privileges.[230] Very quickly, too,
first-generation provincials came to recognize that Whitehall's placemen
frequently lacked knowledge of, or desire to serve, the interests of the
colonial community. Provincials soon developed more confidence in the
abilities of their elected representatives and in their own judgments on
public affairs than in those of their governors. That sense of competence and
self-confidence grew rapidly in the eighteenth century as the assemblies
built up a fund of political and governmental experience. With the growing
complexity of New York and Pennsylvania, an "array" of issues (including
"defense, the need for a medium of exchange, Indian relations, transportation facilities on a . . . [broad] scale, intercolonial relations, and the regulation of competing economic, ethnic and religious groups") appeared that
were beyond the scope of local government and unsuitable for adjudication
in London.[231] As the assemblies proved themselves capable in handling
these problems, "colonists turned increasingly to them to get things
done."[232] In the process of "respond[ing] . . . to . . . constituent demands,"
the assemblies matured as institutions, and the relationship between representatives and their electors became more regular.[233] The increasing prominence of the assemblies in turn confirmed New Yorkers and Pennsylvanians
in the belief that their legislatures *should* be more prominent.

The record of both the New York and Pennsylvania assemblies, then, was
one of persistent promotion of popular power—to the point where New
York's Lieutenant-Governor Clarke publicly raised the question of whether
"the Plantations . . . [were] not without Thoughts of throwing off their
Dependence on the Crown of England," and the Pennsylvania cartographer
Lewis Evans could quietly raise the same possibility in a matter-of-fact
discussion of the character of provincial society.[234] Their point was that
during the early eighteenth century, the assembly in each colony had "devi-
ate[d] from the Example of Parliament" by seizing new powers.[235] Thereafter, they went far beyond the English model. Their refusal to grant a permanent revenue to governors, their determination to control all government
expenditures, and their appropriation of a number of governmental functions that by British standards belonged to the executive, created colonial
constitutions considerably closer to republicanism than the English model
seemed to sanction. And the development of assembly prominence and
competence in provincial affairs (although far more analogous to parliamentary activity) simply reinforced the perception that the two colonies
were developing a more autonomous form of government than was consistent with subservience to Great Britain.

Similar as the New York and Pennsylvania experiences were, there were also important contrasts. One, of course, was the differing temper of provincial politics in the two provinces. Whereas various episodes of conflict among royal governors and a variety of scrappy, well-heeled provincials tended to underline the contentious character of New York politics, the nurturing, protective, and collaborative efforts of William Penn (short-lived as they always were), and the frequent ineffectiveness of the proprietary family, softened the tenor of political affairs in Pennsylvania. What exaggerated that difference was the apparent narrowness of New York provincial politics compared to the relative "populism" of popular politics in Pennsylvania. And, as we might expect, there were different rhythms to the provincial politics of each colony. Whereas the earlier, rather than later, decades of New York politics produced more sustained contention, in Pennsylvania the most marked periods of conflict tended to occur after midcentury, once Thomas Penn had taken control of the proprietorship.

Overall, of course, the Pennsylvania Assembly outstripped its New York counterpart in its accretion of power. That was largely a consequence of their different systems of government. Because New York was a royal colony with no prospect of gaining some of the exceptional popular powers Pennsylvanians won from their proprietor, the New York assemblymen could never hope to tie up their governor to the degree Pennsylvanians could. With an unchallengeable power to prorogue, dissolve, or prolong the life of any assembly (this was subject to a seven-year limitation after 1743), New York governors always possessed a means of both punishing and rewarding the peoples' representatives. In Pennsylvania, on the other hand, with annual elections stipulated and the assembly claiming control of its own adjournment, the best any governor could do to pressure the House was to harass members by continually calling them into session.[236]

Another related issue was the power of royal disallowance. New York laws were to go to Great Britain within three months of their signing and they could be vetoed anytime thereafter.[237] Should disallowance occur, governors were ordered not to sign any similar bill the assembly might subsequently draft.[238] In Pennsylvania's case, Penn's Royal Charter allowed much more room for colonial maneuver. According to the terms of the charter, the proprietor was to forward Pennsylvania laws to Whitehall within five years of their passage, and, once delivered, the Privy Council had but six months either to confirm or to veto them. A veto, however, did little to abate provincial pressure on the governor. Because there were no royal instructions demanding that the Pennsylvania governor refuse to sign bills similar to the disallowed acts, the assembly could simply draw up a new bill essentially the same as the old act and present it to the chief executive at its next sitting. Pennsylvanians also became adept at wringing the most out of the five-year period of grace; the assembly could pass a series of temporary laws knowing that a statute might well have lapsed and been renewed by the time the proprietors sent the laws to the Privy Council.[239]

The character of politics in New York also differed from that of Pennsylvania because there were important inducements in the former colony, which did not exist in the latter, to lead popular politicians to compromise with their chief executive. The institutional strength of the governorship was the most important of these, but there were others. One was the continuing tradition of popular co-option that had begun with James Stuart's arbitrary regimes and continued both under unpopular governors such as Fletcher, Cornbury, and Cosby and under the more respected Hunter, Burnet, and Monckton. A set of the most outspoken proponents of assembly power during Cosby's administration, for example, found it easy to argue that being a "Courtier gives no scandal under a wise and good Administration," once they had cozied up to Cosby's successor, Lieutenant-Governor Clarke.[240] Perhaps the best indicator of the receptiveness of popular politicians to the lure of executive favor was the willing way in which they lined up for a say in the appointment of justices and militia officers.[241] By doing so, they attested to a belief that the administrative and coercive side of government could live in harmony with popular needs and demands. And these circumstances also gave some substance to the view that New York public norms included a place for venality.

Strong reinforcement of these ideas and practices came from the attention New Yorkers paid to the parent English society. Unlike Pennsylvanians, New Yorkers had no fundamental charter to help them develop a strong sense of separate identity. As a result, they fixed their attention on the British constitution as the best guarantor of popular powers. In this manner they came to see, not only how to build and consolidate assembly powers, but also how administrative and legislative personnel could comfortably camp together on common ground. As long as executive/legislative collusion did not traduce the representatives' sense of fundamental commitment to local interests and power, cooperation might be a possible and desirable end.

Another feature of British polity that drew New York's political leaders to much the same conclusion was its famous mixed constitution. According to contemporaries, the genius of the British constitution lay in the fact that the three social orders—monarchy, aristocracy, and commons—all participated in the legislative functions of government, and that such a combination was essential for good government.[242] The problem for New Yorkers was that there was no colonial aristocracy to provide the wisdom that tradition claimed for that estate. Always ready to fill any political vacuum, popular New York leaders characterized themselves as ambidextrous colonials, capable of providing both the popular and mediating roles that came from separate English social orders. They could thus legitimize their social emulation of Britain's upper classes and surrender to their psychological need for inclusion in the larger imperial power structure without cutting themselves off from the popular base that conferred power in a North American colony.

In both their quest for autonomy and their relationships with executive/proprietary representatives, Pennsylvania's popular political leaders were much less equivocal than their New York counterparts. Once past the turn of the century, the executive had little leverage with which to force or persuade assemblymen that accommodation was either necessary or desirable on any grounds other than the assembly's own. Rather than line up for justiceships or military appointments (during the very brief periods when the latter were available), elected politicians walked the other way. By the 1740s, few persons who held such positions could hope for election to provincial office.[243] And in comparison with New Yorkers, Pennsylvanians seemed to adopt strong objections to the unseemly pursuit of wealth at the public's expense.

What alienated popular politicians from proprietary/executive power was a whole series of conditions, including Quaker antiauthoritarianism, hatred of proprietary land policies, the cultivation of a popular sense of provincial identity based on Quaker aspirations, and the perception of Thomas Penn as an enemy conspiring to undermine whatever autonomy the province had won. There were simply no countervailing forces of any magnitude in Pennsylvania society or government strong enough to draw popular politicians toward the executive in a sustained or even intermittent fashion. Short of offering administrative positions to a few prominent individuals, there was little the proprietors could do to moderate the thrust of popular politics.[244]

One other characteristic of the New York and Pennsylvania assemblies is worth mentioning, because related differences suggest something of the distance between the two political orders. Following seventeenth-century English precedents, each assembly saw itself as something of a judicial body as well as a legislative authority. There was no widely shared theoretical separation of the two functions and the assemblies intermingled judicial hearings (or other acts interpreting colonial law) with their law-making activities.[245] The general drift of colonial affairs in the eighteenth century was for the various assemblies to extricate themselves from judicial affairs, because the English model suggested that Parliament's judicial functions would be located largely in the House of Lords and in executive oversight of the courts.[246] Because of New York's status as a royal colony, and because of its interest in following English ways, the governor and council became the primary focus of provincial judicial affairs in the eighteenth century. Which is not to say that the New York legislature abandoned its courtlike claims to the respect legislative bodies felt they should have in their corporate capacity. To the end of the colonial period, members of the New York Assembly were prepared to deal harshly with those it judged guilty of contempt.[247] But the New York Assembly never pressed, as did Pennsylvania's, to be recognized as the "Grand Inquisitor" of the colony.[248] Without a council that it recognized, and determined to gain the right to oversee the behavior of judicial appointments, the Pennsylvania Assembly fostered its pretension as a court, until finally in the late 1750s, Whitehall made a point of strongly reprimanding it.[249] Pennsylvania's political leaders were less willing than their New York counterparts to allow inchoate notions of a separation of governmental functions to diminish their vision of what popular provincial government should entail.

These differences notwithstanding, in both New York and Pennsylvania, provincials asserted as much political control over their circumstances as they felt they could consistent with their always-changing views of what was acceptable within the British colonial empire. They accomplished this primarily through the agencies of their respective assemblies, which undertook, if in piecemeal and uneven fashion, to establish an electorally based hegemonic influence in colonial government. In directing this development, popular political leaders were rarely single-minded, and in doing so they frequently revealed that their political world was a complex one. But if the proving of popular power through the assemblies was only one expression of the processes of political self-definition that both colonies undertook in the eighteenth century, it was clearly of fundamental importance.

Chapter Three

The Pursuit of Popular Rights

NO CONCERN was of greater public importance to British North American colonists than popular rights. The rhetoric of rights ran through colonial discourse with incomparable frequency, for the public believed that the major responsibility of their political representatives was to safeguard those popular rights guaranteed by the contract that in the dim past had supposedly given birth to English government. The English constitution "originated" colonial rights, and its primary purpose was to protect them.[1] That the rights of the people were primary followed ineluctably from the widespread notion, fundamental to popular sovereignty, that the people had inaugurated government for their own benefit.[2] When Crown or proprietary spokespersons occasionally challenged this view by suggesting that popular privileges were a matter of grace rather than right, they merely strengthened the general colonial view that English rights were theirs by unimpeachable processes of social inheritance.[3]

Not surprisingly, the most vocal proponent of colonial rights in the various British North American provinces was the assembly. Its very existence depended on the right of representation, a right guaranteed by the original contract establishing first government, a right grounded in centuries of English practice and perceived as the "Chiefest Birthright" of all Englishmen.[4] Because they owed their creation and continuance to a fundamental right, and were composed of community representatives, it is understandable that the assemblies gained overwhelming recognition as the voice of the people. To New Yorkers and Pennsylvanians alike, their provincial legislatures were "properly the Guardians of all the Peoples Rights, and therefore . . . under the strictest Obligations of Justice to take Care that there be no Infraction made on any Privilege that belongs to . . . [the people]."[5] As for the liberties of the provincial representatives, they were "the Great Guard and Security of all the People's Liberty."[6] When the rights and liberties of the assembly were in jeopardy, so were those of every member of the body politic.[7]

And what were these rights that colonists referred to so much, and the assemblies repeatedly emphasized? In the midst of a controversy with Lord Cornbury, New York assemblymen defined what they meant as clearly as any group of colonials. By rights they "mean[t] . . . that natural and civil Liberty, so often claimed, declared and confirmed by the *English* Laws, and which they conceive every free *Englishman* is entitled to."[8] That definition is less rigorous than we would prefer, but its very imprecision conveys two certainties. First, colonists knew very well what basic rights were integral to their claims and these needed no cataloguing. Liberty meant freedom from arbitrary power, while the achievement of that goal meant equal access with the British to the latter's well-known traditional rights.[9] Logically, it is possible to establish some order among these rights by focusing on what we might call political rights, such as representation, redress of grievances, freedom to petition, taxation by representation, and a whole range of substantive and procedural privileges and powers associated with representative government; or on legal rights such as trial by jury, habeas corpus, and due process of law.[10] But colonials made no such distinctions. What rights they chose to group together at any given time depended on their immediate perspective; when they spoke in general terms of the "unalienable Rights of the People," or of their "Civil and Religious Liberties," they referred to an unsegmented and capacious grab bag, randomly stuffed with minor and disputed, as well as major and uncontested, English rights.[11]

Second, just as colonists assumed a familiarity with English rights that denied a need for full explication, they recognized that no advantage could come from attempts to enumerate them. The value of a general claim to English rights was that it established basic principles, which were then capable of application to a great variety of local situations and needs. No one could anticipate what the future might hold. Hence, it was impossible to elaborate general principles into particular permutations that would cover all possibilities. Often it was the inventive challenge of prerogative or proprietary power that startled colonists into recognizing the implications of general rights. We, of course, see that process a little differently. Some claims for old rights were, in fact, a bid for new rights. What some popular politicians argued to be a reestablishment of old rights, we see as novelty. But however the process is perceived, imprecise rights boundaries clearly offered the option of expanding—or as the colonists would have it, reaffirming—rights at any time.

The lack of precise contemporary analysis of English rights notwithstanding, New Yorkers and Pennsylvanians were ardently interested in establishing a sizable stable of colonial rights suitable for service in their expansive new-world environment of popular politics. They imported into their respective colonies the heightened rights consciousness that was a product of the fierce constitutional and military struggles against centralizing monarchs in the British Isles and western Europe during the late seventeenth century. In New York, that feeling was intensified by the sense of being deprived of rights that James Stuart's policies produced, and by the prerogative powers royal governors paraded on paper. In Pennsylvania, it was fostered by the promise that provincials should enjoy more rights than even the English enjoyed, and by the threat of uncontrolled proprietary privileges.[12] In both colonies, rights consciousness was further encouraged by the respective assemblies' fight for institutional integrity and an enlarged sphere of governmental competence. While the chief thread of legislative continuity was the proving and consolidating of popular power, legislators continually posed their case, not in the language of power, but in that of rights. Throughout the late seventeenth and early eighteenth centuries, when the assemblies fought some of their most important battles against prerogative and proprietary privilege, they continually filled the air with cries of liberty and the people's rights. Assembly rights were popular rights, and popular rights were both represented by, and integral to, assembly rights.

Once rights awareness became entrenched in both the conception and rhetoric of popular politics, as it had by the early eighteenth century, it remained a central part of provincial political culture throughout the remaining colonial years. Popular politicians in New York and Pennsylvania took a leading role in exploring and attempting to extend or consolidate the terrain of popular rights. In New York, the best illustration of this impulse was the conflict over freedom of speech; in Pennsylvania, that over liberty of conscience.

Freedom of Speech and the Zenger Trial

The most important exploration of the boundaries of civil rights in colonial New York concerned the issue of freedom of speech. Arising out of New

York provincial politics in the late 1720s and early 1730s, popular concern about freedom of speech crystalized around the well-known trial of John Peter Zenger, a printer, in New York City in 1735. The immediate circumstances that led to the Zenger case began with William Cosby's appointment to the governorship of New York in 1731.

Cosby was one of those royal representatives whom Lewis Morris, Jr., described in words that smile sardonically from the page: "Governours . . . do not come here to take the air"; they "generally" come, he continued, "either to repair a shattered fortune, or acquire an Estate."[13] Cosby had barely arrived in August 1732, when he turned his attention to fattening his purse. Ignoring his royal instructions, which forbade the acceptance of legislative presents, Cosby pried a £1,000 gift from the assembly to compensate for his self-attested lobbying effort on New York's behalf prior to his departure from Britain. He quickly initiated the practice of demanding for himself or his nominees one-third of all lands included in new patents, and, compared to his recent predecessors, began to profit excessively from his right to pay and supply the four companies of British troops in the province.[14]

Cosby's avarice quickly towed him into dangerous waters. Determined to have all he could lay his hands on, he demanded half the perquisites of the governor's office from the time of his predecessor's death in July 1731 until his own appearance in New York. The problem was that the provincial council had already agreed that an ambiguity in royal instructions allowed the interim chief executive, the council president Rip Van Dam, to avoid reserving half his executive income for the new governor. Van Dam stood fast on the council's recommendation, and when Cosby began to push, Van Dam responded with his version of a compromise: Van Dam would relinquish half of the income of nearly £2,000 he had enjoyed if Cosby would split the reputed £6,400 Cosby had taken in as governor while still in Britain. Stalemated, Cosby decided to proceed with a lawsuit in an appropriate equity court. Unhappily for the governor, the only equity court in the province was the Chancery Court over which he presided. To accept a case in which he was both judge and plaintiff required too much effrontery even for Cosby. His solution was to create a Court of Exchequer by executive ordinance, over which the existing supreme court judges would preside, and to which he would submit his case. By December 1732, this had been done, and in April the Cosby/Van Dam case came up before a supreme court composed of three judges who enjoyed tenure during the "pleasure" of the Crown. Since he was the Crown's deputy in New York, it appeared that Cosby could start to count his money.[15]

First appearances were, however, deceiving. The key figure in the lawsuit was Chief Justice Lewis Morris. Colonel Morris, as even his close friends called him, was at an important juncture in his own career.[16] After nearly twenty years of riding haughtily through New York on the flanks of Governors Hunter and Burnet—of playing the chief advisor to governors and leading assemblymen, and of successfully sponsoring relatives and friends to high offices—the chief justice had watched New York's turbulent political currents cut away his power bases. Popular perceptions of him as too much a governor's man lost him his assembly seat in 1728. Ironically, this occurred just as new gubernatorial appointments cost him his former influence. William Cosby's predecessor, John Montgomerie, allied himself with Morris's opponents, Adolphe Philipse and Stephen DeLancey, and in the process expelled Morris's son Lewis, Jr., from the provincial council. When Cosby took over as governor of both New York and New Jersey, he made no discernable effort to return Morris to favor. Piqued, Morris insulted the status-conscious Cosby by forcing the new governor to wait over an hour beyond the prearranged time at which Morris, the senior New Jersey councillor, was to surrender the seals of that government.[17] With Morris's career on the skids and personal animosity between governor and chief justice, the question that intrigued politically aware New Yorkers was whether Morris would play cat's-paw for Cosby in the Van Dam case. What added an additional twist to the case was the knowledge that if Morris's court decided for Cosby, the governor might well come after one-half the perquisites that the chief justice had recently pocketed as interim chief executive of New Jersey.

Morris was a hard-drinking, arrogant, disputatious man who had a talent for turning adversity to advantage. His long-range goal remained the same as it had been since his entry into colonial politics four decades earlier: to win the highest possible public offices for himself and his sons. In the midst of his current dilemma, he glimpsed a long-shot way to pursue that end, and to repair the loss of political advantage he had recently suffered. Using his power as chief justice to dictate the grounds upon which the Cosby/Van Dam dispute would be argued, Morris opened the hearing with a ruling that the court would entertain no arguments about the particular case, only arguments as to the legality of the supreme court acting as an exchequer court. A confounded attorney-general, representing Governor Cosby, was reduced to ineffective extemporizing. But Van Dam's counsel, James Alexander and William Smith, Sr., whom the devious Morris had forewarned, cut into the court's structural timbers with a well-honed critique. When they tired, the chief justice completed the demolition with a prepared address arguing that all colonial equity courts required legislation, not gubernatorial ordinances, to legalize their existence. When the second and third supreme court judges, James DeLancey and Frederick Philipse, disagreed with their senior colleague, Morris's response was to condemn their reasoning as "weak and futile" and stomp out of the court, vowing never again to participate in equity proceedings.[18] The surprised Cosby dithered for four months before firing Morris in mid August 1733 and elevating the second justice, James DeLancey, to the chief justiceship.[19]

The fact that Cosby hesitated before throwing Morris out of office indicated that the former chief justice's tactics had been worth the gamble. Morris's forthright attack on equity courts gave him immediate community support as champion of a very popular cause. Unlike common law courts, which provided for jury decisions, equity courts were legal tribunals in which either the governor or his appointed justices decided the case. Both large and small landowners, many of whom were far in arrears for the annual quitrent payments they owed the Crown, feared these courts because of their potential for vigorous collection of back rents. Morris had hoped that leadership of a popular cause, combined with his long record of service under the Crown, would force Governor Cosby to deal with him on his own terms and allow Morris to dominate the governor. It was an audacious play for power that might have worked had Cosby long remained paralyzed by the tentativeness that occasionally plagued him.

Cosby saw the danger Morris represented and resolved his doubts about about how to respond through his recognition that in any direct confrontation with the old chief justice that involved an appeal to England, he, as incumbent governor, had the upper hand. Once, when one of his advisors reproached the governor for suggesting an illegal action, Cosby allegedly replied, "How gentlemen, do you think I mind that . . . I have a great interest in England."[20] It was that interest, centering on his brother-in-law, the earl of Halifax, and his cousin by marriage, the duke of Newcastle, that Cosby relied on to carry his colors in any race to influence the Board of Trade.[21]

As Cosby expected, Morris appealed his loss of office to that body, for it could recommend to the Privy Council that Cosby be reprimanded, replaced, or ordered to reinstate the former chief justice.[22] But the appeal in itself would not be enough. Knowing that he could not hope to match Cosby's connections at Whitehall,[23] Morris set out to outmaneuver him in New York. First, he ran a noisy, successful by-election campaign that restored him to the assembly in October 1733.[24] This allowed Morris to spearhead intragovernmental opposition to Cosby and to mask personal attacks on the governor with parliamentary privilege. Second, he and a small number of his supporters, led by the politician and lawyer James Alexander, backed the printer John Peter Zenger in publishing the *New-York Weekly Journal*,[25] a newspaper whose raison d'être was to attack the governor. The conspirators hoped that an aroused public would raise such a clamor against Cosby that the governor's English masters would have no choice but to replace him. Finally, Morris traveled to England himself in late 1734 to press for a Board of Trade hearing into his dismissal, lobby for reinstatement, and negotiate with British politicians for some reform of New York politics.[26]

The background of the Zenger case had other dimensions as well, which went beyond the person of Lewis Morris, Sr. A sprinkling of Morris's close friends, who also had become accustomed to claiming popularity with the electorate, as well as influence with provincial governors, were concerned about their loss of both during the late 1720s and early 1730s. Their chief opponent, Adolphe Philipse, had managed to identify himself and his supporters with a long tradition of popular hostility to New York's governor-run chancery court, with the considerable discontent, inspired by Governor Burnet's efforts to shut off fur trade–related commerce with the French in Canada and with numerous other popular issues.[27] Stealing a second leaf from the Morris/Alexander political handbook, Philipse had then successfully gained intermittent advisory status with Governors Montgomerie and Cosby.

Outflanked politically, a number of the Morris/Alexander faction also felt that Governor Cosby had singled them out, to bear the weight of his cupidity in connection with a particular land grant known as the Oblong Patent, or Equivalent Lands.[28] This 50,000-acre patent lay along the New York–Connecticut border and was ceded by Connecticut to New York as the "equivalent" of southwestern Connecticut (see map 3). That part of Connecticut had originally lain within New York's boundaries, but because it had been settled by New Englanders, New York was willing to give it up in 1683 on promise of future recompense. Because of the cost of surveying the Equivalent Lands, nothing was done until 1730, when a group of investors, most of whom were Morris/Alexander allies, agreed to finance the survey themselves in return for a patent.[29] Governor Montgomerie acquiesced, but in the meantime a disaffected New Yorker, Francis Harison, who "thought himself slighted in not being consulted & taken into that Scheme," organized a group of English notables to petition the Crown in England for the same land.[30] The English group received its patent a month before the New York speculators gained theirs. Despite the fact that the legal description Harison had given to the English patentees was faulty, they commenced a suit against their New York counterparts to be tried in New York's chancery court. That Governor Cosby would preside over the case, that Francis Harison had become one of Cosby's chief confidants, that Cosby's attorney-general initiated the suit, and that Cosby's greed indicated that the governor would like nothing better than to break the 1730 New York patent and regrant the land, securing shares and granting fees for himself, stirred the Morris/Alexander crowd into a veritable frenzy.[31] As Cadwallader Colden observed with uncharacteristic understatement, "this created him [Cosby] many Ennemies who not only oppos'd him as in other cases & as others did from the general opinion of his avaricious ill principles but out of Interest which generally works with the greatest force on mens passions for many & several of good Estates & of the most considerable men in the Province had shares in that patent."[32]

Unhappy with their continuing loss of influence in New York politics and the costs that forced them to bear, the Morris/Alexander men fought back. First, they tried to wrest from Adolphe Philipse the mantle of people's defender from prerogative courts. They attempted to exploit the Cosby/Van Dam case to that end, and once the Equivalent Lands controversy seemed headed for the provincial chancery court, they did their best to make the case speak on behalf of all New York's landholders. Should Cosby favorably rule on "a suit to break and anull a Patent in this Country where all the Titles in the country depend upon Patents, . . . No man could . . . [have] any security for his Estate."[33] When Cosby dismissed the initial objection of the Equivalent Lands' New York patentees to the proceedings in chancery, they presented a petition to the assembly challenging the legitimacy of prerogative courts.[34] But on this issue Adolphe Philipse would not give ground. It was *his* committee of grievances that took the petition under consideration and publicly pronounced that a "Court of Chancery . . . under the Exercise of a Governor, without consent in General Assembly" was "contrary to Law. . . and of dangerous Consequences to the Liberties and Properties of the People."[35]

In the face of such travails and the problematic nature of their connections in England, the Morris/Alexander mob put considerable emphasis on the *New-York Weekly Journal* when they began its publication in November 1733. What would help them, they knew, was that they had a very easy target. Cosby was a man who made "little Distinction betwixt power and right."[36] A combination of English arrogance and the military habit of command led Cosby to push his executive power beyond whatever ill-defined boundaries provincials expected him to observe. Moreover, he was always well accompanied on such forays, for some leading colonials often found even the questionable use of gubernatorial influence quite tolerable if it accompanied their personal preferment. The majority of the council always supported the governor, the leaders of the assembly were in league with him, ordinary assemblymen accepted influence in the appointment of justices of the peace and militia offices as the bounty of acquiescence, sheriffs were willing to run elections as Cosby directed, and a variety of both local officials and private citizens were prepared to ignore some excesses in the use of executive power if they could share in its exercise and profit from its application.[37] Thus, when Peter Zenger's press opened fire, not all of its editorial snipers aimed directly at Cosby:

> Let's scorn the tools bought by a sop,
> and every cringing fool.
> The man who basely bend's a fop,
> a vile insipid tool.[38]

The chief figure in organizing the *Weekly Journal*'s attack on Cosby and his cohorts was Councillor James Alexander. Alexander was one of those rare lawyers who was equally at home amid legal logic chopping or contemporary political philosophy, and he despised "Sailor" Cosby, whose idea of proper address to disapproving councillors was a "God Dam ye!"[39] For Alexander, whose distaste for personal confrontation could prompt narcissistic musings, the newspaper was an ideal way of putting his distaste for Cosby at arm's length, and at the same time indulging his journalistic pretensions. By April of 1734, six months after the *Weekly Journal*'s first issue, Alexander had built up a persuasive case against the Cosby entourage. The governor had sanctioned illegal activities by his councillors, lawyers, and appointees, used the chancery court to intimidate landholders, disqualified voters who met property and residency qualifications, undermined the independence of council and judiciary, destroyed property rights, and flirted with treason by allowing French traders into New York harbor. Even allowing for partisan exaggeration (of which there was a good deal), it was a substantial indictment.[40]

The *Weekly Journal*'s steady barrage of criticism and the attendant effusion of pasquinades wore at the nerves of Cosby and his associates.[41] The local hostility and ridicule that soon spread beyond the narrow Morris/Alexander circle was threatening in its immediacy, while it simultaneously undermined Cosby's interest with English Whig politicians, who put a high value on peaceful provinces. After unsuccessful attempts to defend themselves in William Bradford's *Gazette,* the other newspaper in town, Cosby and his advisors "resolved to make use of the authority with which they were vested to crush what they were not able to do by Argument."[42] The means of accomplishing this was the law of sedition and libel. All Cosby and his cronies had to do was to initiate prosecution and secure conviction.

On the surface, that did not seem particularly difficult. A right of freedom of speech did exist, grounded originally in the privileges that members of Parliament had claimed in order to protect themselves from punitive-minded monarchs, and that extended to the colonies through analogous assembly claims. In the process, that right had expanded to pertain to all freeholders. In addition, it had become coupled with the collateral right of freedom of the press when, after the English Licensing Act had been allowed to lapse in the mid 1690s, and colonial governors and councils ended their attempts to force prior approval on publishers in the early 1700s, the traditions of polemical writing, which developed in England and the Low Countries, began to find expression in the North American colonies.[43]

Yet freedom from prior censorship did not mean one had an unqualified right to speak or publish as one wished.[44] Everyone was subject to the common law that provided for the punishment of those who libeled, not only other individuals and God (blasphemy), but also public authority. This latter category, known as seditious libel, provided for the prosecution of those who defamed or ridiculed the government. Whenever government officials felt they or the institutions for which they spoke had been publicly maligned, and wanted legal retribution, they had two courses open to them. One was to have the chief justice bring the issue to the attention of a grand jury in hope that this public inquisitorial body would return a true bill against the alleged offender. The second was to have the attorney-general bypass the grand jury and file an "information," or direct charge. Should the government be determined not merely to harass the alleged libeler, but actually to press charges, the trial was to be by jury. That circumstance, however, meant little even to those defendants who had strong community support. By law the jury had only the right to decide if the defendant was the actual person responsible for the offending words and if those words, in fact, referred to the persons or institutions that the prosecution alleged. Whether or not the language actually constituted a libel was not for the jury to decide. That was the province of the presiding judge.

In light of the law of libel, then, freedom of speech or the press meant only the right to criticize in an innocuous way. Any publication of words that administration officials could construe as tending to bring the government into ill repute constituted a crime. An additional characteristic of libel law made it very difficult for the defendant to establish any kind of effective defense. According to the law, the truth of the alleged libel could be no defense. In fact, judges were usually guided by precedents stating that the truth of a libelous statement, far from exonerating it, only *exacerbated* the offense. A truthful statement was more likely to bring discredit on the government, and thus threaten the public peace.

Cosby, of course, took a personal hand in the effort to silence his critics. Twice in 1734, he had new Chief Justice James DeLancey wave the *Weekly Journal* and the law of libel in front of the New York City grand jury, but in each case, the jury refused to frame a true bill against Zenger. In November 1734, the governor had his council order the New York Court of Quarter Sessions to burn in public selected issues of the *Weekly Journal*, only to meet defiance. Subsequently, the council ordered Zenger imprisoned, and when the grand jury again refused to indict him in January 1735, Cosby had his attorney-general bring a direct charge, an "information," against the printer.[45]

While William Cosby set the stage for the Zenger trial, the lead actor on the administration side was the newly appointed chief justice, James De-Lancey. DeLancey was a second-generation colonial with a first-rate English legal education, high political aspirations, a strong network of British connections at his disposal, and a leading New York merchant-politician for a father. Elevated to leadership on the supreme court after Lewis Morris's dismissal, DeLancey was determined to keep the post. His dislike of Morris for the humiliation Morris had heaped on him and his fellow justice Frederick Philipse during the Van Dam/Cosby case, along with filial loyalty to his father, Stephen DeLancey, one of the assembly's two main pro-administration leaders, were other reasons why DeLancey cooperated with the Cosby camp. Any further rationalizing he needed, he accomplished by convincing himself that the *Weekly Journal* was tending to undermine the local social order. The young DeLancey viewed respect for government and its officials as a precondition for a civilized provincial society.[46]

In the Zenger case, DeLancey was prepared to assert informally some of the power that inhered in his social and judicial position in order to protect the government he represented. Prior to the trial, the new chief justice made clear what his opinion would be, through what Councillor Cadwallader Colden termed "an exorbitant stretch of power."[47] As councillor, DeLancey had voted to burn a number of Zenger's printings; as chief justice, he charged three grand juries to return presentments against the *Weekly Journal;* as a private individual, he had railed at Zenger on the street; and as presiding judge on the occasion of the printer's arraignment, he set bail at an unjustifiably high £400.[48] As for the jury, whose task it would be to decide the facts of the case (in this trial, whether or not Zenger had printed the seditious material), DeLancey tried more direct intimidation. He declared in public prior to the trial that any jury acquitting Zenger would be guilty of perjury.[49] Tactics of intimidation were common enough in New York politics that, to this point, DeLancey felt he had sacrificed neither personal popularity nor his independence to the extent of jeopardizing his long-term political ambitions. Blatant manipulation of the jury in such a high-profile trial was, however, another matter. Unwilling to risk himself further, De-Lancey overrode the Cosby-appointed court clerk when he tried to pack the jury with men beholden to the governor, including his "baker, tailor, shoemaker, candlemaker, joiner, etc." DeLancey insisted that a more fairly selected jury be impaneled.[50]

At the time of the Zenger trial, DeLancey was just thirty-two years old, with only four years' experience on the supreme court. The one possibility he feared was prolonged courtroom confrontation with seasoned defense attorneys. Zenger's lawyers were William Smith, Sr., and James Alexander, a duo who immediately proved their reputation on their first appearance for

Zenger. At the presentment hearing on April 15, 1735, they moved to intro-
duce arguments against the legality of DeLancey's commission, and hence
against the current proceedings. Able to construe this line of argument as an
attack on the legitimacy of government, and knowing that arbitrary disci-
plining of lawyers would generate little popular hostility, DeLancey took a
step intended to protect himself from a vigorous defense. Accusing Smith
and Alexander of bringing the issue "to that point that either we must go
from the bench, or you from the bar," he suspended the two defense attorneys from further practice before the supreme court.[51] DeLancey then appointed a less formidable, Cosby-sympathizing barrister, John Chambers,
to represent Zenger, and set the trial date for August 4th.[52]

When the Zenger trial opened on the appointed day, DeLancey quickly
realized he had outfoxed himself. Seated amidst the packed audience was the
Philadelphian Andrew Hamilton. A man of "art, eloquence, vivacity and
humor" and a "confidence which no terrors could awe," Hamilton enjoyed
the reputation of being the best colonial lawyer of his day.[53] DeLancey's
suspicion that James Alexander had engaged Hamilton for the defense was
quickly confirmed. After John Chambers had opened the defense, Hamilton
rose and with the help of his cane, carefully picked his way forward. "May it
please Your Honor; I am concerned in this case on the part of Mr. Zenger
the Defendant."[54] After the chief justice acknowledged him, Hamilton
swiftly took the case away from the attorney-general.[55] Admitting that
Zenger had printed the cited *Weekly Journal* articles, he argued that contrary to the accepted law, truth should be a defense in actions for libel and
moved to have witnesses admitted who might attest to the veracity of Zenger's charges. It was early enough in the trial for DeLancey to try to contain
the damage. The chief justice refused Hamilton's request, reiterating that
the truth could be no defense for libel. Blocked at that point, as he clearly
expected to be, Hamilton quickly changed his tactic. He engaged the prosecuting attorney, Richard Bradley, and Chief Justice DeLancey in a discussion of the jury's need to understand the innuendo of the alleged libel, and
when DeLancey again tried to hold Hamilton back, stating, not quite accurately, that the only issue that concerned the jury was whether Zenger
"printed or published" the offensive material, Hamilton challenged the
bench: "I know . . . [the jury has] the right beyond all dispute to determine
both the law and the fact, and where they do not doubt of the law, they
ought to do so. This of leaving it to the judgement of the Court *whether the
words are libelous or not* in effect renders juries useless."[56] Hamilton's certainty in his equation of the right to a jury trial with the right of the jury to
bring in a general verdict, and the current of excitement that he aroused in
his audience with this audacious claim, froze Chief Justice DeLancey in his
chair. He simply abdicated to the mesmeric figure before him.[57]

Once in command of the stage, Hamilton launched into an impressive defense. Why should a jury rather than the judges decide what constituted libel? Because judges were appointed by the allegedly libeled administration, and thus were influenced by considerations of power. Juries on the other hand, were community members who were best informed about the circumstances surrounding the charge, and they felt the obligation to maintain the lives, liberties, and estates of their "fellow subjects."[58] Why were the harsh precedents of English libel law inapplicable in New York? Because they had been forged in a monarchical English past where the king's government was at stake. In the New World, where governors were but "fellow subject[s]" and the colonies were but corporations, threats to authority were of far less "dangerous consequences" to the social order.[59] What were juries better able to judge in the colonies? Whether or not the alleged libels were defensible. How could the jurymen tell? The basic test should be that of the truth. (Hamilton smuggled this in whenever he could and implied it throughout his presentation.) How strong public criticism of government might be depended on the degree to which any administration abused power and infringed on the people's rights. Citizens always had the "natural right" to remonstrate, a right that included sharp public criticism used purposefully to mobilize public opinion.[60] Given the extreme difficulty of arraigning high colonial officials, the only effective way to protect colonial rights was through the public exposure of misdeeds. Free speech was as fundamental as representation to the integrity of the colonial constitutions.

Scattered through Hamilton's long monologue were other appeals pitched to bring jury and audience to his side. He mocked the concept of seditious libel in a society where a man could "make very free with his God, but . . . must take special care what he says of his governor."[61] He played with the Bible to show how easily Scripture might be turned by innuendo into a libelous statement. Finally, in a riveting peroration, Hamilton coupled the Zenger case with mythic heroes and the libertarian tradition they represented: "The question before the Court . . . is not of small or private concern, it is not the cause of a poor printer, nor of New York alone: . . . No! It may in its consequence affect every freeman that lives under a British government on the main of America. It is the best cause. It is the cause of liberty."[62] In the hush that followed Hamilton's summation, Chief Justice DeLancey collected himself enough to flatly recapitulate the law to an unhearing jury. Moments later, the foreman pronounced John Peter Zenger "Not guilty!" and jubilant "huzzas" rang through the hall.[63]

As recent commentators have pointed out, far from being men of principle, the sponsors of Zenger's newspaper were chiefly self-serving opportunists.[64] They amounted to "a somewhat narrow-minded political faction seeking immediate political gain."[65] It was their loss of popularity and influence and the hope of regaining both that led them to sponsor the *Weekly Journal*. Inspired by examples of closely directed opposition newspapers on the periphery of English politics, the *Weekly Journal*'s editors hoped to integrate such an exercise in partisanship and controlled conflict into the mainstream of New York politics.[66] And for a time they were successful, for the mocking and occasionally biting criticism *Journal* writers leveled at Cosby and his alleged tools provoked the Zenger case, which in turn gave the Morris/Alexander crew an unequaled podium from which to present themselves as spokespersons for the rights of the people.

Born of political rivalry, unbridled ambition, and personal animosities, the Zenger case revealed more in the way of the interest-based, competitive impulse in New York politics than of high passion for principle. Moreover, the character of the case itself by no means placed it alone in the vanguard of libertarian thought. The conflict between the Morris/Alexander faction and the Cosby administration had already been "scripted" in England, where opponents of Sir Robert Walpole were pleading liberty of the press against the long-established legal power of the government to prosecute its critics.[67] In New York, the Morris/Alexander writers simply took those facets of English opposition polemics that best served their purpose, interwove them with the peculiarities of local circumstance, and waited to see if the administration would initiate the standard repressive response. The freedom of speech for which the Morris/Alexander faction contended was not what we understand as freedom of expression, but what critical minds were already advocating in England—that an opposition press should be acceptable, but only when it did no damage to the body politic.[68]

Only in Andrew Hamilton's defense did some hint of greater breadth appear. In his presentation, Hamilton stressed two points. One was that the truth should be no libel, and the second was that the jury should be allowed to render general verdicts, rather than have their competence confined to the facts of the case (in this situation, whether or not Zenger had published the questionable material). In the former, Hamilton echoed the "maverick" idea that the English radical Whig writers John Trenchard and Thomas Gordon had suggested in their *Independent Whig,* that the truth should be no libel.[69] In the latter, he exploited the hallowed common law right to jury trials, local belief in the importance of community members as arbiters of acceptable standards of behavior, and the tension that always exists between judge and jury over their relative competence to shelter scurrilous, but popular, criticism of the existing government. But until the end of the eighteenth century, the courts would have none of this argument. Protective of English precedent, their power, and the governments that had secured them their places, subsequent judges rejected Hamilton's argument out of hand.[70]

Yet it is important not to sell the Zenger case too short. Subsequent to the trial, royal courts never succeeded in convicting any colonial of libel, and, although in comparison with England the range of political debate in the colonies was relatively narrow, if anything, the ineffectiveness of Crown prosecutors in this and subsequent cases encouraged partisan writers to test the boundaries of critical commentary.[71] And while Andrew Hamilton's defense of Zenger is often viewed as being short on law and long on rhetoric, the rhetoric itself was of considerable significance. The Zenger case became one of the best-known episodes in the public affairs of the North American colonies precisely because, to many colonials, Hamilton's defense expressed some sense of what justice meant, no matter what the law laid down. By the second quarter of the eighteenth century, most politically aware New Yorkers were convinced that popular criticism of administrative officials should take precedence over pleas by executive and judicial officers of a traditional state right to protect itself from negative comment. Public opinion, not Crown-appointed judges, should decide issues of libel, and the jury represented that community right in a trial. Extensive adherence to this idea by the time of the Zenger trial owed a good deal to past development in the practices of representative government. As they asserted their power in the language of the people's rights, the assemblies fostered the notion that what was truly salient, not only to the legislative sphere, but also to the executive and federative facets of government, was popular opinion. Assertions of popular right and popular power thus fed off each other, reinforcing the belief in popular sovereignty and spreading the notion that if government was truly to serve the interests of the people, those who spoke for a self-proven popular cause always had a self-evident legitimacy.[72]

Liberty of Conscience and Provost William Smith

To contemporaries, the most remarkable feature of William Penn's colony was its guarantee of liberty of conscience. Penn considered freedom of religion to be, as he put it in drafting his first Pennsylvania constitution in 1681, "the fi[r]st fundamentall of the Government of my Country. . . . [E]very Person that does or shall reside therein shall have and enjoy the Free possession of his or her faith and exercise of wors[h]ip towards God, in such way and manner As every Person shall in Conscience beleive is most acceptible to God and so long as every such Person useth not their Christian liberty to Licentiousness."[73] The first article of the Charter of Privileges reiterated that promise in 1701. No one who "acknowledge[d] one Almighty God" should be "molested or prejudiced in his or their person or Estate because of his or their Consciencious perswasion or Practice."[74]

What Penn and his Quaker supporters meant by liberty of conscience and how their fellow Pennsylvanians came to see that right is an important question.[75] On the simplest level, the Quakers meant that there should be no established church in the colony, and that no resident should be compelled "to frequent or maintain any Religious Worship, place or ministry contrary to his or her mind."[76] That meant that church attendance should be voluntary and that no tithe to support the clergy of a theoretically all-encompassing church would be required of anyone. To Quakers, liberty of conscience meant the "unalterable . . . free Exercise of their Religious Perswasion in the Public Worship of God" and "freedom from being compelled to do or suffer any . . . Act or thing contrary to their Religious Perswasion."[77] Penn originally designed such freedom as "an instrument of Christian salvation," but in fact Pennsylvanians tolerated both Catholics and Jews.[78] And although liberty of conscience was not intended to encourage religious or denominational indifference, those who did want freedom from the demands of organized religion found Pennsylvania a congenial residence. As Christopher Saur observed soon after his arrival in Pennsylvania, "everybody may believe what he chooses."[79]

Along with the freedom to practice religion as an individual saw fit went an important implicit right. That was the right to express openly idiosyncratic religious views in the process of defining doctrine and reasoning out modes of religious worship.[80] In practice, that meant the right to contend for religious truth. As Friends' foes would eagerly attest, Quakers were among the quickest of seventeenth-century sectarians to resort to rhetoric and the pen for the furtherance of their cause. Although the prophetic, proselytizing strain in Quakerism was already beginning to weaken during the later days of the century, many of those involved in Pennsylvania's founding, including William Penn, recognized that a promise of freedom of religion meant little without the right to unfettered religious discussion.[81] Penn, of course, hoped that the acrimony that often accompanied religious debate in the Old World would moderate under the influence of Quaker benevolence, reason, and tolerance in Pennsylvania.[82] There were, however, important considerations that suggested otherwise. The very conception of a religiously diverse society peopled by the religiously concerned promised spates of intense religious debate. More important, there were features of Quakerism that were bound to generate disagreement when given expression in government.

The difficulties Quakers would face in trying to fulfill William Penn's visionary ambitions began with Friends' conception of their religious obligations. To Quakers, life was a continuous testimony to truth. Constant observance of a plain style of dress and of plain speech, as well as consistent refusal to swear oaths or to bear arms were simultaneously substantive and symbolic statements of Quaker determination to carry the principles of truth, as they perceived them, into all facets of their lives. That dedication to a particular form of religious observance was bound to be reflected in any Quaker government, for Friends assumed that *"Government . . . [was] a part of religion itself."*[83] In rejecting old-world Erastianism—the belief that the church should serve the state—they turned it completely on its head: governmental activities, like all activities, were to enhance spiritual life. For Quakers, there was no distinct pattern in the social fabric that set apart civil concerns from religious behavior. Civil and religious affairs were of the same cloth, woven to the same large design.

The result was potential conflict between the theoretical religious liberty that Penn promised to all and the peculiarities of Quaker belief that were reflected in their governmental policies. The most important area in which Friends' religious beliefs intruded on what non-Quakers perceived as their rights was that of waging war. Quakers had long professed personal pacifism, but their control of the Pennsylvania government raised the question of what military measures, if any, a Quaker colony might take. Because the British were at war with France from 1689 to 1697, and from 1702 to 1713, this was no academic question. During these years, Pennsylvania was in occasional danger from pirates or from enemy privateers who entered the Delaware River, and Great Britain made sporadic demands upon Pennsylvania's financial and manpower resources for new-world campaigns. Quakers were divided about what their obligations were, but over the years worked out compromises that satisfied most Friends' sense of integrity, yet acknowledged some obligation to the empire. There should be no militia law, even if it exempted conscientious objectors without exacting a fine. If an invasion threatened, Quakers argued that the governor, in his capacity as captain-general, could call out a voluntary militia to defend the colony under his and his officers' directions. Beyond that, as an expression of loyalty, Quaker legislators could vote money to the "King's Use," which could be spent by the chief executive on whatever military or quasi-military project the governor or the British minister had in mind.[84]

For many non-Quakers, however, these limited concessions to the realities of a war-ridden world did not go far enough to respect their rights. In 1702, Governor Andrew Hamilton put the case that Presbyterians were most likely to articulate: "for if those who profess themselves under a scruple to bear arms would think it a hardship to be forced to it, so (I hope) they'll also think it one to Invade the principles of others by Disabling them to Effect what they in Conscience ought to do, which is to Provide, under God, for ye Defence of ye Inhabitants against the Insults of an Enemy."[85] Others argued that they had a natural right to a government that provided adequate defense.[86] To all the Quaker critics, that right entailed a strong militia law and a willingness on the part of the legislature to raise money generously for fortifications, privateers, cannon, provincial troops, and both support services and manpower for British-directed campaigns.

Amid Pennsylvania's first wartime crises, colonists came to realize there was no way to reconcile their conflicting demands. What Quakers saw as an expression of liberty of conscience in their province, non-Quakers and some none-too-conscientious Friends saw as an invasion of theirs. William Penn expressed the dilemma as clearly as any. He had come "thither to lay the Foundation of a free Colony for all Mankind, that should go thither, more especially those of my own profession; not that I would lessen the Civil Liberties of others because of their perswasion; but skreen and Defend our own from any Infringement upon that Account."[87] To conscientious Quakers this was no sophistry but a straightforward invitation to promote their own vision of liberty of conscience. To others, of course, it was a blatant contradiction. All the contending parties could do was to argue with each other in hope of gaining greater political advantage in Pennsylvania and a measure of support from Whitehall.

The right to argue openly with Friends on the issue of defense was one that non-Quakers claimed during every colonial war. After a long period of peace following the Treaty of Utrecht in 1713, they reasserted that right during King George's War (1739–1748). Again, a Quaker assembly was prepared to give minimally to the King's Use, but not to provide a militia law or military initiatives to protect the exposed Delaware waterway. After a raiding party from a French privateer occasioned a severe fright in July 1747, Benjamin Franklin took the initiative with his pamphlet *Plain Truth* and organized a voluntary militia.[88] That action brought about a new round of public sparring between Friends and their critics. The arguments of the non-Quakers followed a familiar refrain. On grounds of conscience and natural right, they demanded a government that would wage war wholeheartedly. The Quakers' reply was their own version of religious freedom; conscience dictated that they go no further than votes to the King's Use, and those only when the need was apparent. Hard as some non-Quakers might press against Quaker policies, unless they could muster the political strength to oust Friends from government, the only right they could exercise was that of the freedom to criticize.[89]

Despite the conclusion of peace in 1748, the problem posed by these conflicting views was not about to disappear. In 1753, French forces occupied the Ohio country and western skirmishes that preceded a new general war soon took place. Beginning in 1754, the Pennsylvania Assembly was under constant demand to provide military aid, first to help the ill-fated Washington expedition, then to support the intended Braddock attack on Fort Duquesne, and finally to defend the province's own frontiers in the fall of 1755. While the Quaker conscience was being squeezed by unprecedented demands and provincial defense needs, the issue of how and to what degree Quaker government might wage war was complicated by Thomas Penn. Aware of the heavy pressure that British requests and local conditions would bring to bear on the assembly to appropriate large sums of money for the war effort, the proprietor was prepared to use the crisis to curtail the assembly's financial autonomy. Penn's governor was to sign no bill that failed to restore the chief executive's power to share in the appropriation of funds voted for the province's defense.

The Quaker assembly was thus caught in a very thorny thicket. If it voted money bills for defense that complied with the proprietor's instructions, the assembly would give up what it considered to be a very important legislative right. If, on the other hand, its defense appropriations bills met with a proprietary veto because it refused to share appropriations power with the chief executive, the assembly's political enemies would try to stigmatize its members as self-centered, faint-hearted Quakers, prepared to offer the blood of their fellow Pennsylvanians to the not-so-gentle goddess of pacifism.

Into this volatile environment came a former tutor and newly ordained Anglican clergyman named William Smith. During a two-year residence on Long Island, Smith, a Scot, had recommended himself to Benjamin Franklin by his educational writings, which complimented Franklin's plans for the newly launched Academy and Charitable School of Philadelphia.[90] During a short visit to Pennsylvania in late May 1753, Smith promoted the expansion of the academy into a college. He also secured Franklin's backing for his bid to head the institution should Smith be able to persuade Thomas Penn to finance a sizable part of the venture. Once back in Britain, Smith soon secured Penn's support for the college and for himself as provost. In addition, Smith established himself as a key intermediary between the Society for the Relief and Instruction of Poor Germans—a British philanthropic organization established in response to the German Reformed minister Michael Schlatter's European appeal for ministers and teachers to serve Pennsylvania's German immigrants—and a select group of Pennsylvanians who, as colonial trustees for the organization, would organize efforts to establish German charity schools in the colony. Such schools would provide employment for some of the schoolmaster graduates of Smith's academy and, at the same time, under Smith's direction, solve what Smith knew many Philadelphians believed to be Pennsylvania's most pressing social problem, the assimilation of a great wave of German immigrants recently arrived in Pennsylvania.[91]

Not surprisingly, the William Smith who disembarked in Philadelphia in May 1754 was rather full of himself. He had come a long way in a very short time, and in the process the confidence and social graces that had brought him success had been transformed into arrogance and duplicity. William Sturgeon, a fellow Anglican priest, characterized Smith as someone with "a High degree of Vanity and a large stock of Pride," which "prompted him to intermeddle in almost every affair."[92] Grace Galloway, one of a number of well-to-do Quaker women who knew a good deal about the province's public affairs, dismissed the provost more summarily: Smith was a "fool by Nature and an Ass by Reading."[93]

Not content with the daunting prospect of organizing the college and promoting German charity schools, Smith decided he would take a hand in setting aright Pennsylvania's political affairs. During the first six or seven months of his Philadelphia residence, Smith concluded that Quaker political power had eaten into legitimate executive functions, threatened property rights, prevented the province from taking a martial stance against the French, and would interfere with himself and other proprietary supporters achieving the kind of leadership role Smith felt was their due in the Penn colony. After his various lobbying ventures in London, he felt he knew the Quakers' Achilles heel—an appeal to British public opinion, which in turn could be focused on the powerful at Whitehall.

In early 1755, Smith's anonymous pamphlet *A Brief State of the Province of Pennsylvania* appeared in London. A scurrilous attack on the Quakers, the pamphlet raised the question of why Pennsylvania was "the most backward" colony in meeting the French invasion of the western territory.[94] After asserting that "most of the Quakers . . . [were] really against Defence from Conscience," Smith went after the assemblymen and the religious leaders of the Society, by accusing them of hypocrisy and deceit.[95] According to the provost, the Quaker insiders had "no mind to give a single shilling to the Kings Use, unless they . . . [could] thereby increase their own Power" in pursuit of their goal of "Independency" and a "pure Republic."[96] The Quakers, Smith further argued, were able to retain their political power in the face of the French danger because of the German vote. Many German sectarians shared the Quakers' pacifist principles, but the remainder were misled by the Germantown printer Christopher Saur.[97] Saur had convinced the Germans, those "ignorant . . . Stubborn Clowns," that a non-Quaker assembly would soon have them fighting the proprietor's wars and cultivating his estates.[98] As for the Quakers, Smith charged them with a fear that the creation of a militia would result in the political mobilization of the soldiers under proprietary leadership.[99] In addition, Smith repeatedly stigmatized both Quakers and Germans as soft on Catholicism, proto-papists with potentially treasonous hearts.[100]

Having identified the problem, Smith was not shy about suggesting a solution. The one way "to prevent the Province from falling into the Hands of the *French*" was for Parliament to apply to Pennsylvania appropriate versions of the same types of laws that had been used to disqualify Friends from holding office in Great Britain.[101] All Pennsylvania legislators should be required to take "Oaths of Allegiance" and a "Test or Declaration" that they would support warlike measures against British enemies.[102] The significance of the oath was lost on no one. Because Quakers would not swear oaths, they would be cleaned out of government. As for Germans, Smith offered a few hackneyed suggestions that had floated around Anglophile Philadelphia circles for some time.[103] Germans should be stripped of the vote until they learned the language—twenty years should do; legal and financial instruments in German should be illegal; no German newspapers or public journals should be allowed; and, of course, Smith's anglicizing German charity schools should be given public support.[104]

Not content with this first effort to bring down Pennsylvania's "haughty masters," Smith followed up his *Brief State* in December 1755 with a second pamphlet, *A Brief View of the Conduct of Pennsylvania for the Year 1755*.[105] In this screed, Smith updated the old themes with new material drawn from the past year. His remarks on Quakerism were just as scathing as before, and, if anything, he was more laudatory of the proprietary position. In Smith's eyes, proprietary demands for executive participation in the appropriation of public monies and for exemption from provincial taxation were just efforts to try to maintain responsibility to king and empire, to restore some balance to the Pennsylvania constitution, and to defend the property rights of all Englishmen. And, of course, the proprietary supporters would ardently defend the province against the French foe without and the papist-leaning fifth column within.

Smith's scribblings exploded in London with incendiary impact. They "raised a general outcry," "poisoned the minds of many, & . . . begot an opinion that a parliamentary enquiry must ensue."[106] To further that end, Smith penned a petition to the king-in-council, signed by a number of influential Philadelphians, which requested royal action to prevent continued legislative dominance by a group of men "whose avowed Principles [were] . . . against bearing arms."[107] Members of the Board of Trade, to whom the petition was referred, were in a receptive frame of mind. They had been influenced by Smith's pamphlets, and primed by Thomas Penn's care in supplying them with the antiwar statements of a small group of Pennsylvania's most uncompromising Quaker pacifists.[108] What made matters worse for the assembly was that British Friends, who had given strong lobbying support in earlier times, were both divided over the nature and merits of the Pennsylvanians' case and becoming less influential in Whitehall circles than they frequently had been.[109] British Presbyterians, on the other hand, operating through the lobbyist Association of Dissenting Deputies, were particularly active at this time, happy to mollify a ministry dissatisfied with the initial uncooperativeness of a number of colonial assemblies (prominent among which were Calvinist-dominated ones), with a Quaker victim.[110] After a short hearing in March 1756, the Board of Trade unequivocally condemned the behavior of the Pennsylvania assembly and recommended that Parliament intervene.[111] Interested parties quickly drafted a "Bill for the Better Defense and Preservation of his Majesty's Dominions in America," the key provision of which was that "none . . . [should] sett [in the colonial legislatures] but those who [would] swear."[112]

Immediately, the London Quakers "mov[ed] . . . heaven and earth" to prevent such an arbitrary end to William Penn's experiment.[113] Capitalizing on doubts they raised in ministry minds, on the clout of one or two friendly and powerful politicians, and on the widespread indifference of British leaders to colonial affairs, the Quakers cut a deal. The disabling legislation would be allowed to founder if Quakers would voluntarily withdraw from the Pennsylvania assembly for the duration of the war.[114] The "Honour and Reputation" of the Society of Friends stood security for the assemblymen's compliance.[115] By the time a representation of London Friends arrived in Pennsylvania in October 1756, to oversee the implementation of the agreement, however, enough Quakers had already withdrawn from government on the basis of their own reservations of conscience to leave the assembly with a minority of Friends, and those who remained apparently had no qualms about supporting a war effort.[116]

While the impact of Smith's writings in London posed the greatest danger to Pennsylvania Quakers, they occasioned more passionate outbursts across the Atlantic in Philadelphia. The *Brief State* "has made a prodigious Noise in this City," chortled Smith to Thomas Penn. Quakers were "never Known to be so vexed before."[117] Sensing that they had the Quakers on the run, supporters of the proprietorship pressed them hard. Governor Robert Hunter Morris, who was in Smith's confidence, if not during the writing of the pamphlet, then shortly after the provost had shipped the manuscript to England for publication, designed his exchanges with the assembly to follow "the same Plan" as Smith's polemic.[118] The governor charged the assembly with duplicity in trying to tax proprietary estates, arguing that they did so in order to "avoid doing what [they] judged inconsistent with [their] Principles."[119] As the leading Quaker Israel Pemberton remarked to his influential English correspondent John Fothergill, "the Governor's assertions are calculated for your Meridian, not for this."[120] Smith joined in the local commotion, too, once Indian raiding parties hit the frontier settlements, by drawing up the petition that eventually took the issue to the Board of Trade in early 1756, and in at least one other local representation that pleaded for strong war measures.[121]

Although Smith and his confidants were careful never to acknowledge his authorship of the *Brief State* outright, by early 1756 it was common knowledge in Philadelphia that it was the provost who had so "basely misrepresented" the Quakers.[122] As Smith's efforts at collective character assassination continued in the new year, it was certainly clear that his reflection on the assemblymen could be construed as scandalous criticism of government, and might hence be considered libelous.[123] Yet Friends did nothing to strike back. They refused to dignify the scurrilous *Brief State* with an answer, and when the Philadelphia Anglican Daniel Roberdeau attempted to get at Smith by revealing a private conversation in which the provost had implied that supporters of the proprietorship and executive were no "Friends of the People," Quakers stayed out of the controversy.[124] London Friends questioned their inaction by forwarding a signed letter Smith had published in the London *Evening Advertiser,* reiterating many of the charges he had levied against Friends in his notorious pamphlets.[125] When the assemblymen read it, they agreed it included "diverse wicked calumnies" and ordered Smith before the bar of the House. After a short hearing, they resolved Smith was guilty of "libelous, false and seditious Assertions," but they put off further proceedings until a "more convenient Opportunity."[126] That moment never did arrive, even for the ensuing 1756–1757 assembly.

Why did the legislature not pounce on Smith when it had him before the bar? There were several contributing factors. The assembly itself cited the press of business and the lateness of the session.[127] Both observations were valid, but they were specious reasons, for unconstrained by the niceties of due process and evidential integrity, the assembly could have jailed Smith on a moment's notice. Granted, there would have been some need for follow-up hearings, but postponements would have taken care of the problem until the end of the current session. Another practical consideration may have been Benjamin Franklin's personal agenda. Franklin was a key member of the assembly at this juncture, and it might be argued that he still hoped to prevent an irreparable breach with Provost Smith for the sake of the College of Philadelphia, which Franklin had been instrumental in establishing.[128] Indications of that, however, are slight.

Much more important than such mundane considerations was the principle of liberty of conscience. The promise of freedom of religion was integral to William Penn's experiment and fundamental to Pennsylvania Quakers' sense of identity and self-worth. Friends had long recognized that adherents of other Christian religions possessed the right to contend for their religious views, and Smith had carefully clothed his assault on Quaker government in the dress of religious freedom and natural right. As the provost was retrospectively to remark, his cause was that of freedom of "Writing and Preaching."[129] Although a half dozen strict Quakers had resigned from the legislature in June, a month before the Smith episode occurred, the assembly was still strongly influenced by conscientious Friends who recognized that belief in religious freedom demanded a willingness to take some stiff body blows from antagonists who were fighting for their version of the same goal.[130] Many Friends did not like doing so, but their concern for their Society prompted them to tolerate such criticism as a testimony to Quaker integrity. Others, much more mindful of how their forebears had proven themselves by suffering (i.e., allowing) their own persecution in late seventeenth-century England, welcomed criticism as one of the challenges that might make the midcentury years in Pennsylvania a "time of distinction as we [conscientious Friends] have not known among us."[131]

For those Quaker leaders possessing a historic turn of mind, the past provided additional guidance in the case of William Smith. It was one of the apparent illogicalities of Quakerism that a religious group dedicated to the principle of liberty of conscience did not, on arriving in Pennsylvania, adopt a rule that kept public Friends (Quaker ministers) out of civil office. There was, in short, no separation of church and state. Quaker ministers served as Pennsylvania magistrates and legislators without apparent qualms. They could so serve, and some clearly felt they *should* do so, because Quakerism was a religion that encompassed all facets of life. Laws, for example, should be drafted and interpreted so as to reflect Quaker attitudes.[132] But what accompanied this willingness to use their influence in government to reflect sectarian ends was an equally strong commitment to "forbearance."[133] They believed there were moments when magistrates and legislators should refuse to use the latent power they held in their hands, and one of those times was the moment at which religious exclusivism encroached on liberty of conscience. Knowledge of the abuses that flowed from English clergymen vested with magisterial authority reminded many of the trust Quaker leaders shared.[134] Not that temptation never narrowed their eyes: when George Keith broke with the Friends in the early 1690s, the minister/magistrates of Pennsylvania's first generation of settlers initially tried to use their power to silence the apostate.[135] But the remaining members of the judiciary stoutly resisted, arguing "*That the matter was a Religious Difference among themselves,* (viz., the Quakers) *and did not relate to the Government.*"[136] The only response the offending magistrates could muster to that observation was the lame reply that their prosecution of Keith encompassed only those parts of their critic's statements that "*tend*[ed] . . . *to Sedition*" and not those that "*relat*[ed] . . . *to Differences in Religion.*"[137] That distinction was a weak one indeed, much too fine to bear the weight of repeated public scrutiny and debate. In the wake of the Keithian dispute, public Friends gradually began to steer clear of direct involvement in governmental office, a trend that eventually led to a rough and informal separation of church and state. And

Quaker notables began to realize that even in Pennsylvania the principle of liberty of conscience could not be defended without suffering some genuine pain.

By the mid eighteenth century, thousands of non-Quaker Pennsylvanians had accepted the Friends' view that religious coercion was morally indefensible and politically unacceptable. Provincial political leaders recognized that they should avoid anything reminiscent of old-world religious intolerance, which would undermine the moral authority of Quaker leadership and the reputation for freedom that had done so much to generate the province's economic growth and prosperity. But despite Quaker efforts to protect liberty of conscience in the practice and observance of religious worship, Friends were vulnerable to critics who felt their religious and natural rights entitled them to a government willing to wage unrestricted warfare when danger threatened. The best that Quaker legislators could do in such circumstances, short of resigning, was to avoid seriously harassing those pro-war protesters who attempted to rouse public opinion to defeat Quaker pacifists at the polls. In the case of William Smith, the last thing Friends wanted to do was to turn the provost, rather than themselves, into the champion of free speech and liberty of conscience. Quakers were having considerable difficulty among themselves divining what their religious scruples allowed them to do in a full-fledged colonial war, and they did not want to take on new burdens. Despite his vigorous attacks on Quaker religion and policy, then, Smith was safe from reprisal. But only in the short run. Once the withdrawal of conscientious Quakers from the assembly separated the issue of religious freedom from that of provincial wartime policy (ironically, what the provost himself tried to effect), Smith and his allies would no longer be able to find shelter behind Friends' commitment to liberty of conscience.

The Character of the "unalienable Rights of the People"

One of the most important characteristics of public life in New York and Pennsylvania was the extensive rights consciousness of the provincial citizenry. Political leaders in the two colonies reflected and shaped that concern for provincial rights by exploring the perimeters of that consciousness in public. In New York, the Zenger defense was highly critical of British law in cases of seditious libel, and made the point that popular critics of a colony's administration should enjoy considerable license. In the case of the Quaker colony, William Penn rejected the English concession of limited religious tolerance and instituted a much broader policy of liberty of conscience that renounced coercion in, and protected the right of individuals to speak freely on, religious affairs. Although similar initiatives took place in other colonies, none posed the issues in quite the dramatic manner or sweeping fashion that distinguished these questions in New York and Pennsylvania.[138]

Rights consciousness among New Yorkers and Pennsylvanians began, as it did for other colonists, with their awareness of English constitutional thought. The rights of colonists originated in the ancient English right to representation, and its transference, along with other rights that Parliament had established over the centuries, to the British settler societies across the Atlantic. As in the case of comparable bodies in Europe, much of the strength of the English Parliament—and by analogy, the colonial assemblies—rested on claims of corporate privilege. Just as various estates or orders in Europe, consisting of an amazing array of nobles, lawyers, colleges, societies, cities, guilds, and companies, claimed rights that were essentially self-serving privileges and exemptions from general laws, the English Parliament rested much of its early strength on the particular privileges that representation gave to the lords temporal and spiritual and the knights and burgesses of the realm.[139] During centuries of change, but particularly during the critical decades of conflict with the Tudor and Stuart monarchs, Parliament strengthened its corporate cachet. And an important part of that process of institutional maturation was the House of Commons's success in asserting what became that well-known collection of English constitutional rights.[140] Although seventeenth- and eighteenth-century legislators frequently claimed these rights in the name of the nation's freeholders, they perceived them primarily as the rights of Parliament, with a much fainter (and frequently limited) application to the broader body politic.

This perception of constitutional rights, centering on their representative institutions, informed colonial as well as British thought. In laying claim to a parliamentary inheritance, and in so successfully asserting their power in the language of rights, the provincial assemblies strengthened the association between their corporate identity and colonials' possession of historic English rights. The fact that representation in the colonies was based on communities or constellations of communities within given geographic areas was a further, if in some colonies faint, reminder of the traditional connection between rights and communal corporatism. In addition, both property rights and the property in rights that colonists believed the British constitution guaranteed them, gained tangible expression within the context of community organization.[141] And residency within incorporated cities such as Albany or Philadelphia, artisan membership within informal fraternal organizations, and the attendant phrasing of rights-concerns in communal terms, occasionally reinforced the corporate view of colonial rights.[142]

While the corporate dimensions of rights consciousness was an important part of colonial thinking, an equally significant strand of rights-awareness centered on the individual. Vaunted English legal rights, conjoined so firmly with the British constitution, were usually expressed in language that suggested individual proprietorship.[143] Certainly the seventeenth-century English social theorists who perceived a developing market economy in the conformation of their contemporary world assumed legal rights to be atomistic, individual-centered claims on society.[144] To what degree, and how long before the seventeenth century, individualistic assumptions permeated English social relations and public thought is uncertain.[145] But from the seventeenth century forward, English legal rights, interpreted as individual possessions, were a fundamental component of the expanding Anglo-American commercial world.

In the colonies, the notion that traditional rights had an individual dimension and a large area of general community applicability was widespread. The acquisitive behavior of many colonists, along with the economic dynamism of various segments of the British colonial empire, gave tangible and multidimensional expression to that belief.[146] Conditions peculiar to the colonies quickly accelerated the trend, observable in early modern England and Europe, toward expanding corporate privileges there to the point at which they became symbolic of larger community rights. The close acquaintanceships that inevitably developed between legislators and their constituents in sparsely populated, contiguous, local communities encouraged the expectation that popular rights should mirror, rather than be subordinate to, assembly privilege.[147] Other characteristics of colonial sociopolitical structure—such as widespread property ownership, relatively low voting barriers, a comparatively extensive sense of economic sufficiency and independence, and the absence of the old and deeply entrenched socioeconomic groups that, in adamantly protecting their established privileges, were such a conservative force in old-world societies—all tended to expand the number of colonists who felt they had a proprietary stake in colonial rights.

The expansion of rights awareness among colonials, no matter how general and widely shared, was not without its ironies. The chief symbol of colonial rights remained the assembly; and as the assemblies augmented their power in the late seventeenth and early eighteenth centuries, they simultaneously raised their profile as protectors of the broad and amorphous cluster of traditional English rights. The assemblies were, as one commentator put it, "the Repository of the People's Priviliges."[148] But in supplementing and consolidating their powers in the name of the people's rights, the colonial assemblies reinforced their predisposition to see themselves as the central institution of colonial government. If, on the one hand, they worked to discredit some prerogative claims and undercut various governors, on the other, they compensated by touting the legislature as an important upholder of governmental integrity and symbol of social order. As a result, the assemblies claimed the right to silence their critics, through charges of contempt and libel, in the name of protecting the parliamentary privileges that lay at the historic heart of the people's rights.[149]

There were numerous examples in the colonies of an assembly "zealously pursuing its prerogative of being immune to criticism . . . summon[ing], interpret[ing] . . . , and fix[ing] criminal penalties against anyone who had supposedly libeled its members, proceedings, or the government generally."[150] The results of the Zenger trial notwithstanding, in the mid 1750s the New York Assembly threw two individuals in jail for critical comments directed at the legislature.[151] And New York assemblymen of all political stripes joined together in 1770 to jail the street politician Alexander McDougall for charging that the legislature had betrayed the public interest.[152] But the most revealing example of the arbitrary use of legislative power took place in Pennsylvania, where the controversy over Provost William Smith entered a new phase.

After Smith's brush with the Pennsylvania Assembly in the summer of 1756, he quieted down for a time.[153] The election of that fall brought a non-Quaker majority to the assembly and a subsequent legislative commitment to join in the French and Indian War. But the Provost's admiration for both the outspoken anti-Quakerism of the Chester County magistrate William Moore and Moore's daughter Rebecca soon headed him for new troubles. Magistrate Moore's history of anti-Quakerism went back to the early 1740s, and in September of 1756, he busied himself locally, just as Smith did in Philadelphia, campaigning to end Quaker political dominance.[154] Shortly thereafter, petitions accusing Moore of extortion and petty harassment began to flood across the assembly clerk's desk.[155] About that time, Smith became a regular visitor to the Moore household, pressing his ultimately successful suit for the hand of Rebecca Moore.

The petitioning campaign against Moore may have been what the Chester County magistrate claimed it to be, simply the personal vendetta of a county legislator. Whatever the exact circumstances, the assembly was prepared to invoke the centuries-old grand inquest powers of Parliament.[156] In its judicial capacity, the assembly inquired into the complaints, and on September 28, 1757, it sent an address to Governor Denny, which it subsequently ordered published in the *Pennsylvania Gazette*, declaring Moore to be guilty of "fraudulent, corrupt and wicked Practices" and asking the governor to remove the culprit from the magistracy.[157] Knowing that the assembly's dissolution for the province's annual October 1 elections spelled the end of its legal existence, Moore quickly produced a very unhumble

"Humble Address" to Governor Denny, explaining his side of the story. Moore castigated the assembly for suppressing evidence, condemning him unheard, publicly humiliating him, and denying him a trial by jury. In the process, Moore accused the House of corruption, "oppressive" behavior, "Slander . . . Obloquy," "Scurrility . . . abuse," "Malice," and acting "diametrically Opposite to the Justice and Humanity which heretofore distinguished their Predecessors."[158] Not content with venting his anger in a private document, Moore went public. He and his friends—including William Smith, who had apparently read and edited the address—arranged to have it published in both the *Pennsylvania Gazette* and the *Pensylvanisch Zeitung*.[159]

Although Moore's "Humble Address" was directed at the defunct 1756–1757 assembly, its successor was not about to let the insult pass. When the new house convened in January 1758, the Quaker speaker, Isaac Norris, Jr., was conveniently indisposed; in his place sat an Anglican, Thomas Leech. Under Leech, there could be no red herring of Quakers persecuting Anglicans, and the assembly immediately arrested Moore on a charge of contempt. During Moore's hearing, it quickly became apparent that the assembly viewed Provost William Smith as the evil spirit behind the aging Moore. Although testimony before the House could not conclusively implicate Smith as a contributing author to the "Humble Address," it was possible to establish that the provost had arranged for publication of the German translation.[160] On these grounds, the assembly charged Smith as a "Promoter and Abettor" of Moore's "Libel."[161]

As the moment of Smith's hearing approached, the assembly established the ground rules for its inquiry. It refused to hear any legal argument on either its authority to punish those guilty of seditious libel or the issue of whether the "Humble Address" actually constituted a libel. That left only the question of Smith's role as an "Abettor" or "Promoter."[162] After three days of hearings, the assembly resolved that Smith was guilty of "promoting and publishing the libellous Paper."[163] Calling Smith before the bar, the assembly ordered his commitment to "the common Gaol" until he gave "Satisfaction" to the House. Sensing a fleeting opportunity for a relatively uncostly moment of martyrdom, Smith irately refused an apology. He had been "singled out as the peculiar Object of their Resentment"; "others, equally culpable . . . had been dismissed unpunished." More to the point, he had done nothing to undercut the constitution or the people's rights. Where there was no wrong there could be no acknowledgement. "Striking his hand upon his Breast," Smith defied the House. "No Punishment they could inflict, would be half so terrible to him, as the Suffering his tongue to give his Heart the Lie."[164] Denied a writ of habeas corpus, Smith sat in jail for the next three months. There he taught his college students, who dutifully attended him for instruction, conversed with his fellow prisoner and soon-to-be father-in-law, William Moore, and put together much of the case that, on his appeal to the Privy Council, eventually secured release for both himself and Moore.[165]

Why did William Smith end up in jail in 1758, whereas two years earlier he had walked away from the Pennsylvania Assembly? Although it is possible that members of Pennsylvania's Quaker Party came to view Smith with more distaste after his electioneering in 1756 and subsequent collusion with Moore, than in the wake of his earlier pamphlet and letter writing, this argument misses the main point. The fundamental changes that took place between 1756 and 1758 were not incremental alterations in Quaker attitudes toward Smith, but a significant transformation in the composition of the Pennsylvania Assembly, the sudden irrelevance of the issue of liberty of conscience in Smith's case, and a shift in the focus of the provost's attention from Quaker influence in government to apparent legislative abuse of power. Whereas, prior to the so-called Quaker "withdrawal" from government in 1756, Friends had accepted Smith's right to criticize their public policies as an exercise of liberty of conscience, their successors were under no such restraint. To the post-1756 Quaker Party coalition of Friends, Anglicans, Presbyterians, and others who had agreed upon warlike policies, no supporter of war could possibly take shelter behind a cry for religious freedom.[166] Recent alterations in the composition of the Quaker Party simply reinforced the strategic changes that the party had sought a little earlier, that of "throw[ing] . . . our disputes from being a Quaker Cause To a Cause of Liberty."[167] Sure that they wore Liberty's fair face, believing in the irrelevance of any Smithian plea for liberty of conscience, and influenced by the sense of coherence, moral purpose, and corporate responsibility that decades of Quaker leadership had bequeathed, the assembly had no compunction about going after the provost with a vengeance when he and Moore condemned its proceedings.

Colonial rights consciousness gained particularly intense expression in New York and Pennsylvania during the eighteenth century. In both societies, the provincial assemblies constantly proselytized on behalf of colonists' rights as they built themselves into prominent authoritative institutions. In both societies, provincials felt the threat of potentially powerful forces (in New York's case, that of the prerogative; in Pennsylvania, that of the proprietary), threats that frequently encouraged them to shore up their protective shield of colonial rights. In New York, with its strong tradition of gubernatorial efforts to maintain centralized administrative presence, and its early experiences of outspoken factional dispute, it is, perhaps, not surprising that the most dramatic incident of rights conflict occurred over freedom of speech.

Similarly, we might expect that in a society like Pennsylvania, committed to an early modern experiment with liberty of conscience, that particular right would also be the focal point of much debate. The full precociousness of New Yorkers who accepted Andrew Hamilton's defense of John Peter Zenger and of the many Pennsylvanians who supported liberty of conscience is less apparent, however, in the fact of those controversies than in their justification of such rights. The British constitution's narrow construction of both freedom of speech and religion predisposed New Yorkers and Pennsylvanians to experiment with the elastic argument of natural rights to support their claims.[168] Natural rights suggested the existence of both a more expansive view of freedom of speech than the English law of libel allowed and an authoritative source of support for liberty of conscience that the Glorious Revolution, the Bill of Rights, and the older statements of English constitutional principle largely ignored. In following this logic, New Yorkers and Pennsylvanians established a legitimate means of pushing beyond old constitutional rights in a way that could be complementary to those traditions but that was also flexible enough to accommodate the aggressive demands of a rights-conscious colonial populace.

Yet despite the potential for better confronting the intellectual and social complexities of the intermingling of community, corporate, group, and individual rights within their respective societies opened up for themselves by New Yorkers and Pennsylvanians, they did not go far in this direction. The Zenger case and both phases of the Smith controversy demonstrated that colonials were only concerned with protecting the rights of those who took a "popular" stand. In this view, Zenger's publications should have been permitted because they represented a popular position in New York. Provincials searched for no general principle beyond the expediency of what was currently popular. In Pennsylvania, Smith's case, too, turned on popularity. His early maligning of the Quakers was unpunished because liberty of conscience was a popular and established principle of Pennsylvania government. But once this plea lost its validity, the Pennsylvania Assembly would punish Smith because it was a popular legislature speaking on behalf of the people. Although "the people [were] . . . more equally divided on their sentiments of the Assembly than . . . usual," in this case the legislators stood their ground.[169] Above all, the Zenger and Smith controversies illustrated the growing prominence of the popular in colonial politics. Those best positioned to plead popularity were those most capable of defending the rights they chose to claim.

Chapter Four

The Organization of Popular Politics

AT THE SAME TIME as the colonial assemblies came to play an increasingly prominent role in provincial government, and as New Yorkers and Pennsylvanians came to assign great importance to public declarations of popular rights, the ways in which groups of elected representatives organized themselves and tried to project collective identities became an equally important defining feature of colonial political structure. During the early decades of colonization, a continual, if variably expressed, popular determination to use assembly power to contain prerogative and proprietary privilege, and an acceptance (even among the Dutch of New York) of the norms of British constitutionalism had to some extent counterbalanced the tendencies toward political fragmentation in colonial New York and Pennsylvania. Common objectives and principles of cooperation, however haltingly expressed, brought some order to public affairs. But once the assemblies became the primary foci of provincial government, the major problem for elected politicians was how to create, and sustain, sufficient political coherence among themselves to maintain control of the legislature.

The problem of popular political organization was particularly acute in New York. As the eighteenth century wore on, traditional localisms and regionalisms grew sturdier roots, and as population grew, the topography of provincial society became more complex. The filling in of the Hudson

Valley counties, the growth in the number of Albany County residents, and the rapid expansion of New York City (and to a lesser extent of other long-settled townships and villages) increased the range of communities that required some degree of political inclusion. There were important developments in the province's ethnic and religious composition as well. In New York City, clusters of Germans, Scotch-Irish, Irish, and Scots appeared alongside the older Dutch, English, and French communities to further complicate the social profile of this polyglot port town. In the countryside, communities had always ranged from narrow, national-group enclaves to culturally interspersed neighborhoods, but immigration increased both the number, ethnic variety, and complexity of these. Simultaneously, New York experienced a parallel process of religious complication. Mainline churches, such as the Dutch Reformed, the Anglican, and the Presbyterian, became stronger in the midst of a growing array of minor congregations owing allegiances to such denominations as the Quakers, Moravians, German Reformed, and Dutch and German Lutherans. Any major coalition of provincial politicians had to be able to accommodate, perhaps to neutralize, possibly to use to advantage, but at least to avoid antagonizing, a broad spectrum of New York's ethnoreligious groups.

As New York developed greater complexity, the relationship between recognizable ethnoreligious groups and the structure of provincial politics became, if anything, more problematic. Ethnically, the segmentation between Dutch and English that gained obvious expression at the turn of the century in conflict between the "English party" and the "meer Dutch," and that was potentially of great importance because of the Dutch plurality in New York, either moderated or was largely ignored in later decades.[1] Sweeping political appeals to either were never again the centerpiece of political debate. Although the Dutch maintained their plurality in New York for some time, and although a large number of them continued to hold elective provincial posts throughout the colonial years, the weakness of Dutch high culture and the comparative strength of anglicizing pressures in the public world led them to assume a subsidiary role in provincial politics.[2] When Anglo-Dutch tensions began to build under conditions of intense political competition, contemporaries acknowledged such stress by either subsuming them beneath other idioms of conflict or expressing them in the context of interdenominational competition, in which Dutch Reformed interests were understood to speak for the domestic-centered, vernacular New Netherlands culture that remained the vital center of Dutch communities throughout New York.[3] Understandably, given the importance of the Dutch Reformed church for the survival of Dutch culture, and the marked need of all New York's major denominations for continuing institutional development and growth, religious divisions possessed greater potential for political conflict than did ethnic or national distinctions. When Lord Cornbury, for example, spearheaded an effort to strengthen the Anglican church in the four counties in which earlier law had created a church establishment, to support its pretensions to privilege in other parts of the province, and to exercise the power to license the Dutch Reformed clergy (who felt that the conquest had brought them promise of an autonomous, if not quite equal, "Sisterhood" with the Anglicans), there were political ramifications.[4] Dutch Reformed antagonism to imperious Anglicanism strengthened New York's early eighteenth-century legislative resolve to clip the wings of its governors and fly the assembly to greater heights. In succeeding decades, other religious conflicts occurred. Dutch Reformed congregations divided both internally and among themselves over clergy and lay attitudes toward evangelical preaching;[5] they chose sides between those who wished to continue close Dutch oversight of provincial ecclesiastical affairs (*conferentie* supporters) and those who wanted the colonial church to be more autonomous (*coetus* supporters);[6] and the large New York City congregation began slowly to pull apart when some church members began to lobby for English-language worship over the objections of those who felt a Dutch service was an essential part of their religious identity.[7] In addition, the Presbyterian church came to be distinguished by both an intermittent anti-Anglican aggressiveness, and by some strong internal disputes over church doctrine and the place of evangelical preaching.[8] These differences did not, of course, automatically or immediately gain sharp expression in provincial politics. They were simply part of the social matrix of ethnoreligious pluralism within which politicians had to work. And their effect depended on the politicians themselves—how these public figures perceived their needs and opportunities, what ends they wished to effect, and to what extent religious concerns ranked high among their personal priorities.

The changes that accompanied rapid growth in Pennsylvania were every bit as dramatic as those in New York. There, too, frontier areas were continuously pushed back and the regular incorporation of new townships within the existing political system complicated a provincial polity already distinguished by considerable variation in local character.[9] Contrary to the situation in New York, late seventeenth and early eighteenth century divisions in Pennsylvania were mainly religious rather than ethnic; Quakers themselves were a fractious bunch and when they were not arguing among themselves, Anglicans supplied a ready opposition. The most bitter of the internecine Quaker squabbles were over by the early 1700s; after another decade and a half, the worst Quaker/Anglican disputes had been laid to rest.[10] That, however, was precisely the point at which Pennsylvania experienced unprecedented immigration that by midcentury had swollen the small late seventeenth-century German component into a major linguistic group in the province, and the early clusters of Scotch-Irish into a sizable ethnic minority.[11]

Structurally, Pennsylvania's diverse communities took shape in much the same way as New York's—as a patchwork of cultural enclaves that underwent continuous change in extent, strength, and composition, and that often shaded into sizable areas of considerable diversity.[12] Not surprisingly, ethnic tensions did appear, most noticeably among Anglophilic Philadelphians, in reaction to heavy German immigration.[13] But as in New York, the Pennsylvania conflicts that had the greatest relevance for political affairs were religious ones. Presbyterian antagonism toward Quakerism, divisions within various churches over evangelicalism and pietism, and disagreements among Friends over the future of their Society, all had potential political implications.[14] While the historic centrality of Quakerism in Pennsylvania, and the deliberate underrepresentation of those backcountry areas in which the most uniform German and Scotch-Irish settlement took place, simplified political considerations in a way that could not occur in New York, the milieu in which Pennsylvania politicians had to organize themselves was, like New York's, a vigorously pluralistic one.

It was within this social context of dynamic growth and marked change, of noisy conflict and quiet accommodation, that New York and Pennsylvania politicians put together two of the most effective political coalitions that ever developed in British North America. The DeLancey/Jones coalition and the Quaker Party dominated midcentury politics in their respective provinces. Each of these political organizations found ways of encompassing the kaleidoscopic social pluralism that distinguished their colonies. In addition, each was challenged by the circumstances of war, which membership in the British overseas empire brought to their doorstep, and religious conflict, which their own distinctive patterns of religious organization occasioned. The way in which the DeLancey/Jones coalition and the Quaker Party responded to these challenges and dealt with the problem of political ossification that their respective long-term success created illustrates the fundamental difference between New York's factional mode of political behavior and the politics of party that characterized Pennsylvania.

The Rise and Fall of the DeLancey/Jones Coalition

Throughout the late 1740s and the 1750s, a political faction led by James DeLancey and David Jones dominated provincial politics in New York. The best known of this duo, Provincial Councillor and Chief Justice James DeLancey, had learned an important lesson a decade earlier in the Zenger imbroglio: the only sure way to sustain personal political power in New York was to secure as much autonomy as possible from the royal overseers Britain sent to the province, and simultaneously to cultivate strong public support. During the short period subsequent to the Zenger trial when the Morris/Alexander coterie held the initiative in public affairs, and when Lieutenant-Governor Clarke headed a conciliatory administration, James DeLancey kept a relatively low profile. He avoided confrontation with the Morris/Alexander politicians and more than repaired whatever damage the Zenger trial had dealt his reputation. As circuit-riding chief justice, he came into close contact with large numbers of provincials, both county men of influence and the many ordinary New Yorkers who appeared before his court. DeLancey's affability, quick mind, air of considered judgment, and the power he could wield in both his public and private capacities, soon gave him an enhanced reputation that rippled out beyond his circles of direct contact.[15] In his political activities he always seemed to champion popular measures. As councillor during Clarke's concessions to the assembly, De-Lancey shared credit for the chief executive's willingness to heed popular legislative demands.[16] When Governor Clinton replaced Clarke in 1743, DeLancey became his chief advisor and immediately fattened his reputation as a popular rights advocate. DeLancey persuaded Clinton to accept yearly appropriations and other legislative innovations, danced the graceful min-uet of principled Whiggism when he inveigled and/or bribed Clinton into issuing a new chief justice commission for good behavior, and carefully cultivated his legislative friends through the convenient joint council/ assembly committees established to facilitate public business.[17] No New Yorker could match DeLancey's ability to raise a toast to the offices of government with one hand while stroking the belly of a none-too-supine provincial community with the other.

The New York Assembly was not an easily managed body, however, and although DeLancey had substantial influence with key residents of New York, Westchester, Albany, Schenectady, and the manors of Rensselaers-wyck and Cortlandt, that was not enough. The late 1730s and early 1740s saw the development of a strong legislative interest, centering on Queens and Suffolk counties, with some sympathetic support from Kings, Rich-mond, and the mid-Hudson constituencies of Orange and Ulster. It was in these areas that the demand for assembly rights was most strenuously voiced; and the leading tenor in the chorus was David Jones of Queens. Jones, a lawyer about whom we know very little, combined his apparent rights consciousness with a studied sensitivity to the parsimony and paro-chialism of his constituents. He was acutely aware that what united such disparate places as Bushwyck in Kings, Brookhaven in Suffolk, and Goshen in Orange was their interest in how responsive the provincial government was to local issues and how effective provincial politicians were in keeping the cost of government low.[18]

While Jones's and DeLancey's political interests coincided at a number of points during the early 1740s, there is no reason to believe that a close working relationship had developed between them at that time. DeLancey liked to bask in the rays that popular legislative gains reflected back on him, but in a number of instances Jones and his supporters clearly turned their backs on the chief justice. Their own interests came first.[19]

The events that altered this relationship came in a rush. In 1744, when France joined with Spain in the latter's war against Britain, DeLancey recognized the difficulties he would face trying to deal with the divergent attitudes toward war that existed, perhaps most markedly in the upper Hudson Valley and in New York City, but also throughout the province. If he was to manage colonial war efforts successfully, he needed support from Long Island and mid–Hudson Valley representatives, whose relative safety and concern for economy would be difficult to reconcile to British wartime demands. Decisive at this point in his career, DeLancey quickly took advantage of the 1745 election. Because the current speaker of the house, the septuagenarian Adolphe Philipse, often went his own way and was a difficult individual for DeLancey to get along with,[20] the chief justice worked hard and underhandedly to defeat this old friend of his father's.[21] DeLancey's success paved the way for a grateful David Jones to succeed to the speaker's chair, and also opened the way to a more effective consolidation of his own personal influence in the New York City and upper Hudson regions.

From the brief 1745–1746 record of relations between the council and assembly, it is difficult to say what the long-range prospects for a continuing close association between DeLancey and Jones actually were.[22] But in late 1746, for reasons that are not altogether clear, Governor Clinton and DeLancey had a falling out; Clinton turned largely to Cadwallader Colden as his chief colonial confidant during the next three and a half years of his governorship.[23] As a result of his decision, Clinton isolated himself along with the loner Colden, facilitating the consolidation of the extensive and popular DeLancey/Jones coalition.

Uncritical acceptance of Clinton's and Colden's testimonies on the events of the 1740s may easily lead to the conclusion that DeLancey was an éminence grise who controlled the assembly through a joint council/assembly committee and superintended council activities from a favorite tavern.[24] These were, however, the exaggerations of men who needed a villain to explain their own ineffectiveness. They were also the ratiocinations of two individuals determined to prove DeLancey unfit for the commission of lieutenant-governor he succeeded in obtaining in 1747, an honor that Colden coveted and Clinton had promised to procure for his new friend. Unquestionably, DeLancey was the senior partner in the popular coalition. He had the prestige of council office, the independent power of the chief justice's commission for good behavior, the connections in Great Britain that could bring him the office of lieutenant-governor, and the stature that members of wealthy families could gain through ability and public service.[25] But none of these could provide legislative leadership in an assembly jealous of its rights and independence.

That was where David Jones fitted in. From 1745 until 1759, Jones was speaker of the New York Assembly, and as Robert Livingston, Jr., pointed out after his long service in the legislature, "a Speaker always has & will have great Influence."[26] Perhaps no one had more than David Jones. As another contemporary testified, "Mr. Jones is one of those extra-ordinary Genius's, to whom Nature both made ample Amend's for the want of a liberal Education."[27] He understood the mechanics of politics and the importance of looking after the small details that could make a large difference in the way in which the public perceived those who served the body politic.[28] And he knew how to use his power in the legislative assembly to manipulate the composition of crucial committees, to speak for the assembly on financial matters, to centralize all correspondence with the legislature's British agent in his own hands, and to maintain a persuasive voice in all deliberations on public policy.[29] It was no accident that when those opposed to the DeLancey/Jones faction raised some sporadic opposition in the early 1750s, the man they most vigorously opposed was David Jones.[30]

If one characteristic of the DeLancey/Jones faction was that the strengths of its co-leaders proved complementary, another was the breadth of electoral support that the coalition enjoyed. Many Anglicans found it easy to keep company with the Anglicans DeLancey and Jones; the bulk of the Dutch Reformed followed along both in the legislature and out-of-doors; constituencies heavily peopled with Presbyterians supported the popular party; and on both Long Island and the eastern side of the lower Hudson Valley, Quaker voters broadened the coalition.[31] What William Smith, Jr., observed of DeLancey, that he was "A Man who laid deep Foundations for Power in his Popularity, . . . who . . . studied to please all Sects, and made the Dissenters confident of his Protection," might equally have been said of David Jones.[32] To be sure, there were always some who resisted the DeLancey/Jones faction, but that opposition had no ethnic or religious monopoly within any one county and no obvious ethnocultural consistency from one county to the next. A few pockets of Dutch Reformed, Quaker, Presbyterian, and Anglican voters sporadically defected from coalition support in the outlying areas of the province, and there was apparently some tension between the wider provincial concerns that frequently monopolized the attention of the DeLancey/Jones leadership and specifically urban interests in New York City in the late 1740s.[33] But that opposition was clearly of a mixed ethnic and religious character and had little prospect of long-term life. By 1752, a rueful Governor Clinton concluded that Oliver DeLancey, James's brother and chief political organizer, could "Sett up his Four Coach Horses" and easily carry any New York City election.[34]

Perhaps the most surprising thing about the formation of the De-Lancey/Jones alliance was that it coalesced during wartime. When clouds began to gather with British/Spanish hostilities in 1739, and finally broke with the engagement of Britain and France in 1744, New Yorkers were a divided lot. Their interests led them to view the conflict in a multitude of ways. In New York City, leading merchants were concerned about the dangers war presented to commerce and the opportunities it brought for privateering. Insofar as city residents turned their thoughts to defense, they were preoccupied with the dangers from a French fleet and with the need to strengthen the harbor's fort and batteries. And insofar as they thought about the overland French and Indian threat, they were far less concerned about any disruption to the old Montreal fur trade than they were with protecting the upriver supply of lumber and agricultural products, in making sure that northern residents and those fur traders directly involved in the Indian trade picked up garrison and fortification costs in Albany, Schenectady, and Oswego, and in avoiding any compulsory militia service on the northern frontier.[35] The provincials who lived on Long Island and in the mid Hudson Valley felt more secure than any other New Yorkers during the war, and their attitudes reflected that. Although some became more concerned about war once New France's Indian allies bloodied both the New York and Massachusetts frontiers in 1745, many residents of these secure areas were, according to the Albanian Philip Livingston, "Narrow lac'd souls that . . . care not what becomes of our frontiers".[36] The "Gentry" who had "their Estates in the Center of ye Country . . . [were] no more Concernd about ye murdurs above Albany than I am to Killd a fatt pigg."[37] If the feeling was unanimous among northern New Yorkers that the rest of the colony did not pay enough heed to the province's frontier travails, that was also where agreement among them ended. Beyond believing that their defense should be a high provincial priority, Albany County and Livingston Manor residents were deeply divided about what was most worth protecting and who was most capable of speaking for upriver concerns.[38]

Aware of the diversity of opinions in their province, the most influential provincial politicians tried to find some middle ground that would be safe for the moment. The assembly responded selectively to the newly appointed Governor Clinton's requests for defense-related expenditures and frequently bargained what support it gave for greater legislative power.[39] Although it fell short compared to that of the aggressive Massachusetts legislators, New York's record of defense expenditures during 1744–1745 was an acceptable one compared with many other colonies.[40] Despite the conflicting views that different perspectives provided, there was enough willingness to compromise through the summer of 1745 that, in his capacity as provincial councillor, even the irascible Cadwallader Colden remarked on the absence of "parties or disputes among us."[41]

That situation, however, had already begun to change. Governor Clinton resented the fame and booty his provincial councillor, Admiral Peter Warren, won at Louisbourg; the leading role Massachusetts's governor, the civilian William Shirley, was playing in the war; and the New York Assembly's "Untowardness" and "Thirst of Power."[42] When the French and Indian foe overran the frontier fort of Saratoga in November 1745, Clinton laid full blame on the assembly and tried to become the forceful captain-general of his gubernatorial fantasies.[43]

But the legislators with whom Clinton had to deal during these months were a wary lot.[44] True, they had been prepared to make some efforts to defend the province prior to the sack of Saratoga, but only within limits. Most representatives wanted to off-load as much wartime expenditure as possible—in the case of protection for the northern frontier, on the fur traders and local residents, and in that of the monies for Indian diplomacy, on the Crown. Mindful of the financial burdens that had come with King William's and Queen Anne's wars, and aware that they were still paying for the financial debacles of those years, New Yorkers were not inclined to rush headlong into heavy new commitments. They insisted that Great Britain pledge to pay a sizable share of any costly campaign against New France, "for unless the Charge is repaid by the Crown, we shall be almost ruined."[45] In addition, many of New York's popular politicians were just as knowledgeable of public affairs in Massachusetts as Clinton was, and their response to those developments was ambivalent. While New Yorkers were happy to have the Bay province fight New France for the benefit of all, they also looked askance at the gubernatorial patronage and influence that accompanied William Shirley's leadership. Cognizant of these tendencies in contemporary Massachusetts politics, aware of Clinton's avaricious ambitions, and mindful of the ways in which prerogative power had abused wartime budgets during earlier times, the New York Assembly determined to keep its governor on a short leash. The fact that in Great Britain, colonial administrators were currently considering ways to strengthen the prerogative in the colonies stiffened the legislators' resolve to give nothing away to executive leadership.[46]

Yet when the situation became perilous in November 1745 with the collapse of Saratoga, the assembly was ready to reinforce the garrison at Oswego, strengthen the fortifications of New York City, build blockhouses above Albany, and support a British-sanctioned expedition against New France. Between July 1745 and July 1746, New York legislators appropriated "something over £70,000 for the defense of the colony."[47] Despite regional differences and parsimonious proclivities, "our Assembly was never more zealous or unanimous than on this occasion to promote the interests of His Majesty."[48] With regard to mounting an offensive against New France, popular provincial politicians were "very hearty in the thing."[49] And among their ranks was James DeLancey, who remained committed to aggressive military action through the summer of 1747.[50] Once the British indicated their intention of sharing the cost of a large-scale offensive against the Canadians, New Yorkers were more than willing to go along.[51]

Just at this point, when there seemed some possibility of cooperative action between Clinton and New York's leading provincial politicians, the reverse happened. Determined to take the leadership role in the war away from Massachusetts, and believing that he should, as much as possible, serve as the sole arbiter of New York's military needs and obligations, Clinton asserted himself as never before. He undercut the province's Indian commissioners and, through the good offices of Sir William Johnson, tried to establish his own reinvigorated Indian policy. He fought with both the provincial council and the assembly over such issues as the allocation of expenses between Britain and New York, the provisioning of the independent companies of British soldiers stationed in New York, the responsibility of the province to advance payment to cover wartime expenses chargeable to Britain, and the deployment, payment, and continued enlistment of provincial troops.[52] As he committed himself to this course, Clinton increasingly relied on the support, advice, and penmanship of Councillor Cadwallader Colden, whose reactionary views of the prerogative and rights of royal officials like himself were extremely impolitic. By trying to assert gubernatorial power and claiming the right to "put Bounds and Limitations, upon . . . [the assembly's] Rights and Privileges, and alter them at Pleasure," Clinton and Colden raised the opposition of every provincial politician who felt either the desirability or the necessity of staying in tune with New York's predominantly Whiggish popular politics.[53]

For its part, once it had committed itself to sizable military appropriations, the assembly was doubly determined to keep a tight rein on expenses, to push as much of the cost of war as possible onto the Crown, and to exercise as much administrative oversight of wartime activities as it could. The more Clinton pressed for an open-ended financial commitment to the war, and the more he emphasized the prerogative, the more the legislators stressed the limits of provincial largesse, the duty Clinton owed, as royal surrogate, to shoulder expenses on behalf of the British government, and the right of the assembly to participate in the administration of the colony on the assembly's own terms. There public affairs remained stalemated during the remaining months of King George's War.[54]

The result of these developments in the mid 1740s was the complete isolation of Governor Clinton and his advisor Cadwallader Colden.[55] True, of course, there were numerous other divisons among New Yorkers during these years, among the most marked of which were differences over the allocation of wartime taxes.[56] But the most significant feature of these conflicts, whether they were fiscal, economic, regional, ethnic, personal, or ideological, was that none was sufficiently strong to give structural definition to popular politics through the creation or perpetuation of major factions.[57] Despite their differences, assemblymen cooperated unprecedentedly to oppose Clinton and Colden. The governor even alienated the majority of his council, including the crucial James DeLancey, but also the important Philip Livingston, who by January 1746 was meeting "Eveningly with [the] Chief Justice & a few others" when Livingston was in New York City.[58] And, as Clinton became more assertive and antagonistic toward the province's representatives, they submerged their various differences to the point where prior to the 1747 election, the assemblymen "a Greed [in] case of a Dissolution to Set up & Joyn so al to Come again in the same body if possible."[59] Solidarity against a threatening governor took precedence over other concerns.[60]

The antagonism that Governor Clinton generated should not, however, blind us to the political acumen of James DeLancey and David Jones. During the early Clinton years, they did not force the pace of politics, but allowed dissatisfaction with the governor to progress at its own gait. Meanwhile, they associated themselves with a mix of policies relating to the war, the province's relationship with Great Britain, the development of assembly powers, and the general concern for governmental austerity, all of which had some breadth of appeal. By the second half of 1746, their light touch had brought them provincewide influence, and as the tension between Clinton and the assembly grew in the ensuing weeks, they gained even greater preeminence as power brokers among New York's county notables. Once the war ended, the DeLancey/Jones coalition continued to broaden its base, capitalizing on disgust with Clinton's continued efforts to shore up the prerogative, and using the advantage popularity conferred to consolidate (frequently in a much more heavy-handed manner than heretofore) their power in various regions of the province.[61] When Clinton finally looked beyond Colden, to try to enlist some provincial politicians to take on the DeLancey/Jones juggernaut, his few supporters met with dismal defeat.[62] James DeLancey and David Jones had done their work well.

By the early 1750s, the DeLancey/Jones coalition seemed unshakable. Clinton finally handed over DeLancey's lieutenant-governor's commission in 1753, after keeping it undelivered for six years (in hopes of gaining its revocation), and carried his complaining tongue back to England. With David Jones firmly in control of the assembly, DeLancey had the opportunity to accomplish what few governors were capable of—composing the rift between assembly and governor in a way that would reasonably reconcile both popular demands for legislative power and perceived needs for executive responsibility in the interests of loyalty, colonial obedience, and good order. But just as DeLancey began confronting this task, the political coalition that would facilitate it was suddenly challenged.

The issue that upset the existing political equilibrium was the establishment of a colonial college. The conflict that took place over the founding of such an institution in New York City was not over the merits of higher education—most civic leaders agreed that the fast-growing mid-Atlantic colonies required their own colleges—but over what religious denomination should control the college administration. Pennsylvania offered one answer. There, Benjamin Franklin's commitment to utilitarian education, and belief that nonsectarian education best suited a society committed to liberty of conscience, produced an experiment in cooperation between Old Light Presbyterians and Anglicans when the College of Philadelphia was grafted onto the Philadelphia Academy in the mid 1750s.[63] But the New York environment was markedly different. There, a group of Anglican clergymen, who had defied their Congregational upbringings to become churchmen, and who served congregations in the New York, New Jersey, and Connecticut hinterland close to New York City, were determined to have an Anglican college. They had failed to crack the Congregational monopolies at Harvard and Yale, and they had been caught flat-footed by a group of energetic Presbyterians who had secured provincial blessing for the College of New Jersey, an institution that genuflected toward that province's ethnic and religious pluralism by promising "free and equal liberty . . . of education . . . notwithstanding any different sentiments in religion," but which, in fact, was run by clergy uncompromisingly committed to New Light standards.[64] The Anglican priests were strongly supported by a group of prominent New York laymen, including vestrymen of Trinity Church and such provincial councillors as Cadwallader Colden, John Chambers, and Joseph Murray, all of whom saw an Anglican college as an essential part of the anglicized social order they hoped would eventually predominate amid New York's diversity.[65]

In addition to the financial support that Trinity Church members could provide, what recommended New York City to these hopeful Anglicans was that alone among the colonies north of the Chesapeake Bay, New York had an Anglican establishment. Granted, it was a truncated and bastardized establishment; but it was the best that existed. Although the English had acknowledged the need to accommodate non-Anglican religious worship immediately after the conquest, in 1693 the ardent Anglican Governor Fletcher succeeded in persuading the assembly to adopt a law that created parishes in New York, Richmond, Westchester, and Queens counties. Non-Anglican legislators accepted the law because they felt they could exploit its vague wording to reinforce the strength of their own denominations in the designated counties. Governors Fletcher and Cornbury, however, used their respective powers to try to consolidate Anglican influence in the four southern counties. They were so successful, particularly once the Society for the Propagation of the Gospel made its resources available to Cornbury, that in later decades some leading New York Anglicans continued to cherish the notion that a more orthodox establishment might eventually encompass much of the province. The proposed Anglican college strengthened such hopes.[66]

If the creation of a limited establishment in New York earned the approval of most Anglicans, it aroused different reactions in other major denominations. Although some Dutch Reformed in New York City resented the taxes that the 1693 legislation required them to pay to support an Anglican clergyman, and others detested Lord Cornbury's high-handed interference in their religious affairs, most Dutch lived in counties unaffected by the Ministry Act. Moreover, various governors, beginning with Fletcher, bought them off with exemptions from the executive's collating power and a willingness to incorporate their churches. The Dutch Reformed church thus gained a privileged position that set it apart from other non-Anglicans, "the next best thing to an establishment of their own."[67] The Presbyterians, however, were far more antagonistic. Cornbury's persecution of a clergyman, Francis Makemie, for preaching without permission in New York City, became a notorious part of Presbyterian folklore. And his placement of Anglican clergy in strong Calvinist parishes brought congregational disobedience in Rye and a bitter dispute in Jamaica, which continued intermittently until the Revolution.[68]

The point is that none of New York's three major denominations interpreted the "liberty of conscience" Governor Sloughter promised in 1691 as the kind of broad-based, voluntaristic religious liberty Pennsylvanians came to associate with the term.[69] During the seventeenth century, the Dutch Reformed and Presbyterians had accustomed themselves to supporting their ministers by community taxation. That practice continued into the eighteenth century in heavily Dutch and Presbyterian communities.[70] And it coexisted in some areas with the local Anglican establishment that the 1693 law brought to the four southern counties. The result was that, unlike

Pennsylvanians, who became accustomed to religious voluntarism, the majority of New York religious leaders retained some taste for coercive church practices. Anglicans hungered for more territory to feed a sharpened appetite for dominance and place. Devout Dutch Reformed adherents thought kindly of any friendly establishment that would promote coherence in the Dutch communities. And numerous Presbyterians both admired the narrow paths of New England Congregationalism and harbored the heat of religious imperialism that fired the souls of so many colonial Calvinists. All of the major New York denominations had their forceful leaders, who coveted the advantages even a weak establishment could provide. That attitude could quickly develop into a deep suspicion of any apparent privilege one denomination might gain over another.

It was against this backdrop that plans for a New York college developed. By mid 1752, the New York legislature had authorized lotteries that raised nearly £3,500 toward the cost of opening the institution, and leading college promoters had persuaded their friends in the assembly to appoint an overwhelmingly Anglican board of trustees to manage the lottery monies and oversee the settlement of the college on New York City lands donated by the Trinity Church vestryboard.[71] Throughout the late 1740s and early 1750s, leading Anglicans simply assumed that the New York institution would be an "Episcopal College."[72]

One of the trustees of the college was the lawyer William Livingston, whose interest in promoting higher education in New York had led to his appointment. Unlike his fellows, however, Livingston was a Presbyterian. And he was not one to remain silent when the course of public affairs displeased him. "There is a thing," he wrote to his former Yale classmate Noah Welles, "which has long been the Subject of my thoughts and which I should be glad to transmit to the Reflector in a course of letters. . . . The case is this—Our future College . . . is like to fall without a vigorous opposition, under the management of Churchmen. The Consequence which will be universal Priestcraft and Bigotry in less than half a Century."[73] The "Reflector" that Livingston mentioned was an essay magazine series entitled the *Independent Reflector,* which he and his fellow Presbyterians and lawyers William Smith, Jr., and John Morin Scott had begun to publish on November 30, 1752.[74] For some time, Livingston, with the fitful help of his two friends and an occasional contribution from others, had built up a series of essays and list of promising topics long enough, he hoped, to sustain a weekly commentary on public affairs.[75] Throughout his early years, the precocious Livingston had been developing a facile, if not diarrhetic, pen. With that went a streak of unshakable intellectual and moral self-confidence broad enough to support his future habit of writing incendiary social criticism. Socially a shy, private individual, Livingston found the essay to be the one way he could best fulfill his intense ambition to instruct, to lead, to correct, and to criticize.

In Livingston's *Independent Reflector* essays, two somewhat contradictory characteristics stand out.[76] One is a rare willingness to hold up established customs for examination and expose their absurdities and inequities; the result was a clear, instructive, but often unsettling commentary, a compelling eighteenth-century version of investigative journalism. The second is a strong ideological derivativeness that mimicked English radical-Whig ideas about the form and dangers of political and ecclesiastical power. At their best, Livingston's ideological writings were well tailored to fit local circumstances and made a telling point; at their worst, they were shrill invectives and formulaic descriptions that reinforced the very type of closed mind that in other circumstances, Livingston prided himself on exposing.

When the *Reflector*'s series of six essays on the "intended" New York college began on March 22, 1753, they included both elements of Livingston's writing.[77] Pointing out that New York was a remarkably diverse society and that many groups had "taxed" themselves through the lotteries, Livingston asserted that such public money should be used like any tax money, for the "Emolument of the Whole," not for some narrow sectarian purpose.[78] Moreover, preference to any denomination in college governance would precipitate widespread social dissension as the favored sect used its power over "tender" student minds to inculcate orthodoxy, thereby stirring others to oppose such efforts to "strengthen and enlarge" its place in provincial society.[79] The way to avoid this predicament was to make the college "a mere civil institution" in which constant questioning and reference to reason would promote true education.[80] Along with this striking approach to New York's college problem went a good measure of anti-Anglican bombast. Livingston castigated the Church of England for its "Thirst for Dominion" and scaremongered with supposed threats of tithes, test acts, and even "Peter-Pence."[81] "Behold," he projected, "the Province overrun with Priest-craft and every Office userp'd by the ruling Party."[82] The Anglicans represented power on the loose and, if possible, the Presbyterian Livingston would deprive the churchmen of their New York victim.

Stung by Livingston's sharp tongue, and particularly incensed by his reference to the College of New Jersey as an example of nonsectarian education (when the atmosphere there was more intensely denominational than anything Samuel Johnson, a leading churchman, had in mind for the New York college of which he was soon to be president), a half dozen of Johnson's clerical friends counterattacked.[83] They swung away at Livingston et al. in the pages of the *New-York Mercury*, declaring *The Reflector* an "atheist" and a "Bigot," guided by the principles of independence and republicanism.[84] Suppose all religions were equal. "What a Scene of Confusion . . . ! What dreadful Convulsions . . . !" The British constitution deliberately preferred one religion above the rest in order to keep a proper "Balance."[85]

Unable to shout Livingston into silence, the Anglicans leaned on his printer, and by November 1753, the "reflector" was left, screeds in his hand, with no place to publish.[86] But a year later the two sides were at it again, filling the pages of the *New-York Mercury* with invective.[87] By this time, however, the issue had changed focus slightly. In November 1754, Lieutenant-Governor James DeLancey had granted King's College its charter, and from that point on, legislative support for the free college bill that William Livingston and his allies had offered as an alternative, and that he had entrusted to his brother Robert, Jr., to shepherd through the assembly, "began to flagg."[88] Thereafter Livingston and his friends hoped to play spoilers. They wanted to stir up sufficient opposition to inhibit the assembly from voting public money to support the Anglican college.[89] They would deal King's College as crippling a blow as possible by blackening its reputation and curtailing its resources.

At this juncture, William Livingston's co-instigator, William Smith, Jr., undertook the most important initiative. Hopeful he could mobilize enough support through public petitions to affect the actions of New York legislators, and aware that any network of contacts he established might be useful in developing an anti–DeLancey/Jones election campaign (should the appointment of a new governor bring dissolution of the assembly), Smith set to work with diligence.[90] More than Livingston, Smith represented orthodox, militant Presbyterianism. He deeply resented the past and present transgressions of New York Anglicans, and while fighting for nonsectarian education in his own colony, could urge New Lights to keep a tight hold on the College of New Jersey in order to secure its place as the "Bulwark of the Presbyterian Interest."[91] What intensified his commitment to the anti-Anglican cause in New York was his deep personal and familial hatred of James DeLancey.[92]

While Smith's puritanically tinged, upper-crust tastes always gave him a hearing among the more educated of New York City society, the parochialism of New York sophistication brought him some decided disadvantages in provincial politics. In his 1754 effort to collect petitions, Smith demonstrated some of these: in his approach to Friends, he evinced no sensitivity whatsoever to the Quaker language of public discourse; initially, he thought that the Anglican Queens County assemblyman Thomas Cornell was a member for Suffolk County; despite its proximity to New York City, he had no contacts in Kings County, which was predominantly Dutch; he failed to find an effective lieutenant in Westchester County, where he had a sizable audience of Presbyterians and Congregationalists; his contact of influence in Richmond was a Clinton supporter who had recently been repudiated by the electorate; he and William Livingston entrusted the task of collecting signatures in the Albany area to a pettifogger, "the Ridicule and contempt of the County," who quickly discredited the cause; and only by accident did he trip over a Congregational minister willing to undertake petition-signing responsibility in Suffolk County.[93]

Yet Smith persevered. His and his father's strong Presbyterianism gave him access to a network of ministers receptive to his message—particularly in Dutchess, Ulster, and Orange Counties. As time went by, he also won the confidence of an occasional Dutch Reformed minister.[94] Gradually, too, he became adept at using what purchase he had through Presbyterian/ Congregational sympathy to move members of the legislature. Thomas Cornell tried to appease the large numbers of Presbyterians and Quakers in his county by supporting the Livingston/Smith initiatives.[95] In Suffolk County, where there were "not 20 Church Families," the Anglican William Nicoll (whose nephew, the Anglican lottery trustee Benjamin Nicoll, was the stepson of King's College's future president, Samuel Johnson) took a more moderate line than his relatives might have wished.[96] Smith benefited too, from the lobbying that Philip Livingston carried out in September and October of 1754 among the New York City Dutch Reformed. As a result, Dominie DeRonde used his pulpit to warn attending Dutch Reformed assemblymen from the countryside that Anglican Arminianism could only be checked by the mobilization of the province's Calvinist forces.[97]

Partly by appeal to what contemporaries perceived as the issues, partly by dint of hard work and manipulative politics, and partly by the accident of divisions among the Dutch Reformed, Smith and Livingston put together a block of assembly votes that held at bay those who wanted to support King's College with public money. Because the Dutch Reformed members of the assembly constituted the majority of that body, they held decisive votes in their hands. Before 1755 they had played their usual retiring and supportive role in provincial politics, in this case largely reacting to Anglican and Presbyterian initiatives; by 1755, however, they began to stir in response to forces within their own communities. With the *conferentie/coetus* split becoming sharper in the late 1740s and early 1750s, the conservative New York City–centered Dutch clergy successfully petitioned to have a Dutch divinity professor added to the King's College faculty.[98] In the meantime, their evangelical opponents had gained considerable support among a group of city Dutch who felt that only the adoption of English-language services could stop their uncomprehending children from deserting their church.[99] This *coetus*-sympathizing group began to argue that only a sectarian college of their own, albeit an English-language one, could preserve their separate identity. Some of their leaders, most notably Theodore Frelinghuysen of Albany, therefore began publicly to condemn any cooperation with the

Anglicans.[100] The result of this convergence of diverse forces was a fairly even split among New York legislators. The hard core of the anti-college coalition consisted of six Dutch Reformed members, two Anglicans, one Dutch Lutheran, and one Presbyterian. On the other side of the question were an equal number, composed of seven Anglican and three Dutch Reformed. Both groups drew on a third six-man contingent of swing voters, consisting of four Dutch Reformed and two Anglicans. It was by successful appeal to members of this group, along with the either purposeful or fortuitous absences of some of their opponents at critical votes, that allowed the anti-college-aid group to push its opponents to a dispiriting compromise in November 1756.[101] At that time, the jaded parties agreed to divide the lottery proceeds between King's College and the City of New York. When the latter decided to use a portion of its share to build quarantine quarters for immigrants and mariners, it seemed a fitting resolution, thought the sour-tongued William Smith, Sr., to divide the money "between the two pest houses."[102]

The Livingston/Smith initiatives clearly shook the DeLancey/Jones coalition. Moderate Anglican and infrequent churchgoer that he was, James DeLancey hated being painted into a corner by the zealots who forced on him the appearance of being an Episcopal stalwart in the context of his approval of the King's College charter in 1754.[103] David Jones, in turn, felt pressured enough by his Quaker and Presbyterian constituents to seek out a public-testimonial by several assemblymen that he had never promoted King's College, an endorsement of which William Livingston made political capital by suggesting that Jones spoke simultaneously out of each side of his mouth.[104] The swell of petitions from the countryside against public support for King's College seemed to impugn DeLancey's and Jones's leadership, and the fracturing of the assembly along unprecedented lines over the same issue signified a loss of coalition coherence where the DeLancey/Jones faction had recently been so strong.

Yet the Livingston/Smith opposition were never able to push their advantage. The general election they hoped for on the arrival of Governor Sir Charles Hardy in September 1755 never took place, and when a New York by-election occurred a year later, the city and county sent James DeLancey's brother Oliver to the assembly. Philip Livingston tested the wind, but feeling no favorable turn, kept his sails furled and watched Oliver DeLancey launch his assembly career "unanimously."[105] When the next general election took place in 1759, in compliance with the terms of the Septennial Act, the turnover was heavy enough (63 percent) to draw notice in the press, but if that result represented any referendum on the King's College brawl, it indicated a repudiation of the Livingston/Smith stance.[106] Of the ten hardcore opponents of public aid for King's College, only one gained reelection;[107] among the ten committed supporters of the college, five were returned;[108] The heaviest turnover took place in precisely those areas in which the anti-college forces had enjoyed greatest support.[109]

There were other indicators, too, that despite Livingston's and Smith's efforts, the Presbyterian/Anglican conflict central to the college dispute was not easily transferred into provincial politics. The New York City Presbyterians were so divided among themselves that William Smith, Jr., could not elicit one petition against college aid from the congregation, while William Livingston complained of their "unnatural feuds which . . . rendered us contemptible to our Enemies."[110] And rural Presbyterians found an alliance with the idiosyncratic William Livingston and the enigmatic William Smith, Jr., somewhat discomforting. Livingston's rationalism and Smith's private touting of Anglican friends, while publicly libeling their religion, was less than reassuring.[111] Although the divisions among the city Dutch Reformed briefly played into Livingston's and Smith's hands, these self-appointed Presbyterian champions were never convincing in arguing the existence of an "English and Dutch Presbyterian" community of interest.[112] Far more English-speaking Dutch were opting for membership in the Anglican church than in the Presbyterian, and no amount of rhetoric proclaiming reformed unity against Anglican tyranny could offset the long-standing Dutch distaste for their Massachusetts and Connecticut neighbors and the association of Presbyterianism with New England Independency.[113] As for William Livingston's notion of a free college, neither hard-nosed Presbyterian nor Dutch Reformed found it any more acceptable than their Anglican counterparts. Still thinking of colleges as quasi-religious corporations and of the edge that establishment-tinged institutions might give their respective churches, they thought a nondenominational college either an absurdity or a Trojan horse. And those denominations, such as Quakers, Moravians, and some Lutherans, who largely accepted religious voluntarism, had no particular interest at this juncture in higher education and little temperamental affinity for Presbyterian zeal.

Finally, it is not at all clear, despite the apparent success of the Livingston/Smith petitioning campaign, that the college issue did much to shape public opinion other than in one or two exceptional areas in which Presbyterian/Anglican conflict had a historic place in the local social geography. As Smith's New York City opponents charged, his petitions were "forced Petitions, from distant Counties, signed by ignorant People, that know not what they are about."[114] Recognizing that the question of the college was a single issue with restricted appeal and a limited life, Livingston and Smith tried to broaden the base of their faction by raising the staple radical-Whig fears of the misuse of power.[115] But in the early to mid 1750s, that was a difficult case to make. The DeLancey/Jones leadership had proven itself repeatedly in the popular antiprerogative wars of the prior decade, and had drawn electoral support from across a wide religious spectrum. Moreover, the major politicians within that faction shared some sense of larger loyalty to their accustomed leaders.

By late 1755, veteran New York assemblymen were anxious to leave behind the religious issue. The two Anglicans who had consistently supported the anti-college position had no desire to fight additional battles for Presbyterians.[116] Unlike their priests and one or two provincial councillors, the Anglican assemblymen were moderate, secular-minded men who deeply disliked the divisiveness of the college dispute and wanted a quick return to normalcy. As for their Dutch counterparts, who often represented areas in which both *coetus* and *conferentie* supporters lived, they had no incentive to continue a battle that had originated within the English-language communities. Most Dutch assemblymen, no matter how they voted on the college issue, continued to share political friendships with their longtime Anglican allies. Both country Dutch and rural Anglican representatives were happy to get back to local issues—the "Destruction of Blackbirds and proclaiming war against Crows and rattlesnakes"—that affected their constituents more directly than any New York City college ever could.[117] Rather than being slowly buried under bucolic concerns, however, the idiosyncratic divisions the college debate occasioned were quickly obscured by the renewal of war in 1755.

The outbreak of the French and Indian War immediately offered the Livingston/Smith duo some opportunity to broaden and reinvigorate their faction. Early in the war, when the college-money question was still unresolved, the anti–King's College legislative coalition used its power in the assembly to establish a new ratio of taxation quotas among the various counties.[118] But the tug and pull of particular interests and the commitment to wartime cooperation engendered by hostilities substantially ended college-inspired legislative divisions.[119] Outside the assembly, fortune momentarily shone on the Livingston/Smith faction. Lieutenant-Governor James DeLancey reacted badly to Massachusetts Governor William Shirley's renewed military prominence in 1755–1756. And capitalizing on their earlier ties with Shirley, a number of William Livingston's relatives and political allies landed the lucrative military supply contracts for the general's northern campaigns.[120] But supporters of DeLancey and Jones took over wartime supply contracts shortly after the British sacked Shirley in mid 1756, and when James DeLancey again became chief executive on Governor Sir Charles Hardy's departure in 1757, the Livingston/Smith campaign trailed off into wordy justifications of its past actions.[121]

As for the DeLancey/Jones wartime policy, it was never as limited as it has sometimes been portrayed.[122] Although neither James DeLancey nor his assemblymen friends had any use for the reforms of the Albany Plan, De-Lancey did offer his "own Plan" for the fortification of the New York frontier and some strategic offensive action against the French.[123] The brief interlude of their opposition to Shirley aside, the DeLancey/Jones coalition pursued the war effectively within their understanding of the realities of New York politics and financial resources. Overall, DeLancey adopted a sufficiently aggressive policy in the former case to placate and in the latter to draw to him two of his most vocal critics from King George's War, Cadwallader Colden and Sir William Johnson.[124] And despite the parsimonious hearts of their constituents, the David Jones–led assembly appropriated over £63,000 for defensive and offensive action before war had even been declared in Great Britain.[125] Once it became clear that the British were determined to devote a major effort to the North American theater, once the supply and paymaster contracts were firmly in friendly hands, and especially once the prospects for victory improved, the dominant faction pushed the war effort with vigor, even at some cost to incumbent popularity in county politics.[126]

The wartime effort was the last hurrah of the DeLancey/Jones coalition, however, for the 1759 provincial election cleaned out the assembly on a scale reminiscent of other major shifts in New York politics.[127] Unquestionably, the most important feature of that election was the defeat of David Jones— and there we must acknowledge the local salience of religious conflict. The bitter dispute between Anglicans and Presbyterians in Jamaica parish, which had begun under Lord Cornbury and had calmed down in the 1730s and 1740s, began "to rise" again coincidentally with William Livingston's anti-Anglican diatribes.[128] By 1754, Queens County Quakers were predicting that unless there was "a Miraculous change in the Minds of the People he . . . ["Mr. Speaker"] never will be Chosen again." But it is important to understand the full range of reasons for that sentiment. The "Clamour" against Jones was not only "in Relation to the College" but also to "some other Matters Respecting this County in Particular."[129] The complexities of local opinion were further underlined by the defeat of Thomas Cornell, Jones's longtime running mate. The Anglican Cornell had been one of the chief contacts on Long Island of William Smith, Jr., he had an impeccable anti-college legislative record, and he was the only assemblyman whom William Livingston openly praised in his polemics as worthy of Presbyterian support.[130] Despite this, Cornell's long association with Jones and his record on local issues were sufficiently distasteful to the bulk of Presbyterian and Quaker Queens County voters for them to send Cornell packing. The Jones/Cornell case demonstrated that large provincial issues centering on religious conflict could have an impact on county politics provided a direct connection could be established between those issues and local affairs. Once set loose and integrated into county perceptions, however, those issues could easily develop an unpredictable logic of their own, depending on the dynamics of the local social environment. But in 1759, with respect to the religious issue, Queens County stood out as the exception.

Of more general concern were considerations related to legislative incumbency and local wartime concerns. New Yorkers repeatedly proved themselves hostile to legislators who strung out their mandate as long as possible, and the big turnover in 1759 certainly owed something to that prejudice.[131] But equally important were the great difficulties representatives had faced in satisfying their constituents during war. Conflicts over taxes, the recruitment of provincial troops, the operation of the militia, the purchase of supplies, the relative need for rangers, guards, and blockhouses, and a number of local issues or special-interest demands not only pitted representatives of one county against those of others but also frequently prompted multiple intracounty interests to raise their voices.[132] Dissatisfaction frequently centered on individual assemblymen, regardless of their record on other provincial issues, and that led to a legislative purge despite the larger wartime success the British and colonists were beginning to enjoy against New France by early 1759.

Important as the 1759 election was in ending the period of DeLancey/ Jones hegemony, it should not be allowed to obscure the fact that the demise of the faction was a protracted event that had begun much earlier, not just in the gradual alienation of various New Yorkers, but in the loss of key personnel. James DeLancey's old associate Frederick Philipse had died in 1751; another reliable friend, the influential Paul Richards, followed Philipse to the grave in 1756; three years later, the New York merchant and De-Lancey/Jones stalwart Henry Cruger resigned from the assembly; and out in Dutchess County, Henry Beekman, a longtime supporter and DeLancey relation, turned over his interest in county politics to his son-in-law Robert R. Livingston. Along with the attrition of age went that of ambition. Between 1758 and 1761, three DeLancey/Jones veterans, John Watts, William Walton, and Oliver DeLancey passed through the influential New York City and County assembly seats to places in the council. The loss of continuity in the city delegation, coupled with the weakening of David Jones's influence among country members, left Lieutenant-Governor James De-Lancey without much legislative clout by the time he died in 1760.

Despite the overwhelming importance of the DeLancey/Jones coalition as a political entity in mid eighteenth-century New York, it had the crucial limitation of all factions. It was the product of a peculiar mix of personalities who could not transcend themselves. Their concerted opposition to Governor Clinton had forged a common understanding of how New York government should work, of the relative places the legislature and executive should hold, of what was tolerable in interregional and interreligious relationships, and of what was an acceptable range of broad goals for New York's wartime efforts. But such agreement was time- and personality-bound. There was no direct spillover into a new generation of ready replacements. Ultimately, the life of the DeLancey/Jones coalition was determined more by the life cycles of its principals than by the viability of its principles.

The Consolidation and Transformation of the Quaker Party

Pennsylvania's Quaker Party first emerged as a recognizable force in provincial politics with the election of 1739. Immediately prior to that event, Andrew Hamilton, the speaker of the Assembly and hero of the Zenger trial, had led a small but important group of Quakers and non-Quakers in retiring from the legislature. Hamilton resigned because of ill-health, but his son James, son-in-law William Allen, and a small number of moderate Philadelphia Quakers apparently did so because they thought that all the knotty public issues of the day had been untangled.[133] No sooner had they announced their intentions, however, than a sizable lobby of "stiff" Philadelphia Friends took over preelection negotiations to settle on candidates for that county.[134] According to William Allen, these activists "were for choosing none but people of that perswasion."[135] Hence the name Quaker Party.

Although the rapidity with which the Quaker Party coalesced caught William Allen and his friends flat-footed, the foundations for the Quaker edifice had, in fact, been laid over an extended period. As Friends became seriously outnumbered in the 1720s and 1730s, they gradually realized that they could no longer afford major political fragmentation if they were to maintain their hegemony in public affairs. And most believed that the Quaker experiment should continue. What facilitated Friends' coming together was the appearance of Thomas Penn in Pennsylvania in 1732. As Penn reorganized proprietary affairs, collected past debts, raised both quitrents and the price of land, and demanded compensation for accepting depreciated Pennsylvania currency for pre-1732 quitrents, the numbers of "grumblers and malcontents" increased throughout the colony.[136] Andrew Hamilton and his allies kept them at bay for some time, because Hamilton's reputation as a popular-rights man allowed him to insist that the Penns' property interests deserved some protection. But once the Penns and the Calverts agreed to settle their dispute over the Maryland boundary, and the Pennsylvania Assembly passed a law compensating the Penns for accepting depreciated provincial currency for their pre-1732 quitrents, there was little to check the ill feelings of discontented provincials.[137] By 1738, these boiled to the surface of Pennsylvania politics with great vigor, finally predisposing many rural Quaker assemblymen (who a decade earlier had been the anchor of the proprietary forces against Sir William Keith's city-based faction) to turn irrevocably away from proprietary influence.[138] At the same time, as an older generation of proprietary Quaker political leaders and administrators died or retired, they left few strong replacements. Fed on tales of a fair and benevolent William Penn (compared to his grasping son), younger Friends saw the new proprietary initiatives as a series of betrayals. Ever opportunists, Quaker politicians began to exploit these feelings, quick to claim that the antiproprietary Friends had inherited the torch of idealism Penn had carried on behalf of all Pennsylvanians.

While Friends were drawing together among themselves, they were also developing a practice of including recent immigrants in Pennsylvania politics. As Scotch-Irish Presbyterians and both German sectarians and German church people interspersed themselves among pockets of old settlers and took up whole townships in frontier areas, Quaker leaders reached out to influential newcomers, connecting them with the existing political framework. In taking the initiative in defending local property rights (as they did against the incursions of Marylanders into southeastern Pennsylvania), and in acting as intermediaries between the proprietor and local settlers, county Quakers built up strong associations with members of other religious groups. In consequence, Friends frequently enjoyed the political support of both Scotch-Irish and Germans. And as the majority of politically active Quakers began to define themselves more clearly as a popular political coalition, German sectarians, who had played only a peripheral role in the earlier factionalized politics of the province, became more active. A Quaker interest tinged with pacifism and Whiggism was one that could easily find sympathy among Mennonites, Dunkers, Moravians, and other religious splinter groups scattered throughout the province.[139]

Coincidental with the emergence of a strengthened, popular Quaker political presence came Britain's War of Jenkins' Ear with Spain, a circumstance of great importance in the consolidation of the Quaker Party. The outbreak of hostilities brought local demands for adequate defenses, including a militia, along with British orders for Pennsylvania to contribute to an expeditionary force against the Spanish West Indies. An enthusiastic Governor Thomas pressed the assembly to respond favorably, and by 1740 was at loggerheads with that body over what he believed was the unwillingness of the Quaker legislature to provide for wartime needs. Popular opinion provided a very different explanation of the dispute, which lasted through 1742. According to this view, the assembly proved its willingness to honor the Crown's request for imperial defense by a conditional grant to support the military campaign against Spain's colonial possessions, and there was no need for any further public action. It was Governor Thomas who, under the guise of providing wartime leadership, was trying to destroy the fabric of provincial society. He disregarded the property rights of masters when he accepted the enlistment of indentured servants for the Cartagena expedition; he threatened the very idea of a Quaker colony when he pleaded to the Crown that Friends should be disqualified from government; and he mounted a frontal attack on the Pennsylvania constitution when he argued that he needed a militia with his own appointed officers in command, a chancery court beholden to himself, power to prorogue and dissolve the House of Representatives, and joint control with the assembly over all appropriations.[140] What made Governor Thomas's actions particularly ominous was that the proprietor, Thomas Penn, at no point disassociated himself from his deputy-governor.[141] The threat to Pennsylvania society was a joint proprietary/executive one.

The major consequences of this period of intense conflict between assembly and governor were fivefold. First, it so entrenched the Quaker Party in the legislature as to make it unshakable. Between 1739 and 1755, Quakers occupied from 71 to 90 percent of the seats in the provincial legislature (compared to 63–77 percent during the preceding decade), and under the leadership of John Kinsey and Isaac Norris, Jr., as speakers, they presented a united popular interest in the face of both proprietary innovations and gubernatorial initiatives.[142] During this decade and a half, Quaker Party dominance ensured the regular return of party veterans in the colony's annual elections and tight party control of committee assignments within the legislature.[143] Despite the overwhelming predominance of Friends in the legislature, however, party leaders never succumbed to the kind of religious exclusiveness that their circumstances seemed to encourage. Speakers Kinsey and Norris both ensured that non-Quakers took an active role in legislative affairs, thereby granting them a voice in party policy.[144] The legislative discipline and breadth of the Quaker Party proved so formidable that even the military threat that reemerged during the last year of King George's War sparked no serious electoral challenge.[145]

A second and closely related consequence of the political conflict of the early 1740s was the creation and immediate emasculation of the Proprietary Party. In 1740, a nucleus of old supporters of the proprietorship and others who approved of Governor Thomas's initiatives put together tickets to oppose the Quaker Party in the annual October election. Having been defeated on that occasion, and after largely sitting out the 1741 election, Proprietary Party leaders decided to challenge their opponents again in October 1742. They organized tickets for each county and tried to mobilize sympathetic voters. Unfortunately for themselves, their zeal outran their judgment. Aided by some ships' captains, a small group of Philadelphia Proprietary Party notables recruited sailors to mingle with the county's intended voters and then, with their clubs, "discourage" Quaker Party supporters from casting their ballots. But whatever finesse was intended to cloak the aggression dissolved with the mist on election-day morning. As proceedings began, a mob of sailors descended on the square, swinging their clubs at the "plain Coats & broad Brims" and their allies the "Dutch *Sons of Bitches.*"[146] Quaker Party supporters retreated, cut their own cudgels, drove off some of the sailors and yarded others to jail. When the flailing ceased and the ballots were counted, one thing was clear: the Proprietary Party had suffered a severe political and moral defeat. Appalled by the aggression, many of those who had intended to vote for some Proprietary leaders scratched their names off the ballot and substituted Quaker Party men. Almost a decade and a half passed before William Allen and his friends again felt strong enough to run for provincial office.[147]

A third major effect of the crisis of 1740–1742 was to reinforce the identification of Quakerism with popular rights and legislative privilege. As early as 1740, Governor Thomas and his Philadelphia supporters saw their rivals as a "Quaker" opposition, and condemned it as such. Supporters of the assembly made the same connection, seeing the cause they backed as the Quaker cause; it was the Quakers, Pennsylvania freeholders concluded, who were best equipped to protect their rights. Anyone of that religious affiliation who joined with the executive's Anglican and Presbyterian supporters was no longer a real Quaker but "an unsteady person."[148] This association of freeholder rights and assembly privileges with Quakerism was to remain strong throughout the remaining colonial years.

Fourth, the crisis of the early 1740s welded politically conscious Quakers together to an unprecedented degree. Prior to this time, Friends had frequently divided politically along proprietary/antiproprietary lines. But that quickly changed. As conflict between Governor Thomas and the Quaker Party deepened, a political upheaval took place, which for the first time in Pennsylvania brought almost all Quakers into a broad coalition. And the change brought conflict. For over two years influential Friends of both sexes involved themselves in politics as seldom before, trying to reconcile their views of the Society of Friends with the affairs of the political party that bore their name.[149] By mid 1743, the fractiousness that accompanied this political realignment had largely died down. Although there were instances thereafter in which disagreements among active Quaker politicians suggested the possibility of a split, in fact, Friends maintained their newfound party consensus through 1755.[150]

Finally, despite the overwhelming preponderance of Friends among the candidates whom the Quaker Party put up for provincial and county offices, the party came out of the early 1740s crisis with an enhanced level of public support among other religious and ethnic groups.[151] Pennsylvania's relatively recent German immigrants were the new Quaker allies most remarked upon. If William Allen is to be believed, their recruitment began in 1740, when Philadelphia Quakers enlisted "about 400 Germans who hardly ever came to elections formerly, perhaps never 40 of them having voted" before.[152] Two years later, members of the Proprietary Party spoke to "ye Heads of ye Dutch" at Germantown, hoping that "ye Dutch cou'd be divided," but it is unlikely that even if the riot had been avoided, the Proprietary Party men would have achieved their goal.[153] While it is undoubtedly true that the various sectarians whose pacifist views were reflected in Christopher Saur's *Pensylvanische Berichte* were the heart of Quaker support among Germans, Quaker popularity also soared among both church Germans and those without clear institutional affiliation. German Pennsylvanians associated the province's "mild government" and liberty of conscience with Quaker dominance;[154] county residents saw no point in paying taxes to defend Philadelphia from an unlikely Spanish attack;[155] the prospect of a militia law appalled those acquainted with the oppressive use of military force in western Europe;[156] and the Quakers offered both a liberal naturalization law and some security of property for the families of unnaturalized newcomers.[157] In a colony in which the German population would soon become the largest component, the spread of such sentiments was crucial to the success of the Quaker Party.

Once past the 1742 election, the Quaker Party faced no sizable challenge until the mid 1750s, when for the first time a British war brought death and destruction to Pennsylvania inhabitants. The descent of Indian raiding parties on the frontiers of the province subsequent to General Edward Braddock's defeat on the Monongahela in July 1755, sent the Scotch-Irish Presbyterians of southwestern Pennsylvania fleeing eastwards for safety and forced the Germans of backcountry Berks and Northampton to huddle together wherever they could find a haven. Faced with the frantic cries of frontier families for military aid, Quakers were divided about what action their party should take. A small number of influential Friends, including some assemblymen, felt that they could not accept even a voluntary militia, nor could they be party to the appropriation and expenditure of money for specific wartime activities.[158] On the other hand, a sizable number of Quaker assemblymen and a majority of Quakers in the province, led by Speaker of the House Isaac Norris, Jr., believed that defensive war measures were consistent with the Quaker mission.[159] The problem for these Quakers was not whether money should be appropriated or not, but who would control whatever monies the assembly chose to raise, and who might be taxed to support the war effort. Thomas Penn insisted through instructions to his governors that the chief executive should have an equal say with the assembly in the expenditure of all money, and that proprietary lands should be exempt from all levies. The Quaker assemblymen believed that they should continue to control appropriations, as they had done for almost three decades, and that they should determine what the provincial tax base should be.[160]

The political scene was further complicated by the growing retinue of influential non-Quakers who accepted the proprietary argument that the executive should be party to any wartime disposal of money, who felt that the Penns should have some say (if not an outright veto on taxation of proprietary lands), and who pressed strenuously for what they considered a regular and workable provincial militia law—one that would provide for executive-appointed, not elected, officers, the enforcement of strict military discipline among troops, and the fining of conscientious objectors.[161] Their demands were animated by a genuine belief that such policies were the only effective way to fight an imperial war, and by a fanciful vision of themselves displacing the Quakers as leaders in the assembly.

Throughout the early stages of the war, representatives of these various points of view groped their way toward positions they were prepared to defend. Despite the doubts they harbored, conscientious Friends initially accepted the need for wartime grants to support the British military effort against France.[162] But once it became clear that this war, unlike earlier ones, was going to require sustained legislative participation in spending wartime levies, continuous oversight of military discipline among provincial troops, and provincial declarations of war against various Indian tribes, pacifist-leaning Friends lobbied their acquaintances in government, encouraged dissent from assembly acceptance of such measures, and ultimately encouraged Quaker legislators to resign rather than compromise a reinvigorated peace testimony.[163]

In the majority of cases, however, that counsel fell on deaf ears. From the fall of 1755 through the spring and summer of 1756, most Quaker assemblymen were willing to sanction war measures. What they were not prepared to do was to give in to proprietary demands on the question of joint appropriation of money, exemption of Penn lands from taxation, and the organization of what proprietary supporters felt would be a regular militia. For these Quakers, no matter what private doubts they harbored, pacifism was not the issue; safeguarding legislative power was.[164] As Isaac Norris, Jr., put it, the assemblymen saw their case, not as "a Quaker cause," but as "a cause of Liberty."[165] That, however, was not an easy distinction to make. From 1754 through mid 1756, they framed a number of bills that Governor Robert Hunter Morris would not sign because they controverted proprietary instructions.[166] Because they drafted a succession of such bills, which they suspected would meet executive rejection (and which did so because of Penn's instructions), the war Quakers laid themselves open to charges of covert pacifism.[167] Their actions could easily be construed as hypocritical, an offering of lip service to frontier defense to hide their first allegiance to the perpetuation of Quaker power and unity.[168]

The Quaker Party's opponents also groped toward renewed political activism. Thomas Penn pursued his interests most effectively by shoring up his support in Britain and by appointing the disputatious Robert Hunter Morris as governor to carry out his policies of regaining lost executive power and protecting the proprietary estate from taxation. As for the proprietor's allies in Pennsylvania, they initially challenged the Quaker Party in some counties in the 1754 election.[169] But not gaining a single assembly seat in that contest, supporters of the proprietorship sat out the 1755 election, hoping that pressure from Whitehall would force the Quakers to resign, and that the Proprietary Party could then easily supplant its old rival. This seemed possible because a number of influential British politicians were prepared to conclude, on the strength of Provost William Smith's charges in his anti-Quaker pamphlet *A Brief State* that Pennsylvania was governed by "An Assembly, principled against military Service."[170] And a Smith-penned, pro-defense petition dispatched to Whitehall in late 1755 was intended to furnish the British with the opportunity to disqualify the Quakers from government.[171]

In the midst of the paralysis this stalemate engendered, Benjamin Franklin established what was to be, henceforth, one of the highest profiles in provincial politics. Well regarded in Philadelphia for his promotion of various civic improvements, increasingly famous overseas for his scientific experiments, and about to be recognized as an imperial constitutional theorist with his contribution to the Albany Plan of intercolonial union, Franklin had, up to this point, played a limited role in provincial politics since his election to the assembly in 1751.[172] Although his closest friends were proprietary-leaning non-Quakers, the freethinking, nominally Anglican Franklin was a longtime fellow traveler of the Quakers, serving as their assembly clerk for almost fifteen years and relying on Quaker Party support to begin his legislative career. As Franklin himself admitted, as late as June 1755, he had "some Share in the Confidence of both" governor and assembly, but unable "to reconcile 'em," he sometimes fell in the middle, "both Sides expect[ing] more from . . . [him] than they ought."[173]

To a man of Franklin's ambition, talent, and practical turn of mind, the crisis in Pennsylvania affairs was as much an opportunity as a problem. Because he was by far the most able writer among assembly spokespersons, and because even those Quakers committed to defensive war were reluctant to take the lead in dealing with military matters, Franklin seized the political initiative in 1755–1756. With his undoctrinaire, matter-of-fact Whig opinions about popular power in Pennsylvania, he argued Governor Morris to a standstill.[174] More important, Franklin took action: he performed feats of legerdemain that allowed the assembly to meet some of the demands of war without much compromising its intransigence over Thomas Penn's instructions;[175] he enhanced Pennsylvania's reputation with Whitehall and put cash into the hands of the province's grateful inhabitants when he mobilized farmers to provide transport for General Braddock's troops in the spring of 1755;[176] he persuaded the assembly to approve a provincial militia much like his Voluntary Association of 1747–1748, and was elected colonel of the Philadelphia regiment;[177] and as assembly leader and advocate of defense, he supervised the fortification of backcountry Berks and Northampton counties.[178] In the course of these activities, Franklin became more convinced that the Quaker government was no impediment to the war effort. As he put it, "the Quakers now think it their Duty, when chosen, to consider themselves as Representatives of the *Whole People*, and not of their Sect only. . . . To me, it seems that if *Quakerism* (as to the matter of Defence) be excluded the House, there is no Necessity to exclude *Quakers*, who in other respects make good and useful Members."[179]

But destroying Quaker government was precisely what Franklin's proprietary acquaintances seemed to have in mind. Provost William Smith's *Brief State* and *Brief View* were attacks on Quakers in government, while Thomas Penn was determined to use his proprietary instructions to keep the pressure on the legislature and to generate anti-Quaker sentiment among war-endangered Pennsylvanians.[180] Gradually a gap began to open between Franklin and Proprietary Party sympathizers. In February 1756, for example, Provost William Smith, whom Franklin had enthusiastically recruited to lead the College of Philadelphia, threw open the doors of the Academy to Proprietary Party supporters who chose to boycott the province's voluntary militia law and to challenge Franklin's leadership of the Philadelphia regiments by organizing their own voluntary defense force.[181] When Franklin questioned Smith's motives, the provost counterattacked with characteristic excess, belittling Franklin and the popular cause.[182] His cruelest rejoinder, however, he saved until May, when Franklin was out of the province; during his absence, Smith and his allies seized the opportunity to push Franklin from the presidency of the College of Philadelphia's board of trustees.[183] Deeply hurt by that blow, Franklin became ever more frustrated with the proprietary position when, in August, Governor Denny arrived in Pennsylvania bearing the same kind of unyielding proprietary instructions that Franklin had so vigorously fought under Governor Morris.[184]

By late summer 1756, it was clear to Franklin that the annual October elections would be among the most important ever held in Pennsylvania.

Pacifist Friends, who had hitherto been an important component of the Quaker Party leadership, had begun to withdraw from the assembly; this development clearly offered opportunity to those who would seize it.[185] Franklin was sufficiently tempted to try his hand at candidate selection for Philadelphia County. Encouraged by his recent high profile ("The People happen to love me," Franklin modestly claimed),[186] and by the fact that the Philadelphians elected in the June by-elections to replace resigning Quaker pacifists were Anglicans who shared many of Franklin's views on provincial affairs, he explored the possibility of sponsoring a coalition ticket in Philadelphia that included both old Quaker Party men and moderate supporters of the proprietorship.[187] What encouraged Franklin to take this gamble was his knowledge of a major Proprietary Party campaign in the outlying counties, intended to capitalize on what supporters of the proprietorship hoped would be a divided and demoralized Quaker opponent. There was the possibility, then, that the new assembly might be sufficiently divided to throw leadership into the hands of those who could work with both Quaker and Proprietary Party men. If Franklin had his own base in Philadelphia, he reasoned, he would be the one individual most capable of building a consensus in the new house.

If Franklin was ultimately wrong about the outcome of the election, he was certainly correct about the Proprietary Party's intentions. Having failed to win seats in the 1754 general election, and again in the June 1756 by-elections to choose successors for six resigning pacifists, and disappointed by the British failure to disqualify Quakers from office, the Proprietary Party was ready by late August to throw its resources into an election campaign.[188] Chief Justice William Allen made sure that the proprietary men were represented on the joint ticket he negotiated with Benjamin Franklin, accepted candidacy for himself in both Cumberland and Northampton counties, and counseled Attorney-General Benjamin Chew to run in York County.[189] But the busiest member of the opposition was Provost William Smith, who was involved not only as a polemicist but as a strategist in Philadelphia and in Lancaster, Chester, and Northampton counties.[190] Like the Livingston/Smith faction in New York, Provost William Smith and his Proprietary Party mounted a strong verbal attack on their opponents (in New York's case, William Livingston's campaign against an Anglican college; in Pennsylvania's, Smith's slanderous screeds against the Quakers), and tried to cobble together a political alliance from what they perceived to be the religious "outs" in the colony. Purposely resurrecting the old seventeenth-century shibboleth that Friends were not Christians, Smith claimed that his goal was to "unite all the [province's] Protestants in one Interest."[191] With his large ego, vaulting ambition, and lack of seasoning in Pennsylvania society, Smith found it easy to conceive of himself as the Moses

of the Proprietary Party. Moreover, as provost of the College of Philadelphia, he held the most important nonpolitical position in Pennsylvania,
an office that was the natural focal point for non-Quaker, interdenominational cooperation in the province.

The College of Philadelphia was as close to an experiment in nondenominational education as can be found in eighteenth-century America.[192] Although Anglicans dominated the college's board of trustees
throughout the colonial years, nondenominational commitment was given
substance by the inclusion of Old Light Presbyterians and Baptists on the
faculty and by the extension of considerable religious freedom to the students.[193] Essentially, the college was a cooperative effort between Anglicans
and Old Light Presbyterians, with Provost William Smith representing the
former and Vice-Provost Francis Alison the latter.[194] Their shared interest
(by the standards of the times) in latitudinarian education and enquiry
rather than dogma, however, gave the college some claim to greater interdenominational breadth. And it was this reputation that Smith wished to
use for political purposes. In this regard he was particularly hopeful, for he
and other proprietary supporters had already made good use of the college's
precursor, the Philadelphia Academy, to focus the cause of interdenominational cooperation upon themselves. That action was their sponsorship and
continuing promotion of charity schools to provide primary education for
the children of Pennsylvania's poorer German immigrants. Although privately contemptuous of the Germans (as his anonymous polemics testified),
Smith felt that the heads of those households whose children benefited from
the charity schools, and whose views might be influenced by the anglicizing
schoolmasters his Philadelphia Academy would provide, might well be predisposed to vote for the Proprietary Party.[195]

The high hopes of both "Franklinists" and the Proprietary Party fed on
the apparent disarray of the Quaker Party, which under the residual influence of strict pacifists remained immobilized through the summer of
1756.[196] Just before the election, however, Old Party supporters came to life.
They put together a series of strong county tickets, and on October 1, they
carried the day.[197] Once he saw how the wind had shifted, Benjamin Franklin tacked accordingly and swept into office again on the Quaker ticket for
Philadelphia burgesses. His one or two non-Quaker friends, whom he had
tried to promote in his compromise county slate, were not so lucky. Quaker
Party candidates swamped them. The Proprietary Party nominees, whom
Smith and others had tried to promote, were no more fortunate. In Philadelphia County, where they had tried to cut a deal with Franklin, the sudden
rejuvenation of the Quaker Party, along with Franklin's swift reaction to that
development, left them dead in the water. Out in the surrounding counties,
where they were better organized, they were simply beaten.[198]

Why, given the unprecedented opportunity, did the Proprietary Party not fare better? One reason was that it did not offer a credible alternative. Although Smith and his friends tried to exploit the differences in attitudes to war that divided sectarians from church groups, the Proprietary Party was never able to persuade large numbers of Pennsylvanians (particularly in the longer settled areas) that Quaker pacifism was the villain proprietary supporters claimed it to be. Despite the certitude with which Smith, Allen, and others pronounced that Pennsylvania's "unfortunate" state resulted from "having an Assembly of all Quakers, whose Principles are against making defence," they were never very convincing.[199] As Isaac Norris, Jr., pointed out, "whatever influence . . . [such views] may have had in England . . . [they] need no answer here where the facts are known clear of the disguises they have been wrap't in."[200] Most provincials believed that the defense issue was one that turned on popular rights, and they did not want to sacrifice the powers of their elected representatives merely for the *possibility* of better defense. "Neither the Quakers nor (if I judge right) any other set who can get elected into the Assembly," averred Norris, "will tamely suffer" "the chains" the proprietor and governor intended "to rivet on the People."[201] The Proprietary Party was trying to make bricks without straw. It had none of the popular principles necessary to create a broad political alliance.

The other major reason for the Proprietary Party's poor showing was its ineffectiveness at ethnoreligious coalition building. Most instructive in this context was the experience of Provost William Smith. To begin with, the alliance between himself and Alison, which symbolized Anglican/Old Light comity, was never very comfortable. Despite their efforts to work together, the two remained far apart: Smith admired the worldliness of the belles lettres, while Alison loved the rigor of classical scholarship; Smith preferred administration and public relations, while Alison's métier was the classroom; Smith was as devious as Alison was unbending; and most important, while Smith thrived on political conflict, Alison hated it.[202] In this case, the vice-provost refused to stoop to partisan scribbling and when his sermons did turn to public affairs, his comments consisted of criticisms of *both* Quaker and Proprietary Party intransigence.[203] That did little to persuade the many Old Light supporters of the Quaker Party that they should become turncoats.[204] Among his own Anglicans, Smith's problems were even greater. In May 1756, the "over Busy and indiscreet" Smith became involved in a public dispute with a fellow Anglican, Daniel Roberdeau. In the course of that disagreement, Anglican vestrymen and even trustees of Smith's college came to Roberdeau's defense, in effect telling Smith to honor the tradition of political noninvolvement that his priestly predecessors had established in Philadelphia during the past quarter century.[205] Later that year,

Richard Peters reported that "two thirds of the Church are gone off from Church Principles & Church Politics," and had no inclination to follow Proprietary Party leaders.[206] As for the New Light Presbyterians, they, too, kept their distance. Despite the fact that Gilbert Tennent had been the most outspoken anti-Quaker theologian in Philadelphia during the previous ten years, contrasting views about theology and religious enthusiasm, competition between the College of New Jersey and both the Academy and College of Philadelphia, and personal feuds among clerics prevented New Light Presbyterians from having much to do with either Old Light Presbyterians or Anglicans.[207] Finally, there was the question of the political efficacy of the German charity schools. What stood out most clearly to those German communities targeted for a school was not the philanthropic dimensions of the enterprise but the overbearing political and cultural intentions of the sponsors. The Germantown printer Christopher Saur quickly pointed out that the schools were intended to produce a particular version of anglicized citizens—ones who would farm, fight, and pay taxes for the benefit of the proprietor and vote for the Proprietary Party. Convinced that Saur's opinions were closer to the truth than was the gloss of proprietary public relations, few parents enrolled their children, and fewer still turned against the Quaker Party.[208] All in all, the anti-Quaker, interdenominational, Proprietary Party coalition came to little.

The major reason for the outcome of the 1756 election, however, was not the weakness of the Proprietary Party but the strength and flexibility of its Quaker opponents. Rather than follow the advice of the handful of high-profile, strict pacifists to boycott the election, the bulk of the province's Quakers continued their traditional political activism. Provincial Secretary Richard Peters complainingly diagnosed the problem: "the Quakers were never more assiduous, nor more of their young People avowedly busy, tho' a few serious and grave men did not shew themselves but of those there were not many."[209] Circumstances were no different in the outlying counties, where long-time Quaker Party supporters flocked to the polls.[210]

Yet in the midst of this success, there was one very important change. Despite the fact that the Quaker Party had won a resounding victory, the number of Friends in the legislature had dropped precipitously. Whereas twenty-seven Quakers had held seats prior to June 1756, their numbers were reduced to a dozen or fewer (depending on the authority) by the end of October of that year.[211] In Philadelphia, Quaker Party managers and voters had exerted themselves "very much in favor of what they call moderate Churchmen."[212] In the outlying counties, again Friends' replacements were predominantly Anglican, but they also included Presbyterians from Chester and Bucks Counties, Dutch Reformed and Baptist members from Bucks, a Swiss-German Mennonite from Lancaster, and a nominal Anglican intermarried with German Lutherans from Berks.[213] The party's recruits had three things in common. First, they were "Quakerized," as Richard Peters called it—that is, they all shared a common ideology of "civil Quakerism."[214] (Penn's placeman and kinsman Lynford Lardner made the point more colorfully: they were all "Bastards begot by the Quakers upon the body politic."[215]) Second, they were all prepared to follow leaders who were "bitter on the side of Party." In particular, what the Quaker Party leaders called "their moderate Churchmen [were] . . . noted for their ill will to the Proprietor."[216] Third, they all accepted the fact that the large numbers of Friends who remained active in politics were clearly committed to waging war in defense of the province.[217]

So sweeping was the success of the Quaker Party (increasingly referred to as the Assembly Party) in restructuring itself and in solidifying community support that the Proprietary Party backed away from further large-scale contests for almost a decade.[218] That did not mean, however, that the remade Quaker Party was without weaknesses. In Philadelphia, Proprietary Party members slashed away at the heels of their opponents until the assembly threw Provost William Smith in jail.[219] ("Our old Inviterate Scribbler has at length wrote himself into a Jail," gloated a self-satisfied Isaac Norris, Jr., to Benjamin Franklin.)[220] More important than these Philadelphia skirmishes, however, was the problem of the west. The long months of terrifying frontier warfare beginning in 1755 and continuing through 1758 embittered some backcountry residents against the Assembly Party for putting its feuds with the proprietor before the welfare of the people.[221] John Armstrong, justice of the peace from Cumberland County, felt he could "forgive everybody except the Assembly and the Enemy Indians."[222] Scotch-Irish critics were more vocal than their German neighbors, but it was a mob of predominantly German backcountry farmers who, in late 1755, dragged a "Waggon-Load of . . . scalped and mangled bodies" to the State House in Philadelphia to underscore their dissatisfaction with assembly priorities.[223] It was all very well for legislative leaders to respond grandiloquently that "those who would give up essential Liberty, to purchase a little temporary Safety, deserve neither Liberty nor Safety."[224] Undoubtedly those who drafted such a statement were sincere. But during such a time of crisis, it was not evident that such a message was persuasive to residents of Pennsylvania's western and northern frontier valleys, who perceived most assemblymen to be cozily insulated in their eastern cocoon.

In the longer run, it was not inadequate and unsuccessful defense in the early stages of the war but the Quaker-sponsored Friendly Association—a philanthropic organization founded in 1756 to promote peace between Pennsylvanians and hostile Indians—that weakened the loyalty of backcountry residents to the Assembly Party. The Friendly Association was the

idea of that small Philadelphia-centered group of "sober" (i.e., highly principled) Friends who had cooperated with like-minded public Friends (i.e.,
Quaker ministers) in orchestrating the partial Quaker withdrawal from
provincial politics. The self-appointed conscience of the Society of Friends,
this minority saw the Friendly Association as a means of demonstrating that
they, not the Quaker assemblymen, were the true heirs of William Penn.
They, not the legislators, were carrying on the tradition of identifying peaceful relations with native Americans as their first priority. Having temporarily
abandoned politics, they were anxiously searching for means of giving public expression to a renewed Quakerism. Vocal, intolerant, and judgmental,
the Friendly Association Quakers embarked on their private crusade, plying
the Delaware Indians with gifts, seeking praise for Quaker land policies of
generations past, and stirring up anger at recent proprietary diplomacy with
the natives. Given the common interest of the Friendly Association and the
renewed Quaker Party in blaming the proprietors for the Indian war against
Pennsylvania, Quaker politicians openly cooperated with the association.
At the Easton Treaties of 1757 and 1758, it was difficult to distinguish the
behavior of assemblymen from that of the association's representatives. By
the end of the war, backcountry residents came to see Quakerism as a
puzzling hybrid, intransigent on the subject of popular rights when the
proprietor or governor threatened assembly power or provincials' sense of
equity, but inexplicably charitable and forgiving to Indians, who sometimes
posed a more immediate and frightening threat to the frontiersmen's lives
and property.[225]

These weaknesses notwithstanding, the most important characteristic of
the Quaker Party during and immediately subsequent to the 1756 crisis was
its instinct for self-preservation. The resignation of the strict pacifists was
enough of a purge to convince the great bulk of traditional Quaker Party
supporters that their party was unequivocally committed to defending the
province in time of war. Popular acceptance of the view "that it was not
the Society of Quakers but the Proprietary Instructions yt obstruct[ed] the
King's Business" meant that the renewed party had every opportunity to
consolidate itself in the late 1750s and early 1760s.[226] If anything, it became
more antiproprietary during these years, determined—even to the point of
soliciting royal government—to try to protect and expand popular powers
in the face of Thomas Penn's continued efforts to reclaim and maintain
executive and proprietary prerogatives. Along with the popular orientation
of their policies, the renewed Quaker, or Assembly, Party continued its
conscious cultivation of non-Quaker and non-English religious and cultural
groups, and its recruitment of politicians who had close ties with those
religiocultural enclaves. Although Quakers who were in good standing in
their Society, along with nominal Friends, regained a slight majority in the

assembly during the late 1750s and early 1760s, they continued to keep close ties to the cultural brokers who represented strong non-English areas in the legislature.[227]

Once Benjamin Franklin fully realized the limitations Quaker Party hegemony imposed upon him, he became a stalwart of and mediator within the revitalized party. His well-known support among the leather-apron men of Philadelphia, his influence with many Anglican city politicians who shared his party loyalties, and his popularity (despite an Anglophile ambivalence about the cultural threat that large-scale German immigration represented) among backcountry Germans, who remembered his defense-related activities of 1755–1756, gave him powerful leverage within the Assembly Party. But the anchor of the coalition remained the speaker, Isaac Norris, Jr., with his conservative Quaker supporters and their non-Quaker allies from Chester and Bucks counties.[228] Although tensions among Norris, Franklin, and leaders like Joseph Fox and Joseph Galloway certainly existed, the refurbished party was no more fragmented than it had been under Speaker John Kinsey, when such prominent individuals as Samuel Blunston, Isaac Norris, Jr., and Israel Pemberton, Jr., had each had his own ideas of how their party should function.[229] What was most remarkable about the new coalition was the way it functioned "like a disciplined regimt"—war pressures, proprietary intransigence, regional tensions, and religious and cultural differences notwithstanding.[230] Throughout its midcentury trials, the Quaker Party not only renewed itself but also retained the internal cohesion that had distinguished it so clearly in earlier times.

"As the twig is bent . . ."

The DeLancey/Jones coalition and the Quaker Party dominated politics in New York and Pennsylvania during the 1740s and 1750s. Amid the improbable circumstances of rapid population growth, continued geographic dispersion, increased socioeconomic complexity, and a strengthening of each province's peculiar tradition of multicultural immigration, these two organizations established considerable control over their respective colonies' political agendas and widespread support among each electorate. Their success in doing so owed a good deal to the particular wartime crises each colony faced in the 1740s. Both Governor Clinton's and Governor Thomas's determination to run their respective colonies' war efforts as they saw fit galvanized the chief politicians in each province into opposition. Their efforts to meet the threat of executive power led these leaders into cooperative political action. In following this course, they committed themselves to a popular political position that their subsequent success, their belief in the validity of such a stance, and the overwhelming public support their appeals elicited encouraged them to sustain both as individuals and as members of collective political entities.

There were, however, important differences between the DeLancey/ Jones faction and the Quaker Party even at their inception. First, the De-Lancey/Jones coalition rose relatively swiftly and without prior indication out of a welter of separate interests that gained political expression in the late 1730s and early 1740s. As the coalition formed, its chief leaders began articulating a dialect of "popular Whiggism," first made familiar to New Yorkers by the Philipse faction of the 1720s and early to mid 1730s (see chapter 6). Building on that tradition, and on their own unsurpassed ability to co-opt county notables and become the political beneficiaries of the strands of dependence that ran through these individuals' hands to surrounding communities, the DeLancey/Jones faction overcame the always-potent centrifugal forces of New York politics. Comparatively, Pennsylvania's Quaker Party had a stronger foundation. Although Governor Thomas's actions triggered the appearance of the Quaker Party in the early 1740s, its coalescence was prefigured in the antiproprietary sentiment sweeping Pennsylvania in response to Thomas Penn's innovations of the 1730s. And the fact that proprietary policies remained a continual factor in the 1740s and 1750s constantly reinforced Quaker Party cohesion and underscored its deep commitment to popular goals. Most important, Quaker Party spokespersons claimed to be the heirs to a generally consistent, antiproprietary, anti-executive stream of popular political thought that had existed since the late 1690s. This idiom of "civil Quakerism" was a powerfully unifying—at times virtually consensual—ideology, which gave the Quaker Party unparalleled political strength (see chapter 7).

The religious profiles of their respective leaders and legislators were a second major difference between the DeLancey/Jones faction and the Quaker Party. In the case of the former, the coalition's leaders were Anglicans who were able to develop and maintain close ties with many Dutch Reformed county leaders. In some cases, these Dutch Reformed notables became legislative lieutenants; in others, they simply filled out the faction's rank and file. The strength of Anglican leadership in the DeLancey/Jones coalition, despite the paucity of Church of England adherents in New York, simply reflected the uncompromising demands of political entitlement in provincial affairs that churchmen had pressed on the Dutch since the late seventeenth century. That pattern of Anglican/Dutch Reformed cooperation was one that had characterized most New York factions since the end of anti-Leislerian politics at the turn of the century.

In Pennsylvania, of course, Friends had always played a central role in popular politics, but unlike the case of New York where the De-

Lancey/Jones coalition represented a continuation rather than a change in the religious composition of popular political leadership, the formation of the Quaker Party began a period in which Quakers dominated provincial electoral office to an unprecedented degree. Given the growing strength of non-Quaker denominations, such a narrow religious base would appear to have made the Quaker Party a fragile entity. Paradoxically, it did not. Because of the very pervasiveness of the civil Quaker ideology, and the strategic vision and tactical expertise of Quaker politicians, its leaders developed the party into the most powerful political organization in early America.

Regardless of the popularity of the DeLancey/Jones faction and the Quaker Party, the fact that both New York Anglicans and Pennsylvania Quakers were religious minorities that wielded a disproportionate share of power through these political organizations meant that the organizations were susceptible to attack. And issues arose in the mid 1750s that triggered heated opposition in both colonies. In New York, the Livingston/Smith faction formed to fight against, first, the establishment of, and then the granting of public support for, an Anglican college. In Pennsylvania, the Proprietary Party reentered electoral politics on the grounds that the Quaker Party's wartime policies were inadequate for the province's needs. In each case, the opposition tried to exploit the issue of religious exclusiveness, arguing that civil policy was being subordinated to selfish denominational interests. In New York, critics portrayed King's College, not as a civic institution designed to serve the general good, but as an effort by the Anglicans to strengthen their stunted provincial establishment. In Pennsylvania, the most notable Anglican and Presbyterian opponents of the Quaker Party placed the blame for perceived deficiencies in provincial defense on Quaker pacifism rather than on proprietary instructions and their own partisan demands for greater executive authority. Both oppositions were simultaneously sincere, bitter, and opportunistic. Anti-college and anti-Quaker spokespersons were certainly committed to different principles of social organization than their opponents. But they were also driven by jealousy of Anglican and Quaker influence, anger at the slights they felt they had received at Anglican and Quaker hands, and a conscious willingness to exploit the license their communities accorded self-proclaimed champions of religious rights to inveigh against religious tyranny. Tired of feeling marginalized, they were committed to cutting down the power of the dominant political leaders by any means at their disposal.

The Livingston/Smith faction and the Proprietary Party hoped to strike at DeLancey/Jones and Quaker Party strength respectively by alienating some of the groups of non-Anglicans and non-Quakers that the latter two had been so successful in attracting, and by building their own coalitions with the help of these potential converts. The Livingston/Smith faction had some success with the former tactic. Despite Anglican/Dutch Reformed affinities, there was a strong, potentially offsetting, provincial tradition of localism and Dutch church autonomy, which encouraged Dutch Reformed leaders to look to their own interests. In addition, the Presbyterians Livingston and Smith were able to divert current, intradenominational Dutch Reformed religious disputes over language and evangelicalism into channels beneficial to their cause. Livingston and Smith were also effective because their faction expressed a secondary idiom of New York politics— that of "provincial Whiggism"—which earned its own legitimacy in provincial discourse in contradistinction to the popular Whiggism of the De-Lancey/Jones coalition (see chapter 6). But despite these advantages, the Livingston/Smith faction had little success (and arguably little sustained interest) in building their own political coalition to the point where they might gain a sizable share of electoral office. Presbyterians had an unsavory reputation among many New Yorkers because of their association with New England and Independency, and once the opportunity for a provincial election disappeared, coincidentally with the college dispute, the Livingston/Smith faction began to lose both shape and momentum.

In Pennsylvania, the Proprietary Party put much more emphasis on forming its own coalition with which to oust the Quaker Party. In large measure, that had to do with the opportunity that annual provincial elections provided, and to the fact that in 1756, large numbers of veteran Quaker assemblymen were sure to resign. But the Proprietary Party leaders failed to understand how closely the ideology of civil Quakerism bound non-Quakers to the Friends, and how anathematical their vision of a Quakerless, proprietary/executive-led provincial government was to most Pennsylvanians. Whereas William Livingston's educational secularism, anticlericalism, and derivative, freethinking rhetoric was far too radical for the conservative, tradition-bound minds of most New York dissenters, the radicalism of Provost William Smith's restructured Pennsylvania was far too reactionary to gain much support in the Quaker colony.

Despite the limited, immediate political effects of the Livingston/Smith and Proprietary Party activities, these nonetheless served to highlight one of the most important morphological differences separating the politics of New York and Pennsylvania. The Livingston/Smith faction encouraged criticism of the DeLancey/Jones coalition, and after the French and Indian War broke out that tendency continued. Just as Presbyterian attacks on Anglicanism played a part in David Jones's defeat in the 1759 provincial election, so other localized criticisms, frequently born of wartime exigencies, wore away at the constituency roots of incumbents in the legislature. Supporters of the Livingston/Smith, anti-college coalition suffered as well as their opponents. But the biggest loser was the DeLancey/Jones faction.

Ultimately, it failed to preserve enough strength to be able to redefine itself around new postwar challenges.

It is possible to imagine circumstances in which a DeLancey/Jones–inspired coalition could have lived on beyond the demise of its original leaders. James DeLancey's brother, Oliver, was still in the assembly in 1760; a member of the friendly Cruger clan, John, gained a New York City seat in 1759; a second DeLancey brother, Peter, continued to represent Westchester; William Nicoll, an Anglican Long Islander with good connections among both Presbyterians and Congregationalists succeeded David Jones as house speaker; and a handful of other coalition veterans returned to the legislature. The opportunity to revive the old antiprerogative popular base of the DeLancey/Jones group was present, too, because the querulous Cadwallader Colden, whose posturings and threats on behalf of Governor Clinton had helped draw the old coalition together, became acting chief executive upon James DeLancey's death. But none of the survivors or new recruits was able to refit the old coalition with policies and structures suitable for new times. So tied to the personalities of its leaders was it that, no matter how coherent and powerful the old DeLancey/Jones coalition had been, it could not live beyond the men who made it. In that respect, the DeLancey/Jones faction was paradigmatic of every political organization to appear in colonial New York.

The direction that the Quaker Party took during and subsequent to the Proprietary Party's challenge was a very different one. Unquestionably, the election of 1756 brought about change. Pacifist Quakers became critics of their old party and frequently nonvoters; Friends became a minority in the assembly; and the Quaker Party pledged to defend the province no matter the nature of the contest. At the same time, however, the party retained its hegemony, and voters of a wide variety of denominations reaffirmed their loyalty to it. Unlike the DeLancey/Jones faction, the Quaker Party adapted to new circumstances. It recruited new members to work alongside veteran leaders and simultaneously remained true to the ideology that had shaped its identity. Rather than die with change, the Quaker Party underwent a reinvigorating metamorphosis. Just as the party had moved from the leadership of John Kinsey to that of Isaac Norris, Jr., in 1750, so it was transmuted from a Quaker Party to a Quakerized one in 1756. Generational change and alterations in political environment notwithstanding, the party lived on.

Chapter Five

The Electorate and Popular Politics

FROM THE EARLY 1690s in the case of New York, and from Pennsylvania's founding in the early 1680s, provincial elections were important events in the public affairs of each colony. Political representation was the preeminent feature of British-American colonial government, the one institution that English immigrants consistently claimed as their "Chiefest Birthright."[1] Once established, the practice of representation through provincial elections became the central feature of eighteenth-century politics, as New York and Pennsylvania societies quickly matured. The increasing power of the colonies' assemblies in governmental affairs drew attention to the importance of electoral decisions; the growing rights consciousness of many colonists, and their close association of popular rights with colonial legislators, reinforced voters' awareness that election day could bring a meaningful choice; the need of factions and parties to mobilize electoral support if they were to gain or retain legislative power, periodically focused public opinion on the trust that freeholders placed in their representatives. Ultimately, the onus lay on the citizenry, through its electoral responsibilities, to determine the character of provincial government.

Vigorous electoral contests first took place early in the colonial history of New York and Pennsylvania and occurred periodically thereafter. Throughout the first three-quarters of the eighteenth century, there were a number of occasions upon which organized groups of politicians competed for voter support and considerable numbers of freemen turned out at the polls.[2] This extended record of electoral engagement notwithstanding, it is only from the late colonial years that sufficient evidence survives to enable us to say very much about the character of voter behavior. By this time, the numbers of potential voters had increased to the point where political organizers resorted more frequently to written communications, and in some cases more to election screeds, to supplement the private meetings, verbal instructions, personal campaigning, and public harangues that still constituted the bulk of election-oriented politics. The higher rate of manuscript survival and the greater quantity of printed sources from the 1760s provide the best evidence we have from the colonial years bearing on the complexities of electoral politics.

As in most of the British North American colonies, there was sharp political conflict in New York and Pennsylvania during the 1760s. In the former colony, concerted opposition to the lieutenant-governor, the Stamp Act crisis, rural riots, and the sharpening of political rivalries among provincials culminated in the two hard-fought elections of 1768 and 1769. In the latter, renewed tensions over frontier defense, the Paxton Riots, the intensification of conflict between the proprietor and the assembly, and the Quaker Party's interest in seeking royal government amid British initiatives (symbolized by the Stamp Act) to reorganize the empire, fueled intense political partisanship in the elections of 1764 and 1765. In each colony, electoral competition was complicated by the injection of religious issues and rivalries into the election campaigns, and by differing degrees of ethnoreligious political clustering. These in turn owed something to the increasing diversity of each colony, yet they varied immensely depending on such circumstances as locale, the changing numbers and organizational strength of various religious and ethnic groups, the occurrence of intradenominational feuds, and group penchants for interdenominational or interethnic cooperation. All told, these four highly contested provincial elections reveal a good deal of the multidimensional character of public affairs in New York and Pennsylvania, and of the considerable impact electoral behavior periodically had on popular politics in early America.

Public Crises and Electoral Conflict

Compared to the decades of DeLancey/Jones dominance, the 1760s were fluid years in New York politics. On Speaker David Jones's defeat in 1759, the assembly chose the Long Island lawyer William Nicoll II as its presiding officer. Nicoll was a legislative veteran with proven compromising ability and no great factional ambitions. Despite offering some support for the establishment of an Anglican college in the early 1750s, Nicoll had managed to keep the confidence of his overwhelmingly Presbyterian and Congregational constituents in Suffolk County. As speaker, he quickly abdicated his claim to be the dominant voice in the assembly's committee of correspondence and devolved responsibility for New York/British relations on the city's four representatives.[3] Clearly a trimmer by temperament, Nicoll had not the will, and perhaps not the talent, to put together an effective legislative coalition out of the DeLancey/Jones remnants that remained in the assembly through much of the 1760s.

Left to their own inclinations, New York's elected representatives were in no hurry to coalesce anew into antagonistic groups. During the 1759–1760 assembly session, for example, William Livingston found he could cooperate with Oliver DeLancey in winding down the war effort, and the New York City merchant Philip Livingston and Captain James DeLancey, Lieutenant-Governor James DeLancey's eldest son and chief heir, agreed to stand with two others as an initial consensus slate for the city and county of New York in the provincial election of 1761.[4] Moreover, neither Cadwallader Colden nor General Robert Monckton, the two men who wielded executive power between 1760 and 1765, provoked factional splits. Virtually all active New York politicians disliked Colden, and none would cooperate closely with him. In Monckton's case, the reverse was true. Everyone wanted to be his friend, and no group of politicians wanted to take the lead against him during the thirteen short months in which he was an active governor.

The popular politicians with the highest public profile during these years, both within the assembly and without, were those who by the mid 1760s were increasingly referred to as the "Livingstons." In the legislature, their influence depended less on the fact that there were four representatives with that surname, and on their occasional alliance in assembly votes, than on Robert R. Livingston's legal and legislative skills and Philip Livingston's growing in-house and public reputation.[5] Among those influential New Yorkers outside the legislature, the Livingstons were most clearly represented by William Livingston and his informal legal partners, William Smith, Jr., and John Morin Scott. This "triumvirate" as they were retrospectively named, were at the pinnacle of the legal profession in New York, and legislators consequently often called on them to draft bills and addresses to serve as the basis of assembly discussion.[6] Moreover, the main issues that pitted Lieutenant-Governor Cadwallader Colden against the assembly during the early 1760s had to do with legal rights that the threesome were determined to defend. This brought them into public debate in such a way as to exaggerate the coherence and popular political influence of the Livingston family.

The two major issues that stirred up Livingston, Smith, and Scott were Colden's determination to grant supreme court commissions only "at pleasure," and to allow the overturning of jury-trial decisions in appeals to the governor-in-council.[7] In the first instance, Colden was very determined to uphold the royal prerogative because of his view that during the late James DeLancey's chief-justiceship, DeLancey had enjoyed a far greater ability to create politically effective dependencies than had New York governors. Colden believed DeLancey had been able to do so because his secure tenure ("for good behavior") as chief justice gave him continuing power in all important matters of property and law, and because the colony's lawyers could only practice in provincial courts on his sufferance, depending for their "bread & fortune" on DeLancey's "Countenance."[8] In Colden's opinion, the lawyers were prompted both by the chief justice's influence over them and by their personal inclinations, as members of families with large landholdings in the province, to collude with the bench in frustrating the attempts by Crown officials to collect back quitrents. Although Colden was irrational in his hatred of lawyers and judges, who he felt had deprived him of a quitrent-funded income during his long tenure as surveyor-general, his diagnosis of the relationship between judges, lawyers, and large landowners was close to the mark.[9] As William Smith, Jr., quietly confessed after opposing Colden's plan to place a well-paid outsider in the chief justice's chair, "the delicate state of the old patents was the true Reason why we gave so little to the Judges, & only from year to year, fearing Hirlings from Home, if we gave liberally & upon a permanent Bottom."[10] Not surprisingly, New York's prominent political leaders wanted a continuation of what they had enjoyed under DeLancey—a chief justice who was one of their own, who understood the dangers a rigorous proving of patents and quitrent collection would pose, and who was impervious, once appointed for "good behavior," to threats from governor, Board of Trade, or Privy Council.

The second instance, again, grew out of Colden's determination to uphold the prerogative, and his deep desire to show up the lawyers who so bedeviled him. When in 1763 Chief Justice Daniel Horsmanden denied a petition for an appeal to the governor-in-council by a defendant wishing to challenge a jury's finding in his case (Forsey v. Cunningham), and was unanimously supported in this decision by New York's other judges and lawyers, Colden determined to "show . . . himself in Law Matters, superior to the whole Body of the Law."[11] The lieutenant-governor prepared a statement in which he denounced the jury system, proclaimed the power of the Crown to set up new courts, and asserted the right of governors and monarch to review jury verdicts. In January 1765, he convened the council as a court, threw open the doors to the public, and before "a hundred or two people" challenged the council and the judges with his rambling exegesis.[12] When they refused to back down, Colden "fell upon" them in a rage, "charging them with Indecency, [and] Want of Respect to the King's Authority. . . . Many sharp Things were Retorted," including thinly veiled threats.[13] Undaunted by the opposition, Colden kept the controversy alive by appealing to the king-in-council for vindication.

As leading members of the New York bar, friends and relatives of judges and other lawyers, intimates of the land-rich, and experienced polemicists, William Livingston, William Smith, Jr., and John Morin Scott were quickly drawn into the initial fray with Colden over judicial tenure. In March 1762, they decided to try to play to the public in the judicial-tenure controversy by launching a newspaper, the *American Chronicle.* For two months they flailed at Colden on both constitutional and personal grounds, trying to breathe political fire into the Whig doctrine of a judiciary insulated from executive pressure.[14] But public response was so weak that the paper soon folded.[15] When leading provincials subsequently found Colden had been armed with new instructions from Britain forbidding any colonial judicial commissions on good behavior, the lawyers and judges realized that further intransigence would yield them no victories. In fact, William Smith, Sr., and Robert R. Livingston, who were on intimate terms with William Livingston, William Smith, Jr., and Scott, accepted the new "unacceptable" commissions after Governor Robert Monckton took over from Colden and oiled his charm over Manhattan's political waters.

In the appeals case, the three New York City lawyers again put themselves in the forefront of protest. William Smith, Jr.,—and belatedly, his informal law partners, Livingston and Scott—mobilized the legal community to defy Lieutenant-Governor Colden's demands that the governor-in-council should hear the appeal. And once Colden referred the case to Whitehall, the three refused to let the issue lie in limbo. Between February and August 1765, they published a series of essays entitled the "Sentinel" in the *New-York Gazette,* reminding colonists of the "inestimable blessing [of rights and privileges] which our ancestors have handed down to us," and publicly articulating the anger people felt toward Colden, whom they accused of "damn[ing] himself & his posterity . . . [so that he might] appear great."[16]

In expressing their concern about recent developments, Livingston, Smith, and Scott also gave vent to anxieties aroused by two new issues. The first and narrower of these concerns stemmed from Colden's about-face on an old and heavily freighted New York problem. Three years earlier, as a conciliatory gesture, the lieutenant-governor had approved an act allowing those who held substantial land tracts in joint tenancy to divide up their common property. Angered by his recent experiences, however, Colden returned to the old logic with which he had opposed such legislation in earlier decades, arguing that partitioning acts defrauded the monarch of Crown land by recognizing property claims originating in questionable first patents, and urging the Board of Trade to recommend disallowance of the legislation he had just signed. By thus turning on his tormentors, Colden gained some personal satisfaction, but only at the expense of further alienating some of New York's most powerful interests.[17]

By the spring of 1765, a second and much broader issue had begun to generate considerable public anxiety. This was the passage of the soon-to-be-notorious Stamp Act. According to the terms of the bill currently headed through Parliament, Great Britain would tax the colonists in an unprecedented manner without the consent of their provincial representatives. From the point of view of maintaining a peaceful New York, this legislation could not have appeared at a worse moment. The hatred that Colden and his recent policies had engendered was, according to the merchant John Watts, "a noble stock to engraft the stamp act upon."[18] The conviction that Whitehall intended "to cram the old man's [i.e., Colden's] Scots unconstitutional doctrinne upon the Colony" in the case of jury-trial appeals, and reports that a boastful British army officer, Major James, had volunteered that he was in New York "to cram down the Stamp act upon them," convinced New Yorkers that acquiescence was insufferable and certainly no way to support traditional rights.[19] Encouraged by the examples of Boston's riots and enraged by Cadwallader Colden's effort to intimidate locals by training the cannon that normally overlooked the harbor on the urban approaches to Fort George, city residents and seamen who were in port took over the streets during the first four days of November, protesting the threat to their rights and effectively preventing the administration of the Stamp Act.[20] Unrest simmered during the ensuing winter months, but by the spring of 1766, the British had removed both grievances.[21]

From 1760 through November 1, 1765, New Yorkers were less overtly divided in their factional politics than they had been for some time, and less than they would ever be again within the current generation's lifetime. Although New York's most outspoken public figures, William Livingston, William Smith, Jr., and John Morin Scott, were deeply influenced by their interests as lawyers and their intimacy with large landowners and speculators, they were also concerned about British administrative and parliamentary initiatives to restructure colonial affairs in the western hemisphere. While their writings centered on the judicial tenure and jury-trial appeal issue, they also registered some concern about the Stamp Act, the extension of admiralty court jurisdiction in the colonies, the new commercial regulations embodied in the Sugar Act of 1764, the currency regulations of the same year, and the dangers posed by British troops stationed in North America.[22] These were issues that longtime political opponents and a range of social groups from merchants to seamen as well as entrepreneurs to casual laborers found relevant to their lives.[23] The antiprerogative and anti-British cast of most colonials' reactions to these issues fostered important feelings of sociopolitical solidarity. It was their sense of satisfaction in this that smirked on the faces of New York's prominent citizenry when a city mob burned Lieutenant-Governor Colden's chariot and sleighs and sacked the house of the infuriating Major James on November 1.[24]

Despite the relative comity with which New Yorkers met the most obvious threats to their rights through November 1st, changes had already begun to take place that would lead to a new polarization in provincial politics. The first of these was the Livingston, Smith, and Scott coterie's loss of reputation as unqualified supporters of colonial rights. Although Scott flirted momentarily with the radical view that British oppression could only convince colonists that "the Connection between them ought to cease," he quickly backtracked to the point where he allegedly castigated as treasonous Patrick Henry's famous Virginia Resolves.[25] And hot as William Livingston had been for traditional legal rights, he was less than uncompromising in his assessment of the Stamp Act.[26] Toward the end of August, as that legislation loomed increasingly large in public affairs, Livingston precipitously shut down the "Sentinel" essay series. His critics interpreted this action as an abandonment of the cause ("in order to look out for himself," they said) precisely when the public most needed leadership.[27]

Those who did take the lead during the Stamp Act crisis were initially a group of ill-defined middling and lower-class New Yorkers, individuals whose occupations, status, and wealth varied enormously, but who saw crowd action as an acceptable way to express their disapprobation of public policy. The "Sons of Liberty," as they soon came to be called, were responsible for the Stamp Act riots, which, once continued beyond November 1, appeared to challenge the credibility of New York's established public leaders. Out of these riots came the nucleus of a tighter central committee known by the same name that coordinated much of New York's street politics between November 1765 and April 1766.[28]

The reaction of William Smith, Jr., to the Sons of Liberty mirrored that of his two friends. In Smith's view the "State of Anarchy" that prevailed threatened to lead to a "general Civil War."[29] Immediately he and his confidants exerted themselves to restore their conception of order. When the Sons of Liberty (who understood something of the hardships that the stoppage of trade caused by the Stamp Act protest was inflicting on middling tradesmen and the working poor) convened a public gathering in late November to push the New York Assembly into giving "Legislative Sanction to . . . transacting Business as usual without Stamps," a clique of conservatives, including Smith and his two close friends, hijacked the meeting and substituted their own request to the assembly to petition Parliament for redress of grievances "in the most respectful . . . Manner."[30] Later on in December, when representatives of the Sons of Liberty confronted the gentlemen of the New York bar and requested them to defy the Stamp Act by returning to business, the lawyers apparently agreed. But no sooner were they left alone than Smith, Livingston, Scott, and colleagues reversed ground and refused to break the law.[31] They followed Livingston's lead in believing that they should memorialize, "casting themselves at the King's feet, imploring his royal protection." They might plead with "Petitions, . . . representations, claims, addresses or remonstrances."[32] But they should not act in defiance.

Once begun, the downward slide of the Livingston-associated lawyers' public reputation continued in 1766. During the spring and summer of that year, land riots broke out in Dutchess, Westchester, and Albany counties where tenants found the will to revolt against their landlords.[33] British troops were used to break the riots, while a special judicial commission that included William Smith, Jr., and John Morin Scott punished nearly a hundred rioters and condemned their leader, William Pendergast, to death. Gubernatorial clemency saved Pendergast's life, but not the property claims of the implicated tenants. William Livingston became the landlord's hired gun, bringing ejectment suits against suspected dissidents.[34] The sympathy of the three lawyers with New York's large landholders and speculators needed no clearer demonstration.[35]

Paradoxically, just as public esteem for the Livingstons began to erode, they gained an apparent ally in the Fort. Soon after his arrival in November 1765, Governor Sir Henry Moore began openly to favor the Livingston family and their associates with his confidence and patronage.[36] Flattering as such attention was, it precipitated a polarization among New York's political leaders, the absence of which had so clearly benefited politicians associated with the Livingstons during the preceding five years. Anytime prominent New Yorkers perceived that one identifiable group among them had gained a near monopoly on the governor's ear, others would consider mounting some electoral opposition. And in the wake of the Stamp Act and land riots, the Livingston-associated lawyers were in a weak position to defend themselves at the hustings.

The individual who first picked up the scent of opportunity in the turn of events beginning in late 1765 was Captain James DeLancey. We know little of this man, other than that he attended English educational institutions, including Lincoln's Inn, fought as a British infantry officer in the French and Indian War, and after his father's death assumed the gentry role of managing the substantial properties that James, Sr., had bequeathed him.[37] In the 1761 election, the twenty-eight-year-old DeLancey was included on a New York City consensus ticket with three political veterans, including Philip Livingston. Although his supporters claimed that "his father's character & memory . . . [was] a Rock" on which he could found his own political career, he was not well known in his own right. When two independents subsequently declared themselves, they both beat DeLancey, pushing him down to last place among the six candidates.[38] The events of the mid 1760s, however, provided DeLancey with the opportunity to improve his political fortunes. Although initially DeLancey was one of those who stood with other conservative merchants and lawyers in frustrating the Sons of Liberty call for radical action in late November, shortly thereafter he threw in his lot with the losers. He willingly served as a member of the citizens' committee that requested the lawyers to defy the Stamp Act, and increasingly he and his close friends made a show of their support for the Sons of Liberty. Although DeLancey never became one of the inner circle in that group, he was closely enough identified with it that shortly after the repeal of the Stamp Act, a number of the Sons of Liberty, led by the influential Isaac Sears, declared that they would back DeLancey at the next assembly election.[39] That was exactly the kind of payoff DeLancey had hoped for. By mid 1766, "the Govrs Neglect of them [the DeLanceys]" was so blatant that Captain DeLancey needed popular political office in order to "raise their Significancy."[40]

During late 1766 and 1767, a number of New York's established political leaders began to feel that they could allow themselves the luxury of an electoral brawl at the next opportunity, and according to the terms of the Septennial Act, that could be no later than early 1768. The threat the Sons of Liberty seemed to pose to traditional leadership ("the Swellings of the great Multitude" as William Smith, Jr., called it) seemed to have largely subsided. The radicals had always been fractious, and by late 1766, they were divided into two opposing groups, one openly associated with the DeLancey interest, the other allegedly with the Livingstons, and each claiming to be the heroes of the Stamp Act resistance.[41] The new imperial issues of 1766 and 1767 that might have roused the Sons of Liberty to renewed activism failed to do so. British demands that New York fulfill the conditions of the British Mutiny Act brought backhanded compliance rather than continued defiance, and despite the imposition of the Townsend Duties in November 1767, the colony had become "the quintessence of moderation."[42] In the absence of street politics that vigorously shouldered men of middling status into positions of political brokerage, the old political leaders were eager to reassert their preeminence through the traditional avenue of electoral politics. Smarting from both imaginary and real slights that had stung them during the past months of social and political turmoil, the old-line politicians hoped that, in attempting to define the issues for the public, in making efforts to display networks of patronal relations, and in reenacting electoral rituals that emphasized the differences between political insiders and the voting public, they could shore up their traditional and recently shaken positions of leadership.

The chief contenders in the 1768 provincial election were a disparate array of city and county businessmen, professionals and gentry, but it was the competition in New York City that dominated the contest. Five serious candidates vied for the four-seat New York City and County riding.[43] Of these five, Philip Livingston was assured of reelection, while his fellow city merchants Jacob Walton and James Jauncey were also strong favorites. (Initially Livingston and Walton announced their candidacies in conjunction with that of Captain James DeLancey, but as the campaign progressed, Livingston distanced himself from the partisan controversy that surrounded the other candidates.)[44] After his poor showing in the 1761 election, and knowing that the only other incumbent seeking reelection, William Bayard, was exceptionally weak, James DeLancey hoped to turn his credibility with the Sons of Liberty into an official prominence that Governor Moore could not ignore.[45] Not to be outdone, the somewhat discredited clique of Livingston-associated lawyers was determined to try to perpetuate the influence it had enjoyed with the last assembly. The group could do so, it hoped, by electing John Morin Scott to one of the vacant seats. Although Walton and Jauncey were factors in the election, and Scott was as much their opponent as DeLancey's, the campaign quickly became a contest between De-Lancey and Scott.

DeLancey's backers (DeLancey was in England at the time), who eventually included the candidates Walton and Jauncey and the merchant Isaac Sears of the Sons of Liberty, quickly took the offensive against Scott, setting up the cry *"No lawyer in the Assembly."*[46] Repeatedly they hammered on the perfidy of Scott, Livingston, and Smith during the Stamp Act crisis, and on the cupidity of New York lawyers. On the former count, they recalled Scott's condemnation of the Virginia Resolves, his associates' maligning of the Stamp Act Congress, the lawyers' collective unwillingness to defy the Stamp Act, and their individual reluctance to "employ . . . even . . . [a] Pen in Defiance . . . [of colonists'] Rights."[47] On the latter, they both railed and ridiculed:

> If men their own advantage understood
> We lawyers are but laboring their good
>   When stript of cash they've little inclination
> Again to enter into litigation.
> . . . .
> Oh! hoh! cries Belzebub, I find you out,
> Your office and my own, beyond a doubt
>   Are both alike;—alike to trick the ninnies,—
> I gull them of their souls, you of their guineas.[48]

In comparison, DeLancey's supporters portrayed their candidate as a spokesperson for commerce, an interest that contributed to broader community prosperity. As Mr. Axe and Mr. Hammer declared "the *Leather-Aprons* . . . are clearly of the Opinion, that it is TRADE, and not the LAW supports our Families:—and honest Jolt the Cartman, says he never got Six-Pence for riding Law-Books, tho' he gets many Pounds from the Merchants."[49]

For their part, Scott and his allies tried to establish some momentum of their own. William Livingston mocked DeLancey's pretensions at every opportunity. In his *Political Creed for the Day,* for example, he offered the following credo: "I believe that none but Merchants are proper to represent the City, and that every Cockfighter, Horseracer and Whoremonger, is in the Politics of the present Day a Merchant."[50] In addition, the three lawyers tried to blunt the most telling attacks against themselves (regarding their behavior during the Stamp Act crisis) by pointing out what selfless past service they had rendered the community, and what such actions indicated they were capable of offering in the future.[51] Finally, there was the religious issue. For some time, William Livingston had suspected that colonial Anglicans were conspiring with their British counterparts to place a bishop in North America; when Thomas Bradbury Chandler, a priest based in New Jersey, openly called for an American bishopric in 1767, Livingston decided to respond with a series of newspaper articles.[52] The election came too early in 1768 for Livingston's anti-episcopal campaign to have much cumulative effect, for the initial article by the "American Whig" (Livingston) did not appear until just before voting day.[53] Despite that, Livingston, Scott, and friends did their best to smear DeLancey as an abettor of high church perfidy. They accused him of traveling to London to solicit an American bishop, implied that DeLancey's election would jeopardize the religious rights of non-Anglicans, and tried to turn the cry "no Bishops" into an anti-DeLancey slogan.[54]

Although Scott's promoters strove hard, they never did take the initiative away from DeLancey's supporters. The issues that arose, however indirectly, out of the Stamp Act crisis struck the most responsive chord among the bulk of the electorate.[55] Not far into the voting, DeLancey surged to second place behind Philip Livingston, and there he stayed. Scott was left in last place, where DeLancey had been back in 1761.[56] There was, however, a final ironic denouement to the contest. Scott thought he was close enough to the fourth-highest candidate, James Jauncey, to challenge him to a scrutiny.[57] In doing so, the Presbyterian lawyers who had tried to build part of their campaign on anti-Anglican solidarity ended up challenging a non-Anglican; Jauncey was a nominal Presbyterian.

The New York City and County election was not the only hotly contested one. Others that we know of took place in Westchester Borough, Schenectady, and Dutchess County. We know little of the circumstances of the first two, other than that they expressed connections with provincial issues through the rivalries of local families or factions.[58] As for Dutchess County, there, as in New York City, another Livingston-associated lawyer lost his case. Vulnerable as a landlord who had participated in punishing the tenant rioters, maligned as a lawyer who prospered on the miseries of others, identified as a social conservative who abhorred the violence of the Stamp Act days, and distrusted as a city man who did not understand the needs of the county, the prominent Robert R. Livingston "so . . . lost the esteem of the Freeholders . . . , that he gave up before half the Freeholders then present had given in their votes."[59] Insofar as the anti-episcopal diatribes of his New York City kinsman and friends adversely affected the Anglican Robert R. Livingston,[60] they merely reinforced an already-conclusive trend. Livingston's obvious talent, his intelligence, his sense of civic responsibility, and his gentle personal side did nothing to offset the electorate's conviction that he had failed them miserably during the recent social and political crises.

The changes that the electorate thrust on the legislature in 1768 were important ones. The presence of Captain James DeLancey, the absence of Robert R. Livingston, the retirement of Speaker William Nicoll II, and the replacement of almost half the old assembly (48 percent) with new members ensured that the new house would differ from the old. But what its character would be was not immediately clear, for Governor Moore put off calling the assembly into session until October 1768. In the meantime, two important sets of circumstances influenced provincial politics.

The first of these was William Livingston's determination to continue his polemics against an American bishop. Through May 15, 1769, Livingston (with the help of William Smith, Jr., John Morin Scott, and a handful of occasionals) published sixty-two "American Whig" essays in the *New-York Gazette*.[61] Livingston believed that the bishopric issue was "of greater importance . . . than the imposition of any customs, or commercial restrictions which affect not the right of conscience," and he was encouraged in such views by the anti-bishopric "Centinel" essays that Philadelphia Presbyterians sponsored from March through July of 1768, as well as by the opinion of a number of mid-Atlantic Presbyterians and Connecticut-based Consociated Congregationalists, who, contemplating the formation of a loose federation in 1766 and 1767, concluded that Anglicanism was on the march.[62] More immediately, Livingston was reacting to his own and his lawyer friends' loss of public reputation during the Stamp Act crisis.[63] Clearly uncomfortable with the secular political issues that had exploded with such force in New York, Livingston wanted to turn public debate onto the anti-Anglican, rationalist, and latitudinarian ground he had so successfully cultivated during the King's College dispute, and on which he felt so much at home. His view that "the generality of the people would more quietly submit to three stamp-acts, than to the exertion of English ecclesiastical hierarchy" was no more than a rationalization of Livingston's own priorities.[64] Of course, the "American Whig" soon roused vocal opposition among the group of northeastern Anglican clergy who had their hearts set on an American bishop.[65] They excoriated the "Whig" with tales of Presbyterian persecution and Independent leveling, and charges of gross bigotry. Soon others jumped into the controversy, and throughout much of 1768 and early 1769, the New York press crackled with charge, countercharge, and rejoinder. As one observer remarked, the "frolic of the fray . . . seems to be a very keen one, for they bespatter one another with great good will."[66]

The second issue that complicated New York politics in the spring and summer of 1768 was the fallout from the imposition of the Townsend Duties. Although differences among New Yorkers over a proposed retaliatory boycott of British goods had the potential to develop into serious conflict, the most immediate problem facing the new assembly was how to respond to the Massachusetts Circular Letter, written in February, criticizing the Townsend Duties and inviting intercolonial protest on behalf of traditional rights.[67] When the British ordered the Massachusetts General Court dissolved on its unwillingness to rescind the Circular Letter, when Whitehall dispatched troops to Boston, and when Lord Hillsborough instructed the colonial governors to dissolve any assembly that should even acknowledge receipt of the Massachusetts Letter, it quickly became clear that the New York Assembly would have some difficulty dealing with the issue.[68]

When the new assembly met on October 27, it lacked both direction and cohesion. A number of representatives were licking the wounds they had sustained in sharp election battles, and they were in no hurry to rush back to the hustings. There was also a tentative air about the House, as veterans waited to see what impact Captain James DeLancey and Philip Livingston, the newly chosen speaker, would have on legislative affairs, and as freshmen members gradually accustomed themselves to their new surroundings. Quickly tiring of the jockeying for position that was taking the place of decisive legislative leadership, New York City street politicians again took a direct hand in forcing the pace of public affairs. As Governor Moore viewed it, "that licentious Rabble . . . the Sons of Liberty" initiated a public demonstration on November 14, drawing attention to the Massachusetts Circular Letter.[69] When Governor Moore and his council reacted sharply and stampeded the majority of assemblymen into concurring in a condemnation of the riot, a group of merchants, which included well-known Sons of Liberty, put a draftsman to work drawing up instructions to the city representatives. Signed by an unknown number of residents and borne to the four representatives by merchants of the town, the instructions labeled Hillsborough's directive an "Insult," and called upon their assemblymen to have the Massachusetts Circular Letter read and answered in the House "in a respectable Manner."[70] Seeing the opportunity to cultivate popular support, Captain James DeLancey and his two close associates Jacob Walton and James Jauncey welcomed the instructions and endorsed their message. In order to prevent DeLancey from becoming the uncontested spokesperson for colonial rights, those who might have preferred to avoid the issue (and their motives varied widely) embraced the popular cause as well.[71] Then they began to prepare for the next election. For this, they did not have long to wait. Governor Moore dissolved the legislature on January 2 and sent out election writs three weeks later.

Like the 1768 election, that of 1769 was characterized by its "warmth."[72] And again New York City and County set the pace with a "hott and pepper" affair.[73] The direction the city contest would take was decided within four days of the January 2 dissolution. In a complicated series of events, Philip Livingston, whom DeLancey, Walton, and Jauncey initially "courted" to be the "Chief and Head" of a consensus ticket, rejected the offer and shortly thereafter accepted the draft of a faction of Presbyterian and Dutch Reformed citizens (Philip's brother William prominent among them), who nominated their own ticket, consisting of Philip, Peter Van Brugh Livingston, Theodorus Van Wyke, and John Morin Scott.[74] For the first time since the Leislerian era, New York voters would be faced with two four-man tickets. The backers of the new ticket did not suppose they could carry their whole slate, but they believed that Philip Livingston's inclusion would cause enough "Cross-Voting" to bring John Morin Scott in on Livingston's coattails.[75] The full ticket was simply another means to accomplish what Scott's backers had failed to achieve in 1768.

Determined not to repeat their mistakes of a year ago, the managers of the Presbyterian/Dutch Reformed ticket quickly tried to take the initiative in defining the election issues. Attempting to build on the religious consciousness the "American Whig" had fostered during the previous year, the Livingston-led coalition portrayed itself as a "Glorius Combination of Dissenters." Inviting those who were old friends of the Anglicans to reexamine the Church of England's past politics, William Livingston pointed out past injustices and then tried to focus attention on the present danger should Anglicans, who already controlled the governorship and council, come to dominate the assembly as well. The "balance" that produced religious liberty in New York would be gone, and the three parts of government would then undoubtedly welcome colonial bishops. Once that step had been taken, the game was lost, for bishops would unceasingly press for the full range of powers they held in England. "Nor are we prejudiced against any episcopalean for his religion" declared Livingston, "it is the politics of the church,—its domineering spirit,—its perpetual strides towards universal dominion,—its pride,—its power and its thirst for domination";[76] that was what Livingston abhorred. Given the chance, other writers charged, the Anglicans would "extirpate all other Denominations," "pul[ling] down" "their Steeples" and "burn[ing]" "their pulpitts & Pews . . . [in] the streets."[77]

Understandably, the DeLancey ticket wanted as little to do with the episcopacy issue as possible. Their spokespersons argued that the Anglican oppressions complained of had long ceased, that in New York liberty "flourished," "Rights of Conscience" were strong, and even in its English form the Anglican church was recognized as a mild religious establishment.[78] And, insofar as they stressed religious affiliation, the pro-DeLancey politicians placed emphasis on their efforts to represent something of New York's diversity. The two Anglicans, one Presbyterian, and one member of the Dutch Reformed Church who composed their ticket had drawn past political support from a range of denominations, and they hoped they could continue to do so despite the attempt of their opponents to polarize the community along religious lines.[79] They ridiculed the "Glorious Combination of Dissenters," pointing out that only representatives of two Presbyterian congregations, the Baptist congregation, and a faction of English-service Dutch Reformed congregations were involved. Where were the Dutch-service Reformed representatives? Where were the Quakers, the Moravians, the French, and the Dutch and German Lutherans?[80] The Presbyterian/Dutch Reformed faction had deliberately sowed the "Seeds of Discord" when it persuaded Philip Livingston to forsake the other old members, and to what end?[81] To give preeminence to "illiberal Independents" who "confin[ed] their Favours and Employ to their own Sect," who fomented faction in other denominations, and who feigned good relations with other churches while they underhandedly behaved like imperious autocrats.[82] And at what Price? That of "divert[ing] . . . [interest] from the important controversy with Great Britain."[83]

For the DeLancey supporters, contrived religious quarrels threatened to obscure the important issues of the day. The real question was not "to what CHURCH or *Meeting* a Candidate belong[ed]; but whether he be worthy of a Seat."[84] More specifically, they stressed their representatives' conduct during the Massachusetts Circular Letter debate. DeLancey, Walton, and Jauncey were the earliest to press for a direct response to it to vindicate colonial rights, openly welcoming instructions from their constituents to push for a spirited reply, damn the cost. If it was "the Duty of Representatives to assert and maintain the just Rights, Liberties and Privileges of their Constituents, and in Consequence thereof, bring on themselves a Dissolution, or any other inconvenience: it . . . [was] equally the Duty of their Constituents to support such Representatives to the utmost of their Power."[85]

As partisans set out the framework of debate, polemicists quickly amplified with detail and branched out into scurrility. "Snake in the Grass" Philip Livingston had rejected constituent instruction. ("Let them that would choose Tools Instrct Them," Philip had allegedly said.)[86] The DeLancey faction's claim to special consideration because it welcomed constituent instruction was spurious, cried Philip Livingston's supporters; the whole house was prepared to answer the Massachusetts Letter, and Philip Schuyler took the lead by introducing the motion to answer it.[87] John Morin Scott was again vilified, for his response to the Stamp Act crisis, for his occupation, and for his social behavior—most notably his "danc[ing] with, and kiss[ing] (filthy Beast!) those of his own Sex."[88] Captain James DeLancey faced the charge of soliciting a council seat for himself while in England, and those who believed in James Jauncey's reputation for charity had to confront evidence that he was a harsh and vindictive creditor.[89] For those who tired of polemical prose, DeLancey writers produced a song with a refrain designed to remind voters that a Presbyterian was really

A raving, ranting,
Cozening, canting
English Independent.[90]

As for slogans, the 1768 cries of "no lawyer" and "no bishop" gave way to "no Presbyterian" and "no Churchman."[91]

Although the backers of the Livingston-headed ticket waged a strong polemical campaign, ticket members failed badly at the polls. Their strategy depended on a strong Philip Livingston, and on election day former supporters deserted him in droves, some apologetically saying they were "Exceeding sorry he should so mismanage the best interest any man ever had in this town."[92] With no Livingston coattails to help his fellow candidates, the whole ticket suffered resounding defeat.

In a number of outlying areas, there were sharp contests as well, for more than on any previous occasion, the 1769 election saw coordinated efforts between factional leaders in New York City and their friends and relatives in various counties. The most striking success that the Livingstons enjoyed was in Albany County. During the internal assembly politics of the November–December 1768 session, Philip Schuyler had come into close association with William Livingston, William Smith, Jr., John Morin Scott, and the Livingston Manor heir apparent, Peter R. Livingston; their support helped Schuyler succeed in his bid to return to the House.[93] Elsewhere, the Livingstons cheered on Lewis Morris III's renewed challenge to Captain

James DeLancey's cousin, John DeLancey (Westchester Borough), expressed hope in Henry Wisner (Orange County), and sent both election screeds and personal assistance in aid of Robert R. Livingston's effort to regain the seat he had lost in 1768 (Dutchess County).[94] In the former case, they were successful; in the latter two instances, their allies failed.[95] DeLancey supporters who reached out to Westchester, Richmond, Dutchess, and Orange counties to encourage friendly candidates were somewhat more successful.[96]

And what were the issues in these county contests? While the evidence is very weak, what there is suggests the Livingstons had difficulties establishing anything like a broad intercounty, religious-based appeal. Out in Queens County, where we know there had been a long history of dissenter/Anglican acrimony, there was no indication that local Calvinists offered much of a challenge to the Anglican and Quaker incumbents.[97] In Albany, where Philip Schuyler had to contend with an ardent Anglican, Sir William Johnson, the religious issue seemed to promise conflict. But Schuyler and his running mate were accommodating enough to avoid opposition.[98] In Westchester Borough, the contest was between two Anglicans, John DeLancey and Lewis Morris III. No religious contest this; rather, it was a new-generational expression of old family rivalry.[99] And in Dutchess County, while Robert R. Livingston's Anglicanism perhaps earned him the continued distrust of county Presbyterians, that was a prejudice clearly secondary to the social and political issues that soured Livingston's tenants on their landlord during the mid 1760s.[100] In Dutchess, like other counties, the relevance of local to provincial themes was much more easily expressed in the secular terminology of rights, responsibilities, and liberties than in highly charged sectarian rhetoric.[101]

Overall, only five new faces appeared in the 1769 assembly, but that belied the changes that the election brought. Captain James DeLancey's place at the head of the New York City and County poll bestowed a clear preeminence on him, and he lost little time in using it.[102] Philip Livingston's defeat left the speakership vacant, and DeLancey's influence quickly secured it for his experienced associate and old family friend John Cruger. And from Orange County came a representative who would make a difference in the running of the legislature. In sweeping the county, DeLancey allies had placed John DeNoyelles in the House, and DeNoyelles's braying, bulldozing mannerisms could be used to effect in whipping diffident members into line on partisan matters.[103] There were still a few Livingston friends in the assembly capable of offering leadership, but the initiative clearly lay with DeLancey and his confidants.

Once in the ascendancy in the assembly when it convened in April 1769, DeLancey was determined to press his advantage. Relatively unskilled as a parliamentarian, and resentful of the way in which his political opponents occasionally outmaneuvered him (just as they had done during the November–December 1768 session), DeLancey resolved to resist seating anyone who might bolster his critics. When Robert Livingston, Jr., the lord of Livingston Manor, had his tenants elect, first Philip (the just-defeated speaker of the 1768 house), and then his cousin, Robert R. (the recently defeated candidate for Dutchess County), the DeLancey gang disqualified each in turn.[104] At one point in the squabble, with a nice vindictive twist, Captain DeLancey threatened to inquire into the Livingston Manor's right to an assembly seat.[105] Before long, he had the anguished heir to the manor, Peter R. Livingston, wailing in distress to his father: "I . . . am Sorry to find that you think the present Politics are a striving whether the Church or Meeting should rule, it is by no means so. But the DeLancey's are striving their utmost to make our famaly rediculous and to keep them out of all Posts of Honour [and] Profit and are determined to oppose everything and every Body that they support which is too hard to bear."[106]

Politically more promising than such complaints were the Livingstons' attempts to build up their own electoral support, much as Captain DeLancey and his friends had done since the Stamp Act crisis. One such effort was William Livingston's continuation, beyond the election, of the "American Whig" essays and his sponsorship, in February 1769, of the Society of Dissenters.[107] Founded by representatives of New York City's Presbyterian and Baptist churches, the society's purpose was to preserve "their common & respective civil and religious Rights and Privileges, against all Oppressions and Encroachments by those of any Denomination whatsoever." They pledged themselves both to enlist other dissenting denominations and to establish local chapters throughout the province.[108] The society's founders unquestionably intended to continue their campaign against episcopacy and hoped to build a provincial network that might prove helpful come the next election. But the bishopric issue was soon subsumed under broader perspectives on public affairs, and the prospect of developing a unified leadership among Presbyterians, let alone facilitating interdenominational cooperation around a Presbyterian core, was never a very promising one.[109] By mid May, Livingston terminated his "American Whig" writings, and there is no indication that the Society of Dissenters functioned beyond a month or so.

Such failures notwithstanding, the Livingston faction soon gained new strength through the extramural activities of the merchant Alexander McDougall and the legislative tactics of such individuals as Philip Schuyler, George Clinton, Abraham Ten Broeck, Nathaniel Woodhull, and Charles DeWitt. When the assembly, under DeLancey leadership, voted money that Whitehall demanded for billeting British troops in New York, McDougall wrote a brief pamphlet entitled *To the Betrayed Inhabitants of the City and Colony of New York*, charging that DeLancey and his friends had given up what colonists had fought so hard to retain during the Stamp Act crisis—the right to self-taxation.[110] The rhetoric and argument of this pamphlet swung the New York City crowd behind McDougall. When governor, council, and assembly agreed that the author should be tried for contempt, critics of DeLancey's leadership multiplied to the point where, on several occasions during the long-drawn-out prosecution, they took over the city streets. Handed hope by this shift in public sentiment, the Livingston-associated faction more avidly began to cultivate popular sentiment by espousing popular reforms. They supported the opening of the assembly gallery to the public; they participated in demonstrations in favor of voting by ballot; they claimed they would end mandatory taxation for the support of Anglican clergy in the four establishment counties and allow non-Anglican churches to incorporate; they proposed to legislate against plural officeholding and initiate a number of other changes to curtail corruption in the electoral and legislative process.[111]

As these issues came to the fore amid continued Anglo-American tension, New York politicians became polarized to an unprecedented degree. In the assembly, the DeLancey- and Livingston-associated representatives repeatedly confronted each other over these and related issues, forming blocs that most visibly correlated with tensions among the province's prominent religious subcultures.[112] Outside the legislature, it seems clear that the Livingston appeal to public opinion met with considerable success, and DeLancey cadres, now reduced in size, were driven back onto the defensive. But, unknown to contemporaries, that meant little, for the customary electoral dimension of provincial politics had already come to an end. Successful in reaching accommodation with a succession of chief executives, and aware of the turn in public opinion, Captain DeLancey prevented another assembly dissolution until the military engagement between Britain and America had begun. The voting trends that registered public opinion in the 1768 and 1769 elections thus had no opportunity for further expression in the familiar colonial setting. Beginning in 1770, it was with the evolving revolutionary committees and institutionalized republicanism, not with the traditional colonial electorate, that the future of representative politics lay.

Riot, Royal Government, and Electoral Competition

The conflicts that the French and Indian War precipitated in Pennsylvania politics, and that occasioned a reorganization of the Quaker Party seemed likely to subside once the British won decisive victories in 1759. But such was not the case. Aggrieved by shortsighted British policies, and desperately hoping to force their monolithic foe into a belated respect for Amerindian integrity, the Ottawa leader Pontiac led a loose alliance of northwestern tribes in a series of attacks on colonial outposts beginning in June 1763.[113] By midmonth the exposed backcountry settlers in Pennsylvania had suffered their first casualties, reawakening a sense of terror that had only just begun to fade.[114] As the Indian incursions increased and the number of casualties rose during the summer and fall, renewed demands for effective protection rang out from the frontier.[115] Provincial and regular troops should be enlisted in numbers; scalp bounties should be posted; Indian towns implicated in the hostilities should be destroyed; and the members of Pennsylvania's two major settlements of Christian Indians should be interned to prevent them from extending clandestine aid to belligerents.[116] With few funds available because of recent wartime expenses, and unwilling to raise new taxes subject to the condition of joint executive/legislative appropriation, which Pennsylvania's governor would demand as the price of his consent, the assembly provided for the enlistment of a small contingent of seven hundred provincial troops in July and added another hundred in October.[117] That was not enough to slow down the carnage on the frontiers.

Despairing of additional aid or adequate leadership from Philadelphia, backcountry volunteers seized the initiative and organized their own raids against concentrations of hostile Indians.[118] In so doing, they forcefully expressed their opinion that voluntary community efforts to exterminate Pennsylvania's Indian residents were a legitimate social goal. In the process of policing their neighborhoods, numerous white residents also came to accept the view that the Christian Indians of Conestoga and Northampton County were traitorous spies in league with the Indian belligerents. These beliefs, in the context of continued Indian attacks on western Pennsylvania communities, precipitated one of the most notorious sequences of crowd violence in eighteenth-century America—the Conestoga massacre and the Paxton riots.

Throughout the hostilities of late 1763, the pitifully small remnants of the Conestoga Indian tribe remained on their land not far from the county seat of Lancaster. Apparently convinced that despite their long-standing friendship with the Quaker colony these Indians were enemy spies, a mob of Lancaster residents decided to deal with them the same way they had dealt with hostile Indian towns. On November 14, 1763, they rampaged through Conestoga Manor and murdered the six Indians who were home. About a fortnight later, on December 27, they repeated their actions, this time killing the fourteen remaining natives, whom authorities had belatedly tried to protect by housing them in Lancaster Borough in the county workhouse.[119]

Bloated with the bravado that riskless victories often foster, the crowd threatened to march on Philadelphia to frighten, if not punish, the Quaker legislators who had been so unwilling to defend the frontier, and to kill a group of Moravian Indians whom the Quakers were trying to protect near Philadelphia. By early February, the threats seemed well on the way to fulfillment. Approximately 250 residents of western Lancaster County marched toward the capital, arriving in Germantown on February 5. Hearing that Governor John Penn had stiffened quivering city spines by reading a new riot act and by encouraging Benjamin Franklin to organize a defense force, the invaders paused for two days. A negotiating committee subsequently met with the rioters, who agreed to disperse peacefully in return for expeditious legislative consideration of their grievances.[120] That agreement ended the threat of domestic violence. But it also opened the way for a war of words.

Eastern Pennsylvanians who identified with Quaker or Quaker-associated legislative leadership were quick to perceive the massacre and march on Philadelphia as flagrant Presbyterian attacks on the principle of Quaker government. Although Scotch-Irish Presbyterians had no monopoly on frontier violence, and although the men who perpetrated the Conestoga massacres were a motley crew of "persons of Various Countries and Denominations," the rioters quickly became known as the Paxton Boys.[121] Unlike the appellations "Hickery Boys" or "Volunteers," terms that a few apologists initially employed to suggest frontier toughness and the heroism of community defenders during the French and Indian War, the "Paxton" designation associated the mob with a long-settled community of Scotch-Irish Presbyterians.[122] Shortly after the Conestoga killings, word filtered back to the frontier that vocal easterners were comparing the murders "to the Irish massacres and reckon'd [the former] the most barbarous of either."[123] While on the one hand, Scotch-Irish leaders were incensed by such absurd exaggeration, on the other, they were prepared to capitalize on such an association both to inculcate fear in their critics and to claim for Presbyterians the popularity that killing the Conestoga Indians had brought them.[124] By the time the rioters orchestrated their march on Philadelphia, the participants *were* largely Scotch-Irish, and they were determined to speak out as such against what they viewed as a predominantly Quaker legislative establishment.

On February 6, the day after the Paxton Boys reached Germantown, they presented a "Declaration" to Governor John Penn that castigated the "Villany . . . of a certain Faction that have got the political Reigns in their Hand and tamely tyrannize over the other good Subjects of the Province."[125] The leader of that "Faction" (in their view, Israel Pemberton, Jr.), "together with others of the Friends" had "enslave[d] the Province to *Indians*," "cherish[ing] . . . and caress[ing]" their favorite natives, who at the same time, remained "firmly connected in Friendship with our openly avowed imbittered Enemies."[126] More specifically, the Paxton Boys charged the Quakers with turning their backs on Pennsylvanians who had been captured during the French and Indian War, failing to protect frontier inhabitants, carrying on trade with Indians regardless of the consequences to western settlers, and even encouraging Indians "to scourage the white People" who defrauded them of land and furs.[127] All told, the "Remonstrance" was the most bitter attack Friends had faced since Provost William Smith's *Brief State.*

Coincidental with the Paxton Boys' articulation of their case against Friends, Benjamin Franklin published his *Narrative of the Late Massacres in Lancaster County.*[128] Although one or two other criticisms of the killings had appeared in print prior to early February, Franklin's pamphlet was the first widely distributed indictment of the Paxton Boys.[129] In it, he elicited sympathy for the Conestoga Indians by identifying each and sketching in the family relationships of the "7 Men, 5 Women, and 8 Children, Boys and Girls."[130] When those in the workhouse were attacked "they divided into their little Families, the children clinging to the Parents; they fell on their Knees, protested their Innocence, declared their Love to the *English* . . . and in this Posture they all received the Hatchet!—Men, Women and Little Children." Who would perpetrate such barbarities, Franklin rhetorically asked. Not "*Heathens, Turks, Sacrens, Moors, Negroes* . . . [or] *Indians,*" all of whom respected the safety of those who sought sanctuary. Only the scripture-quoting "CHRISTIAN WHITE SAVAGES of *Pechstang* and *Donegall.*"[131] Although he avoided mentioning the word Presbyterian throughout his pamphlet, Franklin's message was unmistakable: Presbyterian zeal endangered civility, and in so bloodying the banner of Christianity, mocked its central precepts.

The Paxton Boys' "Declaration" and Franklin's *Narrative* set the tone for what followed. Between February and October 1764, Philadelphia printers produced a parade of polemics that pitted "Presbyterian" champions against "Quaker" counterparts.[132] Emotions ran high, and each camp was determined to abuse the other with whatever scurrilities it could concoct. There were occasional efforts, mainly on the part of Quaker partisans, to point out that the actions of a few should not be used to discredit entire religious societies.[133] Some Presbyterians turned out to defend Philadelphia against the Paxton Boys; some also were critical of the Conestoga killings.[134] And the activities of the Society of Friends were not to be confused with those of the Friendly Association or, in fact, with the post-1756 legislature, for despite continued Quaker participation in government, a number of important leaders in the Society of Friends no longer sanctioned such public service.[135] These objections against overgeneralization were important because they remind us that reality was not simply the rhetoric of the times. But such qualifications and distinctions were too fine to bear much respecting among self-selected polemicists whose chief interest was in blackening their Quaker or Presbyterian foes.

The wellsprings of Presbyterian/Quaker hostility did run deep, and the circumstances of the time prompted defenders of both denominations to tap into them. By the early 1760s, the Presbyterians felt strong enough to flex their muscles. The union of Old and New Synods in 1758 gave them confidence, the outpourings of Presbyterian clergymen from the College of New Jersey provided them with invigorated institutional leadership, the growing number of Scotch-Irish immigrants made them, they thought, "the most numerous . . . of any one Denomination" in Pennsylvania, and their prominent place both as sufferers and soldiers in the recent Indian wars gave them a right to have a large say in the formulation of public policy.[136] Puffed up with a new sense of self-importance, Presbyterian champions were also frustrated by the ineffectiveness of their past efforts to shake the credibility of Quaker leadership. Gilbert Tennent's occasional past sermons against pacifism had never shown any signs of galvanizing the electorate to throw out Quaker legislators, and frontier petitions never initiated wartime tactics aggressive enough to satisfy their instigators. Presbyterian partisans believed that Quaker principles were antithetical to government, especially during wartime. They believed the Friends had only masqueraded at withdrawing from government, for Quakers continued to hold sway through their political allies and through the influence of the Yearly Meeting, the Friendly Association, and well-connected merchants. Above all, prominent Presbyterians could not fathom the symbolic importance of good Indian relations to many leading Quakers. They did not understand why the imagery of William Penn's peaceable kingdom had become so compelling among Quaker reformers, who were determined to include benevolent relations with the remnants of the province's Indian tribes in their redefinition of Pennsylvania's Quaker mission. To the hard-bitten Scotch-Irish Calvinists, such notions were as preposterous as pacifism.

Among prominent Philadelphia Friends, there was little sympathy for the Scotch-Irish frontier residents. In remarking that their predicament was "their own fault," James Pemberton spat out some of the resentment against backcountry Presbyterians that choked many members of his circle.[137] Just as galling to the frontiersmen as this overt prejudice, which they felt was reflected in public policy, was Quaker aloofness and arrogance. Because Pennsylvania had long been their province, Friends felt that rather than criticize and protest, members of other religious societies should acquiesce to Quaker paternalism. After all, in moving to Pennsylvania and accepting the benefits of Quaker government, the Scotch-Irish and Germans signified their acceptance of an implied contract, binding the newcomers, not to challenge, but to support the existing foundations of provincial society.[138] The resulting tendency to disdain debate with those who broke the understanding was reinforced by the Quaker commitment to consensus. Troubled by the differences that Pennsylvania's midcentury crisis had sparked among members of the Society of Friends, many Quakers worked to avoid confrontations that would intensify controversy and thereby exacerbate internal divisions. As a result, they were not willing to enter the public lists more than minimally against the Presbyterians.[139] Although the reputation and policies of Quakers were at the center of public affairs in 1764, the Society of Friends authorized only one pamphlet, a direct address to Governor John Penn, defending Friends against the allegations in the Paxton Boys' "Remonstrance."[140] Presbyterians interpreted this silence (among members of a sect that not long before had produced some of the most ardent controversialists in Great Britain and the colonies) as contempt for their critics. The anger that such dismissal brought was heightened by such pious Quaker platitudes as "having the Testimony of our Consciences to recur to for our Innocence, We hope thro' Divine Assistance we shall be enabled to bear Reproaches."[141] Knowing they were right, Quakers seemed to be saying, they needed no defense. Righteousness and long-standing dominance in public affairs had bred a smugness among upper-class Philadelphia Friends that drove Presbyterians into paroxysms of rage.[142]

One additional facet of the Paxton imbroglio contributed a great deal to the embitterment of Quaker-Presbyterian relationships. Outspoken Presbyterians often voiced suspicions that Friends were less than sincere in their pacifism and the Paxton riots at last gave them evidence of that. When Philadelphians organized to defend the city against the frontiersmen, over two hundred young Quakers apparently turned out for service. Although their actions mortified the Society's leaders, none was disowned. Their actions were treated as an unfortunate excess of uncomprehending youth.[143] Not surprisingly, the Presbyterian pamphleteers rubbed the Quaker noses in their "*pretended* Scruples against War and Fighting."[144] Friends had long declared pacifism, with a "pious Air, and meek Countenance," but when "their Fellow Subjects . . . [became] obnoxious to . . . [them] we then see the Quaker unmask'd, with his Gun upon his Shoulder . . . thirsting for the Blood of . . . his Opponents."[145]

> . . . Feuds and Quarrels they abhor 'em,
> The LORD will fight their Battles for 'em
> In this of late they were so staunch
> As not to move against the *French*.

> But now the Case is alter'd quite,
> And what was wrong, is chang'd to Right.
> These very Drones, these sluggish Cattle,
> Prepare their Guns and Swords for Battle.[146]

Of course, the Presbyterians emphasized this episode out of all proportion, but more than any other aspect of the Paxton Boys confrontation, it wore away some of the rock of Quaker credibility. Those who had been capable of granting grudging respect to principled consistency looked again, and those who had always suspected Quakers of hypocrisy stridently proclaimed their vindication.

Stung by the vehemence of the anti-Quaker screeds, Quaker apologists were quick to answer back. Even the understated Society response to the Paxton Boys' "Remonstrance" had some bite. It impugned the Presbyterians for misrepresentation, slanderous reports, invidious reflections, and malice toward Friends.[147] Other authors, unrestrained by Quaker scruples, picked up on the obsession with Presbyterian malevolence that some prominent Philadelphians had begun to display in their private discourse. "*Presbyterianism* and *Rebellion* were twin sisters," pro-Quaker polemicists charged, and the Paxton riots were just another example of Presbyterians' unwillingness to accept any government but one that they ran.[148] Civil insubordination had been a hallmark of Scotch-Irish behavior in Great Britain and Ireland, and the series of Presbyterian challenges to Quaker government was a colonial mutation of the same disease.[149] Suppose the Presbyterians became the dominant group in Pennsylvania, what kind of governors would they make? Oppressive ones, without a doubt. It was the "Piss-Brute-tarians (a bigotted, cruel and revengeful sect, sprang from the Turks)" who had put Quakers to death in New England and who were responsible for the Scotch and Irish massacres of the seventeenth centuries.[150] "They . . . tolerate no other profession or Opinion but their own, and never cease till they establish themselves in such a Manour, so as to exclude all other Sects . . . witness *Scotland* and *New England*."[151] And witness, too, the College of New Jersey with its intolerant New Light airs and narrow strictures on students.[152] Put power in their hands and Presbyterians would "drive on Jehu-like," over the humane Quaker policies of liberty of conscience that had originally brought them to Pennsylvania.[153] Once ensconced in the seats of government, the Presbyterians would establish their own church, collect tithes for Presbyterian ministers, and end freedom of religion for other denominations.[154] To the very marrow of their bones, Presbyterians were infected with the disease of persecution. And as for hypocrisy, the Quakers had no monopoly on that. What was Christian about the Conestoga killings? How could anyone involved in such brutal acts claim they were "fechting the Lord's battles"?[155] Christianity was founded on charity and civility, and neither on gratuitous violence rationalized as vengeance nor on Old Testament commands to extirpate the heathen. Repeatedly, commentators mocked the Paxton Boys' heroics, contrasting claims with deeds:

As to their Bravery no Body will ever dispute it, that has heard of their gallant and loyal Behaviour at *Lancaster;* where only fifty of them compleatly arm'd were able to vanquish a numerous Company of eight Men and Women, and seven small Children, all disarm'd and coop'd up in a Gaol.—The Fame of this noble Exploit ought surely to be recorded in the Annals of America for the Honor of the religious, Christian *Presbyterians.*[156]

While a good deal of the animosity that fueled the Paxton controversy was rooted in historic Quaker/Presbyterian strife, and in perceptions of the current relationship of each of these denominations to the Pennsylvania legislature, there was an additional source of social conflict in Philadelphia that fed into the pamphlet wars. That was the College of Philadelphia. From its beginnings, the collaboration of Anglicans and Old Side Presbyterians had been "Oil and Vinegar, jaring . . . [components] which . . . never agree[d] cordially with one another."[157] Despite the efforts of the Anglican provost, William Smith, and the Presbyterian vice-provost, Francis Alison, to compromise for the sake of the liberal education they both believed in, the college seemed to breed animosities within its walls.[158] Among the most important contributors to the Paxton writings were a tutor, Isaac Hunt, and Professor Hugh Williamson. Hunt was an Anglican who deeply resented Presbyterian influence in the college. He, a handful of other Anglicans, and Benjamin Franklin, acted as surrogates for Friends who believed some polemical involvement was necessary on behalf of Quakers but who had no desire to defy the pressures of Quaker strictures against controversy or to risk meeting censorship. On the other side was the Presbyterian Williamson, who felt that Episcopalian interests, whether educational, religious, or political, were frequently inimical to those of Presbyterians. It was thus incumbent on capable Presbyterians to do battle against both Quakers and Anglicans when spokespersons for the latter denomination cooperated in political affairs with those of the former to disadvantage their Calvinist foes.

While Williamson and other Paxton Boys' apologists placed much of their emphasis on familiar backcountry grievances—the assembly had spent far too much effort protecting Indians and too little fighting them, far too much money on trying to buy the goodwill of frontier tribes and far too little on relief for their white victims—they also broke new and important ground. During the crisis of the mid 1750s, Quaker critics had occasionally mentioned the inequitable apportionment of seats in the provincial legislature, but they made nothing of it.[159] By 1764, however, the backcountry population had grown markedly. The Paxton Boys believed their defense problems would soon disappear if the principle of equality of representation among counties were observed, so that the distribution of seats in the assembly reflected either the wealth or the population of the western counties.[160] They argued that their "natural Privileges of Freedom and Equality" and the 1701 Charter of Privileges promised them sufficient legislative strength to protect their lives and properties.[161] The charge that Friends had deliberately underrepresented more recent immigrants, so that "they must ever wear such a yoke as a Quaker . . . [might] please to shape for them," put the Quaker Party on the defensive.[162] Although the 1701 charter said nothing about the future, its careful allotment of an equal number of representatives to each of the original counties did suggest that William Penn had some principle of equity in mind. Moreover, Quaker Party men had, in fact, deliberately created new counties with only one or two representatives so that church Germans and Scotch-Irish Presbyterians would not be able to challenge eastern power.[163] More to the point, they had no intention of altering that situation. Pressured to address the issue, Quaker apologists tried a number of tacks. One was deliberately to understate both the numbers and wealth of the westerners. By one such set of calculations, the east was actually underrepresented.[164] Another was to argue that those who were most heavily represented should pay the greatest tax load and then assert that most westerners were happy to trade less representation for lighter taxes.[165] The most effective answer the Quakers had, however, was to point out that even in areas where Germans or Scotch-Irish were numerous, electors quite frequently chose Quakers to represent them,[166] and to explain, based on the usual eighteenth-century conceptions of government in British colonies, that the primary responsibility of the legislature was to protect the liberties of the people.[167] Regardless of the allocation of its members, the assembly was a corporate body that represented all Pennsylvanians in the most important struggle of all, the ongoing battle with proprietary tyranny.[168] And it was undeniable that, overall, Pennsylvania Quakers had a sterling reputation as popular champions.

From the perspective of the Quaker Party, then, the central issue in the current crisis was not the apportionment of representatives but the overwhelming threat of proprietary encroachment upon popular privileges. In 1763, the assembly was in the midst of a standoff with Governor Hamilton over the issue of taxation of proprietary land. During the latter stages of the French and Indian War, the assembly had bribed Governor Denny to ignore Thomas Penn's instructions forbidding Denny to sign any tax bills that placed levies on proprietary lands. Penn appealed to the Privy Council, but because the currency funded on the taxes had already been spent to finance the war effort, annulment would have created great hardship and extreme inequities.[169] What the Privy Council ordered was that in the current case, the Pennsylvania Assembly should pass amending legislation, and in all future tax bills incorporate within the act six rules of taxation designed to ensure fair assessment of proprietary land.[170] Although its agents, Benjamin Franklin and Robert Charles, agreed to the conditions (they had little choice), the assembly argued that the old legislation had treated the proprietors fairly and refused to pass amending acts. Governor Hamilton badgered them to do so and the disagreement between executive and legislature continued into the first months of Pontiac's war. That was one reason why the assembly did not move with alacrity to defend the frontier. Any attempt to raise new funds would likely lead to renewed conflict over the terms of taxation.[171]

British demands for military support from Pennsylvania to carry the war to the western Indians, new rumors that if aid was not forthcoming, the Paxton Boys would soon be on Philadelphia's back porch, and some sympathy for the plight of the backcountry people obliged the assemblymen to frame a new taxation bill despite their reluctance. When they did so, they met with yet another surprise. John Penn, who had recently been appointed governor, upheld an interpretation of one of the six Privy Council conditions for taxing proprietary land that outraged legislators.[172] The relevant clause stated "that the Located uncultivated Lands belonging to the Proprietaries shall not be assessed higher than the lowest Rate at which any located uncultivated land belonging to the Inhabitants shall be assessed."[173] The assembly took this to mean that land in similar circumstances belonging to proprietor and other individuals should be similarly taxed, whereas John Penn argued it meant the best proprietary land in the richest townships should be taxed only at the rate applied to the least productive land in the poorest part of the province. In the ensuing uproar, the assembly caved in. But this time what the Quaker Party took to be Thomas Penn's duplicity in trying to reinterpret Privy Council decisions to avoid equitable taxation pushed them too far.[174] In the past, popular politicians had occasionally tried to blackmail the proprietors by threatening to petition the Crown to repossess Pennsylvania as a royal colony. Always before, they had held back. But not this time. On March 24, 1764, the House of Representatives passed twenty-six resolves criticizing Thomas Penn's attempts to dictate policies for Pennsylvania from afar, cataloguing his efforts to undercut traditional rights, and "praying" George III "to take the People of . . . [the] Province under his immediate Protection and Government."[175]

The moving spirit behind this initiative was Benjamin Franklin, who had been led to it by his experiences over the preceding eight years.[176] Left to their own devices, Franklin's Pennsylvania confederates would have been unlikely to solicit royal government, but given his encouragement and leadership, they were quick to support the cause. A number of veteran assemblymen, the most talented of whom was Joseph Galloway, were exasperated by the strain of always having to work around proprietary instructions. To the envious eyes of Pennsylvania's popular leaders, it appeared that assemblies in royal colonies had a comparatively easy time persuading their governors to ignore Whitehall's instructions. Crown policies were far less rigorously enforced than were proprietary edicts. Assembly Party insiders saw other attractions as well. Anglicans welcomed a closer association with the Crown, while Quakers had a long history of looking to royalty for protection. Both Anglicans and Quakers, represented by such leading figures as Joseph Galloway, John Hughes, and James Pemberton, saw the Presbyterians as the greatest current threat to the old Pennsylvania political order, and they felt that a royal governor would provide a needed counterweight to the aggressive Calvinists.[177] Under royal government, it might be easier to resist the expansion of backcountry representation; in royal colonies that power was part of the Crown's prerogative.

Once the assembly passed the March resolves, the Quaker Party began an intensive public relations campaign to persuade the public to support its position. The resolves were published, and Franklin wrote a set of "Explanatory Remarks on the Assembly's Resolves," which appeared in the *Pennsylvania Gazette* three days later.[178] In April, as Hugh Williamson began to draw together opinion against the Quaker Party, its treatment of the Presbyterians, and the change of government with his "Plain Dealer" pamphlets, Franklin and Galloway encouraged those sympathetic to innovation with *Cool Thoughts on the Present Situation of Our Public Affairs* and *An Address to the Freeholders and Inhabitants of the Province of Pennsylvania*.[179] After the assembly had reconvened in early May and had drawn up a formal petition to the king requesting royal government, Joseph Galloway again went to the press in order to refute the objections of the eloquent young legislator John Dickinson.[180]

The argument that the advocates of royal government advanced was simple enough. In a proprietary form of government, contention was endemic, because private interest rather than the good of the public guided the executive branch of government. It was only with the greatest effort that Pennsylvanians had been able to preserve their rights from proprietary encroachment, but the conflict that accompanied that effort was ripping the social fabric apart—witness the Paxton riots. Faced with a loss of privileges and possible anarchy, the colony had no way to rescue itself short of royal expropriation, for proprietary instructions turned the assembly into a "French Parliament, with only the Power of forming and registering . . . [our] Master's Edicts."[181] Pennsylvanians needed to realize that their greatest obstacle to overcoming the shackles of proprietary government was their baseless fear of change. There was no reason to believe that a royal government would annul traditional provincial privileges. Only an act of Parliament could do that, and parliamentarians were defenders of the rights of Englishmen. Certainly if there were any hints of an abridgment of rights in discussions with the Crown, the assembly's representatives would break off negotiations.

To John Dickinson, who conceded to Franklin and Galloway that the proprietary form of government did leave something to be desired, the prospects of retaining Pennsylvania's vaunted rights should the Crown take over were not so clear. To make such claims, Galloway would need to possess "a spirit of divination . . . [that could] penetrate . . . into the region of *contingencies*—and fix . . . with infallible *confidence*, the *uncertainties* of the times to come."[182] Dickinson argued that the surrender of charters should only be contemplated in circumstances in which traditional privileges could be "perfectly secured."[183] Unlike Quaker Party stalwarts, Dickinson believed that the times were dangerous for such negotiations, and that the good judgment of his opponents had been overridden by "ambitious projects and personal resentments."[184] What he meant by this was that Franklin's and Galloway's motives were ambitions for royal appointments in the new regime and hatred of Thomas Penn, not the devotion to provincial rights that they professed.

Whereas Dickinson's writings were relatively restrained and reasoned, those of other opponents to the change of government were incendiary. The most effective of these pundits, Hugh Williamson, saw the whole business as an elaborate Quaker ruse. He countered Franklin and Galloway by observing "that Quaker politics and a Quaker faction," not proprietary policies, had "involv'd this province into almost all the contentions, and all the miseries under which we have so long struggled."[185] Disagreements that had paralyzed the province since Governor Thomas's time could be traced to Quaker selfishness, and the current conflict was no exception.[186] "The majority of this province" had been "depriv'd of their share in legislation . . . because they . . . [were] not fairly represented in Assembly."[187] This "grievance" had its origin in the determination of the Quakers to keep government in their own hands, and its results were the desolation of the frontier and the Paxton march on Philadelphia. The underrepresentation of the backcountry and the safety of westerners were the real issues. "It is cruel," Williamson charged, "to deprive people of their liberties, and when they cry for justice, immediately raise a counter-cry, and set the province in a ferment about another affair, lest the groans of the injur'd should be heard."[188]

Because the advocates of royal government introduced their plan to the public in the midst of the bitter argument over the Paxton riots and the defense issue, it is hardly surprising that the new issue perpetuated existing animosities. In fact, Quaker Party loyalists had already done their best to tie the Paxton riots to the proprietorship in order to discredit them both.

Franklin's friends had pointed out Governor John Penn's reputed solicitude for the Paxton Boys' leaders, and that he had made little effort to bring the killers to justice.[189] Although Proprietary Party men were loath to defend the frontiersmen's actions during February and March, once their opponents opened their attack on proprietary government, they countered with vigorous assertions of Presbyterian integrity and frontier rights, as well as apologies for the proprietors.

During the eight weeks between the assembly's passage of its anti-proprietary resolves and its reconvening on May 23 to request George III for royal government, the Quaker Party set out to draw the electorate into its scheme by collecting as many petition signatures as possible to demonstrate popular support. Public harangues, door-to-door solicitation, free liquor, misrepresentation, and fear all had a place in the Quaker Party's bag of tricks.[190] Eventually, party members turned in approximately 3,500 signatures.[191] Taking these as evidence of solid public support, the House of Representatives voted 27–3 to seek the end of proprietary government.[192] That vote seemed to settle the matter, for no one seemed to think that further and more effective opposition might develop in the colony.

Until the end of May, the Quaker Party's political enemies did little to oppose Franklin's plans. The Proprietary Party had a tradition of electoral inconstancy and a not-unrelated absence of internal cohesion. While the usual friends of the proprietorship sat in their plush homes stunned by Franklin's audacity, however, a troika of Philadelphia Presbyterian ministers forcefully spoke out. Acting with uncharacteristic unity, New Light Gilbert Tennent and Old Lights Francis Alison and John Ewing sent out a circular letter (their enemies called it a "Presbyterian Bull") to Presbyterian congregations, advising congregants not to sign the Quaker Party petition.[193] The reason the three clergymen took such action was not because of any affection for the proprietary family or for the form of proprietary government. They thought that the advocacy of royal government might be "an artful Scheme . . . to *divert* the Attention of the injur'd Frontier Inhabitants from prosecuting" their own grievances, including underrepresentation. Observing that "the Heads of . . . [the] Society [of Friends]" had not endorsed the "Change of Government," they thought it might be "a *Trap* laid to ensnare the unwary . . . *Presbyterians* for . . . attempting to ruin the Province." Finally, if the plan to petition for royal government was genuine, it was "not *safe*" to proceed so "rashly; Our Privileges by these means may be greatly *abridged,* but will never be *enlarged.*"[194] Already angry at the Quakers for their defense policy and at Franklin for his attacks on the Paxton Boys, many Presbyterians heeded the pleadings of the Philadelphia ministers and refused to sign the petitions.

They were not alone. Although the Quaker Party brandished the 3,500 signatures as evidence of popularity, the truth was that most of their support came from Philadelphia. A large number of Pennsylvanians of various religious backgrounds sympathized with the Paxton Boys and disliked Quaker Party attacks on them.[195] And even larger numbers, both in country and city, associated their rights and liberties with the existing provincial constitution. Pennsylvania's proprietary charter and the 1701 Charter of Privileges were what had guaranteed liberty of conscience, freedom from military service, and numerous elected officials. There were many Anglicans, Quakers, German churchmen, and sectarians, as well as Presbyterians, who were loath to sign a document seeking the end of their renowned charters.[196]

Gradually it began to dawn on the chief proprietary politicians that the Quaker Party had handed its longtime adversaries an issue of great popularity. One of the first to recognize this was Provost William Smith. Smith had arrived back in Philadelphia in June 1764, after a two-and-a-half-year sojourn in Great Britain soliciting funds for the College of Philadelphia, and he quickly hit on a way to embarrass the Quaker Party. He initiated a proprietary-led petitioning campaign to counter the Old Party's. It proved a resounding success. By September, Smith's friends claimed to have collected 15,000 signatures, dwarfing the results of their opponents.[197] Encouraged by such support, the proprietary men laid plans to contest the October 1 election with slates of candidates committed to rescind the petition for royal government. In the politics of Philadelphia County, Smith was particularly important. He set out to court the numerous German voters by pressing the governor to appoint additional German justices of the peace, by arranging for the payment of naturalization fees for prospective German voters, and by ensuring that German churchmen, in the person of Henry Kepple and Frederick Antis, were included on the Proprietary ticket for assemblymen.[198] Presbyterians were active, too, as never before. A committee of Old and New Light Philadelphians tried to encourage political unity among their fractious fellows and to organize correspondence committees in other counties.[199] The Old Light Philadelphia merchant Samuel Purviance served as provincial coordinator, while the committee's strategist, William Allen, lent credibility to the Proprietary Party's collective denunciation of a change of government through his reputed findings (during a recent trip to Great Britain) that royal government would likely bring restrictions on Pennsylvania's constitutional rights.[200]

The relative success of the Proprietary Party in organizing opposition tickets in 1764 should not obscure the fact that it was an unstable collection of dissidents. There was considerable strain between leading Anglicans and Presbyterians. Presbyterians distrusted Provost William Smith, whom they suspected of a secret ambition to become America's first bishop.[201] Enmity between Anglicans and Presbyterians associated with the College of Philadelphia was deeper in 1763–1764 than it had ever been before, and even the relationship between Vice-Provost Francis Alison and Provost William Smith was coming unglued.[202] While Smith was certainly the least-trusted of the proprietary leaders, he was not alone in this regard. John Dickinson, or "Johnny Vain," as his enemies nicknamed him, had been "long hated by some, and disregarded by the rest of the Proprietary Faction."[203] They welcomed his eleventh-hour conversion on the issue of royal government but were not about to forget their old animosities.[204] Another high-profile leader of the proprietary coalition was the Quaker notable Israel Pemberton, Jr., "The Quaker-Presbyterian Indian Colonel," as his detractors called him.[205] Since 1756, Pemberton had been a loose cannon in political affairs, and his efforts to join the Proprietary Party in discrediting the campaign for royal government seemed another example of his unpredictable character.[206] All told, it was a strange collection of collaborators.

The major issue in the 1764 election was the proposed change of government; the contest was a virtual referendum on it. But each party was quick to bring into the campaign all of the provincial controversies of the previous year. The assembly's dismissal of backcountry grievances, its woeful performance in defending the frontier, the Paxton Boys' killings and march on Philadelphia, and the antagonism between Quakers and Presbyterians were all grist for polemicists pleading their parties' causes. Those intent upon exposing the long-lived malevolence of their opponents reached back into the past and plucked incidents from the 1740s and 1750s that seemed to prove their point. The Quaker Party men tried to build a cumulative case that condemned proprietary tyranny, exposed the continual malevolence of their proprietary opponents, and justified the request for royal government. On the other side, the proprietary writers underscored what they viewed as the impossible contradictions of Quaker government and the self-serving policies that the Quaker Party had frequently espoused.

Given such aroused feelings, it is not surprising that party writers often ignored the issue of royal government in favor of vituperation. Benjamin Franklin, for example, was charged with selling out the province's rights in order to fulfill personal ambition, squandering the public's money during his days as an ineffectual agent in Britain, using and then discarding those who befriended him, showing disdain for Quakers, Germans, and Scotch-Irish, and, finally, "cruelly suffer[ing]" the alleged mother of his illegitimate son William "TO STARVE."[207] Not to be outdone, Quaker Party writers charged their proprietary opponents with toadying to Thomas Penn and conspiring to defraud Pennsylvanians of their rights. One individual whom they singled out was Provost William Smith, a "P[ederast]" who also had "strong Itchings to Illegal V[ener]y."[208] In comparison with Benjamin Franklin's well-taken-care-of son William, "the illegitimate Progeny of

[Franklin's] Adversaries . . . [were] so *numerous* so *scandalous* and so *neglected* that the *only* concern of the Parents . . . [was] least their *unhappy* By-Blows should commit Incest."²⁰⁹

The intensity of the election campaign foreshadowed the heavy voter turnout that occurred. Outside of Philadelphia City and County, however, that did not mean bad news for the incumbents. Chester and Bucks counties continued to be dominated by the Old Ticket politicians, and even in the western counties, inroads into Quaker Party strength were limited. Only about half of their ten representatives were strongly anti-Quaker. At first glance, such results appear bizarre, because countryfolk were notoriously opposed to a change of government.²¹⁰ But in light of a comment by William Allen after the election, they become much less mysterious: "in the Country, all but Northampton, the Quakers had the address, or I might say, Craft, to delude the Dutch by false Storeys, so that they . . . were induced to oppose our friends, and carried the elections against them. They were made to believe that, if they changed the Assembly, the Government would be changed."²¹¹ Blaming the artful Quakers and their German dupes for their election defeats was an old Proprietary Party saw, which, in reality, had always meant that rural voters shared their representatives' predilections for popular government. The circumstances were no different this time. However they had done so, Quaker Party candidates continued to stress their traditional role as champions of popular rights.²¹² They, not their opponents, were most likely to keep faith with the values clustered together under historic Quaker Party guardianship.²¹³

The Philadelphia City and County results were the reverse of those in the outlying counties. Although support for the royal government petition had been at its strongest in and around Philadelphia, the Proprietary Party stalwarts carried both city seats and six of eight in the county.²¹⁴ Among the losers were the Old Party leaders Benjamin Franklin and Joseph Galloway. In considering this major upset, Franklin put his finger on the main electoral shift responsible for his defeat. The Proprietary men "carried (would you think it!) above 1000 Dutch from me, by printing part of my Paper . . . on Peopling new Countries where I speak of the *Palatine Boors* herding together, which they explain'd that I call'd them a *Herd* of *Hogs*."²¹⁵ Yet in pointing to the use his opportunistic opponents made of his careless comment some fourteen years earlier, Franklin was identifying the symptom rather than the cause of his defeat. If prejudice against Germans had been the issue, the Proprietary Party men would not have received a vote. Provost William Smith had maligned the Germans at length in his *Brief State* and *Brief View*, and other Proprietary Party leaders shared his views.²¹⁶ But when Quaker Party writers reminded Germans of this, their readers turned a deaf ear. They picked up on Franklin's comments because they wanted to vote against him, and imputing prejudice to him made that easier. In fact, Philadelphia Germans were among the most appreciative of the benefits they enjoyed under the 1701 charter, and they did not want to risk losing them.[217] German-language campaign literature stressed the folly of offering up the best constitution in the world for an unknown royal alternative. Even Christopher Saur, Jr., traditionally a friend of the Quaker Party, was of the opinion that Franklin and Galloway should be tossed on the dunghill of discredited legislators.[218] Convinced that Franklin was wrong, flattered by the Proprietary Party, which placed two German churchmen on their Philadelphia County ticket, and promised more justices of the peace in the future, Philadelphia County Germans were softened to the point of being receptive to scurrilous charges. Evidence that Franklin was condescending to Germans confirmed their suspicions of his judgment, and justified the feelings of disgust that sprang from perceptions of political betrayal.

Philadelphia County Germans were certainly not the only residents of Pennsylvania who shifted their political support to the Proprietary Party because of the Assembly Party's ill-conceived policy. On election day, the Proprietary Party's entourage swelled beyond recognition with large numbers of English-speaking provincials who cherished their existing constitution. The Proprietary Party politicians were the lucky recipients of a windfall; they had success thrust upon them in a cause they had long despised. The irony of the situation made Benjamin Franklin shake his head:

Pleasant, surely it is, to hear the Proprietary Partizans, of all Men, bawling for the Constitution, and affecting a terrible concern for our Liberties and Privileges. They who have been, these twenty Years, cursing our Constitution, declaring that it was no Constitution, or worse than none, and that Things could never be well with us, 'till it was new-modell'd, and made exactly conformable to the British Constitution. . . . Wonderful Change! Astonishing Conversion! Will the wolves then protect the Sheep, if they can but persuade 'em to give up their dogs?[219]

The election clearly demonstrated that the vast majority of voters were committed to maintaining the kind of popular rights, assembly power, and executive weakness that had long distinguished provincial politics. Only a clutch of proprietary placemen defied this popular orthodoxy, and in the interest of the electoral success that had long eluded them, they abandoned their long-standing critique of the Pennsylvania constitution and defended the old order—in effect, buying into a version of the Quaker Party's ideology of civil Quakerism.[220] What divided the provincial electorate, then, were not different perceptions of the province's sociopolitical order, but different opinions about how best to protect the province's traditional rights and privileges. For decades the Quaker Party had enjoyed an unrivaled role as the people's party. In moving to secure provincial rights through royal government, however, Franklin and his friends inadvertently created a rank-

and-file opposition, one that had gained its political education and its sense of values under the aegis of the Quaker Party, but that was unable to accept the Old Party's judgment that the proprietary charter could be exchanged for something better.

The unprecedented electoral success of the Proprietary Party intensified conflict between it and the Quakers in the months that immediately followed the 1764 election. A "Majority of the last assembly remain[ed]" to be marshaled in the House by the Quaker Party stalwart John Hughes and directed from outside by Franklin- and Galloway-led "private meetings & cabals."[221] When the assembly moved to proceed with the petition for royal government with "the Utmost Caution" and appointed Benjamin Franklin agent for the negotiations, a minority of ten legislators broke with tradition and publicly stated their dissent.[222] Because the ten criticized Franklin so heavily as the "Chief Author of the Measures" designed to secure royal government, and because they mistrusted him as having personal interests and prejudices unbefitting a provincial agent, Franklin wrote a scathing retort that maligned William Allen and the other supporters of the proprietorship.[223] Although Franklin left for Great Britain in early November, partisan political tracts continued to appear through the winter of 1765. These scurrilous attacks and counterattacks perpetuated the differences between the Quaker and Proprietary parties that the political battles of 1764 had initiated.[224] Spring, however, brought some respite. The Proprietary Party leaders were increasingly confident that the petition would go nowhere, and that the Quaker Party's commitment to royal government was more equivocal than it admitted. In fact, many of the Old Party members simply wanted to use the threat of royal government to force the proprietor to negotiate on the issue of his instructions, and by early 1765, negotiations with Thomas Penn were under way.[225]

The temper of Pennsylvania politics also changed because, for the first time since the end of the French and Indian War, imperial issues began to command attention. Throughout 1763 and 1764, Franklin and Galloway had played down the importance of imperial innovations such as the raising of a revenue on colonial trade and the stationing of British troops in the colonies.[226] Although the Pennsylvania Assembly, under Franklin's brief speakership, took a strong stand against the British presumption that Parliament had the right to tax the colonies, Franklin was quite prepared to promote an imperial loan office, analogous to the Pennsylvania land bank, that would provide a general colonial revenue to the British.[227] Once Franklin arrived in London, he straddled the fence in much the same way, lobbying against such legislation as the Stamp Act and the Quartering Act, but willing to suggest alternatives or modifications, and ultimately willing to participate in the enforcement of new laws.[228] As he wrote to the Philadelphia merchant Charles Thomson, a Presbyterian friend of his, "We might as well have hinder'd the Suns setting . . . [as prevent the passage of the Stamp Act]. Let us make as good a Night of it as we can. We may still Light Candles."[229] One of the Philadelphia candles he had in mind was the Quaker Party chief John Hughes, for whom Franklin secured the Pennsylvania stamp distributorship. When popular protests against the Stamp Act began to build in the colonies, Franklin urged Hughes to execute the office "with Coolness and Steadiness."[230] While the Quaker Party leaders haltingly began to practice what one commentator has aptly called "the politics of ingratiation" in order to prove that their colony deserved royal government, the proprietary men were uncertain what public stance they should take on imperial issues.[231] Despite his conservatism, William Allen had leveled a barrage of criticism against British innovations in order to give weight to his contention that royal government would mean far more restrictions than the proprietary variety had occasioned.[232] His political allies were far less adventuresome, until news began to pour into Philadelphia in August 1765 of the anti–Stamp Act protests and riots in other colonies. At that point, well-known Proprietary Party men joined with other Philadelphians in demonstrating against the impending parliamentary legislation and trying to force John Hughes to resign.[233]

The most perspicacious of the Proprietary Party leaders saw the Stamp Act crisis as a means of holding together their political alliance and of striking a second and more serious blow at the Quaker Party. The 1764 coalition was proving fragile at best. The Presbyterians Allen and Alison were constantly suspicious of Provost William Smith;[234] John Dickinson felt unappreciated and, with the thin-skinned petulance he was to show for many years, repeatedly announced he would not stand for election in 1765;[235] and Israel Pemberton, Jr., lived up to his reputation by offending some of his most recent political allies.[236] But if the Proprietary Party could claim the cause of colonial rights as its own during the current crisis, it might arrest its disintegration and deal the Old Party a mortal blow. Events certainly helped the Proprietary Party's cause. The Quaker Party could be portrayed as an enemy of American rights after its members made a determined effort in the House of Representatives to prevent Pennsylvania representatives from attending the Stamp Act Congress.[237] The fact that Franklin and Hall's *Pennsylvania Gazette* refused to print many reports of Stamp Act protests, or of Franklin's nomination of Hughes as stamp officer, implicated the London agent.[238] Local street politicians needed no more evidence to set up the cry that a corrupt and ambitious Franklin had "pland the Stampe achte."[239]

In the face of these charges and mobbish threats to pull down the houses of Hughes, Franklin and others, the Old Party leaders defended their men's reputation and property. The latter was the easiest to do, for the Old Party commanded the loyalty of a large number of Philadelphia mechanics, whose devotion to Franklin was intense. Peace reigned in Philadelphia when other colonial communities were torn by violence because, as Galloway bragged, he and his lieutenants could "Muster ten to . . . [the protesters'] one."[240] As for the issues, the Old Party tried to play down those that sapped their strength. They stressed that protests against the Stamp Act should be peaceful and respectful, not violent and defiant. Beyond that, they chose to emphasize the old, familiar causes—the antiproprietary complaints that had precipitated the petition for royal government, the grievances that had furnished the substance of Pennsylvania politics for decades. They wanted a Penn family willing to accept equitable taxation, a land office independent of the proprietor, and justices appointed for good behavior. Because the Quaker Party had been invincible on these issues in the past, they felt most comfortable with them now. At this critical juncture, when they needed to nip Proprietary success in the bud and reseat Galloway in the legislature, Old Party supporters placed their confidence in the familiar appeals that had long rewarded them.[241]

Knowing that appeals to the issues rarely won elections on their own, the Old Party leaders turned their hand to organizational matters. Stung by charges that they had ignored German churchmen in the past, Philadelphia leaders recruited Michael Hillegas, a second-generation German merchant, to run on their county ticket, and paid the naturalization fees of a large number of German immigrants in order that they might be eligible to vote.[242] While Quaker Party writers tried to turn voters against the Proprietary Party men with scurrilous blasts, others turned to more practical tasks.[243] During the election, Old Party managers bought support with alcohol and then solicitously guided their unsteady charges to the State House to vote.[244] Never had the party wheelhorses worked so hard.

Faith in the efficacy of hard work may have inclined Quaker Party men to be optimistic about the election. Nonetheless, it was with some relief that the Philadelphia merchant and party leader Thomas Wharton could understatedly report that their "Labour . . . [was] not Lost."[245] The Old Party swept Philadelphia County and dominated most other parts of the province. In doing so, it purged from the legislature half of the ten representatives who had opposed Franklin's agency, and secured a Philadelphia County seat for Galloway. Of course, the Stamp Act remained an issue in Pennsylvania until its repeal, but the Quaker Party continued to control both the protests against the act's implementation in the fall of 1765 and celebrations of its repeal in the spring of 1766. Politically conscious Pennsylvanians were so deeply immersed in their local disputes of 1765 that emotions and issues raised by the Stamp Act were largely subsumed under existing divisions. As the Sons of Liberty of Philadelphia confessed, "Our Body in this City is not declared Numerous, as unfortunate Dissentions in Provincial Politicks keep us rather a divided People."[246]

Preoccupied with their woes, Philadelphia's Sons of Liberty failed to sense that the deep electoral divisions they bemoaned were already on the wane. The issue of royalization quickly lost its explosive force once word spread that British ministers had little interest in taking over Pennsylvania. And repeal of the Stamp Act rendered ineffective the efforts of a few Quaker Party opponents to discredit Franklin, Galloway, and Hughes as promoters of the tax.[247] The 1766 election brought only token opposition to the Old Party in Philadelphia City and County, and the voting turnout plunged precipitously from its record levels of the two preceding years.[248] Immediately thereafter, the Quaker Party faced only limited electoral challenges as Galloway took closer control of the assembly and attempted to entrench eastern county control within it.[249] Governor John Penn and William Allen both counseled peace with the Quakers. The former thought the Quakers were a "Macedonian Phalanx," impossible to defeat; the latter thought his elitist interests best served by a closer understanding with "the better sort of Quakers."[250] Among the numerous recent opponents of the Quaker Party, many came to agree with the Presbyterian minister Francis Alison that colonial "contests with the commons of England made Harmony . . . necessary."[251]

The well-known localized political conflict in Philadelphia in the 1770s notwithstanding, the most active phases of colonial electoral competition had come to an end.[252] Uncertain of the future, and rarely inspired by the political choices either conservative or radical leaders offered them, many Pennsylvanians opted out of the electoral process; of those who did continue to cast ballots on election day, the majority reflexively endorsed the still-active remnants of the regime they had long found so familiar. As in New York, the future of Pennsylvania's electoral politics no longer lay with the colonial experiment but with the Revolution and the republicanism of the new order.

"However they will, the people must decide . . . "

Despite the obvious differences in the circumstances and timing of the major electoral battles in New York and Pennsylvania during the 1760s, there were important points of convergence, which reveal a good deal about the character of electoral politics in colonial America. One of the most obvious of these was the high profile Presbyterian spokespersons and apologists established on behalf of their denomination in the polemical literature of each colony. In New York, the most vocal critics of Anglican leaders and of their allies in the Dutch and French Reformed communities were Presbyterians. And in Pennsylvania, Presbyterians frequently led the hue and cry against Quaker influence in provincial politics.

Unquestionably, Presbyterian rhetoric had a significant impact on public affairs in both colonies. As the New York lawyer Peter Van Schaack pointed out in 1769 in addressing Presbyterian fears of Anglican oppression, "the Apprehensions expressed by the Pres[byteria]ns are I believe in Truth a chimerical but with Respect to *themselves* they are *real*, because they *think* them so."[253] Such suspicions, raised and reinforced by polemical posturing, clearly encouraged some Presbyterians to make a more conscious connection than they had hitherto done, between their denominational affiliation and their political allegiances. In the New York City and County election of 1768, only 18.6 percent of the votes of Wall Street Presbyterian Church members went to the three leading Anglicans (Bayard, DeLancey, and Walton) compared to 49 percent that went to the two Presbyterian candidates, John Morin Scott and James Jauncey.[254] In the 1769 sequel, 78 percent of Wall Street voters favored the ticket headed by Philip Livingston, which included two Presbyterians, and only 8 percent the DeLancey ticket with its one Presbyterian.[255] Although we have no poll lists for Pennsylvania on which to base a comparable analysis, a few contemporaries did suggest that some Presbyterians made similar efforts to express their denominational consciousness in political affairs.[256] Apparently the mud-slinging between Presbyterian champions and Quaker apologists did precipitate a few cases of concerted electoral activity among some Presbyterians.

It is important, however, to note what did not happen as well as what did. And the ubiquity of Presbyterian polemics notwithstanding, there was no great tide of Presbyterian political mobilization in elections in either New York or Pennsylvania in the 1760s. In New York City in the 1768 and 1769 elections, the percentage of (male) Wall Street Church members who voted was 34.9 and 29.4 respectively. That was only slightly more than one half of the rates (65.9 percent in 1768 and 56.55 in 1769) at which members of the Collegiate Dutch Reformed Church participated in the same elections. While many of those Presbyterians who did vote registered some denominational consciousness, there were a very large number of their co-religionists who proved indifferent to the religious issues designed to draw them to the polls. Nor was New York alone in this regard. In Pennsylvania, not only did Presbyterians remain fractured among themselves during the mid 1760s (according to one contemporary, they "were a laughing stock . . . to all other denominations on account of the divisions among them"[257]), they also demonstrated no evidence of unprecedented mobilization in areas in which they were sufficiently numerous to have made their way into office.[258] In both colonies, the rhetorical prominence of a Presbyterian cause belied the fact that many members of Presbyterian congregations remained inactive, divided, or both, in the four strongly contested provincial elections.

If Presbyterians were not quite the highly mobilized, unified core of electors that contemporary apologists either hoped they would become or perceived them to be, what denominations were at the heart of political affairs? Although the evidence is not all that it might be, what there is indicates that amid the increased mobilization of voters, members of those religious groups with deep roots in their respective colonies—the "charter" churches, as it were—tended to remain at the center of political activities in the long-established counties. There are indications that many adherents of the Anglican church in New York City and County were politically active during hard-fought contests. The Anglican church was old, rich, and venerable. It was associated with British colonial rule, and in its pews sat many of the colony's important political leaders. Above all, the establishment and anglicizing character of the church encouraged members to affirm their special preeminence through political activity. In addition, we know that members of the Dutch Reformed church were about twice as likely to vote as Presbyterians. Despite its polyglot origins, the Manhattan Dutch community had retained considerable coherence into the late colonial years, and members of that ethnic group had continuously played an important role in the colony's economic and social development, had largely controlled city government, and had always been able to exercise some influence in provincial electoral politics when they felt so inclined.[259] Although divided among themselves, in differing degrees the large, old-line Anglican and Dutch Reformed congregations (and possibly the French Reformed) appear to have dominated the public stage and kept the Presbyterians, German Lutherans and Reformed, and other later and less numerous churches somewhat on the periphery of political affairs.

It seems clear that substantially the same generalization holds true of Pennsylvania. In the old eastern counties, Friends remained at the center of politics through the Revolution. They completely dominated politics in Bucks and Chester counties, and in Philadelphia City and County, they ensured the victory of the remade Quaker Party in 1756 and fought back in 1765 to avenge the one substantial defeat they had suffered in the preceding year. There is every indication, too, that, as in New York, many Philadelphia Anglicans were also quick to turn out to assert their old and sometimes prominent stake in provincial society. From their earliest days, Anglicans had taken a leading part in public affairs, and, if anything, they grew stronger as the eighteenth century progressed.

Philadelphia County also harbored the one apparent exception to the correlation between political mobilization and both sustained and prominent denominational presence. There, members of the German Lutheran and Reformed churches took an important hand in the 1764 and 1765 elections; it is arguable that in comparison with the Quakers and Anglicans, they were relatively recent arrivals in Pennsylvania. Granted that supposition, however, it is worth noting something of the circumstances attending these mobilizations of German voters. According to contemporaries, German freeholders from the county gathered in Germantown before proceeding to Philadelphia to cast their ballots. That they did so is quite important. First, it was there that Christopher Saur, Jr., the voice of sectarian Germans through his newspaper and printing establishment, connected the leadership of the old German sectarian community with church Germans in urging a common stand against changing the Pennsylvania Charter for royal government. Second, Germantown was the symbol of a German participation in the Quaker experiment dating back to the seventeenth century, and the village had always served as the center of German political activity in the county, however sporadic and peripheral that had been. Because spokespersons for the Lutherans, such as Henry Melchior Mühlenberg, wanted to claim that members of their church were the critical voters in the Proprietary Party's success of 1764 (a claim that is certainly sustainable), and because of German church leaders' hostility to Saur and the sectarians, they refused to acknowledge the importance of the Germantown connection. But the mobilization of unprecedented numbers of German church voters depended as much on the sectarians' efforts to include church people in the historically sanctioned Germantown claim to political influence, and on the willingness of churchmen to exploit that situation, as on the independent activities of first-generation churchmen like Mühlenberg.[260]

Even when we pay due regard to the long-standing political centrality of such religious groups as the Dutch Reformed, Anglicans, and Quakers, one of the obvious features of the four intense electoral competitions of the 1760s is the extent to which contemporaries used religious and, secondarily, ethnic distinctions both to plead partisan positions and to describe what they thought they perceived. Presbyterians saw themselves as an important political interest; Anglicans defended their public prominence; Quaker apologists emphasized the many benefits Friends' guidance brought to provincial society; New York commentators anecdotally related the activities of "Irish" and the "Germans" electors;[261] and various participants in Pennsylvania's wild contests drew attention to activities of "the Dutch" (i.e., Germans), Presbyterians, and Baptists.[262] The existence of such evidence inevitably raises the question of how prominent religious and ethnic considerations were in shaping late colonial New York and Pennsylvania politics.

The ethnoreligious dimensions of New York politics were perhaps the most complex.[263] One reason for this was the existence of powerful tensions within the Dutch Reformed church, which affected local congregations in diverse ways. Differences linked to the Leislerian disputes, to the conflict between advocates of pietism and orthodox approaches to religious worship, to the disagreement between *coetus* supporters who wanted more autonomy for the colonial church and their *conferentie* opponents, and to discord over the desirability of holding English-language services fissured county communities in ways that had important political implications.[264] In New York City and County, the area for which we have the best evidence, the dispute over offering English-language services had the greatest political salience. This disagreement, which began in the mid 1750s, came to a head a decade later and gained clear political expression in the 1768 and 1769 elections. In the former contest, voting members of the English-language faction of the Collegiate Church overwhelmingly supported the English-language faction member Philip Livingston and the Presbyterian John Morin Scott.[265] In comparison, voting members of the Dutch-language faction placed Livingston and Scott at the bottom of their list of preferences among the six serious candidates.[266] In the 1769 election, 72 percent of the English-language faction voted a straight Philip Livingston–headed ticket, while 73 percent of the Dutch-language faction supported the foursome led by De-Lancey. This situation appears to be a classic case of negative–reference group politics, in which intrareligious group differences over narrow, group-specific, but highly charged, issues appear to have influenced larger political choices.[267]

There were, as well, other ethnoreligious dimensions to New York City politics closely related to the split in the Dutch Reformed church. On the one hand, important bridges ran from the Dutch to the Anglican church on the strength of some members of the former's respect for the establishment character of the latter, and an appreciation of both the latitudinarian and liturgical dimensions of Anglican practice.[268] The knowledgeable Peter V. B. Livingston concluded that by the late colonial years, "the greater half of Trinity Church consist[Ed] . . . of accessions from the Dutch Church."[269] On the other hand, a taste for evangelical religion and personal connections developed over several decades seems to have drawn other members of the Dutch Reformed church toward the New Light variety of New York Presbyterianism. Rather than defect to an English-language church, as those Dutch who became Anglicans had done, the English-language faction of the Dutch church remained (with some notable exceptions) a part of its old congregation, still traditionalists of a sort, but strongly tied to some prominent New York Presbyterians.[270]

Yet there is evidence that such considerations were not as forceful as they might have been even among the New Yorkers whose politics seem to have been most shaped by ethnoreligious tensions and affinities. Of all the voting members of the English-language faction of the Collegiate Church who strongly favored Livingston and Scott, for example, over one half (52.8 percent) voted for the Anglican Captain James DeLancey in 1768. And overall in that election, 38 percent of English-language faction votes went to the three Anglican candidates, Bayard, DeLancey, and Walton. Then there was the case of those Dutch whose politics clearly reflected other priorities. A substantial number of Collegiate Church members had avoided direct involvement in the language dispute.[271] Among voters from their ranks, only 15 percent exclusively supported *either* the three leading Anglican candidates *or* the Dutch Reformed/Presbyterian duo of Livingston and Scott.[272] The majority spread their votes in ways that clearly cut across the most prominent ethnoreligious fissures.[273]

Beyond the confines of the New York City Dutch Reformed community, there were other indications that ethnoreligious differences were only one part of a complex political scene. In the case of New York's numerous mechanic voters, what evidence we have suggests little correlation between any obvious religious or occupational groupings and political behavior.[274] While there may indeed have been strong religious communities among some lower-middle-class city residents, it also seems very clear that there were large numbers of poorer artisans who developed few of the close communal attachments that are integral to strong ethnoreligious identity.[275] On a broader scale, the comparative rate of political participation in the 1768 and 1769 elections is also revealing. In 1768, when religious themes were less developed, electoral competition was pluralistic, and secular concerns evolving out of the recent crises were ubiquitous, voter turnout was relatively high. One year later, when Presbyterian politics was an issue and the organization of two tickets tended to polarize competition around ethnoreligious considerations, voting plummeted by 13 percent, despite unprecedented efforts to mobilize the electorate.[276] There were, of course, a number of reasons for that development, but attempts to catalogue these should include, foremost, the obvious desire of many New Yorkers to boycott a competition encouraging the kind of ethnoreligious polarization they were either indifferent to or wished to avoid.[277]

There is no question that ethnoreligious rivalries played an important part in New York's electoral politics of the late 1760s. Tensions within the Dutch Reformed church, the efforts of a small group of Presbyterians to focus public attention on religious issues, and the loss of a midcentury orientation in public affairs that had structured provincial politics around popular and provincial Whig traditions all encouraged such a development.[278] But as important as such considerations were, the peculiar ethnoreligious strains that developed out of the highly unique socioreligious mix in each New York county and gained expression in the idiosyncratic politics of each county community never took over the political agenda. They did not do so because, despite ethnoreligious divergences, different groups were predisposed to foster a civic consciousness expansive enough to accommodate considerable diversity.[279] Consequently ethnoreligious imperatives were always intertwined both with a great variety of political, social, and economic issues and with the often obscure, but crucial, personal dimensions of community relations. From this melange, contemporaries inferred what they called "political tenets"—that is, political principles and predispositions in public affairs that both office seekers and voters intimately connected with the larger issues of provincial politics.[280] And in the late 1760s, what swung most New York voters behind the emerging DeLancey faction were largely the secular issues, relating to traditional popular powers and rights, that the various public crises of mid-decade had brought to the fore.

Although the absence of poll lists for Pennsylvania prevents the same kind of analysis that illuminates voter behavior in New York, it is still possible to draw conclusions about the relative importance of ethnoreligious politics in the Quaker colony from the available evidence. As in New York, the religious issue undoubtedly strengthened the connection, particularly among some Presbyterians, between their denominational affiliation and their political choice. It also seems clear that, as in New York (depending on the historic patterns of ethnic and religious development and the character of that mix in the 1760s in different communities), ethnoreligious conflict could vary considerably in form and in intensity from county to county.[281] And, as in New York, compelling examples of ethnic political mobilization demonstrated that ethnoreligious factors did have political relevance. In the 1765 election, for example, the Lutheran minister Henry Melchior Mühlenberg reported that "about six hundred German citizens assembled in and before the schoolhouse [in Germantown] and [then] marched in procession to the [Philadelphia] *courthouse* to cast their votes."[282]

But the point is to find the most appropriate *level* of relevance for such evidence of ethnoreligious activity. While Mühlenberg's example may be used to argue that political coherence existed among various congregations of German church people, and hence that ethnoreligious considerations played some part in structuring county politics, it does not at all demonstrate that ethnic and cultural factors determined the political choices voters made.[283] And in this situation there is every indication that what motivated such a sizable group of Germans to support the Proprietary Party was the voters' determination to protect the colony's royal charter, its Charter of Privileges, and the customary rights inherent in the Pennsylvania constitution.[284] When the most immediate threat to provincial liberties seemed to subside, as it did in 1766, this new bloc of German voters largely dissolved.[285] Had intra-ethnic antagonisms against the large numbers of sectarian and church Germans who continued to support the Quaker Party been the primary focus of the 1764 and 1765 election contests, it is very unlikely that Mühlenberg's Germans would so quickly have given up the field or mingled with many of their recent opponents as they did during the late 1760s. As for Mühlenberg and other like-minded ethnic leaders, the test of their ethnoreligious generalship was not in the 1764 and 1765 elections, when they enjoyed a popular issue and the support of Christopher Saur, Jr., but in the immediately subsequent years, when they had neither. Despite claims of ethnoreligious solidarity, when the Proprietary Party's German leaders looked around in 1766, they saw few of their recent cadres still in the field.

As in New York, ethnoreligious considerations clearly played a part in structuring local politics in Pennsylvania. Such an outcome is hardly surprising in any pluralistic Western society with a relatively broad franchise. But, at the same time, ethnoreligious factors certainly did not play as determinative a role in Pennsylvania's provincial politics as they did in the Hudson River colony. Presbyterian rhetoric and ethnoreligious consciousness notwithstanding, electoral competition between the tickets of the Quaker and Proprietary parties mainly centered on the political, constitutional, and secular dimensions of public issues. Perhaps the most distinctive feature of Pennsylvania society was the penchant provincials had for developing and bringing to bear on their public affairs a highly distinctive and capacious brand of civic consciousness. For decades political activity in Pennsylvania had revolved less around ethnoreligious considerations than around an ideology of civil Quakerism; and the electoral politics of the mid 1760s continued largely in that vein.[286]

Part II

*Articulating Early American
Political Culture*

Chapter Six

Factional Identity and Political Coherence in New York

DIVIDED BY geographic, economic, and cultural imperatives, and by the seventeenth-century experiences of military conquest and explosive political conflict, eighteenth-century New Yorkers were notably fractious. Contemporaries frequently tried to find some political order in their colony by taking notice of constitutional and political distinctions that they felt would simultaneously promote both provincial coherence and the political fortunes of their own faction. When they stressed the order that replicating English constitutional and legal precepts might bring, they emphasized the problem as much as they reassured themselves. In attempting to import "landed/mercantile" and "court/country" models of political behavior from Great Britain in order to explain and give a larger legitimacy to their various cliques, they exaggerated the very factiousness they tried to explain.

When New Yorkers could not find political self-definition in narrowly applied intellectual constructs imported from Great Britain, they discovered political order in their own provincial experiences. During the mid eighteenth century, they developed a far greater sense of political identity as they came to understand public affairs in terms of a division between popular and provincial Whig traditions. Beneath the rhetorical emphasis on landed/mercantile and court/country distinctions, provincial politics in the late 1720s and early 1730s was, in fact, distinguished by the organization of the

Philipse popular Whigs and the Morris/Alexander provincial Whigs. Later the demise of these two factions permitted the coalescence of the DeLancey/Jones popular Whigs and the Livingston/Smith provincial Whigs. By mid-century, when New Yorkers found their provincial politics defined by the second generation of popular/provincial Whig factions, they had far less need to justify their political partisanship in terms of the English models upon which they had drawn. Their world continued to be a highly competitive one, with its own style of shrill, "cantish" polemical debate. But, delineated as it was by the increasingly familiar popular and provincial Whig traditions, it was a known world, which created context and instilled a sense of public order into the political community.

With the demise of the DeLancey/Jones faction, the fragmentation of its provincial Whig counterpart, and the changing circumstances of imperial politics, New York politicians became disoriented. Bitterly competitive but uncertain of the tradition they represented, and unclear about how to apply past principles to new exigencies, New York's political factions of the late 1760s constructed a rationale for themselves based predominantly on family identity. Although such thinking served their needs of the moment by again creating a semblance of order in provincial politics, it was no more than a brief holding action in a rapidly changing political environment.

Constitutionalism in Colonial New York

In coming to terms with their eighteenth-century provincial society, New Yorkers faced a particularly complex political scene. The social, economic, and geographic diversity of the colony, the various strategic and financial considerations that provincials faced during wartime, and the personal and political divisions that arose out of conquest and revolution in the late seventeenth century clearly encouraged political factionalism.[1] According to the canons of early modern English thought, however, factional politics posed a grave danger to any society, signifying the preeminence of private over public interest and perhaps presaging a slide into the abyss of anarchy. Like others of their intellectual heritage, New Yorkers tended to stress the fundamental institutional features of their colony that promised to promote a well-ordered world.

Politically conscious residents of New York were unanimous in identifying the British constitution as the basic guarantor of public order. Because of its stalwart character and marvelous combination of mixed government with a balanced structure, the constitution promised the possibility of constructing a society characterized by ordered liberty and restrained authority. Of the two main features of the British constitution, mixed government was the most difficult to understand. Implicit in the idea were two notions. One was that the constitution included elements of the three pure Aristotelian types of government: monarchy, aristocracy, and democracy; their mixture checked the propensity of each of these types in singular form to degenerate, respectively, into tyranny, oligarchy, and mob rule. The second notion was the far vaguer idea that the three British social orders (monarchy, aristocracy, and commoners), or more specifically the various prominent estates (monarchy, lords spiritual and temporal, and knights and burgesses), all participated to some degree in the functioning, particularly the legislative functioning, of government. While mixed government was wonderful in theory, "its benefits . . . were achieved in practice by the balanced constitution of King, Lords and Commons."[2] These three institutions of government had their own powers, yet they were all connected through a series of delicate checks and balances that prevented any one of them from dominating. Together they represented sovereign authority; and the comity they brought to the exercise of ultimate authority promised political harmony and social order.[3]

Aware of the blessings the British constitution bestowed at "home," New Yorkers were quick to claim the same for themselves. "The Constitution of the Colony . . . is a picture in Minature of that of Great Britain."[4] "It is the great Happiness of the People of the Province of New York that the Government is form'd as near as may be upon the same Plan with that of our Mother Country."[5] Others joined in the tub thumping with a chorus that was repeated in virtually every statement about the structure of colonial government. The colonial constitution was "similar" to Great Britain's because of its balanced character.[6] New York had a governor "representing" the king, a council "resemaling" the House of Lords, and a General Assembly that was the counterpart of the House of Commons.[7] Another writer expressed the congruence in a slightly different fashion. There was a "Delegation" of kingly power to the governor, the "Form" of the House of Lords in the council, and a "Resemblance" of the House of Commons in the assembly.[8] Regardless of the wording, the point was always the same. New York's constitution provided for three legislative voices, which in their asserted similarity to British counterparts evoked the vision of mixed government and a balanced constitution.

The determination of New Yorkers to identify with what they thought to be the positive features of British government pushed them beyond mere paeans. Most legislators, lawyers, and judges believed that the colony "should be governed by the Laws of England; and [that] in this Province these . . . [were] better known, and more strictly adhered to, than in any other."[9] Court procedures followed a similar bent. "In all our courts," observed William Smith, Jr., "the practice at home is more nearly imitated in this and New Jersey, than in any other Province upon the continent."[10] So pleasing was the British analogy to provincial political leaders that they wove it into their language where they could: "we have no other news in Town but Parliamenteering" wrote the well-known New York City politician Henry Holland prior to the 1761 New York election.[11] By attempting to bring provincial laws into close conformity with British statutes, by replicating British legal procedures, and by describing colonial election scrambles in terms designed to invoke the dignity and authority of Parliament, New Yorkers tried to reassure themselves that they could share the blessings of ordered liberty that the British constitution apparently could bestow.

The considerable attention members of New York's elite paid to their constitution did not arise solely from their hopes of checking their contentious politics with mixed and balanced government. They believed that as a royal colony, and as a strategically located outpost of British authority among the northern colonies, New York had a particular obligation to represent British society at its best. Moreover, because English speakers were a minority in late seventeenth-century New York, they feared for their identity and aggressively pushed their vision of an anglicized society on a large Batavianized population.[12] British dominance in the eighteenth century did little to arrest old apprehensions, and breast-beating Anglophilia thus continued to have a prominent place in public dialogue.

Another fear of New York's politically literate elite also went back into the seventeenth century and had to do with the colony's origins. New York was, in fact, a conquered province; common law traditions essential for the adoption of mixed government and a balanced constitution could come to a conquered land only through appropriate treaties, charters, and grants. As the Virginian John Randolph pointed out, it was not at all clear how such a foundation had been poured in post-conquest New York.[13] Frightened by the implications of such reasoning, New Yorkers rarely addressed the issue and collectively tried to brazen their way to safe ground.[14] Boldly they asserted, as though there could be no legitimate questioning of the position, that New York was no different from any colony of settlement in which "English[men] . . . [carried] as much of law and liberty with . . . [them] as the nature of things [would] . . . bear."[15] Judged by the frequency and vociferousness of their claims, New Yorkers believed unquestionably that the British constitution was in part theirs, and that mixed government and a balanced constitution were part of the same heritage.

While their claim to the British constitution seemed to promise New Yorkers a respectable orderliness in political affairs, standards—or the expectation of such—were all it in fact offered. Consensus on the broad outlines of colonial government and on the desirability of an orderly public could not in itself bring the harmony that many hoped would follow. Disagreements began with efforts to think through the application of the precepts of mixed and balanced government to New York, and went from there. Even a quick glance could lead to reservations about the congruence between the constitutions of Britain and New York. There was no range of estates or social orders that provided the underpinning for mixed government, and governor, council, and assembly were simply not the same as king, lords, and commons. As for the balanced constitution, conflicts over the relative power of the governor and the assembly wracked the province for decades.[16] Lawyers argued over which institutions and powers actually came to New York with British custom, what place the colonial legislature should play in modifying British tradition, and how recent British statute law might be adopted by a colony.[17] The very determination of New York lawyers to draw on British statutes willy-nilly could produce confusion rather than order, for as John Randolph cautioned his New York friends, once "we wade into the Statutes, no Man can tell what the Law is."[18] Amid the efforts to apply British constitutional and legal doctrine to New York, some individuals acknowledged their difficulties. "The constitution of the Plantations at Present, I own I do not understand," lamented Cadwallader Colden—perhaps the only admission of incomprehension he ever made in a very long life.[19] Others offered a rationale for the dilemma. The province was young, and "the Constitution of . . . [the] Country . . . [was] not yet settled."[20]

There were, of course, some prescriptions offered. New Yorkers should worry less about popular rights and put their faith in the governor, because local privileges ultimately depended on the prerogative.[21] Or they should redouble their efforts to take the "Laws of England for a Pattern," for that would lead to political behavior "more consistent" with "Sense and Prudence."[22] But most public figures came to realize that agreement on the desirability of mixed government and a balanced constitution, and a desire to emulate the British in constitutional and legal affairs, would not bring the kind of political harmony it seemed to promise. New Yorkers needed to look elsewhere for concepts that might provide order and legitimacy in their singular world.

The Relevance and Irrelevance of the Landed/Mercantile Distinction

Colonial New Yorkers frequently tried to look beyond the principles of the British constitution to other value-laden concepts drawn from the English political lexicon, thereby to secure for themselves some of the legitimacy those terms conferred. Responding to such clues, historians have focused on those terms occasionally to suggest that they reflected larger organizing principles for New York's diverse sociopolitical world.

"Landed," "mercantile" (alternatively "commercial" or "trade"), and "monied" interests constituted one of the important sets of categories in English public thought during the first half of the eighteenth century. The last of this threesome was almost always a term of opprobrium, used to designate those involved in the stock-jobbing of London's financial markets. The other two described important, time-honored national interests representing the productive capacity of the nation. The landed interest was closely connected with the idea of civic virtue. Independent landowners had a responsibility to withstand the corrupting social and political influence of society's monied men and thereby preserve the traditional liberties that the British constitution conferred. The mercantile interest was not as pristine as its landed counterpart, for commercial activities could easily take a surreptitious slide into the world of finance. But overall, mercantile activities were perceived as benign, either because traders practiced a frugality that was an expression of virtue, or because they were essential to the vitality of contemporary society. In either case, merchants were associated in a positive way with the protection of English liberties.[23]

During the late seventeenth and early eighteenth centuries, New Yorkers were looking for language that would help transform their recently revolutionary society into an orderly part of the Anglo-American world. Because of the positive connotations of landed and mercantile interests, and also because these terms seemed to capture some of the tensions that existed between New York City and its hinterland, they readily entered the New York political vocabulary.[24] The most intense focus upon the landed/mercantile dichotomy began in 1713, when Governor Robert Hunter and his friend Lewis Morris, Sr., publicly condemned a land tax as regressive, and argued that taxes on imports were a far more equitable way of meeting the colony's financial needs.[25] When Hunter, Morris, and Robert Livingston subsequently put together a legislative coalition pledged to pay off New York's accumulated debts and provide the administration with a five-year revenue, they did so without resort to a land tax. The Public Debt Acts were funded on an excise and on import duties to run through the 1730s, and the Revenue Act on import levies and a tonnage duty.[26] The chief opposition to this settlement was a group of politicians, led by a handful of prominent New York City merchants, who finally ousted many of Morris's allies from the assembly in 1726 and who in turn dominated the provincial government through 1737.[27] The merchants were far more critical of taxes on commerce than the Morris-led faction had been. When they gained power in the mid 1720s, they cut the number and amount of import duties, but they refused to remove the tonnage duty on trading vessels entering New York harbor and added a land tax component to the Revenue Act.[28]

Despite the surface evidence and occasional contemporary references to landed and mercantile interests, there is still reason to be skeptical of any fundamental political division between the two. For example, the reputed landed leader Lewis Morris, Sr., had no compunctions about drawing up bills that shifted more tax weight from commerce to property. In the six years during which Morris and Robert Livingston ran the assembly under Governor Burnet (1720–1726), they raised twice as much money on land taxes as the allegedly mercantile faction did during the ten subsequent years in which the latter dominated the legislature (1726–1737).[29] On the merchant side, there is considerable evidence that the supposedly mercantile faction led by Adolphe Philipse represented more than New York City and Albany countinghouses: after a brief experiment with a small land tax, they refused to renew it in 1728; three years later, they withstood Governor Montgomerie's urgings to pass a land tax from which to fund Indian trade expenses and instead passed an ultimately ineffective sumptuary tax on wigs; in the early 1730s, they decided that a tonnage duty was not such a bad idea after all, for they reimposed that alleged bane of the merchant community; and during the same November 1734 session, they levied unprecedented import duties on cider, pork, and beer to cover defense expenditures that had hitherto always been funded by land taxes.[30] To return to the supposed landed interest, once their representatives regained some influence in 1737, the only change they made in taxation was to cut the import duty rates on wine and spirits.[31]

If we choose to look at the personnel of the two factions, the differences between them become even less clear. While it is true that Lewis Morris, Sr., had little truck with commerce, Morris was the exception that probes the rule.[32] Land-tax opponents such as Robert Livingston and his sons were involved in a range of commercial activities, and the Philipse clan, which was predominantly associated with the mercantile faction, was one of New York's well-known landed families.[33] The resources of landownership spilled over into commerce, and mercantile profits were often ploughed into land. Knowledgeable contemporaries were no better at establishing clear-cut economic distinctions than historians have been. The provincial councillor George Clarke was sure that the elevation of Adolphe Philipse to the assembly speakership in 1725 ensured that the legislature would become "mercantile interest oriented."[34] Surveyor-general Cadwallader Colden was equally sure that "the leading Men" of the "present [1726] Assembly" were among those deeply interested in the "large Tracts" of New York land patented in earlier days.[35]

Disagreement over land taxes and import duties had a much more ragged character than any imputed socioeconomic distinction between political factions suggests. The issue first came to the fore in 1713 because Governor Robert Hunter and Lewis Morris, Sr., chose to make it an issue.[36] They were intent on generating a revenue for the executive, yet New York had already been burdened with land taxes during Queen Anne's War. (Between 1706 and 1711, the provincial government levied over £30,000 in land taxes on provincial residents in order to finance the war with France.)[37] The only way for Hunter to get his revenue, then, was through a reimposition of the import duties that colonials believed had been subject to such abuse and had become so unpopular under Cornbury. The way Hunter and Morris set out to overcome this legacy was ingenious. They took to the press and to the hustings, setting up a clamor that there were politicians in the community who *would* impose a land tax.[38] In order that freeholders might avoid the malevolence of such men, Hunter and Morris advised them to choose representatives willing to acquiesce only in the taxation of commerce.[39] In working to make "the very name Land Tax . . . odious," the outspoken duo cast themselves as local heroes, bringing many New Yorkers around to the view that a revenue from imposts was the lesser evil of taxation alternatives.[40] Nor were Hunter and Morris entirely insincere. Both men apparently believed that land taxes were more onerous for most New Yorkers than any set of commercial duties.[41]

Those who eventually opposed the Hunter settlement made up an odd legislative rump that demonstrated how fragmented New York politics could be. One outspoken opponent of the Public Debt and Revenue Acts was Suffolk County merchant Samuel Mulford. While we cannot be sure how large Mulford's following was, it is clear that he spoke for traditional New England parochialism. The aged Mulford was an ethnocentric English provincial of Puritan intensity, old commonwealth leanings, and a deep distrust of unelected officials. To Mulford, Hunter was far more dangerous than the haughty Cornbury had been, because Hunter hid gubernatorial venality under affability and an apparent honesty. Mulford was sure that once the legislature handed the governor a customs revenue, Hunter would become as tainted as his predecessors. While it was impossible to control the appetites of placemen like Hunter, it was possible to keep them hungry. Because a land tax was a direct tax, and because the existing land tax occasioned by the recent wars with New France was still so burdensome, assemblymen would never grant an additional land levy at a rate higher than the minimum necessary to support government. In turn, the governor would never have sufficient revenue or power to bribe assemblymen into furnishing a more lavish gubernatorial income. Mulford wanted only land taxes, not because customs duties impeded commerce but because taxes on land

and chattels were the only effective means of controlling executive power.[42]

Mulford's political allies were strange bedfellows for a man so gnarled by austerity and moral rigor. The handful of New Yorkers who joined him (in far less vocal fashion) to resist the Hunter settlement and suggest a preference for land taxes were some of the city's most affluent and worldly men. Governor Hunter observed that the core opposition to his Debt and Revenue Acts were a few individuals who recognized that the increased liquidity that the issuance of paper money under the Public Debt Acts promised would undermine their economic hegemony. Prior to this legislation, they enjoyed a virtual monopoly of credit in New York City, and they had used that power to keep competitors from challenging their preeminence.[43] Some who opposed Hunter and Morris had additional commercial reasons for their opposition to imposts. Stephen DeLancey's heavy involvement in the wine trade, for example, meant that he would be hard hit by tonnage and impost duties.[44] Other opposition welled up from a variety of sources, including the old Leislerian/anti-Leislerian battlefields and the peripheral places some individuals currently occupied as political "outs." Whatever peculiar mix of motivations moved the Hunter/Morris opposition, its ranks did not represent anything like a unified mercantile interest. New York's merchants were clearly divided in their attitudes toward the Revenue and Debt Acts and the efficacy of a land tax.

After a brief hiatus, provincial taxation again became a contentious issue in the late 1720s and early 1730s.[45] A recession had devastated the New York City economy, and politicians were searching for some response to the crisis. The Philipse faction decided to cut taxes, hardly a difficult decision, given the fact that prior good times and population growth had produced a budgetary surplus.[46] One of the noteworthy features of the subsequent legislation[47] was its termination of the £1,200 per annum land tax that lawmakers had imposed as part of the Revenue Act two years earlier.[48] This action, and the subsequent legislative reimposition of the tonnage duty, certainly cut the ground out from under the Morris/Alexander faction, whose leaders were in favor of both changes.[49] But had the Morris/Alexander group wished to, they might have used the well-known 1733 Westchester County by-election (in which Lewis Morris, Sr., stood successfully for an assembly seat) to reassert their claim to be the chief defenders of landed interests.[50] They felt, however, that they could gain greater advantage by trying to impose English court/country distinctions on local politics and by appropriating what they judged to be a compelling country position for themselves.[51] In a bizarre scene on the Westchester town green, the supposedly anti–land tax Morris/Alexander faction rallied behind the English country, anti-Walpolian cry of "No Excise" (the Excise tax in New York was universally agreed to be an acceptable tax, despite the scandalous way in which it was administered),[52] while the supposed mouthpiece of mercantile New York, the Philipse faction, chanted "No Land Tax" in reply.[53] Four years later, in the heated battles of 1737, the Morris/Alexander leaders confirmed their apostasy; a little-noticed part of their platform was "an easing" of imposts "by a land tax."[54] But that was the swan song of the land-tax issue in its old form.

By the 1730s, insofar as New Yorkers raised questions about taxation, they framed them in the context of disagreements over the apportionment and assessment of taxes on real and personal property, not over whether land taxes were a just means of generating revenue. All New Yorkers recognized that the renewal of British-French warfare in the 1740s and 1750s meant onerous land taxes (that is, taxes on visible estates, including land); that was the only way enough money could be raised to fight the war. Compromises over who would pay how much were hammered out in the assembly, where the various land taxes were apportioned among counties, and within the counties themselves when quotas were assigned to constituent towns, manors, and precincts.[55]

On three occasions the issue of tax assessments bobbed to the surface. It did so because New York land taxes customarily excluded unimproved land, and some rightly perceived that the chief beneficiaries of this were well-to-do investors and manorial lords who tied up huge tracts of land in hopes of future sale or development.[56] Among other campaign proposals during the mid 1730s, the Morris/Alexander group suggested taxing unimproved land, but no debate is recorded.[57] The first time the issue drew comment was in the early 1750s, when a writer, probably associated with Cadwallader Colden, who was then surveyor-general, attacked the tax break large landholders enjoyed.[58] Finally, in the mid 1760s, rumors that Parliament might impose a colonial land tax made the issue a point of contention among political factions that sought advantage from drawing attention to ostensible landed/commercial divisions.[59]

Aside from Colden and one or two others, however, there were virtually no New Yorkers who openly and unambiguously addressed the question.[60] In fact, taxation of unimproved land was a non-issue in most of the colony. Those who would have profited most from such a policy—artisans and the working poor in both town and country—were never able to break into the public dialogue enough to articulate whatever desire some may have had to soak the rich landowners. Small-to-middling landholders, whose farms, leaseholds, and speculative holdings frequently included unimproved acreage, were unwilling to press for a reform that would cost them pence, even if it would bring pounds to the public coffers from the purses of large landowners. Finally, there was no merchant community sufficiently separate from, and antagonistic to, the owners of large land tracts to raise the taxa-

tion issue. Many merchants themselves were deeply involved in land speculation, while those who were not were likely to have business partners,
family, friends, potential in-laws, and political allies whose assets included
unimproved land.[61]

Insuperable difficulties thus confronted any effort to make the distinction between landed and commercial interests central to New York politics,
but it is important to emphasize that contemporaries did use the terms in
revealing ways. Politicians in New York City and Albany who had genuine
mercantile roots displayed them proudly and worked them for the advantages they bestowed. And they were quick to drape the mantle of mercantile
prestige around the shoulders of political allies whose genteel life experiences included no bona fide commercial credentials.[62] Moreover, they were
equally adept at defining the limits of the commercial community in such a
way as to exclude political adversaries of various backgrounds.[63] Because
their place at the apex of the urban social hierarchy proclaimed success, and
because wealth gave them a large stake in the community, public-minded
merchants felt they had a right to political prominence. And once a collection of merchants had seized the initiative and successfully asserted themselves as the political voice of the commercial community in provincial
affairs, others were often reluctant to criticize or consciously undermine the
credibility of mercantile leadership.[64] But when differences among merchants became too intense to be muffled, the issue of who spoke for the
merchant community was worth squabbling over because of the cachet
custodial claims could carry.[65]

That influence was rooted, not simply in merchant power, but in society's
usual willingness to accept the special character of commercial qualifications
for leadership. Mercantile accomplishments apparently entailed a breadth of
vision, and independent observation could ostensibly verify that merchants
provided the entrepreneurial efforts, capital, and employment vital for New
York's economic success. Merchant apologists proffered, and freeholders
occasionally quaffed, drafts drawn from the springs of British public
thought that complimented mercantile accomplishment and credited commercial activity with major contributions to the superior character of British
society. Because of the fine aura that hovered about the notion of a commercial or mercantile interest in the minds of New Yorkers, aggressive politicians frequently introduced the terms in public debate, hoping to manipulate them to advantage.

Mention of a landed interest was far less frequent in the later colonial
years than that of its commercial counterpart. Because large landowners
were frequently involved in the kinds of commercial and entrepreneurial
endeavors that would develop country estates into complex economic enterprises, they never acquired the one-dimensional socioeconomic profile that

merchant interests did.[66] Yet the notion of a landed interest was ever present in political discourse. Large landholders were such a prominent feature of New York society they could not be overlooked, and the idea of landowner-ship was an essential component of the various currents of early modern Anglo-American thought that flowed through the colony. If pressed, many colonials would have agreed that land was the foundation of independence, a bastion of English liberties, and a guarantor of civic virtue. Given the positive values associated with landownership, it is not surprising that large landholders viewed themselves as a particularly important component of New York's body politic.[67]

Nor was that sense of self-importance confined to the major landholding branch of any family. Despite the diverse occupations and varied circum-stances of members of collateral branches of prominent landed families, many manifested a strong sense of identification with the ancestral estate.[68] This produced a landed consciousness among different groups of New Yorkers that extended far beyond the confines of manor life and inspired considerable confidence among spokespersons for landed property and privilege.[69] At the same time, however, there was never any indication in New York that major landholding families were capable of coming together to form any durable political alliance. On the contrary, New York history is rife with examples of intermittent conflict among the scions of the prov-ince's original land barons.

Unquestionably, both landed and commercial interests did exist in colo-nial New York, and public debate frequently recognized that fact. In refer-ring to such groups, pundits were not only acknowledging a reality but trying to impose some sense of sociopolitical order on provincial affairs by describing New York society in terms that derived a degree of legitimacy from their place in British public thought.[70] In so doing, contemporaries oversimplified and distorted. They offered no compelling rationale for their colony's political divisions, and they failed to provide analytical categories of much more than marginal use in the retrospective analysis of New York politics.

The Relevance and Irrelevance of the Court/Country Dichotomy

The distinction between court and country has come to be perceived as one of the most important organizing principles of early modern Anglo-American politics.[71] Originally used to distinguish between supporters and opponents of the Stuart monarchs during the early decades of the seven-teenth century, the terms gained new life with the discrediting of the Tories and the establishment of Whig ascendency in Parliament after 1714. During much of the early and mid eighteenth century, divisions between court and country constituted one of the main fissures in British national politics. Contemporaries distinguished between, and often identified themselves in relationship to, court and country interests. The former was composed of courtiers filling executive and administrative posts, who from the purchase they gained thereby tried to control the popular institutions of government to their own advantage. The latter was made up of gentry and a smattering of ideologues who had no interest in assuming power and who believed that their self-imposed obligation of using their parliamentary influence to criticize the court and defend English constitutional principles was essential for the preservation of liberty.

The British court interest was closely identified with the vast changes that had transformed English government between the Glorious Revolution and the Hanoverian succession. During these turn-of-the-century decades, the financing of European warfare had prompted the court to cooperate with London financiers in establishing the Bank of England, which greatly increased the financial resources of the government, allowing the Crown to establish a standing army, increase the bureaucracy, and augment the ranks of placemen and retainers. According to their self-evaluation, courtiers pursued these policies in order to preserve British liberty and advance the national interest of Great Britain. Increased governmental power was necessary to assert Britain's international interests, and domestically to prevent anarchy, promote order, protect property, and guarantee freedom. The extension of court patronage among members of Parliament was meant to overcome whatever objections they might have to these and other liberty-enhancing Crown policies.

The country view of the court was a far more jaundiced one. In the eyes of the country interest, recent government policies had been a disaster. The public prominence of financial interests, the political influence of money, the burgeoning bureaucracy, and the standing army seriously threatened English liberty. These innovations, and the resulting ability of the court to seduce parliamentarians with patronage, constituted a system of corruption that threatened Britain's balanced constitution. The corruption of the court was the corruption of power seeking to augment itself, to undermine country autonomy, and to demoralize those who stood for the verities of independence, selfless service, and guardianship of the ancient constitution.

In counterposing themselves to corrupt court minions, the country spokespersons offered a vision of national politics dominated by civic virtue. By definition, country politicians would not seek office. Their purpose was independent service in Parliament, wherein they could maintain high standards of rectitude, provide careful, disinterested consideration of local and national affairs, and, above all, work to preserve Britain's mixed and balanced constitution by containing the contagion of court corruption. Given their way, the countrymen would have insisted on substituting a well-regulated militia for a standing army, instituting sufficient electoral reform to make it more difficult for court interests to buy elections, and passing place bills that would have impeded the ability of government retainers to sit in Parliament. The purpose of these changes was to weaken the forces of corruption and augment the power of the gentry. But such preferences in fact posed little threat to the court, for the aversion in the name of virtue of the independent gentlemen politicians to the compromises office entailed ensured their confinement to the backbenches of Parliament.

To the court, not surprisingly, the country view of politics was misguided, if not absurd. It ignored the needs of the modern state, encouraged license among members of the body politic, and would create an unworkable system of government, in which the Crown would be unable to carry crucial legislative initiatives through Parliament. This brought the court back to its own view of itself. It was the court-sponsored modern system of British politics, not a romanticized vision of a mythic past, that guaranteed English liberty.

The conception and language of the court/country dichotomy came to North America along with many other facets of British political culture. The focal point of the court interest was, of course, the colonial governor. Unlike the situation in Britain, where a system of ministerial power and corruption had replaced the prerogative as the main threat to liberty, the royal colonies were confronted with representatives of the Crown whose prerogative claims were reminiscent of seventeenth-century English monarchical powers.[72] While it seems logical that a more extensive prerogative should have made the colonial court interest more dangerous than its British counterpart, that was not in fact so. The reasons for this were twofold: first, the strong popular sentiment that supported the assemblies' countervailing claims of power kept the governors relatively weak; second, the chief executive and his advisors had few of the means that the British court had at its disposal to seduce popular politicians.[73] There were few rotten boroughs, and no Bank of England, financial interest, standing army,[74] secret service fund, permanent revenue, or extensive civil list. The rewards a governor had at his command to bestow on malleable assemblymen were a few provincial offices that brought high status, easy access to land grants, and a few local patronage positions—hardly the stuff of a bloated court interest. Nonetheless, condemnation of the court did not fade away. Some popular politicians found the self-image that the country rhetoric offered deeply compelling. They were attracted to a language of self-portrayal that emphasized their independent character, their selfless service, their triumph over the passions, their steely resistance to temptation, and their determination to defend popular rights and the time-hallowed principles of the English constitution. In vociferously claiming for themselves a monopoly of civic virtue, they simultaneously condemned the colonial court (such as it was) for large-scale corruption. Country virtues and court vices were two sides of the same coin. Would-be country politicians could show how virtuous they were by emphasizing the snares the governor and his friends set out.

The way in which the court/country distinction affected New York's political factions is best illustrated by referring to the period when it was most frequently used by contemporaries. In the 1730s, James Alexander, Lewis Morris, Sr., and Jr., and a number of their allies sponsored John Peter Zenger's *Weekly Journal* to mount a country attack against what they viewed as Governor Cosby's court faction—led by Cosby himself, the provincial secretary and councillor George Clarke, Speaker Adolphe Philipse, and Francis Harrison, a placeman. The paper drew attention to Cosby's disrespect for colonial property rights, his alleged fraternization with the French for personal gain, and his demands for kickbacks from land patentees. Most insidious were his attempts to corrupt the New York constitution by stacking the supreme court with supporters, creating equity courts by decree, influencing the legislative council in its deliberations, and rewarding his supporters with various local patronage appointments.[75] In criticizing these court excesses, the Morris/Alexander faction laid claim to being a country opposition. They were for an independent judiciary and an autonomous legislative council; they supported the creation of a court system by assembly, not by executive fiat; and they championed liberty of the press and protested against the arbitrary dismissal of local officials. Morris/Alexander supporters coupled these demands with others intended to produce a more open assembly, free from influence: triennial elections, elected sheriffs, place bills, and equal representation.[76] Finally, by advocating reimposition of a tonnage duty on foreign ships, a reduction in the official interest rate, a provincial loan office, and bounties for various provincially produced commodities, they appealed to the economic self-interest of the many New Yorkers who had been hurt by a long depression.[77]

Given the breadth of appeal of the Morris/Alexander country platform, it is not surprising that the faction gained popular support. But it was a tough battle. The chief reason for this was not that Governor Cosby's court influence was particularly great (it was not), but that New York freeholders had a longer memory than Morris and Alexander would have preferred. During the decade and a half prior to the founding of the *New-York Weekly Journal*, the Morrises, James Alexander, and others had constituted as much of a court faction as New York would ever know.[78] As Bradford's *New-York Gazette* reminded the public, their earlier careers hardly squared with present claims. Members of their faction had accepted a chancery court as long as a friendly governor presided over it; they had never challenged the governor's right to sit in the legislative council as long as the governor was their ally; they had attacked the assembly's right to decide its qualifications for membership and its claim to decide supreme court judges' salaries; they had worked to make Governor Hunter's and Governor Burnet's influence pervasive among judges, councillors, and assemblymen; and they had encouraged Governor Burnet to prolong the life of the notorious "long Assembly" for ten years in order to continue their influence in that body.[79] As their opponents argued, there was considerable difference between the current "Shew" and past "Reality."[80] These men were "Demogogues," not the country "patriots" they pretended to be.[81] Lewis Morris, Sr., had made a career out of heading popular protests, only to lose his enthusiasm once he had achieved his personal goals. And James Alexander was hardly cut from populist cloth. Alexander was as rich and conservative a lawyer as one could find in the colonies; his initial response to the two Morris's differences with Governor Montgomerie was that they should have tried ingratiation for a time rather than mounting an immediate attack.[82] Even in the midst of their dispute with Cosby, the Morris/Alexander crew were prepared to fold up their tents of protest if they could gain a minimum of face-saving concessions and readmittance to the governor's confidence.[83]

While contemporaries were somewhat skeptical of the country credentials of the Morris/Alexander faction, they also harbored reservations about the *Weekly Journal*'s characterization of Adolphe Philipse as a court whore. James Alexander and his friends hated Philipse (they referred to him as "Ape") for upstaging them in provincial politics.[84] And that is the point. Philipse had opposed them with *popular* policies when the Morris/Alexander cabal constituted Governor Burnet's inner circle.[85] No matter his current collusion with Cosby, Philipse was on record as being against a court of chancery, for more frequent elections, and in support of revenue grants of shorter duration.[86] Nor did his record end with assembly rights. During his speakership, Philipse had refused to renew the taxes on salt and molasses sponsored by Morris and Governor Burnet—taxes that always pinched hard on middling tradesmen, small farmers, and especially the working poor.[87]

The question of just how "country" the Morris/Alexander group was hung over the faction until the 1737 election. In the new assembly of that year, the group apparently gained a slight preponderance. James Alexander headed a successful New York County slate, while Lewis Morris, Jr., was elected speaker of the house.[88] Once in control (if precarious control) of the assembly, the Morris/Alexander faction self-destructed. True to form, Lewis Morris, Sr., abandoned the faction that had worked so hard on his behalf.

When he received an offer from the Crown to head New Jersey's government in 1738, he sailed across the Hudson to become a prerogative-conscious, court-minded governor.[89] Morris's son, Lewis, Jr., did his part to destroy the faction's credibility as a country party, principled against arbitrary dismissal of government officials, by exploiting Lieutenant-Governor George Clarke's willingness to change all the judicial and militia officers in Westchester County for Morris's nominees.[90] Only James Alexander stayed the course to stand for reelection in 1739. But his halfhearted efforts in that contest demonstrated his desire to distance himself from contentious electoral politics and ease his way back into a council chair and his once-lucrative law practice.[91]

Weekly Journal editorials reflected the changed circumstances. The paper that had so recently arraigned gubernatorial power and court behavior quickly developed a new theme. Lieutenant-Governor Clarke, whom the *Journal* had recently characterized as "a true politician, so that when he said anything, you might be sure he would do the contrary," had become a "man of brains" who promised exemplary leadership.[92] Because good government was the essential underpinning of liberty, those who had been elected in opposition to Cosby and his "Tools" had a duty "to agree" with the lieutenant-governor.[93] "The word Courtier . . . [could give] no Scandal under a wise and good Administration."[94] In "*always* be[ing] for his Country," "a good Common Wealth's Man" might "*sometimes* . . . [be] for the Governor."[95] Just like King William's and Queen Anne's courtiers, Lieutenant-Governor Clarke's supporters would be remembered as "Honourable" men.[96]

As for the assembly session that followed the 1737 election, it produced some important legislation. Reforms included a triennial act (which the Crown disallowed in 1738), an annual, rather than multiyear grant of revenue to the governor and civil officers of government, a loan office from which cash-short freeholders could borrow against their real estate holdings, and an unenforceable lowering of the official interest rate on loans to 7 percent.[97] Frequently, these innovations have been credited to the Morris/Alexander faction, but once Adolphe Philipse regained a New York City assembly seat in a by-election, hard on the heels of the 1737 general election, he was as much in the forefront of legislative change as anyone. Telling, too, is the observation that once the Morris/Alexander and Philipse faction leaders shared assembly power, *neither* was too willing to embrace the rash of reforms that propagandists had promised during the preceding few years.

So who was court and who was country? It depended on the time and the observer. For much of the Hunter and Burnet governorships, the Morris/Alexander group implied that they were court and their opponents country.[98] James Alexander admitted as much in 1728 when he compared

Adolphe Philipse to the well-known Massachusetts Bay politician Elisha Cook, Jr.[99] In the early 1730s, however, the sponsors of the *Weekly Journal* made a strenuous effort to alter perceptions; the Morris/Alexander faction was to be country, the Philipse group court. By the late 1730s, Alexander still preferred to keep the hard-fought-for country designation, but to no avail. His sometime confidant Cadwallader Colden concluded that since the Morris/Alexander rapprochement with Clarke, the Philipse faction had become an "Anti-Court party."[100] Colden was unwilling to call the Philipse faction a country party, but his implication was that the Morris/Alexander crew had returned to the court mold. The second lord of Livingston Manor, Philip Livingston, was more direct. Noting that the seating of Adolphe Philipse in the assembly after his by-election victory was "ag't ye Inclination of [?] Some of ye Court Party," Livingston went on to observe that, in politics, "we [New Yorkers] Change Sides as Serves our Interest best not ye Countries."[101] That remark reinforces the point that the editor William Bradford tried to make in his *New-York Gazette* to his counterpart Peter Zenger of the *Weekly Journal*. Those who wrote for Zenger, Bradford charged, "found Fault only because others . . . [were] In and they . . . [were] Out."[102] The Morris/Alexander writers took umbrage at this, but they had always asserted much the same of their opponents, whom they accused of being "woolen Mittens that . . . [would] fit either Hand."[103] New York's political situation was not as simple as that, of course, for opposing factions did emphasize somewhat different policies, expressed themselves in dissimilar ways, and projected contrasting political styles, whether they were in opposition to or in the confidence of the governor. But the element of raw opportunism was ever present as well. There were few New York politicians who were not prepared to throw the "ins" out for the sake of their own advancement.

The distinction between court and country in early modern British politics is an important one, because it encompasses some of the fundamentals of both political thought and behavior. The terminology was widely used, and the issues that divided court from country were frequently aired. On the one hand, many individuals defended court policies and fully accepted the position that the Glorious Revolutionary settlement, and hence British liberty, depended on powerful ministers with strong financial and military resources and considerable control over the body politic. On the other, less numerous, but sharp-tongued, country radicals perceived modern British political development as a threat to traditional liberties under the constitution. Beneath the rhetoric lay corresponding behavioral differences. Court politicians who supported the turn-of-the-century revolution in governmental practices, and who vied among themselves for major political offices, were the dominant figures. They were surrounded by smaller fish, who hung round the edges of the eddies churned up by the powerful professional politicians, happy to deliver their school of parliamentary votes in return for the tidbits of place and pensions that the political sharks let come their way. Round about, in calmer waters, the country politicians watched, some with close interest, others with indifference. They were an odd collection of species, but one thing was certain: their values precluded metamorphosis into ministers or court minions.

The political waters of New York, in contrast, were murky, characterized by whorls and eddies of change, and filled with creatures whose relationships seemed to alter with the current. The court/country terminology fluctuated markedly in frequency of use and was often ambiguous in application. The political squabbles of the mid 1730s to some extent revolved around the court/country dichotomy, but thereafter the terms were integrated only sporadically into public debate. One important reason for this was that while politically literate provincials knew very well what the court/country designation meant in British public thought, and tried to use that ideology to advantage, it did not fit comfortably with the factional features of New York politics. During the 1730s, the Morris/Alexander and the Philipse factions shared a taste for both court life and popular credentials. Later on in the century, application of the court/country categories could produce truly bizarre results. Orthodox British canon had it, for example, that the country should be unsparing critics of court corruption and the use of a standing army. In New York, however, we find, not a country faction, but Governor Clinton's court hounding the popular DeLancey/Jones faction for the latter's creative use of public funds.[104] And during the 1750s and mid 1760s, those provincial politicians who tried hardest to associate themselves with English country thought had no interest in those parts of the tradition that went beyond philosophic radicalism. Despite relishing his role as a social critic, William Livingston defended nonresident voting and never pushed for either annual assemblies or a more equitable distribution of assembly seats.[105] Far from stressing the country canon of "no standing army," Livingston and his friends appreciated the presence of royal troops and welcomed their use in putting down the riots of the 1760s.[106] Moreover, it was the commission for good behavior of Livingston's bête noire, Chief Justice James DeLancey, that was the most important symbol in New York of the country principle of an independent judiciary.

There is, admittedly, a certain logic to the view that there always had to be a court/country split in New York. Whatever faction cooperated with the governor became a court faction, and whatever opposition developed, by virtue of its opposition, became a country faction. But it is equally true, and far more revealing, that between 1705 and 1775, no self-acknowledged court faction—that is, a faction that justified itself as a governor's party—met with any success in electoral politics. Structurally, the most courtlike faction to appear in New York during the post-Cornbury decades was the coalition that Governor Robert Hunter put together with the assistance of Lewis Morris, Sr., and Robert Livingston. Hunter's pleasing personality and adept political horse-trading were important ingredients of his success. By gilding his office with charm, emphasizing his British Whig leanings at appropriate times, relinquishing important gubernatorial powers, and spreading around the immense largesse of the Public Debt Acts, Hunter was able to quiet assembly opposition. But equally important for the success of his efforts to salvage part of the royal prerogative was his ability to establish a credible public agenda capable of drawing attention away from his court inclinations. In a cunning act of political prestidigitation, Hunter and Lewis Morris, Sr., portrayed themselves as redoubtable champions of a landed interest, and their slicing attacks on the merchant faction convinced many New Yorkers that Hunter's foes were too malevolent to represent the public at large.

Subsequent to Hunter's administration, there was but one effort to build a governor's party.[107] In the late 1740s and early 1750s, a rag-maned collection of raced-out nags from the Morris/Alexander faction and a sprinkling of gaunt-framed, coltlike neophytes occasionally worked on behalf of Governor Clinton.[108] They failed election miserably, not only because they were an ill-matched team, but also because they developed no effective public appeal for popular support. Voters would simply not endorse the political ambitions of those whose chief interest seemed to be a defense of the court.

The chief problem with the court/country typology as an explanatory device for New York politics is its reductionist nature. For the sake of symmetry with British politics and standardization in the colonies, it ignores the important differences between the colonies and Britain, and the sociology of politics peculiar to each province. One of the most important differences between Great Britain and New York was that in the former, county magnates who sat in Parliament were usually secure in their local eminence. Their social prominence, their paternalistic hegemony, and their control of local patronage were not things they came to through elected office; rather they were what put them into the House of Commons. In New York, however, county politicians faced a different world. Granted, social and economic power were prerequisites for provincial office, but election could considerably augment their preeminence, and, above all, the acquisition of local patronage power frequently *depended* on election. Because of this there could be no diffident, independent country politicians analogous to those in Great Britain. New York's provincial politicians vied among themselves, on antiprerogative and other popular grounds, for electoral support. But their commitment to the electorate was never a promise of unqualified and continuous opposition. Loyalty to the Crown, and a desire for the increased local eminence that legislative influence could bring, meant that they would cooperate with various persuasive leaders whose aims were to establish an acceptable relationship with the colonial governor. The dominant paradigm of political behavior in mid eighteenth-century New York was not a court/country polarity but the partisanship implicit in the organization of popular and provincial Whig factions.

Popular and Provincial Whigs

From the 1720s through the early 1760s, New York politics was dominated by factions of "popular" and "provincial" Whigs.[109] Both repeatedly tried to gain control of the legislature by stressing their commitment to English rights and liberties. But once in command of the assembly, their members were usually prepared to work with the governor (assuming his receptivity) and to enjoy the perks of office. The existence of two types of factions does *not* mean that there were two continuous factions, one of each type. Discrete factions *always* dissolved with either the death or political eclipse of particular leaders. Nonetheless, there was enough similarity in the concerns of successive factions within each of the two groups, and in their language and style, to demonstrate significant continuity.

A popular Whig faction first coalesced under the leadership of Adolphe Philipse during the 1720s. The faction began as an opposition to Governor Burnet, Governor Hunter's successor, who continued his predecessor's close association with Lewis Morris, Sr., and Robert Livingston. Whereas Hunter had been smart enough to keep the very capable Adolphe Philipse neutralized by membership in the council, Burnet was not. He threw Philipse out of that body in 1720 for taking too active a hand in running New York government between Hunter's departure and his own arrival.[110] Philipse immediately began to build a popular political base. He entered the assembly in a by-election in 1722, took over the speakership from the terminally ill Robert Livingston in 1725, and gained reelection at the head of a strong legislative following when Burnet dissolved the infamous "long assembly" in 1726.

During the 1720s, Philipse emphasized several popular issues. Two of these were explosive ones that related to the governor's power. Knowing that extended revenue grants to the executive, and the continuation of a friendly assembly contributed to the governor's autonomy, Philipse demanded revenue bills of short duration and frequent provincial elections.[111] A third and related issue centered on New York's chancery court. Authorized by executive decree and presided over by the governor, the chancery court was a symbol of the personal, unfettered power of the chief executive. What made the chancery court so dangerous was that it had the power to interpret land patents in a restrictive fashion and to enforce quitrent payments.[112] Once in control of the assembly, Philipse prompted the legislature to raise an outcry against the governor's exercise of chancery powers. According to Philipse and his followers, only an act of assembly could establish provincial courts.[113]

While Philipse's political prominence owed much to his espousal of popular causes, he also profited immensely from his close association with Stephen DeLancey. DeLancey was a New York City merchant who had arrived in the colony with other Huguenot émigrés in the 1680s and quickly allied himself through marriage with the rich, eminent, and numerous Van Cortlandt family.[114] DeLancey represented both the New York merchants who were dissatisfied with existing taxes on commerce and those New York and Albany traders who opposed Governor Burnet's efforts to stop the flow of Indian trade goods from New York City through Albany to Montreal. But DeLancey was more than the voice of one or two commercial factions; he had important popular credentials of his own. His suit was the one that had put the infamous Lord Cornbury in jail for debt.[115] He had provided security for the irascible Samuel Mulford when Governor Hunter's gang sicced the law on the old republican.[116] He was involved in a dispute with Governor Burnet over the latter's authority to intercede in a religious dispute in the French church.[117] And his argument with Chief Justice Lewis Morris over DeLancey's citizenship was integral to the assembly's claim of a right to jurisdiction over its own membership.[118] DeLancey thus became a symbol of both resistance to executive tyranny and assertion of immigrant rights. Rather than working to Philipse's disadvantage, DeLancey's reputation strengthened the speaker of the assembly, for DeLancey was an eighteenth-century rarity, an eminent politician willing to let others take the lead. Although excitable and disputatious in affairs that touched him personally, he gracefully gave way to Philipse on larger public issues.

Once in control of the legislature and rid of Governor Burnet, the Philipse faction was in a position to move from opposition into the confidence of the governor. And that is precisely what it did under Governors Montgomerie and Cosby. Philipse and his friends procured as much local patronage as they could, acquiesced in Governor Cosby's land kickback schemes, and supported the governor in his disputes with other provincial politicians. Philipse had his nephew, Frederick, and DeLancey his son, James, placed on the supreme court bench. When these two argued against Chief Justice Lewis Morris, Sr., for the legitimacy of a chancery court division in the supreme court in the Van Dam case, Adolphe Philipse and Stephen DeLancey said nothing about their earlier claim that executive decrees could not originate New York courts.[119]

While it supported Governors Montgomerie and Cosby, the Philipse faction maintained its popularity in the early 1730s. Its leaders continued to support frequent elections, handed out some tax relief, and, above all, revoked the invidious salt and molasses taxes that bore so heavily on the middling and lower classes.[120] When in the 1737 election the Morris/Alexander faction attacked the Philipse faction's record, the former group found it difficult to move beyond Catonic-tempered generalities.[121] They cited the depression of the early 1730s as evidence of Philipse's lack of concern for his country, and claimed that he had "advance[d] some of his Friends into Places of Profit and Honour" and "protect[ed] others . . . in their Oppresions and Injustices."[122] Yet support for the Cosby administration did prove more damaging to the Philipse faction than any of its leaders anticipated. Governor Cosby's determination to silence the *New-York Weekly Journal,* and the willingness of the Philipse-sponsored placemen to support him, tarred many of them with the brush of repression.[123] While Philipse and a few of his friends retained a good deal of personal popularity, his faction slowly disintegrated. By the end of the 1730s, it was clear that future definitions of popular politics would have to come from a new generation of leaders.

The politicians who finally pushed Philipse aside and took up the mantle of popular Whiggism were David Jones and James DeLancey. Both were associated, Jones in the assembly, DeLancey in the council, with legislative efforts to curtail the royal prerogative when it was under the custodianship of Lieutenant-Governor George Clarke.[124] And when Jones became speaker of the assembly in 1745, and DeLancey pried a chief justice's commission for good behavior from Governor Clinton in 1744, they were well positioned to lead a popular campaign against the governor. In their opposition to Governor Clinton during the latter part of King George's War, they engineered an assembly takeover of a number of powers that theoretically belonged to the Crown. In consultation with DeLancey, Jones and his assembly cohorts controlled military appropriations, determined who would build fortifications and supply troops, and tried to influence the management of Indian affairs. The assembly took over the nomination of various civil officers, voted whatever sums it wanted for services it alone valued, and continued to keep the officers of government on a short rein with annual appropriations and the voting of compensation to individuals rather than to offices.[125] Certainly the DeLancey/Jones faction used the wartime opportunity to augment the assembly's power, and in doing so it artfully practiced popular politics. Better the people's representatives should control the peculation a sumptuous military budget always occasioned than that a governor should threaten liberty by filling all the chairs at such a feast.

Although he was a member of an appointive rather than elective body, James DeLancey played a leading role in the popular politics of the 1740s.

He had the resources in council to turn it into a second house of opposition against a very unpopular governor and chief advisor. He was adept at working with and through others, as he demonstrated innumerable times in his relationships with leading assemblymen.[126] And he was a master at turning his judicial appointment into a symbol of commitment to popular power. By insisting that his commission be for good behavior rather than at pleasure, DeLancey personified the cause of an independent judiciary. Secure in his office, the chief justice was in a position to orchestrate carefully selected episodes of popular politics. In 1749, for example, when gunfire from a British man-of-war accidentally killed a New York woman, he claimed jurisdiction over the case for the supreme court.[127] By doing so, DeLancey asserted the preeminence of New York's civil courts over British-controlled military tribunals.

The most difficult test of the DeLancey/Jones partnership, and of DeLancey's commitment to popular politics, began with his appointment as Lieutenant-Governor. As the Crown's representative, he had to reconcile specific royal instructions to strengthen the prerogative with assembly claims that DeLancey himself endorsed under Governor Clinton. By exercising a patient dexterity, exploiting the coincidence of a new war, and winning the acceptance of Governor Charles Hardy when Hardy interrupted DeLancey's lieutenant-governorship, DeLancey encouraged British ministers to tolerate, if not become reconciled to the major gains the assembly had made vis-à-vis the governor since Lieutenant-Governor Clarke's days. Beyond that, DeLancey was able, just as Adolphe Philipse had been under less difficult circumstances, to associate himself with popular events and policies. During the French and Indian War, DeLancey managed to avoid blame for major catastrophes and bask in the reflection of such military highlights as Colonel William Johnson's victory at Lake George in September 1755. When the British military sparked cries of outrage over their billeting demands in Albany, DeLancey could say little officially, but he was most effective at communicating his support for the Albanians through his trusted spokespersons.[128] In situations in which he thought there would be no serious accounting to the British, DeLancey flouted his instructions with impunity. Despite orders to the contrary, for example, the lieutenant-governor extended the life of the provincial loan office that provided cheap mortgages to New Yorkers.[129]

The DeLancey nose for a popular issue was evident in other instances as well. Early in his tenure of office he supported legislation to prevent nuisance suits for "Trespass, Batteries and other Misdemeanors."[130] In doing so, he repudiated the arbitrary process by which the attorney-general could prosecute by information rather than through the more open procedure of a grand jury presentment.[131] Of greater significance, however, was his outspoken championing of the £5 Act. Through the mid 1750s, magistrates had summary jurisdiction over cases involving 40 shillings or less. If the case involved a larger sum, it had to be tried in a provincial court, where the fees of lawyers and court officers could dwarf the actual suit.[132] Recognizing that expansion of magistrate jurisdiction to the £5 level was a reform "the People" of New York had "so much at heart," David Jones and his legislative allies plumped for the change, and DeLancey was strong in support.[133] In this manner, the lieutenant-governor portrayed himself as an attentive dispenser of cheap and accessible justice, willing to sprinkle salt on the parasitic lawyers and court officials who leeched blood from the middling and poorer sort of citizen.[134]

Just as in the case of Adolphe Philipse, however, James DeLancey and David Jones found that they could not completely reconcile power with popularity. While the Philipse faction foundered on the Zenger trial and advancing age, the DeLancey/Jones coalition ran against the King's College controversy, local dissatisfactions with the war effort, and the political atrophy that frequently besets parties in power. After Speaker David Jones met electoral defeat in 1759, James DeLancey was left during the last months of his life much as Adolphe Philipse had been during his last years, a man still dressed in his popular Whig attire, but in clothes carefully cut for yesterday's ball.

Although they were two distinct factions, the Philipse and DeLancey/Jones coalitions had enough in common to demonstrate political continuity. Each faction was built on a strong popular base, each was able to reconcile power with popularity for substantial periods, each mounted strong attacks against provincial governors, each was committed to the expansion of assembly powers, and each brought a healthy dose of pragmatism to the political arena along with its Whiggish ideas. Similar in their approach to politics, as well as in many of their ideas, the Philipse and DeLancey/Jones factions established a strong tradition of popular Whiggism in mid eighteenth-century New York politics.

As in the case of the popular Whigs, two distinct factions of provincial Whigs played an important role in New York politics. The first of these was the well-known Morris/Alexander group, which existed for approximately a decade, beginning in the late 1720s. This faction was distinguished by the heavy emphasis it placed on preserving English rights and the piercing, Catonic tones in which its members expressed their concerns. Emphasis on the rights issues flowed naturally out of the political struggles of the time. When Governor Cosby set up a new exchequer court and removed Lewis Morris, Sr., as chief justice, James Alexander and his allies sprang to the attack, arguing that provincial courts could be established only by act of government, and that supreme court judges should be given the same tenure on good behavior as their English counterparts.[135] When Governor Cosby responded to criticism by indicting the newspaper editor Peter Zenger for libel, the Morris/Alexander cabal trumpeted the cause of freedom of the press. While the provincial Whigs did not ignore other traditional English rights, such as trial by jury, frequent parliaments, and redress of grievances, they referred to these rights largely to make the point that the whole roster of rights safeguarded by the British constitution was threatened when any one right was placed in jeopardy. If the governor laid siege to one right, he endangered them all.[136]

The language best suited to make the case that Morris and Alexander wanted to plead was the rhetoric of the English country opposition. Inspired by contributors as disparate as the real Whigs John Trenchard and Thomas Gordon and the Jacobite-tainted Tory Henry St. John, Viscount Bolingbroke, the country ideology could be compelling in its simplicity. Its main thrust, a biting critique of power, was so elastic that it could easily stretch to fit circumstances in the colonies.[137] According to the Morris/Alexander partisans, power had corrupted Governor Cosby and his "tools," and the rights of New Yorkers were at stake.[138] The closer Morris and Alexander purported to look, the more they apparently perceived a system of corruption emanating from the governor out into the body politic through the agency of his "under Tyrants."[139] Patronage, bribery, threats to private property, the avoidance of elections, incompetent placemen, and abuse of judicial powers, all bore witness to the imperiled state of liberty.

Although the provincial Whigs' countrylike litany included appeals to reason, its strength came from insistent claims to exclusive political understanding. There was no built-in tolerance for dispassionate inquiry. The provincial Whig strategy was to launch a friendly newspaper on an effusive stream of praise for the well-known English country writers. Thereafter, provincial Whig writers largely supplanted English texts with a flood of pieces that examined local politics in the light of a carefully selected and restricted list of country standards. What emerged was a strident, repetitive condemnation of governor and supporters: their intentions were malevolent, their corruption unbridled, and the consequences of their action the destruction of colonial liberties.

Of course, the provincial Whigs knew how to stop that process of corruption. What the Morris/Alexander faction advocated was more frequent elections, less financial autonomy for the governor, independent judges, and autonomous courts.[140] Because the Philipse cabal had sold out to power and were incapable of self-generated reformation, the Morrises, James Alexander, and their friends would seek office. Once elected or reappointed to government office, they would clean the Augean stables.

In 1737, they had their opportunity. After winning over a sizable number of legislators in the newly elected assembly, the Morris/Alexander coterie spearheaded the successful effort to tie the governor down to very specific annual appropriations, and it also supported the ill-fated Triennial Act. But the most important feature of the politics of the late 1730s was how quickly the Morris/Alexander faction changed its recent tastes. Its members shut off the spring-water spigot of select country effusions at Peter Zenger's door and turned once more to slake their thirst with the heady wine of place and office.[141] By 1739, the disintegration of the provincial Whig Morris/Alexander faction was complete.

Unlike the case of the popular Whigs, a long hiatus occurred before a new provincial Whig faction formed. It was not until the early 1750s that the partnership of William Livingston, William Smith, Jr., and John Morin Scott formed the nucleus of such a group. The one issue that fused the Livingston/Smith faction together was its rejection of public aid for an Anglican college. The group believed that a provincially supported Anglican college would strengthen New York's partial Anglican establishment and lead to both religious repression and political tyranny. If Anglicans could strengthen their interest, many would be tempted to extend the parish system throughout the province. Dissenters would be forced to pay taxes to Anglican clergy, church and state would embrace each other to augment their respective strengths, and Anglican placemen would swarm over the colony. Livingston and his friends offered as an alternative a publicly supported nondenominational college that allowed students to worship as they pleased, ensured that college governance was shared by representatives of different religions, and emphasized civic responsibility in its curriculum. A free or nondenominational college best suited the religious diversity of New York society.[142]

While the college dispute and the resulting antagonism between some Anglicans and various groups of dissenters was the main vehicle Livingston and Smith used to mobilize citizens against the political supporters of Lieutenant-Governor James DeLancey and David Jones, their campaign against King's College was only one part of a cacophonous critique of public affairs. In November 1752, Livingston and his partners had established their own journal, the *Independent Reflector*. The publication was more high-brow than Zenger's *Weekly Journal,* but it was just as partisan and just as influenced by some features of the English country ideology. In the first issue, Livingston promised that nothing should "deter" him "from vindicating the *civil* and *religious* RIGHTS of my Fellow-Creatures: From exposing the peculiar Deformity of public *Vice* and *Corruption;* and displaying the amiable Charms of *Liberty,* with the detestable Nature of *Slavery* and *Oppression.*"[143] Livingston was true to his promise. The pages of the *Independent Reflector* and the corpus of other polemical writing that he and his friends produced during the 1750s were filled with condemnation of religious and political tyranny, warnings of the expansive nature of power, and fretful urgings that men should mind their liberties. By cultivating the fears of power that the college disputes generated, and that the tribulations of the French and Indian War later emphasized, the provincial Whigs hoped to humble their popular Whig opponents.[144]

If the Livingston/Smith and Morris/Alexander factions clearly shared a provincial Whig heritage, there remained obvious differences between the two groups. Neither Livingston nor Smith had anything like the appetite for office that goaded the Morrises to a frenzy. And nominal Anglicans like Morris and Alexander were indifferent to the religious concerns that so preoccupied the Presbyterians Livingston and Smith. Most important were their different approaches to politics. Morris cut his teeth on turn-of-the-century politics, in which leaders combined radical and often egalitarian mobilization tactics with extreme claims to personal preeminence.[145] Morris dragged this unstable combination into the 1730s when he, his son, and James Alexander inspired one of the most radical movements in eighteenth-century colonial politics. With the help of appeals to economic and class interests, the Morris/Alexander faction raised a lower-class political interest in New York City that helped to push them into power.[146] Once they had achieved their goal, however, they quickly pulled down their vibrant radical colors, just as they toned down their country-tinged rhetoric and asserted their elitism in defense of social and political stability. As for Livingston and Smith, they had no use for gutter politics. They were social conservatives whose idea of radical politics was to manage petitioning drives. While Morris and Alexander were principally preoccupied with the worship of interest and how best to exploit their personal influence, Livingston and Smith were mainly fascinated with the logic of their own arguments and the potential power of social criticism. Only by dint of their literary efforts, in which they mingled specific issues of religious and educational freedom with some of the main nostrums of English country Whiggism did Livingston and Smith become factional leaders of note.

Different as the Morris/Alexander and Livingston/Smith factions were, their most important features were ones they shared. Both established themselves as credible political opponents to those in power by stressing their connection with Catonic standards. Both proselytized on behalf of threatened English liberties, both castigated officeholders for their depravity, their bent for power, and their encouragement of luxury and corruption, and both identified themselves as paragons of virtue. Neither faction saw any need to sacrifice themselves permanently to the self-denying standards of the English country movement. The Morris/Alexander group accepted office the moment it had the opportunity, and William Livingston was quite willing to spend his brief two years of service in the assembly (as one of the leading House members cooperating with old DeLancey/Jones foes) in winding up the French and Indian War. The selective way in which the Morris/Alexander and Livingston/Smith factions drew on country Whig discourse and the peculiar competitive framework of New York political life ensured that like their counterparts the popular Whigs, the two provincial Whig factions would create create their own clear tradition in New York politics.

The Character of Mid Eighteenth-Century Politics

The existence of popular and provincial Whig factions provided a rough order in New York politics during the mid eighteenth-century decades, for despite their common Whig orientation, they created two distinguishable political traditions. Foremost among their differences was the emphasis each placed on provincial rights. The popular Whigs made much of their concern for assembly rights, which stood, symbolically, of course, for the various rights colonists claimed under the British constitution. When the Philipse faction defended New Yorkers' right to answer the law in common law courts rather than plead in chancery, it did so by arguing that the establishment and regulation of provincial courts was a legislative responsibility, not a royal prerogative. The one time the DeLancey/Jones faction loudly pronounced the glories of freedom of speech, it did so on behalf, not of any individual radical or cabal of irksome social critics, but of the assembly, when Governor Clinton tried to prevent the printing of one of its representations.[147] In comparison to the popular Whigs, their provincial rivals demonstrated a willingness to strike out into controversial gray areas of civil and religious rights. The Morris/Alexander faction made its reputation defending John Peter Zenger's right to publish freely. The Livingston/Smith faction rode the cause of religious liberty to prominence during the King's College controversy.

The difference of emphasis on rights issues between popular and country Whigs was partly a product of the former's ability (an ability the provincial Whigs were never able to duplicate) of holding power for sustained periods. Because popular Whig factions frequently wielded power, they clearly tried to avoid raising potentially uncontrollable rights issues that might easily be turned against them. Conversely, because provincial Whigs were almost always in some state of opposition, they were far less constrained. Unburdened with the immediate responsibilities of protecting assembly rights and of the need to consider working out a modus vivendi with governor and council, their opportunism led them to try to stage epic confrontations that might move public opinion in their direction—hence the attraction for them of the potentially explosive issues of freedom of speech and religious liberty.

The fault line between popular and provincial Whigs, however, was by no means completely dictated by political circumstances. The popular Whigs' narrow focus on assembly powers and related constitutional rights reflected a predisposition toward a traditional way of thinking that conceptualized rights as privileges inherent in corporate integrity. The assembly's corporate weight was, in turn, the fundamental guarantor of other basic rights. While provincial Whigs did not reject this idea, they also saw rights as a general heritage shared by society members at large, although practically to be claimed only by those with the solid clout of status and wealth. In so doing, the provincial Whigs gave public expression to some of the strains of individualism that coursed through their provincial society.

A second difference between popular and provincial Whigs was the language in which they chose to demonstrate their rights' consciousness. Overwhelmingly, the popular Whigs expressed their concern for popular rights by means of constitutional and historical language that stressed the seventeenth-century British conflict between Parliament and Crown. The prerogative, they felt, was the preeminent threat to colonial liberties, and they concentrated on finding constitutional precedents and local legislative customs on which they could string their catch of governors.[148] The provincial Whigs usually fished an adjoining stream. Rather than subsuming colonial political conflicts under the old seventeenth-century English paradigm of Commons versus Crown, they incorporated both current colonial and historic English battles into the "modern" interpretation of court versus country. Whereas the popular Whigs straightforwardly argued their case from the principles of the British constitution, the provincial Whigs put a good deal of emphasis on the corruption that the modern court brought to bear on colonial virtue.[149]

A third difference between the two traditions was a matter of emphasis as well as language. Both popular and provincial Whigs drew on a common appreciation of natural law and natural rights. But when occasion demanded examination of the basis of authority, popular Whig spokespersons stressed the contractual relationship between magistrates and people, and the right of resistance should that contract be breached. The contract was straightforward, and the right to resist was a logical conclusion to be stated simply and clearly.[150] The provincial Whig approach to the same issue was somewhat more complicated. To be sure, provincial Whigs accepted the contractual relationship between rulers and ruled as fundamental. Their religious and political philosophies were firmly anchored in natural law. But when they left off religious and philosophic topics and turned to the political, they very often took the notion of contract for granted and focused more directly on the relationship between power and rights. Provincial Whigs never tired of pointing out that power was continuously conspiring against liberty, and that freeholders needed to respond with constrained resistance to tyranny within the existing set of constitutional relationships. More than their counterparts, the provincial Whigs simply assumed the contractual aspect of government and focused their attention on the immediate dangers that corruption, vice, and luxury presented to civic virtue.[151] Temperamentally, then, a number of New York's provincial Whigs were ideologues, much more so than their popular Whig counterparts. The provincial Whigs were represented by some of the colony's most persuasive writers, and they, in turn, tended to attract others who found catchphrase political argument to have great appeal.

If intellectual differences divided popular from provincial Whigs, their contrasting political styles broadened the gap between them considerably. The leaders of the two factions of popular Whigs were what the name implies, popular men who moved with éclat through their New York world. James DeLancey cultivated a reputation for love of wine and conviviality, his brother Oliver for tavern brawling, and Adolphe Philipse for excessive sexual appetites.[152] While the popular Whig leaders were arrogant in their elitism, they were also expansive in their social relationships, ready to share conversation and a bottle in all parts of the province.[153] When Frederick Philipse, Adolphe's nephew and James DeLancey's companion on the supreme court bench, died in 1751, he was lauded as "extremely social, . . . a good companion . . . [whose behavior] procured him a more unfeigned Regard than can be purchased with Opulence, or gained by Interest."[154] David Jones could charm any small gathering and even the austere Stephen DeLancey was known to make free with his "Mederra" for the sake of political companionship.[155] From the limited evidence we have, it seems clear that these men liked earthy metaphors, jocular irreverence, and a quick tongue.[156] James DeLancey clearly felt more comfortable trading army camp quips with General Monckton than he did writing official correspondence. "My Compliments to old Gates," DeLancey wrote, "as he has now no opportunity of seeing any Women, I hope he will recover his Eye sight."[157] Adolphe Philipse had no more love for the pen than did DeLancey; "his Deeds and Actions were always louder than his Words."[158] Far from being intellectuals, these politicians were men of practical affairs who lived robustly and delighted in their provincial eminence. As they swaggered through town and country, frequently flirting with violence, never shy about asserting their authority, and ever ready to join in the gaming pleasures of the day, they always seemed to trail a fetching cloak of affability. They sported a style of life that not only came into sympathetic touch—in taverns, brawls, and cockfights—with lower-class mores, but also appealed to many of the rough, self-made middling sort who rounded out New York's developing society.[159] It was not a style that would walk far in Philadelphia, but New York was no Quaker city.

The provincial Whigs were cut from a different cloth than their popular Whig cousins. Lewis Morris, Sr., it is true, enjoyed good conversation, fine wine, and a lively fiddle, but he loved a crowd only when he needed it. On various occasions during his public career, he worked hard to cultivate a following of common folk, but in every case, once his immediate political goal had been accomplished, either he turned on them or he cut them dead. As Cadwallader Colden remarked, Morris "was far from being a popular man. Nor was his Temper fitted to gain popularity."[160] And what was true for Morris was also true for all the leading provincial Whigs. Lewis Morris, Jr., was as haughty and "querulous" as his father.[161] The tightfisted James Alexander was "delicate in his Sense of Honour, . . . strict, . . . temperate," and concerned about social standards of propriety.[162] William Livingston was shy and awkward. Unwilling to seek, and probably unable to attain, any elected office outside his brother's "pocket-manor," Livingston was quick to disparage "Popularity" as a true indicator of any man's inclination to be "a Lover of Liberty & the Public Weal."[163] William Smith, Jr., was a prude whose interests in wealth and propriety precluded any kind of common touch.[164] When the Morris/Alexander faction needed a credible street leader during the 1737 New York City by-election between their man, Cornelius Van Horne, and Adolphe Philipse, it had to turn to Lewis Morris, Sr.'s son-in-law, Matthew Norris, a British naval officer, temporarily stationed in New York.[165] Later on, the Livingston/Smith faction relied on John Morin Scott to win the crowd.[166] But for some reason—perhaps he telegraphed too much "Pride and Haughtiness of Soul," perhaps ill feeling against well-heeled lawyers was too pervasive—Scott never developed the combination of charisma and clout that distinguished his political adversaries.[167]

Aside from their lack of flamboyance, what most distinguished the provincial Whig leaders was their interest in philosophic and political issues. For all of them a good evening was not backgammon and bumpers but conversation with other educated men. Morris and Alexander were intolerant of those who had no intellectual bent, and when Livingston and Smith graduated from college, they sought out the company of Alexander and William Smith, Sr., in preference to younger, less serious minds.[168] More than anything, it was their intellectual capabilities that made the provincial Whig politicians a powerful force in New York public life. When they took up a political cause, their primary tactic was to use the press to win over public opinion. They tried to bury their opponents under a barrage of polemics, and justified their attacks by praising their own concern for the public welfare. Unable and unwilling to match the popular Whigs in their practice of personal politics, the provincial Whigs relied on their writings to help them recruit the second tier of political leadership necessary for campaign victories. What they found was that intellectual leadership, selective adherence to the canons of English country thought, and single-minded promotion of a cause could, on occasion, make up for their weaknesses, and could, in fact, raise them to a level of public prominence that their intellectual arrogance assured them they deserved.

But persuasive and powerful as the provincial Whig writings were, they could also have a perverse effect, for in their public condemnations of popular Whigs, they frequently contributed to the mythology that made their opponents so formidable. In designating Adolphe Philipse as "Ape" or "Baboon," the Morris/Alexander crowd simply emphasized the sexual prowess that made Philipse an object of wonder.[169] In drawing attention to Oliver DeLancey's tyranny of New York City streets—he carried "his Elections by the Numbers . . . [he] horsewhipped," his critics complained—they encouraged the kind of perverse respect that physical intimidation could earn in a brutal society.[170] In trying to blacken James DeLancey for his "popularity," they generated awe of a man who could, with "affability and ease," command the allegiance of scores with his "adroitness at a jest," "a smile . . . , a promise, or a bottle."[171]

The differences between popular and provincial Whig factions were important ones. Frequently, when they expressed their concerns about public affairs, members of the two types of factions spoke in their own peculiar manner. Different perspectives on the nature of colonial rights, the institutional and social context of such rights, dangers to public order, and the relevance of select strands of English country thought to colonial affairs produced distinct popular and provincial Whig dialects that largely dominated political discourse in colonial New York. And those fissures of conception and political language were emphasized by contrasting political styles between the leading spokespersons for each dialect.

We can, of course, make too much of those differences. As good Whigs, representatives of both New York factions emphasized the importance of the post–Glorious Revolution political settlement, the mixed and balanced constitution, and traditions of natural law and natural right. Both advocated the very important goal of keeping the executive in check, and it would be difficult to decide (and foolish to try) which variety of New York Whiggism was the strongest strand in the rope that tethered successive colonial governors. Both were committed to parsimonious government, for their constituents demanded nothing less.[172] Both were also willing to make confusing, cross-tradition borrowings. When popular Whig spokespersons on occasion felt it would strengthen their case, they were not reluctant to pick up bits and pieces of the English country lexicon and use them to condemn their antagonists.[173] For their part, provincial Whigs could be eclectic opportunists, quick to appropriate popular Whig policies that seemed to have some appeal.[174] Finally, representatives of both popular and country Whigs proved that they would modulate their voices if they found themselves with some power in the House of Assembly. Influence in government was the ultimate leveler.

The obvious opportunism of New York politics, combined with the intense personal animosities that often divided popular and provincial Whig leaders, resulted in a shrill, accusatory mode of political discourse, to which both politicians and freeholders soon became accustomed. Factional spokespersons castigated their adversaries as "bigots," who defended themselves and attacked *their* opponents with the most specious varieties of "cant."[175] Participants in public affairs frequently felt that raising a "Noise and Clamour . . . [was their] best Policy."[176] Or as William Livingston (who on occasion could be as brutally objective as he could be self-deluding on others) advised his brother that, when challenged, he should answer "cant with cant."[177] Indeed, if we were to coin a word to offer insight into mid eighteenth-century New York politics, it might be "cantentious." Acrimonious exchanges and aggressive posturings were pervasive.

The tendency of New Yorkers to perceive the arguments between popular and provincial Whig factions as "cant" owed much to the intellectual proximity of the disputants and the clamorous style of their punditry. Moreover, the way in which provincial Whigs drew on select facets of English country rhetoric also worked to that end, for the logic of country thought demanded an antinomic relationship with an identifiable court faction. Yet at no point did New York's provincial Whigs have a clear-cut court opponent. In electoral politics, they always confronted a popular Whig faction that, no matter how tainted with power, continued to have an integrity of its own, not on court grounds, but on its past and continuing representation of popular rights and constituent interests. Thus, both popular and provincial Whigs continually vied in exaggerated terms to claim concern over colonial rights and liberties as their exclusive property, and tie the can of tyranny to the tail of their opponents.

In addition, provincial Whig leaders always managed to debase their coin as the principled voice of opposition. The Morris/Alexander faction treated its choice list of English country professions like a throwaway when its members met with the opportunity for office in 1737. And in the mid 1750s, after some initial success, William Livingston so emphasized the relatively unpopular anticlerical and latitudinarian facets of English country thought that he tended to marginalize the impact of that rhetorical tradition. Paradoxically, although New York produced two factions that at times did draw heavily on English country inspiration, and although facets of that language of politics were widely diffused through provincial Whig loquaciousness and popular Whig borrowings, in the context of New York's factional battles, that rhetoric was frequently perceived as little more than self-justifying "cant."

The result of this circumstance was a New York political culture not particularly sensitive to the moral dimension of the English country paradigm. According to that view, a society's continued integrity depended on the virtue of an ever-vigilant citizenry. If members of the community, and especially its political leaders, abandoned standards of integrity, honesty, independence, and selflessness, the social and constitutional order itself would begin a downward spiral into luxury, decay, and ultimate chaos. Evidence certainly existed to show that New York was in such danger. Governors had the potential resources to buy political support;[178] kickbacks were often part of the traffic in office and land titles;[179] patronage was blatantly distributed;[180] large landowners tampered with juries;[181] voters faced intimidation during elections;[182] and crass commercialism was rampant.[183] But because the spokespersons for the English country critique of New York were themselves so compromised by their personal leadership in the society that accepted these practices, their larger social criticism— always aimed at their opponents of the moment—was widely dismissed as self-serving rhetoric.

The prevalence of rhetorical conflict in New York did not, however, mean that the province's political relationships were particularly fragile. Forged in a demanding environment, they were tough enough to withstand ongoing abrasion from rasping tongues. Leading popular and provincial Whigs were part of a provincial oligarchy, and they operated within the framework of a broad social consensus. It was precisely because they shared so much that they could join in such furious debate. Intellectual cousinry tended to encourage political argument in intense but stylized ways.[184]

If the rhetoric of New York's political environment was heated by Whiggish "cant," its effect was often mitigated by local cynicism or indifference. Most New Yorkers understood that politics was a competition for power, that interests frequently determined the conformation of partisanship, and that principle would bend in office. There was, as well, considerable indifference to the pristine logic of *any* narrow, English political ideology. Many New Yorkers who culturally were New Netherlanders, or who were influenced strongly by their Dutch neighbors, played important supporting roles in provincial politics. But they were motivated more by considerations peculiar to their own communities than by any affinity for particular models of idealized English political behavior.[185]

The tendency of New Yorkers to think and act on their own terms was also evident beyond the confines of the Dutch communities. The term "commonwealthman," for example, has drawn considerable notice as representing a particular strand of radical-Whig republicanism within the English country tradition.[186] It has come to signify a heightened political awareness expressed through ideological consciousness, and defined by opposition to those in power, and deep commitment to the public, as opposed to private interest. But in New York, while a "good Common Wealth's Man" would "*always* [be] for his Country" he also might be "*sometimes* for the Governor."[187] At the very moment those who expressed this opinion stressed their understanding of, and allegiance to, radical-Whig ideology, they also denied it by placing a commonwealthman alongside the governor, who, of course, was the symbolic repository of unrestrained prerogative power. Just as revealing was another admission that a commonwealthman need not be the public-minded, independent citizen standing virtuously against the potential ravages of commerce. He might simply be an entrepreneur, an individual who "bought and sold a great deal very fairly, and employed many Men, who . . . [he] generally paid very punctually."[188] Such a person was virtuous but he proudly earned his virtue through his pursuit of private interest in his capacity as an honest businessman. The rich texture of New York society ensured the development of both its own logic of political behavior and its own standards of linguistic relevance.

There is evidence, too, that some New Yorkers preferred sardonic self-deprecation to the moralistic outrage of the English country perspective. When, in the 1748 New York municipal election, for example, two prominent aldermen (who anticipated that the governor would elevate them to the offices of mayor and recorder) began to lobby outside their respective wards for other aldermanic candidates determined to survey the city's "Out Ward," they presented a classic case of political corruption. The twosome were intent on undermining the representative system in order to advance themselves politically and economically. They would do so by preempting traditional pasture rights in the Out Ward common, an action that would bear heavily on the less well-to-do City residents, who could never replace such a valuable customary benefit. But rather than rail at them in English country-style phraseology, critics chose the ridicule of ironic conclusion. "The common people, . . . lose its true, the pasture of their cows, but then Bakers expect more money for their bran. Thus, you see, the clamors against itinerant aldermen are without cause."[189] Despite its factionalism—or perhaps because of it—New York had a far more relaxed political culture than the abundant writings of a few doctrinaires would suggest.

Finally, there is the issue of factionalism itself. Factions, as most politically literate New Yorkers knew, were alleged to consist of "private Dealers in Politicks," "Combinations" that pursued self-interested ends to the exclusion of any concern for public welfare.[190] But few contemporaries seemed troubled by their involvement in contentious political episodes that might be called factious. Rather than handling the rhetoric of faction gingerly, with a touch of introspection, political leaders threw it around with abandon in hopes of blackening their opponents. In their highly competitive political world, New York politicians needed verbal means by which they could dismiss their opponents and thereby elevate themselves. The language of faction fulfilled that need. Rather than signifying a particularly anxiety-ridden society, then, the language of faction became a rote form of dismissal, simply a commonplace language of New York's peculiar provincial culture of partisan politics.

All in all, it is very clear that the character of New York politics was much more complex than the country tradition that historians have so intimately linked with the later, Revolutionary republican ethos. In this vigorous new-world society, politics revolved around a distinctive provincial culture of structured factionalism that encouraged an acute awareness of the self-serving ends of public rhetoric, a pragmatic attitude toward office and political power, a frank acknowledgment of self-interest, an uninhibited irreverence in redefining an ideologically charged old-world vocabulary to suit provincial values, an unreflective ambivalence about corruption, and a marked penchant for interpreting virtue in multiple ways.[191] Rather than serving as a major signpost to republicanism, the political culture of colonial New York pointed in another direction—it signaled, in an inchoate, provincial way, the development of characteristics integral to an emerging American liberalism.[192]

The Factionalism of the Late 1760s

Compared to the relatively clear profile that popular and provincial Whig factions provided during the midcentury decades, the political divisions of the late 1760s quickly became confusing. One obvious reason for this was the impact of imperial affairs. The reorganization of the British empire following the conclusion of the French and Indian War had a profoundly unsettling effect on the American colonies. The efforts of the British to control colonial expansion, tighten up the trade of the empire, and tax the colonies directly, along with their willingness to use parliamentary power to effect these ends, fundamentally altered the relationship between metropolis and province. Accustomed to a loose halter, most provincial politicians felt they should try to rid themselves of the hackamore the British had suddenly dropped over colonial heads. The expectations of many free-holders that their representatives should resist put factional leaders under considerable pressure to think innovatively and to achieve a new level of political dexterity. Colonial politicians had to placate their outspoken constituents, while simultaneously convincing the British that the colonies were peopled by loyal subordinate subjects.

One of the most conspicuous changes in New York society between the early to mid eighteenth century and the late 1760s was the increased level of social, economic, and political conflict. The Stamp Act riots and the tenant rebellions of 1766 arrayed some of New York's middling and lower-class residents against the defenders of great wealth and privilege;[193] the cyclical woes of the provincial economy set economic groups at each other's throats;[194] and the increased politicization of the populace—"the Swellings of the Great Multitude," as William Smith, Jr., put it—rocked New York's political leaders back on their heels.[195] During the late 1760s, many assemblymen learned what it was to live in fear of their constituents.[196] The political results, in the shape both of rapidly changing circumstances and of the fears those changes engendered, intensified short-run opportunism. From the perspective of New York's established leaders, the only rock in a turbulent sea was office.

A second circumstance that contributed to the murky texture of New York's late colonial politics was that the old distinctions between popular and country Whigs had faded away during the early 1760s. James De-Lancey's death, David Jones's electoral defeat, and the gradual attrition of time had worn away the popular Whig coalition that dominated New York politics through much of the 1740s and 1750s. The William Livingston/ William Smith, Jr. provincial Whig faction of the 1750s had faded less, but it had lost much of its vitality. Livingston, Smith, and Scott were still young and active enough to constitute a significant political force in the early 1760s, but they made their presence felt largely as a professional interest group, a faction of lawyers. The larger network that Livingston and Smith had built up during the King's College controversy had atrophied as the principal leaders focused their attention on more narrowly legalistic matters.

During the late 1760s, however, new imperial policies, two provincial elections, the apparent favoritism of Governor Moore for Livingston family members and friends, and both the revival of old and the development of new public rivalries produced a period of intense political expediency.[197] By that time, the senior figures in what was frequently to be called the "Livingston" faction were recognizable as much for their rank conservatism as for an older heritage of provincial Whiggism. The able pen of New York's foremost ideologue William Livingston, it is true, continued to play an important role in defining the public position of any faction to which he might adhere. But excepting his religious and philosophic radicalism, Livingston was unadventuresome, if not reactionary. He played down the significance of the Stamp Act legislation and refused to become involved in any protest against it other than by petitioning.[198] He actively supported New York's landlords against their truculent tenants and identified with Massachusett's prerogative-conscious governor, William Shirley, to the point of advocating an independent income for New York's chief executive as a counterweight to the popular Whigs.[199] Rather than worrying about the abuses of a standing army, Livingston and his friends welcomed the intervention of British troops in civil affairs to promote order and protect property.[200] As for the other partisans of the Livingston faction, William Smith, Jr., was prepared to bolster New York's governors with an exchequer court and an independent income;[201] John Morin Scott condemned outspoken attacks on parliamentary authority as treasonous;[202] Philip Livingston would have nothing to do with constituent instruction of assembly representatives;[203] and Robert R. Livingston exerted himself against popular demonstrations in New York City during the Stamp Act riots.[204] Several had a nose for high office as well. William Smith, Jr., accepted an appointment to the council, and it seems likely that Robert R. Livingston and John Morin Scott would have done likewise had the opportunity arisen.[205] Robert R. Livingston accepted a supreme court commission "at Pleasure" and opposed any place bill that might have disqualified high court judges from assembly membership.[206]

Spokespersons for what was to become widely known as the DeLancey faction quickly perceived opportunity in their opponents' conservatism. Polemicists pummeled the lawyers for their role in the Stamp Act crisis and their self-interested record in public affairs.[207] DeLanceyite writers hinted that their faction would welcome a change to voting by ballot, and would throw open the doors of the assembly so that auditors might better take the measure of their representatives.[208] Captain James DeLancey personally associated with the Sons of Liberty, endorsed the idea that constituents should instruct their legislators, and, in an unprecedented step, refused an appointment to the council so that he might take a leading role in the 1769 election.[209]

Once the 1769 election put more power in the hands of the DeLancey faction, however, its zeal abated. Its members dragged their feet on structural political changes that would place more power in the hands of the electorate,[210] preferring that New York City decisions on such issues as the boycott of British-manufactured goods be made by a merchant-directed, house-to-house canvassing, rather than at open town meetings.[211] Of course, they were strong supporters of the effort to bring Alexander McDougall to account for libel when McDougall published a broadside accusing the DeLancey men of betraying provincial freeholders by voting supplies for British troops stationed in New York.[212] In hopes of offsetting the unpopularity of these stands, the DeLanceyites picked through and carried away what they could from the old English country Whig boneyard. Assemblymen introduced "freedom of religion" legislation that would end taxation of non-Anglicans for support of Church of England clergymen in the four establishment counties. They supported a place bill that would disqualify supreme court judges from the assembly, and took the position that nonresident representation of constituencies should no longer be allowed. Although these last initiatives were blatantly directed at the Livingston family and manor, the DeLanceyites tried to maintain some semblance of impartiality by applying the same standards to their supporters.[213]

In the face of the DeLancey faction's backpedaling and its forthright attacks on Livingston interests, William Livingston's crusade against Anglican episcopacy was hardly an adequate response. Recognizing this, others put together a remodeled opposition. Impetuous Peter R. Livingston, the recently radicalized John Morin Scott, and the stung but unchastened Philip Livingston turned their attention to the kind of aggressive politics that the DeLanceyites had recently used to their advantage. They worked out a rapprochement with former DeLanceyite Sons of Liberty Isaac Sears and John Lamb, and, along with Alexander McDougall, took to the streets to organize an out-of-doors opposition to the DeLancey faction. They encouraged town meetings to demand the ballot, pushed for a continuation of nonimportation of British goods until all of the Townsend Duties were repealed, and supported McDougall in his attack on the DeLancey-led assembly for provisioning British troops.[214] Robert R. Livingston underlined the Livingston faction's new receptiveness to popular politics when, in defending his election to the assembly seat representing his cousin's manor, he argued for constituents' right to instruct the assembly.[215] Neither this popular opposition nor that of a handful of sympathetic legislators in the House of Representatives did much to weaken the DeLanceyite hold on the assembly. But the combined pressure did occasionally bring the DeLancey men to heel, and it prompted a number of feral counterattacks that contributed to the embitterment of contemporary politics.

The division between the DeLancey and Livingston factions during the late 1760s and early 1770s was a deep and angry one that defies easy classification. Unlike the factions of the mid eighteenth century, neither of the later counterparts distinguished themselves with the kind of consistent self-definition that creates a unique character. Both factions were willing to play to the crowd with promises of popular political reform. Neither had compunctions about working with the various political street generals who had emerged during the Stamp Act and Townsend Duties crises in order to turn out the electorate or organize a town meeting when such behavior suited their purposes. Both drew on English country Whig ideas when they were useful and ignored others that were inconvenient. Neither appeared to be more in tune with mainstream British Whig thought than its opponents. Both fielded a respectable team of polemicists who were equally at home in the idiomatic world of contemporary British ideologies or in the detail of local scurrilities. As for political styles, both factions covered the spectrum. At one end were Captain James DeLancey and Philip Livingston. The former, a "Cockfighter, Horseracer and [reputed] Whoremonger," combined swagger and gentility in a way that appealed to many New Yorkers;[216] the latter built the "best interest that any man ever had" in New York City on his "rappid . . . bluster[ing]" affability and his gambling success in the macho privateering circles of the French and Indian War.[217] At the other end, representing the DeLanceys and the Livingstons, were respectively, the aged and conservative Crugers and the cautious, society-conscious William Smith, Jr.[218] More than at any previous time, the political contests of this era were simply games of leapfrog, with the "outs" trying to o'erleap the current "ins." Yet it was no friendly game, for the antipathies contemporaries felt appear to have been stronger than anything New Yorkers had experienced since the turn of the century. In part, it was the very intensity of interfactional hatred that impelled the ins to continue kicking their off-balance rivals, and determined the outs to do whatever was necessary to displace their foes in the confidence of the electorate.

The later 1760s saw an urgent need for a fresh political breeze to bring a sense of order and respect for the body politic, for the smog of cynicism that had always laced New York air thickened with the soot of so much opportunism. In the course of fighting their battles, politicians strained to establish credentials as spokespersons for the public welfare. Partly this was reflected in the attempts of both factions—but perhaps even more among Livingston supporters—to draw on English country nostrums.[219] For the most part, however, that effort entailed emphasizing connections with interests that had long been legitimate components of New York society. One theme that DeLancey writers stressed was their connection to the province's "commercial" interest, for the merchants had always claimed accolades as key contributors to provincial growth and prosperity.[220] When charged with too close an association with parasitical lawyers, the Livingstons defended themselves by pointing out how practitioners of the law had been chiefly responsible for securing many of the rights New Yorkers felt were theirs.[221] Other interests that carried some legitimacy in provincial society were religious organizations. Churches were an essential underpinning of the social structure, strong pillars that supported the weight of state and society. The Livingston faction's strategy of brazenly claiming that it was the political voice of all dissenters was an attempt to transfer some of the moral authority that always accompanied religious causes to the slippery secular world of contemporary politics.[222] The DeLancey faction resisted its opponents, but only to a degree. Its members wanted to avoid being labeled solely an Anglican interest. If they could establish themselves as champions, not only of the Anglican church, but also of its "sister" denominations, while stigmatizing their opponents as Presbyterians or Congregationalists rather than as a dissenter interest, the advantage would lie with them. In either case, members of both factions recognized that they could enhance the stature of their partisan politics by donning the clothes of established and well-regarded interests.[223]

Of all the efforts the politicians made to distinguish their factions, the most revealing, and arguably the most successful, was their tendency to describe the rivalry as one between the DeLancey and Livingston families. Of course, this was not an accurate description of the current political divisions. The DeLancey faction was a loose confederation of individuals among whom the DeLanceys were important but not unchallengeable.[224] On the other side, those who were in the front rank of the Livingston faction were frequently divided in their actions and judgments.[225] And, as William Smith, Jr. pointed out (without revealing his own notion of what constituted the Livingston faction), political activities "under the name of the Livingston party did not always proceed from motives approved of by that family."[226] It is also true that there had been no long-standing and simple bifurcation of New York factions into DeLancey- and Livingston-centered groups.[227] Both families had developed disparate interests over the decades, and representatives of the two families had engaged in cooperative as well as competitive activities. But such observations, while worth brief mention, miss the point. When individuals such as Peter R. Livingston made sweeping (and misleading) statements castigating the opposition as "a party that has from the beginnings of this Province opposed our famaly," they were attempting to sanction the present through manipulation of the past.[228] It was much easier to create a past than to control the present, and if the past were interpreted to include a family-centered political struggle of mythic proportions, tradition could place some order in, and offer some justification for, current political partisanship.

The tendency of many contemporaries to interpret New York's late colonial political divisions in terms of family rivalries was not accidental. Family had always been integral to the way in which provincials conceived of their political relationships. Unlike Pennsylvanians' political dialogue, in which words like *family, connections,* and *relations* seldom appeared outside of proprietary circles, that of New Yorkers was peppered with the terms.[229] DeLanceyites and Livingstonians overtly acknowledged the important role that some family members played in mobilizing the electorate and in protecting each other from blindside attacks by their political opponents. Family consciousness among politically prominent third- and fourth-generation New Yorkers was reinforced by their knowledge of what well-connected British relations had accomplished for their colonial forebears, and of the important role consanguinity continued to play in the appointment of political placemen. Just as in Britain, members of collateral lines of important provincial families were conscious of which clan they belonged to, frequently thinking that such connections should confer status, if not more tangible benefits. For many of the politically prominent and their far-flung relations, place within the colony's huge network of old families provided a more revealing perspective on New York politics than any other vantage point.[230]

Ultimately, the appeal of a familial interpretation of New York's late colonial politics rested on its ability to provide some satisfactory sense of order amid any current spate of factionalism. The cutthroat opportunism, the lack of principled differences, and the duplication of political styles that characterized contemporary politics sent New Yorkers on a search for distinctions that would grant some larger meaning to the squabbles of the moment. Contemporaries had neither the perspective, nor the analytical frame of reference necessary to explain midcentury provincial politics in terms of a distinction between popular and provincial Whigs. They did, however, feel the *absence* of such clear divisions, and they sensed that they could enfold themselves within that ordered political tradition by stressing *select* family connections. On the one hand, the current crop of DeLanceys, Waltons, Joneses, Nicolls, Ver Plancks, and Van Schaacks were growing up in the protective shade of older uncles and cousins who had been in the field with James DeLancey and David Jones during the most recent popular Whig heyday. On the other, the middle-aged Livingstons, Smiths, Morrises, and Alexanders educated their young allies by relating current political battles to past experiences of provincial Whig factions. Because animosities between families had always been a feature of New York politics, and because family connections had always been an important component of the organization of political affairs, recasting the past in terms of family rivalry was a natural and convincing way of recapturing some of the sense of order that had pervaded mid eighteenth-century politics.

Although the explanation of the New York political divisions of the late 1760s as an expression of family rivalries did tap into the vital wellsprings of legitimacy that nourished New Yorkers' sense of autonomy and well-being, that success was only momentary. No such view could encompass the diverse political forces that were building up pressure within provincial society. During the 1770s, intermittent constitutional, cultural, and sociopolitical conflicts escalated; as they did, they became the principal focus of divisions among the politically active.[231] While the familial view of New York public affairs was briefly useful in allowing established political leaders to create some semblance of order during the unsettling events of the late 1760s, it had no ability to address the emerging fundamental issues of New York politics. In essence, it was a reaffirmation of colonial oligarchic values—the last hurrah, as it were, of the old political system. And by reminding many New Yorkers of the strength of that tradition, its advocates simply intensified the reaction against it in the years that followed.

Chapter Seven

Understanding Quaker Pennsylvania

MORE THAN ANYTHING, the establishment of Pennsylvania as a proprietary Quaker colony determined the character of provincial politics. Because of the special powers and privileges that successive representatives of the Penn family gained from their colonial possession, the proprietors were repeatedly in the foreground of public affairs; their respective policies imparted a distinctive rhythm to Pennsylvania politics. Initially, William Penn's immense presence encouraged the development of a powerful anti-proprietary brand of popular politics. This abated somewhat during his wife Hannah's custodial decades, only to revive under son Thomas's hard-nosed proprietorship. In the face of what they perceived as proprietorial exploitation, provincial Quakers tried to exercise as much control over popular politics as they possibly could. Convinced that they, not the proprietors, were the true stewards of the colony, Pennsylvania Friends believed that the provincial government was and should be theirs to direct in ways consistent with the "holy experiment." And despite proprietary power, a heavy inflow of immigrants, which soon made Quakers a minority in their province, and various divisions among themselves, Friends remained largely in control of Pennsylvania's popular politics and continuing overseers of many governmental policies.

Because of their central role in Pennsylvania politics, Friends and fellow travelers were the chief authors of social and political thought in their province. Beginning with their opposition to William Penn, Quakers evolved a highly distinctive strand of constitutional thought, which celebrated Pennsylvania's plethora of popular rights and unique governmental structure. These ideas dominated popular thought at the expense of the other important English Whig principles of mixed government and constitutional balance. Building on this firm foundation, the Quakers developed the provincial political ideology of civil Quakerism, which centered on the particularly valuable character of the Pennsylvania constitution, liberty of conscience, provincial prosperity, loosely defined pacifism, rejection of a militia, and resistance to the arbitrary powers of proprietors. Civil Quakerism dominated public thought in the province, becoming the single most important underpinning of Friends' political hegemony. In refining their ideas and in reaching out to bring others under the aegis of the Quaker Party, Friends developed civil Quakerism into a unique language of politics—a provincial political dialect as it were. So compelling and powerful a persuasion was it that the idiom of civil Quakerism completely dominated political debate in the colony, forcing others to come to terms with its grammar and the assumptions its syntax expressed.

Just as the persuasive and ubiquitous nature of civil Quakerism makes Friends' political dominance during the mid eighteenth century comprehensible, so does it explain much of their continuing strength in the late colonial years. Although Friends weakened themselves by a series of well-known unaggressive stands in the course of colonial confrontations with Great Britain, their Pennsylvania opponents were unable to take much advantage of these. And when they did, it was largely because these opponents themselves became defenders of proven civil Quaker tenets. While some of Friends' sizable residual political strength resulted from the weakness of their political opponents and a marked underrepresentation of the provincial backcountry, continuing political loyalty to the old regime rested to an overwhelming extent on many Pennsylvanians' deep internalization of the ideology of civil Quakerism.

Proprietors and Politics

Throughout the colonial years, the most coherent periods of provincial politics coincided with specific phases of proprietary family control. During the first thirty years of colonization, William Penn was at the center of all Pennsylvania affairs; a second period extended through the years of the proprietary interregnum, a span of time that arched from Penn's incapacitating stroke to the settlement of his estate; the third and last ran roughly from the beginning of Thomas Penn's proprietorship until the Revolutionary upheaval. Corresponding changes took place in popular politics, as the public moved from preoccupation with William Penn's policies, through a less focused period, on to intense concern with Thomas Penn's priorities. Movement through these three distinct stages of proprietary ownership gave a rhythm to Pennsylvania's public affairs.

During the first three decades of Pennsylvania's organization, the dominant theme in political affairs was the antiproprietary reaction of provincials to William Penn. Certainly there were numerous divisions among Quakers, and between prominent Friends and leading non-Quakers. Occasionally these erupted in political factiousness, but the prevailing winds were antiproprietary, and it was their consistency that contoured popular political consciousness in Pennsylvania.

Initially, William Penn had been most solicitous of potential settlers. They had been "principally Encouraged . . . [to undertake 'the Difficulties and hardships Incident to the Settlment of New Collines in these wilderness partes of the world'] by the great Liberties, Franchises and immunities promised . . . [them] in Diverse papers published to the world by Wm penn proprietor."[1] Thereafter, Penn seemed to prove himself a most perfidious man. As governor, he had dumped the 1682 Frame of Government at the first opportunity and reneged on promises of popular control over judicial officers. After conveying important powers to the assembly in the 1701 Charter of Privileges, he immediately tried to limit them by claiming a proprietary veto over legislation and contesting the assembly's power to adjourn as it wished. As a landlord, the colony's founder seemed just as untrustworthy. Penn had arbitrarily changed the terms of land purchase, demanded quitrents where he had promised none, preferred the cash of new purchasers to the interests of existing landholders, attempted to establish arbitrary powers in his property managers, and allowed his appointees to run the land office like a fiefdom. Finally, as an English lobbyist and protector of the colony, Penn had done little to redeem himself. In the eyes of many provincial Quakers, the proprietor failed to protect the province from royal officials, seemed to make no headway in persuading the English to accept a universal substitution of the affirmation for the oath, appeared ineffective in settling the boundary dispute with Maryland, and risked the property rights of all Pennsylvanians with his personal financial irresponsibility. All told, it was an impressive indictment.[2]

Of course there were those who held more favorable opinions of their proprietor. Penn's return to the province in 1699 evoked some positive response, and more moderate politicians gained legislative clout in 1705 and again in 1710.[3] But at no point did they relinquish any of the significant popular powers that antiproprietary leaders had gained in their various vendettas with Penn and his governors. That was unthinkable. Most politically conscious settlers simultaneously gave considerable credence to Penn's critics and accepted the flattery that was the other side of the popular politicians' antiproprietary pitch. The first settlers and their progeny were the real custodians of the "holy experiment." The province was theirs because of their willingness to risk their lands and meager fortunes, and because Penn, speaking as a fellow settler, not as the absentee landlord he had subsequently become, had originally promised it would belong to the Quaker community. Anything that took from an absentee proprietor and increased the power and autonomy of representatives of the people was a laudable step in fulfilling the promise of Pennsylvania.[4]

With Penn's illness and death, those who had exploited the proprietary threat this gigantic man seemed to pose lost much of their ability to whip up public ire. Between 1712 and the early 1730s, there was only one instance in which proprietary claims sparked popular anger reminiscent of earlier times.[5] Stung by Governor Sir William Keith's cavalier disregard for the advice and authority of councillors and proprietary officials such as himself, James Logan took his complaints to William Penn's widow, Hannah, who was managing proprietary affairs while English courts untangled the legal mess William had left behind. When he returned to Philadelphia in 1724, Logan brought a letter of instruction from Hannah Penn to Keith requiring the governor to heed the majority of a provincial council stacked with her supporters. Keith refused, asserting that here in new uniform were the familiar old bashaws fronting for proprietary tyranny. David Lloyd joined in to argue that the 1701 Charter of Privileges and the Royal Charter of 1681 located legislative power solely in the hands of the proprietor and the freemen or their delegates. Moreover, the popular fear of the hard-money convictions that Logan and his friends allegedly harbored increased the political tension surrounding the argument, which lasted from mid 1724 until early 1726. The councillors might well use their veto power to stop further emissions of paper currency intended to alleviate the severe economic depression that the bursting of London's South Sea Bubble had precipitated in the early 1720s.

Aside from this year and a half of dispute over the nature of the Pennsylvania constitution, the issue of proprietary power was overshadowed by the specter of royal government. When William Penn commissioned Charles Gookin as governor in 1709, Penn expected the seasoned military officer to bring the kind of order and respect to the governor's office that his predecessor, the young, impetuous John Evans, had been incapable of providing. Instead, Gookin brought rapacity and ineffective opportunism. Once convinced that William Penn would sell his rights of government to the Crown (negotiations were all but complete when Penn suffered his stroke in 1712),

Gookin turned a blind eye to proprietary interests and tried to cultivate connections that might secure him a royal governorship in Pennsylvania or the three Lower Counties. One of the last documents Penn signed, with the guidance of his wife's hand, was the commission ending Gookin's faithless trusteeship and replacing him with Sir William Keith (1717–1726). Keith's ambitions were not unlike Gookin's but his tactics were far different, befitting the charming, intelligent man that he was. Through 1726, he ingratiated himself with popular politicians in both Pennsylvania and the Lower Counties, hoping to convince locals that as a royal governor he would be solicitous of their interests, and to demonstrate to Whitehall that he would be effective in converting proprietary allegiances into royal ones. Immediately after his dismissal in 1726, Keith proved himself a master of improvisation. He headed a slate of Philadelphia County candidates for the assembly with the idea of becoming speaker of the house. Denied that goal by a former ally, David Lloyd, Keith incited his followers to create as much political turmoil as possible. While they churned provincial waters, Keith headed back to London, hoping to convince Whitehall that Pennsylvania's political discord required his presence as royal governor. Failing that, he hoped to gain such an appointment to the Lower Counties. Despite Keith's energy and ingenuity, the Penn family kept control of Pennsylvania, and his little faction of Keithians had faded away by 1729.

Because of the cloud over the proprietary title, and Gookin's and Keith's somewhat aberrant reactions to the possibility of royal government, the 1710s and 1720s produced some strange alliances and bizarre political battles. Nor did other related conflicts in public life do much to clarify the period. While fear of gubernatorial power remained strong during these years, the assembly acquiesced in Governor Keith's decision to set up an equity court over which he could preside as chancellor. Quakers were willing to promote some anglicization of their province by modifying their liberal laws to bring them into closer harmony with England's harsh criminal code, but, at the same time, they continued to plead distinctiveness, pushing hard for the right to substitute an affirmation for all oaths. Many Friends seemed happy to encourage the political radicalism of the Anglican Keith, even though Quakers were heavily outnumbered in Keith's Philadelphia bailiwick and his success might weaken Quaker political power in the long run. Others, Friends from the surrounding counties and a few from the city, had begun to recognize the need for Quakers to pull together if they were to stay masters in their own house. David Lloyd's country-based coalition, which had battled the Keithians into submission by 1729, was the first Quaker political group to react to the implications of large-scale non-Quaker immigration and the slow growth of Quaker meetings.[6] Other larger circumstances, such as the growing maturation of Pennsylvania's social structure and the changing nature of British politics, may have contributed to less contentious provincial politics, but the connection is very difficult to establish.[7] The fact that this was the one period under the Charter of Privileges when councillors found it possible to achieve election to the assembly simply demonstrates the point.[8] Popular hostility to the proprietorship was less focused at this time than at any other. Without the polarity a strong proprietary presence imparted to provincial affairs, and as long as governors were acquiescing to popular demands, Pennsylvania politics could be anything from quietly cooperative to eccentrically contentious.

By the early 1730s, members of the proprietary family had sorted out their differences. William and Hannah Penn's three sons, John, Thomas, and Richard, owned both government and property rights to Pennsylvania. As the eldest, John was the senior partner, but upon John's death in 1746, Thomas became the majority owner, adding John's one-half interest to his own quarter. In fact, Thomas was the principal architect of proprietary policy from 1732, for from that date until 1741, he resided in Pennsylvania, attempting to reorganize proprietary affairs. Although Richard's two sons served in the Pennsylvania government during the 1760s and 1770s, Thomas Penn remained the central proprietary figure through the Revolution.[9]

The reappearance of proprietors in Pennsylvania did not immediately set off an antiproprietary reaction. The turmoil that Hannah Penn's instructions occasioned had subsided, and the passage of a quarter century since the episodes of conflict under William had killed off old combatants and dulled aged memories. Many Quakers shared a vague fondness for John Penn, "the American," by virtue of his Pennsylvania birth during William and Hannah's brief residency, and they also anticipated some financial demands from the Penns, given the train of outstanding proprietary debts that trailed back into earlier times. A number of provincials were also acutely aware of their need for proprietary support. Subsequent to William Penn's death, the neighboring Calverts had begun to encourage settlement under Maryland patent in what Pennsylvanians regarded as their southern and southwestern borderlands. By the 1730s, violence had broken out in the contested areas; the only hope for clarification of land titles lay with negotiations between the Penns and Calverts. This was no time for Pennsylvanians to turn on their proprietors. Finally, there were the inclinations of Andrew Hamilton, Pennsylvania's dominant popular leader during the 1730s. Although Hamilton was, in important ways, an intellectual radical and a critic of social pretense, he also had conservative tendencies.[10] He believed in the sanctity of property, argued that the proprietary family should be compensated for accepting the devalued Pennsylvania currency in lieu of sterling quitrent payments, and remembered that he had been the recipient of proprietary largesse in earlier times.[11]

While all of these circumstances conspired to keep overt antiproprietary appeals out of popular political discourse, the controversy over Pennsylvania's court of chancery proved more indicative of the direction that Pennsylvania politics would soon follow. Gubernatorial power exercised through chancery had become the focal point of political controversy in neighboring New York, and with a new proprietor roaming the province, Pennsylvanians paid heed to the issue.[12] Their concern grew as Thomas Penn acted to encourage, rather than deny, "whisper[s] that we intend to make use of the Court to recover our arrears" in quitrents and land-purchase money. Penn believed that such rumors might encourage debtors to "think it more proper to comply."[13] The assembly's response was to shut down the old chancery court, which had existed on sufferance, and refuse to legislate a replacement. His support for proprietary interests notwithstanding, Andrew Hamilton led the popular disavowal of the prerogative courts.[14]

Thomas Penn's attitude toward a provincial chancery court indicated his priorities. His primary purpose in coming to Pennsylvania had been to begin recouping the fortune his father had lost, and he began vigorously to sort out affairs at the land office. He quickly found that his problems were cumulative ones. First, there were irregular titles and outstanding debts from William's day. Second, because of the litigation over the proprietary title subsequent to William's death, the land office, with very few exceptions, had been unwilling to grant proper deeds for the preceding fourteen years. As a result, hundreds of settlers had property claims based on squatters' rights, warrants, or surveys on which little or no purchase money or quitrents had been paid. Although Thomas Penn hoped he could quickly convert all of these rights into regular titles and collect the outstanding debts, he found that impossible because of a third problem. Those with claims in the southeast had no intention of paying up, because the continuation of the Pennsylvania/Maryland boundary dispute prevented Penn from granting clear title. In fact, as the border conflict escalated during the 1730s, Penn found himself increasing the number of irregular claims by offering unofficial property rights to settlers willing to occupy parts of the disputed area.[15]

Despite these circumstances, Thomas Penn established his terms of settlement where he could. As of 1732, land prices were to increase by approximately 50 percent in order to compensate for the depreciation of Pennsylvania currency against sterling. Quitrents, an important component of Penn's projected long-term income, would double and would be paid in sterling. Staring these new terms in the face, many landowners argued that their pre-1732 property claims should be settled under the old rates. For those who had shown some willingness to pay the proprietors by taking out a warrant or completing a survey, Penn had sympathy. But he did demand that either they pay their back quitrents at rates equivalent to sterling or the assembly compensate him for accepting Pennsylvania currency at face value. For those who had no proof of honest intention, Penn had no charity. They would pay the new rates.[16]

Throughout the mid 1730s, Pennsylvania settlers did not feel the full effect of Thomas Penn's policies, but circumstances changed swiftly. By the end of the decade, Whitehall had established a temporary boundary line between Pennsylvania and Maryland, and Pennsylvania legislators had passed a law compensating Penn for accepting an artificially low exchange rate on his pre-1732 quitrents.[17] In anticipation of these events, Thomas Penn came as close to glee as he ever would. He would "lose no time to seize on the tenants and use all methods the laws allow to make a speedy collection of the whole."[18] He was as good as his word, for by December 1739, he could report that Receiver-General James Steel had "for eighteen months past gone through more business than ever he did for two or three years past."[19] But there was a price to pay for this. When the Donegal Presbytery examined Reverend Samuel Thomson of Pennsborough in September of that year for writing a letter "containing some things which are very offensive to the honourable proprietors," he replied that they were "not his thoughts but the thoughts of the people."[20]

Popular distaste for Thomas Penn's land policies did not accumulate for long before it gained political expression. When Governor George Thomas broke with the Pennsylvania Assembly in 1740 over what he construed to be the unwillingness of Quaker legislators to provide for colonial defense, public opinion held a different view. Thomas had encouraged the enlisting of indentured servants to serve in a British military campaign against the Spanish; to many provincials such action was tantamount to attacking the property rights of the servants' masters. As the dispute escalated, evidence appeared that Thomas's intentions were far more malevolent even than his opponents first suspected. Governor Thomas wrote to Whitehall that Quakers should be disqualified from government, a proper militia law passed, a chancery court established, and the chief executive given powers to prorogue and dissolve the assembly, as well as joint control with the assembly over all appropriations. This was a prescription for destroying the whole concept of a Quaker colony and for emasculating the provincial constitution. At no time during the conflict between governor and assembly did Thomas Penn dissociate himself from the sentiments of his governor; given Penn's later advocacy of all of Governor Thomas's suggestions (with the notable exception of disqualifying Quakers from all public offices), there is every reason to believe that the governor and the future chief proprietor were in fundamental agreement. Pennsylvanians certainly believed so, for it was Penn, not Thomas, whom Philadelphians hanged in effigy at election time in October 1741.[21]

The coalescence of antiproprietary anger in mid eighteenth-century Pennsylvania took place for much the same reasons it had in William Penn's time—because of the unpopularity of both proprietary land policies and political priorities. But in the last thirty-five years of the colony's existence the shape of proprietary/antiproprietary rivalry was to be much different from what it had been in the first thirty-five. Whereas Pennsylvania's early years were frequently characterized by factional fluidity and significant divisions within the predominantly Quaker political community, the latter period was distinguished by conflict between the Quaker and Proprietary parties.

The long-lasting polarization between proprietary stalwarts and Quaker critics, although conceived in the 1730s, was born in the early 1740s. Tired out from his efforts to reconcile proprietary and popular interests, Andrew Hamilton turned his back on provincial politics in 1739, and a number of his old friends did likewise.[22] Subsequently, but before the annual October election, word arrived that Britain was at war with Spain. Expecting that non-Quakers would use this occasion as an opportunity to push for a militia and defense preparations, a large number of Friends and their sympathizers were "for choosing none but people of that Persuasion."[23] Advocates of defense backed off from an electoral contest, perhaps fearing defeat, but also thinking that a Quaker assembly, "do[ing] nothing but trust[ing] in the Lord," would make an easy target in the future.[24] In this they were wrong. Governor Thomas's ill-advised recruitment of indentured servants and his attacks on the Pennsylvania constitution quickly became the central issues of the day. But supporters of the proprietorship and executive felt that was a sham. They believed that Quaker leaders were exploiting whatever opportunity they could to mask their pacifist leanings. Consequently, they redoubled their efforts to characterize the assemblymen as an enclave of Quaker intransigents.[25]

The proprietary men's decision to focus their attack on the Quakerness of their opponents was one of two crucial errors they made during the 1740–1741 defense crisis. Since the 1720s, Friends had become increasingly conscious of their minority status and recognized that if they were to maintain their political dominance, they could no longer afford the kind of internecine warfare that they had been a party to in the past. When Governor Thomas and his Philadelphia allies attacked Quakers, the Quaker presence in government, and the Pennsylvania constitution, they made it easy for Friends to come together in a Quaker political alliance. It also promoted the association of popular rights and privileges with the Quaker Party, which in turn strengthened the appeal of Quaker leaders to growing numbers of non-Quaker freemen.

The second error Proprietary Party leaders made was to tolerate, if not encourage, a plan of electoral intimidation in the Philadelphia county election of 1742. Angered by their opponents' popularity and frustrated by their own failure to win assembly seats the previous year, proprietary sympathizers recruited a large gang of mariners to try to control access to the ballot box. A riot broke out, in which the sailors set on the "Quaker *Sons of Bitches*," trying "*to knock down the broad Brims*."[26] Speaker of the Assembly John Kinsey, a man the New Yorker James Alexander assayed to be hungry for "popularity applause & to be Esteemed a Patriot," was not about to let this opportunity pass.[27] He launched an inquiry, which pinned blame for the riot on proprietary stalwarts. Not only did the proprietary men lose the election, they lost their reputations as well. The "knock-down" election became a symbol of the Proprietary Party's willingness to undermine the Pennsylvania constitution, and the stigma stuck to them for the next thirty years.[28]

During the 1750s and early 1760s, feelings against Thomas Penn ran as high as they ever had done against his father. Once he became chief proprietor in 1746, he advocated all of the changes in the Pennsylvania government for which Governor Thomas had pleaded a decade earlier. Penn wanted a regular militia, a chancery court, a greater say in the appointment of public officials, and "the first cause of all," as he put it, joint appropriation with the assembly of all revenues.[29] His tenacious adherence to the latter demand in his unyielding instructions to his governors earned the proprietor the intense hatred of various popular provincial leaders. "The Proprietor has no Bowels," lamented Benjamin Franklin, "he never relents."[30]

There was nothing but vinegar in Penn's land policies as well. On becoming chief proprietor, Thomas Penn reorganized the land office, ordering distraints for rent, the ejectment of squatters, and the burning out of homesteaders on unpurchased Indian land. By mid 1757, Penn was taking in more money than at any time since his Pennsylvania residency. But while the proprietor was uncompromising in his pursuit of wealth, and Pennsylvania residents were paying unprecedented taxes to support the French and Indian war effort, Penn was doggedly resisting assembly proposals to tax proprietary land. Even his generosity had a false bottom: a proprietary gift of £5,000 to support the war effort was to be paid out of quitrents collected during the hardship-filled war years. Such policies brought the proprietary family both scorn and hatred. When Richard Penn's eldest son, John, arrived in Philadelphia in 1753 for a short visit, prominent country Quakers refused to make even a token courtesy visit.[31]

Under these circumstances, the division between the Quaker and Proprietary parties became more pronounced. Quaker Party leaders found that they continued to have a broad constituency of political supporters. Those who were antagonized by the policies and distrusted the intentions of the proprietor gravitated toward the remade Quaker/Assembly Party, which dominated the House of Representatives after 1756. That restructuring of the party notwithstanding, the proprietary men continued to emphasize the "Quakerness" of their opponents. At the beginning of the French and Indian War, as in the early 1740s, the Proprietary Party tried to convince Pennsylvanians that Quakers, including those who sat in the assembly, were "principled against military service."[32] When they learned through the continued participation of numerous Quakers in political affairs that such was not the case, but that there was disagreement among Friends over the definition of and priority that should go to peace testimony, proprietary spokespersons made little effort to adjust their views. To them, the antiproprietary party remained the home of "Quaker plot[s]."[33] "The *Ruling Party*" was a Quaker entity, and Friends were behind its Machiavellian tactics.[34] These divisions between the Proprietary and Quaker parties, which went back to Thomas Penn's early days, persisted through the later stages of the French and Indian War and found renewal in the electoral rivalries of the mid 1760s. Although they weakened somewhat thereafter, it took the Revolution to alter the patterns of political partisanship significantly.

Throughout nearly a century of colonial history, proprietary activity was an important determinant of political affairs in Pennsylvania. Despite their different situations, both William and Thomas Penn structured Pennsylvania politics by adopting unpopular policies and thereby becoming lightning rods for colonial discontent. When the proprietorship lay in limbo between the first and second generations, provincial politics were less focused. But as important as this proprietary-induced cycle was in establishing an understandable order in Pennsylvania political affairs, proprietary policies, or their absence, provide only a limited perspective on the character of popular politics. For a more revealing view, it is necessary to turn from the proprietors to the Pennsylvania populace.

Quakers in Politics

The most important influence on political behavior in early Pennsylvania was the Quaker character of the colonial experiment. Friends had planned the enterprise as a Quaker haven, and they predominated in public affairs during the first decades of settlement. Their expectation of prominence was clear, for example, in their reflections on governance. "*Governmant*," ruminated William Penn, "seems to me a part of *Religion* it self, a thing *Sacred* in its *Institution* and *End*." His further assertion that government was "capable of *Kindness, Goodness and Charity*," and "that the Care and Regulation of many . . . Affairs, more soft and daily necessary, make up much the greatest part of *Government*," suggest the kind of benevolent superintendency that Quakers imagined exercising in their enlightened new world.[35] At the same time, William Penn was sincere in his expansive promises "to lay the Foundation of a free Colony for all Mankind, that should go thither."[36] He simply assumed that outsiders would become Friends or adjust their own values to Quaker standards of law and decorum. In either case, they would accept the public tutelage that leading Friends were eager to offer.

While simple in theory and uplifting in concept, the Quaker vision proved difficult to implement. How could a people principled against violence protect colonists? Would Quaker legislators appropriate money for war against France? Should Quaker officers of government administer capital punishment? If Quakers were unable to fulfill all the requirements of civil office, such as administering oaths, what right had they to hold such positions? On reflection, some Friends thought "government so ill-fitted to their principles" that they were willing to turn their backs upon it.[37] The problems appeared to be so intractable, and acceptable compromises so improbable, that the light Friends might shine in administrative affairs seemed not worth the candle.

By far the majority of Friends, however, held a different opinion. Firmly believing that the "colony and constitutions of government [had been] made by and for Quakers," they felt that Pennsylvania was rightfully theirs and that they had a consequent obligation to defend their inheritance.[38] The first Quaker settlers had come to the Delaware valley voluntarily, under a contract that promised to make them "more free and Easy than they were in their Native Countreys."[39] In their first years as colonists, they enjoyed civil rights that they had been denied in the Old World, and recognized the possibility of developing a warm, caring, domestic life of "holy conversation" within the confines of a Quaker province.[40] But such felicity seemed threatened at many turns. Pennsylvania Anglicans used Friends' rejection of oaths to discredit Quaker government and deny Friends access to courts.[41] Next door, Delaware Anglicans demonstrated what more their Pennsylvania counterparts would do given the chance. During Queen Anne's War, the Lower Counties passed a militia law that refused conscientious objector status to Quakers.[42] Frightened by such turns, most Quakers reacted with determination. "It is not to be thought we intended no easier nor better terms for ourselves, in going to America, than we left behind us."[43] The way for Quakers to protect their heritage was not through quiescence, but through effective and purposeful political involvement.

Resolved though they were to stay in control of Pennsylvania's government, Friends realized that the relationship between government and Quakerism could not be a static one. The old vision of a colonial utopia, which the proprietor and his co-planners had founded on an all-encompassing Quaker paternalism, was outdated by the mid 1690s. The Keithian schism discredited the theocratic tendencies of Quaker government by publicly exposing its worst features. As the first generation of minister-magistrates died off, younger public Friends began to steer clear of administrative and judicial appointments. Fights between the Keithians and their opponents, and the subsequent public brawls between David Lloyd's supporters and more conservative Friends who backed the proprietorship did even more to separate politics and religion into two related but separate spheres.[44] Whereas Quakers were prepared to accept political leaders who were uncompromising, outspoken, and contentious in pursuit of popular power, they chose quieter, far less secular-minded men and women as their spiritual leaders.

Coincident with this change were others that worked to strengthen the Quaker commitment to continued influence in politics. Perhaps the most important of these was the growing worldliness of Quakers. Pennsylvania's rich land and resources brought material well-being to scores of thrifty Quaker farmers, artisans, and merchants, many of whom became more preoccupied with keeping their worldly possessions than with movings of the spirit. To such individuals, Quakers in government were their best guarantee of continued prosperity and protection for their property.[45]

Other contributions to a growing secular-mindedness came from within Quakerism itself. However tribalistic Quakerism would become by the second quarter of the eighteenth century, early Pennsylvania Quakerism had an inclusive nature. Once settled in the New World, English, Welsh, and Irish immigrants who had been nominal Friends, or simply friends of Friends, in the British Isles flocked into Pennsylvania's new meetinghouses, imparting a substantial "local content" or "made in Pennsylvania" component to Delaware Valley Quakerism.[46] The result of this infusion of new blood, once families had established themselves and gained whatever weight long-standing meeting attendance conferred, was to dilute the collective memory of old-world "sufferings" that symbolized Friends' historic unwillingness to compromise with the world. To many Pennsylvania converts and second-generation Quakers, the exercise of political power seemed the most important historically sanctioned way to protect their sectarian integrity.

Friends' determination to control as much of Pennsylvania's political destiny as possible found expression in both the exclusive and inclusive tendencies within Quakerism. In the early days of the "holy experiment," the former predominated; a small group of Quaker ministers, magistrates, and councillors jealously guarded their growing power against outsiders from the Lower Counties and proprietary influence. But by the early eighteenth century, necessity, opportunity, and inclination turned the heads of some Quaker leaders in a different direction. The Keithian schism and spontaneous immigration in the late 1690s so increased Pennsylvania's non-Quaker population that James Logan estimated in 1702 that only one-third of Philadelphia residents were Friends.[47] In 1697, the dissident Quaker Robert Turner put together a coalition of "dutch sweed[s] Fene[s] . . . Baptist[s] Endependant[s] Presbitterian[s] . . . [and] church of England" men to test the political strength of the dominant Quaker leaders.[48] A few years later, David Lloyd was so successful at combining a strong following of Friends with a sizable group of non-Quakers that he and his confidants became the dominant force in Pennsylvania politics. Outsiders were subsumed, politically, by an inclusive popular Quakerism.[49]

Throughout the first three decades of the eighteenth century, leaders of different political factions put more or less emphasis on the exclusive or inclusive character of Quakerism, depending on the nature of their constituency. It was a measure of David Lloyd's opportunism, for example, that the popular faction he organized in the mid 1720s against Sir William Keith was far more exclusively Quaker than his earlier coalitions; Lloyd was forced to build his new faction on rural footings, and the townships in Chester, Philadelphia, and Bucks were predominantly Quaker.[50] This later Lloydian organization, however, was singular in its narrowness. Other respectably sized factions formed during the first quarter of the eighteenth century were a more eclectic combination of Quaker and non-Quaker elements.

In the 1730s and 1740s, Pennsylvania's popular political leaders moved to a new level of sophistication by drawing the exclusive and inclusive characteristics of Quakerism into a symbiotic relationship that was to last until the final colonial years. This development was largely a response to Friends' recognition that they were becoming a shrinking minority amid a burgeoning non-Quaker population. If they were to maintain their monopoly of popular political power, they had to find a renewed commonality of purpose and combine it with a broad appeal to those beyond the walls of Friends' meetinghouses. That they were successful in doing so is a matter of record. Friends strengthened their own sense of political identity by forming what became known as the Quaker Party in 1739 and simultaneously establishing long-lasting political ties between themselves and a variety of out groups in the province's different counties.[51]

The close linking of Quaker exclusivism to a broader political inclusiveness may appear paradoxical, but the process of social maturation in Pennsylvania facilitated such a political development. Provincial prosperity brought wealth and social status to Quakers, reinforcing their perception of themselves as a particularly fortunate people. At the same time, social stratification had not developed to the point of unduly isolating successful Friends from their neighbors.[52] The same kind of duality flowed from Friends' emphasis on loving family relationships. On the one hand, the great emphasis Quakers placed on the quality of their domestic life worked to create tight community nuclei composed of families deeply committed to "loving conversation." On the other hand, love worked against isolation. Hundreds of families had children marry outside the meeting to partners of different denominations or of no particular religious affiliation, while others had relations who left the Quaker meeting for social, economic, religious, or idiosyncratic personal reasons. The continuation of affective relationships, despite religious apostasy or indifference, took the care and concern of Quakers out of their religiously defined community and built a multiplicity of small bridges into the wider colonial world.[53]

Friends' deep commitment to Quaker control of the Pennsylvania government remained strong during midcentury controversies. When, after close to thirty years of peace, King George's War broke out in 1739, Friends had a sharp retort for those who condemned the Quaker aversion to preparations for military conflict. Quakers felt they had a moral right to continue "the free Enjoyment of Liberty of Conscience, for the Sake of which . . . [their] Fore fathers left their native Country."[54] Non-Quakers who had immigrated to Pennsylvania had known when they did so of Friends' disinclination to participate in warfare. If those of other religious persuasions disliked that condition of settlement, they might "go elsewhere."[55] Implicit in Quaker politicians' defense of their political preeminence was a sentiment William Penn had articulated long before: "if the coming of others should overrule us that are the originals, and made it a country we are unhappy."[56] Most of Penn's successors were not at all willing to contribute to their own disenfranchisement.

The most severe challenge to Friends' political dominance came, not from outside their society, but from within. During the wartime crisis that French and Indian attacks on the Pennsylvania frontier precipitated in 1755–1756, strict pacifist Friends began a reformation of their society by renouncing the by then long-hallowed tradition of Quaker involvement in government. Emphasizing the exclusivist side of Quakerism, the reformers argued that the Society of Friends had been corrupted by the worldliness that Quaker inclusiveness had encouraged. The essence of Friends' religion was their responsibility to bear testimony in all facets of their daily life to Christian precepts; that was impossible for Quaker politicians and officials to do. During the preceding years, conscientious Friends had uneasily accepted the kind of assurances that politicians such as the prospective sheriff Mordecai Lloyd gave, that "not withstanding his profession he would fully execute his office in all respects."[57] Now war would lure politically involved Friends into deeper water. They would soon be beyond wading depth, lost in a torrent of activities supportive of violence. Their performance of such tasks would contravene the spirit and intent of their religion to an intolerable degree. Even ordinary Quaker citizens should take a stand, many argued, by refusing to pay taxes intended to finance warlike activities.[58]

While the mid eighteenth-century Quaker reformation was ultimately of great significance in the future of the Society of Friends, it was of far less consequence for the immediate future of Quaker political power.[59] The most eye-catching incident of the crisis, of course, was the retirement from electoral politics of a number of high-profile Quakers. But the pacifist reformation was sharply limited by its character as a revolution from the top. The strict Quakers may have dominated such high-profile gatherings as the Meeting for Sufferings and the Philadelphia Yearly Meeting, but they did not have the minds of the people. By the end of 1756, a public Friend, John Churchman, reported that even in the self-consciously Quaker county of Chester, only about thirty individuals had refused to pay provincial taxes earmarked for the Crown's use.[60] Why, country Friends asked, should they balk at such a tax when English Friends paid impositions specifically levied for the support of war?[61] A year and a half later, Israel Pemberton, Jr., a strict Friend, lamented new developments. The fact that those individuals appointed "to levy, assess & collect the [wartime] tax in the 3 old counties . . . [were] generally such [i.e., Friends]" meant, in Pemberton's view, that Quakers were willing to persecute other Quakers.[62] If that were so, it was likely because the tax men expected to meet few neighbors willing to undergo sufferings for a dubious redefinition of Quaker morality. Israel Pemberton's brother James summed up the situation succinctly when he admitted that "there . . . [was] indeed a majority amongst us who show[ed] little regard to the principles of their profession."[63]

Had they been more appreciative of their own tradition of political involvement, reforming Friends would have been better prepared for its strength. Most Pennsylvania Quakers thought well of the relationship between their religion and their government, and felt it was absurd to relinquish such a connection. In the intense dispute over the narrow ethical question of Quaker legislators' voting money for the Crown's use in wartime, Speaker of the House Isaac Norris, Jr., offered a compelling justification for Quaker traditionalists. In concluding that "money . . . [could] and ought to be given to the Crown," Norris pleaded the past. "I have been particularly careful to follow Precedents where men of the closest understanding & reputation among us have been the immediate actors from the first settlement of the Province."[64] In larger arenas of public debate, apologists for a politically active Quakerism were equally direct. Pennsylvania was Friends' "birthright and possession." "Because they had been the first settlers," Quakers had a right to govern the province. "Because by good government they had shown themselves fit persons to run the colony," they had an obligation to extend their stewardship.[65]

In their effort to justify Quaker political hegemony, the most useful ally popular political leaders turned up was William Penn. By the 1720s and 1730s, contemporaries were choosing to forget the antiproprietary sentiments and factionalism of the early days and had begun to mythologize the past.[66] Negative judgments of the colony's founder, which their predecessors had passed so freely, became infrequent;[67] encomiums began to abound. Penn was a "great Man," whose "whole Conduct [was] governed by, an inexhaustible Stock of Humanity and Benevolence to Mankind."[68] He was "OUR late honourable and worth Proprietor, *to whom the Province of* Pennsylvania *must . . . be under the deepest obligation.*"[69] Most important, Penn's life bespoke a commitment to political activity. He was "justly [to be] compared . . . to the great *Lycurgus*" in "his Wisdom and Policy" in granting "so excellent a Form of Government" and his deep involvement in governmental affairs.[70] As Pennsylvania's popular leaders saw it, Penn's life was an endorsement of Friends' participation in public affairs.

It was against this tradition that the self-styled "sober sort" of Friends rebelled subsequent to the outbreak of the French and Indian War. Convinced that involvement in government led to moral bankruptcy, the Quaker reformers tried to come to terms with Pennsylvania's past by arguing that the vital part of William Penn's experiment was his promise to "settle . . . a perpetual Friendship" with local Indians.[71] That was in keeping with the reformers' belief that personal pacifism, and the goodwill to all humans that such a doctrine entailed, lay at the heart of Quaker benevolence. But as morally intimidating as the reformers could be, they were never very effective in promoting their alternative vision. Far more compelling was the tradition of Quaker political involvement that William Penn had apparently endorsed. Rather than giving ground to the reformers, some Quakers may have found the case for political involvement stronger than ever before. Whereas William Penn had served "as an Agent and an Advocate for his People, [determined] to defend and secure their Rights and Privileges, . . . his Successors [had tried] to abolish and destroy them."[72] Not only had the second generation of proprietors broken faith with their people, they had also broken faith with the Lord. The true heirs of William Penn's vision of a Quaker polity were not his apostate sons—Thomas Penn was a lapsed Quaker, and Richard was an Anglican—but the posterity of his old partners in settlement. Pennsylvania Friends were the only ones who could truly carry the torch of the Quaker past into the unlit future. Pennsylvania gave Friends the freedom to practice their faith *because* the colony was run by colonial Quakers.

The best indicator of just how dominant Friends became in the popular politics of colonial Pennsylvania was the character of the Pennsylvania Assembly. The convening of the House of Representatives in Friends' Phila-

delphia Meetinghouse during the 1690s showed the close connection between Quakerism and government.[73] The unicameral legislature of the
1700s was in some ways an analogue of the Quaker meeting. It was "a
common practice for them [i.e., the legislators] to sit in silence awhile, like
solemn worship, before they proceeded to do business."[74] Later, in the
more cosmopolitan atmosphere of the State House (now better known as
Independence Hall), the old ways continued. The speaker might well end
debate by declaring the sense of the House rather than calling for a vote;
divisions, when they occurred, were infrequently recorded; and members of
the House might issue a meetinglike pronouncement to testify to the good
behavior of one of their fellow representatives.[75] As late as 1774, a young
Philadelphian described the "scurvy appearance" of our HONOURABLE
HOUSE. . . . it was enough to make one sweat to see a parcel of Countrymen
sitting with their hats on, in great course cloth coats, leather breeches, and
woolen stockings in the month of July;—there was not a speech made the
whole time, whether their silence proceeded from their modesty or from
their inability to speak I know not."[76] The "broad brimmed hats planted
firmly upon . . . [Friends] heads, and . . . [the] long silences, . . . inner
dialogues . . . central to the Quaker decision making process," those were
the observable signs of a continuing Quaker ascendancy.[77]

Nor were appearances deceiving. Throughout the entire colonial period,
Friends were constantly at the center of political power in the assembly. The
speakership of the assembly was always occupied by a Quaker, a nominal
Friend, or someone willing to concede a great deal to Quaker influence.
Prior to 1756, Quaker legislators were in a majority and dominated assembly
committees. During and after 1756, when Quakers constituted a sizable
minority in the House of Representatives, they formed the core of an evolving coalition that kept its majority through 1774. So thoroughly entrenched
was Quaker legislative power that it took a revolution to destroy it.[78]

A Unique Constitution

Because of their dominance in Pennsylvania government, Quakers and their
close political allies were the chief authors of provincial constitutional
thought. Friends' interest in constitutional matters began with first settlement, for they arrived in Pennsylvania strongly determined to take whatever
political action they felt necessary to protect the sectarian integrity they had
developed amid old-world persecution. Consequently, they were receptive
to political innovation as no group of North American colonists had been
since the Puritan migration. Their primary political concern was fidelity, not
to the orthodoxies of British political theory, but to the logic of the "Holy

Experiment"; the result was one of the most distinctive strands of constitutional thought in any British colony.

One of the most important determinants of the course of constitutional thought in Pennsylvania was the popular understanding of the "Compact" that William Penn and his first purchasers concluded prior to immigration.[79] In England, the parties had negotiated an agreement; the 1682 Frame of Government, along with its accompanying liberal laws, set out the terms of the bargain mutually agreed upon. Even though the original frame of government met with immediate modification in the New World, original principles such as substantial popular participation in government, liberty of conscience, and an enlightened penal code remained conditions of the contract.[80] To political leaders like David Lloyd, Penn's promises to accept popular control over judicial and administrative officials were a part of the unwritten provincial constitution, as binding after the adoption of the Charter of Privileges in 1701 as in the years before.[81] Moreover, Penn's guarantee of specific rights was quickly metamorphosed into a general promise of "Enlarged" popular privileges.[82] Pennsylvania's first settlers, "men of Sobriety and substance," were "Induced [to immigrate] Chiefly by the provincial Constitution, Which by Compact with the Proprietary was . . . so Established as that the purchasers and adventurers were to have *greater*[83] Privileges than they Enjoyed in their native Countreys."[84]

Although popular leaders frequently took William Penn to task for what they perceived as his backsliding on their settlement contract, when it suited their purposes, community members would also emphasize occasions on which the proprietor appeared as the most unreserved supporter of popular rights. The adoption of the 1701 Charter of Privileges was the best known of these episodes. Knowledge of Penn's acceptance of "the Charter . . . primarily . . . to shelter . . . [Pennsylvania] against A violent or Arbitrary [i.e., royal] Governor" prompted many Pennsylvanians to view their new constitution as a proprietary gift, signifying a commitment to deed to the people "all the Power he could."[85] This view, that Penn had finally passed on to the Pennsylvania Assembly all the legislative power reserved for "the freemen of the . . . Countrey . . . or of their Delegates or Deputies" in the Royal Charter of 1681, was confirmed by the text of the Charter of Privileges.[86] The slight 1701 constitution only briefly considered the legislative powers of the governor and the assembly, but provincial politicians quickly interpreted the absence of any specific legislative mandate for the provincial council as incontrovertible evidence that legislative authority was divided, not into three parts, "but [into] two states or Branches."[87] Because there was nothing resembling a middle estate vying for power with the assembly and governor, there appeared to be fewer constraints on popularly elected representatives. Granted, the governor was still a force with which to contend.

But a unicameral legislature that could claim to be the voice of all provincial residents soon made itself into a structural embodiment of Pennsylvanians' dedication to the fullest expansion of popular privileges.

Because they were convinced of the special nature of their enterprise and of the uniqueness of their constitution, Pennsylvania's early political leaders found the issue of their constitutional relationship with Great Britain a delicate one. All were quite prepared to "claim" and "enjoy all the Common Rights and privileges of freeborn English subjects."[88] In order to possess more rights than Englishmen, Pennsylvanians had to be blessed with the existing ones. But usually the discussion of rights arose in the context of a debate over assembly powers, and that inevitably raised the slippery question of how analogous the Pennsylvania constitution was to its Westminster counterpart. In the heat of argument, exuberant popular spokespersons would sometimes voice sweeping generalizations that ignored the different circumstances of colony and mother country. They might claim an unqualified "Right to parliamentary Privileges," or "that the Assemblies in the *English*-Plantations . . . [were] formed on the Plan of an *English* Parliament."[89] Occasionally, legislators would go to great lengths to develop an extended parliamentary analogy that they thought would bolster their case in a heated argument with a governor over a specific power.[90]

Most of the time, however, pundits were far more circumspect. "The Constitution of England & ours much differ," they argued.[91] While "the method of Executing . . . [legislative] Power, always was as near as could be in a Parliamentary way," the actual allocation of legislative power in Pennsylvania was between proprietor and people, not among king, lords and commons.[92] No authority could "bind" Pennsylvania's assembly to parliamentary precedents. "Only as they . . . [were] found by the House convenient and consistent with the Constitution of this Government [were] they . . . admitted; and frequently altered and adopted to the particular Circumstances of the Colony."[93] While it was true that Pennsylvania's inclusion within the British realm and general adherence to a British constitutional order provided guidelines for what "Proper Incidents . . . though not expressly granted" should attend the exercise of legislative power, popular leaders were determined that they should decide what these "Proper Incidents" were.[94] And always they would interpret such powers in ways that reinforced the unique character of the Pennsylvania constitution. Local leaders were acutely aware that their provincial government had "the Advantage of the British Constitution" in a number of respects, and they were determined to protect those features.[95]

The belief that the Pennsylvania constitution was both peculiar and peculiarly attractive gained great currency during the first half of the eighteenth century. Utilizing William Penn's supposed promises, select elements of

English political tradition, and the structure of their proprietary government, popular political leaders gradually put together a political theory that proved to be an immensely persuasive interpretation of Pennsylvania's constitutional order.

The most important stimulus to innovative constitutional thinking in turn-of-the-century Pennsylvania was the adoption of the 1701 Charter of Privileges. The omission, purposeful or not, of any clear legislative mandate for a governor's council allowed the assembly, under David Lloyd's unyielding leadership, firmly to deny any formal advisory role to the council. As Lloyd put it, the council's power went no "further than as a Council of State, & . . . [was] no part of the Legislative power of . . . Govermt."[96] The consequences of this situation, as one critic of Pennsylvania's government derisively snorted, was to make the council "only a name."[97] During the first quarter of the eighteenth century, William Penn's young, tendentious proprietary secretary, James Logan, tried his utmost to bring the council into the legislative process through the back door.[98] As he later explained, the charter's failure to describe the council as a functioning upper chamber in a bicameral legislature had been an oversight occasioned by William Penn being "under a great pressure of Affairs," and that as soon as the proprietor had realized the omission, he "established a Council," with standard conciliar powers, "by Letters Patent under the Great-Seal."[99] Logan's efforts, however, were counterproductive. The ensuing controversy between assembly and proprietary officials simply attested to what David Lloyd had always maintained, that councillors with a direct legislative role in government would use their authority to curtail popular power.

Two decades later, the council again became the focal point of political debate. In hopes of easing his way to a royal governorship of Pennsylvania should William Penn's death precipitate the demise of the proprietorship, the current proprietary-appointed governor, Sir William Keith, made common cause with assembly politicians, completely disregarding the advice of his councillors. In order to bring Keith to heel, William Penn's executrix, his second wife Hannah Penn, sent instructions commanding Keith make "no Speech, nor send any written Message to the Assembly . . . nor pass any . . . Law[s], without the Consent of a Majority of . . . [the Council] Board."[100] Not surprisingly, this effort to give the council legislative authority by proprietary instruction occasioned angry resistance. Popular spokespersons responded that the council could not "legally be understood to be any other than a Council of State, to advise, and be present, as solemn Witnesses of the Governor's Action."[101] So intense was the protest against alteration by proprietary ukase that James Logan and a handful of his Philadelphia friends were soon feverishly backpedaling, trying to explain away their earlier statements and salvage a few shreds of political influence.[102]

Informally, of course, council members did play a role in Pennsylvania government, giving advice to the governor and on occasion serving as an interim executive board between gubernatorial appointments. Building on what they perceived to be their intended similarity to both the British House of Lords and councils elsewhere in the colonial realm, apologists for the Pennsylvania council occasionally tried to dress themselves up as a special, if ill-defined, estate in Pennsylvania. Their order was composed of "men of Substance," whose wealth distinguished them as new-world aristocrats.[103] In their view, they brought the wisdom to Pennsylvania government that the aristocratic element theoretically supplied to Britain's mixed constitution. Such pretension, however, few Pennsylvanians would abide. "Gentlemen who form the Council," observed the cartographer Lewis Evans, "have no Interest of Privilege above the Freeholders nor are they delegated by the People."[104] Other critics believed that wealthy and influential councillors personified predatoriness, not wisdom, and that any group so thoroughly self-deceived was no worthwhile candidate for a special and permanent role in provincial government.[105] Moreover, there were no local customs that suggested the councillors' claims were more than rank opportunism. Council members had never disqualified themselves from voting in provincial elections, or, in fact, from sitting simultaneously as assembly representatives. In England, members of the aristocratic estate did not meddle in electoral politics. More important, while the British constitution made provision for lords temporal and spiritual, the Pennsylvania Charter of Privileges appeared to deny the existence of a separate conciliar order. Governor and assembly were acknowledged, but there was no provision for a "third" legislative "State."[106]

The efforts of a few outspoken council members to find a rationale for their inclusion in the legislative process met with little success. The public at large recognized what Hannah Penn openly admitted, that the council was a clutch of proprietary "friends."[107] The prevalence of that view during William Penn's proprietorship prevented the council from gaining stature as a distinct governmental institution with legitimate provincial interests to represent. Once control of Pennsylvania passed to the second generation of Penns, a greater distance opened up between proprietors and councillors. But the council was so burdened with its reputation as a proprietary rubber stamp, and so frequently put into the position of having to defend Thomas Penn's odious policies, that it became, if anything, a less prestigious body by the mid eighteenth century than it had been some decades earlier.[108]

Pennsylvanians' rejection of a bicameral legislature meant that legislative power was "lodged solely in the Governor and Assembly," the "two parts [of] our legislature."[109] Strictly speaking, the governor was the proprietor, but with the exception of the few months of his Pennsylvania residencies when William Penn personally exercised gubernatorial power, he and his successors always appointed a deputy (referred to in this book as governor) to reside in Pennsylvania and exercise executive power. Shortly after the adoption of the 1701 Charter of Privileges, William Penn tried to claim that, as proprietor, he retained a separate veto power over any legislation upon which his deputy and the assembly agreed. Even his hand-picked councillors, however, would have nothing to do with that idea.[110] Proprietary failure to gain a veto made the appointment of a governor particularly important for the proprietary family. The province's chief executive was the only official with power to protect proprietary interests from assembly encroachments.[111]

Proprietary surrogate though he was, the Pennsylvania governor was also a representative of the Crown. Incumbent governors tried to capitalize on that connection, recognizing that they could benefit from the royal cachet. But that was not easy. Most locals felt that "the Royal Prerogative as exercised in England . . . [could] no more be understood to accompany . . . Sovereignty, than all the other [English] Laws [could]."[112] Pennsylvania had its own constitution, and under that set of arrangements the governor was overwhelmingly the proprietor's man. The Penn family appointed him, sent him instructions, placed him under a performance bond, and in the late seventeenth and early eighteenth centuries even paid him. Proprietary privileges and gubernatorial powers were inextricably entwined. Executive authority over the Pennsylvania system and over court personnel, for example, was, simultaneously, proprietary patronage power.[113] Proprietary demands that Penn land be exempt from taxation took the form of gubernatorial insistence that, as one part of the legislature, the chief executive had a right to amend tax bills.[114] Although William Penn was willing to give his governor somewhat more leeway to depart from proprietary instructions than his son Thomas was, the public always felt that on issues of executive power and proprietary privilege, the governor's first inclination was to heed the voice of those who had commissioned him.

The close association of Pennsylvania's governors with the proprietary had a profound impact on popular attitudes toward the provincial constitution. The most important consequence was the belief that the gubernatorial half of the legislative process was dominated by private interests, most notably those of the proprietary. "The Proprietaries . . . [themselves comprised] a separate Branch of the Legislature" and "the Proprietary Estate and Interest . . . [was] separate" from those of the people.[115] Penn family concerns constituted "an Idol to which, they . . . long sacrifice[d] the Public Weal."[116] Rather than allow their governors to participate in the give-and-take of legislative compromise, the proprietary family mandated specific policies, to the point where under Thomas Penn's suzerainty they could be accused of "oblig[ing] . . . [the assembly] to make Laws [favorable to the proprietor] by Direction."[117] Under bond as he was, the governor appeared to be little more than "the Proprietaries Tool," an agent whose charge it was simply to implement proprietary instructions.[118]

On their own account, Pennsylvania's governors were not above self-interested activities. As everyone in Pennsylvania knew, "men . . . don't commonly, make use of all the Friends and Interest they have, to get themselves appointed Governors, merely for an Opportunity of doing good to the people they are to govern."[119] And the governors were always surrounded by advisors whose positions belied their disinterest. Councillors were, on the one hand, proprietary and governors' favorites, "chosen as Men do Horsewhips, for being neat and pliant," and, on the other, "a sett of private men" with their own agendas.[120] There was little reason to think that considerations of public interest would prevail over the cacophony of private demands that ceaselessly echoed through the frequently rather vacuous minds of Pennsylvania's governors.

Popular political leaders responded in a variety of ways to the perceived dominance of private interests in the gubernatorial portion of the legislative power. During periods of intense political conflict, they frequently condemned what they believed to be specific instances of selfish behavior. When the rich council members lobbied against a land bank in the early 1720s, they were declared guilty of sacrificing the public good to private gain.[121] When Thomas Penn insisted on exempting his land from taxation during the French and Indian War, he demonstrated how the unrestrained pursuit of private advantage could thoroughly corrupt.[122] Powerful figures such as Penn and James Logan required continuous and close scrutiny, for they artfully maintained a specious pretense of public good while pursuing their interests as "private persons," "infring[ing] . . . on the Properties [of provincial landholders,] and opress[ing] the Freemen of Pennsylvania."[123]

On balance, however, Pennsylvanians avoided wholesale condemnation of private interest. Jaundiced against proprietary government though he was, Joseph Galloway summed up a half-century of political experience when he described private Interest, not as an enemy, but "like some restless Friend, . . . always alive, . . . ever active."[124] As Pennsylvania's popular leaders clearly recognized, the secret of reducing the toll that gubernatorial surveillance could exact was to induce the restless friend inside each chief executive to work on behalf of, rather than against, popular interests. The conservative councilman Isaac Norris, Sr., pointed out the means of doing so when he reduced the essence of government to an exchange. "Government ought to be supported, the Governor maintained, and the necessary public charges defrayed: But then the people must have Privileges granted and laws made."[125] Simply put, the way to induce a governor to pick up a pen (with which to sign popular legislation) was to put money in his purse. In the early eighteenth century, the assembly took over from the proprietary the financial responsibility of maintaining their governor and thereafter became quite adept at buying the goodwill of numerous chief executives.[126] Even the proprietor occasionally proved amenable to such tactics. In the late 1730s, Thomas Penn accepted legislation allowing freeholders to pay their quitrents in depreciated Pennsylvania currency rather than in sterling in return for a compensatory stipend.[127] By the mid eighteenth century, most popular political leaders could agree that the "Practice of purchasing and paying for Laws . . . [was] interwoven with our *Proprietary* Constitution."[128] It was possible to experience sustained good government under a proprietary regime if the assembly tended to the public good and the governor stood, not by his commission, but by the hand that fed him.

The most important result of the close association of private interest with gubernatorial power was a diminution of the authoritative aura of the chief executive, and a related tendency for the assembly to gain widespread recognition as the *only* institution of government capable of speaking for the public interest. If the governor was, "in a sense, not even a public officer at all, but the agent of a private person or group of persons . . . charged . . . with the defence and protection of distinctly private interests," he could not possibly speak for the public good.[129] When Governor Evans tried to shore up his position by claiming that he had "the chief command of all the People in the Province, . . . [and was] theirs, & therefore their Representatives Superiour," the assembly would not yield.[130] They claimed a "Concurrent Authority," an "Equality" that flowed from the establishment of "two states or Branches in the Legislative authority of . . . [the] Province."[131] Ordinary legislators were "in as near Relation to the Crown as any . . . [could] pretend to be in this Govrmt."[132] In the hand-to-hand encounters of political debate, popular pundits repeatedly cut into gubernatorial pretension with derisive ripostes.[133] Governors were "our Fellow-Subjects," "Proconsuls" who "strut and king it away in the Provinces, and who usurp the Title appropriate to their royal Master, by calling themselves God's Viceregents, to which they have just as much Right as the Parish Constables, who as well as the others execute their Office in the King's Name."[134]

Occasionally, as a matter of practical politics, popular leaders would retreat from their belittlement of the governor. In times of war, Quaker assemblymen were frequently willing to put the monkey of preparedness on the governor's back. As captain-general and "Head of the Legislature," the governor bore responsibility to react to danger.[135] Military defense was the duty of those in whose hands "the executive powers of government" lay.[136] In the face of other, less conventional crises in which they needed the governor, elected representatives could be far more creative. When legislators tried to initiate impeachment procedures against James Logan, and later against Provost William Smith, they argued that the governor could "be deemed to supply a middle state, Resembling (though in Inferiour Degree) that of the [English House of] Lords" and thereby empowered to serve as judge in such an action.[137] That bizarre notion, however, was the closest any popular politicians ever came to suggesting that the governor had a claim to an elevated status under the Pennsylvania constitution. To an overwhelming degree, the effect of popular political rhetoric was to disparage the governor's ability to transcend a narrow private interest (one that was particularly inimical to those of Pennsylvanians), and thereby discredit him as a spokesperson for the public good.

In place of the governor as the traditional leader of the community, popular politicians proffered themselves, through the agency of the Pennsylvania Assembly. In their view, the assemblymen represented the "whole Province," or more specifically the "whole Body of the People."[138] Because there were no separate estates in Pennsylvania, those who paid taxes, owned property, and qualified to vote were part of a provincewide "Body Corporate, and every Person thus situated, a real Member of that Body."[139] In representing "the Whole people," legislators assumed responsibility for reconciling or discounting private interests to the point of discovering the public good.[140] As the province's custodian, the assembly's obligation was plain: to be an effective initiator and guarantor of good laws. Elected representatives composed a "Body of Delegates, impowered by their Constituents" to legislate "for the general interest and utility of the whole Body Politic."[141]

Critics responded that their opponents occupied indefensible ground. William Penn, who knew his old friends well, quietly stated that they were courting anarchic consequences by trying to "mak[e] . . . themselves the whole Legislative," and thereby, putting executive powers under the control of an "uncertain collective body."[142] Others were less restrained. The assembly failed to acknowledge that it represented only "a part" of "the People of Pennsylvania," not them all.[143] By taking the lead in government, the House of Representatives strove "to invert the order of Govmt," and politically conscious Pennsylvanians either encouraged them or quietly acquiesced, "allow[ing] the Legislators [i.e., representatives] to be Head of State."[144]

Pennsylvania's popular leaders were sensitive to these charges that they were closet republicans with "democratical aspirations."[145] Thus, they were always willing—and, it is important to note, sincerely willing—to acknowledge some kind of vague symbolic subordinance. The governor appointed by the proprietor was at the "Helm of Government";[146] Pennsylvanians were in a dependent relationship with Great Britain;[147] in urging governors to ignore proprietary instructions, the chief executive should look to "his

Majesty's Interest" and "the Good of his Subjects."[148] In time, popular spokespersons became adept at turning charges of constitutional radicalism back on their opponents. "Such a conduct [Governor Morris's intransigence over a taxation bill] in a Governor, appears to us the most likely thing in the World to make People incline to a Democracy, who would otherwise never have dreamt of it."[149] But, in fact, their critics were not so far wrong. Popular political thinkers were inspired by the conviction that Pennsylvania had been founded by "MUTUAL COMPACT" among prospective settlers, including William Penn, who intended to place "the WHOLE legislative power . . . where it . . . [was] always safest lodged, *in the hands of the People.*"[150] The responsibility for implementing this contract to promote the public interest clearly lay with the people's representatives.

Because of the uniqueness of the Pennsylvania constitution, public discourse over its character differed considerably from constitutional debate in other colonies. There were a handful of intellectual traditionalists and social conservatives who, with little sense of the irony of their situation, argued for radical change. James Logan believed that Pennsylvania's constitution "Blemish[ed]" the countenance of Britain's colonial empire.[151] Only the adoption of a mixed government would guarantee the kind of conformity that Logan craved. Provost William Smith was another well-known figure whose distaste for his adopted province's "Independency" gained expression in his cries for "mix't Forms" of government.[152] But Logan, Smith, and a few fellow travelers drew on assumptions that were outside the mainstream of political thought in Pennsylvania; they further marginalized their intellectual impact with ill-advised pronouncements that the Charter of Privileges was "not worth so many pence," or that the provincial constitution was an "absurdity."[153] To the vast majority of politically conscious Pennsylvanians, such sentiments were ludicrous. Mixed government had been traded off for a frame of government that provided more rights than Englishmen enjoyed. To argue that "the government of . . . [the] province . . . [was] defective, as far as it want[ed] . . . an exact Resemblance to that of our Mother-Country" was unreflective mimicry of a "laudable partiality in *Britons,* to prefer their own Constitution, as the most perfect of all others." "It . . . [was] altogether as absurd to prescribe the same form of government to people differently circumstanced, as to pretend to fortify all forts . . . on the same model."[154]

Not surprisingly, Pennsylvania's popular leaders also dismissed traditional notions of balanced government. To be sure, the issue of balance did arise in mid eighteenth-century Pennsylvania. But the balance in question was not the legislative equilibrium that king, lords, and commons maintained in the idealized English constitution. One tendency was to see the Quakers as a balance wheel in the political relationships of the various religious denominations and linguistic groups in Pennsylvania.[155] Another, although this but rarely, was to imply the need for some balance between the proprietor as a "separate estate" and the interests of the people.[156] But the most common use of the term *balance* (and even this was infrequent) was in the context of the "Great" John Locke's division of governmental power into "Legislative, executive and federative."[157] Although acknowledging this tripartite scheme, Pennsylvanians primarily concerned themselves with the balance of power between the legislative and executive branches of government.[158] Used in this context, balance offered a rationale for both proprietor and assembly. Thomas Penn and his supporters availed themselves of this logic more than anyone else. Penn felt entitled "to get the power of Government more equally divided," for in his view the Pennsylvania constitution promised him "one Half the legislative power."[159] Popular politicians perceived this as a second-generation proprietary plot "to recover the Privileges their father gave in order to settle his Province without any charge to himself or the Crown."[160] Assembly spokespersons occasionally used the argument of balance in support of their resistance to proprietary efforts to reposition the fulcrum that lay between executive and legislature.[161] But in the larger sense of pleading for a legislative equilibrium between the traditional three estates, the idea of balance had no relevance for Pennsylvania politics. "BAL-LANCE OF POWER," snorted Andrew Hamilton, "that was much talked of . . . *Nonsense,* when applied to a Democratical Government" like that of Pennsylvania.[162]

Convinced that Pennsylvania had "a quite different Frame and Constitution . . . than *Great Britain,*" and that such distinctiveness was the single most important reason why they enjoyed more rights than the English, the majority of popular politicians were predisposed to dismiss out of hand structural criticism based on standard categories of English constitutional thought.[163] While it was true that a half-century after its founding, Pennsylvania's "Constitution [was] not old enough to plead Perscription," its foundations were much stronger than the "simple conjectures" that contemporaries relied on to elucidate the English past.[164] William Penn, for example, had left a clear record of what he had intended. The 1701 Charter of Privileges reinforced the 1681 Royal Charter by placing a great deal of power in the unicameral legislature, and the 1682 Frame of Government promised the representatives of the people sweeping powers of appointment and review over executive and judicial officers.[165] These documents, along with Penn's selectively remembered ancillary promises, provided a thorough set of guidelines for the provincial constitution. Contemporaries could examine their provincial traditions to determine if their constitution had decayed or deviated from its standards.[166] Alternatively, they could look to the past to help them identify powers that needed to come under assembly control in order to fulfill Penn's alleged vision of a model commonwealth. And if the past was not as clear as it might have been, Pennsylvania's political thinkers could look elsewhere for help. Not to Great Britain, not to the inappropriate standards of mixed government and a balanced constitution, but to "their reason."[167] "Reason" and the logic of "natural Right" were the obvious means of illuminating relationships between the assembly and the proprietor.[168] Quiet, reasoned appreciation of Pennsylvania's unique constitutional development would do much more than anything else to clarify and promote the political goal that William Penn had long ago singled out, *"to support Power in Reverence with the People, and to secure the People from the Abuses of Power."*[169]

The Ideology of Civil Quakerism

From the first years of settlement to the end of the colonial period, Quakers and a handful of individuals in close association with Friends dominated the Pennsylvania Assembly and defined the character of the provincial constitution. Yet from the early eighteenth century on, Friends were in a minority, and by 1757 Provincial Secretary Richard Peters estimated that only one-eighth of the province was Quaker.[170] That circumstance raises the very important question of how the Quakers maintained their political dominance.

The best point at which to begin considering this problem is with the admission of Isaac Norris, Jr., that Friends safeguarded their political influence through what he called "the Quaker System."[171] In the narrowest sense, Norris meant by this the Quaker ability to exploit both the divisions within other denominations and the rivalry among them. The Anglican, Presbyterian, and German Lutheran and Reformed churches all experienced some localized or regional divisions during the mid eighteenth century, and the animosities among factions of different denominations worked against the appearance of any large, popular non-Quaker political alliance. As the Friends archenemy, Provost William Smith, saw it, the Quakers had "made it their invariable rule (agreeable to the Maxim, *Divide* et *impera*) to divide and distract all other Societies, and to take off some men among them."[172] Both Norris and Smith recognized, although Smith made too much of it, the deliberate, manipulative side of Quaker politics. Continuation of the "Quaker System" of politics required intentional exploitation of the advantages that religious pluralism provided.

Another important part of the Quaker strategy of maintaining political power was to gerrymander county boundaries and to underrepresent new counties in the assembly. When Berks and Northampton counties were established in the early 1750s, the Quaker Party carefully separated the new German-settled backcountry areas of Philadelphia and Bucks counties from the long-established Quaker communities of the southeast.[173] The practice of decreasing assembly representation to new counties had begun sometime earlier. When Lancaster County was created in 1729, it received four assembly seats. Twenty years later, York was given two seats. When Berks and Northampton were established in 1750 and 1752 respectively, each was assigned only one seat. The progressive decline in the representation of backcountry counties was a deliberate assembly policy designed to ensure the continued dominance of the three old Quaker counties and Philadelphia, with their combined total of twenty-six legislative seats. The "Quaker System" entailed keeping political power where it began in Pennsylvania, in the long-settled Quaker communities close to the Delaware River.[174]

A third way in which popular Quaker leaders consciously enhanced their political influence was to exploit the patronage possibilities that assembly powers offered. As the House of Representatives asserted itself against governor and proprietors, more and more powers came their way. Trustees of the loan office, currency signers for Pennsylvania's paper money, collectors of the excise, inspectors of flour, staves, and lumber, collectors of tonnage duties and import duties on criminals, servants, and slaves, and provincial commissioners to direct the expenditure of various funds—all were creatures of the assembly. These were just some of the perquisites that popular leaders divided among the more voracious of their followers.[175]

Finally, there was the opportunity that the proprietary presence itself created. The "Quaker System" of government rested, to some degree, on the cultivation of antiproprietary sentiments. Popular leaders were prepared to distill the discontent proprietary policies engendered and to use the potent mixture for their own political purposes. In so doing, they acted consciously, deliberately, and pragmatically. They took note of corrupt surveyors, land office favoritism, and increasingly heavy quitrent exactions, and tried to exploit the resentfulness such awareness produced when the Quaker Party faced immediate threats.[176] Non-Quakers or Friends, backcountry residents or easterners, countryfolk or urbanites, it made little difference. Most Pennsylvanians responded positively to the popular tactics of blackening the proprietary. So intoxicating could the sentiments behind popular politics become that on occasion even Thomas Penn's own attorney-general could not be counted on to defend charter-based, proprietary privileges.[177]

But the relationship of Pennsylvania residents to the proprietor was never simply a matter of political opportunism. Day-to-day conflicts between proprietor and people were also a catalyst to a broader range of thinking about the nature of the Pennsylvania polity. Differences between William Penn and his fellow first settlers, as well as those between his son Thomas and second-generation Pennsylvanians, raised the question of what the Quaker experiment was to be. How was it to be carried out? How governed? What values would it reflect? What might it hope to achieve? By posing such questions, proprietary/popular conflicts created a context in which Quakers were forced to define themselves and their mission in Pennsylvania. Because the Society of Friends was a religious organization, we tend to think of Pennsylvania Quakers in religious terms—the universal potential of the Inner Light, personal pacifism, the avoidance of oaths, a plain style of life and address, and various other testimonies. We forget that Friends had already largely succeeded in establishing a powerful religious identity prior to their immigration. What preoccupied them far more on their arrival in Pennsylvania was their need for supplementary, and very extensive, self-definition as participants in, and governors of, a new worldly experiment.

The introspection that the assumption of governmental responsibility occasioned, sharpened by continuing conflict between proprietors and their Pennsylvania opponents, produced a reasonably coherent cluster of popular beliefs that may best be referred to as an ideology of civil Quakerism.[178] More than anything else, this ideology defined the character of Pennsylvania's popular political community, providing the glue, as it were, that held together the "Quaker System" of government. After a few short decades in Pennsylvania, Friends found themselves identifying so closely with the ideology of civil Quakerism, and giving it such precedence in their conception of community purpose, that they strongly resisted even the instruction of Quaker reformers whose interests were far more focused on the Society's religious integrity.[179] Nor was the appeal of this ideology limited to Quakers. One of its strengths was that it brought others into the "Quaker System" through a process of "Quakerization."[180] Contemporaries meant by this that non-Quakers accepted Friends' standards of judgment on many public issues and embraced many of the political goals identified by popular Quakers. Quakerization was shorthand for the political consensus that the ideology of civil Quakerism tended to produce.

The cluster of interrelated political beliefs that identified the ideology of civil Quakerism appeared piecemeal in the reflections of both Friends and their non-Quaker allies on the nature of the Pennsylvania experiment during their experiences in public affairs. One observation that frequently prompted speculation about the principles of Quaker government was the type of comment the New Yorker John Watts made in 1774 on considering the Pennsylvania he had come to know. "'Tis an amazing Colony that, for increase and wealth."[181] How was it possible to explain the colony's growth, its demonstrable riches, and the fact that those "among us who are in other Places called *the common People*" could search the "Whole Globe" and find no place "to compare for *Ease, Freedom, Sufficiency* of Necessaries, and a general Equality?"[182] Andrew Hamilton had an answer that other Pennsylvanians echoed innumerable times:

It is not to the Fertility of our Soil, and the Commodiousness of our Rivers, that we ought chiefly to attribute the great Progress this Province has made, within so small a Compass of Years, in Improvements, Wealth, Trade and Navigation, and the extraordinary Increases of People, who have been drawn hither from almost every Country in *Europe*; a Progress which much more antient Settlements on the Main of *America* cannot at present boast of; No, it is principally and almost wholly owing to the Excellency of our Constitution, under which we enjoy a greater Share both of civil and religious Liberty than any of our Neighbours.[183]

There it was. At the heart of the ideology of civil Quakerism, was Pennsylvania's unique constitution, with its "Charter of Privileges . . . a Monument of . . . [William Penn's] Benevolence to Mankind."[184] The essential character of the Pennsylvania constitution had nothing to do with the mixed government and balanced constitution that was the centerpiece of political thought in Great Britain. Rather, the Pennsylvania document presented an array of particular powers that the representatives of the people had come to enjoy under the Charter: the council had no ability to veto legislation, provincial elections were annual, and sheriffs were elected, while the assembly sat on its own adjournments, raised and disposed of public money, named its own treasurer, appointed many of the officers of government, and controlled the salaries of others.[185] Although there were a few isolated Philadelphians who claimed that their fellow-citizens enjoyed a surfeit of privileges, the vast majority of politically aware Pennsylvanians thought that, if anything, assembly powers should be increased, not checked.[186] In a Quakerized polity, guided by the view that government should be "limited," and accustomed to perceiving authority as arising from a deeply internalized ethic of self-restraint, the concentration of political power in the hands of the people's representatives was nothing to fear.[187]

The other major feature of the Pennsylvania constitution that Andrew Hamilton emphasized in his paean was its guarantee of liberty of conscience. William Penn considered freedom of religion to be, as he put it, "the fi[r]st fundamentall of the Goverment of my Country. . . . every Person that does or shall reside therein shall have and enjoy the Free Possession of his or her faith and exercise of wors[h]ip towards God, in such way and manner As every Person shall in Conscience beleive is most acceptable to God and so long as every such Person useth not their Christian liberty to Licentiousness."[188] All of Penn's early constitutions granted religious liberty, and in 1701 the first article of the Charter of Privileges reaffirmed that promise. No one who "acknowledge[d] one almighty God" should be "molested or prejudiced in his or their person or Estate because of his or their Consciencious perswasion or Practice."[189] Stated as it was, in emphatic tones, and contrasting markedly with prevailing practices on both sides of the Atlantic, Penn's promise of religious liberty echoed loudly through the dissenting religious communities of the British Isles and western Europe. The Presbyterian Francis Alison immigrated "because of the charter that protected every religion and . . . [granted] equal privileges of citizenship."[190] German sectarians were drawn to Pennsylvania by assurances that "children of God" would find a haven "secure from outward persecution."[191] Once resident in Pennsylvania, individuals were, if anything, more appreciative of their religious freedom. Locals reminded pretentious Anglicans that "by Pens Charter" "all Religions are free in this Province," and when the corporation of Philadelphia welcomed Thomas Penn to Pennsylvania in 1732, it thanked him, "*above all* [192] . . . [for his] religious care . . . in securing that Natural Right *Liberty of Conscience* and Freedom from Spiritual Tyranny."[193] Many Pennsylvanians could easily agree with the German immigrant who pointed to Pennsylvania's religious freedom as the most important reason why he "did not repent . . . [his] immigration."[194]

There were, of course, differences over what religious liberty entailed. During the late seventeenth and early eighteenth centuries, Anglicans challenged Quakers over the latter's demand that affirmations should replace oaths, and claimed that religious freedom entitled them to the same establishment benefits they enjoyed in England.[195] As for Friends, their spokespersons frequently felt that responsibility for the maintenance of civil order and for the good reputation of their society placed an onus upon them to distinguish the practice of religious liberty from that of licentious behavior.[196] The most serious disagreements, however, occurred over pacifism. Many Friends believed that liberty of conscience entailed some limitation on wartime commitments, while many non-Quakers felt that God's injunctions to defend themselves required provincial laws facilitating active belligerence.[197] But such disagreements rarely produced any qualifications to the widely shared judgment that Pennsylvania's "chief virtue" was "the wholesome Laws of . . . [the] Province, by which all Men, without distinction, are protected from Injury and Persecution, on Account of any religious Opinions."[198]

Without question, most Pennsylvanians believed they lived in a favored world. "We are distinguished," their representatives wrote, "above any others of the King's Subjects abroad."[199] And most were equally convinced that they owed their enjoyment of Pennsylvania's political and religious privileges to the Quakers. William Penn had provided the frame of government and the ideal of a benevolent society open to immigrants of varied background; other Friends had dedicated much effort to securing the popular privileges that the assembly had gained and the Quaker Party was determined to defend. While many non-Quaker Pennsylvanians lauded freedom of conscience, no religious group earned the kind of association with that principle that Friends enjoyed. Liberty of conscience, the most essential of all Privileges, remained first and foremost a Quaker issue.[200]

Like the constitution and liberty of conscience, prosperity, too, was coupled tightly to Quakerism. Of course, it was happenstance that placed William Penn's colony in a "healthful Climate" and "productive Country," but many colonists were prepared to see even that as the bestowal of divine favor on a secular Quaker enterprise.[201] And the more apologists emphasized the connection between prosperity and the Quaker constitution, the more the promotion of economic opportunities seemed, in itself, to be a principle of Quaker government. Most important, the assembly's sponsorship and management of the provincial loan office seemed to be incontrovertible evidence of the Friends' commitment to the province's economic well-being.

The Pennsylvania loan office came into existence in 1723, when the assembly tried to ameliorate the effects of economic depression by printing a provincial currency. The currency provided a number of benefits. It primed the economic pump by allowing public works expenditures to be financed on the expectation of future government income. It raised a public revenue through the interest payments borrowers made, and thus contributed to Pennsylvania's ability to avoid provincial property taxes through the beginning of the French and Indian War. It provided a local circulating medium of exchange in an economy frequently short of specie, and hence relieved some of the pressure on debtors, whose lack of liquidity, rather than lack of assets, threatened them with serious losses. Most important, the loan office was a land bank that extended moderate-sized loans to residents who could offer as collateral realty or personalty valued at twice the amount of the loan. The fact that the interest rate was a flat 5 percent, with no consideration given to risk, drew thousands of Pennsylvanians to the loan office door. While it is obvious from the collateral requirements that the provincial loans were no subsidy to the working poor, they did allow a wide range of farmers and small businessmen to purchase land and invest in improvements that ultimately raised productivity. By offering below-market interest rates, and thus subsidizing capital formation, the Pennsylvania government facilitated the economic expansion and prosperity that so clearly distinguished the colony.[202]

In the thirty-odd years during which the loan office was effective, Pennsylvanians closely associated it with popular Quaker leaders and the Quaker Party.[203] When the assembly first broached the idea of a loan office, the proprietary family and its Pennsylvania voice, James Logan, strongly resisted it, correctly viewing the plan as inflationary. Eventually, Thomas Penn came around to the view that the loan office was a necessary evil, facilitating the liquidity he needed in order to sell land and collect quitrents. In the public mind, however, he remained the enemy of paper currency.[204] From the beginning, assemblymen were the chief sponsors of the loan office, and it was the popular politician David Lloyd who, in 1729, persuaded Governor Patrick Gordon to break his proprietary instructions against further emissions.[205] Thereafter, the Quaker-dominated assembly spearheaded both the successful campaigns to increase and re-emit loan office funds in the 1730s and 1740s, and the ill-fated, prolonged effort to persuade Thomas Penn to agree to augment the currency in the late 1740s and early 1750s.[206]

In the organization of the loan office, political sponsorship was just as clear. Under Andrew Hamilton's speakership of the assembly, Hamilton himself was also acting trustee of the loan office. John Kinsey followed in Hamilton's footsteps in both offices, and when Isaac Norris, Jr., became speaker, his brother Charles took over the loan office. The four additional trustees appointed to represent the three old counties and the southwestern backcountry were without exception close allies, who thus acquired the power to oversee property evaluations, to order the waiting list for mortgages, and to decide against which delinquent debtor legal proceedings might commence.[207] There was no appeal from their recommendations, and clearly they made some enemies. One anonymous petitioner charged that the "station of a Trustee of the General Loan Office . . . [was] attended with such influence and power upon the persons and estates of the Inhabitants . . . and upon the votes in elections, that it . . . [was] highly unreasonable they should sit or act as Representatives in the General Assembly."[208] But complaints were few. By all accounts, the loan office was lenient and the wait for those in line worthwhile.[209] Obviously, the trustees granted loans and administered their office with one eye on the politics of their decisions. But blatant patronage merely underlined what everyone knew, that Pennsylvania's popular politics were Quaker politics.[210] And the loan office symbolized one of the most admired characteristics of public-spirited Quakerism—an innovative, facilitative turn of mind, willing, within what we now recognize as conservative economic parameters, to enhance Pennsylvania's reputation as "the best poor man's country."[211]

While the bulk of contemporary comment attesting to Pennsylvania's attractiveness centered on the provincial constitution, liberty of conscience, and economic opportunity, other features of the Quaker colony were by no means overlooked. "Neither Soldier nor mercinary Bonds of any other Denomination burden or injure us," wrote one individual. "The Natives . . . we have always livd peaceably with and they love us. We have none of those opulent powerful Men, which are in some Parts of the World, to oppress or enslave us."[212] Some chose to stress the ethereal side of the provincial heritage, "the hand of Brotherly Love, Forbearance and meekness" that attended Quakerism.[213] Others turned to the practical. Pennsylvania was free of "racking Rents for Lands, oppresive Taxes, Tythes, and Military Appointments."[214] Whatever their specific concern, and no matter how fragmentary, such statements enhance our understanding of the peculiar popular political ideology that distinguished the Quaker Party.

One of the values that contemporaries most frequently associated with colonial Pennsylvania was peacefulness. Quakers were committed to harmonious relationships among all human kind, and their North American experiment was intended to foster "mutual forbearance" and respect, tolerance, and charity.[215] Whereas to be "Presbyterianized" was to demonstrate an "uncharitable temper" in public affairs, to be Quakerized was to be predominantly concerned with establishing amicable relations.[216] It was the Quaker influence in Pennsylvania that was responsible for producing what William Livingston of New York identified as a quiet "medley of all kinds of People and of all denominations" in comparison with the dissonance of his own multicultural colony.[217] While Friends' desire for social harmony was implicit in their advocacy of religious tolerance, it found clearest expression in the principle of pacifism. Quakers were widely known to eschew warfare, and Pennsylvania was intended to be a peaceable country. Many non-Quaker immigrants welcomed such a policy; they, or their parents, had seen too much of warfare in the Old World. One indicator of how persuasive pacifist sympathies had become in Pennsylvania by the outbreak of the French and Indian War was the bellicose Governor Robert Hunter Morris's recognition that he needed to play to that gallery. "I and the People of Pennsylvania," Morris disingenuously proclaimed, "have been used to Peaceable principles."[218] By using this language, Morris was trying to identify himself with the many Pennsylvanians who yearned for a continuation of peace, and who felt aggrieved by their loss of blood in the province's first real war. He hoped to bring round "soft" pacifists to support aggressive military policies.

But Quakers, too, recognized that the advent of war created a new situation. And new situations required a clarification of old standards. While the well-known Quaker reformers, with their formulation of a new strict pacifism and withdrawal from politics (although not from all political activity), frequently commanded the attention of outsiders, the majority of Friends believed they could retain their personal pacifism and still participate as citizens, local officials, and legislators in the war effort.[219] At the local level, within the context of the community in which non-Quakers usually came to know their Quaker neighbors, there was plenty of evidence that pacifism did not always mean what its Philadelphia critics charged. Out on the frontier areas of southwestern Pennsylvania, there were Quakers who had been closely enough involved in the Pennsylvania-Maryland boundary fracas to lay to rest any rumors that they would sacrifice their community to strict pacifism.[220] And incidents during the French and Indian War and Pontiac's Rebellion pointed out that the tradition of tough-minded frontier Quakerism continued on. The well-known Quaker Wright brothers, James and John, busied themselves procuring military transport;[221] Thomas Minshall supported defensive measures; and the Warrington Monthly Meeting rebuked John Pope and John Blackburn for their aggressive response to Indian attacks.[222] "Four leading Quakers," among others, supported the recruitment of a local force of rangers after York County faced repeated attacks;[223] in Northampton County, Friends were prepared "to be security for all [the arms] that should be loss or broke or stolen" in order to encourage their delivery.[224] As practiced, Quaker pacifism was by no means a simple, one-dimensional faith. Rather, it was a predisposition that in wartime could accommodate a variety of actions contributing to community safety, provided, of course, they stopped considerably short of personal violence. Non-Quakers perceived those gestures of community commitment as meaningful in themselves, but also as symbols of goodwill that validated Friends' claim to conscientious objector status.

Given their views on warfare, it is not surprising that most Pennsylvania Quakers were opposed to the establishment of a provincial militia prior to the French and Indian War. They believed that the governor, in his charter-sanctioned capacity of captain-general, could issue commissions and call out a voluntary militia if he wished.[225] Governors Evans and Thomas both availed themselves of that option when warfare seemed to threaten the province.[226] Another alternative was for citizens to take the initiative (as they did in Benjamin Franklin's famous Association of 1747) and having organized themselves into military companies, place themselves under the command of the governor.[227] Both of these options allowed the bellicose to organize and defend themselves without creating laws that might result in punitive action against pacifists.

Once the French and Indian War broke out, the reorganized Quaker Party was prepared to break with tradition, but only slightly. It would pass a militia law, provided there be no compulsory turnout, the men choose their own officers, and the elected officers write the articles of discipline.[228] Outsiders viewed such a law as a "Joke on all military Affairs."[229] But to Pennsylvanians, the principles involved were a matter of conviction. The assembly would not relent even when the Crown repealed the province's voluntary militia law in 1756. Thereafter, those Pennsylvanians who did fight in the French and Indian War did so largely as paid provincial enlistees, serving for short periods under officers whom the governor commissioned and subject to the discipline of the British Mutiny Act.[230]

For Pennsylvania's popular politicians, the issue of the militia certainly touched on the problem of protecting pacifists. The passage of a militia law in the three Lower Counties that required all able-bodied men to enlist, provide arms and ammunition, and attend exercises under threat of fine, again demonstrated that persecution was never far off.[231] But the Quaker Party leaders also understood that conflict over the organization of a militia was a quarrel over political power. In the highly polarized atmosphere of the day, the governor would appoint only his supporters as officers, and Quaker Party leaders feared that the militia would thus become an instrument of political change. Back in Governor Evans's day, the voluntary militia had taken upon itself the right to intimidate electors, and that specter remained.[232] In his polemic *A Brief State*, Provost William Smith set out a blueprint for a political revolution by proposing that militia patronage, indoctrination, and intimidation be used to build up a strong governor's party, dedicated to increasing executive and proprietary power and establishing a mixed constitution. The only sure way to frustrate such a nefarious scheme was to keep the choice of militia officers in the hands of the troops. As Richard Peters observed, the principle of election was one that the Quaker Party would "never" give up.[233]

Prejudice against any militia law that had a whiff of punitiveness or coercion about it ran far beyond Quaker circles. During the early 1740s, for example, German settlers were likely to see a militia in the context of both proprietary land policy and their European past. A governor controlled by a proprietary family might well use the militia to "eject . . . poor people out of their possessions," or to force the many Pennsylvanian land claimants who were tardy in paying fees or purchase money to take out regular patents immediately.[234] The militia itself might be exploited as a source of labor to build forts.[235] Quaker Party supporters warned their fellow Germans that following the Proprietary Party would only "bring the same Slavery upon us, for which we fled from our Native Country."[236] When the French and Indian War crisis broke, Quaker Party leaders continued to play on these same fears. Benjamin Franklin was a master at this. He evoked images of old-world tyranny by accusing Thomas Penn of "reducing a free People to the abject State of Vassalage."[237] On reconsideration, Pennsylvanians would be worse off than that, for "Vassals must *follow* their Lords to the Wars . . . : our Lord Proprietary would *send* us out to fight *for* him."[238] Penn's willingness "to stile himself *absolute Proprietary*" was indicative of his intentions.[239] He wanted provincials "not only to *defend* . . . [proprietary] Lands, but to *plough* them: For this . . . [his] Lieutenant . . . [might] alledge the *Usage and Custom* in *Germany* . . . [for by the mid 1750s the province was] chiefly [composed of] *Germans*."[240]

How much such skillful innuendo and rhetorical flourish affected public opinion is difficult to say. Isaac Norris, Jr., was already sure of German sympathies in the spring of 1755, certain that they would "joyn . . . [with the Quaker Party] in dread of arbitrary Government."[241] That Norris knew his neighbors well, Governor Denny confirmed over two years later. "When I hastened . . . into the County of Berks," he recounted, "to encourage the raising . . . [of a local defense force] I met with an unexpected Obstacle. The Country People . . . woud not serve under Provincial Officers . . . but insisted on chusing their own; . . . cry[ing] this up as a most valuable Privilege, and it is generally deemed so, and obstinately persisted in."[242] Like other Quakerized Pennsylvanians, church Germans as well as "soft" pacifists (such as Christopher Saur, Sr., had become in 1755) might accept a militia under the dread of Indian attack, but they would do so only under the terms of a noncoercive, elective militia law.[243] Suspicion of standard defense organizations and those associated with the military continued throughout the war.[244] Ultimately, Pennsylvania's governors had to give up on a militia law and settle for defending the province with hired guns who sold their services for short periods of enlistment. Because these men would only serve under neighbors whom they knew and trusted, and who frequently shared many of the same popular political assumptions as their troops, the proprietary supporters' hopes of establishing militia-based cadres for their party came to nothing.[245] Even Conrad Weiser, a well-regarded military leader who supported the governor's party, found it impossible to translate his military influence into electoral support.[246]

Although civil Quakerism gained its distinctive character largely from its few fundamental conceptions—the sanctity of the provincial constitution, liberty of conscience, provincial prosperity, a loosely defined pacifism, and no regular militia law—Quaker Party supporters frequently stressed other appealing ideas consistent with their main tenets. One of the most attractive of these was low taxes. Building on their view that a tithe-free society promised cheap government, popular Quakers quickly broadened their position to oppose public levies that were for the support of superfluous placemen. William Penn had originally promised to take care of the expenses of government, and some onus to do so remained on the proprietary family even after his death. As for the general populace's contribution to public revenue, that should be as little and as painless as possible. In fact, until 1755, Pennsylvania had no provincial tax on wealth or property, a circumstance that lent credence to popular belief in the beneficence of Quaker leaders and in good prospects for prosperity under their care.[247] After the French and Indian War broke out and taxes skyrocketed, the Quaker Party could no longer make such sweeping claims, but it compensated somewhat by stressing its commitment to equitable taxation. If Pennsylvania freeholders were going to pay unprecedented taxes, popular leaders would do their best to see that the proprietors did likewise.[248]

A related area in which Quaker and Quaker Party leaders took some interest was property rights. As we might expect of those who shared a strong belief in the sanctity of property, they were careful never to question the proprietor's right to purchase Indian land and to set land prices, quitrent rates, or settlement covenants. But they did take the view that community interest and individual property titles needed some protection from proprietary capriciousness. That conviction lay behind the assembly's willingness to pay compensation to the proprietary for accepting pre-1732 quitrents in Pennsylvania currency at a pegged rate.[249] If the proprietors demanded sterling, the exchange rate would fall further, injuring all Pennsylvania consumers. It was that conviction, too, that prompted the Quaker Party to push for public access to the proprietary land office. Because the real property rights of all Pennsylvanians were dependent on the records of that office, it was intolerable that these documents were not open to scrutiny, and that the office could be opened or closed at the whim of its secretary.[250]

Although these were quite specific Quaker Party policies, they reflect a larger dimension of civil Quakerism. This was the general tendency of Quaker leaders to try to put power that had obvious public implications under the control or oversight of popular representatives or institutions. The land office should be put in the hands of assembly appointees, individuals who would regard themselves as public, not private, trustees. The governor should never be given the power to preside over a chancery court. Governors were proprietary appointees, and many chancery cases would involve proprietary land claims.[251] Such cases should, instead, go to the common law courts, where juries could represent the community's voice. Juries, however, were not enough in themselves. Magistrates could be petty tyrants in summary hearings, and they could overawe juries not of firm resolve. The assembly, then, should have the right to remove magistrates, for those who once broke "over the Verge and Confines of Law . . . [to] rove in the Field of Oppression . . . [were likely to] never stop."[252] The important thing about these ideas was neither their individual distinctiveness nor their Whiggish cast, but that they complemented the general tenor of civil Quaker thought so well.

Civil Quakerism as a Political Idiom

The ideology of civil Quakerism, composed as it was of a deep appreciation of Pennsylvania's unique constitution, liberty of conscience, provincial prosperity, loosely defined pacifism, rejection of a militia, and resistance to the arbitrary powers of proprietors, was a compelling persuasion. It began with early Quakerism, gained clear expression in David Lloyd's creative hands, and matured into an orthodoxy under the Quaker Party. And it won election after election for its most articulate spokespersons. Like all ideologies, it was subject to manipulation. Popular political leaders such as David Lloyd, Andrew Hamilton, and Benjamin Franklin exploited the prejudices that belief entailed. But they were able to do so with such effectiveness because they, too, held some faith in the main tenets of civil Quakerism, or, at least, in their efficacy, and combined that faith with their political bent for pragmatic ways.

The powerful hold that civil Quakerism maintained over the majority of the Pennsylvania populace was in part explicable by the talents of popular leaders. It also owed something to the inherent difficulties of the proprietary position and the incompetence of proprietary leaders. But its greatest strength was its coherence. For Friends, the main tenets of civil Quakerism gave expression to two of their most important concerns—their Quaker identity and their autonomy. The former dictated the need for the latter; the latter allowed them to pursue the former. Civil Quakerism was the synergistic offspring.

A related process took place among non-Quakers. Take, for example, the case of Pennsylvania's numerous German population. Whether they were of sectarian or church leanings, Pennsylvania Germans centered their public discourse on liberty of conscience, freedom from taxation, the absence of coercion, and both the experience and expectation of prosperity—ideas that merged easily with the primary tenets of civil Quakerism. This conceptual congruence, along with a shared tolerance for shifting positions on pacifism, and a parallel emphasis among the large numbers of southern German immigrants and among Pennsylvania Quakers on the importance of the indwelling spirit and of domestic life, encouraged the Germans' appreciation of civil Quakerism, and, to the extent that cultural and linguistic barriers permitted it, their inclusion within that discourse. Provincial Germans were reflecting their acculturation to the dominant political norms as much as their own experiences when they praised Pennsylvania as a unique land, unsurpassed in its provision of privileges.[253]

Among Pennsylvanians generally, no matter their ethnic background, the logic of the "Quaker System" was in itself persuasive enough to bring many outsiders into a Quakerized political relationship with Friends. But that development was immeasurably strengthened by a simultaneous and interrelated process of socioreligious Quakerization. During the early eighteenth century, for example, James Logan reported that "the affirmation is looked upon by the generality of the people who are not of our persuasion to be as binding as an oath";[254] by midcentury there were always a significant number of non-Quaker assemblymen who qualified by affirmation rather than by oath;[255] and in the 1760s, Joseph Galloway testified that those who scrupled to swear oaths included "*Quakers,* the *Moravians, Men-nonists, Dumplers,* and a great Number of the *Irish* and *Dutch* Presby-terians."[256] Just how far the outer limits of Quakerization extended can be seen in the case of the Pennsylvania Presbyterians, whose attitudes toward work and leisure were patently Quaker, and by the gentlemen "who call . . . [themselves] Quaker[s] but hath not the least apparance of one of that Stamp either in Garb, Conversation, or Behaviour."[257] Extensive accultura-tion to Quaker norms was evident in the complaints of clergy that their parishioners were indifferent to the sacraments of baptism and communion, in the ease with which outsiders attended Quaker meetings, in the number of Friends who married non-Quakers, and in a host of instances of neigh-borly interchange.[258] The persuasive power of the Quaker example was enormous, and the large numbers of Pennsylvanians who were "Friendly," although not Friends, were the result.[259]

A small episode in Andrew Hamilton's career illustrates how pervasive and subtle the Quaker influence could be. In 1738, when Hamilton was once again nominated speaker of the House, he refused to disable himself—that is, go through a ritual disparagement of his abilities prior to the governor's recognition of him in that capacity. "As that Piece of Modesty is [in] general look'd upon to be meerly formal, and far from Sincerity, he was not desirous to be censur'd, as saying that with his Mouth which was not agreeable to the Sentiments of his Heart." Although he "fell very far short" of perfection, "his large Experience" inclined him to "thankfully accept . . . the Trust."[260] In this vignette, the Anglican Hamilton put parliamentary precedent to the Quaker test of honesty and found tradition to be lacking. In so doing, he illustrated how acculturation to Quaker social norms could have important implications for political behavior. Overall, socioreligious Quakerization and political Quakerization were mutually supporting and facilitating. They worked together both to expand the perimeters and to increase the cohesion of the civil Quaker ideology.

The very pervasiveness of the ideology of civil Quakerism gave it enor-mous resilience during the mid to late colonial years. To its declared ene-mies, the supporters of the proprietorship and executive, its popularity frequently defied understanding. The complexity of the proprietary place-man Lynford Lardner's attempt to explain Quaker political power illustrates how baffled some commentators felt. The Quakers kept their influence, Lardner opined, because "their yearly meetings, their economy, their indus-try, their unanimity—in short their riches, to say nothing of their craft and subtlety . . . [gave] them advantages." "Their whole plan," Lardner went on, finally glimpsing the true dimension of the problem, was "to keep clouded the minds of the common people, in other words the majority."[261]

Others, less prone to seeing the world in manipulative terms, might also on occasion glimpse the Proprietary Party's difficulty in trying to weaken Quaker influence. The Quaker Party had the "ears" of the electorate and the "affections of the People."²⁶² By such an admission, Proprietary Party leaders were not only drawing attention to the way in which popular politicians cultivated the electorate, but also acknowledging how extensively Pennsylvanians had internalized the values that civil Quakerism entailed.

So compelling were the tenets of civil Quakerism that even when some groups had occasional doubts about specific Quaker Party policies, they continued to affirm their belief in Quakerized leadership. When a group of Philadelphia and Chester County petitioners requested the assembly to work out some adequate means of defense in the early stages of the French and Indian War, Speaker of the House Isaac Norris, Jr., put the hard question to them. Should the assembly "give up any Righ[t]s, which, in the Opinion of the House, the People were justly entitled to? . . . No, they answered, [what] *they wanted was that some Expedient might be fallen upon.*"²⁶³ By the same token, many German settlers in the exposed areas of Lancaster and Berks counties agreed that it was sensible for them to pick up arms and push for more effective government action in the face of Indian warfare. But such actions implied neither a rejection of the "Quaker System" nor a repudiation of the notion that pacifist-tinged politicians served society well in normal times.²⁶⁴

As the central ideas of civil Quakerism diffused through Pennsylvania society, they lost some of their sharpness and took on multiple meanings. But that characteristic became, in itself, a strength. Differences in understanding exactly what peaceable principles meant allowed Friends to muddle through the exclusion crisis, and gave their non-Quaker friends the opportunity to accommodate whatever differences they had with their neighbors. Similarly, some non-Quakers could write off the extreme solicitude of the "sober set" of Friends for the Indians as an aberration. Most Quakers were far less concerned about charity to natives than they were about maintaining traditional political rights and privileges. Perhaps the best indicator of the great strength of the civil Quaker ideology is to be found in the elections of 1764 and 1765. When Benjamin Franklin and his fellow Philadelphians appeared to turn their backs on the Pennsylvania constitution, the centerpiece of the "Quaker System," numerous Quaker Party supporters briefly abandoned their leaders. If the price for defending Pennsylvania's superior political system was continued proprietary government, the defectors would pay it. On the other hand, adherents of the Quaker Party saw themselves as reaffirming their faith in the special character of the Pennsylvania experiment through the new policy of seeking royal

government. Quaker and Proprietary party leaders were effective in mobilizing competing cadres of voters precisely because both appealed to beliefs shaped by civil Quakerism.[265]

So powerful and pervasive was the ideology of civil Quakerism that it
structured the language of political debate in Pennsylvania and gave the
province its own idiom of political discourse. The best means of illustrating
this development is explicitly to compare key passages in the language of
civil Quakerism with those of the country, or classical republican, paradigm
that reputedly molded eighteenth-century British-American colonial political language so powerfully in its own image.[266] What emerges from such
close comparison is a view rather different from the conventional one: while
country thinkers focused mainly on promoting a mixed and balanced constitution, arguing over the legitimacy of a religious establishment, advocating a militia rather than a standing army, and asserting the corruption of the
post–Glorious Revolution Anglo-American political system, Pennsylvanians had somewhat different priorities.[267]

At the center of political discourse in Pennsylvania was the provincial
constitution, a constitution that the colonists had strenuously built to guarantee themselves far more privileges than the British enjoyed. Far from
advocating the mixed form of government, Pennsylvanians overwhelmingly
rejected it. They dismissed the council, and treated the proprietary as a
powerful private interest, even though the Penns represented one estate
through their control of the governorship. In taking the view that only the
democratic branch of government truly considered the public interest,
Pennsylvanians turned their backs on the traditional categories of British
constitutional thought and struck out on their own. They masked their
temerity by continuing to talk about the British constitution, assembly
rights, and occasionally about balance in government. But if we look closely
at what they were saying, we can see that theirs was no traditional English
political discourse. Most references to the British constitution were general,
suggesting that it was a wonderful creation that provided important, but
nonspecific, guidelines for the structuring of colonial government. Most of
their attention went to rights, particularly assembly rights, but the important point here is that Pennsylvanians perceived the enjoyment of popular
rights (far beyond those sanctioned by the British constitution) as the
primary means by which they might attain social and political harmony.
And, finally, the ways in which provincials used the term balance was determined by local context. When remarked upon in a positive way, the term
meant something very different from what it did in Great Britain.[268]

The most widely known distinguishing feature of the Pennsylvania constitution was its guarantee of liberty of conscience. Fulfillment of that promise had important implications for political discourse, because so many

old-world countries and their colonies still supported state churches. Complaints against tithes, indictments of state-church pretensions, and criticism of establishment worldliness were staples of eighteenth-century Anglo-American thought. Such writings served as a self-congratulatory reminder to Pennsylvanians of their province's enlightenment, but they were of little relevance to local politics. What took their place was public discussion over what liberty of conscience meant in a society that was committed to such a goal. Answers to that question included some general reflections on the character of natural rights, but because the Pennsylvania sponsors of religious freedom were Friends, political exchange inevitably centered on the problem of pacifism. The apparent clash of Quaker values with what others frequently considered to be the duties of government was a recurring theme in public affairs. (To what extent should conscientious objectors be required to support the government in wartime? What right did Quakers have to prevent non-pacifists from enjoying governmental leadership in defending themselves?) As the moral equivalent of the church/state debate, it became a major component of the popular political idiom.[269]

No issue demonstrates more clearly the distinctive nature of political thought in Pennsylvania than the disagreement over the colonial militia. In the majority of British North American colonies, residents seemed to accept that the maintenance of a well-ordered militia was a crucial underpinning of liberty, a canon of English country thought. Militias preserved rights, standing armies betrayed them. Yet most Pennsylvanians saw a regular militia as anything but a benefit; it was, in their view, a malevolent force, a threat to the province's most cherished liberties. For pacifists, the very organization of a militia would transgress their religious rights; for both conscientious objectors and their non-pacifist political allies, an active militia was a specter of proprietary tyranny. What they hit on for defense (in place of the various unworkable voluntary militias) were local hirelings, enlistees whose services the province bought for relatively short periods of time, and who could be expected to disband once the assembly stopped their pay. There were also Pennsylvanians who clearly had no fear of a standing army and gave indications that they would welcome a permanent complement of British soldiers to keep the peace.[270] In opting for these solutions to their military needs, and in vigorously rejecting a customary militia, Pennsylvanians broke free of English country thought and blazed their own trail through new-world thickets.

Finally, there was the issue of corruption. While it is true that colonial Pennsylvanians did on occasion use country language, which suggested that an expanding subculture of corruption was systematically poisoning British society and threatening to precipitate a cycle of decay in British liberty, attitudes and conditions were so different in Pennsylvania that such ideas had little relevance.[271] The financial revolution in Great Britain that encouraged luxury and venality among public figures had no counterpart in Pennsylvania. Popular politicians controlled the colony's paper money and kept taxes low. Patronage appointments were few, and because the assembly filled a considerable portion of these, there was no clamor for the kind of place bills that British reformers constantly demanded. Nor was the English country cry for annual parliaments of any relevance in a colony with yearly provincial elections. While English radical-Whig writers viewed commerce with some reservations, Pennsylvanians were far less equivocal; they recognized commerce as their life's blood and felt that a broadly shared prosperity was likely to enhance both public and private virtue.[272] The pessimism of the radical-Whig ideologues was not at all appealing to those schooled in the optimistic universalism of Quaker theology, convinced that Pennsylvania's material prospects were overwhelmingly favorable, and ebullient about the rights they enjoyed under the Pennsylvania constitution. When Pennsylvanians did show signs of what we today might call paranoia, it was directed at various denominations, not at some distant source of corruption.[273] Granted, Thomas Penn was perceived as a potential tyrant, but the dangers he posed were much more comprehensible in the context of Pennsylvanians' ongoing struggle with proprietary privilege than in that of a British culture being overcome by luxury and vice.

The point is, that far from mimicking any particular strand of Anglo-American thought, Pennsylvanians formed their own distinctive political dialect. Unquestionably, they drew on the country tradition.[274] But their discourse reflected several other traditions as well. The most discernable of these was the seventeenth-century constitutionalist tradition, which, because of the institutionalized conflict between governor and assembly, periodically informed public debate.[275] Others, to name the obvious, were the traditions of English common law, Lockean liberalism, work-ethic Protestantism, and various strands of natural jurisprudential thought.[276] Present, too, in somewhat more amorphous form was the court tradition of mainstream Whiggism.[277] However precisely focused or diffuse these various strains of Anglo-American thought were, they all shared one thing in common in the Pennsylvania context: they were subordinate to, rather than determinative of, civil Quakerism. Pennsylvania's distinctive political idiom drew on an English heritage, but that is only to say that Pennsylvanians shared a capacious conceptual and linguistic currency with all Anglo-American societies. What created a peculiar political idiom in Pennsylvania was the proprietary presence, the unique provincial constitution, and the continuous political leadership of Quaker and Quakerized politicians.

The fact that the idiom of civil Quakerism played such an important part in structuring political discourse in Pennsylvania had significant implications for the tenor of provincial politics. In comparison with New York, political debate in Pennsylvania was far more focused on the peculiar policies associated with civil Quakerism than on the "Cant-Words" of Anglo-American politics.[278] For example, politicians made only minimal efforts to gain advantage from the court/country distinction;[279] those categories fitted so poorly with the realities of Pennsylvania politics that by the mid to late colonial years, contemporaries were searching for alternatives, such as "friends of the People," "the Party of the People," or the "popular side," to supplement the standard Quaker Party nomenclature.[280] This means neither that political argument was unfailingly principled nor that cant was absent. Provost William Smith, for example, would dress himself in whatever clothes came in handy, and cant phrases abounded in the polemical literature of the 1720s and 1760s.[281] But despite the excesses of partisan writing, political debate had a fundamental shape, a basic integrity that came from the substantive questions at issue. Popular Quaker leaders had no need, and no desire, to represent themselves as heirs to any particular fashionable strand of British political thought. They were comfortable in their own Quaker traditions and thus forced their critics to differentiate themselves in the most disadvantageous way possible, through their opposition to the main tenets of civil Quakerism.

Moreover, the moral dimension of Quakerism reinforced this characteristic. As numerous commentators pointed out, Friends had their own "stile," particularly in the poorly recorded political world of personal meetings and community gatherings.[282] Occasionally, we get a glimpse of this, in petitions, in remonstrances, or in a casual comment.[283] It is clear that in politics, as in business and religion, Friends valued directness and honesty. The diffusion of this concern for public integrity among non-Quaker political allies was part of the larger process of "Quakerization," and it reinforced the tendency of spokespersons for civil Quakerism to focus their attention on issues that mattered the most to themselves and their peers. There was no honesty in looking east across the Atlantic for political euphemisms; the important questions could best be addressed in the context of Quaker belief and Pennsylvania tradition.

Continuing Quaker Dominance

During the last ten years of the colonial period, the Quaker Party leaders seemed to lose their unerring touch for popular politics. They ended up on the wrong side of the Stamp Act controversy; they had little sympathy with the hard-line non-importers who wanted to extend Philadelphia's embargo against the Townsend Duties beyond 1770; in the early 1770s they lost the support of numerous Philadelphia mechanics, shopkeepers, and merchants who wanted a stronger patriotic response to Great Britain and more input into a political process from which they felt excluded; and they did little to build an effective interest in the fast-growing frontier areas of western Pennsylvania.[284] Yet they remained in control of provincial politics. Those upper-class individuals who gained prominence as anti-British, "patriot" spokespersons could only gain an occasional perch in the assembly.[285] Mechanics and lesser merchants from among Philadelphia's street politicians met with even more sparing success.[286] And longer-lived legislative critics of assembly speaker Joseph Galloway's policies were among the most moderate of men.[287]

The fundamental reason for the continuing power of the Old Party in the assembly and the moderate character of most successful opposition initiatives, both within the legislature and in the street politics of Philadelphia, was Pennsylvanians' deep attachment to their constitution and the "Quaker System" of politics. Pennsylvania residents continued to be deeply appreciative of their province's enviable reputation as a place blessed by more popular privileges than any other society; that gave the ideology of civil Quakerism a continuing vitality that the Quaker Party's arteriosclerosis tended to obscure.[288] Take, for example, the views of the two most prominent public figures in Pennsylvania during the late colonial years, John Dickinson and Joseph Galloway.[289] Both were legal-minded traditionalists, whose well-known determination to perpetuate Britain's connection with her colonies illustrates how severely each was enmeshed in the web of British constitutional thought. Yet their social and intellectual conservatism led them to defend Pennsylvania's constitutional integrity *despite* its incongruence with British assumptions. Dickinson turned a blind eye to the standards of mixed government when he defended his province's constitution as an exceptional repository of popular privileges. Many of the rights that he emphasized were at the heart of civil Quakerism.[290] As for Joseph Galloway, he simply dismissed objections to his efforts both to strengthen assembly power and emasculate the proprietorship with the bland assurance that "considered as a Charter-Government," Pennsylvania was "as near the mix'd Form, as Wisdom and Prudence could direct."[291] He might doff his hat to these fundamental assumptions of Anglo-American political thought, but his first allegiance was to Pennsylvania's peculiar brand of constitutionalism.

Just as Pennsylvania's distinctive popular political ideology lived on, so did the process of Quakerization. Back in the early 1740s, an anonymous German writer had defended Friends' political influence by rhetorically demanding, "what hurt have we received of them? don't they appear to be good and peaceable as Neighbours and made us partakers of such privileges as they enjoy themselves . . . both in Temporal and Religious Affairs."[292]

Overwhelmingly, non-Quakers answered the question in the affirmative; they continued to do so in the 1750s, when Isaac Norris, Jr., observed that Lancaster County always elected Quakers "tho' there . . . [were] scarcely one hundred of that profession in the whole county."[293] And amid the stress of the mid 1760s, that pattern continued in a number of western areas.[294] In fact, the Quaker Party had always recognized a need to speak to some backcountry concerns, even during times of conflict between east and west, and that tradition continued on some important issues.[295] Which is not to say, however, that Quakerization overwhelmed the province the way it once had, for the social roots that sustained the process were gradually dying. As the Quaker reform movement gained strength, the most outward-looking, secular-minded Friends (poor Friends but good Quakerizers, as it were) were disowned, and the Society's leaders began to shepherd their flock into more enclosed pasture.[296] More and more Pennsylvanians lived in areas remote from Quaker residents, and that prevented the kind of community interchange essential to Quakerization. In the Philadelphia area, attitudinal barriers that separated the Quaker elite from "the Yahoo Race" seemed to grow higher, a concomitant of wealth- and class-induced social isolation.[297] Yet in the old rural areas, including Lancaster and Berks counties, traditional patterns of political behavior continued to have tremendous strength. Even in the hotbed of Philadelphia, the loyalty of many city mechanics to the Quaker Party through the early 1770s attested to the persistence of Quaker influence.[298]

If the Quaker Party was slow to weaken in the 1760s and early 1770s, part of the reason was the character of its opponents. Despite its electoral success in the mid 1760s, the Proprietary Party refused to take further runs at the Assembly Party; subsequent to the 1765 election, the two began to develop a passively cooperative, if bickering, relationship. What facilitated that on the Proprietary Party's side was the moribund state of the campaign for royal government, the assembly's acceptance of a modus vivendi with the proprietors on the fundamental issue of taxation of proprietary land, and joint appropriation of governmental revenues. On the Quaker side, old antagonisms stemming from proprietary land policies in the eastern counties had died away, and supporters of the proprietorship were clearly willing to let Quaker Party loyalists have their way in electoral politics in the three old counties. The prevailing feeling among leaders of both old parties was that, given the uncertainties of the imperial relationship, they wanted to avoid public rivalries that might encourage significant political mobilization. Some Proprietary Party men had felt very uncomfortable in their mobbish opposition to the Stamp Act and were happy to support the efforts of Old Party leaders to restrain boisterous public protests against British policies. Many members of both established parties also looked askance at the growing numbers and vociferousness of Presbyterians. The old combatants felt more comfortable with each other than they did with what they viewed as the unpredictability of some of the current spokespersons for mid-Atlantic Calvinism.[299]

Although historians sometimes assume that the Proprietary Party served as an important vehicle for the expression of the discontent of western Pennsylvania with the Quakers, there is little evidence of such a development. Far from supporting the proprietary interest, western settlers hated the Penns. All of the animosity stemming from proprietary quitrent policies, favoritism in land grants, and land office corruption and ineptitude, which had once emanated from eastern Pennsylvania and turned so many Quakers against William Penn, currently centered in the more recently settled western areas and soured frontier families on those with proprietary connections. The Scotch-Irish again and again demonstrated their abiding hostility to Penn claims and exactions. In the 1730s and 1740s, they fought for their homes in Paxton, Derry, and Donnegal against the land-purchase terms Thomas Penn demanded. In the 1750s it was the Scotch-Irish assessors of Cumberland County who stung the proprietors by overassessing Penn lands, thinking as Provost William Smith reported to Thomas Penn, that it was "justice to do him injustice."[300] In the 1760s and early 1770s, those same Scotch-Irish left upper Lancaster and Cumberland counties to support Connecticut's claims to the Wyoming Valley, and joined with Virginians in Redstone Valley on the Monongahela River and at Fort Pitt to resist the hated Penn terms for land. And the antipathy was mutual. Back in the 1750s, proprietary placemen were just as anxious to hive off recent immigrants into minimally represented new counties as their Quaker counterparts were.[301] The low esteem in which the governor's friends held frontier settlers was reflected in their attitude toward western county assemblymen. As the Presbyterian minister John Elder lamented in soliciting the "best Offices with the Govr" through his old acquaintance Richard Peters,"It's well-known that Representations from the back Inhabitants, have but little weight with the Gentlemen in power, they looking on us, either as incapable of forming just notions of things, or as biass'd by Selfish Views."[302] The extent to which that attitude permeated the ranks of both Proprietary and Quaker parties and drew them together became clear in the 1760s, when members of both parties considered denying the fundamental English right of local trials to whites indicted for murdering Indians. Their perception of justice and concern for law and order overrode whatever sympathy either party had for western grievances. Rather than serve as point men for westerners' attacks on the Old Party, many Proprietary Party men preferred to help the Quakers defend their mutually shared eastern redoubt.[303]

As the Proprietary Party gradually drifted toward détente with the Quakers, a few Old Party leaders began to comment on a new opponent, an amorphous entity they called the Presbyterian Party.[304] Rather than a fundamental realignment in electoral politics, the appearance of this appellation reflected the state of mind of a few prominent Quakers and Anglicans.[305] Presbyterians seemed on the ascendancy because of the increase in their numbers in backcountry areas, the steady stream of New Light ministerial graduates from the College of New Jersey (Princeton), the intercolonial cooperation of some Presbyterians and Congregationalists through the Sons of Liberty protests against the British, and talk of one great Calvinist union between mid-Atlantic Presbyterians and New England Congregationalists. Also, they were distrusted as the historic persecutors of Friends, as inveterate critics of Pennsylvania's Quaker government, and as vicious opponents of recent Quaker Party policies.[306]

Yet such concerns expressed fears of what might be, not of what was. Despite their numbers, Presbyterians were in political disarray. The western Scotch-Irish had only the most tenuous political links with easterners, and those became weaker once Chief Justice William Allen appeared to prefer his old proprietary connections to the interests of his fellow Presbyterians from across the Susquehanna.[307] In all parts of Pennsylvania where sizable numbers of Presbyterians gathered, incessant religious squabbles precluded sustained political cooperation. In the outlying areas of the province, New Lights, Old Lights, seceders, and covenanters fragmented Scotch-Irish communities.[308] In Philadelphia, where cooperation was essential for political success, the range, frequency, and duration of the conflicts between Old and New Light church members portrayed groups far more interested in being right than in being elected.[309] As one interested party observed, "some denominations openly insult us as acting without plan or design, quarreling with one another, and seldom uniting together, even to promote the most salutary purposes."[310] Even among those who were politically minded, counsel differed. Some wanted to rail on against Friends, others were "so much more apprehensive" of Anglican efforts to acquire a bishop for North America and to promote the establishment of their church in all the colonies, that they were "fully determin'd to meet the Q[uaker]s half Way, shake Hands and be Friends."[311] Those who were of different mind contributed to the stigma Presbyterians needed to overcome if they were to broaden their political support—that they were too narrowly sectarian to merit trust in Pennsylvania's multicultural society.

Divided as they were, and in some instances deeply distrusted, Pennsylvania's Presbyterians were incapable of establishing their own political party. In Philadelphia, they composed several shards of an increasingly fragmented electorate; in old rural areas in which they resided in numbers, most continued to be either actively or passively Quakerized;[312] out in the underrepresented reaches of Cumberland County, they simply represented, as best they could, their frontier interests. Despite the network of Presbyterian congregations that honeycombed much of Pennsylvania and seemed by its very presence to demonstrate the existence of a Presbyterian Party, nothing galvanized any faction of Presbyterians to make common cause with their counterparts in the electoral politics of the late 1760s and early 1770s.[313]

Although the continued vitality of civil Quakerism, the appeasement of the Proprietary Party, and the influence of Presbyterians are important in explaining the continuing nature of Quaker Party political power in the late colonial years, it is arguable that one feature of the Pennsylvania political system, the underrepresentation of the backcountry, was the critical variable that allowed the aforementioned factors to come into play. From the early 1750s on, backcountry champions occasionally raised the issue of the inequitable allocation of assembly seats, and of course, during Pontiac's Rebellion, apologists for the Paxton Boys tried to make a cause célèbre of the issue.[314] The question is a difficult one with which to deal because conclusions so clearly depend on the particular assumptions we make.[315] Had *all* the counties been given the same eight assembly seats that each of the three old counties had, there is no question but that Pennsylvania's post-1750 politics would have worn a different face. Ultimately, Quaker Party influence was determined by residency patterns, and aside from the existence of a few small pockets of influential Quakers in Lancaster, York, and Berks counties, western settlement took place beyond the Friends' effective political perimeter. The sheer weight of western representation under such a scheme would have established new centers of western power.

Given prevailing attitudes, however, it would have been most unlikely (short of revolution) for contemporaries to make such a radical change. A more likely scenario would have been a partial reapportionment to reflect some changes in the geographic distribution of wealth and numbers. Had such reform taken place, strong centers of Quakerized politics like Philadelphia City and Philadelphia, Lancaster, and Berks counties, would have been the chief beneficiaries, along with the neglected Cumberland and Northampton counties.[316] It is possible, of course, that such change would have differed little from those produced by more radical reapportionment. Perhaps the pressure of expanded representation in the city and county of Philadelphia and Lancaster County, in particular, might have exploded the Quaker system and unleashed powerful anti-Quaker, and possibly more egalitarian, political forces.[317] But such a hypothesis substantially discounts the momentum of decades of Quakerization and the continuing influence of civil Quakerism. Such change would surely have created more political conflict, but it is unlikely that it would have brought the continuing power of the old Quaker coalition to a quick end.

Simply put, the Quakers remained so entrenched in power in the late colonial years because they continued to have the minds of the people. The Quaker system of politics and the ideology of civil Quakerism continued to have unrivaled persuasive power even in such uncertain times. For close to a century, Friends and their political allies had been the custodians of a social experiment designed around contemporary ideas of benevolence, liberty, and prosperity. Although self-serving, Friends' characterization of Pennsylvania as a society uniquely favored among western countries was, for the most part, accepted as accurate. Convinced of their good fortune, and concerned about the changing tenor of private and public life in Pennsylvania, most politically active citizens would not easily or hastily turn their backs on the political leaders who had been the traditional defenders of their province's rich heritage.

Chapter Eight

Some Comparative Dimensions
of Political Structure and Behavior

BY MID EIGHTEENTH CENTURY, New York and Pennsylvania possessed political cultures of considerable complexity. There were a multitude of ways in which provincial politics intersected both with institutional features of government and with habits of social behavior to contour society in both the Hudson and Delaware River colonies. In the interests of analysis, however, it is necessary to simplify. We may derive important observations about the political cultures of the two colonies by viewing them from the following four perspectives: the imperial politics of place, which centered on Crown and proprietary appointments; the organization of electoral politics; the confluence of local government and provincial politics; and the relationship between observable social values and provincial politics in each society.

The politics of place and of electoral practice were the two areas of public activity most obviously connected with each colony's political culture. The former of these, which encompassed each colony's connections with Great Britain, the character of their respective governors' offices, and the nature of the two provincial councils, had some influence in shaping political life in both New York and Pennsylvania. But as significant as these factors were, they were clearly overshadowed by the institutionalization and practice of electoral politics. The profiles of highly contested elections reveal important patterns of political behavior, not the least of which was the overwhelming prejudice in favor of popular government in each colony. In addition, the organization of political campaigns, the mobilization of voters, and the long-range consequences of such activities reveal a good deal about the relatively stable, competitive political conditions that constituted such an important part of political culture in New York and Pennsylvania.

Beyond the boundaries of imperial and electoral politics, there were two other major determinants of political behavior. The respective relationships between local government and provincial politics in the two colonies constituted one of these: in New York, a hardy tradition of local exceptionalism and independence had numerous ramifications; in Pennsylvania, a greater sense of standardization and provincial communalism left its mark. The second had to do with the way in which articulated social values impinged on politics. Upper-class emphasis on hierarchy in New York and the Quakers' embrace of equality in Pennsylvania each had a significant impact on political life. Converging on some grounds, diverging on others, the political cultures of the two colonies attest, not only to the intricacies of each, but also to the tremendous vitality of the collective political personalities present in mid eighteenth-century colonial America.

The Politics of Place

The most obvious structural feature of colonial government in New York and Pennsylvania was one they shared with other contemporary settler societies in America: their subservience to old-world monarchs. In all the new-world empires, including that of Great Britain, the fundamental means of demonstrating colonial submissiveness was through the institutionalization of political dependency. The British claimed, and their colonists accepted, an ongoing metropolitan right to have some say in the running of provincial governments. The way in which that was done obviously had implications for colonial politics.

In New York and Pennsylvania, the particular relationship of the respective colonies to Great Britain encouraged somewhat different tendencies in provincial politics. As a royal colony, New York had little to buffer it from the demands of English politicians who viewed North American affairs primarily as an opportunity to strengthen their influence at home. They tried to achieve their ends by securing as many provincial appointments (such as governor, attorney-general, provincial secretary, or naval officer) as they possibly could for their slavering relatives and political allies.[1] The fact that the most important patronage decisions relating to New York were made in England did not, however, turn leading provincials into mere bystanders. In the late seventeenth and early eighteenth centuries, New York politicians frequently tried to play off different groups of British relations, friends, business connections, and political acquaintances, hoping thereby to turn the tables on the British and put pressure on court notables, who much preferred to settle patronage matters unobtrusively among themselves.[2] New Yorkers pursued such tactics in order to protect their own provincial interests, ranging from minute details of patronage to large constitutional issues. In either case, New Yorkers willingly contributed to a continuing interpenetration of British and provincial politics.

The most easily observed result of the close linkage between high-level provincial and metropolitan politics was its occasional tendency to encourage factionalism in New York. After cabals of New Yorkers met with local defeat, they could play their English card. A classic example of this was the Cosby/Morris dispute.[3] When Governor Cosby fired Lewis Morris as chief justice, Morris went off to England to seek reinstatement. The political cohesion of Morris's New York confederates, which had remained reasonably strong through the first months of Morris's absence, was noticeably strengthened in November 1735, when Governor Cosby on his deathbed suspended Morris's ally, Rip Van Dam, from the provincial council.[4] Cosby's purpose was to prevent Van Dam from asserting his right as senior councillor to take charge of New York government on the governor's death.[5] By suspending Van Dam, Cosby opened the way for a moderate ally, George Clarke, to become president of the council and titular head of the colony. The questionable nature of Van Dam's suspension inspired the Morris/Alexander faction to defy Clarke's authority by having Van Dam appoint his own slate of New York City officials in September 1736, as if Van Dam were running the provincial government. What made the dissidents willing to risk what Clarke called treason was the expectation that Lewis Morris would bring news of his own reinstatement and a repudiation of Clarke from London. Only when the English card had been fully played—that is, when a disappointed Morris returned in October and Clarke's leadership was confirmed with a lieutenant-governor's commission—did the crisis in New York politics begin to abate.[6]

While such episodes illustrate how royal government could exacerbate political factionalism in a colony, too much can be made of them. Close connections between British and New York politics did not always provoke factionalism. There were occasions when provincials were able to mobilize their British influence in order to consolidate their power and prevent local opposition from escalating into a significant threat.[7] And although conventional wisdom has it that the truncated powers of New York's governors encouraged factionalism, that is by no means clear.[8] In a society in which "Governors . . . [could] neither draw nor drive Assemblies, or people, from their Obstinate Wayes of Thinking," increased gubernatorial powers, short of the impossible goal of attaining a full panoply of British "prime ministerial" powers, would most likely have intensified rather than diminished political factionalism.[9] The very weaknesses of New York's governors gave factions of the popular and provincial Whig varieties the opportunity to come to terms with each other. They were far more comfortable with the uncertainties of popular politics than with the unpredictable egocentricity of governors with increased executive power.

While New York's status as a royal colony did, if in limited measure, encourage New York's factional proclivities, Pennsylvania's peculiar relationship with Great Britain had a somewhat different effect. Because Pennsylvania was a proprietary colony, most administrative positions in the province were filled by the chief proprietors. William and Hannah Penn and their sons, John and Thomas, were careful to use their influence at Whitehall to oppose any ministerial encroachment in matters of policy and personnel vigorously. Frequently there were differences between the proprietors and individual placemen, and occasionally a considerable gulf developed between the Proprietary Party and the proprietors. But there was no alternative source of overseas power to which discontented Pennsylvania officials might turn in order to further their ambitions. Rather than encouraging factionalism, the transatlantic structure of Pennsylvania's proprietary government worked to curtail it.

Pennsylvania's old-world Quaker connections also tended to reinforce structure in Pennsylvania politics. During the early eighteenth century, British Quakers developed one of the most highly organized and effective outsider political lobbies of the day.[10] With the death of William Penn, "the last of the seventeenth-century generation of great individual lobbyists," the London Meeting for Sufferings "hesitantly" began to intercede in British politics to gain important political and religious rights for Quaker colonists.[11] Beginning in the early 1740s, however, as Pennsylvania Friends came under attack for their wartime policies, and as the second generation of Penns drifted away from Quakerism, spokespersons for the London Meeting threw their full weight behind Pennsylvania's Quaker Party against proprietary and Proprietary Party attacks. There was always some tension between Pennsylvania and British Friends, but leading London Quakers did, in fact, shield Pennsylvania's Quaker Party from the vagaries of British ministerial policies.[12] The protection they offered encouraged Quaker Party leaders to stand firm against proprietary demands, thereby facilitating the structuring of Pennsylvania's provincial politics along Quaker/Proprietary party lines.[13]

Just as the general character of New York and Pennsylvania's transatlantic connections had some long-term effects on the patterns of political behavior in both colonies, so did the peculiarities of each province's governorship. As the chief administrator and political connection between Whitehall and the colonies (and, of more relevance, in the case of Pennsylvania, between the Penn family and their proprietorship), the governor was always one important focus of provincial affairs. Beyond the broad structural similarities that membership in a common imperial enterprise entailed, the most significant feature of the New York and Pennsylvania governorships was the disparity in their incomes and in their powers, both formal and informal. The New York governor enjoyed an income bloated by fees and graft from the colony's commerce, land grants, and military affairs.[14] Numerous patronage possibilities lay close by if the governor could exploit them, and the powers of proroguing or dissolving the assembly were largely in his hands.[15] In Pennsylvania, on the other hand, proprietary government brought the colony's chief executive little cream with his morning's milk. Although fees grew substantially during the late colonial years, the governor's income was largely dependent on the assembly's annual salary grants. There was relatively little opportunity for graft or patronage, and little control over annual assemblies convinced that they could adjourn themselves at will.[16]

As important as these contrasts were in contributing to the different temper of politics in New York and Pennsylvania, we should not lose sight of the way in which royal and proprietary regimes simultaneously fostered political convergence. In New York a distended prerogative incited provincials to strip away those claims and develop an encompassing political culture centering on popular representative government; in Pennsylvania, the weakness of the governor determined colonists to keep his office that way. The fact that in both colonies governors were almost always British placemen and not provincials further animated popular predilections.[17] Rather than serving as the cement of empire, the governorship—whether royal or proprietary—was frequently a catalyst for provincial self-awareness. And that self-awareness, formed in part by reference to colonial neighbors, tended, as the eighteenth century wore on, to encourage a common high level of popular political prejudice.

The imperial connection and the transatlantic patronage connection notwithstanding, politically aware New Yorkers and Pennsylvanians forged their own sets of provincial relationships, which were most important in bequeathing their distinctive characters to the two colonies. Of the various provincial institutions in which colonial politicians were represented, the British intended the governor's council to have a high profile and an important hand in shaping provincial politics. In New York, the council was composed of no more than twelve appointees, who served as a privy council, an upper legislative house, and a high court of appeal.[18] Despite the council's reduced prominence (after being New York's sole governing body prior to the establishment of representative government in 1691), many well-established New Yorkers aspired to membership throughout the colonial years. There were numerous reasons for this, not the least of which was the cachet that membership continued to confer. As Admiral Peter Warren pointed out, councillorship was one of the few ways New Yorkers could demand a "little rank above the commoner sort."[19] After all, councillors were advisors to the Crown's representative, and in their legislative capacity, they could claim some functional similarity to England's peers. The most status-conscious councillors and their wives emphasized the precedence (after the governor, lieutenant-governor, and president of the council) they enjoyed on social occasions.[20] Others, however, were more appreciative of the opportunities membership brought. Council membership placed them at the center of public affairs, intimates to all that contemporaries recognized to be of public import. And it could bring them advantage: some say over commercial regulations; insider knowledge about impending public policy; influence over patronage appointments; the opportunity to land lucrative government contracts; and the clout to acquire licenses allowing themselves and their friends to purchase Indian lands.[21] Although the community denied councillors the kind of public trust assemblymen enjoyed, there was an offsetting advantage. Once appointed, councillors were relatively secure;[22] they could savor their place, knowing they would never have to confront the "uncertain" "breath" of the people.[23]

Under Pennsylvania's 1701 Charter of Privileges, the office of councillor was considerably less attractive than it was in New York. Although the council's advisory role gave incumbents the opportunity to become perpetual insiders in public affairs (and membership conferred the same social precedence as it did in New York), the fact that the council had no legislative role under the Pennsylvania constitution diminished its prestige.[24] The public's perception that the councillors were largely a collection of proprietary cronies whose primary obligation was to protect proprietary privilege and implement unpopular proprietary policies brought hostility rather than respect. Moreover, council membership failed to bring the kind of tangible benefits it could provide in New York. Patronage appointments were more dependent on timely good relations with men such as Richard Peters, William Allen, Benjamin Chew, and Thomas Penn than on council service to the governors. And given Thomas Penn's determination to grant a substantial number of appointments to Quakers, councillors could sometimes end up in line behind their political opponents. Land grants did not so easily come their way either, because the land office was an administrative entity separate from the council. Again, friendship with land office officials, including deputy surveyors, was more important in gaining access to prime Pennsylvania land than was faithfulness at the council table. As for government contracts, the assembly had far more patronage at its disposal than did the chief executive. All of these circumstances were reflected in the constant difficulty the Penns faced in finding strong individuals who would sit in council.[25]

In neither New York nor Pennsylvania did the provincial council play a determinative role in provincial politics. In New York, it is true, councillors could develop a good deal of influence, but they were able to do so primarily because of the power their friends and relations wielded in the assembly, and that they themselves could exercise, in one or two cases, as supreme court justices. In fact, most councillors gained their appointments because of sponsorship by popular leaders;[26] a few placemen aside, the complexion of the council usually reflected divisions among popularly elected politicians. To the extent that the council directed political affairs during the 1740s, as some historians have argued, it did so within parameters dictated by assembly politics.[27] In Pennsylvania the council was much more one-sidedly partisan than in New York; and it was on the wrong side. Stigmatized by its proprietary complexion, the council was frequently irrelevant to the course of popular politics and thus marginalized to a degree that its New York counterpart was not.[28] Different as the New York and Pennsylvania councils were, however, to an overwhelming extent both were limited and shaped by the forces of popular politics. And these forces frequently depended on the outcome of electoral contests.

Electoral Politics

The chief distinguishing feature of colonial government in the first British empire was the prominent role elected representatives played in public affairs. While representation was a basic English right, it was also a very important means of reconciling colonials to the operation of provincial, county, and township government. The idea of representation, the fact that many individuals served the community in a wide variety of local offices, and the sense of inclusion that representative government extended to the many males eligible to vote fostered feelings of loyalty among each colony's body politic and promoted the legitimacy of their respective systems of government. Of the various levels of representative government in New York and Pennsylvania, by far the most important was the provincial. Once provincial houses of representation were established, assemblymen quickly gained a preponderance of power in both provincial governments, and they also controlled the circumstances under which many of the local officers of government carried out their responsibilities. Because of the important role assemblymen played in the colonial political structure, the electoral politics that placed them in power was one of the most important features of the colonies' political cultures.

An obvious place to begin a search for insight into electoral politics is with those colonial elections in which voter turnout was particularly high. These were the critical moments of electoral politics in which candidates and their closest supporters scrambled for popular support; in doing so, they encouraged provincials to enter actively, if briefly, into public affairs. Because of the way these intense political experiences cut through apathy and roused colonials to testify to their sense of community integrity, the concerted competition and considerable voter participation of the day reveal a good deal about the structures of provincial politics.

In New York, two of the three instances of largest electoral turnout took place in 1737 and 1761.[29] The former case was a by-election between the popular Whig leader Adolphe Philipse and the provincial Whig Cornelius Van Horne. The fact that Philipse's immediate political fortune was at stake identified the contest as a pivotal one; both factions, still hot from the general election three months earlier, poured all of their resources into the fray. The 1761 election had important competitive dimensions as well. In the early stages of the election, a group of political managers organized a four-man ticket, including three assembly veterans and young Captain James DeLancey. There was little disagreement over the choice of the three incumbents, but Captain DeLancey was a controversial choice because of his youth, his educational and career-related absences from the city, and his familial association with the old DeLancey/Jones popular Whig coalition. Unwilling to see a new DeLancey grab the brass ring so soon after an asthma attack had rid New Yorkers of his father, the provincial Whig John Morin Scott announced his own candidacy. He was followed by William Bayard, a moderate, who apparently sensed some distaste for a De-Lancey/Scott restaging of yesteryear's political wars.[30] The result was an enthusiastic three-cornered contest among old popular and provincial Whigs and those who wanted to escape the shadows of the past.

Why, we might ask, did the 1737 and 1761 elections occasion the largest voter participation rate in New York's colonial history? The answer to that question has to do with the character of New York politics during the mid eighteenth century. This was a period in which the distinctions between popular and provincial Whig factions gave a clearer, more sustained structure to provincial politics than at any other time.[31] Voters were attracted to candidates, not just as personalities in their own right, but as individuals who either represented familiar currents of political thought and behavior or, as in the case of Bayard in 1761, rejected the traditional lines of polarization. Of course, voters were drawn into election-day activism because of the intense huckstering of the candidates' friends, but many were simultaneously willing participants.[32] And although the intense localism that distinguished New York politics continued unabated, a broader dimension of political understanding was clearly evident. The electorate was salted with individuals who shared some sense of inclusion in the ongoing political debate between popular and provincial Whigs. However haltingly, these men believed that participation in current provincial politics was a worthwhile dimension of community life and felt convinced that New York's peculiar traditions of political discourse allowed them to understand and identify with the positions that their chosen candidates represented. That was more the case during the midcentury decades than earlier or later, and the consequences were clear at the polls.[33]

Just as in New York, the highest voter turnout in Pennsylvania elections took place when the contending candidates represented clearly differentiated positions. In 1764 and 1765, debate centered on the fundamental question of whether or not Pennsylvania should seek royal government.[34] From 1740 through 1742, defense preparations and executive power were the issue.[35] In each of these two situations, the issues transcended personalities and encouraged potential voters to respond to the cajolery, enticements, and posturings of party organizers. Debate was more focused in these Pennsylvania elections than in their New York counterparts, but given the sharp differences between the proponents of civil Quakerism and its critics, compared to the frequent assonances of New York's popular and provincial Whig dialects, that should hardly be surprising.

If there was a similarity in the way in which relatively structured oppositional politics encouraged voter participation in New York and Pennsylvania, there was also one very important difference in the character of these high-turnout contests. The New York City and County elections featured competing individuals, while the Pennsylvania contests favored opposing slates of candidates. Despite the potential for the development of competing slates of candidates, which its four-seat assembly representation gave New York, only twice (in 1699 and 1769) did such a development take place (see map 3). Other than in those two instances, contested elections were between two or three serious candidates for one or possibly two seats.[36] Politically engaged New Yorkers might be eager participants in the public debates between popular and provincial Whigs, but they refused to push their partisanship to the point of offering two clear-cut tickets where the winner might take all. This behavior suggests that despite continuities in factional strife and traditions of ideological differences, many politically active New Yorkers resisted too great an explosion of divisive electoral politics. It was one thing for a handful of high-profile factional leaders to risk themselves; they could always make a comeback. But others wanted no part of a polarization that might significantly reduce their ability to cut deals

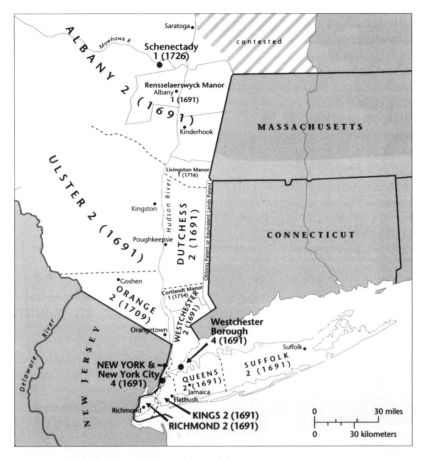

MAP 3. New York, Distribution of Assembly Representatives, 1734–1772. Drawn by Eric Leinberger based on maps in *Atlas of Early American History: The Revolutionary Era, 1760–1790*, Lester J. Cappon, ed. (Princeton, 1976), 2, 4, and Montgomery Schuyler, *The Patroons and Lords of Manors of the Hudson* (New York, 1932), 3–4. Dates refer to the years in which electoral districts first received representation.

should they have the good fortune to be elected. Respect for that way of thinking was reflected in the actions of factional leaders who, rather than pressing for complete tickets, practiced the electoral strategy of first attempting to knock out a key opponent or two and then trying to lead the assembly "over to a right way of thinking" by personal persuasion.[37] The circumstances of a given election were a related consideration. Prominent factional adherents recognized that the advantage in an election always lay with the Whig faction that could most convincingly portray itself as the champion of popular rights. In the one or two cases in which both popular and provincial Whig factions felt they had good title to such a claim, public interest became deeply engaged and the number of voters soared. But these occasions were few. Determined to maintain their viability, New York's popular and provincial Whig factions avoided frequent all-out electoral contests that might have exposed their fragilities and hastened their disintegration.

In contrast to New York, Pennsylvania's high-turnout elections invariably featured contests between opposing slates of candidates. One of the reasons for this was structural. The size of both the counties themselves and of the delegations of representatives from each of the old counties (eight) invited cooperative election campaigns (see map 4). And unlike in New York, where a citizen might legitimately vote for fewer candidates than there were electoral vacancies, in Pennsylvania incomplete tickets were deemed spoiled ballots.[38] The reluctance of individuals to vote for either a political adversary or an undeclared fill-in just to validate their ballot encouraged party managers to organize complete tickets. More important, however, were the preference of Quakers for consensus and their belief that politics should reflect the shared purpose that underlay their colonial venture. Friends always preferred a common approach to public issues, be they religious or civil.

Because of the cohesion incumbent assemblymen in Pennsylvania usually displayed, and because of the popularity of the tenets of civil Quakerism, opponents saw little hope of gaining legislative power through piecemeal action. The New York strategy of electing two or three leading dissidents, who might then bring the assembly around to their views was useless in Pennsylvania. The Proprietary Party notable William Allen found that out during his lonesome years in the House of Representatives in the late 1750s and early 1760s. A few other members would drift in Allen's direction when it served their immediate purposes, but just as surely they floated away again with a slight change in the political breeze. As a consequence, the serious critics of both the incumbent Quaker factions of early Pennsylvania history and the Quaker Party of later decades usually restricted their electoral efforts to occasions on which they felt they could organize widely enough to win a majority of the assembly. That required issues, and the recruitment of slates of candidates to meet the tickets of their opponents. As Sir William Keith demonstrated in his futile attempts during the 1720s to take over the assembly with his ten out of twenty-six seats, there was little opportunity for compromise once outsiders decided to take on the Quaker monolith.[39] The challengers had either to win an immediate majority (which none ever did) or to give up the fight.

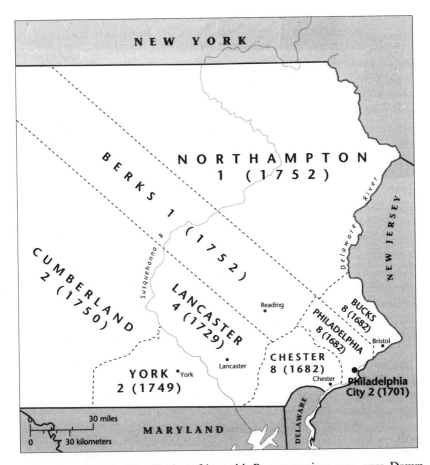

MAP 4. Pennsylvania, Distribution of Assembly Representatives, 1752–1771. Drawn by Eric Leinberger based on maps in *Atlas of Early American History: The Revolutionary Era, 1760–1790,* Lester J. Cappon, ed. (Princeton, 1976), 4, and Alva Burton Konkle, *The Life and Times of Thomas Smith, 1745–1809* (Philadelphia, 1904), 20–21. Dates refer to the years in which electoral districts first received representation.

Hard-fought campaigns that produced a high voter turnout were not the only kind of election contests that took place in New York and Pennsylvania. There were others in which the public's response was less than optimum. In New York, these contests took various forms. Some were county elections in which pairs of candidates faced off against each other;[40] others were three-cornered competitions in which a trio of candidates tried to eliminate one of their number;[41] some involved larger numbers of participants—six or seven individuals competing for four seats, or five hopefuls for two seats—and some fewer.[42] In Schenectady, in Westchester Borough, and twice in a manor, the rivalry was always (so far as we know) between two aspirants for the single assembly seat.[43] In Pennsylvania there was variety as well. Perhaps as many as six or seven candidates might vie for the last three seats of an eight-person delegation;[44] or perhaps two aspirants might fight it out for the one available seat both in counties entitled to one representative and in those with two, four, or eight seats in which incumbents had a lock on the rest.[45] The most important observation to make here is that such single-slate competition took place *within* the ranks of early popular Quaker factions or of the Quaker Party, not between these groups and their proprietary rivals.[46] When we look at these elections, it is clear that a number of circumstances could explain why they occasioned only mild to moderate voter interest. Managers were less adept at getting out the vote, the candidates were less attractive than they might have been, or perhaps "Cloudy or Rainy Weather," a "cold Morning," or "some trifling business" kept folks at home.[47] But it is also likely that constituents perceived the elections neither to be crucial to their rights nor so closely aligned with, or symbolic of, the main political fissures in their respective colonies.

No matter how parochial some election contests seemed to be, the fundamental predisposition of voters in both New York and Pennsylvania was to support candidates who at any moment seemed the most believable exponents of popular rights. There were numerous indicators of this in New York. If we look at the rate of turnover of assemblymen in New York, we find that the lowest rate of change took place in elections between 1743 and 1752 (average 23 percent) and in 1769 (22 percent), when as a body the assembly was closely identified (through its confrontations with provincial governors) with the cause of popular rights. Conversely, the highest rates of turnover occurred in 1726 (46 percent), 1737 (48 percent), 1759 (63 percent), and 1768 (48 percent), after assemblies of seven to ten years' duration in each case.[48] During these long periods, legislators were tempted to grow fat, grazing on the eminence and patronage power they enjoyed. Once elected, many assemblymen seemed to forget their earlier concerns for frequent elections, and the very partisanship that gained them office all too often seemed to narrow into capriciousness rather than broaden into disinterested service. Popular skepticism of incumbent legislators grew quickly during the days of Fletcher and Cornbury, and reached an apogee in the early 1720s. The excesses legislators committed were epitomized in the infamous "long assembly" (1715–1726), during which assemblymen paid off themselves and their friends under the provincial Debt Acts, gobbled up local patronage appointments, and stood off constituent demands that they submit to reelection. Currents of constituent distrust ran through all of New York's prominent communities thereafter.

The results of this charge to New York's political atmosphere was apparent in numerous instances. Given a clear choice, New Yorkers always voted for the outsider of the moment. During the late 1720s, the electorate supported the most credible champions of popular rights, the Philipse faction. Once that group had begun to consolidate its power, Lewis Morris became the outspoken champion of New Yorkers' liberties, and he easily won the well-known Westchester by-election of 1733. When the Morris/Alexander faction gained a dominant position in the 1737 election, the just-discredited Adolphe Philipse immediately regained enough acceptance as the standard-bearer for popular rights to prevail in the 1737 New York City and County by-election. The same dynamic operated out in the hinterlands. Untoward efforts to exploit patronage power immediately before an election always worked to the disadvantage of those currently holding power.[49] And if a sitting member clearly proved himself more attentive to the cause of popular rights than to the perquisites of his office, his constituents were not only effusive in their praise but also enthusiastically returned him to the next assembly session.[50]

In Pennsylvania, the public's support for popular rights was apparent at every turn. The antiproprietary legislative factions of Pennsylvania's early years and the Quaker Party of the mid to late colonial decades dominated provincial politics because they were widely perceived as synonymous with popular liberties. As Governor George Thomas observed, "the people . . . [were] always fondest of those that opposed the Gov't."[51] When there was some political disagreement over how Pennsylvanians' rights should be protected (such as occurred during the mid 1760s), citizens turned out in numbers to vote protection for their provincial heritage. Equally significant was the degree to which other less-noticed political contests also turned on the issue of popular rights. One of the county officers of government who was of "great importance" was the sheriff, and unlike the situation in New York and other major North American colonies, Pennsylvania's sheriffs were elected. Not only was the sheriff "the very chief weight whereby all . . . [was] moved and turned in the courts," he was also the critical figure in the running of elections.[52] Because of the political sensitivity of this office, one of the voters' major considerations was the candidate's ability to "Shew good inclination to Select a few persons that can Oppose a Certain Interest if Occasion . . . [should] require."[53] A properly disposed sheriff would make sure that election inspectors, and jurors sitting on proprietary land suits, were firmly antiproprietary. It should not be surprising, then, that on occasion the contest that "drew the greatest numbers to . . . [an] election" was that for sheriff, not the one for assemblymen.[54] And because the sheriff held the position for three years, it was important to select those whose popular disposition would wear well in office. In quiet times, the sheriff's election served as a periodic refresher course on the fundamentals of popular politics.

If widespread concern for popular rights characterized high-turnout elections, it did not automatically lead to political mobilization. Citizens might eagerly attend "a Merry Making, a Husking, a Christening or what they call a 'Bee,'" but if they thought their neighbors would satisfactorily tend to elections or that political affairs would take care of themselves, they would as often stay at home as turn out to vote.[55] The result was that candidates for political office often had to overcome their constituents' apathy. They had to induce countrymen to travel to the county seat and city dwellers to mingle intimately in the election-day crowds.

The mobilization of the electorate began with the conscious decision on the part of the office seekers to "make" interest.[56] Everyone, of course, had an "interest" by their potential to influence family, friends, acquaintances, and even strangers. The trick was for the candidate to enlist as many and as influential backers as he could as active supporters. One of the best examples that we have of this process of "making" interest is a letter of the Chester County, Pennsylvania, notable John Morton to his old acquaintance Joseph Pennock, Sr., in which he admitted being "prevailed on in favour of . . . [Morton's] Kinsman Mr Philip Ford," who "[had] a Mind to Use his [Ford's] own Interest and that of his friends to procure him the Office of Sheriff." Morton went out of his way to assure Pennock that Ford was "A Steady friend to Liberty & the Constitution." To colonials in New York and Pennsylvania, that assurance was always of great importance, but it also meant vastly different things, depending on the circumstances in which it was used. In Chester County's political parlance of the hour, it meant that Ford was of an antiproprietary bent, that he would respect tender-conscienced Quakers in carrying out his official duties, and that he supported the continuation of Pennsylvania's constitution rather than the current campaign for royal government. Pennock could also find confidence in Morton's declaration that Ford's "Principles . . . [were] honest" and that he would grace office with "Candour Generosity and Integrity." Morton knew that Pennock had "not Troubled . . . [himself] to Attend Elections some years past," and he did not ask the old gentleman to do so. What Morton requested was Pennock's "Interest respect and opinion about home when Opportunity Suits"—that is, "to drop Something now and then for him [i.e., Ford]." Morton went on to say that "if . . . [Pennock's] family . . . [could] be Engaged in his favor . . . [Ford felt he would be very] Strong in . . . [their] Quarter." Finally Morton reassured Pennock that no election-day embarrassment lay down the road, for Morton "believe[d] that Ford's "Interest . . . [was] good throughout the County."[57]

There were few variants of this first level of "making" interest. Once a candidate decided, in consultation with his politically minded friends, to stand for election, or was drafted by them to participate on a ticket, the candidate and his political associates and managers turned to their family and friends to tout their cause. Those "connections" in turn reached out to others.[58] Some, like Robert Livingston, Jr., could on occasion round up considerable support. In 1761, Livingston felt he could deliver fifty to eighty votes downriver from his manor to his political friends in Albany.[59] But in tight contests, even small gains were valuable. In one instance, Arent Stevens, a business acquaintance whom Sir William Johnson had pressed into service to round up support for the candidates of Johnson's choice, reported the results of a hard morning's lobbying: "I have prevail'd with Nicholas Velie to Vote but he must be taken care of, and not suffer'd to be talked to by the other side."[60]

The continuities of factional and party politics facilitated the process of making interest in New York and Pennsylvania. Because of ongoing allegiances in both colonies, the candidates who were acceptable to any faction or party immediately fell heir to a preexisting network of political influence. In Pennsylvania, in particular, where Quaker Party allegiances were rock-solid, the number of representatives from some of the old counties was large, and party candidates were occasionally not agreed upon until the eve of the election, a relatively stable core of party loyalists in each county bore the brunt of interest-making. It was thus possible for some candidates, such as John Smith and Isaac Norris, Jr., to play the diffident gentlemen—above soliciting office or votes on their own behalf—even during contested elections and still win seats.[61] They could do so, however, because they were unqualified partisans. Because of past associations and active interest-making at earlier stages in their lives, they had legions of the party faithful out working for them. Far more characteristic of affairs in both New York and Pennsylvania were candidates who played a leading role in reactivating and trying to extend the interest networks of their respective factions and parties. The veteran New York politician Henry Beekman kept himself in the forefront of interest-making in Dutchess County, New York. Despite his ascetic side, Beekman's son-in-law, Robert R. Livingston, did the same.[62] The New York lawyer John Morin Scott benefited from his close association with longtime provincial Whigs, but that was not enough; he tried to strengthen his interest by adding an element of street politics to his appeal, going "in Person, from House to House, to solicit votes."[63] In Pennsylvania, all of the major party leaders (with the exception of Isaac Norris, Jr.) took pains to be in the forefront of electioneering, tirelessly trying to extend and consolidate their electoral support. Out in the provincial hinterlands, relatively unknown candidates tried to do the same. In the Northampton County election of 1754, James Burnside went "from place to place" bawling his support for the Quaker Party and "beating his breast" to prove his determination to "serve the County to the utmost of his power."[64]

The testimony of James Burnside's opponents is a reminder that not all interest-making was through private correspondence and quiet conversation. Speeches and pamphlets were an important facet of election campaigns. In Philadelphia, Israel Pemberton, Jr., "harangue[d]" the crowd, while in New York, Oliver DeLancey traveled up the Hudson to Esopus in Ulster County, bringing with him "all the songs & faction papers" of the day to "read . . . in the tavern."[65] Such preelection efforts were important, not only because they encouraged voters to turn out on election day, but also because the writings continually extended into rivalries of the moment the various political discourses and interpretive frameworks that colonists used to make order of public affairs. New Yorkers and Pennsylvanians turned out large numbers of screeds and editorials during the eighteenth century, and each wave of electioneering material provided context for succeeding conflicts.[66] Political partisans did their best to manage the news—to spread both information and disinformation in ways that would benefit them come the next election. In Pennsylvania, the party proponents of civil Quakerism commanded the "ears" of the country people; in New York, factional contests for the public mind were much more common.[67] At one point in 1747, Henry Beekman, a popular Whig, was in the assembly with a number of others "when [it was] not siting." Cornelius Van Horne was railing at Governor Clinton's orders to send New York City troops to Albany, and about the unwillingness of the detachments to go without an act of assembly, when Beekman apparently interjected in a "Jocular Manner" that Oliver Cromwell had gotten his men to march by shooting one or two. The next thing Beekman knew, Dutchess County politicians who had ties with the remnants of the old Morris/Alexander faction of provincial Whigs were trotting the anecdote around the county to prove that Beekman was not as friendly to the people's rights as he and his associates professed to be.[68] In New York, it was hard to tell: little incidents could turn out to be significant in future electoral battles.

Connection, argument, and propaganda all played an important part in mobilizing voters, but partisan politicians were rarely willing to let it go at that. Making interest involved not only polite overtures to friends but also attempts to use the leverage that socioeconomic power provided. The existing sources for New York and Pennsylvania suggest that contemporaries were well aware that the power wielded by trustees of the loan office, supreme court judges, justices of the peace, lawyers, creditors, business partners, employers, and the socially preeminent could be turned to political ends. At their subtlest, these relationships could find expression in the offering of a vote as "Recompense" for "Private Favours."[69] They could also take the form of blunt threats. One of the "GREAT MEN (as they are called)" had "come into our neighborhood" pushing a particular ticket, complained one Philadelphian, and if the complainer and his neighbors did not fall in line, "he threatened to sue some of us."[70] In New York, one well-known resident, Peter Van Schaack, told of an acquaintance who wrote "a Number of Letters to his Tenants or Debtors or Dependants . . . in order to intimidate them to vote as he wanted them to."[71] At its extreme, intimidation could become outright violence. Twice, county elections in Pennsylvania erupted into violence when one side determined to drive its opponents from the polls.[72] But these were aberrations in what was normally a well-ordered scene. Lynford Lardner, a relative of the Penns, reported that election riots, "such as happen at almost every Election in England, . . . [were] here to[o] rare not to be made the most of by the opposite party."[73]

On balance, however, politicians recognized that the carrot was more attractive than the stick. Candidates and their close supporters offered loans to individuals, donated money to charities, promised transportation or to stand travel expenses to bring voters to the polls, and paid naturalization and freemanship fees to those who would pledge their support.[74] Most commonly, they treated all comers to food and drink. Overall, the most cost-effective bribe was alcohol, the chief lubricant of all election machines.[75] Votes were bought and sold in taverns; when, in highly contested elections, party and faction runners brought in "The Deaf, the Blind, the Young and the Old," their price was most frequently not that of the "Stockings," "Shoes," and "Breeches" of which the poor were in need, but enough drink to dull the aches and bitterness that the hard turns of life had brought their way.[76]

Not surprisingly, when colonial politicians were prepared to make such strenuous efforts on their own behalf, they were also determined to seek every advantage they could at the polls. The key figure in any effort to control an election was the sheriff. In New York, the sheriff's office was an appointed one; because New York's governors abandoned all but minimal efforts to have their own men in local administrative posts, county politicians could, under favorable circumstances, have great influence over their sheriff.[77] That was apparent in the way sheriffs tilted the scales toward one faction or another. As overseers of elections, they could disallow votes on technicalities; they could raise questions about the qualifications of some voters and overlook the shortcomings of others; they could give brief notice of an impending poll to some townships and ignore others; they could arbitrarily change the election venue; and they could shut down a poll quickly or keep it open until distant precincts had sent in their last man.[78] No wonder William Corry smacked his lips at Sir William Johnson's claim to renewed influence with Lieutenant-Governor James DeLancey in 1757: "you can now get us a sheriff—that is the first grand point."[79]

While Pennsylvania's sheriffs were just as embroiled in partisan politics as sheriffs in New York, their elective status gave them a consistent political bias that their northeasterly counterparts did not share. With only one or two exceptions during the late colonial years, Pennsylvania sheriffs were antiproprietary politicians in their own right. That meant that anti-Quaker challengers faced uphill battles, for in Pennsylvania, too, the sheriffs could influence the choosing of election inspectors or close the balloting down prematurely.[80] Because of the regularity of Pennsylvania elections, along with the tradition of holding elections at county seats, Quaker colony sheriffs had less latitude for creative politics than New Yorkers. But in both colonies, active politicians recognized that the circumstances of the election could be as important in determining the outcome as voter turnout, and representatives of all parties and factions wanted to avoid election losses because of the "wrong management" of their campaigns.[81]

As exciting as electoral battles might be, as fulfilling as partisanship might feel, and as sweet as victory could taste, political veterans always viewed contested elections with considerable ambivalence. "Unforeseen . . . turn[s] of popular humor" were always a threat, and the best-laid plans could fall afoul of poor management.[82] The result of these fears (reinforced in Pennsylvania by the Quaker distaste for overt conflict) was that leading politicians often wished to avoid a contest. As Abraham Ten Broeck pointed out when election writs reached Albany in early 1768, "Every body is averse to a poll."[83] In New York City, and in Pennsylvania generally, during the mid 1740s and early 1750s, there were virtually no contested elections, largely because of the overwhelming popular antagonism to Governor Clinton in New York and to the Proprietary Party in Pennsylvania. But these exceptions aside, the available evidence suggests that political cleavages were usually too great to bridge, for electoral competition of some kind—within the Quaker Party, among locally oriented county notables in New York, or between clearly identifiable representatives of the two colonies' respective factions and parties—was most characteristic of politics on the Hudson and Delaware rivers. There was certainly no pattern of dramatic shift from contested to uncontested elections similar to that in England in the 1720s, which historians have associated with the seismic cultural shudders that preceded a relatively stable political landscape in Great Britain through 1832.[84] And the number of uncontested elections in New York and Pennsylvania seems likely to have been considerably less than the 65 percent Virginia experienced between 1728 and 1775.[85]

That does not mean, however, that New York and Pennsylvania were without some structural stability in their respective political systems. One indicator of this is the rate of turnover of colonial assemblymen. In both New York and Pennsylvania, there was a significant drop-off in the turnover of legislators during the early eighteenth century, a change that suggests the emergence of a more "settled, coherent and predictable" political environment.[86] In the case of New York, the duration of assemblies tended to reinforce that development. During the first twenty-five years of royal government, New York had sixteen assemblies, but during the next forty-five, only twelve.[87] During the turbulent turn-of-the-century decades New York politicians were divided by their own quarrels, frequently at odds with their governors over fundamental constitutional issues, and felt encouraged by the English Triennial Act to expect frequent elections. But as the main outlines of an acceptable provincial constitution began to emerge, factions became more cohesive and governors less willing to subordinate their personal financial interests to a defense of strict prerogative claims. Most important, the dominant political factions found that it was possible to work out compromises with governors and still, because of the gains in power the assembly had made, not entirely forgo the public esteem they needed in order to secure reelection.

Finally, there were two important structural features of electoral politics that underline the functional integrity of the respective political systems of both colonies. The first of these is the pattern of voter turnout in provincial elections. The high points of voter participation fell in clusters, as far as we know, during the middle decades of the eighteenth century, when the factional and party structures of New York and Pennsylvania were most clearly defined.[88] It is, of course, possible to emphasize the absolute number of voters that participated in elections and use that record of slow growth to argue for a linear model of political development in the colonies.[89] But a much more revealing indicator of political behavior is the record of voting *percentages*. Despite a fast-growing population, New York experienced *no* appreciable percentage gain in voter turnout between the 1730s and the early 1760s.[90] And despite Philadelphia's unparalleled growth, the percentage of voters who turned out between 1750 and 1775 in the county elections actually *declined* slightly, to an average of 23.2 percent (down from 25 percent between 1725 and 1750).[91] What we have, then, is not a linear model of voter mobilization but an episodic one. Voters tended to turn out at what contemporaries perceived to be crucial political junctures, both in response to their own sense of public priorities and to the promptings and inducements of competing politicians. The considerable willingness of settlers to take an active hand in politics when significant issues and symbolic confrontation distinguished elections suggests they were members of well-integrated political systems, in which many residents tended to identify with and incorporate themselves within their respective provincial political cultures.[92]

The second structural feature of electoral politics is the extent to which members of the early established, or charter, ethnoreligious groups in New York and Pennsylvania shaped traditions of vital, competitive popular political activity. The heirs of seventeenth-century immigrants formed the bulk of the mobilized electorate in the older counties. Members of the Dutch Reformed church had a lock on New York City politics throughout the colonial years, and when the elections of 1761, 1768, and 1769 took place, members of the Dutch Reformed church turned out in higher proportion than any other denomination for which we have records.[93] The Anglicans may have matched them, but the Presbyterians, who have so often been identified with the politicization of late colonial politics, were among the least active voters.[94] In Albany, too, it is clear that rivalry among various Dutch factions was what brought out the vote.[95] Rather than always practicing cosy, paternalistic politics, the Dutch joined with the offspring of some of New York's early British settlers to engage periodically in the competitive electoral episodes that strongly influenced the political texture of the province's two most important centers of population. While there are no Pennsylvania voting records that reveal the participatory patterns of provincial voters, there is every reason to believe that early residence in given areas spawned stable traditions of polarization. Even in Philadelphia, where Quakers were quickly outnumbered, Friends and their German allies formed the core of the Quaker Party.[96] Despite the sporadic participation of voters from one election to the next, the patterns of political participation that developed in the late seventeenth and early eighteenth centuries in both colonies imparted a continuity to electoral politics that continued throughout the pre-Revolutionary years.

Government and Politics

Just as it is essential in assessing the character of popular politics in New York and Pennsylvania to have some understanding of the relationship of the imperial authorities to the colonies, of the place of the council in provincial affairs, and of the tenor of electoral politics, it is necessary to know something about local government in the two colonies in order to come to grips with the subtleties of their respective expressions of colonial American political culture. In both societies, the character of county and local government contributed to the legitimation of colonial regimes. Colonists most frequently came into contact with their governments through the administrative procedures of caring for the poor, developing a transportation system, providing for public buildings, licensing taverns and public houses, probating wills, registering claims to land and chattels, and the legal processes of the civil and criminal courts. By participating in parochial public affairs, whether as petty officials, interested parties, or observers, New Yorkers and Pennsylvanians recognized their governments' claims to their allegiance and thereby imparted strength to them.[97]

But if the processes of legitimation were similar in each colony, their expression was often somewhat different. Compared to Pennsylvania's, the most important feature of New York's local government was its varied and parochial character. During the sixty-seven years of European settlement prior to the establishment of representative government in 1691, "localism took root . . . [in 'random' fashion] and flourished in all parts of the colony."[98] On Long Island, the dozen and a half Dutch and English towns "began with completely different forms of government, and were given different degrees of autonomy."[99] Even among English towns there were variations, depending upon their early status as either New York or Connecticut possessions. Up the Hudson River, almost a dozen towns were scattered in Westchester, Dutchess, and Albany counties, each with its own sense of propriety and community identity.[100] In addition to the towns, there were the two prominent city corporations of New York and Albany and the handful of well-known Hudson Valley manors. The characters of the two cities were distinct, and there was considerable variation in the manorial ethos of the colony's great estates.[101] With the establishment of representative government in 1691, all these areas were included in counties, and there was subsequently some effort to standardize. Established towns and manors, as well as the precincts into which most newly settled sections of the counties were divided, were all to elect supervisors. These officials, with the assistance of elected assessors, collectors, constables, and overseers of the poor, were intended to take over the administration of the bulk of local affairs from county court officials.[102] But this process was never more than a compromise with the forces of individuation. Some manors resisted integration;[103] some county courts refused to hand over all their administrative responsibilities to the supervisors;[104] and most towns retained an institutional, and possibly a sociopolitical coherence unmatched by precincts.[105] Moreover, New Yorkers continued to tolerate exceptions, allowing the creation of new towns and the granting of assembly seats to favored towns and manors.[106] In New York, the traditions of localism persisted strongly throughout the colonial period.

Pennsylvania, of course, had nothing like New York's tangled thickets of hardy localisms. Areas on the Delaware dominated by pre-Pennsylvania settlers had either been sloughed off with the Lower Counties in 1704 or swamped by the new arrivals who poured into the colony beginning in 1682. Although William Penn professed to prefer the establishment of closely knit agricultural villages, what he got was dispersed settlement.[107] There were no strong towns and town officials, no proprietary control over township lands, and no clear congruence between township boundaries and religious congregations.[108] Penn's manors had no effective jurisdictional integrity, and when it appeared that areas such as Germantown or the Welsh tract might possess a social base predisposing them toward significant local autonomy, powerful Pennsylvanians would have none of it. They revoked the Germantown charter in 1707 and divided the Welsh tract by redrawing the Chester-Philadelphia county line in 1691.[109] Philadelphia had a strong corporate identity and assembly representation of its own, of course, but the City of Brotherly Love was a singular place.[110] Of the three other municipalities that gained charters, and the half dozen county towns that Thomas Penn laid out during the last quarter century of the colonial period, none rose to distinction save as administrative centers for county affairs.[111] As county seats, they anchored a uniform system of county government that was by far the most important focal point of local affairs. From the first days of Pennsylvania settlement, all townships were included within extensive counties, with each county run largely by a handful of county justices and then, increasingly after 1718, by three popularly elected county commissioners and their half-dozen assessor associates.[112] (While some conflict accompanied this change, it was a change from one relatively centralized and uniform system to another.) There were no pockets of townships whose existence antedated the counties, and hence no communities determined to assert the kind of special privilege that institutionalized parochialism in New York. In Pennsylvania, as new areas became settled, new townships were established, with exactly the same powers as the first ones on the shores of the Delaware River. And as clusters of townships formed far to the west, they constituted new counties similar to the old ones.[113] Each county was in itself a powerful unit serving as a major focal point for local activities. But with the single and very important exception of assembly representation for the counties, Pennsylvania's organization of local government was a far more standardized system than its counterpart on the Hudson.

The differences in the historical development of local government in New York and Pennsylvania had important concomitants in political affairs. One of the most significant of these was the character of patronage politics in county government. Conditioned by their sense of regional autonomy, and prompted by their belief that local power should be protected, New York's assembly representatives tried to gain as much control over the appointment of justices of the peace, militia officers, and other local officials as they possibly could. By 1715 they had had considerable success. Their ability to "make and unmake Officers in their several Counties" soon became so well recognized that county residents frequently referred to "the sitting members" as "*the present administration.*"[114] The security of that privilege varied from time to time and place to place. On occasion a governor might try to regain some of the power his predecessors had traded away.[115] And councillors such as Cadwallader Colden and Sir William Johnson were sometimes successful in their efforts to channel appointments through themselves.[116] Yet even in such circumstances, the elected county representatives were rarely shut out, and certainly they never relinquished their claim to appointive influence.[117]

The devolution of patronage authority in New York had important consequences. One was that having control of county appointments strengthened local politicians and inflated their sense of self-importance. With influence on both the elective and appointive side of the political ledger, assemblymen easily came around to the view that their county was their fiefdom. And the cumulative effect of that was to reinforce the parochial basis of provincial politics at the expense of the tendencies toward centralization that accompanied the province's growing experience with representative government.

A second consequence had to do with the way in which assemblymen used their "right" over local appointments to consolidate their political support. In the case of militia appointees, they demonstrated a modicum of restraint. Senior militia appointments were of some importance: although such officers had lost a considerable power they enjoyed early in the century, that of choosing which troops might be sent on duty to the frontier, and although it was widely recognized by the mid eighteenth century that the officers did little even in wartime, the title of "colonel" or "captain" could carry some prestige.[118] Assemblymen occasionally tried to procure these titles for themselves, and much more frequently for their friends. But in doing so, and in appointing lesser officers, the legislators were constrained by practical considerations. Citizens would only cooperate with officers who had their trust, and the number of commissions was limited by demographic constraints.[119]

In the case of justices of the peace, however, local politicians abandoned all pretense of evenhandedness. Justices were to "herd with the common people," to "hail fellow well met with them over a mug of ale," and, with the influence they gained thereby, to bring them to the polls in support of the incumbents at the next election.[120] In order to increase their political support, provincial politicians expanded the commission of the peace as much as they could. Henry Beekman's 1744 list of thirty-nine appointees for Dutchess County provided a justice for roughly every one hundred sixty people.[121] By comparison, Berks County, Pennsylvania, had a ratio of justices of the peace to residents of approximately 1:1,300 in 1769.[122] Put another way, the thirty-nine magistrates Beekman proposed to name in one year were only nine short of the total number of justices commissioned for Chester County, Pennsylvania, for all the twenty-five years between 1729 and 1755![123] Dependent as they were on political goodwill, the lifetime òf New York magistrates' commissions could be very short. William Smith, Jr., claimed to know of one situation in which the county commission was changed three times in one year. If assemblymen perceived their judicial appointments to be lacking in loyalty, the justices could quickly be stripped of their office and "superseded" in another extensive list.[124] When Deputy Provincial Secretary Goldsbrow Banyar was asked for information on justices of the peace, he threw up his hands in disgust. He had no idea where the current justices resided within their counties, or if they had even qualified to serve.[125] Not only did the structure of New York's patronage politics promote localism, it also clearly exacerbated the rivalries that centered on county affairs.

The fact that Pennsylvania had nothing like New York's historically entrenched local governments was reflected in the character of the patronage relationships that did emerge in the Quaker colony. One of the most important sources of patronage in provincial government was the Pennsylvania loan office. It was a highly centralized institution. A small group of four or five assemblymen, headed by an acting trustee, looked after the allocation of mortgages and the valuation of property offered for security throughout the entire province. There was some regional representation, for the committee was composed of one representative from the backcountry and at least one from each of the three old counties. But the assembly as a whole decided who those individuals should be.[126] When New York undertook to establish a similar institution in 1737, its organizational structure contrasted sharply with its Pennsylvania counterpart. Each New York county had its own loan office representative, and that officer was chosen, not by the assembly, but by the township supervisors with the concurrence of three justices of the peace.[127] While New York's politicians gave the ponies of parochialism their head, Pennsylvania's Quaker Party was adept at keeping them pulling along well-rutted roads. In Pennsylvania, such appointments were highly partisan, of course, but that partisanship was overwhelmingly provincial in its orientation.

The comparative degree of centralization that distinguished the Pennsylvania Assembly's patronage also characterized the judicial appointments for which the proprietors bore responsibility. Unlike the situation in New York, the composition of the commission of the peace was always decided in Philadelphia by the chief proprietary advisors, with the usually perfunctory concurrence of the governor. Although Pennsylvania magistrates always carried the stigma of being proprietary placemen, proprietary officials, prompted by Thomas Penn, refused to indulge their partisan proclivities overly much when making up the commission.[128] They took seriously names suggested by the existing members of the county bench.[129] They solicited the opinions of those who, like Reverend Samuel Finley, "care[d] not what party they [the justices] belong[ed] to." Finley, a Presbyterian, recommended both a Presbyterian and a Quaker, the former "a man of strong judgment, firm purpose, strict justice and impartiality," the latter "a good natured, candid, sensible man."[130] Knowing of Thomas Penn's conviction that Quakers as well as other religious groups should be represented in the ranks of the magistracy, that the majority by far of well-qualified individuals were Quaker, and that Quaker politicians frequently knew country personalities better than themselves, proprietary officials sought the advice of their political opponents as well as their friends.[131] Proprietary advisors showed no inclination at all to debase the judicial coin by flooding the country with men who could easily be bought. On the contrary, they believed that the only way to further the proprietary interest was to appoint magistrates who knew "how to maintain the dignity of . . . [their 'place'] by the proper exercise of authority."[132] Occasionally there were minor purges of a county commission, but when those occurred, they were as likely to be the result of delinquency of duty or less-than-exemplary personal conduct as of political opposition to the Proprietary Party.[133]

Unlike in New York, where town governments antedated the provincial assembly and local peculiarities continued to be granted institutional and statutory expression well into the eighteenth century, local interests in Pennsylvania were either subordinate to or well integrated with the more centralized notions of what the Quaker experiment entailed. Stalwarts of both the Quaker and Proprietary parties were imbued with this expansive provincial perspective, which counteracted many of the centrifugal political forces occasioned by parochial loyalties. With respect to patronage appointments, the results were clear: a brake both on the autonomy of regional spokespersons and on partisanship of a distinctly local kind.

Given the character of settlement patterns in New York, and the perceived legitimacy of local concerns, it is not surprising that assemblymen from various counties, towns, and manors frequently shared their constituents' belief that local problems were unique and required legislation speaking directly to their needs. A good part of a representative's public reputation depended on his ability to hear and respond to the right combination of local interest groups.[134] Attentiveness to the "little interests of the particular counties" was a far more efficacious way of demonstrating self-importance than was searching out similar problems and suggesting colonywide solutions.[135] Even for those who did have broader horizons, there was a compelling logic behind solicitude for local interests. While acknowledging that specific community demands pandered to parochialism, it also brought legitimacy to and acceptance of the provincial government. And in a society that had a tradition of viewing central authority as an intrusive force, that was an important consideration.

The results of parochial power and the thinking that accompanied it were evident in the New York statutes. There were separate laws providing for the extirpation of wolves in Albany, Dutchess, and Orange counties.[136] Regulations for laying out highways required special treatment in Suffolk, Albany, Ulster, Westchester, and Dutchess counties.[137] Kings County required a particular act to safeguard its sheep;[138] Hempstead one to prevent rams from running loose and breeding at random;[139] and Claverack precinct in Rensselaerswyck Manor one to protect local property from foraging swine.[140] Another indication of New York legislators' concern for their locale was the number of place-specific acts. Between 1701 and 1770, 117 acts were specifically aimed at New York City. (During the same period, fewer than a third as many Pennsylvania acts dealt only with Philadelphia.)[141] In their demonstrable solicitude for local self-importance, New York assemblymen offered the same public gesture of respect for parochialism to their towns and districts that British legislators frequently extended to the entrenched private and quasi-public interests of their idiosyncratic constituencies.[142]

New Yorkers' concern for local interests had other important consequences when the issue of taxation arose. Rather than adopting a uniform tax rate for the province, legislators willingly jumped into battle with their peers in order to assign quotas to the various counties.[143] All shared the same motive of trying to push as much of the tax burden as possible onto other counties, and thus ingratiate themselves with their constituents. Nor did that competitive mode of behavior stop at the provincial level. A county's share of taxes was in turn distributed by quota among towns, manors, and precincts during a free-for-all among their supervisors.[144] That kind of rivalry injected an irascible element into New York localism, ruffling relationships among provincial politicians and increasing the difficulties they faced in forging a consensus among their disparate constituent communities.

While New Yorkers put a premium on their local roots and traditions, Pennsylvanians emphasized their participation in a shared new-world experiment. Most Quaker leaders had no desire to promote an order of settlement and local government at odds with the kind of rationality that the gridlike plan of Philadelphia symbolized. New Yorkers felt the need to extend assembly representation to nine counties and manors in 1681 in order to respect community variety, but Pennsylvanians originally set out only three counties to encompass all their townships. The large size of the counties, the equality of representation accorded each, and a sense of shared purpose, encouraged Pennsylvania assemblymen to form large legislative committees that cut across differences rather than give legislative expression to idiosyncrasy. Decades later, when the new backcountry counties were badly underrepresented, the tradition of having large legislative committees continued. Politically, of course, that was a means of maintaining Quaker control, but it also had the effect of continuing the kind of legislative standardization that distinguished many of Pennsylvania's statutes on local affairs. In New York, the practice of accepting one- or two-man legislative committees served parochial interests, and also encouraged them. In Pennsylvania, the refusal to accept such narrowly based committees worked against the proliferation of highly individualized acts of legislation.

Pennsylvania's relative preference for the simplicity of statutory standardization was obvious. When Quaker assemblymen provided bounties for wolves, they did so, not in individual county acts, but in one paragraph of the Act for Raising County Rates and Levies.[145] Laws covering matters of intense local concern, such as the laying out of highways, and irritations like foraging swine were always given uniform applicability.[146] When nearly a dozen Anglican churches scattered throughout the colony needed help raising funds, the assembly dealt with all of them in one enabling act.[147] A related feature of Pennsylvania legislators' behavior was their refusal to slide into the kind of antagonistic parochialism that distinguished New Yorkers' negotiations over taxes. When provincial taxation was necessary in the Quaker colony, representatives set a rate that applied to all eligible provincials, irrespective of their place of residence.[148] On the local level, there was no direct pitting of township against township. Given the size of the counties (Lancaster and Chester counties, for example, had thirty-three and fifty-two townships respectively in 1759), negotiations among township representatives over tax quotas would have been impractical. It was up to the small number of justices of the peace and, later, county commissioners to make tax decisions to conciliate the many local communities within their jurisdiction. If these men hoped to maintain their positions and reputations, they could not afford to be open or overeager advocates for any township, village, or borough.

While the different local government experiences of New York and Pennsylvania in some measure explain the plethora of parochial statutes in the former case and their comparative scarcity in the latter, they do not come close to accounting for the very great disparity in the number of acts that the two colonies promulgated. Between 1701 and 1770, New York averaged a little over eighteen acts per year, and Pennsylvania averaged a little under half that.[149] This pattern was consistent for the number and duration of periods in which no legislation was passed. In New York there were only four such times, all less than two years long.[150] In Pennsylvania, there were a dozen hiatuses in legislative enactments, three of which were from three and one half to five years long, three from two to three and one half years, and six from one to two years.[151] How can that disparity be explained? What do these differences tell us about the character of government and politics in each society?

In the case of New York, the legislative record indicates that despite some heated differences between assembly and governor, political leaders shared an underlying belief that their society required constant regulation. Because New York's frontiers demanded militia vigilance, but no chief executive could be trusted with an open-ended militia law, annual renewals had to be authorized. The colony's complex of revenue acts needed continual refinement and updating. Fortifications needed tending, and annual governmental salaries had to be paid. Above all, most assemblymen believed that duly passed laws were the primary means of establishing the legitimacy of their colonial government, for statutes were the primary symbols of provincial authority. Regulation by statute was the most secure validation local interests could gain, and acceptance of a claim to regulate was the strongest confirmation of the right of provincial leaders to govern. In a society such as New York, with a past checkered by conquest and a present plagued by frontier foes, yet peopled by settlers who in large measure preferred order to uncertainty, the desire to prove legitimacy through legislation was one that all assemblymen shared.

Pennsylvania differed considerably. The early years of settlement brought flurries of legislation, as Quaker legislators established the administrative, political, and legal framework for their experiment.[152] But thereafter their perceived need for regulation diminished. The justices of the peace and county commissioners assumed much of the responsibility for the pressing local matters that accompanied rapid population growth and economic development. Quaker pacifism meant that there was no need for annual militia laws and constant attention to colonial defense. Provincial taxation was infinitesimal during the early decades of settlement, and when provincial needs increased, the loan office and excise provided ample income, with only periodic statutory change. The power of the House of Representatives and its financial resources meant that much provincial business could be dealt with by assembly resolve rather than by legislative act.

More important even than these practical considerations in constricting the volume of Pennsylvania's laws was Friends' attitude toward their government. Whereas to New Yorkers the essential means of establishing and proving legitimacy was the exercise of legislative power, to Quakers the sources of legitimacy were largely internal. Friends believed that in the past the exercise of civil authority had almost always been an impediment to truth, and would remain potentially so in Pennsylvania even under Quaker custodianship. Worldly demands, including those of legislators and magistracy, would constantly threaten the purity of the Inner Light. Only by keeping secular voices to a minimum and by periodically stilling them, both in meeting and in civic affairs, could Quakers fulfill their larger obligations to God. Morality, good order, and civility were dependent, not on external regulation, but on internal commitment to "holy conversation," to Quaker testimonies to truth, to a family life suffused with charity, and to the mutual forbearance that adherence to the golden rule produced.[153]

The results of these beliefs were the antithesis of the kind of extensive regulation our acquaintanceship with Puritan New England has accustomed us to expect from colonials of intense religious conviction. Reckoning that power was dangerous, Quaker legislators accumulated it to prevent its abuse, while simultaneously expressing their ethic of self-denial by refusing to use it.[154] Knowing that the legitimacy of the Pennsylvania experiment rested on internal sources, not external ones, they were under no compulsion to prove their authority by the frequent exercise of the law. When disputes with governors eluded settlement or brought legislative paralysis to the provincial government, Quaker representatives felt under little pressure to compromise for the sake of social order. They knew that county government and the courts would answer most local government needs, that the established framework of provincial law never required much in the way of immediate change, and that society was in no danger of disintegration. Proof of this lay in the colony's past. Had not the community been able to continue an orderly life with no provincial constitution at all?[155] Could not the courts function smoothly without legislative sanction?[156] Proof lay, too, in the character of the colony's social relations. Had not many Pennsylvanians, regardless of their religion, become Quakerized, clearly sharing Friends' attitudes toward government and accepting the right of Quakers to lead the way?[157] Only when the problem of war wracked the colony did the Quakers' authoritative aura dim and the interior pillars of public legitimacy show signs of crumbling.[158]

More than the politics of place and the patterns of electoral behavior, the structure of local government in New York and Pennsylvania and the attitudes of their respective citizens toward the sources of governmental authority reveal something of the individual character of the two colonies' political cultures. Were we to look no further than to the strictly political and governmental, however, we would miss a number of other important insights into the process of sociopolitical individuation that operated in New York and Pennsylvania. Some of the most telling features of the two colonies' respective political cultures were neither narrowly institutional nor directly political, but were related rather to the broader social values current in each province. These can be found only by focusing on the conjunctive relationship between politics and society.

Between Politics and Society

One of the most important characteristics of New York society was the emphasis many prominent colonial leaders placed on emulating the English. In a conquered province with a sizable Dutch population and tough-rooted traditions of local diversity, self-conscious anglicization was the obvious and easiest way for leading colonists to emasculate the foreign element that threatened to dwarf them, and to create a larger sense of provincial coherence. That New York was a royal colony after 1685, that it soon became well integrated into the British patronage network, and that it occupied a critical geographical location in Britain's North American rivalry with France all encouraged emphasis on a cultural transfer from mother country to colony.

There were numerous illustrations of New Yorkers' intense efforts to structure their society along English lines. They reacted to doubts about the character of their provincial constitution by exaggerated assertions of its comparability to the British model.[159] The New York bench and bar stressed their faithfulness to English models and argued that their province would show greater "Sense and Prudence" if only provincials would be more determined in adopting "the Laws of England for a Pattern."[160] Those families with close connections to powerful English and Scottish politicians, those recent arrivals from Great Britain whose traditional values remained strong, and those who needed to prove their colonial world by old-world standards all stressed the need to establish another "new" England on the Hudson.

One of the local circumstances that encouraged New York Anglophilia was the colony's late seventeenth-century land policy. Early New York governors granted immense tracts of land to favorites in order to bolster executive power.[161] By the early eighteenth century, however, the governor's position had changed markedly with the increase in assembly power, and New York's large landowners became far more concerned with consolidating their patent and manorial land claims, and with expanding their own bases of popular power, than with showing gratitude to the Crown. The establishment of large landed estates in various New York counties created one of the most highly visible underpinnings of an old-world style gentry; that was a social image that had immense appeal to the large landowners and to their political allies. New York's land-rich were acutely aware of how unscrupulous their forebears had been in expanding the boundaries of their land grants, how the sanctity of their landed property depended on their own continuing influence and political power, how new and unformed their society was, and how uncertain its rules were.[162] Analogies between themselves and the hallowed English gentry distracted attention from the questionable sources of their wealth and fostered the legitimacy that New York's "grandees" needed for long-term survival.[163] Not surprisingly, conscious self-promotion of their gentry status was pervasive among the province's large landholders. The proprietors of Rensselaerswyck were referred to as "patroon," "lord," or "lord patroon"; proprietors of manor lands promoted themselves as "lord proprietor"; and Robert Livingston (of Clermont), was known as "King" Robert.[164] The close association of "Sir" William Johnson and "Admiral" Peter Warren with New York emphasized an apparent transferability of English social distinctions from the Old World to the New, and in so doing encouraged colonial defenders of social hierarchy. The predilection of prominent New Yorkers to think this way is best illustrated by the Long Islander William Hick's reference to the Pennsylvanian Thomas Wharton, a Quaker Party stalwart, as the "duke of Wharton," and Robert Hunter Morris's tendency to see Pennsylvania politics largely in terms of localized "interests and connections."[165] On the rare occasions on which New Yorkers considered Quaker colony leaders, they rendered Pennsylvania's political culture comprehensible, not by attempting to untangle its subtleties, but by transforming its political personalities into caricatures and describing its features in ways that made sense within the context of their own system of politics.

The notion that New York's political culture was, and should be, similar to England's was reinforced by two important features of the province's political organization. The first of these was the fact that, unlike other major British North American colonies, New York had a number of anomalous units of provincial representation along with its standard counties. The manors of Rensselaerswyck, Livingston, and Cortlandt, and Westchester Borough had much in common with those English pocket boroughs in which one or two patrons could frequently decide who would represent the community.[166] The second was that, like England, New York had viva voce voting. Voters in a given constituency were required to declare the candidates for whom they wished to vote openly in front of the assembled freeholders.

The effect of large landholders' gentry pretensions, along with the existence of provincial pocket boroughs and of viva voce voting, was to encourage leading New Yorkers to think of their provincial politics in terms of the patron/client relationships that were central to the English sociopolitical order.[167] According to the old-world canons of hierarchy, status was in part determined by the number of dependents an individual or family might have.[168] New York landowners and merchants who cared about their public personas were thus acutely aware of their influence among their tenants and the tradesmen, retailers, entrepreneurs, and laborers with whom they dealt. A good part of the trick for New York's upper classes was for them to act like patrons and thereby assert the influence they felt they should have by right. Such behavior was most regularly in evidence among the members of New York's manor families, because tenant status so clearly symbolized the kind of dependency upper-class provincials liked to envision for less prominent mortals. But patronal attitudes existed elsewhere in New York in various situations in which individuals accumulated large concentrations of socio-economic power. Some of the best examples that we have of these senti-ments come from the Mohawk Valley, where Sir William Johnson set the standard for patron/client relations.[169] Johnson fostered strong ties be-tween himself, his tenants, laborers, and business associates, and at election time, he voiced his anticipation that they would "all as one Body . . . Stand by me."[170] The same sort of assumptions informed the lesser landlords within Johnson's sphere of influence. Just before one important election, an old acquaintance, William Corry, assured Johnson that Corry had "directed *my people* to vote on your side."[171] In the minds of New York's upper classes, political affairs *should* be settled by those who could speak of "my folcks."[172] And in turn, those "folcks" *should* cooperate.

Another good illustration of how patron/client relationships were inter-twined with politics occurred in Dutchess County during the 1730s and 1740s. There, the landed magnate Henry Beekman tended his patronal influence with both private attention to detail and considerable extrava-gance. Beekman took a personal hand in the selection of such local officials as justices of the peace, militia officers, coroners, and supervisors;[173] he impressed on his county lieutenant, Henry Livingston, the need always to heed Beekman's personal philosophy, never "slight" or be "forgitfull" of "your frends";[174] he cultivated the county sheriffs assiduously, for he under-stood that their goodwill was essential for the "artful . . . Joabbing" neces-sary to fill juries with friendly clients whose brand of justice would reflect Beekman's county dominance.[175] The other side of Beekman's behavior was his ability and willingness to play an expansive, openhanded role as regional patron. At election time, he entertained the county with barrels of cider and rum, "100 Loves" of bread and "Beef, Porck & Backin . . . Buylt a Day or 2 before ye Election."[176] The motivation for such entertainment was less one of bribery (although food and drink could serve that purpose in the country as well as in the city) than it was Beekman's desire to show hospitality commensurate with his assumed patronal stature. Like English magnates of an earlier era, Beekman may have thought of himself as not so much "per-suading electors . . . [as] acknowledging supporters."[177] Beekman the benevolent country gentleman complemented Beekman the local fixer. Each role facilitated the other. Together they made Henry Beekman one of New York's high-profile politicians, an exemplar of gentry leadership.

Evidence of New Yorkers' efforts to replicate some of both the substance and the style of seventeenth- and eighteenth-century English patron/client politics took various forms. In the manors, in the relatively insulated county of Suffolk, and periodically, in quiet times in other constituencies, New York elections might show signs of what they had been in early seventeenth-century England: a ritual in the social ordering of the community as much as a political event.[178] Vestiges of the English past might also be seen even in such vigorously competitive locales as New York City and County, where, on the rare occasions in which unanimity prevailed, confirmation of those agreeing to stand for the assembly was by "shout," "three Huzzas" from the assembled crowd signifying the electors' consent.[179] More prominent, however, were provincial practices that reflected more current English electoral politics. Extravagant donations to charitable causes, promises to forgo payment as assemblymen, purposeful lobbying for votes, and intense cultivation of select constituents, were all prominent characteristics of New York electioneering with English counterparts.[180]

One of the most important reasons why leading New Yorkers put as much emphasis on their patronal influence in political affairs was that viva voce voting held that influence up to public scrutiny. The ability to mobilize a retinue of supporters who would speak out for their patron at the poll was a measure of the man. Robert Livingston, Jr., for example, was a proud man when it turned out that some eighty voters agreed to follow him to Albany in 1759. But when Livingston's candidates refused to force a poll, robbing him of the chance to head such a parade, his pride turned to bile. His allies' failure to push for a vote not only cost him a triumphal role in Albany politics but could also be interpreted as reflecting his allies' doubts whether he could deliver the Kinderhook vote.[181] That, Livingston felt, was a public affront. Ordinary freeholders, as putative clients, did not have as much at stake as recognizable patrons. But there is some indication that considerations of honor were important to them too. As one participant in the 1768 preelection campaigning in New York City put it:

Since sundry moneyed Gentlemen of this City, have been generous enough to open the Strings of their Purses, to furnish Belly-Timber during the present Election: Let us Eat heartily, tho' temperately; Drink liberally, tho' cautiously; Sing jovially, tho' modestly; applaud disinterestedly, tho' generously: And under the protection of Bacchus, let those Gentlemen know, that we love their Bread and Wine, but despise the Imputation of being influenced by either.[182]

Come the day of choice, there were those who were quite ready to "Stand by" their man and openly profess their political allegiance.[183] As one Richmond County freeholder put it, he welcomed the opportunity "to shew his

Integrity." Many New Yorkers believed that demonstration of civic integrity could best be accomplished through the celebration of both clientism *and* independence that viva voce voting occasioned.[184]

Because of the open nature of voting, and the desire of patrons to flaunt their influence, sanctify the electoral process, and make it easy for free-holders to join their cadres, New Yorkers put a great deal of emphasis on ceremony and public display. The best-described example we have of this is the Westchester by-election of 1733. That episode gives us some idea of the nature of election-day drama. In this contest, Lewis Morris, Sr., ran as a provincial Whig seeking to reenter the assembly after losing his seat five years earlier. Because Morris was running in his own backyard and had already staked out appealing positions on the questions of the day, the outcome was a foregone conclusion. The opposing Philipse faction put up a relatively weak candidate, an Anglican schoolteacher, William Forster. The Morris entourage entered the Eastchester green "at Sun rising" on the day of the election: "first rode two Trumpeters and 3 Violines: next 4 of the principal Freeholders, one of which carried a Banner; on one Side of which was affixed in gold Capitals, KING GEORGE, and on the Other, in like golden Capitals LIBERTY & LAW; next followed the Candidate LEWIS MORRIS Esq: late Chief Justice of this Province; then two colors." Later Forster arrived: "next him came two Ensigns, born by two of the Freeholders, then followed the Honorable *James DeLancey,* Esq; Chief Justice of the Province of *New York,* and the Honorable Frederick Philipse, Esq: second Judge of the same Province and Baron of the EXCHEQUER . . . and . . . they entered the Green on the *East* side, and riding twice round it, their Word was *No Land-Tax.*"[185] The pageantry at this election was by no means singular. Other contests had their parades, their slogans, their songs, their banners, and their drums.[186] Their purpose was twofold: to accentuate the impression of patronal power, and to encourage freeholders to join in the excitement of events and, in doing so, validate the colony's sociopolitical order.[187]

In retrospect, what stands out most markedly about New York political leaders was their exaggerated efforts to be "gentry" and to try to replicate in their various locales the kind of patron/client relationships they associated with English society. Much of their self-consciousness stemmed from the fact that they were never entirely what they thought they should be, and they rarely gained the kind of unchallenged local hegemony they felt they should have. By the standards of the Chesapeake Bay gentry, many New Yorkers were "aggrandized upstarts," overly assertive of their assumed status because they had neither the "opportunity" nor the "capacity to observe the different ranks of men in polite nations, or to know what it . . . [was] that really constitute[d] . . . that difference of degrees."[188] Looked upon with some condescension by their southern counterparts, New York's upper classes were made more sensitive by their patronal shortcomings. Some elections, for example, laid bare their pretensions by proving that the outright purchase of votes was far more effective than any of the subtle ties of patron/client relations. In 1761, Robert Livingston, Jr., reported that many of the Hudson River German freeholders, who had a long association with the Livingston family, would follow his lead in the Albany election only if they received forty shillings a head.[189] Although such bribery was a feature of the eighteenth-century English electoral scene, and thus was and is capable of being explained as simply more evidence of anglicization, in fact, there was a very important difference between the two societies. In England, what were soon to be called "rotten boroughs," with their tiny electorates, were the centers of bribery.[190] In New York, however, a few comparably small manor and county seats are the best examples we have of peaceful, patron-dominated constituencies. It was the large counties that were centers of the commercial politics of vote buying.[191] And these were the constituencies that were the backbone of New York's political system. Convinced that an anglicized colonial order was essential, but faced with uncertainties of status and attenuated patronal influence, New York's gentry reacted with intense and repeated affirmations of their belief in a hierarchical society, and used whatever means they could to try to demonstrate their leading place in it.

In comparison with New Yorkers, Pennsylvanians' sense of sociopolitical identity depended far less on English standards. They had their own charter, their own constitution, their own political tradition and their own sense of place and purpose derived from the province's proprietary/Quaker past. Which is not to say that Pennsylvania politics were completely idiosyncratic. Obviously they were not. Electoral competitions in the Quaker colony shared many features with their New York counterparts. Old seventeenth-century English practices, such as deciding the winners of elections "by view" of the candidates' supporters, occasionally emerged in vestigial form in Pennsylvania in the choosing of election inspectors.[192] Other British concerns, such as maintaining personal honor in public affairs, also characterized politics in Pennsylvania and New York.[193] But there were also a large number of distinctive features in Pennsylvania politics that gave the province a rather different profile from that of New York.

To begin with, there was nothing in Pennsylvania comparable to New York's manor families and large patentees. Pennsylvania's proprietors, of course, held immense tracts of land, but most of their acreage was for sale. There were many Pennsylvanians who bought and sold either unsettled or improved land, and some real estate barons, merchants, and professionals did develop country estates.[194] But gentry status did not have the baronial connotation it had in New York. Granted, Pennsylvania had its "great men," but unlike in New York, where the provincial "grandees" frequently *were* the leading provincial politicians, the term "great man" was usually employed in the Quaker colony to dismiss or diminish proprietary supporters who were already at the periphery of popular politics.[195] Patron/client relationships were always a part of colonial society, but there were no Pennsylvania patrons with the highly visible reach that some of the New York magnates appeared to possess. Although numerous, tenants in Pennsylvania were perceived as being autonomous, clearly expected to be treated as such, and in many cases were very independent.[196] No Pennsylvania landlord that we know of instructed *his* people how to vote or marched them to the polls; only in the peripheral counties was there even a hint of the kind of one-family influence that distinguished the manors and other small, or isolated, constituencies in New York.[197] There is no indication, either, that patrons in Pennsylvania ever ventured beyond the admittedly flexible standards of "treating" to consider purchasing votes.[198] Nor did Pennsylvanians organize the kind of processions, rallies, and celebrations that occurred in New York. An individual or two might harangue a crowd, but there was little in the way of public preening and parading.[199] The one exception to this was a telling one. In 1726, former Governor Sir William Keith celebrated his election to Pennsylvania's House of Representatives amid "Mobs, Bonfires, Gunns [and] Huzzas—a Keith for Ever," organized "Itinerations and processions," so his disgruntled opponents claimed, of "Butchers, porters & Tagrags," and a fortnight later headed a cavalcade, some eighty strong, into Philadelphia preparatory to his bid to become speaker of the assembly.[200] But Keith was a British outsider, insensitive to Quaker norms and unpersuasive in his innovations. His English-modeled electioneering practices departed with him.

Another important and obvious reason why the character of Pennsylvania politics differed markedly from New York's was that Pennsylvanians voted by ballot rather than viva voce. Quakers believed that voting was a public matter, but that the choice should be private. And the adoption of the ballot was a repudiation of precisely the kinds of political patronalism that distinguished Great Britain, and that some principals tried to foster in New York.[201] In theory, the ballot was an endorsement of a voter's right to exercise freedom of choice without pressure or threat of reprisal.[202] In practice, however, secrecy could not easily be achieved. Ballots were frequently written out in advance of the election to be distributed by faction or party insiders, and presumably they were identifiable. Still, various voters indicated that they did exercise the freedom to make a "private decision" by writing out their own tickets, and on occasion large numbers of freeholders crossed out one or two names and added substitutes.[203] Others "pretend[ed] they vote[d]" for one candidate while actually casting a ballot for another, a strategy some German voters allegedly refined into something better:[204]

> But the *Dutch* was so wise, they put on Disguise,
> To deceive those poor Tools in their Folly,
> Themselves they did provide, with Tickets on both Side,
> Tho' . . . it drove those poor Slaves melancholy.[205]

Given the evidence, it is quite possible that colonial Pennsylvania had the closest thing to a secret ballot that any colony or state enjoyed prior to the adoption of the Australian ballot in the United States in the late nineteenth century. The direct results of this were two. First, there was little public parading of the patron/client hierarchy, and second, voter intimidation took very direct and immediate forms. One Philadelphia freeholder reported such an experience: "I stood amazed at the *Tann'd* Impudence of a Fellow two Years ago, who stood upon the Stairs [leading to the ballot box] with Heaps of prepared Tickets: . . . he took . . . [mine], look'd on't, and then told me it was not right, would have kept it; and offer'd me another, as it seems he had managed several."[206] But the fact that the voter "with some Trouble . . . got" his ticket back "again" and used it as his ballot also shows how ineffective even such brazen interference could be.[207] The only way one party could be sure of carrying an election was, literally, to drive anyone who was not a known supporter away from the ballot box. That, and the fact that the Quaker Party's pacifism made its members easy targets for thugs, explains why, on occasion, election-day riots took place in Pennsylvania rather than in more raucous New York.[208]

There were other important differences in the temper of political affairs in New York and Pennsylvania that had little to do with any specific institutional variation in the colonies. Whereas New York's upper classes constantly spread the gospel of social hierarchy, Pennsylvania's social leaders articulated a considerably more complicated set of community values. No matter how worldly leading Friends became, and no matter how pervasive the values of England's "better sort" became in other mainland provinces, Pennsylvania society was shot through with Quaker egalitarianism.[209] The sense of partnership that William Penn had cultivated with his first purchasers, and the feelings of religious fraternity that drew Friends together were unique. Try to imagine Robert Livingston or some other early New York proprietor speaking to his friends, but social inferiors, as William Penn addressed Robert Turner—as a man "whose shoes lachets I am not worthy to unloose"![210] And the communal purpose that the first settlers had emphasized in order to strengthen their control of the province lived on in Pennsylvania's public ethos. That was most obvious in Pennsylvanians' rejection of pretense and their distaste for various manifestations of authority. Andrew Hamilton expressed this very well. On the one hand, Hamilton was a gentleman who believed in prerogatives for wealth and status when capacity earned them; on the other, he despised posturing and empty ritual in public affairs.[211] Despite being Pennsylvania's leading public figure in the 1730s, "it was not . . . [Hamilton's] natural disposition to be on the side of those who . . . [were] accounted Great or in Power."[212] Although his own temperament was one that could not "easily brook" slights, Hamilton "hardly . . . [uttered] a sentence without Dog, Rogue be Damn'd and the Like" and "he took pains to Unmask the Hypocrite, and boldly censured the Knave, without regard to Station, or Profession."[213]

Hamilton's disregard for authority and his questioning of the icons of political tradition were far from unique to him. Despite the pains propri-etary leaders took to recruit respected citizens as magistrates, Quakers har-bored a deep distrust of dependent judicial officers, an "inveteracy . . . against the Magistracy" that never abated.[214] Friends constituted the vast majority of those well enough educated and of sufficiently strong local reputation to merit appointment as justices of the peace, but as the eigh-teenth century wore on, fewer and fewer were willing to compromise their popular reputation and their scruples for a questionable judicial appoint-ment.[215] In other situations, expressions of irreverence might appear in a much more haphazard manner. The Bucks County Quaker William Biles dripped contempt for authority when he dismissed the newly appointed Governor Evans as "but a boy . . . not fit to be . . . Governor. We'll kick him out."[216] Benjamin Franklin both reflected and emphasized leading Pennsyl-vanians' willingness to poke fun publicly at English standards that their New Yorker counterparts would never have questioned. "A pecuniary grati-fication," Franklin puckishly wrote, "is offered to any of the learned or unlearned, who shall *mathematically* prove, that a Man's having a Property in a tract of land, more or less, is thereby entitled to any Advantage *in point of understanding* over another fellow who has no other estate, than THE AIR . . . *to breath in,* THE EARTH . . . *to walk upon,* and ALL THE RIVERS OF THE WORLD . . . *to drink of.*"[217] Irreverence for old-world cultural tradi-tions, whether seriously or humorously expressed, was a vital part of the Pennsylvania perspective.

The highly original twist that Quaker thinking gave to Pennsylvania society is clearly observable in the character of the provincial legal culture. Whereas the contemporary system of English law legitimated upper-class rule by the public dramaturgy developed around the concepts of majesty, justice, and mercy, the Pennsylvania legal system institutionalized a very different set of values.[218] Rather than emphasizing the majesty of the law with court-day "spectacles" of judicial haughtiness, so as to "by word and gesture . . . fuse terror and argument into . . . [an] amalgam of legitimate power," the early Pennsylvania courts brought their proceedings down to a common level of understanding and experience with simple pleadings, few lawyers, unschooled judges, and unpretentious courthouses.[219] Rather than trying to enhance "Justice" as "a power with its own claims" on the basis of "punctilious attention to forms" and an "absurd formalism," Quakers worked to "demystify the law" by eliminating legal fictions, simplifying procedures, and making the courts easily accessible.[220] Rather than trying to enhance the "psychic force" of the law by juxtaposing the terrors of "exemplary hangings" under a harsh and extensive criminal code with paternalistic pardonings as "acts of grace," the Pennsylvania court system cut down on capital punishment and "presented incentives for the accused to show repentance, confession, and reformation."[221] In short, "the legal ideology of the Delaware Valley prized substance over form, simplicity over complexity, and reform over retribution."[222] Even though the influence of the established English legal ideology began to seep into the Pennsylvania legal system by the second decade of the eighteenth century, the Quaker-built foundation of the provincial legal culture remained solid.[223] Comprehension, rationality, and simplicity were more the guiding norms in Pennsylvania courts than in those of any of Britain's other North American colonies.

Other revelations of the differences between the political cultures of New York and Pennsylvania took place on the infrequent occasions in which they came into contact. One of these incidents occurred in the early 1750s when William Smith, Jr., who was trying to build a political coalition against James DeLancey, approached Queens County Quakers for their support. Smith did get a sympathetic hearing, but in the process he revealed how little he understood the moral imperative that underlay the "Plain Stile" of Quaker language and Friends' unwillingness to compromise honesty for the sake of the silky compliments that upper-class New Yorkers viewed as buttressing social order.[224] About the same time, Thomas Penn appointed a member of one of the oldest "gentry" families in New York and east New Jersey, Robert Hunter Morris, as governor of the proprietary colony. Pennsylvanians hated Morris's haughtiness, his contemptuous dismissal of Quaker ways, his duplicity, and his authoritarian attitudes. Anyone with Hudson River or east "Jersey Airs" was ill suited to deal with the much more matter-of-fact and self-confident provincial culture that had developed on the west side of the Delaware.[225]

The unique character of Pennsylvania's sociopolitical order was something observers occasionally sensed, and it could make them feel quite uncomfortable. Most tended to respond by dismissing Pennsylvania as being too "republican."[226] That was a reassuring stock answer, for it placed the

Quaker colony on a spectrum of political behavior that was widely known; and certainly some important features of Pennsylvania's political behavior were best understood in those terms.[227] But telling, too, were the commentators who strove to dismiss Friends in gender-related terms, as individuals ill fitted for public leadership because their religious society encouraged much of what current male orthodoxy defined as feminine weakness.[228] In taking this tack, such critics pointed out an important perspective on the ways in which Pennsylvania differed from New York.

In both provinces, of course, women occupied a central place in the domestic and religious life of their respective families.[229] Beyond that, it is possible to argue that an apparent favoring of the economic interests of children and creditors over those of widows in Quaker Pennsylvania, versus a Dutch cultural elevation of women's property rights and a more active female presence in business affairs in early New York, granted a greater sense of individual empowerment to New York women than to their Quaker counterparts.[230] But if this was so, any large-scale sociopolitical consequence of this tendency is difficult to perceive. On the other hand, it is certain that Quaker women in Pennsylvania occupied an extremely elevated social position, which was clearly discernable and had an observable impact on public affairs. Historically, Friends' belief in the universal accessibility of the Inner Light, along with the prominent exemplary leadership of Margaret Fell, prompted early English Quakers to accept both women's meetings and female ministers or "public Friends."[231] As women ministers built reputations traveling through the various Anglo-American societies, they gained the kind of experience, worldly wisdom, and aura of authority that could not easily be dismissed. And within local communities Quaker women carved out important areas of supervision and discipline among themselves. In doing so they became "vital partners in the activities of their inner faith," which were perceived as the "primary business of the Society as a whole."[232] Because the moral imperatives of Quakerism extended to all aspects of community life, and because Friends placed so much emphasis on maintaining the unity of their collective socioreligious experience, barriers between the political and the religious, between the public and the familial, were consistently breached even as they were created.[233] Governance in all its dimensions was based on interlocking gender relations, for "women had no power independent of the men," but neither did "men claim . . . authority separate from women."[234] As "spiritual mothers" within this partnership, then, women could have considerable influence on the politics of the day.[235]

The conjunctive authority of Quaker women and men was something that many colonials found deeply offensive and threatening. While most critics focused their attention on Quaker pacifism as entirely inappropriate for public affairs, it is clear that the issue was also a powerfully symbolic one at the visceral level, going far beyond the principle involved.[236] Pacifism was a feminine characteristic, and its influence in public policy both reflected the influence of Quaker women in social affairs and represented the tendency of Friends consciously to extend values born of religious and family experience into the larger public arena. Although pacifism was the most obvious example of the organic connection between domestic life and larger community values among Quakers, there were others. Friends' emphasis on love-centered marriages, on ensuring the independence of their children, and on recognizing that the pursuit of Truth in some cases *required* youth to rebel against adults—all conspired to offend by propagating an air of social egalitarianism in public, as well as in private life, that contradicted a number of dominant Anglo-American social assumptions.[237] Because of the ubiquity and tenaciousness of paternalistic values even in the Quaker colony, the influence of Quaker women was never all that it might have been. But it was enough to raise the ire of many of the more orthodox, and to play a part in distinguishing Pennsylvania from its neighbors.

The point is that Pennsylvania's Quaker women played a part in public affairs that had no counterpart in New York society. Nor was it anything like the role that women played in English elections, where property ownership, family patronalism, social-inversion rituals and the vote-getting efficacy of sexual enticement occasionally involved women in electioneering.[238] In Pennsylvania, Quaker women were power brokers, not a titillating sideshow, and they were power brokers, not because of a familial property right in some rotten borough, but because they were part of a mixed male/female network of respected public leaders. Various women participated in the traffic of political confidences along with their male acquaintances:[239] women such as Jane Hoskins of Chester County were involved in negotiating county tickets prior to elections;[240] and on one occasion that we know of, the well-known Susanna Wright of Lancaster County took a "stand . . . in an Upper Room in a public House and . . . [had] a Ladder erected to the window and there distribute[d] Lies and Tickets all day of the election."[241] A further example of how women entered into public affairs occurred in 1755 when Catherine Peyton, an English public Friend, insisted on a ministerial meeting with Quaker assemblymen, and was among those ministers with whom the legislators met for advice as Pennsylvania stood on the brink of war.[242]

The assembly, of course, was the most respected institution in both Pennsylvania and New York. And to whom provincial representatives, as a group, would listen, is an important indicator of provincial values. In the case of Pennsylvania, not only did Quaker legislators give a hearing to Peyton and her near allies, but also in 1748, the assembly (including non-

Quakers) opened its doors to the Quaker minister John Churchman to listen to his concerns about public policy.[243] Compare that to New York, where legislators lampooned pacifism, strutted a macho image with their titles as militia colonels and captains, and would invite only city lawyers to advise them in the assembly chamber.[244] Male and Anglophile, representing social hierarchy and pleading prescription, the New York City bar personified the most prominently paraded public values of provincial New York. New York leaders might envy Pennsylvania's economic success and relative autonomy, but they clearly found nothing seductive about the aura of Quakerization that crowned their Delaware River neighbor.

The contrast between New York and Pennsylvania is most marked in the ill-understood twilight zone between social behavior and politics. Taken by itself, of course, the distinction between the New York emphasis on hierarchy and Pennsylvanian solicitude for equality can be misleading, for the two societies were complex. But only when we appreciate the respective sociopolitical temperaments of the colonies is it possible to understand the strengths and weaknesses of each regime in the changing politics of the late decades of the colonial period.

Chapter Nine

Oligarchical Politics

ONE OF THE important questions about any particular political regime is to what extent deep structural conflicts in society have an observable impact on the political order. In societies such as colonial New York and Pennsylvania, in which representative institutions were so prominent, changes in the personnel and character of popular government can reflect the extent to which contemporaries perceived those social conflicts to be political or to have major political implications. Three of the most prominent indicators of social crisis that historians have identified as having considerable implication for mid eighteenth-century colonial politics are those of general economic distress, crowd or mob activities, and ineffective courts. Although each of these factors did affect both the short- and long-term conduct of political affairs in ways both obvious and subtle, none had a sufficient impact on the political structures of either New York or Pennsylvania to alter the fundamental character of the colonies' respective regimes.

In retrospect, the most compelling feature of popular politics in both New York and Pennsylvania was its oligarchical nature. This was clearly reflected in the prevailing patterns of provincial representation, as well as in the organization of factional and party politics in the two colonies. What kept these provincial oligarchies secure at the centers of political systems distinguished by a strong commitment to popular politics was more the

accessibility of officeholders within their respective communities of intimate citizenship than any pattern of political deference and/or patronalism.
The most successful provincial politicians were well grounded in their local
communities and felt many of the same concerns that touched their neighbors. Commitment to the circumscription of capricious power, the pursuit
of parsimonious government, the service of community needs, and the
maintenance of capable political leadership, along with the need to face
periodic reelection, effectively reconciled the oligarchic with the popular in
mid eighteenth-century New York and Pennsylvania politics.

No matter the vitality of this particular sociopolitical hybrid, it was not
impervious to change. Alterations in the relationship between the colonies
and Great Britain, coupled with increasing social tensions in the provinces themselves, created problems that the old oligarchies were not well
equipped to address. In raising fundamental questions about the distribution of power, the Stamp Act protests and land riots in New York and the
Paxton riot in Pennsylvania dealt a severe blow to the colonies' respective
oligarchies. Leaders could no longer speak for the most dynamic forces in
their society when those forces challenged the oligarchs' own hegemony,
and the recurring extralegal attacks on British authority further undercut
oligarchic power. As a consequence, both New York and Pennsylvania regimes became more defensive, arbitrary, and conservative during the last ten
years of colonial rule. By the beginning of the 1770s, they were ripe for
revolutionary change.

Political Discontent

Like their more modern American counterparts, colonials frequently recognized that politics was confined neither to the legislature nor to the election
and appointment of public officials. The purpose of government was to
serve the community and thus, when citizens experienced, or thought they
experienced, sharp socioeconomic change, or when they felt that they were
the victims of an unjust or overly predatory officialdom, they were likely to
give political expression to their discontent. We have no clear idea of exactly
where eighteenth-century New Yorkers and Pennsylvanians located the
boundary lines between what they considered to be political and nonpolitical phenomena. Quite likely there would have been some variety in their
answers. In general, colonists had a less expansive view than current generations of what constituted a political statement or agenda. But it is clear that
colonials did make important, if erratic, connections between some social
and economic dimensions of community life and the course of political
affairs.

One of the beliefs that many colonists shared was that government had some obligation to promote the economic well-being of the community. A flourishing provincial economy might be cited as evidence of good government and equitable social relations; a deteriorating one could suggest a political order overrun by the private concerns of self-centered men. Picking up on these concerns, and more particularly on the expressions of socio-economic grievance that appeared during a few periods of economic distress, some historians have suggested that class conflict engendered a radical political consciousness of significant dimensions. They have argued that an undercurrent of laboring-class mutuality and antagonism toward the selfishness of the rich ran continuously beneath public affairs and on occasion broke to the surface, partly on its own and partly on the invitation of upper-class politicians competing for popular favor.[1]

There is no question that voices claiming to speak on behalf of New York and Pennsylvania mechanics did roil the political waters of both colonies during the most acute economic crises. The clearest examples of this occurred during the late 1720s to mid 1730s in New York and the early to mid 1720s in Pennsylvania, when depression hit the economies of the two colonies hard. In both cases, socioeconomic grievances became part of the rhetoric of political discontent.[2] Political propaganda proliferated as competing factions sought to control the public agenda. In New York City, "Timothy Wheelwright" spoke either to or for the many artisan groups when he complained of hunger amid the "Entertainment[s]" of the rich and the inequities of the law. "Great Men" might flout the law, and if tradesmen complained to the grand jury or county representatives, why "Fiddle faddle, give the Goose more Hay . . . what signifies that? mayn't great Men do as they please for all them and us too? Suppose any great Man should . . . whip you through the lungs . . . or Knock your Brains out, and he should be presented to the Grand Jury, pray what Notice would be taken of it? . . . very little." The best that mechanics could do to improve their situation was to elect "poor honest" or "midling" men rather than "rich Knaves."[3] Not to be outdone, advocates for the artisans and farmers of Pennsylvania drew on a strong provincial tradition of egalitarianism, and trained their tongues on the rich with homely turns of phrase. "It is an old saying with us," wrote Roger Plowman, "that we must never grease the fat sow in the Arse, and starve the Pigs."[4] In both colonies, too, the effects of depressed economies went beyond rhetorical sallies against the rich. New York legislators espoused reforms such as triennial elections, lowering official interest rates, the creation of a loan office, and bounties to stimulate the production of various commodities.[5] Pennsylvania assemblymen responded to their own situation in a similar manner, and espoused export inspection laws and a paper currency in their efforts to stimulate the provincial economy.[6]

The intensity of the language of class conflict during these times of economic distress suggests that tensions between rich and poor were always present to some degree in the colonies. In western European settler societies in which disparities of wealth quickly appeared, it would be surprising if there were no such burning resentments and if the coals of animosity did not flicker occasionally into flame, as the rich, the middling, and the poor jostled each other in the public places of colonial society. The question, however, is not whether privately and publicly expressed class-related animosities existed or not—clearly they did[7]—but to what extent the resulting tensions determined the patterns of political conflict and political change.

There are several important pieces of evidence from pre-1764 New York and Pennsylvania that bear on this issue.[8] First, there was no *necessary* connection between hard times and radical politics. During the first decade of the eighteenth century, and again during the late 1740s and early 1750s in both New York and Pennsylvania, for example, depressions occurred. But they created little spontaneous political mobilization among the laboring classes.[9] Moreover, if we look carefully at the major incidents of political change and conflict, they do not correlate particularly well with either structural economic problems or divisions over economic policy.[10] Take, for example, the cases of the greatest political upheaval in assembly membership. The 1759 New York election brought the biggest turnover in the colonial years, over 63 percent.[11] Yet 1759 was in the midst of a period of prosperity in which no particular issue germane to class conflict or prompting a rethinking of the postulates of political economy wracked the province. By the same token, if we look at the four occasions of greatest political change in New York, the principal common denominator was not socio-economic strain but the longevity of the preceding provincial assemblies.[12] The high turnover following a long provincial assembly is best understood within the context of New Yorkers' political ideas, rather than as their response to short-term economic cycles. The same may be said of political change in Pennsylvania. In 1710, for example, an election occurred that became the standard for every other episode of radical political change. In that year the electorate rejected every incumbent and chose an entirely new assembly! Far from turning on economic issues, this revolution clearly spun on a political and religious axis.[13] In fact, if we look at the major episodes of public conflict in Pennsylvania—the confrontation between popular political leaders and the proprietary in the early eighteenth century, and between the Quaker and Proprietary parties in the early 1740s, the mid 1750s, and the mid 1760s—they all centered on facets of civil Quakerism.[14] Overall, economic depression and inequities in the distribution of wealth were never of more than secondary importance in bringing on either sustained political conflict or considerable political change in the two colonies.

If there is no direct connection to be made between economic hardship and radical politics, the circumstances of the New York and Pennsylvania experiments with radical politics in the 1720s and 1730s are nonetheless revealing. Judging from both colonies' experiences, the appearance of overt class-based political appeals required both significant splits among the established political leaders and a willingness on their part to tap into the existing reservoirs of economic discontent and class tensions in order to bolster their respective positions. In New York, vigorous competition between the Philipse and Morris/Alexander factions prompted their leaders to seek support among city tradesmen. In Pennsylvania, Sir William Keith wanted to build up his popularity among Philadelphians in order to defy the Penn family and further his hopes of having Pennsylvania royalized under his leadership. Although in each situation leading politicians tried to capitalize on the socioeconomic grievances of the middling and lower-class mechanics and farmers, and claimed to be against the "great men" of their day, in fact, they discouraged anything in the way of outsider political participation other than as voters. In Pennsylvania, the Keithians "engross[ed] . . . the Management of . . . [elections] into the hands of a small number" of Sir William's upper-class friends.[15] And in New York, the Morris/Alexander crew, often regarded as one of the most radical pre-Revolutionary political factions in the colonies, made an explicit part of their election campaign the caution that electors should choose as representatives those who were not only well affected toward "Liberty" but who also had "a considerable Interest in the Property of this Colony."[16] Clearly electors heeded this advice, for it is hard to imagine a group of New Yorkers more filled with themselves and their upper-class status than James Alexander and his confidants.[17] Even in the much-noticed New York municipal elections of 1734, there was little evidence of artisanal precociousness. The socioeconomic backgrounds of incumbent city officials and their challengers were very similar, and their profiles indicate little to suggest they shared, or wanted to share, very much with the working men of their neighborhoods.[18]

All told, it is clear that "no homogeneous artisan political community" developed in either New York City or Philadelphia to make a distinctive mark in political affairs.[19] Small producers there were aplenty, but there is little evidence of a distinctive small-producer mentality that prompted many to seek direct access to the seats of provincial political power. Despite efforts to portray the colonial experience as a tableau illustrating "ordinary people . . . striding to the forefront of politics," the actual politics of conflict left a record of the laboring classes' political "ambivalence" and fitfulness.[20] The primary reason for this was that despite their sizable numbers (as many as half the taxable males in New York and Philadelphia), "at no time were . . . [they] a unified body, identifying themselves as a class or united interest group."[21] In terms of wealth and status, mechanics ranged all the way from the lower levels of the social structure to the upper middle ranks; because of this, they merged and overlapped with retailers and entrepreneurs of various bents. Classification of artisans in terms of wealth or craft also tends to underemphasize the fluidity of socioeconomic relations in early New York and Philadelphia. Economic and demographic growth, the differential rates at which journeymen could advance to become independent producers, increasing specialization among mechanics, the relative informality of craft organizations, divisions among journeymen, apprentices, and masters, and conflict within artisan groups, as well as among related crafts, created a dynamic social structure in which many of the relationships that might have created class cultures were in considerable flux. In England, economic specialization created craft enclaves such as occurred in Nottingham in 1754, where over one-quarter of local voters were framework knitters.[22] The common experience of such a sizable single-craft fraternity could produce a kind of lower-class cultural milieu impossible to duplicate in the eighteenth-century American experience. In the more fluid, ethnically diverse, and substantially less dense new-world lower-class environment, there was more of a tendency toward the atomization of artisan society than we might expect, and a greater acceptance of such circumstances in the local communities that mechanics and laborers forged.[23]

Despite the absence of any clearly defined artisanal or "lower sort" political consciousness, the laboring classes did have an important impact on colonial politics. Their most significant influence on the structure of New York and Pennsylvania politics was the fact that they shared with many members of the entrepreneurial, professional, retail, and merchant classes a marked prejudice in favor of popular rights. It was artisan votes as much as any that tended consistently to support the New York Whig factions that were the most credible current champions of popular privileges, and anti-proprietary, anti-executive politics in Pennsylvania. Harder to gauge, because it had no verifiable impact on officeholding, was the fact that spokespersons for the lower and middling classes could, and on occasion did, articulate the language of class conflict. The poor did have a case against the rich, and the passions that socioeconomic division could generate were never too far from the surface. Both New Yorkers and Pennsylvanians simply had to live with the obvious, that their respective provincial social orders always possessed a delicate quality along with their considerable strengths.

The activities of colonial crowds are one important illustration of how out-of-doors community activism could generate a sense of fragility in New York and Pennsylvania, notwithstanding the overall political stability of these two societies. Historians who place mobs close to the center of their treatment of political behavior tend to see crowd activities in one of two ways. The first of these involves an emphasis on mobs in which at least a sprinkling of well-to-do and respected citizens joined with a preponderance of middling and lower-class men and women to assail targets such as local officials or naval press gangs. These mobs claimed to speak for the community, and as such, they have been perceived as an expression of extra-institutional governance rather than as an anti-institutional form of subversive behavior. According to some interpretations, they supplemented, rather than challenged, the existing political order.[24]

Mob behavior of the second type is seen as taking the form of plebeian riots. In this view, when the "sociological oppositions peculiar to eighteenth-century society" forged a "reintegration" of "fragmented elements of older patterns of thought" among laboring people, a smouldering lower-class consciousness sometimes flared up into "insurgent direct action."[25] The crowd defended traditional rights relevant to the circumstances of different laboring groups, tried to protect the common interests of its members as consumers and victims of power, and spoke out for time-sanctioned privileges that symbolized justice to the participants.

One problem with both these hypotheses is that *prior to* 1764, few crowds in New York and Pennsylvania appear to fall into the designated categories. The most easily classified examples of such behavior occurred in New England, where vigorous local traditions, English homogeneity, considerable isolation, relatively dense concentrations of population, and an atavistic turn of mind encouraged it.[26] Some expressions of both all-class and lower-class protest spread west and south into New York and New Jersey, frequently through migrants from New England, but also as part of an old-world emigrant response to the peculiar experiences of each colony. These were sporadic, however, and their impact was marginal.[27] Further south in Pennsylvania, they virtually petered out.[28]

Secondly, even though those who emphasize the classlessness of colonial crowds and those who view mobs as the voice of the lower orders offer very different interpretations of colonial society, they both emphasize the degree to which "their" mobs represented "community." In the former case, the mobs are conceived of as vertically integrated crowds speaking for the community; in the latter case they are depicted as agents of a lower- and lower-middle-class community articulating long-hallowed standards of justice and morality. Both hypotheses tend to see the crucial dynamic of crowd action as a conflict between the mob, representing a community, and the objects of its anger, who, while earning that wrath, defined themselves or were defined as outsiders. In the former case these were most frequently negligent or ill-intentioned officials; in the latter, they were upper-class pariahs who ignored their larger obligations to society.

By choosing to accept the mobs' claims that they represented communities, and by focusing largely on the mobs' apparent aims, apologists for both types of crowds ignore the obvious: violence almost always fractured colonial communities in a variety of ways. Just as important as the division between the mob and its objects were the divisions between those who participated in mob activity and those who did not. If we pay attention to the boundaries of the mob, we soon see that many citizens from the same classes as the rioters recoiled from involvement and refused participation. They may have acquiesced to the mob, but there is no reason to assume that acquiescence meant approval. Clearly, too, not all occupational groups were equally represented in the crowd. Members of some occupations were more predisposed to riot in a given situation than others, a behavioral difference that suggests important attitudinal variations.[29]

The problem of cross-community, cross-class divisiveness amid violence is frequently difficult to untangle because of the very few examples of "community" crowd actions that we have in New York and Pennsylvania and because of the sparseness of records surrounding these episodes. But there were a number of other types of mobbing incidents for which we do have better evidence. These illustrate that polarization rather than consensus—but polarization of a non-class specific kind—most frequently attended mob action. Take, for example, the well-known boundary dispute violence in both New York and Pennsylvania. Although a limited class dimension distinguished the conflicts in northeastern New York during the early to mid 1750s, the harassment, clubbings, shootings, and deaths that actually occurred took place largely between prospective neighbors whose chief concerns were how best to advantage themselves in the competition for productive land.[30] The similarities between New York's rural violence, whether on the Massachusetts or the New Jersey frontier, and that intermittent along the Pennsylvania/Maryland boundary far outweigh the dissimilarities embodied in the different systems of landholding and land alienation procedures in the two colonies. In Pennsylvania, as in New York, competition for cheap land and the violence that accompanied it testified to the fragility of community relations and to the various ways in which communities in the process of formation could be fractured in expanding settler societies.[31] But land issues were, of course, not the only focus of group violence in the two colonies. There was, for example, the violence that occasionally broke out at elections. In York County, Pennsylvania, in 1750, the community split into two warring groups and resorted to "Clubb law" to settle their dispute.[32] In the well-known Philadelphia election riot of 1742, the immediate perpetrators of violence were a crowd of mariners from other home ports, who thought that beating on pacifists would be a fine "Frolic."[33] The main consequence of their action was to divide the community for years along lines that had nothing to do with differences between the lower and upper classes.[34]

There were other mobbing episodes, too, that exposed more of the fault lines in colonial society. In New York City in 1712, rioting blacks killed several whites and attempted to fire the town.[35] Approximately thirty years later, on rumors of a similar rebellion, whites visited their wrath on suspected black conspirators. Although the courts were the main vehicle whites used in order to go after the suspects, the inquisition had an air of mob violence about it, as thirty-four inhabitants were put to death.[36] Although New York Jews never experienced such intense persecution, they did face considerable harassment. Small groups of New Yorkers included the humiliation of Jews on their list of entertainments and ways to make merry.[37] All told, the preeminent characteristic of mob activity in New York and Pennsylvania was its tendency to fracture local or provincial communities in a variety of ways—but with the exception of the election riots, almost always in ways that had few clear and demonstrable political implications.

The multifaceted nature of colonial mobs, in fact, serves to remind us of how fragile the colonial social order may from time to time have appeared to contemporaries. Not only did most New York and Pennsylvania mobbings signify social divisiveness, but mobs were also unpredictable. The emphasis historians have sometimes placed on the ritualized characteristics of commemorative celebrations and popular holiday activities tends to obscure the capricious side of public events, "frolics," and "merry" making.[38] When viewed anthropologically, for example, the "rites of passage" license that some communities apparently gave to young men to harass others, or to fight and destroy property, may appear relatively benign.[39] But for participants it was the aphrodisiac of imminent conflict and the excitement of facing the unpredictable that made those forays attractive. For other members of society, regardless of class, it was precisely the element of unpredictability that always lurked around the mob's perimeter that could be so threatening. There, on the outskirts of the crowd, participant met nonparticipant face to face; there, those with a grievance met the property of those less committed to protest; and there, crowd consensus became frayed—as new recruits joined in and the half-hearted or exhausted dropped out, as alternative agendas came to mind in the swirl of action and events, as personal friendships and hatreds reconstituted themselves under the pressure of social activism, and as differences of occupation, ethnicity, religion, and race found ways of asserting themselves. Whether they were ritualized urban mobs, election riots, or rural confrontations over property rights, crowd mobilization could carry with it a peripheral capriciousness that was frequently of frightening dimensions.

To concentrate too heavily on the disruptive aspects of crowd confrontations, however, is to oversimplify. There is little evidence that the conflict and fears that violence generated put New Yorkers or Pennsylvanians into a continual state of sociopolitical nervousness. Certainly, the ritualized character of some crowd activities could work to limit anxiety, whether within the larger community or within the potpourri of the colonial laboring classes. But given the low frequency and geographic dispersion of large-scale communal crowd activities in New York and Pennsylvania that is easily overemphasized. Far more important is the simple fact that eighteenth-century colonists were inured to low-level violence. From what we know of criminal justice procedures and the offhand reporting of the use of force, colonials were frequently casual in their attitudes toward incidental fracases. Many were "resigned . . . to living in a violent world" and not particularly interested or concerned about "alter[ing] the violence of their society."[40] Colonials' insensitivity to recurring episodes of personal violence suggests that even large-scale mobbings may have telegraphed far less in the way of sociopolitical tension than we sometimes think. Prior to the mid 1760s, there are no clear examples in either New York or Pennsylvania of an episode of mobbing resulting in significant changes in electoral outcome.[41] In a violent age, violence was not invariably freighted with serious implications for political affairs. Connections may have existed, but most were far too subtle for us to pick up at the distance of two and a half centuries.

Questions about the relationship between socioeconomic and political structures in New York and Pennsylvania inevitably raise the issue of the relative political stability of each colony. At first glance, New York certainly appears to have been the more fragile. Strong and idiosyncratic traditions of localism based on geographic, ethnic, religious, economic, and historic differences could work against the political integration of the province. The colony's partial religious establishment was a compromise that occasionally exacerbated conflict among imperious spokespersons for various denominations. The execution of Jacob Leisler and his friends in the late seventeenth century hung for some time like a pall over New York, reminding eighteenth-century political leaders of how volatile public life could be. The charge of "treason" was one that New Yorkers continued to use in their factional battles as late as the 1730s.[42] The slave rebellion of 1712, followed by the alleged black conspiracy of 1741, suggest a society prone to periodic fits of fright. And the incidence of violence, both in land riots and attendant upon the continuous contact between members of the four independent companies of the British army stationed in the province and various provincial communities, certainly reinforces that perception.[43] Yet Pennsylvania also had its obvious weaknesses: a provincial legislature that appeared to avoid wielding power; a government that refused to sanction warfare in a war-filled century; a dominant sect that maintained its electoral power partially through the underrepresentation of backcountry settlements; and a number of local communities that were occasionally wracked by violence.

In order better to compare levels of governmental legitimacy and the related sociopolitical resilience of Britain's North American colonies, a number of historians have turned to court and legal records.[44] There has been an especial interest in New York's legal history, and research has turned up some important evidence that strengthens our perception of that colony's social and political order as a particularly fragile entity. Overall, from 1691 to 1775, approximately 37 percent of criminal indictments simply trailed off into inaction, while only 47.9 percent of the remaining cases resulted in conviction.[45] The fact that many of the Dutch apparently disputed the right of court officials to enforce the law, along with the increase in offenses of personal violence in New York City, and riot in the countryside after 1750, suggests a society in which authority was tenuous.[46] There is a difference, of course, between the attitudes of those suspected of criminal activities and the attitudes of the general population toward political authority. But in colonial New York, there were also important connections between court officers and politics.[47] Local law-enforcement officers were partisan political appointees and rejection of their authority could have had political implications. The rapid turnover of court officials that took place in some counties could undermine the legitimacy that frequently attends continuity in officeholding.[48] And the turning of justices of the peace, sheriffs, and other court officers into the political agents of the dominant county politicians seems to have downgraded the quality of those willing to accept such positions. Many of these political appointees had little interest in their office beyond its perfunctory administration and their profits.[49] The results were unenthusiastic courts and disrespect for incumbent officers.[50]

When we turn to civil court actions, which were far more numerous than their criminal counterparts and more revealing of the way in which contemporaries dealt with interpersonal conflict, the evidence is less clear. It is arguable that the high incidence (50 percent) of unresolved civil cases that came before the New York Supreme Court at midcentury simply reflects the same indifference of, and disrespect for, the courts that the languishing criminal cases apparently indicate. It appears on closer examination, however, that circumstances such as poor recordkeeping, the death of one party to the dispute, out-of-court settlements, or the substitution of private arbitration for further court proceedings may have accounted for many of these unresolved cases. Moreover, the extensive use of arbitrations rather than suits at law, church-sponsored mediation between antagonists, and the relative absence of court actions from the heavily Dutch area of Kings County suggest that local communities were quite capable of handling their disputes internally.[51] In the case of the Dutch communities, there was little incentive to go to court, because the "tedious Examinations, by Interpreters" made the process very costly both in time and money.[52] No matter how many criminal actions remained unresolved, there is much evidence that

New York society retained considerable coherence, and that local community members were adept at resolving civil disputes among themselves, the vagaries of the province's court system notwithstanding.

Unfortunately, we do not have the same quantitative evidence for Pennsylvania as for New York, and that makes comparison more treacherous than it might otherwise be. In the early years of Delaware Valley settlement, county courts and Quaker meetings teamed up very effectively to promote social order and to draw the settler population into a willing recognition of governmental legitimacy.[53] Certainly, there are indications that the courts in the older settled areas of the Quaker colony continued their early colonial activism in criminal matters into the mid eighteenth century.[54] And Quaker meetings in particular, but also other churches as well, were bulwarks of social order, in that they frequently arraigned their members for breach of discipline.[55] Arbitration was such an integral part of Friends' approach to social relations that it significantly influenced the judicial system,[56] and there is every reason to believe the practice became widespread, a highly visible product of the Quakerization process. Andrew Hamilton, for example, is alleged to have done something no one ever suggested his New York counterparts even contemplated—that is, spend "more time in hearing and reconciling Differences in private, to the loss of his Fees, than he did in pleading Causes at the Bar."[57] Among Presbyterian leaders, there were numerous efforts to discourage their "People" from "going to the Civil Magistrate & to Issue such personal Injuries and affronts, as may be among them."[58]

But the Pennsylvania court record is by no means unambiguous. There is evidence that local officials exercised a great deal of discretion in carrying out court orders, even to the point of ignoring judgments.[59] This would suggest that the number of unexecuted judgments and unresolved cases may have been far closer to the New York figures than first impressions suggest. Just as in New York, ethnic tensions could discourage local officials from doing the courts' bidding, but in Pennsylvania such circumstances were not quite as simple as the Dutch-English confrontations on the Hudson. There were incidents of Welshmen standing off the English, and of the Scotch-Irish defying Germans.[60] In Lancaster County, for example, the election of a German, John Barr, as sheriff produced protest:

The Irish Presbyterians being disappointed in not having one of themselves elected to that office, refused to serve on either Grand or Petty Juries, tho' regularly summoned by the sheriff, because he was a Dutchman. So that there was a failure of justice last term in that county. The sheriff, in endeavoring to serve a process on one of those people, was violently assaulted, had both ears of his horse cut off, and was obliged to fly to save his life.[61]

Of course, Pennsylvania's courts did not suffer from the same cheapening of justice of the peace appointments that took place in New York and undermined the court's prestige there, but Quaker colony judges had their own problems.[62] Invariably, "any other magistrates except Quakers . . . [were] thought to be dependants on ye proprietaries"—that is, partisan appointments.[63] And that meant that their authority was periodically undermined by the waves of antiproprietary sentiment as they washed through the colony.[64]

All in all, it may well be that there was slightly more tension over the legitimacy of provincial and county government in New York than in Pennsylvania. Even if this is so, it is nonetheless possible that the former had more potential for flexibility than the latter in the event of any serious crisis challenging the existing colonial regimes. But throughout the mid eighteenth century, there were no such crises. Socioeconomic disturbances were limited in their impact, class conflict was sporadic and inconsistently expressed, and the provincial courts worked adequately, if not perfectly, amid both cynicism and supplementary, informal methods of resolving disputes. In short, the socioeconomic weaknesses and the testing of authority that occurred in New York and Pennsylvania are unlikely to have been more severe than occurred in other reasonably stable colonial societies, and the political oligarchies in each of the two colonies enjoyed a relatively free hand to exploit their respective strengths.

Accessible Oligarchies

Popular political leadership in both New York and Pennsylvania was unquestionably oligarchical. In both societies, relatively small groups of individuals and families wielded political power throughout the colonial years.[65] For much of the eighteenth century, New York and Pennsylvania had the smallest number of assembly representatives per adult white male of any of the British colonies in North America and the West Indies.[66] From 1700 to 1734, New York's assembly expanded from twenty-one to twenty-seven seats, where it remained through 1773. During that same three-quarters of a century, the province's population multiplied almost ten times.[67] Pennsylvania had twenty-six provincial representatives from 1701 through 1729; thirty from 1729 to 1749; and thirty-six from 1752 to 1771. The Quaker province's population multiplied approximately fourteen times during that same period.[68] The degree of tight political control that members of these relatively small legislatures exercised is emphasized by the low turnover rate in their ranks.[69] The most complete study we have of this aspect of politics is of Pennsylvania, and there the proportion of assembly seats filled by incumbents and veterans from earlier sessions appears very high.[70] Although we have no comparable statistics for New York, it is likely that the entrance of newcomers into the assembly was even more restricted than in Pennsylvania. Between 1726 and 1758 only 62 new members sat in New York's House of Assembly; that was exactly one half the number of neophytes who entered the Pennsylvania legislature between 1726 and 1754.[71]

There were several other circumstances that emphasized the exclusivity of legislative office in the two colonies. Physically, for example, the small size of the assembly halls encouraged intimacy and a clubbish sense of fraternity. Picture the New York House of Assembly as James Duane briefly described it, an "ornamented" "Chamber" "on the first Floor of the City hall . . . [with] the Members tak[ing] . . . their place round a Table fixt on the Floor . . . [and] occupi[ng] . . . about two thirds of the Room"; or the Pennsylvania assemblymen sitting in Quakerish silence waiting for inspiration.[72] Comfortable in their cocoons, both New York and Pennsylvania representatives tried to insulate themselves from outside pressures as best they could. There were no visitors' galleries (although visitors were occasionally admitted to hearings involving members of the public), and unlike those of the Chesapeake colonies, the New York and Pennsylvania assemblies kept the door shut to outside auditors until just before the Revolution.[73] They emphasized the extent to which the assembly was a corporate body representing the entire colony and tried to prevent the use of the public record against themselves by only infrequently publishing division lists.[74] To most assemblymen, their office was an "Exalted . . . Station," and once elected, many found it difficult to "shake off" what one disgusted conscientious Quaker termed their "Raggs of Imaginary honor."[75] Because of the closed, consensual orientation of the Quakerized Pennsylvania Assembly, it was somewhat more of a "Conclave" than the New York legislature, but both were self-conscious bodies, whose occasional imperiousness reflected the success they had enjoyed in checking governors and in building up their own power.[76]

The primary means by which assembly incumbents kept themselves and their friends in the seats of power was their control of the nomination of candidates. Those who were in the forefront of politics and who saw themselves as political leaders and power brokers were always quick to seize the initiative in organizing electoral affairs. And once they were active, their agreements and disagreements determined the character of the ensuing contest. In New York, the most frequent method of nomination was the candidates' own announcement of their intentions. In New York City, that might be by newspaper advertisement, while in the counties it might simply be by peremptory public announcement. In Albany, in 1761, one individual asserted that the "old Candidates" were about to announce their intentions to stand for election "without the advice of any of the Citysens."[77] To many outside observers, nominations may have appeared that cut-and-dried, and in the manors and during quiet times in Suffolk and Kings counties, they may have been. But in most of the constituencies there was a good deal of interest-making behind the scenes, to which only a few were privy. In New York City, there was little taste for the kind of divisive contest that split the electorate in 1737, and in most elections, both before and after that contest, a nucleus of assemblymen and their close friends worked to establish an orderly succession or limited contest when any of the incumbents died, retired, or became an electoral liability.[78] When David Clarkson died in 1751, for example, those in the know "talked of" two possible successors, John Watts and William Walton.[79] But there was no immediate announcement of candidacy, and the two reached an agreement that prevented a contest. Walton got Clarkson's place and Watts gained a preeminent claim to the next vacancy on New York's four-person delegation.[80]

It is impossible to know how many brokers were involved in the Walton/Watts negotiations, and thus in the related nomination procedures. But evidence from elsewhere is suggestive. We know that Henry Beekman could settle his own candidacy in Dutchess County, for example, in consultation with not more than a half dozen people.[81] And for the 1761 Albany election that William Johnson's informant judged settled by the impending announcement of two candidates, we have a detailed account. In that case the two "Old Candidates" did not initially act in concert as the first observer surmised.[82] Ultimately, three autonomous candidates appeared, and the major reason for the contest was that negotiations between the seven or eight major power brokers in the area were fraught with intrigue, indecision, and deceit. The three eventual candidates jockeyed for the best possible position vis-à-vis the other two; Sir William Johnson and Robert Livingston, Jr., were unclear as to what their full intentions were; and one major player who "made a Low Bow in token of Consent" when one candidate asked for his "vote and interest," apparently broke his word.[83] It is possible that Albany (and, one might add, Schenectady) politics were perpetually more byzantine than anywhere else. Agreement over nominations may have been more easily arrived at elsewhere, or alternatively the fissures between leading politicians may have been more consistent and sharply defined. But the Albany record is the best evidence we have of the extent of meaningful participation in the nomination procedure. Key players were the "principal people" of the county, and that select group is unlikely to have gone much beyond a dozen or so individuals, even in New York City.[84] When politicians made a show of securing broader community support, what they always sought, and received, was crowd assent to a preselected slate, not nominations from the floor.[85]

Just as in New York, nomination procedures in Pennsylvania were restrictive processes. The most convincing evidence of close political control

368 / EARLY AMERICAN POLITICAL CULTURE

comes from the crises of 1710 and 1755–1756, when the Philadelphia Yearly Meeting directly addressed provincial politics and clearly had some impact on the selection of candidates in the three original counties and in Philadelphia.[86] But those situations were exceptional. The counties varied considerably in political temperament, and in normal times each protected its own autonomy.[87] Ticket selection was up to the political activists in each county, not imposed from above.

When we turn our attention to the respective counties, the most surprising observation may be that what frequently passes for the most radical political faction in early Pennsylvania, the Keithians, may well have practiced the most tightly controlled nomination procedures of any of colonial Pennsylvania's factions or parties. A distinguishing feature of Keithian politics was the way in which "a small number of Philadelphians," "a select Club" "engross[ed] . . . the Managemant of elections."[88] They acted as though they had been "appointed by Law to make the Tickets, and the People had only a Right" to confirm that choice.[89]

In comparison with both the practices of the Keithians and the county politics of New York, Pennsylvania's Quaker Party certainly canvassed a greater number of people. In Philadelphia, there were relatively large numbers involved in choosing the main county slate for the 1739 election, and in the early 1750s, the politician John Smith admitted attending meetings "of a pretty many people" to settle the assembly ticket.[90] In Chester County, nomination meetings were large enough and open enough to be held at taverns.[91] One activist identified a group of "the Buisy friends," a collection of "Modern [Moderate?] and Sensible Quakers," a subset of that group who formed a "Clubb," and several influential individuals, all of whom felt they should have some say in the county ticket for 1743.[92] Yet there also could be exceptions outside the three old counties. When in the early 1740s, "Friends at the River" (namely, Samuel Blunston, John Wright, and the latter's offspring, Susanna, James, and John) sang out the names of their preferred candidates for Lancaster County, the local notables usually joined in with a strong supporting chorus.[93]

To the extent that broader participation in the nominating process occurred in Pennsylvania than in New York, and the evidence does suggest such a conclusion, it was prompted by two circumstances. The complex tickets that needed to be cobbled together were the most obvious of these. Unlike New Yorkers, who most frequently voted for one or two assemblymen in isolation, most Pennsylvanians voted on the same day for four to eight assemblymen, three county commissioners, and six assessors, as well as for county sheriffs and coroners. The numbers and variety of officers invited participation on behalf of numerous interests. If a given geographical area could not get an assembly nomination, perhaps it could get a commissioner or assessor; if five or six assemblymen were agreeable to all, there was room for disagreement over the last two or three. When we add to these practical considerations the Quaker-inspired strand of equality that wound itself through Pennsylvania's cultural fabric, we can understand why political management could have a broader participatory dimension than existed in New York.

But absent one important caveat, that conclusion can also be misleading. Despite their various efforts to include Quakerized Pennsylvanians within their ranks, most Quaker Party fixers also gave strong political expression to their cultural tribalism.[94] The old first purchasers and prominent contemporaries of William Penn were revered in memory as they rarely had been during their lives. And that reverence was a legacy their sons and daughters inherited. James Wright, for example, may occasionally have raised his fellow legislators' hackles because of his willingness to put farming before politics, but despite that, his public reputation was assured not only "by his own merit" but also "in gratitude to the memory of his father, who serve[d] . . . [the province] diligently and faithfully."[95] Mordecai Lloyd deserved the office of sheriff in part because he was the son of a first purchaser, Thomas Lloyd.[96] A Chester County candidate for sheriff was questionable because he had "no Claim to Such an Advancement from the merritts of his Progenitors," and his election to that post would be "the highest Injustice" to many "Gentlemen of Probity and Approved fidelity . . . (the descendents of the ancient Settlers who merritted much in their time) . . . [who were] So Very Capable of Serving."[97] This broadly shared concern to keep what Pennsylvania Quakers called "Mussroom" politicians from gaining too much influence in the county areas of concentrated Quaker settlement inevitably constricted the range of candidates that even sizable groups of Quaker Party nominators might offer the electorate.[98]

Whatever their differences in nominating procedures, the political results in New York and Pennsylvania were quite comparable. In New York a small handful of "principal men," often including the incumbent assemblymen, had to set their imprimatur on aspiring candidates in order for the electorate to take them seriously.[99] In Pennsylvania, preelection consultation may have included a greater number of people, but ultimately political control was just as constricted. The clusters of "merchants, lawyers, millers and farmers" who controlled Pennsylvania's political affairs were formidable in their dominance, for as one Philadelphia witness testified in 1770, it was "customary" for "a certain Company of leading Men to . . . settle the Ticket for Assemblymen without ever permitting . . . a Mechanic to interfere."[100] Because of their Quakerism, Pennsylvania's political leaders had less of the pretension, showiness, and ostentatious veneer of a gentry political style that characterized Anglophile New Yorkers. But despite their differing values, procedures, and styles, both groups were intuitively oligarchical and instinctively tenacious of their political power.

Given the oligarchical nature of politics in provincial New York and Pennsylvania, the question that has bothered generations of "democratically" conditioned historians is why the colonial electorate tolerated such circumstances. Because of the relatively wide distribution of wealth and low property qualifications for voting, anywhere from 50 percent to 80 percent of white adult males may have been eligible to vote.[101] That was approximately three times higher than the percentage of eligible voters in England during the eighteenth century.[102] Why did such a large number of colonists with unparalleled access to voting rights willingly acquiesce to oligarchical rule?

The fashionable answers to that question for the past three decades have been "deference" and "patron/client" power relationships. To take the former first, historians have placed a great deal of emphasis on the ideas of hierarchy and order that prevailed in the eighteenth-century Anglo-American intellectual world and reputedly found strong expression in the sociopolitical behavior of the colonists. In particular, the classical theory of deference, which was an integral part of the English country ideology that allegedly suffused the colonies, demanded that deference "be spontaneously exhibited." The division between "the elite" and "non-elite" should take place "naturally, voluntarily and spontaneously," largely inspired by the recognition of the non-elite that the elite were "of a superior status and culture of their own"—clearly a "better sort" of people. The "wealth and birth, leisure and property, liberality and education" that distinguished upper-class "culture . . . [should] be recognized by the *demos* as part of the superior natural capacities" that qualified citizens for political leadership. In this theory of deference, two features stand out: the onus was firmly on the non-elite to *thoroughly* and *naturally* recognize the superior qualities of members of the upper classes, and social deference was inextricably intertwined with political deference.[103]

Problems with this theory of deference as an explanation for colonial political behavior begin right there. In New York and Pennsylvania, those who were the most strenuous advocates of "better sort" superiority were always of the upper classes. But even among their ranks, there were those who occasionally invited questionable characters to share in the exercise of political power.[104] And if we survey the multiple borderlands in which contact between the upper classes and their lesser neighbors took place, we see a great deal of evidence irreconcilable with a pervasive deferential political ethic.

In both New York and Pennsylvania, the extensive articulation and demonstration of anti-authoritarianism suggests far more attenuated notions of deference than the classical model prescribed. In New York, the authority of government was repeatedly challenged by those who "did not value the Courts . . . order[s] a fart."[105] And the expected recognition of a natural order in society was undermined by the "levelling Sentiments of the People" and the rough "equality in point of condition" of so many countryfolk.[106] Perhaps the most revealing examples of the weakness of deferential attitudes among New Yorkers took place in the case of an individual often perceived as exemplar of deferential politics. Robert R. Livingston was a classic case of the man who had it all—intelligence, presence, personal warmth, professional accomplishment, religious sensibilities, and "Something of the Gentleman" in his manners.[107] He was also a large landowner with many tenants, and he possessed a family pedigree second to none. Yet Livingston never received the kind of deferential reverence in Dutchess County that his station seems to have demanded. When his friends first suggested him as a candidate for the assembly, others objected that his city upbringing had made him "ignorant of the affairs of the Country."[108] Service to the county was of crucial importance to them, not Livingston's array of entitlements to social deference . For a while Dutchess County residents did swallow their reservations and elect Livingston to represent them, but a revulsion against landlords, punitive judges, and Anglicanism, on top of reservations about Livingston's ability to represent county needs, soon swept him from office. Of course his opponents were no lower-class radicals, but they did not have the same array of deference-inspiring attributes that Livingston clearly possessed.

The same sort of indifference to deferential entitlements also existed in Pennsylvania. In July of 1763, Joseph Shippen, the secretary to the Provincial Council, desperately needed to get supplies to Fort Augusta, and he ordered a wagoner to redirect the goods the carter was hauling, originally destined for Harris's Ferry, to the fort. Although Shippen made his demand in the governor's name, the teamster "did not seem to regard that much" and simply turned around and went home to Germantown.[109] Such attitudes were particularly strong in Pennsylvania, because Quakers invited egalitarianism by discouraging any words or signs of respect tainted by artificiality or insincerity. Their political leaders made a point of denying the overt deference that various status-conscious officials felt was their right.[110] Picture David Lloyd, hat on, in the midst of a conference with the governor and council, refusing "to stand when speaking as all others there did." When Governor Evans rebuked his behavior as "affrontive" to his authority and demanded "a due Deference," Speaker of the Assembly Lloyd refused. As he continued to slouch in his chair, Lloyd argued that the "mouth of the Countrey" deserved an "Equality" the governor denied.[111] Friends' refusal to use flattering ornamental language, their determination not to offer "hat honor," and their unwillingness to pay particular regard to proprietary officials indicated a commitment to an expansive culture of common humanity as much as their quiet respect for their ancestors and commercial success communicated approval of an ordered society.

Among the upper-class members of the two provincial societies, Pennsylvanians were clearly more at ease with anti-authoritarian attitudes than their New York counterparts. On one occasion Charles Norris laughingly recounted to Susanna Wright how "our poor little G———r, the other day, had like to have got a drubbing on the High way by a rude Carter who would not turn out of a deep & hollow road, or more properly turn back, for he could not get up the sides with his loaded waggon."[112] Norris was not at all alarmed by the carter's "uppityness," nor did he suggest that the drayman's assertiveness was exceptional.[113] Norris's humor turned on the juxtaposition of a new governor, accustomed to old-world standards of propriety, with the relatively egalitarian ethos of Pennsylvania society. Compare that incident with a similar situation in New York: Governor Cosby, "out in his Coach & meeting a loaded Waggon in which one of the Planters sat with his Wife . . . order'd his Coach man to whip him because the man did not drive so quickly out of his way as he expected."[114] Cosby symbolized the attitude of many upper-class New Yorkers who, rather than accept the assertiveness or offhand indifference of their less prominent fellow citizens, tried to command deferential behavior by their assertion of power, swagger of personal intimidation, and purchase of political support. Cosby was only the best-known New Yorker quick to reach for his whip. During Chief Justice James DeLancey's days, Governor Clinton charged James's brother, Oliver DeLancey, with "carrying his Elections by the Numbers he has horsewhipped in ye City."[115] And the mercurial Peter Livingston well understood that one way to enhance his personal political fortunes was to have "Brusers" at his beck and call.[116] Also, it should be no surprise that in a society in which the commercial ethic was so strong, in which wealth was both revered and coveted, in which administrative officers frequently demanded payoffs, and in which governors could sell political offices with impunity, the province's political leaders viewed "money . . . [as] the Senues of [political] war."[117] The important thing for New York's highly self-conscious, politically involved gentry was to show up at elections with an entourage. The means of mobilization was less important than the fact of a following. Like the proverbial emperor's suit of clothing, pecuniary-induced political support might be paraded as deferential finery. The issue was how the political leaders saw *themselves.*

The classical model of deference, then, was no more than a set of ideal relationships that some members of the upper classes felt *should* inform their provincial worlds. In reality, colonial politics took place in a far more complicated behavioral and ideological matrix. To begin with, the political arena was dominated by those who sought out political power. They were a self-selected group that increasingly became recognizable in the eighteenth century as the politically engaged, in contradistinction to various clusters of prominent economic and social leaders who either stayed out of politics or remained on the political periphery.[118] What determined political success was not some relative ranking of deference entitlements, but rather a wide variety of peer-group and constituent considerations. An individual's willingness and ability to pursue commonly agreed upon political goals, his abilities (or "capacity" as contemporaries would have said), the nature of his personal connections with established families and prominent economic interests, his experience in public affairs, his place of residence, his personal drive and commitment, his sense of integrity, the nature and extent of his resources, the reach of his detractors, and whether or not his name was worn "smooth Enough to go down in a General way," all played a part in the process of political selection.[119] Multidimensional, reciprocal, and developmental relationships among individuals (as agents) and the existing power structures—that is, among various political, religious, economic, and social agglomerations of power—determined the peculiar character and evolution of each colony's oligarchical political system.[120]

Which is not to say that deference did not exist. Clearly, respect for such characteristics as the aforementioned was an important and dynamic part of the colonists' social relations. (It is, in fact, impossible to imagine a relatively complicated Western society operating peacefully without some expressions of *social* deference.) And those deference entitlements played a part in politics as well. Those who enjoyed upper-class advantages, and who had the inclination to assert them in the competition for political power, could preempt the field. But as William Smith, Jr., testified when he described the New York legislators as "plain, illiterate husbandmen, whose views seldom extended farther than to the regulation of highways, the destruction of wolves, wildcats, and foxes, and the other little interests of the particular counties which they were chosen to represent," and as an anonymous Pennsylvanian pointed out when he identified the Quaker oligarchy as one of "merchants, lawyers, millers and farmers," there was no widespread belief that gentry "culture," "property," and lifestyle were the essential requisites of political leadership.[121] Frequently, constituents felt "in mighty dread" of political power in the hands of those of polished gentry style, whose manner and leisure concealed larcenous hearts; given a choice they frequently preferred representatives conversant with "Piggs and foul / What biggness Stallions out to Strou'l."[122] Witness how "Haytime & Harvest" either shut the legislatures' doors or left numerous seats empty.[123] Moreover, as both the statements and the political behavior of numerous lower-class and middling colonists illustrated, there was always considerable "ambivalence" toward the existing authority figures.[124] "Acceptance [of the existing order] and alienation [from it] exist[ed] very often in the same persons."[125] A carter or farmer might acquiesce to authority in one situation and respond with rudeness in another. There was simply no deep and consistent commitment to the kind of hierarchical society that traditional ideas of deference implied. That fact was underlined in politics, for although the same carter or farmer might on one occasion support the unanimous reelection of an influential gentleman legislator, at the next opportunity he might vote for a less imposing figure. At the heart of New York and Pennsylvania politics was partisanship based on ideology, issues, local service, and traditional factional divisions. The very salience of such considerations diminished the importance of the deference entitlements that were the bedrock of any *system* of deferential politics.[126]

A second and related way of explaining the electoral support New York and Pennsylvania voters gave to their respective oligarchies is to emphasize the strength of patron/client relationships. Large landowners, merchants, and entrepreneurs, the argument runs, recruited their political support from among those over whom they had "an ascendant"—that is, their tenants, the artisans and laborers they employed, and the retailers and professionals with whom they dealt.[127] In its softest form, this argument posits that acceptance of patronal political leadership was one part of the unstated contract that bound principals and dependents together in a network of reciprocal obligations.[128] Dependent on their patron for various social and economic favors, clients would acquiesce to his wishes in political matters. The harsher version of this position argues that in societies of relative scarcity, dependence fostered a coercive relationship in which landlords and merchants used their economic power to *force* their clients to accept upper-class political suzerainty.[129]

It is in New York, of course, where this model is most applicable, but also where the limitations of that interpretation become most clear. It is possible, for example, to cite occasions when tenants trotted to the polls in support of their landlords.[130] Clearly at times there was an appearance of great landlord/tenant comity. But there were also many important examples of tenant independence. Robert R. Livingston lost the 1768 Dutchess County election overwhelmingly, "tho' he had every thing in his favour, which power could give him."[131] Again in 1769, Livingston met defeat at the hands of his and his relatives' tenants, "notwithstanding all the pains . . . [he took] with them."[132]

There were several reasons why such a repudiation could take place, beginning with the weakness of the patronal system in rural New York. The principal foundation stone of strong patron/client relationships in any new society is a close and continuous connection, expressed in frequent face-to-face dealings between patrons and clients.[133] While that may have been the norm in one or two instances, such as Philipsburgh Manor, it was far from the case elsewhere in New York.[134] The entrepreneurial Livingstons made a practice of distancing themselves from their tenants, impersonalizing much of their manor business and failing to encourage the development of the kind of community infrastructure necessary to consolidate themselves as "legitimate local leaders."[135] And Robert R. Livingston and Henry Beekman demonstrated the tendency of the large landlords to emphasize their status by insulating themselves rather than constantly cutting a figure in the county. Robert R. was always more a big-city lawyer than a county magnate; despite his openhanded election-time treating, even the attentive Beekman waited years before courting the "principal and most Leeding [Quaker farmers] . . . in . . . [Dutchess] County."[136] In eighteenth-century English society, in which the feudal past had etched traditions of "obligation," "favour," and "acknowledgement" into the country landscape, and where the ripe scent of privilege laced every breeze, the gentry may have benefited from distancing themselves from their tenants.[137] In sequestering themselves behind the "high palings" of large estates, in dealing with tenants and tradesmen through intermediaries, and in carefully orchestrating their public appearances, the English gentry masked both their rapaciousness and their disdain for many paternal responsibilities.[138] But in a new land like New York, only persistent *personal* attention to the patron-client relationship could ward off the corrosiveness of a liberating social and physical environment.

A second support that was crucial to the strength of the patron/client relationship was the church. But again in New York any church/landlord connection was relatively weak. In England, parsons *belonged* to the county magnates, and the clergy were among the most important local figures in conditioning farmers and tenants into obeisance, in persuading farmers that civil and religious authority were closely connected, and in pressuring voters to turn out in support of their patron.[139] In New York, the multiplicity of religious groups and the distance between church and state in the Hudson Valley counties simply made impossible any such continuous prostitution of religious influence to patronal purposes.[140]

In the midst of these structural impediments to the development of strong patron/client relations were ideas that had the same effect. Dependence, which was at the heart of the patron/client relationship, was excoriated in public thought, while independence was held up as an individual's most prized possession.[141] One of the hallmarks of independence was an ability to form an opinion on public affairs.[142] That produced differences and encouraged partisanship. And partisan politics in turn undermined the political deference that accompanied the patron/client dyad. Unlike the case in England, where many tenants "would not think of selling their landlord," New York farmers periodically raised the question of why they *should* give their political allegiance to their landlords rather than to someone else.[143] The mere asking of that question pointed out the attenuated character of patronal power in the Hudson Valley.

When we shift attention from the countryside to New York City, it is clear that a case may be made there for the political salience of a harsh, exploitive variety of economic clientage. In the city, merchants, entrepreneurs, and professionals would apparently bully, bribe, or flatter those over whom they had any kind of economic leverage in order to achieve their political goals.[144] There was a raw element to all this (matched in the countryside by the bald purchase of votes) that was alien to the more subtle behavior and quieter language of traditional patron/client relationships. Contemporaries recognized this, for already in the mid to late eighteenth century, New Yorkers were beginning to use the term *boss*.[145] Usually associated with the patronage-ridden and corrupt politics of the next century, its origins lay in eighteenth-century New Yorkers' need to describe those who held masterful power over their employees and associates, and more particularly those grandees who exploited their various sources of power for political purposes. But however heavy-handed some of these New York politicians became, the important thing was that there was too much slack in the existing social and economic system for exploitive economic clientage to *determine* political affairs. The mid-Atlantic New World had nothing like England's intricate web of dependency relationships. Moreover, there were many bosses in local areas, frequently in competition with one another, and their economic dependents were quite adept at shopping around for a better deal.[146] There were always, too, a good number of professionals, merchants, and businessmen whose "thoughts . . . [were] confined to the Scripture & the Selling of Goods" and who stayed out of politics.[147] On occasion they could provide alternative sources of employment and credit. The very fluidity of a growing city like New York meant that the ties of economic dependency were frequently loose and obscure, and consequently difficult to exploit in the short periods before elections.[148] Finally, critical issues did have a marked effect on factional allegiances. In 1768, for example, the New York City merchant Philip Livingston was acknowledged to be the strongest politician in his constituency. A year later his support plunged and he failed election to the assembly. In that short year, it was not Livingston's position as a boss that had changed, it was his failure to meet community demands with regard to the issues of the day.[149]

If patron/client relationships were less important to New York politics than we have sometimes thought, they were of even less significance in

Pennsylvania. Tenants and farmers were known for their independence, and voting by ballot protected them against the worst excesses of political pressure. Some Philadelphia merchants undoubtedly tried to influence the votes of their employees, but there were few complaints of this and no overt political actions that testified to its prevalence.[150] The chief distinguishing feature of Pennsylvania politics was its party character, and that was antithetical to the whole cluster of dependency relationships that distinguished the eighteenth-century Anglo-American model of patron/client politics.

If deference and/or patron/client relationships do not explain the longevity of the New York and Pennsylvania oligarchies, what does? The answer is a straightforward one, yet one that rests on a complex set of social and political circumstances and imperatives. Simply put, the two provincial oligarchies were accessible. Both were open to community influence, both reflected important elements of community opinion, and both made selective efforts to respond to many of the major political concerns of their constituents.

In order to understand how such conditions could obtain, we must first comprehend how political relationships in colonial New York and Pennsylvania were shaped by the broadly shared circumstances of "intimate citizenship" that characterized colonial society.[151] No matter the conflicts of class, the segregation of socioeconomic stratification, the separation of ethnic enclaves, or the pretensions of leadership, the character of life in interconnected, developing, and (by modern standards) relatively sparsely settled colonial communities fostered certain important, widely shared perspectives. Take the issue of power. Most eighteenth-century colonists wanted to be free of what they regarded as the arbitrary power of, and excessive taxation by, monarchical governments. Colonial prejudice against prerogative power was so pervasive that the advocacy of popular, antiprerogative measures was essential for sustained influence as an elected politician.[152] And the cry for public frugality was so unremitting that it could never be ignored.[153] New York and Pennsylvania politicians were sensitive to such demands, not only because they were forced to seek periodic reelection, but also because, as products of their provincial communities, they had internalized the same prejudices as their constituents. In New York, county leaders such as Henry Beekman were quick to cry out against "Arbetrary power," while in Pennsylvania, Quaker assemblymen made a sustained effort to finance their provincial government without resort to any direct levies on the bulk of the provincial population.[154] The results of such thoroughgoing commitment to popular policies was evident in each case. Because of its tradition, and the long-standing competition between factions to champion that tradition, New York was in the forefront of colonial opposition to British attempts to curb provincial autonomy and tax without colonial consent between 1764 and 1767.[155] As for Pennsylvania, the legislative leaders tried to push the proprietor as far from governmental powers as possible, and "oppose[d] everything that . . . Governor[s] or . . . [their] friends propose[d]."[156] By expanding their assembly powers and confining prerogative privilege, by the second quarter of the eighteenth century, Pennsylvania legislators had come as close as was practically possible to building a republican colony within a monarchical empire.

Another imperative that tended to keep both the New York and Pennsylvania oligarchies accessible was their concern for community service. Each colony's oligarchy began with the self-promotion of a small number of individuals who, having asserted themselves as provincial leaders and insiders, entrenched themselves in power. They then passed on the torch (sometimes willingly, sometimes with reluctance) both to family members and to unrelated associates who constituted self-selected groups of the next generation's politically minded leaders. But what made this oligarchic succession possible was legislators' recognition either of the prudence of listening or of an obligation to listen to their constituents. On one level that commitment showed up in assembly concerns about executive power and parsimonious government. On another, however, it reflected the place county politicians felt they occupied on the public stage. And that perspective was different in New York than in Pennsylvania.

In New York, the same strong traditions of localism that affected the structure of provincial government also conditioned many county magnates to identify themselves with their county's particular needs and to try to strengthen their individual claims to local preeminence by providing "Service for their Respective places."[157] Political leaders frequently saw themselves in the patron role, no matter the weakness of deferential attitudes and patron/client ties, and they tried to act accordingly. They wanted to be able to claim responsiveness to parochial needs, even if they preferred to gather local opinion through agents rather than through their intensive personal canvassing of county communities.[158] What reinforced this predilection for attentiveness was that it was often easy for a legislator to promote his personal interests along with those of county communities. Government services were frequently directed toward the development of the counties, and with a little guidance, a well-connected legislator could ensure that the process of settlement and growth benefited himself as well as parts of the larger community. Power brought demands for service, but service could substantially augment power.

The same concerns for service to the community occurred among Pennsylvania politicians, but there it wore a somewhat different face. Because of their belief that political leaders should serve a broadly rather than narrowly defined community, Quakers gained an enviable reputation throughout the

Delaware and upper Chesapeake regions as public custodians.[159] Following this lead once the "Holy Experiment" began in Pennsylvania, Quaker leaders there put emphasis not just on parochial county needs but increasingly on a civil Quakerism capable of fulfilling the larger needs of the colony's diverse peoples. The confidence the Quaker oligarchy soon had in its provincial establishment, and in its ability to articulate policies, adopt administrative structures, and establish provincewide regulations that would satisfy large numbers of Pennsylvanians, was reflected in the ease with which its members interacted with their constituents. The records are filled with evidence of legislative intent to seek "the Minds of. . . [their] Constituents" either in forming some policy or for retrospective judgment.[160] That the sense of obligation was intense is evident from the Quaker assemblyman David Cooper's pledge "to study the good of my Constituents (& next to my duty to my Maker) preserve it with all my Might."[161] When challenged, Cooper's counterparts put the issue directly to their critics: with "anniversary [i.e., yearly] Elections," assemblymen found themselves regularly "mix[ing] with the People"; if their "Constituents" felt legislator "Conduct . . . [to be] inconsistent with their Sentiments, they . . . [would] supply [the incumbents'] Places" with new representatives.[162] Much of the strength of Pennsylvania's civil Quaker ideology rested on the fact that it did speak to what many non-Quakers felt were their public needs. Which in turn meant that its partisans could strengthen that ideology further by making overt and repeated solicitations of constituent opinion a ritualized part of what was, in reality, oligarchic politics.[163] Such circumstances gave the language and idea of constituent service a prominence in Pennsylvania that New York's localism and efforts at patronalism could not quite match.

Finally, there was the issue of political competition, both within parties and factions and within the larger community itself. Political rivalry meant that the performances of incumbent politicians were always subject to critical review. And that meant that members of both the political establishment and the electorate were always looking for the "fittest" individuals, those of "capacity," "extraordinary Genius," "Integrity and Public Spirit," and "Wisdom and Ability,"[164] who might bolster the fortunes of a faction and strengthen the legislative leadership of the two colonies. Great advantage lay with the politically ambitious relatives and close friends of existing leaders, but the door was never closed to the self-educated, or to those "tho' not learned, of Strong Natural Parts."[165] Accessibility, then, meant some degree of openness, not just to the concerns of the community but also to individuals of considerable ability who could reinvigorate the connection between political leaders and the body politic.

In their efforts to pay some attention to community opinion, both New York and Pennsylvania politicians quickly found out that, in fact, most colonials wanted very little positive legislation from government. Settlers were preoccupied with their private lives; what they wanted most from their assemblymen was a commitment to protect or enlarge the spheres of social and economic activity that were immune from capricious, expensive, or enervating public demands.[166] Given that protection and a minimum of facilitative encouragement to order and develop their communities, many colonists were content to remain politically apathetic. None of the waves of Dutch, English, German, or Scotch-Irish immigrants carried traditions of broad political participation into the middle colonies, and as long as legislators reflected their fundamental opinions about the shape government should take, settlers had no particular or sustained incentive to become a highly mobilized electorate. Yet they were quite capable of becoming so. And did so frequently enough (if episodically) to reinforce commitment to both particular principles and practices of popular government, thereby continually strengthening the foundations of what was becoming a formidable and distinctive early American political culture. Nor was that development impeded in any crucial way by the occurrence of voter apathy. The popular political rhetoric of the colonial oligarchies and the strong institutional basis of participatory politics militated against such results. Of additional importance was the way in which colonials both extended and elaborated their sociability through the activities and organization of voluntaristic groups. Ranging from neighborhood associations and religious organizations, through community libraries, fire companies, and craft associations, to Masonic lodges, fraternal benevolent orders, and urban improvement societies, these groups promoted a sense of civic-mindedness throughout provincial society. And exercising both power and restraint in the capacious social expanse that lay between the governmental and the strictly private, their members continually practiced politics without being overtly political. Infused with the politics of voluntaristic and civic consciousness, numerous colonial citizens found it easy to transform themselves, when occasion demanded, into the politicized participants of provincial election campaigns. The movement from apathy to political involvement was less elite than a side step from one expression of community and civic consciousness to another.[167]

Needless to say, existing political oligarchies tried to insulate themselves from future episodes of electoral activism. They used their monopolies over information to advantage whenever possible in order to extend their political hegemony; they used patronage to try to entrench themselves in power; they exploited their experience and their traditions of service; and they frequently tried to force a strengthening of deferential attitudes and patron/client bonds. But the fundamental issues of protecting provincials from capricious public power, ensuring parsimonious government, serving community needs, and maintaining a capable political leadership prevented accessible oligarchies from turning into intolerably oppressive ones.

The character of New York's and Pennsylvania's oligarchies is perhaps best symbolized by colonial ambivalence over the relationship between assemblymen and constituents. Assembly apologists very carefully defended the institution as a corporate body "representing the Whole" body politic.[168] Within that institution, representatives were to follow the "dictates of . . . [their] own Conscience & Understanding," not that of any group of "leading men" within the assembly or any "active" out-of-doors lobby.[169] But there was also a countervailing strand of thought that ran strongly through the political cultures of both New York and Pennsylvania. As David Lloyd put it (drawing on William Penn's writings from earlier times), there was "no *Transessentiating* or *Transsubstantiating* of Being, from People to Representative."[170] Representatives were simply individuals responsible to their constituents. As the Long Islander Benjamin Hinchman put it, "I think it but . . . [the assemblymen's] reasonable duty when they know our minds, to do it."[171] In the sporadic sparring that took place between the champions of assembly corporatism and constituent instruction, colonials acknowledged that their provincial political cultures were no havens of rational consistency.[172] But the tensions that they generated were frequently creative. The occasional challenges that constituent spokespersons directed toward assembly pretension served as periodic reminders to the political leaders of both New York and Pennsylvania that their long-term oligarchic survival depended on continued accessibility.

The Limits of Colonial Oligarchy

By the mid 1760s, the two oligarchies that had served their provinces and themselves so well during earlier decades began to show their limitations. Structural changes in the relationship between the colonies and Great Britain, and within each provincial society, created problems that the old oligarchies could not effectively address. As will frequently happen in such situations, conflict appeared at the weakest point in each society.

In New York, the 1760s brought threats to various old land patents, a postwar recession that caused considerable hardship, and attacks on the basic English rights of trial by jury and self-taxation. The resulting social tensions appeared most clearly in New York City in the Stamp Act crisis of 1765. When Lieutenant-Governor Cadwallader Colden seemed determined to enforce the Stamp Act on the eve of its November 1 implementation date, his authority was instantly challenged in what began as a classic case of pre-Revolutionary, all-class community mobbing. Over the years, the long-lived lieutenant-governor had alienated almost everyone of note, and members of the city's upper and middle classes were happy to get at the "old man" who preferred prerogative and parliamentary power to provincial rights.[173] But in the course of the rioting that followed, prominent New Yorkers began to feel the warmth of lower-class resentment of wealth and privilege, and of an oligarchy of political leaders who seemed increasingly ineffective in guarding traditional rights and unsympathetic to the working poor in tough economic times.[174] Although members of the upper classes did retain a great deal of influence in the days ahead by means of their judicious cultivation of various middling street politicians, they had never felt so vulnerable. Once the class consciousness of the politically marginalized gained lucid, if intermittent, expression, New York's political oligarchy began to lose credibility as spokespersons for the entire society.

The specter of class conflict was most apparent, however, not in the streets of New York City but in the Hudson Valley. There a small number of avaricious manor lords were determined to have every acre they could possibly screw out of the imprecise wording of their families' first patents.[175] Much of this land was on the eastern boundaries of New York, and groups of New England settlers and speculators, who found encouragement among Massachusetts officials, periodically tried to claim title to the same acreage on legal grounds frequently as tenuous as those of the New York magnates. Squatters from both New England and New York, as well as tenants upholding various landlord claims, moved into the contested areas, and some had carved out valuable improvements there by the mid 1760s. At that time, a number of New York landlords began to try to bring the eastern reaches of their putative claims under control. They mounted a serious effort to throw the alleged squatters off their improvements and replace these recalcitrants with tenants beholden to themselves. These ejections met with serious resistance in southeastern Dutchess County in the fall of 1765, and thereafter the anti-landlord movement spread until it became the "Great Rebellion" of 1766.[176]

In late 1765, those who felt most aggrieved against their landlords were encouraged to voice their discontent by three circumstances. The first was the success of a group of Dutchess County squatters in controlling the eastern section of Philipse Highland Patent and holding at bay landlord claimants; the second was the success of the Stamp Act rioters in the cause of "Liberty"; and the third was the belief that the Stamp Act defiance had cast the normal procedures of law enforcement into abeyance. "The people are [of the] opinion that there is no Law and very freely Say So upon account of the Ditestable Stamp Act," wrote one observer who was well acquainted with county affairs.[177] Abruptly, tenants on Cortlandt Manor in upper Westchester County, who had long been plagued by particularly odious estate-management practices, raised the flag of rebellion. Toward the end of April 1766, the combined forces of the Westchester and Dutchess County insurgents marched on New York City to force John Van Cortlandt to "grant forever" the Cortlandt Manor lands, to rescue a few Dutchess County dissidents from the city jail, and to seek an alliance with the city's Stamp Act rioters in order to inaugurate a new, just provincial era under the aegis of rural and urban "Sons of Liberty."[178] A month later, tenants and squatters on the eastern boundaries of Livingston and Claverack Manors, who had gone through a long period of the same sort of border-related, New England versus New York conflict that their Dutchess County counterparts had experienced, also asserted themselves. They marched on the manor house of Robert Livingston, Jr., and tried to terrorize tenants loyal to John Van Rensselaer. In all cases the rebels soon fled the field. Meeting a New York City determined to fight off the rural marauders, and urban Sons of Liberty convinced that "no one . . . [was] entitled to Riot but themselves," the main concentration of some five hundred farmers straggled back to their homes.[179] Subsequently, Governor Moore ordered civil magistrates to enforce the law, called upon the British military to hunt down the offenders in both southern and northern centers of rebellion, indicted over sixty protesters for riotous behavior, and struck a special court of oyer and terminer to sentence to death a later-pardoned leader of the Dutchess County traitors, William Pendergast.[180]

The Great Rebellion is a difficult event to interpret because of the complexity of New York society. To begin with, the conflict was no thoroughgoing replica of old-world class conflict between poor tenants and gentry. The New York rebels were not "peasants" in any meaningful sense. Some were poor, but others were reasonably well-off farmers, so long as they could make good their property claims.[181] And those of tenant status in any manor or county were always divided about how they could most efficaciously protect what their sweat had earned. Some were prepared to work with their landlords, while others opted for confrontation.[182] For their part, the landlords whose interests were directly involved in the riots were hard-driving, profit-conscious entrepreneurs who kept their tenants at a distance, hired unforgiving estate managers, and, where they had some prospect of success, were as intent on establishing land claims in the conflict-ridden no-man's-land between New York and Massachusetts as were their farmer opponents.

Despite the fact that the motives of the contending parties were not as far apart as we might at first think, the battle still had all the intensity of a class confrontation. Many Hudson Valley tenants may have been "petty landed bourgeois," but most also believed that "no matter how good the terms, leaseholding was not as desirable as freeholding."[183] Because of that belief, the landlords were right: tenant protest threatened not just isolated parts of their manors but, given the weakness of their original titles and the willingness of some royal officials to challenge their claims, "the entire tenancy system."[184] And despite their acquisitive predilections, rebelling tenants appeared to echo the moral overtones of English lower-class rioters against gentry authority.[185] "Poor Men were always oppressed by the Rich," and in this case the landlords only too frequently "turn[ed] . . . people out of possession . . . [because the tenants] had an equitable Title but could not be defended in a Course of Law because they were poor."[186] As for the landlords, they had little enough of the gentry in their backgrounds, but they were determined to develop what they could of a patrician status by defending a large-scale, landlord/tenant system that might sustain their pretensions. In doing so, the large landlords contributed to perceptions of themselves as an oppressive class, for manor life rested on the privilege of such extensive landownership and collateral civil power that it appeared to deprive less fortunate families of the kind of freehold ownership and independent citizenship many viewed as the right of those who applied their labor to uncultivated land.[187] Most commonly in the colonies, polarization between agrarian dissidents and landlords was either marginalized by its peripheral geographical location, and/or small scale, or mediated by the complexities of a more developed social structure. But in New York the historic prominence of the manorial system and the strategic nature of the Hudson Valley corridor exaggerated its impact.[188] Idiosyncratic in its morphology, and restricted in actual scope, the rebellion of 1766 signified much more than its actual events entitled it to.

Unlike in New York, the fundamental weakness that showed up in Pennsylvania was not class division. Rather it was the peculiar nature of the Quaker regime that had dominated the Delaware River colony since its inception. And that weakness had two primary characteristics. The first was the way in which Quaker strength was delimited by residential patterns. Because Friends did not move into backcountry areas in any strength, Quakers denied themselves the organizational base and attendant influence they had in the east. And because they were weak in the newly settled areas, Quakers cut off the new counties they created from anything approaching proportional representation in the assembly. That circumstance in itself was not a fatal flaw, for many backcountry settlers could still easily identify with the Quaker Party, and Friends acknowledged an obligation to serve the fundamental development needs of the west. But there was a second and related weakness in the Quaker regime. The bulk of western settlers did not take pacifism seriously, particularly in any conflict with Indians. When colonial expansion into the interior triggered the French and Indian War and Pontiac's Rebellion, even the loosely defined pacifism of civil Quakerism seemed an inadequate answer to the western settlers' requests for defense. And when the strident voices of Quaker reformers called for a new strict pacifism among members of their sect, numerous Westerners were convinced that the Quaker system was in need of change.

The chief manifestation of Pennsylvania's sectional weakness was, of course, the Paxton Rebellion.[189] The march of the frontiersmen on Philadelphia to assert their right to better representation of their interests in future frontier wars was just as frightening for the Quaker leaders as New York's Great Rebellion had been for its grandees. Just as in New York's case, Pennsylvania's rural rebels met with preparations for self-defense rather than sympathy in the capital city. But unlike their New York counterparts, the Paxton rebels did gain a hearing, and none met with prosecution. These circumstances may be explained by the more conciliatory tone of Pennsylvania society, the peculiar nature of the colony's party politics, and the fact that in this instance, sectional feelings rather than class bias predominated among the personnel of the county courts. Yet the rebellion was a great shock, a frightening challenge to the Quaker oligarchy. As Richard Peters observed, many Paxton apologists questioned the legitimacy of the old regime: "the Government failing to give the people that protection they were bound to do; the Compact between them, is broke."[190]

The rebellions in New York and Pennsylvania were important events because they thoroughly frightened members of the existing oligarchies and threatened them in ways that they could not effectively address. Both regimes had been able to maintain their place because their constituents accepted the leadership they gave and had never questioned the premises of oligarchic power. Once the rebellions raised the issue of the distribution of political and socioeconomic power in the two colonies, the existing regimes were on the defensive, for they could not act as spokespersons for forces that challenged their hegemony. At the same time, they lost the ability to take the lead in imperial politics. When the British instituted policies that could be effectively resisted only by extralegal means, the New York and Pennsylvania oligarchies were placed at a severe disadvantage. Previously, they had been able to draw on the unpopularity of arbitrary British acts to shore up the institutional basis of their power. But sustained extralegal activism undercut the very system that had produced and protected them. And repeated attention to questions of right and power, in the circumstances of the late 1760s and early 1770s, inevitably raised questions, not only about the legitimacy of British rule, but also about the right of the provincial oligarchy to continue to monopolize legislative office.

Not surprisingly, given their peculiar characters and the different threats they faced, the two oligarchies responded to their respective late colonial crises in slightly different ways. One reaction of New York's provincial leaders was heavy-handed intimidation. They used the courts to punish many of the 1766 rebels and showed no constitutionally based reservations about calling out the British army to hound rioters from the province and terrorize the communities that gave them support.[191] In New York City, upper-class politicians tried to keep control over their neighbors on some issues by personal canvasses, in which they could face down dissenters, rather than allowing open challenges in public meetings.[192] In circumstances of threatened violence, community leaders might mobilize "the discreet Inhabitants" to patrol the streets in the cause of civil order.[193] And when Alexander MacDougall, a ship's captain, published a broadside charging the colony's legislators with betraying New York by voting to supply royal troops in late 1769, the assembly threw him in jail and initiated prosecution for libel.[194] At the same time, the long-standing factional character of New York politics prompted competing parties to try to use what they could of the issues of the day for partisan purposes. The main thrust of that activity was negative, as each set of New York's provincial politicians tried to characterize the other as the greatest threat to colonial liberties. So virulent did that competition become at one point, that the DeLancey-led coalition starkly revealed its essentially *nouveau* character, which both it and its oligarchic opponents had tried to keep concealed beneath their upper-class finery. When the DeLancey faction began to enquire into the right of Livingston Manor to representation, it threatened the thin cloak of new-world prescriptive rights in a way that seriously jeopardized old-world norms.[195] But the impetus that partisan politics gave to upper-class radicalization through such incidents was halting because it was insincere. By 1768, the New York oligarchy's attitude toward imperial affairs was "the quintessence of moderation," and "the only leadership it subsequently manifested [against Britain] was in the movement to abandon . . . [resistance] by being the first colony to relinquish [the intercolonial] nonimportation [agreement]."[196] The oligarchs' ultimate concern was to save as much of their power as they possibly could.

Like their New York counterparts, Pennsylvania's political leaders reacted strongly to the threats they faced, but they did so in their own way. Rather than strike out at their opponents, they tended to withdraw, to circle the wagons as it were, around their traditional areas of strength. When the Stamp Act crisis began to break, Quaker Party leaders showed their colors by calling together, neither the entire legislature nor spokespersons for various interest groups, but the assemblymen from the old eastern areas to give their informal opinions on the legislation.[197] And once Joseph Galloway took over leadership of the Quaker Party in 1766, he began to isolate the party in unprecedented fashion. As speaker of the assembly, Galloway concentrated more and more of the legislature's power in the hands of Quaker politicians from Chester and Bucks counties, paid less and less attention to radicals from Philadelphia and critics from the west, and gave no thought to the important role that Quakerization had played in the party's success in prior decades.[198] At the same time, rather than flirting with the new forms of anti-British politics, the Quakers followed the logic of their own brand of traditional radicalism by seeking the end of proprietary government. The result was that the Old Party spent much of its waning influence on the hopeless task of trying to protect Pennsylvania's peculiar provincial constitutional rights through appeasement. Because of the antiproprietary logic of Quaker politics, the inability of the pacifist ethic to accommodate popular demands for aggressive resistance to imperial reform, and Friends' intuitive impulse "to preserve the appearance of an union in ye Society of Pennsylvania" above all else, the Quaker oligarchy withdrew into its existing political fortresses and hoped to wait out the forces of change.[199] It was not by accident that the strongest stand the Quaker Party took against the British was not on taxation but on Lord Hillsborough's threats to adjourn the Pennsylvania legislature. The assembly was the principal symbol of the province's Quaker-built system of government.

The unfamiliar ghettoization of the Quaker Party occasioned results that compounded the oligarchy's problems. One of the most important features of earlier Quaker politics had been the easy commerce between representatives and constituents. Quakers knew that they served the community well, that they were popular, and that, consequently, they could invite constituent judgment and advice. But once the Quaker oligarchy refused to take a leading role in the politics of protest against imperial reform, it could no longer play the role of a receptive legislature. Rather than inviting constituent activism, Quakers found themselves discouraging it, lobbying against town meetings and quietly canvassing in favor of political quiescence.[200] Constituents, long used to invitations to speak out to their representatives on community affairs, were angered by these changing attitudes precisely when, in the minds of many, the times demanded outspoken political participation as never before. As more Pennsylvanians perceived the Quaker leaders to have forsaken their traditional role and to have become increasingly preoccupied with the retention of oligarchic power, class-based objections to the old regime began to surface. And the Quaker response to these, which was to reach out for support to their old proprietary enemies, only reinforced the impression that the Quakers were putting class before community. The demoralization and creeping paralysis that afflicted the old Quaker oligarchy were clearly reflected in the assemblymen's response to the kind of libels that had made earlier legislatures bridle and landed offenders in jail.

When Joseph Galloway was harshly criticized in the press for his politics in 1771, the assembly merely responded with a statement that the charges were "false, scandalous, & malicious, a daring insult to & a breach of the Priviliges of . . . [the] House."[201] Once among the most prickly of political establishments in British North America, by the late colonial years, the Quaker oligarchy had become a demoralized, if still powerful conservative force.

Beginning in the mid 1760s, the colonial worlds that had proven so friendly to the New York and Pennsylvania oligarchies quickly developed a momentum inimical to their interests. Violence was not restricted to the Stamp Act crisis, the landlord/tenant riots, and the Paxton Rebellion. During the last decade of colonial rule, there was a proliferation of both all-class riots and their class-oriented counterparts.[202] The French and Indian War increased the number of indigent in the densely settled areas, while sharp fluctuations in economic cycles fostered feelings of vulnerability among all manner of colonists.[203] The conflicts between and among various socioeconomic groups and geographical groups were unprecedented. Accompanying these conflicts was an increased politicization among the colonial populace. Although there is no way to measure this development accurately, it seems likely that given the proliferation of town meetings and the development of committees to meet the various crises in imperial affairs, and an increase in the outpourings of the press, that political awareness increased considerably.

All of these developments posed insuperable problems for the New York and Pennsylvania oligarchies. As the range of public activities that people perceived as political increased, as disagreements took place over what the important public issues were, as the purview of political opinion broadened on those issues, and as various groups held more intensely to their own viewpoints, the ability of the old leaders to serve large numbers of the community diminished significantly. That was most clearly evident in the elections of the late colonial years. Through Herculean efforts, voter turnout in Philadelphia was higher in 1764 and 1765 than it had ever been. But thereafter in Pennsylvania, and despite the fierce factional competition in New York, also in that province, voter participation in colonial politics declined from earlier highs.[204] The colonial population was undoubtedly more politicized than it had ever been, but the establishment politics of the existing provincial oligarchies increasingly failed to speak to colonial concerns. That fact was underlined by increased citizen demands for constituent instructions and for candidate pledges to respond to particular socioeconomic and political needs. Most important, an ominous popular note resonated through local communities with far greater intensity than ever before. "The Good People of this Province," wrote John Harris, "will not suffer Tamely their Liberty's & Privilidges to be Taken from them, By their Representatives."[205] The enemies of the colonists were not simply the old bogeymen—neither the governor, nor the proprietor, nor influence run riot. They could on occasion be the legislative oligarchies, who in the bright glare of crisis-lit America, seemed more preoccupied with protecting themselves than with the welfare of their provincial communities.

Chapter Ten

The Legitimation of Partisan Politics

FROM EARLY in their existence, the societies of colonial New York and Pennsylvania were varied, dynamic ones distinguished by a diversity of interests. Traditional thinking, premised on the view that society should be an integrated, organic entity, had only a limited capacity to accommodate such a development and the interest-group conflicts that accompanied it. Ideas centering on corporate distinctiveness, religious identity, and a demarcation between the better and poorer sort proved of limited value to contemporaries trying to comprehend the character of their respective provincial worlds. More promising were the notions some shared about the relevance of self-interest and individualism. But even when coupled with other ideas that we now recognize to be components of a liberal worldview, such perspectives were inchoate and never articulated with the clarity that might have offered New Yorkers and Pennsylvanians greater understanding of the social processes structuring their respective societies.

They did, however, have much greater success dealing with the political rather than the social facets of interest-group proliferation. Competing interests produced partisan politics in both New York and Pennsylvania, a partisanship that public-minded residents of each colony soon came to view as acceptable. Although Anglo-American Whig rhetoric condemned partisan politics, and although many New Yorkers and Pennsylvanians continued to observe this convention publicly, they simultaneously began to develop an informal discourse of politics that described the existing practices of provincial politics much more accurately, and accepted the partisanship those practices entailed as a normal feature of political life.

In New York, political changes capable of encouraging a distinction between party activities and factional behavior occurred only partially. The perpetuation of a number of features of electoral politics that tended to encourage the factionalism frequently seen as typical of New York tended to retard such thinking. These very circumstances, however, prompted many New Yorkers to view the strife that factionalism entailed as an expected and normal aspect of their provincial affairs. Turning old words to new uses, they developed an *informal* perspective on their provincial politics that assigned functional value to political conflict and was powerful enough to intrude upon the established *formal* Whig orthodoxies condemning such behavior. In a different but related process, Pennsylvanians distinguished themselves in an equally innovative way. They developed an *informal* discourse of politics centering on the recognition of party as a legitimate, nonfactional category of political behavior. A complex of circumstances ranging from the Quaker concern for consensus to the earned integrity of Quaker Party symbols encouraged Pennsylvanians to see first Quaker Party activities and then those of other parties as an acceptable way of addressing the various interests of community members. And in the course of directing their attention toward party politics, Quaker colony residents began to invent the terms of a new political language suitable to their needs. Together, the political experiences of New York and Pennsylvania demonstrated an impressive level of conceptual innovation, providing the foundation for a new level of political understanding that clearly gave expression to the character of an unfolding American society.

Interests, Polity, and Party

One of the most important facets of the socioeconomic development of New York and Pennsylvania from the late seventeenth century through the pre-Revolutionary years was the proliferation of interest groups. As New York matured, local and regional interests became entrenched, and as Pennsylvania grew, sectional and intraregional identities became more pronounced. Colonial records are filled with public demands from specific towns, townships, precincts, counties, and regions.[1] Fundamental to the structure of provincial society, too, were various imprecisely defined classes. While contemporaries acknowledged that there were upper, middling and lower classes, they also recognized that most social interaction took place among a larger plurality of socioeconomic classifications or classes. Merchants, large landowners, ministers, lawyers, and educators inhabited the upper reaches of society.[2] Further down the social scale, city, town, and country artisans constituted a variegated collection of laboring classes.[3] Farmers were another group that might be thought of as a "class," and even broad, cultural groups such as German Pennsylvanians might occasionally draw that designation.[4] Most frequently, however, religious and ethnic groups were identified simply as such. Denominational, ethnic, national-group, and cultural designations were part of the working vocabulary of all New Yorkers and Pennsylvanians who ventured beyond the confines of their own ethnoreligious enclave, or who thought at all about provincial affairs. Finally, there were a large number of local voluntary associations, ranging from the unique (such as Franklin's Association for Defense) to well-known social organizations (such as the Masonic Temples and the nationality-based charitable associations), various craftsmen's fraternities (such as those of the joiners and the saddlers), and a plethora of nameless social clubs and local improvement associations that are often only casually remarked upon.[5]

The multiplication of these various socioeconomic groups in New York and Pennsylvania had a profound effect on both the developing stratification and the value systems of the respective colonies. Immigrants knew that rank had been of great importance in the Old World, and some settlers and their offspring continued to give it respect. But in New York and Pennsylvania, legitimate associational groups, drawn together by common interests, could frequently obscure rather than clarify the minutiae of vertical social distinctions. Already weakened by rapid economic growth, the simplification of social distinctions that accompanied first settlement, and the absence of both institutional support and long-standing traditions, the provincial systems of stratification remained ill defined and were easily challenged. A general population not particularly inclined to observe deferential niceties was even less encouraged to do so when the dynamics of interest-group relationships were as important an element in their lives as concerns about rank. On one level, contemporaries solved the problem by referring to the composition of society in the broadest possible terms; the Presbyterian minister Francis Alison, for example, indiscriminately mixed vertical and horizontal social classifications when he addressed his audience as "all ranks and denominations of Christians" in Pennsylvania.[6] But that very indefiniteness could cause problems when more precision was required. In situations in which damages for personal injury were to be awarded in court, "Age, Rank or Office," were acknowledged criteria, but how were the latter two to be applied in societies that were essentially voluntaristic?[7] No one knew for sure.

Given such circumstances, a great deal of social conflict characterized both provinces. Within the same two societies that supported powerful oligarchical systems of provincial politics, there were intermittent, cacophonous whirls of contention—frequently marked by a mean-spirited and surly exchange or by shrill shouts, vibrant with nervous anxiety.[8] Status demands might meet with denial and could come into sharp conflict with associational allegiances. Interest groups continually warred over religious or cultural issues, local loyalties, or economic differences.[9] Beneath these various group conflicts lay the heavy commitment of New Yorkers and Pennsylvanians to principles of private interest. James Alexander testified to its great power when he observed reflectively near the end of his life that "Interest often connects people who are entire strangers, and sometimes separates those who have the strongest natural ties."[10] Not surprisingly, New Yorkers were well known as a collection of contentious and avaricious people; and Pennsylvanians inhabited a world of "many jarring and opposite Interests and Systems" with "Every body here in a Scramble for Wealth and Power."[11] Recognition of a multiplicity of interests and their frequently conflicting nature became part of a distinctive middle colony outlook.[12]

The major task that thoughtful New Yorkers and Pennsylvanians faced amid the disparate interests of their provincial societies was to come to terms with the "exclusive companies" and "combinations" that pluralism brought to their respective societies.[13] One direction in which they might have been expected to turn for some inspiration as to group behavior was to the strand of Anglo-American thought that acknowledged the legitimacy of corporate power. But they did not. Although legal corporatism had once been strong in England, and continued to be so in New England, in the mid-Atlantic colonies it was on the wane, and few thought it worth reviving. The colonial assemblies, whose imputed origins lay in the medieval English practices of corporate representation, and whose leaders vigorously protected privileges grounded in that tradition, were, of course, the great exception. But some of their privileges were beginning to meet with occasional *popular* criticism, and eighteenth-century legislators put a great deal more emphasis on the assemblies' parliamentary character than on their corporate nature, for corporate status implied "a Power of a lower Order."[14] Corporate rights did remain a bulwark of localism in some of New York's towns and manors. But once into the eighteenth century, power-conscious governors made few additional grants of corporate privilege to units of local government, and they were very reluctant to grant even the minimal autonomy attendant on the incorporation of religious congregations.[15] In Pennsylvania, only a few incorporations were ever granted, and the most prominent of these, the corporation of Philadelphia, became stigmatized by an association with proprietary privilege.[16] These provincial circumstances, a general disparagement of corporations in English Whig thought, and the fact that corporatism seemed backward-looking, anchored in a traditional hierarchical world of special status and privilege, rendered it ineffectual as an intellectual tool for exploring the more fluid interaction of interest groups in the middle colonies.[17]

Another direction in which colonial spokespersons turned to try to account for social conflict was toward religious pluralism. The great diversity of religious groups in both New York and Pennsylvania, the frequent involvement of religious leaders in public disputes, the noticeable impact religious differences had on political debate, and the use of denominational organizations for the mobilization of voters suggested to contemporaries that the character of public affairs might best be understood in terms of rivalries between religious groups. Hence the perception of "Quaker" and "Presbyterian" parties in Pennsylvania and the tendency on the part of some public figures in both New York and Pennsylvania to try both to exploit the potential inherent in denominational differences for partisan purposes and to explain political divisions in those terms.

Seductive though this approach was to explain public conflict in both New York and Pennsylvania, ultimately it was more befuddling than useful. The fundamental difficulty with it was that it offered too narrow an answer to a very broad problem. Although religious divisions were prominent, the matrix of public affairs was composed of numerous variables. Religious identities were subsumed under local loyalties, large issues arose that had little to do with religion, the secular dynamic in colonial society ebbed and flowed, and a multitude of nonreligious interest groups asserted themselves in pursuit of their particular goals.[18] Unquestionably, religious stereotyping and sweeping generalizations about the influence of particular denominations provided psychic satisfaction to some contemporaries, for it helped them create a type of orderly world they could encompass. But rarely did such perceptions mesh very well with the ongoing dynamics of political life. And rarely, too, has such an approach led to clear retrospective understanding of the intricacies of colonial politics. It may be demonstrated, for example, that within specific electoral units both intra- and interdenominational rivalry contributed to voter mobilization and partisan behavior, but in such instances religious differences were usually subsumed under, or connected with, broader issues.[19] At the same time, no one set of religious conflicts could explain provincial political behavior at the voter or leadership level because each county was its own module of religious dynamics.[20] And a narrow focus on religious differences often precludes serious consideration of other conflicts. Although an innovative initiative, efforts to find intellectual grounding for colonial interest-group conflict in religious diversity frequently failed to advance the political goals of contemporaries and have often lacked significant explanatory power in the hands of later historians.

Another strand of thought that New Yorkers and Pennsylvanians tried to apply to their situation came with strong parental recommendation. Like the English they admired, upper-class colonists blamed social conflict on the fact that the civil "better sort" of people like themselves lived symbiotically with the restless ranks of the "lower sort."[21] According to such logic, the turmoils of society were largely produced by lower-class people who would not keep to their place. The lower orders pushed against social and institutional constraints and defended their economic interests with pugnacious assertiveness. The attractions of this explanation of colonial disorder are plain enough. First, the provincial upper classes felt they strengthened themselves by emphasizing their societies' cultural similarity to England. Second, by stressing the cultural differences between upper and lower classes in their respective provinces, the colonial leaders felt they were encouraging lower-class deference. Third, by blaming their colonies' bouts of contentiousness on the poorer sort, the upper classes absolved themselves of complicity in them. Moreover, toward the end of the colonial period, the upper classes' continuous stress on the distinctions between themselves and the lower sort seemed vindicated when, aided by the growing stratification and economic dislocation of the later colonial years, the bipolar interpretation of colonial society seemed a more appropriate fit than ever before.

However appealing it was for the colonial upper classes' understanding of their societies, the distinction between the better and the lower sort was far too simplistic to encompass the varieties of sociopolitical conflict in New York and Pennsylvania. In the case of England, there was arguably an organic relationship between earlier forms of social organization and polarization in the early modern era into two classes, creating a bipolar eighteenth-century social matrix from which the middle class emerged. The mid-Atlantic colonies, however, found the past foreshortened and the future hurried.[22] A fundamental feature of New York and Pennsylvania societies was their rapid commercial development and the strength of "the Middling Sort of People," whether defined by possessions or by attitudes.[23] Contemporaries frequently acknowledged the strength of the middling social element in both town and countryside.[24] Even those wedded to the better/poorer perspective recognized that there was some difference between "the low class" and "the middling People, the Farmers, shop-keepers and Tradesmen."[25] In New York and Pennsylvania, where as everyone knew, even provincial councillors were "each man [but] a leather apron Lord," it was not the middle classes but the better sort who had to struggle to assert a cultural identity.[26] In simplified settler societies, the trick was for farmers, millers, entrepreneurs, and merchants aspiring to higher status to *distinguish themselves* from their middle-class peers.[27] The struggle over clientage, such as it was, was not carried on by the middling people to free themselves from upper-class dominance, but by the self-proclaimed upper classes to establish some semblance of control over their middling neighbors.

The prominence of the middling elements in New York and Pennsylvania was only one of the most obvious problems with the bipolar perspective. There were other ways in which the theory did not fit at all well. One of the ways in which New York and Pennsylvania distinguished themselves, for example, was by the extent of the divisions among their respective social and political leaders. The upper classes of both colonies were frequently split into contending factions; that condition could not be ignored, for it was a fundamental component of the conflict in each province. But such divisions had no substantial place within the traditional upper-versus-lower-class social model, even when these divisions were perceived to be economic ones. Most telling, however, was the absence of any means of dealing with the great religious, cultural, local, and regional differentiation that was so strongly felt in colonial society. Conflicts arising from such divisions could penetrate all of the various socioeconomic levels of society and were frequently aired with great passion and intensity. The establishment of a proper relationship between upper and lower classes would do little to sort these out in an intelligible manner.

The most direct way in which New Yorkers and Pennsylvanians tried to deal with their fluid, conflicting public worlds was in their piecemeal attempts to come to terms with what historians now recognize as an emerging liberalism.[28] Retrospectively, it is clear that if liberalism had any home in colonial America, it was in the middle colonies. Provincial polities that either embraced liberty of conscience or experienced considerable toleration quickly came to accept voluntarism as an important principle of social organization. Representatives of diverse cultural groups found that they could retain their distinctiveness and still interact as members of one provincial society by finding accommodation, on what many might perceive as rational, pragmatic grounds, around belief in the importance of such notions as individual property rights. Rapid economic development invited acquisitiveness, and emphasis on the promise of the marketplace allowed proud entrepreneurs to claim to be commonwealthmen.[29] Easy, relatively unrestricted access to land encouraged the pursuit of self-interest amid a larger environment of ethnoreligious clustering. And all of these characteristics tended to foster individualism. Such tendencies were reflected, not only in the behavior of New Yorkers and Pennsylvanians, but also in the extent to which they hailed the benefits of free association, appealed to reason, embraced the principle of popular consent in government, incorporated contractual language in their public discourse, expressed political issues in commercial metaphors, openly acknowledged acquisitive concerns, spoke unabashedly of interest as a "restless Friend," and repeatedly voiced solicitude for individual accomplishment, right, and integrity.[30]

But the problem for those on the ground floor of liberalism in America was that they did not know they were beginning a tradition. Colonists were too restricted in their vision, and too sensitive to their provincial status, to envision a worldly philosophy of such dimensions. There was no overt recognition of the overall coherence of that ideology, no farsighted ability to articulate it as an integrated interpretive tool in contemporaries' efforts to make sense of their respective societies. Intimately implicated in the creation of the normative conceptual units of political imagination, which would only later be understood as features of a coherent political doctrine, New Yorkers and Pennsylvanians were blinded by their myopic engagement in the processes of innovation.[31]

Which is not to deny that colonists picked up on and elaborated important strands of British liberal thought. Influenced by the ubiquity and acceptance of interest in public affairs, and by seventeenth-century English free-market thought that emphasized the good consequences of rational, self-interested activities, numerous New Yorkers and Pennsylvanians were prepared to assert that "every passion, every view that men have is selfish in some degree. . . . when it does good to the public in its operation and consequences, it may justly be called disinterest in the usual meaning of that word."[32] Self-interest could occasion beneficence, and could result in harmonious social relations provided it was the product of independent action.[33] And interest could be a legitimate form of influence that individuals could quite properly use to advance their private fortunes and public reputations.[34] So thoroughly did the logic of self-interest permeate segments of New York society that the radicals' agenda of discontent during the pre-Revolutionary years was deeply imbued with it.[35] And it infiltrated the orthodoxies of civil Quakerism so completely in Pennsylvania that Joseph Galloway could not imagine *any* repository of public power, even the Crown, as being devoid of "private Interest."[36] But at the same time, there were always a number of vocal critics who emphasized the propensity of "Interest . . . [to] Tyrannise" and ideologues like William Livingston who stressed the importance of detached wisdom for good government and castigated "Private interest" as "the Whore of Babylon."[37] For many colonists, the unrestrained pursuit of self-interest continued to pose ethical problems of considerable proportions.

Another facet of liberal thought that New Yorkers and Pennsylvanians stressed in their efforts to come to terms with their respective societies was individualism. In neither colony, for example, was there European and English-style "Interest of Privilige"—that is, special entitlements that conferred a superior status on some citizens. "In America," wrote one observer, "the highest rank is freeman, and any man . . . [able to qualify for the vote] is such."[38] The high proportion of men who, compared to the English norm, could meet the franchise requirements encouraged the view that the provincial societies were relatively egalitarian. While from one perspective the assembly continued to be a restrictive corporate body, the community it actually represented expanded sufficiently to allow the illusion of inclusiveness on a common footing. In such an environment, it is understandable why even spokespersons for the radical Morris/Alexander faction might conclude that "the Community is but an Aggregate of private persons."[39] That this statement came from a group of opposition politicians interested at the time in the electoral mobilization of their less affluent neighbors suggests the comment was less an attempt to duck traditional community responsibilities to the poor than a revelation of widely shared philosophical convictions about the character of colonial society.[40] The widespread reverence for freeholder independence, preoccupation with the many private spheres of social life, the centrality of the individual in reformed Protestantism, the vestigial character of crowd activities associated with old-world corporate consciousness, the attenuated and underdeveloped state of new-world clientage relationships, and the attendant atomization of urban, lower-class society, and other circumstances, all contributed to the tendency of colonials to perceive their provincial societies as composites of individuals.

But as in the case of self-interest, emphasis on individualism raised serious problems. As most contemporaries recognized, colonial society was at its most dynamic when individualistic striving coexisted with a larger community ethic. The most vibrant segments of New York and Pennsylvania societies were frequently the religious and ethnic enclaves that were influenced by private, family-oriented value systems, but that allowed their members to move easily back and forth between individualistic endeavors in the larger society and their safe havens of communal support. In such an environment, the scale and intensity of conflict—"Convulsions" as one commentator described them—could be particularly intense.[41] And that was a major impediment to the unqualified acceptance of liberal values. Apparently, individualism exaggerated conflict rather than promoting long-term social harmony. Until colonists could develop new perspectives on that difficulty, liberal social ideas would remain inchoate.

The most innovative way in which New Yorkers and Pennsylvanians came to confront the problem of interest-group conflict was not in social but in political terms. And that innovation came out of the dilemma created by the ongoing juxtaposition of classical republican political standards with the predominant patterns of colonial political behavior. Well represented in the public prints of New York and Pennsylvania are republican demands that political leaders be disinterested, that only those who could still their selfish desires and rise above the passions of the day were fit for public office. Only those gentlemen whose independence, demeanor, and capacity indicated their predisposition to serve the public good should be elected to political office. And such emphasis on disinterest and independence ineluctably led to a condemnation of faction and party as the political expression of selfish views and servile dependence.[42] Yet the outstanding feature of political life in New York and Pennsylvania was obviously not gentlemanly disinterest, but the partisan character of their respective political cultures. From the establishment of representative institutions until the Revolution, provincial politics were steeped in the kinds of partisanship that produced the very faction and party that the classical republican discourse deprecated.

To a limited extent, the English country tradition of politics could accommodate conflict. Eighteenth-century pamphlets and newspapers are filled with examples of political antagonists seizing the high ground of principled independence and disinterest and castigating their opponents as fomenters of discord. But the conventions of the country tradition also had serious failings. Its extreme polarization of political behavior as either virtuous or corrupt resisted any kind of modulation, and no participant in public debate could avoid periodic tarrings at the hands of his antagonists. Most seriously, repeated exchanges of such rhetoric cast doubt on the intrinsic worth of colonial politics. And that simply did not reflect how most colonists thought about their provinces. Popular leaders in both New York and Pennsylvania were generally proud of their societies and confident of their own competence in public affairs. The colonies' experience of growth and expansion, their surfeit of freemen, and their record of protecting rights and extending popular privileges, bespoke sound public mores and vital political cultures.[43]

The inability of the country language to describe, in anything but condemnatory terms, the partisan politics that were integral to societies in the very forefront of English libertarian practice prompted leading colonists to find their own ways of expressing the norms emerging from their political experience. The most revealing evidence of this was their movement in the direction of developing their own informal language of politics, centering on the expression of more positive attitudes toward party politics.[44] There had always been crosscurrents in the main flow of country rhetoric that had acknowledged the salience of party divisions in public affairs.[45] More important, as English historians have come to realize, party allegiances forged in seventeenth-century England continued to play a major role in the structure and language of English county politics through the mid eighteenth century.[46] The point is that English immigrants to New York and Pennsylvania during the late seventeenth and early eighteenth centuries had far less reason to be inhibited, either intellectually or practically, from viewing party as an acceptable aspect of political life than a strict emphasis on the main tenets of country ideology would seem to suggest. Following this lead in their informal discourse of private correspondence and conversation, many New Yorkers and Pennsylvanians began unabashedly to acknowledge that they were partisans in a partisan political world. Unashamedly they spoke of "our party," "my party," "their party," "your party," "our side," "my side," "the other side," "the other party," "your side," "the opposite party," and "our Members" of the assembly, designations that conveyed none of the opprobrium that characterized the formal anti-party rhetoric of the time.[47] In associating *themselves* personally with parties, in frankly attributing party allegiances to *themselves*, colonials indicated that they had passed over a very important divide both in their personal and in their group thinking. Many had come to accept partisan activities expressed through party associations as a legitimate form of political activity.[48]

The willingness of New Yorkers and Pennsylvanians informally to acknowledge the fundamental place of party activities in their respective political cultures was an important development. It accommodated some of the political expressions of liberalism and served as a baseline from which they could work at creating a fuller rationale for their systems of provincial politics. And in this case, as in others, New Yorkers and Pennsylvanians traveled this route by somewhat different paths.

New York and the Politics of Contention

In taking the important step of informally acknowledging party activities as an acceptable feature of political behavior, New Yorkers were influenced by various characteristics of their provincial politics. One of the most important of these was the existence of intercounty networks of family, interest, and like-mindedness in public affairs. The long and intergenerational association of popular and provincial Whig factions created a rough, if ill-defined, order in provincial politics that suggested durability and consistency of public purpose. The longevity of, and apparent continuities in, the political differences that divided New York's oligarchy conspired to convince participants that they were more "parties" to ongoing disputes than factions in pursuit of transient goals.

The intercounty dimensions of provincial politics were most clearly revealed during elections. Frequently, friends from surrounding areas would come to their allies' aid in election contests and exert themselves in various precincts or townships where they thought they had some influence.[49] Actually, the laws governing New York elections encouraged this sort of collusion, because the sheriffs of the various counties had considerable freedom in setting the election date. This allowed for the staggering of election dates so that prominent city residents, for example, might attend the elections in Richmond, Queens, and Westchester counties as well as their own, or that Albanians might have some say in Rensselaerswyck Manor and Schenectady affairs as well as in the city and county of Albany. Outsiders often had a claim to electoral influence, not just on the basis of their friendship with or relationship to a candidate, or because of their provincial eminence, but because landownership in various counties might entitle them to a vote in each of those electoral districts.[50] The law against nonresident voting notwithstanding, the vote in New York went to all qualified landowners in any jurisdiction, regardless of their place of residence.[51] Electoral custom thus encouraged intercounty cooperation among New York politicians, and whenever the elections of neighboring jurisdictions were scheduled for the same day (the purpose being to weaken the political alliance with the strongest out-of-county support), shouts of complaint echoed through the province.[52]

Despite the interaction among "activists, officials and voters"—a requisite of modern participatory politics—New Yorkers never did fully develop the kind of persisting group consciousness and symbols of political identity essential to the practice of "party" politics.[53] The primary preoccupation of New Yorkers with short-run factional politics rather than with the continuities in the popular and provincial Whig traditions was reflected in the names they used to refer to their political divisions. References to "Morrisites," "Cosbyites," and the "Livingston" and "DeLancey" parties tell a tale of personality-dominated, factional politics. By the late 1760s, New Yorkers still had found no clear way to designate such alliances as "the DeLancey's, Crugers, & Church Interest" beyond describing them in those terms, or using a shorthand version such as the "DeLancey Party" or "Church Party."[54] At the same time, there was no development of effective party organizations. Although some "management" always occurred, and was particularly noticeable in the relatively complex four-seat riding of New York City and County, it is clear that whatever intercounty electoral cooperation did take place among politicians, it was too intermittent to gain much strength.[55] And while factions did adopt symbols and slogans, there was little carryover from one contest to the next.[56] The reasons for this were both institutional and cultural. Elections were held infrequently. For all anyone knew, there might be a decade—or, after the Septennial Act, seven years—between elections. And the venues were predominantly double- or single-seat constituencies.

The paucity of electoral offices, coupled with the gentry pretensions of provincial politicians, tended to turn elections into contests between a handful of leading men vying for power and status within their counties. That preoccupation was reflected in the way in which individuals referred in the first person possessive to their respective political followings. Abraham Yates of Albany and Robert Livingston, Jr., for example, came from very different backgrounds and represented very different tendencies in New York political life. Yates was a classic case of a man on the make. He began his employable years as a cobbler's apprentice, moved on to clerk in an Albany law office, and after serving in some minor town offices, gained appointment as sheriff of Albany County during the later 1750s and early 1760s.[57] Robert Livingston, Jr., on the other hand, was born to the provincial purple and gained as much as his narrow intellect could absorb from a college education and long association with other New York oligarchs. Despite their differences, however, Yates and Livingston shared a common perception of how New York's party politics worked. Each described electoral competition in terms of "my party" and detailed how their respective loyalists could best achieve their goals in competition with the "parties" of other individuals.[58] What that reflected was the propensity of leading New Yorkers to think in terms of patron/client relationships and to conceptualize both intra- and intercounty political cooperation largely as a convenient coalition of provincial "grandees."[59]

It was this individualistic and local outlook of New York's prominent leaders that, more than anything else, militated against the development of cohesive, long-lived provincial parties. Egocentric conflicts between Robert Livingston, Jr., and respectively, John Morin Scott, Philip Schuyler, and John Van Rensselaer, for example, prevented any kind of tight party organization from developing around the "Livingston" interest of the late 1760s.[60] The individualistic focus of provincial politics was both reflected in and reinforced by New Yorkers' rhetorical use of the "patriot" tradition of English country thought.[61] Patriots were singular men committed to serving the public through disinterested leadership; they were autonomous "Pillars of the Earth," with "ye world ['set'] upon them."[62] And it was in this context of ongoing competition between a handful of self-justifying and influential county strongmen that we can best understand Philip Livingston's often-quoted comment, "We Change Sides as serves our Interest best."[63]

The type of highly personalized, county-based party competition that characterized New York politics goes some distance in explaining the penchant of New York politicians, relative to their Pennsylvania neighbors, to controvert election results.[64] This is not to deny the mimetic element in New York's political culture, which possibly encouraged provincials to imitate defeated politicians in English elections. A very high proportion of losing candidates in England petitioned the House of Commons against the results if there was any chance of disqualifying enough of their opponents' votes to reverse the decision, or of having the election set aside on grounds of corruption.[65] Nor is it intended to lessen the importance of viva voce voting in explaining the incidence of election petitions. Voting by poll meant that a checklist of voters and their choices was available after the election, and an opponent's supporters could be challenged on such grounds as inability to meet the property qualification or lack of citizenship. In short, the records of viva voce voting created the best opportunity for a challenge to election results. The motive, however, was frequently competitive excess.

Not surprisingly, there was some clustering of election petitions during times of intense provincial conflict and high legislative turnover.[66] But even during these years, such conflicts as the Ulster and Orange petitions of 1737, or the Schenectady, Richmond, and Queens petitions of 1761, should be viewed along with the more sporadic ones, primarily a result of intracounty rivalry between local and often individual party interests. In elections, local magnates put their influence on the line in a very direct and highly visible manner, and losing was always a blow to their prestige. When the vote was close, of course, petitioning was the next logical step, but when it was not, there were always irregularities in elections that offered the temptation to strike back against an opponent. If nothing else, a petition offered some measure of revenge, for the whole process of assembling and examining suspect voters could be as costly a procedure as a prolonged election poll.[67]

New Yorkers' recognition that personality-centered group competition was a normal feature of their political life was expressed in the language of party that infused much of their informal political discourse. That language, and the concept of controlled competition within a defined sociopolitical world, came easily to politicians whose lawyer leaders and friends viewed a conflict-filled world of "party" disputes as a perfectly acceptable aspect of social relations. But, paradoxically, that very propensity to understand party in terms of personal and local loyalties militated against the development of a strong provincewide party consciousness. On the provincial level, the conflict between a limited number of strong individuals who led personalized factions seemed to reinforce Viscount Bolingbroke's view: "Faction is to party what the superlative is to the positive: party is a political evil and faction the worst of all parties."[68] The tendency to conflate faction and party was so reinforced by the highly visible and nearly continuous conflict in New York's provincial politics that such anti-party rhetoric continued simultaneously with the personal acceptance and approbation of party activities right through the colonial years. William Livingston and his coterie might at one moment attempt to distinguish between party and faction and at the next, lapse into mimicry of those parts of the English country monologue that stridently asserted the common roots of faction and party and the undesirability of both.[69] Another prominent provincial, Sir William Johnson, was the head of an extensive political family, in which the language of political expression was largely the idiom of partisan politics. But at the same time, Johnson frequently associated himself with country norms by denying that he ever "prostituted" his interest "meerly to party."[70] The predominance of one perspective over the other in respect to New York's partisan politics depended on the inclinations of each individual and his political circumstances of the moment.

But the impetus toward justifying New York's system of provincial politics was much too strong to be stymied by the difficulties in making a clear distinction between party and faction. Rather than spend their intellectual energies drawing overly fine distinctions, New Yorkers turned to confront the characteristic that seemed most to typify both party and factional politics directly. That characteristic was contention.

When Robert R. Livingston set out to examine the relationships that existed between New York's various socioeconomic interests in the mid eighteenth century, he flatly asserted that they were "always at war."[71] The casual way in which Livingston made this observation, simply positing it as a given in his colony, illustrates the extent to which New Yorkers accepted ongoing sociopolitical conflict as a fundamental feature of their society. Most politically aware colonists believed that "a just clamour" in public affairs was always welcome, while partisans never had trouble convincing themselves that their cause was "just."[72] As Cadwallader Colden retrospectively put it toward the end of his long life, "Opposite Parties have at all times and will exist in this Prov[in]ce."[73]

As New Yorkers became accustomed to the kind of political contention and party rivalry that characterized their province, and as they came to view party competition as normative, they sought for ways both to rationalize and to dignify their politics. One of the two most important of these attempts was rhetorical, narrowly self-justifying, and traditional in its orientation. It involved claiming "patriot" status for partisan politicians. In the eighteenth-century Anglo-American world, a patriot was understood to be an individual free of prejudice, ambition, and avarice whose overriding concern was "to promote the Welfare . . . [of the] Common Wealth."[74] An integral part of the English country tradition, the language of patriotism was itself a party cry, and for this reason, as well as for its content, it appealed to both sides of New York's family of factions. As one New York writer observed, "there is scarce anything so much talked of and so little practiced as Patriotism."[75] Leaving aside the question of practice, the commentator was certainly correct. There was a variety of patriotism for everyone. "Red-hott Patriots," "real Patriot[s]," "zealous Patriot[s]," and "flaming Patriots" were those who pushed to the point of public contention or vociferously advocated popular liberties.[76] Ordinary or "true Patriots" were those who more quietly stood up for both the people's rights and "Submission to the Laws."[77] So prevalent did patriotic claims become in mid eighteenth-century New York, that skepticism also began to appear. There were "Pretended Patriots," "modern Pretended Patriots," and "nominal Patriots," whose outspoken concern for liberty was only a "tickling [of the] Ears, with empty sounds."[78] The prevalence of the terminology was not the result of accident or random mimicry. Its attraction was that it offered a label of legitimacy to all the Whig factions of New York. They could, and did, claim that their own actions represented the best of patriotic intentions, while others fell short. The patriot terminology provided politicians with a means of justifying their partisanship and thereby helped to put them at ease with the factional world they created and worked to perpetuate. Most important, the language of patriotism was one that could be openly expressed. It could be publicly used in subtle ways by the political press to couple patriot practices with specific public figures, and to suggest a rationale for partisan behavior.[79] In short, it was an effective, if indirect, means of publicly acknowledging the factional political world with which New Yorkers were becoming increasingly comfortable.

The second strand of New Yorkers' efforts to rationalize their politics was conceptual and highly original. It constituted an effort to appropriate established idioms of traditional Whig discourse to assist them in expressing the innovative ideas that their new attitudes toward party and partisanship had engendered. This was most clear in the way in which New Yorkers drew on the notion of balance that was associated with the mixed and balanced constitution. One of the basic ideas that provincial thinkers shared was that their colonial constitution should replicate the British constitution. Largely ignoring the differences between colony and mother country, provincials never tired of publicly proclaiming how "the Constitution of the Colony . . . [was] a Picture in Miniature of that of Great Britain," and how that structure created "balance[d]" government.[80] As New Yorkers became reconciled to their contentious politics, and as they saw political power seesaw back and forth on the fulcrum of electoral competition, they began to transpose the idea of balance into the context of their provincial politics. By coupling party to constitutional ideas of unquestioned value, New Yorkers found a way to redeem themselves and their political parties. Listen for a moment to Peter Van Schaack, writing to his brother Henry:

How do you like the Event of this Election? It is I own very agreeable to me and yet it throws rather too much Weight into a Scale which I wish, indeed *rather than any other* to predominate; but in general my Sentiments are in Favour of a Ballance of Power—In a Constitution like that of Great Britain, there will be (I wish never to see the Day when there shall *not* be) *Parties*—the Bulk of the People, will be divided & espouse one or other Side—from the very Temper of Man when he gets Power he will be inclined to abuse it . . . but while each Party continues formidable to the other and upon an equal Footing neither will dare to attempt because neither *can* oppress."[81]

Respect for colonial ways *as well as* for English values led Van Schaack to turn traditional thought on its head. Under colonial constitutions modeled after those of Great Britain, what guaranteed liberty was, not public unanimity (for in a society in which interests were constantly at war, peace meant subservience), but the partisanship and party activities that gave expression to political differences.

Peter Van Schaack's wholehearted endorsement of the efficacy of political rivalry was singular in its clarity, but along with the tendency of many New Yorkers to attribute party activities to themselves, it indicated how thoroughly many provincials had internalized new standards of political behavior based on their provincial experiences. The strength of this tradition, and of the informal political discourse that gave it expression, was further revealed by the way in which the new thinking occasionally broke into the formal world of public prints. William Livingston, of course, has often been identified as one author who was willing to write publicly what others were only prepared to write and say privately. In leading the battle against an Anglican King's College, Livingston argued that far from being a desirable state of affairs, political harmony could indicate "a Combination of Roguery."[82] Rather it was "the Jealousy of all Parties combating each other, [that] would inevitably produce a perfect Freedom for each particular Party."[83] But in giving voice to these sentiments, Livingston was not the soloist he was on other occasions. There were others who praised the salutary nature of *"parties, cabals,* and *intrigues."* One writer claimed that "some opposition, tho' it proceed not entirely from a public spirit, is not only necessary in free governments, but of great Service to the Public. Parties are a Check upon one another, and by keeping the Ambition of one another within Bounds, serve to maintain the public Liberty."[84] Another argued "that Parties in a free State ought rather to be considered as an Advantage to the Public than an Evil. . . . [They] warn the Public of any Attack or Incroachment upon the public Liberty."[85] By the later colonial years, many New Yorkers clearly thought of their politics in terms of a "contrariety of . . . Interests" and of their provincial constitution as one that "suppose[d] an Opposition."[86]

A fundamental feature of the development of any new political discourse or language of politics is the "borrowing" of concepts from older paradigms and turning them to new uses in contemporary affairs.[87] And that was precisely what New Yorkers did when they shifted the familiar old notion of balance from its traditional, anglocentric constitutional and social matrix to a political context of conflicting parties and interests. Accustomed to the clash of provincial parties and having accepted their own involvement in party activities, yet deeply respectful of tradition, politically aware New Yorkers were eager to accommodate their political behavior to old verities. By emphasizing their faith in the efficacy of balance, they could still worship at the shrine of English liberty. But they did so according to a liturgy that was a new-world innovation.

Pennsylvania and the Politics of Party

Although it shared many similarities with New York, provincial politics in Pennsylvania adjusted to the diversity of colonial society in its own particular way. Whereas New Yorkers tended to perpetuate their factional politics while attempting to organize them, Pennsylvania politics quickly became known by their party character. More than in any other British-American province, Pennsylvania colonists not only structured their political activities along party lines, but also accepted such behavior as normative.

Party consciousness in Pennsylvania began with the notion of "broad bottom." In the Quaker colony, this was never the kind of "cant word" that it became in the 1740s in Britain, when it was identified with efforts to create a coalition government of various Whig and Tory factions.[88] Rather, it was a means of expressing both William Penn's policy of religious inclusiveness and a related commitment of popular Quaker politicians to include as many interests as possible within their antiproprietary parties.[89] The Quaker mission was, of course, central to the Pennsylvania experience, and Friends assumed a widely recognized entitlement to preeminence in public affairs.[90] But, as James Logan reminded second-generation Friends, "the Proprietor's own Invitation was general and without exception."[91] Penn's principles and his province's rich land brought numerous non-Quakers to Pennsylvania, and as part of the body politic, they deserved some representation in public affairs. On the one hand, Quakers were recognized as appropriate political leaders in provincial affairs, and to some extent their sectarian self-assurance made many Friends indifferent to other religious groups.[92] But on the other, politically active Quakers recognized that if they were to maintain their reputations as evenhanded custodians of the public welfare, and continue to tap the electoral support of non-Quaker residents that granted them power, they had to create "broad bottom" coalitions that both reflected and fostered the sociopolitical processes of Quakerization.

The initial vehicle for gathering together the various interests of the Pennsylvania community was the assembly. Because the proprietary was a private interest and Pennsylvania's governors were proprietary deputies, spokespersons for the assembly asserted that the House of Representatives was the only institution capable of isolating the public interest. As a "Body," the "People" through their representatives could "not be supposed to judge amiss in any essential Points; for if they decide in Favour of themselves, which is extremely natural, their Decision is just; in as much as whatever contributes to their Benefit, advances the real publick Good."[93] In practice, the assembly repeatedly reflected this kind of hubris. For example, its leading members might arrive unannounced at the governor's "Chamber" and demand "to know if he had any . . . [business] to offer them."[94] One governor's sarcastic enquiry "whether in this Province, it were the custom for ye Govr. to call the Assembly, or ye Assembly the Govr." was no more than a helpless confirmation of how much Pennsylvanians assumed their legislature should take the leading role in formulating the public policy.[95]

By midcentury, these attitudes had become deeply embedded in Pennsylvania's political culture. Assembly spokespersons emphasized how the "whole Powers the House were invested with were derived from the People themselves," and because of the close ties between representatives and people, "we can have no Motive but the good of the People."[96] But by that time, such sentiments were identified not merely with the assembly as an institution but with the "Assembly Party." And that designation was used interchangeably with the "Quaker Party." As divisions opened up in the Pennsylvania community over such issues as pacifism, defense, and Thomas Penn's second-generation proprietary policies, the Quaker Party appropriated for itself the entire popular tradition associated with their assembly and with William Penn's idealism. Quakerism was so intimately connected in the popular mind with Pennsylvania's well-being that the pejorative connotations of "party" were pushed further and further from mind. The wrapping of the authoritative aura of such words as "Quaker," "assembly," the "country," and the "people," around "Party," through their conjunctive use inevitably worked to make the latter both a respectable ideograph and an acceptable way of thinking about political relationships.[97] In the minds of many, strong allegiance to the general interest of a Quaker-led community became synonymous with Party. As Quaker assemblymen retorted when Governor Thomas charged them with deceiving the people, "the Party we are of is our Country."[98]

Two other prominent circumstances also made important contributions toward the legitimation of party activities. One of these was the impetus that religious pluralism gave to innovative thought. By early in the eighteenth century, spokespersons for Pennsylvania's various religious denominations accepted the fact that "by the settlement of Pennsylvania all professions of the Christian religion . . . [were] to be on the same footing."[99] The result was that religious parties were ubiquitous and normative, and contemporary usage tended to throw the word "party" into the same heap as "denomination," "sect," "society," and "nation," as perfectly acceptable expressions of partisan allegiance and concern.[100] The second development was the tendency of Pennsylvanians to dissociate party from faction. The crux of the difference between the two was made clear in a contemporary's definition of factious as "Quarrelsome, Riotous, Rebellious, [or] dissatisfied with the Publick Establishment."[101] To most Pennsylvanians (and unlike the case of New Yorkers, who tended to see both party and faction as fraught with contention), party in the Quaker colony could coincide with peaceful government.[102] This does not mean that there were no times when contemporaries stressed the factious nature of party conflict, nor that there was a total absence of Pennsylvanians who felt with New Yorkers that "constant Debate & faction" was an invaluable source of liberty.[103] But overwhelmingly in Pennsylvania, the Quaker Party was identified with peace. Friends' attitudes toward public affairs were grounded in a discourse of "Love and Unity," which put a high premium on conciliation, "mildness of temper," and consensus.[104] Family relationships were grounded in an ethos of "Holy conversation" that stressed loving relationships.[105] Friends tried to avoid disagreement over unsettled issues, discouraged individual initiatives in public affairs, and fostered unanimity whenever possible.[106] Within the context of Pennsylvania's religious diversity, they saw the Quaker Party as the "balance" wheel serving to keep order among Anglicans, Presbyterians, German church folk, and sectarians of various stripes.[107] Even in contested elections, Quakers were known for making "no stir . . . than by their Votes" and avoiding "heat," "confusion," and "quarreling."[108] In short, the association of the Quaker Party with good government and Friends' preference for quiescence gave the lie to the idea that party meant factional discord.

Perhaps the best indicator of how much Pennsylvania's political culture was bound up with party politics is the extent to which the Quaker Party shared the characteristics of more modern parties.[109] The most striking features of the Quaker Party were those previously discussed: an ideology of civil Quakerism that shaped opinion and promoted political cohesion;[110] an ability to transcend policy crises, defections, and generational changes in leadership;[111] a determination to hold power; and an organization sufficiently coherent to achieve success in electoral politics.[112] But there were two other features that were equally significant and that provided important underpinnings for the party itself.

The cooperative dimensions of Pennsylvania politics, which contrasted markedly with New York practices, constituted the first of these. Pennsylvanians never used the term "my party" to refer to a group of political loyalists committed to the support of one individual.[113] There were no county magnates who saw themselves as heads of their own parties and capable of determining political affairs on their own with an opportunistic, short-term alliance with one or two counterparts. Pennsylvanians thought in terms of "our party," a larger entity that subsumed individual loyalties, and that had some degree of autonomy and an integrity larger than any cabal of its members. Perhaps the most important reason for the difference between New York and Pennsylvania in this respect was structural. Unlike New York elections, which most characteristically focused attention on twin county seats, Pennsylvania elections involved tickets for assemblymen, county commissioners, assessors, sheriffs, and coroners. The very complexity of negotiating such tickets promoted a more communal approach to politics and discouraged individuals from running their own course with the bit in their teeth. Moreover, the issues of provincial politics were frequently deemed relevant in the election of county commissioners and sheriffs, as well as in the choosing of assemblymen.[114] In such instances, cooperation became the watchword of electoral politics, and cooperation promoted Quaker Party identity.

One indicator of how much more emphasis centered on the Quaker Party rather than on the individuals composing it was the paucity of election disputes. Far more remarkable than the peculiar circumstances of the four election petitions that were drawn up in eighteenth-century colonial Pennsylvania was the simple fact of the losers' unwillingness to contest the results.[115] Even in closely contested elections, in which the difference between success and failure was a dozen votes, candidates were unwilling to call for a recount.[116] Again there were important structural reasons for this: vote by ballot meant that there were no poll lists for candidates to challenge. But despite that problem, most commentators agreed that there were always grounds for nullifying election results, for voting by the unqualified was undeniable and ballot stuffing occurred regularly in some counties.[117] What militated against election petitions was not simply the vote by ballot but that losers saw their defeat largely within the cooperative context of party relationships. Unlike their New York counterparts, Pennsylvania politicians were guided more by an overarching party ethos, which was in turn reinforced by a Quaker aversion to litigiousness, than by any individual wish for vindication or immediate vengeance.

Finally, there is the question of party identification through "a common name and symbols."[118] More than any other colonial party (and perhaps more than a number of later counterparts), the Quaker Party maintained a symbolic integrity that brought leaders and followers together. Although the party had three interchangeable names, "the Quaker Party," "the Assembly Party," and "the Old Party," its identity was unalterably rooted in the "plain style" of Quakerism. Everywhere Friends and their Quakerized allies were known as "the Broad Brims of Pennsylvania."[119] When the Proprietary Party recruited sailors to go after its opponents in the 1741 election, the mariners had no trouble distinguishing the "Quaker *Sons of Bitches*."[120] They were the *"Men with broad Hats and no Pockets."*[121] In public affairs, Quaker Party members were always discernable by their "broad brimmed beaver hats, undyed and uncorked," their plain "shadbelly" coats with few pockets, and an absence of the "deep cuffs, false shoulders, [and] super-fluous buttons" that signified pride and showcased sexuality.[122] Shared pref-erences for muted colors and homespun fabric, the traditional honor ac-corded leather aprons and breeches, the aversion of upper-class Friends to showy periwigs, and both the melding of Quaker peculiarities with the plain characteristics of other sectarians and the diffusion of that style throughout the broader provincial community, graphically symbolized the common interests that drew Quaker Party leaders and their supporters together.[123]

The "party" perspective that the Pennsylvania Quaker experience pro-duced was one that markedly influenced Pennsylvanians' approaches to other political groups. With the significant exception of the mid 1760s, the Proprietary Party was never much more than a faction, a loose aggregation of proprietary placemen riven with rivalry and pretension, and with little in the way of consistent and effective leadership.[124] As Isaac Norris pointed out, "it is indeed absurd to call the opposition a party; a few men only compose it."[125] But call it the "Proprietary Party" or "Governor's Party" they did.[126] Partly it served the purposes of Quaker Party politicians to emphasize the coherence, and hence, the threat, that the Proprietary Party represented to popular power; but partly, too, it indicated that the propri-etors' private interests could have a legitimate role in public affairs. And that legitimacy, whatever its cost, required acknowledgement as a party interest. The same kind of judgment underlay the willingness of many Pennsylva-nians to recognize the political precociousness of a handful of Presbyterians during the mid 1760s. As soon as a few Old and New Lights attempted to encourage some intercounty political organizing among their fellows, even those Pennsylvanians on the periphery of provincial politics began to see the Presbyterian initiative as an effort "to become a Party."[127] Like the propri-etary interest, the Presbyterian interest had every right to assert itself as an autonomous force in provincial politics. Perhaps the best indication of how persuasive this logic was came from the Pennsylvania Germans. When, in 1772, Philadelphia Germans established a "Political Society" to speak to the perceived public needs of the day, they "openly identified" their association as a "Parthey." Such terminology clearly demonstrated that party endeavors were an acceptable means of pursuing the public interest.[128]

But the extent to which others accepted the party ethos that Pennsylva-nia's popular Quaker politicians pioneered can best be appreciated by look-ing westward to Lancaster County in the 1760s. There, in loose association with their more erratic eastern counterparts, opponents of the Quaker Party

412 / EARLY AMERICAN POLITICAL CULTURE

created a "New Party" or "New Side" to challenge the local "Old Side" chapter of the Quaker Party.[129] The New Side partisans were individuals who had long stood outside the Quaker Party. As spokespersons for traditional mainstream Whig and English country ideas, and as frequent critics of civil Quakerism, they might have been expected to reject vigorously the party thinking of their Quaker opponents. But they did not. Following the lead of their Quaker Party counterparts, they tried to create their own "broad bottom" coalition.[130] They were painstaking in their efforts to balance geographical and religious interests on the complex ballots that elected fifteen officers each year.[131] Steeped in partisanship, the New Siders could deride even those individuals closely connected with their own Proprietary Party who insisted on strutting to the tune of the disinterested gentleman. Such actors were "playing the independent man," a charge suggesting that in Pennsylvania's partisan political environment, *non*partisanship was widely perceived as artifice.[132] But more important, it was through the prism of party politics that they saw the spectrum of crucial issues in Pennsylvania politics. The campaign for royal government, the authority to tax, the nature and direction of public works, and the splitting up of western counties into new administrative units were all hues on the party palette that made up the Lancaster landscape.[133]

In dealing with these issues, New Side partisans illustrated that they were participants in forging a powerful new discourse of party politics, one that provided a very different context of political understanding from that with which we habitually associate the formal writings of English country ideologues. As we might expect with such a discourse, there were important consistencies in language usage and innovations in terminology. Nowhere in their exchanges about political affairs did the New Side writers mention faction. They did not consider it an appropriate word with which to describe either themselves or their opponents. Both were parties. But their own party was no longer simply "our party"; occasionally it became "the Party," the definite article suggesting an autonomy and an integrity that outstripped the institutional strength of the organization.[134] Yet there were important organizational developments as well. The party did extend beyond the "principal men" in Lancaster Borough to outlying areas.[135] Township "deputies" were partisan members of their communities who had some weight in party affairs.[136] By designating them "deputies," New Side spokespersons put to party purposes a term that in New England parlance and early Pennsylvania custom meant the representatives of the people. Amid such partisanship, it should not be surprising that the term "electioneering" came into use to describe the various forms of interest-making that accompanied elections.[137] And although candidates might still "set up" for an election contest, it was not unheard of for others to "run" or "to be run" for "tickets" their acquaintances put together.[138] What these innovations illustrate is the ability of Pennsylvania's party politicians to begin to develop an informal language of party politics by "generating idioms from within the activity of its own discourse" and, in so doing, testify to the normative character of partisan politics in the provincial experience.[139] New practices and new habits of thought gradually began to forge new forms of political expression, expressions that indicated the revolutionary character of Pennsylvania's political culture.

Toward a New Politics

In both New York and Pennsylvania, the public response to the development of variegated societies with considerable levels of political partisanship was to develop a new understanding of, and a new set of norms for, political behavior. In their respective ways of doing so, New Yorkers and Pennsylvanians were simply opposite sides of the same coin. Pluralistic societies without powerful, traditional governments and time-sanctioned, social orderings were fraught with interest-group conflict. And in order for what we would recognize as a functional political theory to emerge in such circumstances, contemporaries had to view that conflict in a positive light in its relationship to society's overarching purposes. In positing that party and factional contention could promote liberty, New Yorkers did just that. But relatively open, pluralistic societies also required the existence of political organizations that were broadly enough based and strong enough in their own right to reconcile different interest groups and give some specificity to public concern for the community's welfare. In creating a viable tradition of party politics, Pennsylvanians filled that need. The result was that, together, New York and Pennsylvania provided the components of a new type of political understanding, tailored to a maturing American society.

In neither New York nor Pennsylvania was there much structural resistance to the development of these innovative ideas. In New York, royal governors could never carry with them the full prestige of the Crown; that made it easy for local parties to characterize themselves as associations of loyal colonials, advocating constitutional positions that in their minds were expressions of British monarchical government. Because of the remoteness of the Crown, it was easy for New Yorkers to develop an oppositional mode of politics, yet simultaneously to associate that with the maintenance of imperial government and monarchical institutions. In Pennsylvania, the Crown was so removed from the ordinary course of provincial affairs, the proprietary interest was so clearly self-serving, and the governors were so obviously proprietary creatures that the process of refining a public interest under the aegis of popular political organization seemed entirely consistent with loyalty to the British empire and the Crown. In neither colony was the hurdle of reconciling popular political parties to the notion of a disinterested, evenhanded Crown nearly as high as it was in Great Britain.[140]

The extent and power of the new paradigms of politics that New York and Pennsylvania offered in their informal discourses of partisan politics have escaped attention. In being overly attentive to colonial expressions of the formal orthodoxies of English country ideas that stressed the standards of disinterested political leadership and equated party with self-serving myopia, historians have frequently slighted the multilingualism of North American colonists. Just as articulate settlers could shift from political to religious discourse, or from one genre of religious thought to another, they could move between varieties of political discourse, depending on their interests and the appropriateness of the audience. William Livingston, for example, asserted in the public prints, with all the righteous fervor he frequently displayed, that he "never was of any Party."[141] Yet he nevertheless reported on the fortunes of "our party" to distant friends and embroiled himself in factional conflict over King's College.[142] In Pennsylvania, Isaac Norris, Jr., might write to his English correspondents in the cliché-ridden aparty language that his image of old-world politics seemed to require.[143] But Norris was partisan to the core. In 1756, he caused a public uproar when, from the speaker's chair of the Pennsylvania Assembly, he made reference to "Our Side."[144] Consensus had it that certain forums were inappropriate for the language of partisanship, and Norris knew better than most that the assembly was one of those sanctuaries. In his reflexive flouting of convention, Norris demonstrated just how deeply the informal language of partisan politics governed his ordinary manner of thinking.

Because the language of partisan politics was predominantly an informal discourse, sparsely represented in the public prints of the time, its significance is easily overlooked. But if we carefully examine the evidence, it is plain that this discourse indicated a way of understanding political affairs that was quite prevalent during the last three or four decades of the colonial period. Although much of our best evidence comes from political managers and insiders, it is clear that New York's and Pennsylvania's informal language of partisan politics, whether focused on issues, personnel, voter mobilization, or patronage, was also a predominant idiom of tavern and crossroads politics. When an assembly enquiry into Pennsylvania politics in the 1740s revealed the street language of the day, there was not a hint of the kind of aparty linguistic texture that we associate with the country rhetoric.[145] There is every reason to believe that in their oral contact with each other over public affairs, contemporaries spoke as much in the language of partisan politics as they did in the "ornamental," high styles of various old-world

Whig discourses.[146] Recognition of colonials' extensive literacy in the language and conceptions of this informal political discourse is of crucial importance because it renders comprehensible the apparently random intrusion of ideas associated with that discourse into those fortresses of orthodoxy, the public prints.[147] When writers occasionally suggested in the newspapers and pamphlets of New York and Pennsylvania that parties and factions, rather than aparty disinterestedness, were coupled with liberty, such writings were not simply "forays beyond the boundaries of accepted thought" nor "forshadow[ings] of the future."[148] They were, in fact, evidence that vigorous provincial political cultures were already flourishing, and that a significant element in those cultures was the practice and acceptance of partisan political behavior. Above all else, innovative politics was the measure of mid-Atlantic America.

Conclusion

THE MOST NOTICEABLE feature of the political cultures of early New York and Pennsylvania is the extent to which they centered on popular politics. Of course, politically active colonists recognized that they were members of a monarchical empire; yes, they appreciated the importance of integrating themselves within the larger administrative and political networks that emanated from Great Britain. But the primary political arena for all but a few upper-level placemen was the provincial one, where imperial ties could best be exploited or circumvented in the interest of North American concerns. And whatever the character of those psychological, social, and material concerns—insofar as they gained integration into political dialogue—they were shaped by the demands of popular politics.

How can we best understand the dynamics of provincial politics? First, there is the issue of context. Judging from the parameters of political debate, the practices of governmental administration, and the range of activities associated with legislative processes, the provincial assemblies were the primary locus of politics in New York and Pennsylvania. The confluence of British constitutional practice, popular belief in the fundamental character of representative institutions, and pointed, if truncated, assumptions about the validity of popular sovereignty all encouraged such an outcome; and the quick development of the New York and Pennsylvania assemblies into two of the most powerful legislatures in the British dependencies guaranteed it. In consolidating and defending their public prominence, and in reconciling their position with gubernatorial privilege and executive demands, assembly spokespersons established themselves as the foremost continuing architects of colonial political culture.

The language in which colonial politicians repeatedly expressed their affinity for popular, as opposed to prerogative, power was an effusive one of rights and liberties, which possessed a momentum of its own. It had the potential to range beyond immediate legislative concerns and encourage the wider development of popular political sensibilities. Such was the case in the controversies over freedom of speech and freedom of religion in New York and Pennsylvania. These were important issues, which expanded the breadth of provincial political debate and illuminated some of the easily overlooked dimensions of colonial rights consciousness. At the same time, however, in demonstrating the explosive potential of libertarian thought, they underscored the problem of maintaining control in a popular political environment. When cast in the language of popular rights, any innovative challenge to authority or orthodoxy was bound to meet with opposition flowing from the accepted ways of thinking about the dangers posed by disorder to the existing structure of politics.

Whatever their positions on specific rights issues, popular politicians were always concerned about order, because only by having a hand in controlling the legislature could they and their friends fulfill their various public ambitions. If they were to be effective in extending or protecting from abuse the power the assembly had accrued, if they were to safeguard the liberties of the people, serve what they believed to be worthwhile interests, and enjoy the eminence elective office could bestow, they needed more than individual effort. They needed to cooperate. To that end, they formed loosely organized political groups, shaped in ways that both reflected and befitted the circumstances of their respective colonies. The conflicts these factional and party organizations generated, the amplification of their views in paper wars, and the engagement of both vocal partisans and auditors in those battles were instrumental in creating the two provinces' political identities.

Although the formation of factions and parties arose mainly from attempts to control the processes of legislative politics, the inevitable result of such a development was to place greater emphasis on the popular aspects of colonial political life. The fate of factions and parties always lay in the hands of the electorate, and provincial elections in which popular politicians proposed and voters chose were frequently the most important occasions for explicating and strengthening factional or party identity. Candidate selection, acknowledgment of factional or party allegiances, the activities of nominators and other partisans, and, ultimately, the activities of voters, periodically reminded contemporaries that the practice of representation was a crucial aspect of their political system. The importance of electoral activities in provincial politics was, perhaps, the most important demonstration of the fact that popular politics lay at the heart of political culture in New York and Pennsylvania.

But if the popular character of politics was a dominant feature of colonial political culture, so too was the restricted way in which power was held. Notwithstanding dramatic demographic change and rapid population growth, most popular politicians in both New York and Pennsylvania were quite content to see their assemblies remain small, fraternal gatherings. Their commitment to representation was overwhelmingly to the system that had brought them electoral success. They understood the eminence that membership in each colony's most exclusive corporate body could confer, and once in the assemblies, they were not averse to emphasizing that exclusivity by occasionally indulging authoritarian tastes in the name of the people's rights and liberties. And, as a group, they recognized the importance of mastering the informal processes of politics. The effective use of patronage, skill at developing an interest, an ability to manage private meetings, a nose for established patterns of public behavior, and some understanding of how best to follow that scent were important requisites of sustained political success. Most important, there was the sense of who belonged "inside" the political world, along with a determination to respect rather than challenge that limitation.

The fact that the political systems of New York and Pennsylvania were narrow does not, however, mean they were simple. In both colonies we can observe the importance of the legislators' corporate awareness, as well as their understanding that the existence of a variety of interests required reconciliation. In both colonies we can appreciate something of the multiplicity of demands for accommodation with, and rejections of, social deference. In New York, provincial political life was sharpened by conflict and contention and shaped by the pretensions of patronalism and attendant localism. In Pennsylvania, we can see something of the effects of consensual values as they were reflected in ideological awareness. And in each province, ethnocultural consciousness clearly found expression both in tendencies toward religious and ethnic exclusivity and in the crosscutting patterns of intergroup cooperation that successful political practice frequently required.

The subtleties of the interplay among the various contextual strands of provincial relationships notwithstanding, the second fundamental feature of colonial politics was never in doubt. An oligarchic temper governed political affairs in New York and Pennsylvania from their earliest to their latest colonial days. In neither case was that oligarchy the product of any set of simple and easily isolated structural features of society. More than we sometimes choose to acknowledge, the popular colonial leaders maintained a distance between themselves and other, nonpolitical elites.[1] Although in profile, popular politicians inevitably mirrored particular socioeconomic interests, their success was, in fact, a product of the forces of *both* structure and agency that emanated from the concentric circles of provincial, regional, and local influence. Cumulatively, these circumstances created different patterns of political leadership in each colony. But no matter these differences, New York and Pennsylvania politicians shared the same oligarchic disposition.

The problem, of course, is how to reconcile oligarchy with popular politics. But in the colonial years, that was not as difficult as it may seem. On the one hand, there was considerable willingness to accept a system that claimed to protect the people's liberties better than any other, there was a widespread belief in the efficacy of virtual representation, and there were no agreed-upon principles by which representation might be made more equitable. The system was what it was, and it repeatedly proved its worth. On the other hand, both the intimate and constricted dimensions of colonial citizenship and the parochial character of government and politics encouraged provincial politicians to be accessible. And the most successful of them made a point of being both accessible and responsive. Tied by common prejudices to their communities, sharing many of their neighbors' values, often construing the obligations of legislators in the same rough way, and desirous of retaining the eminence that elective office had brought their way, provincial politicians found that they could both serve their constituents and retain their oligarchic ways. Forced as they were by the demands of a representative system to participate in popular politics, the former, in a sense, became a precondition of the latter. Put another way, it was the restricted scope of provincial politics and the very strength of provincial identities that reconciled the two sides of political behavior and fused the popular with the oligarchic temper.

While the context of politics is one basic issue, a second, equally important one is that of the political text. What do we find when we look at the continuous interplay between political rhetoric and behavior in New York and Pennsylvania?

One of the most striking features of political culture in colonial New York and Pennsylvania is the way in which both "countries" developed distinctive political profiles and related political dialects. While traditional patterns of British political discourse and behavior were equally available to all Atlantic provinces, ready for colonial adoption, in practice, the most significant feature of the New York and Pennsylvania record was the varied and flexible ways in which they combined their British heritage with their colonial experiences to create innovative patterns of provincial politics. More than Pennsylvania, New York displayed noticeable streaks of Anglophilia, based on some prominent provincials' desire to transform superficial resemblances to Great Britain into a more substantial similitude. In keeping with that urge, they clearly drew on the language of seventeenth-century English opposition in order to facilitate forging a strong popular political tradition centering on their provincial assembly.[2] And from time to time, different groups of New York politicians deliberately drew on English country thought when they felt it strengthened their hands.[3] But the most striking feature of New York politics was ultimately the way in which contemporaries combined the experiences and the cultural influences they felt most germane to the establishment of their own unique behavioral and discursive identity. Challenged by their notorious predilection for political fragmentation, New Yorkers tamed that tendency largely by structuring an oppositional relationship and an intermittent dialogue between successive factions of popular and provincial Whigs.

As for Pennsylvania, in that colony the innovative cast of mind was, if anything, more pronounced. Religious sensibilities of a radical sort, coupled with a proprietary form of government, produced a pride in provincialism and a way of approaching politics that not only distinguished Pennsylvanians from New Yorkers but also freed them more completely from the orthodoxies of British political paradigms. The language of seventeenth-century English opposition was, of course, useful to Pennsylvanians, just as New Yorkers found it efficacious in building the foundation for a strong assembly in the early eighteenth century. But because of the growing strength of their own provincial constitutional tradition, Pennsylvanians found the opposition rhetoric less serviceable in its unmodified, or mimetic, form than did New Yorkers. Of even less importance was the country tradition. Its lexical components were there, of course, interspersed in political dialogue, but never with sufficient power to shape the course of public debate. Psychologically more autonomous than their New York neighbors, Pennsylvanians brought order to their provincial politics less through the exploitation of specific British political paradigms, than through the expansive influence of the Quaker Party and the broad appeal of the tenets of civil Quakerism. Both colonies distinguished themselves far less by their selective and frequently background mimicry of seventeenth-century English opposition thought and of country nostrums than by their creative amalgamation of different political experiences into vital political cultures.

The evidence that New York and Pennsylvania developed related, but unique, patterns of political behavior confirms what Benjamin Franklin observed in 1760, that no two of the mainland British colonies were much alike. "Not only [were they] under different governors, but [they] have different forms of government, different laws, different interests, and some of them different religious persuasions and different manners."[4] Rather than repeatedly dispute this conclusion for the sake of some arresting, but simplifying, generalization and a tidy "American" history, we might give it more thought. There is every indication that, if not in the case of every colony, then at least in major regions, colonists developed distinctive provincial expressions of their varied political experiences.

Take the case of New England, or, more specifically, Massachusetts. In comparison with New York and Pennsylvania, several characteristics stand out in eastern society. One is the far more pronounced emphasis New Englanders gave to the relationship between the rulers and the ruled. The emphasis on magisterial authority basic to this concern, which was strongly rooted in seventeenth-century Puritanism, lived on with provincial vitality into the era. Rhetorically stressed in election sermons, and given ubiquitous acknowledgement in the intermixture and overlapping of legislative and judicial responsibilities, this tradition was deeply ingrained in the structure of Massachusetts society and in the social consciousness of its colonials.[5] In the context of a society that put great emphasis on maintaining a Congregational religious establishment (historically having believed government to be "the coercive arm of the churches"),[6] accorded great prominence to ministerial families, demanded the enforcement of strict standards of moral discipline, coerced youth into deferential niceties, and paid weighty respect to the aged, it suggests a very different political dialect from those further west and south.[7] So, too, does New England's well-known corporatism. What stands out about the eastern corporate experience from a vantage point outside the region is not the oft-played-out declension away from corporatism to individualism. Rather it is the transition "from an inclusive public communalism to a series of exclusive functionally specific corporations which often mimicked aspects of the earlier structure."[8] The texture of a society in which the "social construction of . . . privatization was not [primarily] individualization," but a variety of increasingly private, along with continuing public, corporatism, is markedly different from anything that distinguished the other colonial regions.[9] And it increases the likelihood that Massachusetts residents—with their rich intellectual heritage and long-standing sense of public identity—expressed themselves in distinctive political dialects reflective of their sense of provincial integrity.[10]

In comparison with New England, the South was less cohesive and is more problematic. In the plantation societies south of Pennsylvania, perhaps the racially based solidarity among whites, coupled with gentry dominance of vestries and county courts, gentry control over the dissemination of information, the established position of the Anglican church, the agrarian-mindedness of the large planters, and the strong lines of connection and dependency that ran between these staple producing areas and England, focused the provincial imagination largely on mimicry of British political paradigms.[11] Arguably, the southern colonial experience, grounded as it was in seventeenth- and eighteenth-century English oppositional ideas, was an exceptionally unified one.[12] Perhaps South Carolina's notable record of public anxieties was both shaped by and largely expressed through English country ideas;[13] perhaps eighteenth-century Virginia is best perceived in terms of mainstream Whig thought, spiced with a dash of country sensitivity to such episodes as the well-known Robinson corruption scandal;[14] perhaps Maryland's proprietary form of government is simply reducible to court/country dimensions.[15] But they are all worth a closer look in the light of the New York and Pennsylvania experiences. Even if they prove to have been the most derivative in their public thought of any of the colonies, that may simply set them off in a differentiated yet familial relationship some distance from their northern counterparts.

The point is that the eighteenth-century provincial political cultures of British America were much too diverse to be depicted in terms of any one-dimensional mimetic process replicating particular strands of English thought. The colonies were, by and large, separate provincial societies, separate "countries" as it were, with their own sociopolitical dynamics. While creating structural similarities to old-world societies, the processes of social and economic maturation simultaneously facilitated the consolidation of regional differences. And the fact of being an overseas adjunct of Great Britain led as much to affirmation of separateness and to political creativity as it did to Anglophile homogeneity. That some colonies were prepared to accept the invitation their circumstances extended seems evident from the New York and Pennsylvania experiences.

And what of the classical republican/liberal tensions so important in American culture? In order to address that issue most directly, it is best to look ahead a little, to the Revolutionary and Early National years on which the controversy has centered, and there consider it in the light of the colonial experiences of New York and Pennsylvania. From one perspective, of course, the existence in British North America of the kind of broad, provincial political pluralism suggested by the study of these two colonies reinforces what recent critics of the classical republican/liberal controversy have been saying: that there were other important discourses in late eighteenth- and early nineteenth-century America that were important components of American political culture.[16] What might be added to this, on the basis of the New York and Pennsylvania colonial past, is a greater recognition of the role regional diversity played in the formation, development, and intertwining of various "American" discursive paradigms. Rather than conflating liberal and republican consciousness in the interest of a consensual past, or sharply limiting the range of political dialects that contemporaries understood, we might take more seriously the plural origins of American public thought.[17] That will only enhance our comprehension of the intellectual synergisms and creativity, as well as the conflicts, parochialisms, misunderstandings, and failed dialogues that were so much a part of the precocious but "unstable" Republic's history through the Civil War.[18] Such observations notwithstanding, however, the classical republican and liberal paradigms continue to be preeminent and are likely to remain so for some time. And the colonial experiences of New York and Pennsylvania do speak to them.

When we appraise America's revolutionary crisis, two observations seem indisputable: first, the leadership of colonial defiance came largely from New England and the South; second, classical republican thinking occupied an important place in the final estrangement from Great Britain. There were areas in New England and the South in which numerous colonials clearly found that important expressions of their regional and provincial cultures could *simultaneously* have meaning in the context of the classical republican paradigm. While different forms of communalism, different religious allegiances, different local government profiles, different styles of political leadership, and different socioeconomic structures, clearly attested to the uniqueness of northern and southern provincial or regional societies, at the same time, leading spokespersons for these societies could agree on the relevance of the classical republican critique of British behavior. From the Stamp Act crisis to the cessation of the Revolutionary War, New Englanders and Southerners were in the lead.

And what of New York and Pennsylvania? Despite their strong traditions of popular government and concern for rights and liberties, New York and Pennsylvania trailed in the rear. Some of the reasons for that were the obvious ones: the conservatism of colonial oligarchies trying to cling to power; New York Anglophilia; Quaker pacifism; the contentment that high-priced grain brought to Hudson and Delaware Valley farmers; and, of course, the way in which their respective behavioral and dialectic political integrity reduced the relevance of country thought. But there were also two additional, interrelated reasons: the north-central colonies' well-known cultural diversity and their predisposition to the legitimation of partisan politics.

The relationship between diversity and the provincial political cultures of New York and Pennsylvania was not a simple one. To begin with, it seems clear that although the political conflict that often accompanies ethnoreligious diversity was a more significant dimension of early colonial public life in New York than in Pennsylvania, it was no more than one of several factors that encouraged New York factionalism. New York had to learn to accommodate the traumas of conquest and rebellion, the stresses of war, sparring between governors and assembly, and the centrifugal thrust of disparate economic and geographical interests as much as it did ethnoreligious diversity in order to develop its popular and provincial Whig traditions and bring some sense of order to its political affairs. In Pennsylvania, the most important consequence of ethnoreligious diversity was less the political conflict those differences generated than the efforts of the Quaker Party to accommodate enough of the province's various peoples to enable the party to maintain its traditional dominance.

A second way in which ethnoreligious diversity became intertwined with New York and Pennsylvania politics was through religious affairs. In New York, religious diversity gained its chief relevance to provincial politics through the partial establishment of the Church of England. That unhappy compromise fed Anglican pretensions and determined others (most notably some Presbyterians) both to resist Anglican claims for greater privilege and to campaign for a broader measure of religious freedom. The conflict over the scope and meaning of religious liberty consequently became an important facet of the popular/provincial Whig dialogue that shaped provincial politics. By contrast, in Pennsylvania, the initial commitment to religious liberty owed nothing to diversity and everything to Quakerism. But in establishing his colony as a religious haven, William Penn created the conditions that fostered diversity; that is, the colony became attractive to those seeking religious liberty. Thereafter, the problem of diversity became the problem of how other religious groups could, or could not, accommodate themselves to Friends' notions of religious freedom. This conflict had to be worked out, either within the dialect of civil Quakerism or in the form of strife between the Quaker and Proprietary parties.

Once irresoluble conflict with Great Britain loomed on the horizon, however, the ethnoreligious dimension of political life began to assume greater importance. Although ethnoreligious diversity had been only one of the contributing factors to the legitimation of political contention and party activity in New York and Pennsylvania, the factions and parties in existence were, in varying degrees, composed of and associated with, members of specific religious and ethnic groups. And once public events began to divide the two provincial political communities in ways that threatened to alter long-standing power relationships among the ethnoreligious components of traditional factional and party associations, increased religious and ethnic consciousness promoted sociopolitical fragmentation. Simultaneously, the key ethnoreligious groups (the Anglicans and Dutch Reformed in New York, and the Quakers in Pennsylvania) that had heretofore been most successful in establishing factions and parties that cut across ethnoreligious lines were incapacitated by the character of the imperial crisis from playing their historic roles.[19]

Combined with the legitimation of partisan politics, the political consequences of these developments were substantial. Ethnoreligious fragmentation tended to exacerbate divisions occasioned by the Revolution and to inhibit provincial unification on "patriot" grounds; at the same time, the predisposition of many provincials to the acceptance of factional or party activities encouraged habits of mind that disinclined them to embrace Revolutionary zeal. But classical republicanism was unequivocal in its Revolutionary prerequisites; it required both an adequate sociopolitical base for its communal ethic and a simultaneous embrace of extremism in the name of liberty. While New York and Pennsylvania each contained groups that could meet one of these demands, neither possessed provincial associations that fulfilled both. The result, by Revolutionary standards, was political paralysis.

Of course, waves of classical republican consciousness swept over both New York and Pennsylvania during the war years, and certainly that discursive paradigm came to influence Revolutionary political cultures in both states. But to assign major emphasis to this is to miss the long-term regional coherence of these two mid-Atlantic societies and their relevance to the liberal experience in America.

However we choose to describe the foundations of liberalism, one point is incontrovertible: liberal politics rest on the acknowledgement of multiple interests in a society, as well as of the legitimacy of the conflict and the accommodation such recognition entails. And it is to the processes of developing those characteristics that New York and Pennsylvania clearly speak. The very complexity of these societies, with their rapid development, growing socioeconomic differentiation, wide geographic range, varied local traditions, and ethnoreligious diversity, rights consciousness, and powerful popular political traditions, meant that New Yorkers and Pennsylvanians had to confront the problems a plurality of interests posed. While they might refuse to contemplate the implications for their private lives, those who concerned themselves with public affairs could not so easily choose avoidance. Their taste for popular political power required that they come to terms with the broader, interest-riven provincial community, an adjustment that resulted in the initiation and exploration of *informal* discourses of politics in both New York and Pennsylvania. In the former case, that discourse emphasized the legitimate role played by competition and contention in the articulation of New York's distinctive political culture. In Pennsylvania, a related, and perhaps slightly stronger, discourse placed more emphasis on the accommodative processes necessary to bring a variety of interests together to form a successful popular political party. Both of these provincial dialects were, to be sure, place-specific rather than broadly theoretical, for they were rooted in the actual conditions of colonial politics. But at the same time, and perhaps because of their deep grounding in provincial practice, they occupied new intellectual ground with enough authority to disregard the ways in which they contradicted some of the important tenets of *formal* English Whig discourses. In doing so, they generated a sufficient sense of their own integrity and worth to guarantee great vitality.

The vigor of that tradition immediately became apparent in the new nation. As New Yorkers restructured their state politics around new contentious issues, they fleshed out their informal language of political discourse, thus giving it greater persuasiveness and coherence.[20] And, at the same time, as they continued to emphasize the legitimate role of contention in political affairs, they began to clarify the distinction between factional and party activities.[21] In Pennsylvania, different changes took place. The organization of Constitutionalist and Republican parties was, among other things, an attempt by Pennsylvanians to reduce the political fragmentation independence had brought and to restore the kind of order they had associated with the politics of party during the colonial years. Revolutionaries reaffirmed what their colonial experiences had told them—that men of integrity *could* be directly involved in party pursuits.[22] Although rancor frequently characterized relationships among partisans, there was also evidence of civility, which in the course of its expression suggested new dimensions of political accommodation within the framework of party politics. Dialogue over the merits of "your republicans" as opposed to "my Constitutionalists" indicated a growing mutual acceptance of party activities and a simultaneous broadening of the informal dimensions of American political culture.[23]

It is hardly surprising, in the face of such developments, that what one observer has labeled "one of the crucial moments—['maybe the crucial moment']—in the history of American politics" took place in Pennsylvania.[24] In a debate in the Pennsylvania legislature in 1786 over the rechartering of the Bank of North America, Representative William Finley stated what had become obvious to those well versed in the traditions of Pennsylvania politics: that interests were ubiquitous, and that the essence of political life was the promotion of those interests.[25] For any confirmation he needed that Pennsylvania was normative, Finley need only have looked around. As the states adjusted to the extreme dislocation of the war, to the new circumstances that exclusion from the British empire occasioned, and to the social upheaval Revolutionary ideals and institutional changes entailed, conflict among different interests appeared to proliferate. And the first experiment with national confederation drew attention to the diversity of the states, their multiple interests, their individual wants, and their various behavioral and dialectic political traditions.

Given these circumstances—ones with which New York and Pennsylvania had long been familiar—and given the particularly intense intermingling of state and national politics in those two states during the Revolutionary and Early National years, it is understandable why the New York and Pennsylvania experiences had such an important effect on the structuring of federal politics. The "First Party System" was largely an extension of many of the features of the political cultures of New York and Pennsylvania to a few other states and their elevation to the more visible stage of national politics.[26] Those who try to reduce the highly variegated and developing American political culture of the late eighteenth and early nineteenth centuries to a stereotypical era of "Antiparty, elite-factional" politics, or who dismiss the Republicans and Federalists as "not modern political parties," or not constituting a "party system," miss the point.[27] Of course, this was not the period of highly institutionalized, national party politics that followed.[28] In order to find out what it was, however, we need to pay less attention to such laggard states as Massachusetts and make less of an effort to prolong classical republican assumptions until the Bucktails of New York could dramatically challenge them.[29] Rather, we should try to comprehend more about the subtle changes that characterized political consciousness prior to the celebrated days of Jacksonian democracy and the more structured era of Whig/Democratic party rivalries.

In the process we may find a far stronger informal elaboration of the assumptions of party politics than we have thought existed. Take William Bingham, for example, a Philadelphian whose lifestyle and public utterances allegedly demonstrated the pervasiveness of the "classical republican atmosphere."[30] Yet here was a man who, even when given the license of diplomatic office to indulge in the rhetoric of public service and disinterestedness, would talk abstractly about party politics. Here was a man who could hypothesize about the conditions under which "a party" could lose its "reputation," and who could diagnose the ills of "our Party" in terms "of [the] Energy & . . . System" it needed to remain strong.[31] Or take the ample public discourse that began to emerge about the relationship of party to government. "It is chiefly by the collusion of parties," wrote one Pennsylvanian, "that public business is pushed forward, with a tendency perhaps different from the views of either party."[32] At the same time, we will find instances of strong aversion to public use of the term "party" and a concerned search for alternatives to describe activities that in themselves contributed to the acceptance of a partisan political tradition.[33] The point is that the nuances of Early National political culture appear in the tensions between informal discourse, public discourse, and the particulars of behavior. Such tensions are complicated matters, and changes during these years were not unidirectional. But one thing they will certainly demonstrate is the strength of an expansive liberal political culture, clearly articulated even during the heyday of classical republican rhetoric, and rooted in long-standing colonial traditions rather than solely dependent on the explosion of social and cultural forces occasioned by the Revolution.

Just as political life in eighteenth-century New York and Pennsylvania illuminates important aspects of the liberal political experience in early America, it reveals something of the origins and character of party politics. During the recent Cold War era of American self-congratulation, historians and political scientists focused a great deal of attention on the "two-party systems" that apparently distinguished American democracy, which some Americans felt were potentially exportable to a "less developed" world.[34] That preoccupation has had consequences for study of the origins of American parties as important as the pervasiveness of the classical republican paradigm for the interpretation of early American political culture. By "party systems" standards, the First Party System was not, in fact, the rivalry between Federalists and Republicans, but the so-called "Second Party System" of the later Jacksonian era.[35] And because of the prominence of the Van Buren Democrats in publicizing the rationale for party competition, whatever attention writers have paid to the roots of American party politics has largely gone to public life in New York.[36]

The model of political behavior eighteenth-century New York offered was unquestionably of considerable significance in the emergence of America's liberal politics. New Yorkers led the way in accepting contention as a fundamental feature of popular politics, and in demonstrating that conflict was a normative feature of any vital new-world political system that embraced a plurality of interests. Of course, the strands of individualism that wound through colonial New York politics inevitably meant that in the expanded context of Revolutionary and Early National political life, coalition politics would play some part. But the factional and party arguments that almost always accompanied such alliances, and the continuing importance of individual county strongmen within factional and party organizations, meant that the accommodative aspects of New York politics were always upstaged by their competitive dimensions. Explosive as the forces of political contention were, however, they did not fragment into random patterns. New York's politics frequently showed how conflict could be channeled into bipolarity, predisposing toward the kind of oppositional politics essential for two-party systems. The New York experience thus presaged, as it were, the two-party future.[37]

There is, however, another component in the development of party politics that often goes unacknowledged, and that the Pennsylvania experience clearly illuminates. Pennsylvanians were the first Americans to distinguish party from faction, and they did so in circumstances far less notable for interparty competition than for one-party dominance. While opposition did exist (and over time it took a variety of forms), a more important feature of colonial Pennsylvania politics was the moral dimension that underlay Quaker Party policies and activities. It was possible for those who sought to serve the public good, and who preferred to conciliate various interests to that end, to do so through the medium of an appropriate political party. (One of the reasons the conflict between the Constitutionalists and Republicans was so bitter was that they *both* laid claim to that heritage.)[38] But the Pennsylvania experience had implications that went beyond state boundaries. Such a view of party resonated with the powerful conformist impulses in American society, thereby facilitating the entry of that view into the communal worlds of New England and the revivalist South and, to a more limited extent, into the hegemonic planter world of the southern tidewater. The acceptance of party in areas of one-party dominance, the subsequent existence of one-party dominance in numerous areas for sustained periods of time, and the curious ways in which that tradition intersected with the better-known "system" of two-party polarization are at the center of the unfolding of America's liberal democratic politics. And that saga began in colonial Pennsylvania.[39]

Finally, there is the issue of what the early New York and Pennsylvania experiences tell us about power relationships in American politics. Not long after the Revolution, the contentious, bipolar factionalism of New York and the party politics of Pennsylvania began to intermingle, forming the underpinnings of national party politics as they evolved from the self-conscious radicalism of Democratic-Republican societies to the full-throated ebullience of the Jacksonian Democrats. Partisan politics, eventually understood as party politics—but never without factional dimensions—became indissolubly connected with liberal democracy. The processes of change by which this development took place have long been celebrated as a fundamental part of the general transformation of American society from its small-scale dependent past to its epic independent future.

Yet the most revealing features of early American society do not consist simply of the laudations of contemporaries or of subsequent observers, but in the tensions that existed among the languages of public celebration and informal discourse, and the many patterns of public and private behavior. We know, for example, that the public rhetoric of equality notwithstanding, informal languages of discrimination flourished. While showering effusions of public praise on their new democracy, Americans were simultaneously sanctioning the spread of slavery, disenfranchising former freemen, and forming barriers to prevent the participation of women in public affairs.

Within the preserve of politics, there was an appositive tension with long-run implications for American political culture. From one point of view, party politics seems so closely associated with liberal democratic ways that it appears to epitomize popular political values. Yet in its first expressions, party politics was an integral part of the respective sets of oligarchic political relationships dominant in provincial New York and Pennsylvania. The tendencies toward oligarchy were obvious, not only in the colonies' restrictive patterns of representation, in the assemblies' corporate sensibilities, and in the legislatures' claims to speak for all rights, but also in the organization of factions and parties and in the tendency of particular ethnoreligious groups to dominate high office, manage elections, and control the informal processes of politics. Of course, the Revolution swept away many distinctive features of the established oligarchic regimes. New standards of equitable representation, modest expansion of the franchise, a heightened commitment to democratic politics, and the discrediting of prominent colonials with Tory inclinations bequeathed an even broader base for popular politics in the new republic. It was one thing, however, to rid New York and Pennsylvania of their old colonial oligarchies, but quite another to eradicate the oligarchic temper that existed *within* the very texture of popular politics. While the Revolution ushered in a new era of liberal democracy, it simultaneously welcomed the intermingling of new and old elites and their fusion into local, regional, and national establishments. And high on the practical political agendas of many of these groups was the modulation of democratic demands and the exercise of control over the various processes of partisan politics, much in the way the old oligarchies had done.[40] What the colonial regimes bequeathed to the new nation, then, was an immensely durable tradition of close linkage between the popular and the oligarchic. This was a tension that was to persist in the new nation just as sharply as it had in the colonial past—a central feature of the distinctively inclusive, yet simultaneously exclusionary, politics of the coming modern America.

Appendix

The Governors of New York and Pennsylvania

Governors of New York, 1664–1770

Governors	Date
Richard Nicolls	Sept. 1664–Aug. 1667
Colonel Francis Lovelace	Aug. 1667–Aug. 1673[a]
Major Edmund Andros	Nov. 1674–Nov. 1677
Lt. Anthony Brockholles, Cmdr. in Chief	Nov. 1677–Aug. 1678
Sir Edmund Andros	Aug. 1678–Jan. 1681
Lt. Anthony Brockholles, Cmdr. in Chief	Jan. 1681–Aug. 1682
Colonel Thomas Dongan	Aug. 1682–Aug. 1688
Sir Edmund Andros	Aug. 1688–Oct. 1688
Francis Nicholson, Lt. Gov.	Oct. 1688–June 1689
Jacob Leisler	June 1689–Mar. 1691[b]
Colonel Henry Sloughter	Mar. 1691–July 1691
Major Richard Ingoldsby, Cmdr. in Chief	July 1691–Aug. 1692
Colonel Benjamin Fletcher	Aug. 1692–Apr. 1698
Richard Coote, Earl of Bellomont	Apr. 1698–May 1699
John Nanfan, Lt. Gov.	May 1699–July 1700
Richard Coote, Earl of Bellomont	July 1700–Mar. 1701
William Smith, as senior Councillor	Mar. 1701–May 1701
John Nanfan, Lt. Gov.	May 1701–May 1702
Edward Hyde, Viscount Cornbury	May 1702–Dec. 1708
John, Lord Lovelace	Dec. 1708–May 1709
Peter Schuyler, President of Council	May 1709[c]
Richard Ingoldsby, Lt. Gov.	May 1709[d]
Peter Schuyler, President of Council	May 1709–June 1709

(*continued*)

Governors of New York, 1664–1770 (Continued)

Governors	Date
Richard Ingoldsby, Lt. Gov.	June 1709–Apr. 1710
Gerardus Beekman, President of Council	Apr. 1710–June 1710
Brigadier Robert Hunter	June 1710–July 1719
Peter Schuyler, President of Council	July 1719–Sept. 1720
William Burnet	Sept. 1720–Apr. 1728
John Montgomerie	Apr. 1728–July 1731
Rip Van Dam, President of Council	July 1731–Aug. 1732
Colonel William Cosby	Aug. 1732–Mar. 1736
George Clarke as President of Council	Mar. 1736–Oct. 1736
George Clarke as Lt. Gov.	Oct. 1736–Sept. 1743
Admiral George Clinton	Sept. 1743–Oct. 1753
Sir Danvers Osbourne	Oct. 1753ᵉ
James DeLancey, Lt. Gov.	Oct. 1753–Sept. 1755
Sir Charles Hardy	Sept. 1755–June 1757
James DeLancey, Lt. Gov.	June 1757–Aug. 1760
Cadwallader Colden, President of Council	Aug. 1760–Oct. 1761
Major-General Robert Monckton	Oct. 1761–Nov. 1761
Cadwallader Colden, Lt. Gov.	Nov. 1761–June 1762
Major-General Robert Monckton	June 1762–June 1763
Cadwallader Colden, Lt. Gov.	June 1763–Nov. 1765
Sir Henry Moore	Nov. 1765–Sept. 1769
Cadwallader Colden, Lt. Gov.	Sept. 1769–Oct. 1770
John Murray, Earl of Dunmore	Oct. 1770–July 1771

SOURCE: Adapted from Patricia U. Bonomi, *A Factious People: Politics and Society in Colonial New York* (New York, 1971), 293–294.

ᵃThe Dutch retook New York in August 1673.

ᵇLeisler assumed the title of lieutenant-governor in December 1689. He was executed for high treason on May 16, 1691.

ᶜSchuyler was acting governor for three days, May 6–May 9, 1709.

ᵈIngoldsby was governor for sixteen days, May 9–May 26, 1709.

ᵉOsbourne took office on October 10, 1753, and committed suicide on October 12.

Governors of Pennsylvania, 1682–1770

Governor	Date
William Penn, Prop. and Gov.	Oct. 1682–May 1684
Council, under various presidents	May 1684–Dec. 1688
John Blackwell, Lt. Gov.	Dec. 1688–Jan. 1690
Council under Thomas Lloyd, Pres.	Jan. 1690–Apr. 1693
Benjamin Fletcher, Gov. under the Crown	Apr. 1693–Feb. 1695
William Markham, Lt. Gov. under the Crown	Apr. 1693–Feb. 1695
William Markham, Lt. Gov.	Feb. 1695–Jan. 1700
William Penn, Prop. and Gov.	Jan. 1700–Nov. 1701
Andrew Hamilton, Lt. Gov.	Nov. 1701–Feb. 1703
Council under Edward Shippen, Pres.	Feb. 1703–Feb. 1704
John Evans, Lt. Gov.	Feb. 1704–Feb. 1709
Charles Gookin, Lt. Gov.	Feb. 1709–May 1717
Sir William Keith, Lt. Gov.	May 1717–June 1726
Patrick Gordon, Lt. Gov.	June 1726–Aug. 1736
Council under James Logan, Pres.	Aug. 1736–June 1738
George Thomas, Lt. Gov.	June 1738–June 1747
Council under Anthony Palmer, Pres.	June 1747–Nov. 1748
James Hamilton, Lt. Gov.	Nov. 1748–Oct. 1754
Robert Hunter Morris, Lt. Gov.	Oct. 1754–Aug. 1756
William Denny, Lt. Gov.	Aug. 1756–Nov. 1759
James Hamilton, Lt. Gov.	Nov. 1759–Nov. 1763
John Penn, Lt. Gov.	Nov. 1763–May 1771

SOURCE: *Minutes of the Provincial Council of Pennsylvania.* Samuel Hazard, ed., 16 vols. (Philadelphia, 1838–1853).

Abbreviations and Bibliographical Note

Abbreviations

AHR	*American Historical Review*
APS	American Philosophical Society
Aspinwall Papers	*Aspinwall Papers,* 2 vols., Massachusetts Historical Society, *Collections,* 4th ser., vols. 9–10 (Boston, 1870–71)
CCLB	*The Cadwallader Colden Letter Books,* 2 vols., New York Historical Society, *Collections,* vols. 9–10 (New York, 1877–1878)
CJS	Correspondence of John Smith
Colden Papers	*The Letters and Papers of Cadwallader Colden,* 9 vols., New York Historical Society, *Collections,* vols. 50–58 (New York, 1918–1938)
Colls. NYHS	*Collections* of the New York Historical Society
CR	*Minutes of the Provincial Council of Pennsylvania,* Samuel Hazard, ed., 16 vols. (Philadelphia, 1838–1853)
DHNY	*The Documentary History of the State of New York,* E. B. O'Callaghan, ed., 4 vols. (Albany, 1850)
DRCNY	*Documents Relative to the Colonial History of New York,* E. B. O'Callaghan and B. Fernow, eds., 15 vols. (Albany, 1853–1887)
FHL	Friends Historical Library, Swarthmore College
HMPEC	*Historical Magazine of the Protestant Episcopal Church*

HSP	Historical Society of Pennsylvania
INLB	Isaac Norris Letter Book
JAH	*Journal of American History*
Journal NYLC	*Journal of the Legislative Council of the Colony of New York, 1691–1775,* 2 vols. (Albany, 1861)
JWLB	*Letter Book of John Watts, Merchant and Councillor of New York,* New York Historical Society, *Collections,* vol. 61 (New York, 1928)
LWC-JFP	Livingston-Welles Correspondence, Johnson Family Papers
MCNY	Museum of the City of New York
NY Col. MSS	New York Colonial Manuscripts, New York State Archives
NYHS	New York Historical Society
NY Hist.	*New York History*
NYHSQ	*New York Historical Society Quarterly*
NY Laws	*Colonial Laws of New York from the Year 1664 to the Revolution,* 5 vols. (Albany, 1894– 1896)
NYPL	New York Public Library
NYSA	New York State Archives
NYSL	New York State Library
NY Votes	*Proceedings of the General Assembly of the Colony of New York, 1691–1765,* 2 vols. (New York, 1764–1766)
PA	*Pennsylvania Archives,* Samuel Hazard et al., eds., 9 ser. (Philadelphia and Harrisburg, Pa.,1852–1935)
Pa. Hist.	*Pennsylvania History*
Pa. Statutes	*The Statutes-at-Large of Pennsylvania from 1682–1801,* James T. Mitchell and Henry Flanders, eds., 15 vols. (Harrisburg, Pa., 1896–1911)
Pa. Votes	*Votes and Proceedings of the House of Representatives of the Province of Pennsylvania,* Gertrude MacKinney, ed., 8 vols., *Pennsylvania Archives,* 8th ser. (Harrisburg, Pa., 1931–1935)
PBF	*The Papers of Benjamin Franklin,* Leonard W. Labaree et al., eds., 30 vols. to date (New Haven, 1959–)
Penn-Logan Corresp.	*Correspondence between William Penn and James Logan, Secretary of the Province of Pennsylvania and Others,* Edward Armstrong, ed., 2 vols. (Philadelphia, 1870–1872)
PHS	Presbyterian Historical Society
PMHB	*Pennsylvania Magazine of History and Biography*
PPOC	Penn Papers, Official Correspondence
PWP	*The Papers of William Penn,* Mary Maples Dunn, Richard Dunn et al., eds., 5 vols. (Philadelphia, 1981–1987)
RPLB	Richard Peters Letter Book

SPG, Letters, B.   Society for the Propagation of the Gospel in Foreign Parts, Letters, ser. B
WMQ   *William and Mary Quarterly*
YUL   Sterling Memorial Library, Yale University

Bibliographical Note

The sources on which this study stands are many and diverse. For convenience' sake, they may be divided into five major groups. First are the published public records of both New York and Pennsylvania. These include collections such as *Documents Relative to the Colonial History of New York*, E. B. O'Callaghan and B. Fernow, eds., 15 vols. (Albany, 1853–1887); *The Documentary History of the State of New York*, E. B. O'Callaghan, ed., 4 vols. (Albany, 1849–1851); *Journal of the Votes and Proceedings of the General Assembly of the Colony of New York, 1691–1765*, 2 vols. (New York, 1764–66); *Journal of the Legislative Council of the Colony of New York, 1691–1775*, 2 vols. (Albany, 1861); *The Colonial Laws of New York from the Year 1664 to the Revolution*, 5 vols. (Albany, 1894); *Ecclesiastical Records of the State of New York*, E. T. Corwin, ed., 7 vols. (Albany, 1901–1916); *Annals of Albany*, J. Munsell, comp., 10 vols. (Albany, 1854–1871); *Minutes of the Common Council of the City of New York, 1675–1776*, 8 vols. (New York, 1905); *Pennsylvania Archives*, Samuel Hazard et al., eds., 9 ser. (Philadelphia and Harrisburg, Pa., 1852–1935); *Minutes of the Provincial Council of Pennsylvania*, Samuel Hazard, ed., 16 vols. (Philadelphia, 1838–1853); *The Statutes-at-Large of Pennsylvania from 1682–1801*, J. T. Mitchell and H. Flanders, eds., 15 vols. (Harrisburg, Pa., 1896–1911); *Minutes of the Common Council of the City of Philadelphia* (Philadelphia, 1847); *Register of Pennsylvania*, Samuel Hazard, ed., 16 vols. (Philadelphia, 1828–1836).

Second, there are a number of useful published collections of private papers. Some of the more important of these are *The Letters and Papers of Cadwallader Colden*, 9 vols., New York Historical Society, *Collections*, vols. 50–58 (New York, 1918–1938); *Cadwallader Colden Letter Books*, 2 vols., New York Historical Society, *Collections*, vols. 9–10 (New York, 1877–78); *Historical Memoirs of William Smith, Jr.*, vol. 1, *1763–1776*, W. H. W. Sabine, ed. (New York, 1956); *Letter Book of John Watts, Merchant and Councillor of New York*, New York Historical Society, *Collections*, vol. 61 (New York, 1928); *The Papers of Sir William Johnson*, James Sullivan et al., eds., 14 vols. (Albany, 1921–1965); *Samuel Johnson, President of King's College, His Career and Writings*, Herbert and Carol Schneider, eds., 4 vols. (New York, 1929); *The Papers of William Penn*, Mary Maples Dunn, Richard Dunn et al., eds., 5 vols. (Philadelphia, 1981–1987); *The Papers of Benjamin Franklin*, Leonard W. Labaree et al., eds., 30 vols. to date (New Haven, 1959–); *Correspondence between William Penn and James Logan, Secretary of the Province of Pennsylvania and others*, Edward Armstrong, ed., 2 vols. (Philadelphia, 1870–1872); *The Journals of Henry M. Muhlenberg*, Theodore G. Tappert and John W. Doberstein, eds. and trans., 3 vols. (Philadelphia, 1942–1958); *Extracts from the Itineraries and other Miscellanies of Ezra Stiles, D.D., L.L.D.*, Franklin B. Dexter, ed. (New Haven, 1916). Two other works that belong more with this group than with the others are William Smith, Jr., *A History of the Province of New York*, Michael Kammen, ed., 2 vols. (Cambridge, Mass., 1972), and Horace Wemyss Smith, *The Life and Correspondence of Reverend William Smith, D.D.*, 2 vols. (Philadelphia, 1879–1880).

Third are the published sources from the colonial years. I have read all the main New York and Pennsylvania newspapers through 1770, and although I have found four or five, such as Zenger's *Weekly Journal* and Bradford's *American Weekly Mercury,* more useful than others, all provide important information. The other essential resource is the American Antiquarian Society's microcard printing of *Early American Imprints,* based on Charles Evans, *American Bibliography,* 13 vols. (New York, 1941–42). Two useful collections of contemporary writings are *The Paxton Papers,* John R. Dunbar, ed. (The Hague, 1957) and William Livingston's *Independent Reflector,* Milton M. Klein, ed. (Cambridge, Mass., 1963).

Fourth, manuscript sources have been of extraordinary importance in helping me form an understanding of New York and Pennsylvania societies. The collections I have used are too numerous to list and many are well known by colonial historians. I can only add that major collections alone are not enough. Often a single document in a miscellaneous, society, or autograph collection provided important clarifications. The custodial archives of this manuscript material are listed in the acknowledgments at the front of the book.

Finally, this study rests on a great mountain of monographs, articles, and dissertations that historians, mainly of early America but also of later times and other locations, have written over the years. I am deeply in their debt.

Notes

Introduction

1. Walt Whitman, *Complete Poetry and Selected Prose and Letters,* Emory Hollo-way, ed. (London, 1964), 5.

2. There are many acceptable definitions of political culture. A simple and useful one is the recognizable "beliefs and expectations that give meaning to the political process and guide . . . the conduct of politics and government" (Richard L. McCormick, *The Party Period and Public Policy: American Politics from the Age of Jackson to the Progressive Era* [Oxford, 1986], 116). For another, see Jean H. Baker, *Affairs of Party: The Political Culture of Northern Democrats in the Mid-Nineteenth Century* (Ithaca, N.Y., 1983), 11–12.

3. Bernard Bailyn, *The Ideological Origins of the American Revolution* (Cambridge, Mass., 1967, and enlarged 25th anniversary ed., 1992); Gordon S. Wood, *The Creation of the American Republic, 1776–1787* (Chapel Hill, N.C., 1969); id., *The Radicalism of the American Revolution: How a Revolution Transformed a Monarchical Society into a Democratic One Unlike Any That Had Ever Existed* (New York, 1991); J. G. A. Pocock, *The Machiavellian Moment: Florentine Political Thought and the Atlantic Republican Tradition* (Princeton, 1975); id., *Virtue, Commerce, and History* (Cambridge, 1985); Lance Banning, *The Jeffersonian Persuasion: Evolution of a Party Ideology* (Ithaca, N.Y., 1978). For a general treatment of the republican-centered literature, see Robert E. Shalhope, "Toward a Republican Synthesis: The Emergence of an Understanding of Republicanism in American Historiography," *William and Mary Quarterly,* 3d ser., 29 (1972): 49–80 (hereinafter cited as *WMQ*); id., "Republicanism and Early American Historiography," ibid. 39 (1982): 334–356.

4. Recent writings have begun to draw attention to the differences among the republican historians. Daniel T. Rodgers, for example, distinguishes between a Harvard and St. Louis tradition ("Republicanism: The Career of a Concept," *Journal of American History* 79 [1992]: 11–38 [hereinafter cited as *JAH*]). Bernard Bailyn has pointed out that he never described "the spokesmen of the Revolution" as "civic humanists" (*Ideological Origins*, vi). And Jack P. Greene argues that there is a marked distinction between Gordon Wood's notion of "public virtue" and J. G. A. Pocock's concept of "civic virtue" (*Imperatives, Behaviors, and Identities: Essays in Early American Cultural History* [Charlottesville, Va., 1992], 208–214, 233–234). These various distinctions notwithstanding (and in the last case, contextualized reading of both of Wood's books (see esp. *Radicalism of the American Revolution*, 104–109) suggests that Greene has overemphasized the *authorial* conceptual gulf between Pocock's civic-minded citizens and Wood's virtuous Revolutionary *leaders*), the chief republican historians remain very close cousins.

5. Joyce Appleby, *Capitalism and a New Social Order: The Republican Vision of the 1790s* (New York, 1984); id., *Liberalism and Republicanism in the Historical Imagination* (Cambridge, Mass., 1992); John P. Diggins, *The Lost Soul of American Politics: Virtue, Self-Interest, and the Foundations of Liberalism* (New York, 1985); Stephen Watts, *The Republic Reborn: War and the Making of Liberal America, 1790–1820* (Baltimore, 1987); Isaac Kramnick, *Republican and Bourgeois Radicalism: Political Ideology in Late Eighteenth-Century England and America* (Ithaca, N.Y., 1990).

6. For some reactions to liberal criticism, see Wood, *Radicalism of the American Revolution;* Lance Banning, "Jeffersonian Ideology Revisited: Liberal and Classical Ideas in the New American Republic," *WMQ,* 3d ser., 43 (1986), 3–19; id., "The Republican Interpretation: Retrospect and Prospect," and Robert E. Shalhope, "Republicanism, Liberalism, and Democracy: Political Culture in the Early Republic," in *The Republican Synthesis Revisited: Essays in Honor of George Athan Billias,* Milton M. Klein, Richard D. Brown, and John B. Hench, eds. (Worcester, Mass., 1992), 91–117, 37–90. Liberalism has often been perceived as a secondary force in public thought during the colonial years (1) because of the difficulty of demonstrating liberal values (see, e.g., the response of James A. Henretta in his "Reply," *WMQ,* 3d ser., 38 [1980]: 697, to James T. Lemon, *The Best Poor Man's Country: A Geographical Study of Early Southeastern Pennsylvania* [Baltimore, 1972], and that of Michael Zuckerman, "Review Essay: Farewell to the 'New England Paradigm' of Colonial Development," *Pennsylvania History* 57 [1990]: 66–73 [hereinafter cited as *Pa. Hist.*] to Jack P. Greene's *Pursuits of Happiness: The Social Development of Early Modern British Colonies and the Formation of American Culture* [Chapel Hill, N.C., 1988]); (2) because of the tendency to forgo discussions about acquisitiveness in favor of those focusing on colonial economic growth and a transition to capitalism (see, e.g., John J. McCusker and Russell R. Menard, *The Economy of British North America, 1607–1789* [Chapel Hill, N.C., 1985], and Allan Kulikoff, *The Agrarian Origins of American Capitalism* [Charlottesville, Va., 1992]); (3) because of the recent discovery of various "traditional" characteristics in colonial societies (see, e.g., Appleby, *Capitalism and a New Social Order,* 7–14, Wood, *Radicalism of the American Revolution,* 11–92, and Kulikoff, *Agrarian Origins of American Capitalism,* 13–33); (4) because of the intellectual attractiveness of classical republicanism as "a predecessor and counterpoint to emergent liberalism" (see Peter Onuf, review of *Liberalism and Republicanism in the Historical Imagination,* by Joyce Appleby, *WMQ,* 3d ser., 50 [1993]: 791); and (5) because of the appearance of a prominent literature of liberalism beginning in 1776 (as symbolized by Adam Smith's *An*

Inquiry into the Nature and Causes of the Wealth of Nations [Dublin, 1776]). John Brooke's *The Heart of the Commonwealth: Society and Political Culture in Worcester County, Massachusetts, 1713–1861* (Cambridge, 1989) is illustrative of this tendency. In describing cultural change in Massachusetts society from the first days of European settlement to the Civil War in terms of an evolving, tension-filled equilibrium between classical republicanism and liberalism, Brooke stresses that classical republican modes of thought and behavior predominated over their liberal counterparts throughout the colonial period.

7. The major statement asserting the ubiquity of the English "radical Whig" or "country" underpinnings of Revolutionary republican thought is Bernard Bailyn's *The Origins of American Politics* (New York, 1968). As Bailyn explains, "It was primarily this opposition frame of mind through which the colonists saw the world and in terms of which they themselves became participants in politics." The rush to embrace republicanism during the 1970s and 1980s produced some modification of Bailyn's thesis, most notably in some acceptance of the argument that "court" as well as "country" thinking played a significant role in the North American colonies. (See, e.g., William Pencak, *War, Politics, and Revolution in Provincial Massachusetts* [Boston, 1981].) But by encouraging such historians as John M. Murrin to place the various colonies along a court/country continuum, such recent scholarship has simply recast Bailyn's original argument in slightly different form—for country ideas only make sense in the context of the court/country dichotomy. See John M. Murrin, "Political Development," in *Colonial British America: Essays in the New History of the Early Modern Era*, Jack P. Greene and J. R. Pole, eds. (Baltimore, 1984), 440. For Murrin's broader application of the court/country model to American politics, see "The Great Inversion, or Court versus Country: A Comparison of the Revolution Settlements in England (1688–1721) and America (1766–1816)," in *Three British Revolutions: 1641, 1688, 1776*, J. G. A. Pocock, ed. (Princeton, 1980), 368–453. Joyce Appleby lays out what she considers to be the English antecedents of American liberal thought in her *Economic Thought and Ideology in Seventeenth-Century England* (Princeton, 1978) and in several essays in *Liberalism and Republicanism*.

8. Focusing on the colonial assemblies (which he had earlier placed at the center of his own explanation of the Revolution in *The Quest For Power: The Lower Houses of Assembly in the Southern Royal Colonies, 1689–1776* [Chapel Hill, N.C., 1963]), Jack P. Greene has voiced the strongest objections to Bailyn's view in "Political Mimesis: A Consideration of the Historical and Cultural Roots of Legislative Behavior in the British Colonies in the Eighteenth Century," *American Historical Review* 75 (1969): 337–360 (hereinafter cited as *AHR*), an important article offering Greene's own single-strand interpretation of colonial politics and questioning Bailyn's tendency to push republican concerns back so far into the colonial period. The dominant political discourse in the eighteenth-century colonies, Greene argues, was that of "the seventeenth-century tradition of opposition to the Crown." Rather than having country concerns uppermost in their minds, he asserts, politically aware colonists were animated by "fear" of the royal prerogative and by a "jealous concern" for the "privileges and authority" of their assemblies ("Political Mimesis," 341, 343). In general, historians have perceived Bailyn's model of colonial politics as capacious enough (because it does include conflict between assemblies and governors) to encompass much of what Greene distinguishes as a separate paradigm. In his *King and People in Provincial Massachusetts* (Chapel Hill, 1985), Richard Bushman offers a noteworthy alternative in arguing that in the monarchically oriented provincial

culture of Massachusetts, the language of seventeenth-century English opposition predominated in popular politics prior to the 1740s, and the republican-informed English country tradition thereafter. For a recent example of a Revolution-determined, reductionist view of colonial politics, see Marc Egnal, *A Mighty Empire: The Origins of the American Revolution* (Ithaca, N.Y., 1988).

9. Exceptions to this seem to occur when historians choose to construct a model of western European "traditionalism" out of the colonial experience in order to magnify the extent of the "transformation" that American society underwent during the late eighteenth and early nineteenth centuries. But this is simply another example of subordinating the colonial past to a Revolutionary or Early National agenda. One recent and glaring example of this is Wood, *Radicalism of the American Revolution*. For a similar tendency from a different ideological perspective, see Edward Countryman, *A People in Revolution: The American Revolution and Political Society in New York, 1760–1790* (Baltimore, 1981).

10. On the paucity of recent interest in colonial "political development" see Greene, *Imperatives, Behaviors, and Identities*, 214–215.

11. Greene, *Pursuits of Happiness*. Although Greene's argument is that, aside from New England, all the British North American colonial regions were structurally similar, and that there was an accelerating convergence among all the major colonies of the first British empire during the middle two quarters of the eighteenth century, much of his evidence indicates immense diversity among the British colonies. See also David Hackett Fischer, *Albion's Seed: Four British Folkways in America* (New York, 1989), and D. W. Meinig, *The Shaping of America: A Geographical Perspective on 500 Years of History*, vol. 1, *Atlantic America, 1492–1800* (New Haven, 1986).

12. J. Hector St. John de Crèvecoeur (pseud.), *Letters from an American Farmer* (London, 1782).

13. Barry Levy, *Quakers and the American Family: British Settlement in the Delaware Valley* (New York, 1988), 8.

14. For this terminology, see, e.g., the *New-York Mercury*, 5 Jan. 1756; Edward Burd to James Burd, 6 July 1776, *The Burd Papers: Selections from Letters Written by Edward Burd, 1763–1828*, Lewis Burd Walker, ed. (Pottsville, Pa., 1899); *The Conduct of the [Eighteen] Presbyterian Ministers . . .* (Philadelphia, 1761), Evans # 8819. For a cartographer's view, see Lewis Evans's "Map of Pennsylvania, New Jersey, New York and the Three Delaware Counties, 1749," in Lawrence Henry Gipson, *Lewis Evans* (Philadelphia, 1939).

15. John R. Dunbar, *The Paxton Papers* (The Hague, 1957), 309; Rowland Berthoff, *An Unsettled People: Social Order and Disorder in American History* (New York, 1971), 25. See also Meinig, *Atlantic America*, 131–144.

16. William Livingston to Messrs. Chapman & Haley, 25 Nov. 1760, William Livingston Papers, Massachusetts Historical Society, microfilm copy, Sterling Library, Yale University (hereinafter cited as YUL); John Watts to John Riddell, 21 Feb. 1763, and to Philip Gibbs, 5 Apr. 1764, *Letter Book of John Watts, Merchant and Councillor of New York* (hereinafter cited as *JWLB*), New York Historical Society, *Collections* 61 (1928): 126, 237 (hereinafter cited as *Colls.* NYHS).

17. Deposition of Luke Mercer, 6 July 1732, *Pennsylvania Archives*, 1st ser., Samuel Hazard, ed., 12 vols. (Harrisburg, Pa., 1852–1856), 1:336 (hereinafter cited as *PA*); James Logan to John Paris, 29 Dec. 1731, James Logan Letter Book, 3, Historical Society of Pennsylvania (hereinafter cited as HSP).

18. I am indebted to John Murrin for this observation.

19. New York and New Jersey shared a common governor until 1738, and Pennsylvania and the Lower Counties were Penn family proprietaries throughout the colonial period.

20. *Historical Statistics of the United States: Colonial Times to 1970*, 2 vols. (Washington, D.C., 1975), 2:1168.

21. Gary B. Nash, "Social Development," in *Colonial British America*, Greene and Pole, eds., 239–240; Alice Hanson Jones, "Wealth Estimates for the Middle Colonies, 1774," *Economic Development and Cultural Change* 18, no. 4, pt. 2 (1970); id., *Wealth of a Nation to Be: The American Colonies on the Eve of the Revolution* (New York, 1980), passim. For the eighteenth-century meaning of competency, see Daniel Vickers, "Competency and Competition: Economic Culture in Early America," *WMQ*, 3d ser., 47 (1990): 3–29.

22. "Letter and Narrative of Father Isaac Jogues, 1643, 1645," in *Narratives of New Netherland, 1609–1664*, J. Franklin Jameson, ed. (New York, 1909), 259.

23. John M. Murrin, "English Rights as Ethnic Aggression: The English Conquest, the Charter of Liberties of 1683, and Leisler's Rebellion in New York," in *Authority and Resistance in Early New York*, William Pencak and Conrad E. Wright, eds. (New York, 1988), 56–94. Joyce D. Goodfriend, *Before the Melting Pot: Society and Culture in Colonial New York, 1664–1730* (Princeton, 1992); Alice P. Kenney, *Stubborn for Liberty: The Dutch in New York* (Syracuse, N.Y., 1975); Donna Merwick, *Possessing Albany, 1630–1710: The Dutch and English Experiences* (Cambridge, 1990); Thomas E. Burke, Jr., *Mohawk Frontier: The Dutch Community of Schenectady, New York, 1661–1710* (Ithaca, N.Y., 1991); William J. McLaughlin, "Dutch Rural New York: Community, Economy, and Family in Colonial Flatbush" (Ph.D. diss., Columbia University, 1981); Edward Henry Tebbenhoff, "The Momentum of Tradition: Dutch Society and Identity in Schenectady, 1660–1790" (Ph.D. diss., University of Minnesota, 1992); Oliver A. Rink, "The People of New Netherland: Notes on Non-English Immigration to New York in the Seventeenth Century," *New York History* 62 (1981): 5–42 (hereinafter cited as *NY Hist.*); id., *Holland on the Hudson: An Economic and Social History of Dutch New York* (Ithaca, N.Y., 1986), 139–171; David S. Cohen, "How Dutch Were the Dutch of New Netherland?" *NY Hist.* 62 (1981): 43–60. For a useful summary of the early Dutch social experience and the view that the Batavianized communities became "virtual islands," see A. G. Roeber, "'The Origin of Whatever Is Not English among Us': The Dutch-speaking and the German-speaking Peoples of Colonial British America," in *Strangers within the Realm: Cultural Margins of the First British Empire*, Bernard Bailyn and Philip D. Morgan, eds. (Chapel Hill, N.C., 1991), 220–223.

24. Michael Kammen, *Colonial New York: A History* (New York, 1975), passim.

25. Joseph E. Illick, *Colonial Pennsylvania: A History* (New York, 1976), passim; Sally Schwartz, *"A Mixed Multitude": The Struggle for Toleration in Colonial Pennsylvania* (New York, 1987).

26. "Governor Dongan's Report on the State of the Province . . . ," in *Documents Relative to the Colonial History of the State of New York*, Edmund B. O'Callaghan and B. Fernow, eds., 15 vols. (Albany, N.Y., 1853–1887), 3:415 (hereinafter cited as *DRCNY*).

27. Doctor Alexander Hamilton, *Hamilton's Itinerarium . . . 1744*, Albert Bushnell Hart, ed. (St. Louis, Mo., 1907), 22.

28. For the issue of regionalization in colonial history and the question of whether or not the middle colonies formed a distinctive region, see Jack P. Greene, "Interpretive Frameworks: The Quest for Intellectual Order in Early American History,"

WMQ, 3d ser., 48 (1991): 515–530; id., *Pursuits of Happiness;* Meinig, *Atlantic America;* Douglas Greenberg, "The Middle Colonies in Recent American Historiography," *WMQ,* 3d ser., 36 (1979): 396–427; Michael Zuckerman, "Introduction: Puritans, Cavaliers, and the Motley Middle," in *Friends and Neighbors: Group Life in America's First Plural Society,* Zuckerman, ed. (Philadelphia, 1982), 3–25; Robert J. Gough, "The Myth of the 'Middle Colonies': An Analysis of Regionalization in Early America," *Pennsylvania Magazine of History and Biography* 103 (1983): 392–419 (hereinafter cited as *PMHB*); Wayne Bodle, "The 'Myth of the Middle Colonies' Reconsidered: The Process of Regionalization in Early America," ibid., 113 (1989): 527–548; John J. McCusker and Russell R. Menard, *The Economy of British America, 1607–1789* (Chapel Hill, N.C., 1985), 189–208; and the articles by Menard, Robert V. Wells, and Susan E. Klepp, as part of a "Symposium on the Demographic History of the Philadelphia Region, 1600–1860," American Philosophical Society, *Proceedings* 133 (1989): 215–233.

One / Seventeenth-Century Beginnings

1. "Articles of Capitulation on the Reduction of New Netherland," 27 Aug. 1664, *DRCNY,* 2:252.
2. Colonel Nicolls to secretary of state, Oct. 1664, *DRCNY,* 3:68.
3. "Grant of New Netherland, etc., to the duke of York," 12 Mar. 1664, *DRCNY,* 2:295–298.
4. Charles M. Andrews, *The Colonial Period of American History,* 4 vols. (New Haven, 1934–38), 4:passim.
5. Robert C. Ritchie, *The Duke's Province: A Study of New York Politics and Society, 1664–1691* (Chapel Hill, N.C., 1977), 25–31; Sung Bok Kim, *Landlord and Tenant in Colonial New York: Manorial Society, 1664–1775* (Chapel Hill, N.C., 1978), 8; E. B. O'Callaghan, *History of New Netherland; or, New York under the Dutch,* 2 vols. (New York, 1845–48), 2:540.
6. Although James's charter stopped on the east bank of the Delaware, a small military expedition had demonstrated the English determination to eradicate all Dutch havens in North America by brutally bringing this little settlement under English control. C. W. Weslager, *The English on the Delaware, 1610–1682* (New Brunswick, N.J., 1967).
7. Merwick, *Possessing Albany,* 68–103. See also Burke, *Mohawk Frontier.*
8. Jasper Danckaerts, *Journal of Jasper Danckaerts, 1679–1680,* ed. Bartlett B. James and J. Franklin Jameson (New York, 1913), 196.
9. "Letter and Narrative of Father Isaac Jogues," 253.
10. Kammen, *Colonial New York,* 74–75.
11. Ritchie, *Duke's Province,* 31–42.
12. Duke of York to Governor Andros, 28 Jan. 1676, *DRCNY,* 3:230.
13. Ritchie, *Duke's Province,* 201; Leonard Woods Labaree, *Royal Government in America: A Study of the British Colonial System before 1783* (New Haven, 1930), 269–270n.
14. Ritchie, *Duke's Province,* 33–34, 96; David S. Lovejoy, *The Glorious Revolution in America* (New York, 1972), 107–114; *DRCNY,* 2:250–253; David William Voorhees, "'In Behalf of the True Protestants Religion': The Glorious Revolution in New York" (Ph.D. diss., New York University, 1988), 62.
15. Ritchie, *Duke's Province,* 34–37.
16. Samuel Maverick to Sampson Bond, May 1669, as quoted in Kammen, *Colonial New York,* 87.

17. Ritchie, *Duke's Province,* 48, 121–122.
18. Ibid., 155–167.
19. Voorhees, "'In Behalf of the True Protestants Religion,'" 62–65; Ritchie, *Duke's Province,* 170–176.
20. Ritchie, *Duke's Province,* 176–197. During that brief period the English began legal proceedings against all other proprietary colonies except the one belonging to James's old friend William Penn.
21. Voorhees, "'In Behalf of the True Protestants Religion,'" 133–139, 243–249.
22. William III to Lt.-Gov. Nicolson, 30 July 1689, *DRCNY,* 3:606.
23. On the destruction of Schenectady during King William's War, see Burke, *Mohawk Frontier,* 68–108.
24. Ritchie, *Duke's Province,* 198–231; Randall Balmer, "Traitors and Papists: The Religious Dimensions of Leisler's Rebellion," *NY Hist.* 70 (1989): 341–372; Donna Merwick, "Being Dutch: An Interpretation of Why Jacob Leisler Died," ibid., 373–404; Thomas E. Burke, Jr., "Leisler's Rebellion at Schenectady, New York, 1689–1710," ibid., 405–430.
25. Ritchie, *Duke's Province,* 198–231; Voorhees, "'In Behalf of the True Protestants Religion,'" 254–263, 338–350.
26. Voorhees, "'In Behalf of the True Protestants Religion,'" 355–365.
27. On the Dutch tradition of city autonomy, see Merwick, *Possessing Albany* and "Being Dutch."
28. For the Schenectady rivalry with Albany, see Burke, *Mohawk Frontier.*
29. Charles W. Spencer, "Sectional Aspects of New York Provincial Politics," *Political Science Quarterly* 30 (1915): 397–424.
30. Voorhees, "'In Behalf of the True Protestants Religion'"; Balmer, "Traitors and Papists."
31. "Loyalty Vindicated," in *Narratives of the Insurrections, 1675–1690,* Charles M. Andrews, ed. (New York, 1915), 387, as quoted in Voorhees, "'In Behalf of the True Protestants Religion,'" 77.
32. "Dying Speeches of Leisler & Milborne," 16 May 1691, *DRCNY,* 2:376–380.
33. Voorhees makes this point most convincingly in his "'In Behalf of the True Protestants Religion.'"
34. Randall Balmer, *A Perfect Babel of Confusion: Dutch Religion and English Culture in the Middle Colonies* (New York, 1989), 34–39; id., "Traitors and Papists." For an emphasis on class division that needs to be read in the light of Voorhees and Balmer, see Gary B. Nash, *The Urban Crucible: Social Change, Political Consciousness, and the Origins of the American Revolution* (Cambridge, Mass., 1979), 46–49, 88–93.
35. Voorhees, "'In Behalf of the True Protestants Religion,'" 15–25.
36. Balmer, *Perfect Babel of Confusion,* 3–30; id., "Traitors and Papists," 353–354. Murrin, "English Rights as Ethnic Aggression," 56–94.
37. On the polarization over consistory elections in the New York City church, see Balmer, "Traitors and Papists," 364–366.
38. Randall Balmer, "Schism on Long Island: The Dutch Reformed Church, Lord Cornbury, and the Politics of Anglicization," in *Authority and Resistance,* Pencak and Wright, eds., 95–113.
39. There is evidence that Leisler himself was not especially sympathetic to some expressions of pietism. Balmer, *Perfect Babel of Confusion,* 18, 26–27.
40. John D. Runcie, "The Problem of Anglo-American Politics in Bellomont's New York," *WMQ,* 3d ser., 26 (1969): 191–217. See also Alison G. Olson, *Anglo-American Politics, 1660–1775: The Relationship between Parties in England and Colonial*

America (Oxford, 1973), and id., *Making the Empire Work: London and American Interest Groups, 1690–1790* (Cambridge, Mass., 1992), 71–72.

41. For a list of New York governors and their terms of office, see Appendix.

42. Lord Cornbury to Lords of Trade, 27 Sept. 1702, *DRCNY,* 4:971.

43. Lawrence H. Leder, *Robert Livingston, 1654–1728, and the Politics of Colonial New York* (Chapel Hill, N.C., 1961); James S. Leamon, "War, Finance, and Faction in Colonial New York: The Administration of Governor Benjamin Fletcher, 1692–1698" (Ph.D. diss., Brown University, 1961); Stanley H. Friedelbaum, "Bellomont: Imperial Administrator. Studies in Colonial Administration During the Seventeenth Century" (Ph.D. diss., Columbia University, 1955); Charles Worthen Spencer, *Phases of Royal Government in New York, 1691–1719* (Columbus, Ohio, 1905).

44. My treatment of land policy under Dongan, Fletcher, and Bellomont is based on Kim, *Landlord and Tenant,* 20–86.

45. King William's War lasted from 1689 to 1697.

46. "Order in Council on the Report of the Lords of Trade of the 19th October," 25 Oct. 1698, earl of Bellomont to Lords of Trade, 22 July 1699, *DRCNY,* 4:411, 535; *Colonial Laws of New York from the Year 1664 to the Revolution,* 5 vols. (Albany, 1894–1896), 1:412–417 (hereinafter cited as *NY Laws*); John C. Rainbolt, "A 'great and usefull designe': Bellomont's Proposal for New York, 1698–1701," *New York Historical Society Quarterly* 53 (1969): 333–351 (hereinafter cited as *NYHSQ*).

47. *NY Laws,* 1:523–525; Jack H. Christenson, "The Administration of Land Policy in Colonial New York" (Ph.D. diss., State University of New York, Albany, 1976), 46–68. Ultimately, the Privy Council refused to accept the New York Assembly's Act of Repeal and upheld the Vacating Act. Board of Trade to Lord Lovelace, 28 June 1708, *DRCNY,* 5:48.

48. *Journal of the Votes and Proceedings of the General Assembly of the Colony of New York, 1691–1765,* 2 vols. (New York, 1764–1766), 1:35 (hereinafter cited as *NY Votes*); Leamon, "War, Finance, and Faction," 219–223.

49. Runcie, "The Problem of Anglo-American Politics," 191–217.

50. "Heads of Accusation against the Earl of Bellomont," 11 Mar. 1700, *DRCNY,* 4:620.

51. "The Burghers of New Amsterdam and the Freemen of New York, 1675–1866," *Colls.* NYHS 18 (New York, 1885), 61–73; Bellomont to Lords of Trade, 29 Apr. 1699, "Heads of Accusation against the Earl of Bellomont," 11 Mar. 1700, *DRCNY,* 4:621, 507–509; Friedelbaum, "Bellomont," 99–103.

52. *NY Votes,* 1:92–143; Thomas J. Archdeacon, *New York City, 1664–1710: Conquest and Change* (Ithaca, N.Y., 1976), 123–146. For coincidental mobilization of Leislerian voters in the consistory elections of the Dutch Reformed Church, see Balmer, "Traitors and Papists," 364–366.

53. Adrian Howe, "Accommodation and Retreat: Politics in Anglo-Dutch New York City, 1700–1760" (Ph.D. diss., University of Melbourne, 1982), 76–77, 104–110, 137.

54. Runcie, "Anglo-American Politics"; Friedelbaum, "Bellomont."

55. Voorhees, "'In Behalf of the True Protestants Religion,'" 388–393, 425.

56. Governor Fletcher to William Blathwayt, 10 Sept. 1692, *DRCNY,* 3:848.

57. Adrian Howe, "The Bayard Treason Trial: Dramatizing Anglo-Dutch Politics in Early Eighteenth-Century New York City," *WMQ,* 3d ser., 47 (1990): 57–89.

58. Ritchie, *Duke's Province,* passim.

59. Murrin, "English Rights as Ethnic Aggression," 56–94. But note difficulty he has dealing with a contemporary's statement that several of the Dutch were in

collusion with the English in pushing for rights. Also Voorhees's revisionist view that *neither* English nor Dutch thought much of the Charter of Rights. See ibid., 71–72, and Voorhees, "'In Behalf of the True Protestants Religion,'" 63–65. For an appraisal of intermittent Dutch-English sociopolitical conflict, see Ritchie, *Duke's Province,* 68–75, 140–143.

60. Bellomont to Lords of Trade, 27 Apr. 1699, *DRCNY,* 4:508; Howe, "Accommodation and Retreat," 21–75; Thomas J. Archdeacon, "The Age of Leisler— New York City, 1689–1710: A Social and Demographic Interpretation," in *Aspects of Early New York Society and Politics,* Jacob Judd and Irwin Polishook, eds. (Tarrytown, N.Y., 1971), 78.

61. Bellomont to Lords of Trade, 27 Apr. 1699, *DRCNY,* 4:508; Howe, "Accommodation and Retreat," 23–25, 76–84, 112–115; id., "Bayard Treason Trial," 61–64.

62. "Heads of Accusation against the Earl of Bellomont," 11 Mar. 1700, *DRCNY,* 4:620.

63. Goodfriend, *Before the Melting Pot,* 40–60, 88, 94–98.

64. *DRCNY,* 4:526–528; John Miller, *New York Considered and Improved, 1695,* V. H. Paltsits, ed. (Cleveland, Ohio, 1904), 54.

65. Archdeacon, "Age of Leisler," 78. Of 224 voters, Archdeacon classifies 133 as Dutch, 111 of whom voted for the Leislerians; 40 of 41 French and 59 of 69 British voted for the anti-Leislerians. Surprisingly, only 2 voters were of unidentifiable nationality. The three groups were also defined to some extent by the Dutch Reformed, French Reformed and Anglican churches.

66. On the structure of the Dutch community, see Goodfriend, *Before the Melting Pot,* 61–76, and Howe, "Accommodation and Retreat," 21–75, but note Archdeacon, "Age of Leisler," 78–79.

67. And secure in office once more, the anti-Leislerians dropped their "English party" rhetoric and appealed to the electorate on other grounds.

68. Howe, "Accommodation and Retreat."

69. Goodfriend, *Before the Melting Pot,* 133–134.

70. Rink, "People of New Netherland," 5–42; Cohen, "How Dutch Were the Dutch," 43–60; Goodfriend, *Before the Melting Pot,* 16, 35–36, 41–46; Voorhees, "'In Behalf of the True Protestants Religion,'" 49–52.

71. For their division, see Balmer, "Traitors and Papists," 364–366. For an Albany-based view suggesting cultural cohesion as the defining feature of the Dutch society of New Netherlands, see Alice P. Kenney, "Dutch Patricians in Colonial Albany," *NY Hist.* 49 (1968): 249–283; id., *Stubborn for Liberty;* id., "Patricians and Plebians in Colonial Albany," *De Halve Maen* 45 (1970), nos. 1, 2, 3, 4, and 46 (1971), no. 1; Merwick, *Possessing Albany;* and David G. Hackett, *The Rude Hand of Innovation: Religion and Social Order in Albany, New York, 1652–1836* (New York, 1991), 9–55. For a very different view of upriver society based on Schenectady, see Burke, *Mohawk Frontier.* For an instructive commentary on New York Dutch community studies, see Karen Ordahl Kupperman, "Early American History with the Dutch Put In," *Reviews in American History* 21 (1993): 195–201.

72. Goodfriend, *Before the Melting Pot,* 81–110, 155–221. For the notion of ethnicization, see p. 219.

73. The "lamb's war" was the spiritual war of the Friends against a carnal world. Some critics, however, including a number of Quakers, saw the founding of Pennsylvania as an abandonment of that war, for the major strategy English Friends had adopted in order to overcome their persecutors was to confront them with Quaker

suffering. Immigration could be construed as avoidance of the suffering necessary to win the war in Britain. On the prosecution of Quakers in England and their resistance, see Craig W. Horle, *The Quakers and the English Legal System, 1660–1688* (Philadelphia, 1988).

74. *The Papers of William Penn*, Mary Maples Dunn, Richard Dunn et al., eds., 5 vols. (Philadelphia, 1981–1987), 2:89 (hereinafter cited as *PWP*).

75. Ibid., 21–22.

76. William Penn to ——, July 1681, Penn Papers, Domestic Letters, as quoted in William R. Shepherd, *History of Proprietary Government in Pennsylvania* (New York, 1896), 175.

77. *Minutes of the Provincial Council of Pennsylvania*, 16 vols. (Philadelphia, 1838–1853), 1:18 (hereinafter cited as *CR*).

78. William Penn to Lord Romney, 6 Sept. 1701, Penn Papers, Granville Penn Book, as quoted in Gary B. Nash, *Quakers and Politics: Pennsylvania, 1681–1726* (Princeton, 1968), 9n.

79. *CR*, 1:19.

80. Ibid., 19–20.

81. Ibid., 25.

82. For a copy of the Pennsylvania Charter, see *CR*, 1:17–26. Also note *PWP*, 2:62–63.

83. Nash, *Quakers and Politics*, 11–47; Schwartz, *"A Mixed Multitude,"* 19–26.

84. *PWP*, 1:387–410.

85. Ibid., 387; Nash, *Quakers and Politics*, 31–32.

86. *PWP*, 2:140–156.

87. Nash, *Quakers and Politics*, 28–29.

88. *PWP*, 2:211–227.

89. Ibid., 216.

90. Ibid., 217.

91. Ibid., 220–221.

92. Nash, *Quakers and Politics*, 39–47.

93. *PWP*, 4:296; *CR*, 2:312.

94. *PWP*, 2:211–228; Nash, *Quakers and Politics*, 39–47.

95. Nash, *Quakers and Politics*, 43–45.

96. *PWP*, 2:504; Penn had his figures wrong. Apparently 2,000 people arrived in 1682 and another 2,000 in 1683. By the end of 1685, the number of immigrants was approximately 8,000. Ibid., 49–50; Marion Balderston, "William Penn's Twenty-Three Ships," *Pennsylvania Genealogical Magazine* 23 (1963): 27–67.

97. *PWP*, 2:504.

98. Ibid., 281–282, 331n.

99. Ibid., 299–300, 318–319.

100. *Votes and Proceedings of the House of Representatives of the Province of Pennsylvania*, Gertrude Mackinney, ed., 8 vols., *Pennsylvania Archives*, 8th ser. (Harrisburg, Pa., 1931–1935), 1:330–331 (hereinafter cited as *Pa. Votes*); *CR*, 1:58–59.

101. *CR*, 1:63.

102. Ibid., 69.

103. Ibid., 60–61; *Pa. Votes*, 1:19.

104. *Pa. Votes*, 1:42.

105. A quorum of the council was twelve. *CR*, 1:43.

106. Ibid., 113.

107. *PWP,* 2:381–383, 471–472, 509–510, 520, 543; Nash, *Quakers and Politics,* 74–77.

108. *PWP,* 2:601.

109. Ibid., 3:59, 68–69.

110. Ibid., passim.

111. Nash, *Quakers and Politics,* 103.

112. For a list of Pennsylvania governors and their terms of office, see Appendix.

113. Ibid., 89–126.

114. Ibid., 181–192.

115. Ibid., 123, 186–187, 192–207.

116. Ibid., 77–81, 92–93.

117. Ibid., 95.

118. *PWP,* 3:247.

119. Ibid., 472.

120. Ibid., 248.

121. Ibid.

122. Ibid., 247.

123. Ibid., 309.

124. Ibid., 309, 507.

125. Ibid., 317.

126. Ibid., 247.

127. Ibid., 350.

128. Ibid., 137.

129. William Penn, "Instructions for Lieutenant Governor Blackwell . . . ," as quoted in Nash, *Quakers and Politics,* 116.

130. *PWP,* 3:356–357.

131. Nash, *Quakers and Politics,* 171.

132. Levy, *Quakers and the American Family,* 21.

133. Horle, *Quakers and the English Legal System,* quotation from p. 268; William W. Spurrier, "The Persecution of the Quakers in England, 1650–1714" (Ph.D. diss., University of North Carolina, 1976).

134. Nash, *Quakers and Politics,* 171.

135. Levy, *Quakers and the American Family,* 112–113.

136. Nash, *Quakers and Politics,* 168–175.

137. William C. Braithwaite, *The Beginnings of Quakerism* (London, 1912); id., *The Second Period of Quakerism* (London, 1919); Rufus Jones, *The Later Periods of Quakerism* (London, 1921); Arnold Lloyd, *Quaker Social History, 1669–1738* (London, 1950); Hugh Barbour, *The Quakers in Puritan England* (New Haven, 1964); Richard T. Vann, *The Social Development of English Quakerism* (Cambridge, Mass., 1969); Melvin B. Endy, Jr., *William Penn and Early Quakerism* (Princeton, 1973); Barry Reay, *The Quakers and the English Revolution* (London, 1985); J. William Frost, *The Quaker Family in Colonial America: A Portrait of the Society of Friends* (New York, 1973); Levy, *Quakers and the American Family;* Richard Bauman, *Let Your Words Be Few: Symbolism of Speaking and Silence among Seventeenth-Century Quakers* (Cambridge, 1983); Fischer, *Albion's Seed,* 419–603; Horle, *Quakers and the English Legal System.*

138. *PWP,* 3:472.

139. William Penn to Council, 19 Aug. 1685, Gratz Coll., as quoted in Nash, *Quakers and Politics,* 49.

140. *PWP*, 3:394, 542, 565.

141. Ibid., 520, 543; Nash, *Quakers and Politics*, 68–69, 73–76, 130–133.

142. Nash, *Quakers and Politics*, 73, 84; *PWP*, 4:296.

143. Nash, *Quakers and Politics*, 68–69, 73–76, 130–133, 201; *PWP*, 3:276, 520, 543.

144. Edward Armstrong, ed., *Correspondence between William Penn and James Logan, Secretary of the Province of Pennsylvania, and Others*, 2 vols. (Philadelphia, 1870–1872), 1:108 (hereinafter cited as *Penn-Logan Corresp.*). There is considerable evidence of the variety of local Quaker communities in Jack D. Marietta, *The Reformation of American Quakerism, 1748–1783* (Philadelphia, 1984). It is also implicit in Levy's *Quakers and the American Family*. In *Albion's Seed*, Fischer pays no attention to the varieties of Quaker migration and distinctions that developed among local communities in the processes of their settlement and maturation.

145. Nash, *Quakers and Politics*, 67–126; Illick, *Colonial Pennsylvania*, 37–43; Schwartz, "*A Mixed Multitude*," 22–29.

146. Quakers did not have ministers in the accepted sense of the term. They rejected ordination and clerical ceremonies, and the notion of a paid, or "hireling," clergy, and believed that no formal education was required for an individual to become a spiritual leader. Quaker "public Friends"—both men and women—gradually gained a reputation as spokespersons on behalf of the "Inner Light" in their local meetings. Established public Friends kept an eye open for those with such talent and recruited them into ministerial meetings and the powerful monthly, quarterly, and yearly meetings. As they followed their "concern" to attend regional, North American, and overseas meetings to testify to "God's Truth," their reputation usually grew proportionately.

147. Endy, *William Penn and Early Quakerism;* Braithwaite, *Second Period;* Jones, *Later Periods.* For a full-length treatment of Keith, see Ethyn Williams Kirby, *George Keith, 1638–1716* (New York, 1942).

148. Levy, *Quakers and the American Family*, 157–172.

149. The following discussion is largely based on Levy's interpretation, but also see Nash, *Quakers and Politics*, 44–180; Jon Butler, "'Gospel Order Improved': The Keithian Schism and the Exercise of Quaker Ministerial Authority in Pennsylvania," *WMQ*, 3d ser., 31 (1974): 431–452; J. William Frost, *The Keithian Controversy in Early Pennsylvania* (Norwood, Pa., 1979); id., "Unlikely Controversialists: Caleb Pusey and George Keith," *Quaker History* 84 (1975): 2–44; Kirby, *George Keith*.

150. Levy, *Quakers and the American Family*, 58–59.

151. Ibid., 59. Refusing to swear oaths, plain manners of dress and speech, and rejection of many conventional signs of social deference were all habits of behavior that set Quakers apart. Ibid., 59–61. See also Bauman, *Let Your Words Be Few*, passim.

152. Levy, *Quakers and the American Family*, 58–59.

153. Ibid., 157–172.

154. Ibid., 161.

155. Samuel Jennings, *The State of the Case* (London, 1694), as quoted in Levy, *Quakers and the American Family*, 159.

156. Levy, *Quakers and the American Family*, 157–172; Butler, "'Gospel Order Improved,'" 436.

157. "Minutes of the Meeting of Ministers, Philadelphia, 4th Month, 17th day, 1694," as quoted in Frost, *Keithian Controversy*, 53.

158. Frost, *Keithian Controversy*, xiii, as quoted in Levy, *Quakers and the American Family*, 167.

159. Jennings, *State of the Case*, as quoted in Levy, *Quakers and the American Family*, 168.

160. Samuel Smith, "History of the Province of Pennsylvania," in *Register of Pennsylvania*, Samuel Hazard, ed., 6 (1830): 280.

161. Levy, *Quakers and the American Family*, 308n.

162. Nash, *Quakers and Politics*, 150–152.

163. Butler, "'Gospel Order Improved,'" 446–451.

164. Kirby, *George Keith*, 86–87.

165. Butler, "'Gospel Order Improved,'" 452.

166. Cooke, Simcock, Richardson, Fox, Carpenter, and George Murrie to William Penn, 18 Jan. 1694, Parrish Coll., Proud Papers, as quoted in Nash, *Quakers and Politics*, 159.

167. Nash, *Quakers and Politics*, 143–144, 158–159.

168. Levy, *Quakers and the American Family*, 169–172; Nash, *Quakers and Politics*, 153–161.

169. *PWP*, 3:510–511.

170. Nash, *Quakers and Politics*, 182–198; Levy, *Quakers and the American Family*, 173–177; Olson, *Making the Empire Work*, 70–71.

171. *PWP*, 3:393, 443–444, 497–498; 4:25–26, 85–87.

172. Nash, *Quakers and Politics*, 217–236.

Two / The Proving of Popular Power

1. The Carolinas, Pennsylvania, New Jersey, and New York were all proprietaries, as was Maryland from an earlier time. Generally on the period, see Wesley Frank Craven, *The Colonies in Transition, 1660–1713* (New York, 1968).

2. Edmund B. O'Callaghan, *Origin of Legislative Assemblies in the State of New York* (Albany, 1861), 5–11, as quoted in Lovejoy, *Glorious Revolution*, 107.

3. Edmund S. Morgan, *Inventing the People: The Rise of Popular Sovereignty in England and America* (New York, 1988).

4. Ibid., 121–127.

5. Michael Kammen, *Deputies and Liberties: The Origins of Representative Government in Colonial America* (New York, 1969).

6. Morgan, *Inventing the People*, 122–148.

7. The governor's commission granted him "all powers necessary for establishing and maintaining a provincial government" (Labaree, *Royal Government*, 8).

8. *NY Laws*, 1:221.

9. Ibid.

10. The basic organizing unit of representation after 1691 was the county. By 1717 only New York City and County, with four seats each, and Albany City and County with three, exceeded the two representatives (or occasionally one) allotted the other counties. Spencer, *Phases of Royal Government*, 75–78.

11. Evarts B. Greene, *The Provincial Governor in the English Colonies of North America* (New York, 1898), 93; Labaree, *Royal Government*, 477–478; Bailyn, *Origins of American Politics*, 66–70.

12. *NY Votes*, 1:186. See also Labaree, *Royal Government*, 174–175.

13. Labaree, *Royal Government*, 174.

14. Lovejoy, *Glorious Revolution,* 106–114; Voorhees, "'In Behalf of the True Protestants Religion'"; Jennifer L. Jopp, "'Kingly government': English Law in Seventeenth-Century New York" (Ph.D. diss., SUNY, Binghamton, 1992), 173–180; John E. Pomfret, *The Province of East New Jersey, 1609–1702: The Rebellious Proprietary* (Princeton, 1962); id., *The Province of West New Jersey, 1609–1702* (Princeton, 1956); Langdon G. Wright, "Local Government in Colonial New York, 1640–1710" (Ph.D. diss., Cornell University, 1974).

15. In Governor Fletcher's words, New York legislators were frequently "bigg with the priviledges of Englishmen and Magna Charta." *Journal of the Legislative Council of the Colony of New York, 1691–1775,* 2 vols. (Albany, N.Y., 1861), 1:39 (hereinafter cited as *Journal NYLC*).

16. *NY Votes,* 1:145.

17. Stanley M. Pargellis, "The Four Independent Companies of New York," in *Essays in Colonial History Presented to Charles McLean Andrews by His Students* (New Haven, 1931), 96–123.

18. Spencer, *Phases of Royal Government,* 97–128.

19. Pargellis, "Four Independent Companies."

20. Spencer, *Phases of Royal Government,* 97–128; Leamon, "War, Finance, and Faction," 247–277; Charles W. Spencer, "The Cornbury Legend," New York State Historical Association, *Proceedings* 13 (1914): 307–320. The best treatment of how governors milked the military budget is Beverly McAnear, *The Income of the Colonial Governors of British North America* (New York, 1967), 21–25.

21. Leamon, "War, Finance, and Faction," 247–277; Spencer, "Cornbury Legend," 314–315; Dixon Ryan Fox, *Caleb Heathcote, Gentleman Colonist: The Story of a Career in the Province of New York, 1692–1721* (New York, 1926), 11–12, 18–19, 27, 31–32, 71–73; Leder, *Robert Livingston,* passim.

22. Spencer, *Phases of Royal Government,* 113–119; Leamon, "War, Finance, and Faction," 147–151, 169–178, 214–217; *NY Votes,* 1:170–171, 205, 213.

23. Labaree, *Royal Government,* 271–283.

24. *NY Laws,* 1:248–253.

25. Ibid., 517–518; Christenson, "Administration of Land Policy," 237 n. 10.

26. Charles W. Spencer, "The Rise of the Assembly, 1691–1760," in *History of the State of New York,* Alexander C. Flick, ed., 10 vols. (New York, 1933–37), 2:166. For customs corruption under Fletcher, see Friedelbaum, "Bellomont," 76–78.

27. Samuel Mulford, *Speech to the Assembly at New York* (New York, 1713), Evans # 1705.

28. Balmer, *Perfect Babel of Confusion,* 91, 205–206; Robert Quary to Lords of Trade, 28 June 1707, *DRCNY,* 5:19.

29. For an extended treatment of the bloated prerogative powers that royal governors possessed, see Bailyn, *Origins of American Politics,* 66–70.

30. For an elaboration of this argument, see Greene, *Quest for Power;* id., "Political Mimesis."

31. Based on his southern model, Greene's view of this process is that it was a much longer, evolutionary development. See Greene, *Quest for Power* and "The Role of the Lower Houses of Assembly in Eighteenth-Century Politics," in *The Reinterpretation of the American Revolution, 1763–1789,* Jack P. Greene, ed. (New York, 1968), 86–109. Greene's argument that the discourse of seventeenth-century English opposition thought dominated colonial politics through 1763 (id., "Political Mimesis") also derives much of its force from that southern model.

32. Beverly N. Bond, *The Quit-Rent System in the American Colonies* (New Haven, 1919), 254, 258.

33. "Additional Instructions for Lord Lovelace," 20 July 1708, *DRCNY,* 5:54.

34. Board of Trade to Lord Lovelace, 28 June 1708, Ibid., 48; *NY Laws,* 1:412–417, 523–525.

35. Armand S. La Potin, "The Minisink Patent: A Study in Colonial Landholding and the Problems of Settlement in Eighteenth-Century New York" (Ph.D. diss., University of Wisconsin, 1974), 63, 77.

36. *NY Laws,* 1:405–408; *NY Votes,* 1:95–96.

37. *NY Votes,* 1:193, 310, 328; Spencer, *Phases of Royal Government,* 88–89.

38. Spencer, *Phases of Royal Government,* 93.

39. Ibid., 87.

40. Greene, *Provincial Governor,* 122–123.

41. *NY Laws,* 1:478–479, 638–653; *NY Votes,* 1:186.

42. *NY Laws,* 1:698–700.

43. Greene, *Quest for Power,* 297–309.

44. *NY Laws,* 1:584–585, 622–623, 665, 667, 800, 835–838, 998, 999, 1033–1034; *NY Votes,* 1:306; Governor Hunter to Lords of Trade, 11 Sept. 1711, *DRCNY,* 5:263.

45. Governor Hunter to Lords of Trade, 28 Nov. 1710, Council of New York to Lords of Trade, 13 Dec. 1711, *DRCNY,* 5:185, 295; Stanley N. Katz, "The Politics of Law in Colonial America: Controversies over Chancery Courts and Equity Law in the Eighteenth Century," *Perspectives in American History* 5 (1971): 273.

46. Lords of Trade to Secretary St. John, 23 Apr. 1717, Governor Hunter to Lords of Trade, 1 Jan. and 11 July 1712, *DRCNY,* 5:333, 300, 344.

47. Governor Hunter to Lords of Trade, 31 Oct. 1712 and 14 Mar. 1713, *DRCNY,* 5:348, 356–358; *NY Votes,* 1:246, 328.

48. Governor Hunter to Lords of Trade, 12 Sept. 1711, *DRCNY,* 5:255–256, 263.

49. *NY Votes,* 1:224; Spencer, "Sectional Aspects," 408.

50. *NY Votes,* 1:423.

51. Robert Hunter, *To All Whom These Presents May Concern . . .* (New York, 1714), Evans # 1641.

52. Mulford, *Speech.*

53. *The Minutes of the Court of Sessions, 1675–1696, Westchester County, New York,* Dixon Ryan Fox, ed. (New York, 1924), 102.

54. Governor Hunter to Secretary Popple, 18 Oct. 1714, *DRCNY,* 5:381.

55. Kenneth Scott, "The Slave Insurrection in New York in 1712," *NYHSQ* 45 (1961): 43–74.

56. *New-York Weekly Journal,* 23 Sept. 1734.

57. Governor Hunter to Lords of Trade, 14 Mar. 1713, *DRCNY,* 5:356–358.

58. "Representation of Cadwallader Colden . . . ," in *The Letters and Papers of Cadwallader Colden,* 9 vols. [*Colls.* NYHS, vols. 50–58 (New York, 1918–1938)], 8:160–164 (hereinafter cited as *Colden Papers*); Cadwallader Colden, "State of Lands in the Province of New York, in 1732," in *The Documentary History of the State of New York,* Edmund B. O'Callaghan, ed., 4 vols. (Albany, 1849–1851), 1:254 (hereinafter cited as *DHNY*).

59. "Governor Hunter's State of the Quit Rents, with the Attourney-General's Opinion thereon," 30 July 1713; Hunter to Secretary Popple, 7 May 1714, *DRCNY,* 5:370–371, 378.

60. Eugene R. Sheridan, *Lewis Morris, 1671–1746: A Study in Early American Politics* (Syracuse, N.Y., 1981), 101–102.

61. *New-York Weekly Journal,* 24 Sept. 1734.

62. Olson, *Making the Empire Work,* 87–91.

63. *NY Laws,* 1:815–826, 938–991.

64. Sheridan, *Lewis Morris,* 110–112, 118–119.

65. *NY Laws,* 1:847–857, 858–863; Governor Hunter to Lords of Trade, 25 July 1715, *DRCNY,* 5:416–418.

66. "Brigadier Hunter's Observations on Mr. Walpole's Memorial," 18 Aug. 1720, *DRCNY,* 5:558–559.

67. Lewis Morris, Sr., to James Alexander, 29 Mar. 1729, Rutherford Coll., roll 1, New York Historical Society (hereinafter cited as NYHS).

68. For a discussion of patronage, see chapter 8. And see Christenson "Administration of Land Policy," 75–76.

69. Cadwallader Colden to Archibald Kennedy, September 1722, in *Colden Papers,* 8:166–170.

70. Most open criticism of the settlement centered on the Public Debt Acts. There were those who saw in that legislation the old pattern of corruption extended to the assembly and beyond. Governor, councilmen, assemblymen, and many freemen had their noses in the public trough. (Mulford, *Speech;* Governor Hunter to Lords of Trade, 2 Oct. 1716, *DRCNY,* 5:480.) A small group of very prominent anti-Leislerian merchants objected to the second Debt Act, fearful that the paper money the act authorized would erode their prominent economic position. Their political allies were the last holdouts against anything more than an annual revenue act. Hunter to Secretary Popple, 3 Dec. 1717, *DRCNY,* 5:494–495.

71. Peter R. Livingston to Oliver Wendell, 2 Sept. 1765, Livingston Papers, Museum of the City of New York (hereinafter cited as MCNY).

72. Ibid.; *NY Votes,* 1:223–224.

73. "Justice Honeywell's Speech to the Grand Jury of Westchester," 1733 [?], John Chambers Papers, New York State Library, Albany (hereinafter cited as NYSL).

74. Stanley N. Katz, *Newcastle's New York: Anglo-American Politics, 1732–1753* (Cambridge, Mass., 1968), 79–80.

75. See chapter 3.

76. For other perspectives on the political divisions of the 1730s, see chapter 6.

77. Christenson, "Administration of Land Policy," 49–51; Samuel G. Nissenson, "The Development of a Land Registration System in New York," *NY Hist.* 20 (1939): 16–42.

78. Henry Beekman to Gilbert Livingston, 12 Dec. 1741, Beekman Papers, box 1, NYHS; Governor Hunter to Secretary Popple, 7 May 1714, *DRCNY,* 5:378.

79. "Governor Hunter's State of the Quit Rents . . . ," 30 July 1713, *DRCNY,* 5:369–370.

80. As did Deputy Provincial Secretary Goldsbrow Banyar. Banyar to George Clarke, Jr., 20 Jan. 1756, Goldsbrow Banyar Papers, box 1, NYHS.

81. La Potin, "Minisink Patent," 55–56, 76 nn. 23, 24; William Smith, Jr., *The History of the Province of New-York,* Michael Kammen, ed., 2 vols. (Cambridge, Mass., 1972), 1:165; Governor Hunter to Lords of Trade, 14 Mar. 1714, *DRCNY,* 5:356–358.

82. Henry Beekman, for example, stopped paying his quitrents in 1731 because he was not forced to do so. Because of the controversy over chancery in the last days

of Burnet's term, Governor Montgomerie refused to convene the Chancery Court. Beekman to Gilbert Livingston, 12 Dec. 1741, Beekman Papers, box 1, NYHS. Katz, "Politics of Law," 274–276.

83. See chapter 3.

84. *New-York Weekly Journal,* 26 Aug., 29 Apr., and 20 May 1734; Alexander Campbell, *Maxima Libertatas Custodia Est* . . . (New York, 1732), Evans # 3511; Robert Dissolution, *A Letter From a Gentleman in the Country to His Friend in Town* (New York, 1732), Evans # 3514; Andrew Fletcher, *Vincit Amor Patriae Virg* . . . (New York, 1732), Evans # 3540. The assembly's desire for greater protection against executive power was clear in its demands for judicial appointments of "good behavior" and an equity court *only* with legislative approval. George Clarke to the Lords of Trade, 29 May 1736, *DRCNY,* 6:63.

85. Edith M. Fox, *Land Speculation in the Mohawk Country* (Ithaca, N.Y., 1949). When Henry Beekman finally began to resume payments of his quitrents after ten years of negligence, he did so not because Clarke pushed for enforcement but because Whitehall ordered the attorney-general to initiate suits on his own. Beekman to Gilbert Livingston, 12 Dec. 1741, Beekman Papers, box 1, NYHS.

86. *NY Laws,* 2:951–952.

87. Lieutenant-Governor Clarke to Lords of Trade, 2 June 1738, *DRCNY,* 6:119.

88. *NY Laws,* 3:38–50; Lieutenant-Governor Clarke to Lords of Trade, 24 Apr. 1739, *DRCNY,* 6:141–142.

89. *NY Laws,* 3:295–296; Labaree, *Royal Government,* 222, 286–287.

90. Robert E. Ziebarth, "The Role of New York in King George's War, 1739–1748" (Ph.D. diss., New York University, 1972), 37–99.

91. "Points in support of Governor Clinton's Application for certain Allowances," 1743, *DRCNY,* 6:246–247.

92. Governor Clinton to Lords of Trade, 22 June 1747 and 15 Nov. 1748, Governor Shirley to Governor Clinton, 13 Aug. 1748, *DRCNY,* 6:353, 466, 432–437; *New-York Weekly Post-Boy,* 24 Feb. 1746; Serena M. Moody, "A Study in Incompetency: Governor George Clinton and the New York Opposition, 1743–1754" (Ph.D. diss., Ohio State University, 1977), 87, 138.

93. Edward P. Lilly, *The Colonial Agents of New York and New Jersey* (Washington, D.C., 1936), 115–119.

94. "Governor Clinton's Report on the Province of New York," 23 May 1749, *DRCNY,* 6:508.

95. *NY Votes,* 2:174–175.

96. Cadwallader Colden to Archibald Kennedy, 7 Nov. 1756, Colden Papers, Box 11, NYHS; Cadwallader Colden to John Catherwood, 21 Nov. 1749, *Colden Papers,* 4:162; Governor Clinton to Lords of Trade, 10 Nov. 1747, *DRCNY,* 6:411. When King George's War drew to a close, the assembly refused to renew the provincial militia law. From 1748 through 1753, New York had no such act. *NY Laws,* 3:1153–1154.

97. See chapter 4, pp. 130–133. For a discussion of the Indian Commissioners, see Thomas E. Norton, *The Fur Trade in Colonial New York, 1686–1776* (Madison, Wis., 1974), 73–82. On Clinton's estrangement from the commissioners, see Bradshaw, "George Clinton," passim.

98. It is possible to follow something of the crooked course of his rationalizations for, and his diagnosis of, his problems in *DRCNY,* vol. 6.

99. Leonard W. Labaree, *Royal Instructions to British Colonial Governors, 1670–1776,* 2 vols. (New York, 1935), 1:190–193; Smith, *History of New-York,* 2:139.

100. Smith, *History of New-York*, 2:133–137.

101. Charles Hardy was governor from September 1755 until July 1757, but DeLancey had considerable influence with him. Ibid., 191–213.

102. Labaree, *Royal Instructions*, 1:194.

103. Quoted in Spencer, "Rise of the Assembly," 194.

104. Ibid., 193.

105. Goldsbrow Banyar to George Clarke, Jr., 1 Nov. 1753, Goldsbrow Banyar Papers, box 1, NYHS; Lieutenant-Governor DeLancey to Lords of Trade, 3 June 1757; and chapter 4, pp. 127–133.

106. La Potin, "Minisink Patent," 59; Christenson, "Administration of Land Policy," 86.

107. *NY Laws*, 1:633–636.

108. Ibid., 882, 1006–1007; 2:329–337; "Mr Colden's Memorial against the Act for the Partition of Lands held in Common," 24 Dec. 1726, *DRCNY*, 5:807–809.

109. Henry Beekman to Gilbert Livingston, 12 Dec. 1741, Beekman Papers, box 1, NYHS.

110. *NY Laws*, 3:209–222, 400–402.

111. Cadwallader Colden to Mrs. Colden, 14 Oct. 1753, *Colden Papers*, 4:407.

112. *NY Laws*, 3:1107–1121.

113. In requesting the legislature to annul the three patents against which the Iroquois had long protested, Hardy was following the orders of the Board of Trade (Lords of Trade to Governor Hardy, 19 Mar. 1756, *DRCNY*, 7:77). DeLancey played a double game on the issue of the patents. In 1754, he was prepared to push for the annulment of the Kayaderosseros Patent because that would be a blow against a number of his Livingston critics and because it was a way of building bridges between himself and Sir William Johnson. But there is no question that once the issue became broader and other patents came into question, DeLancey sided with "the wealthiest, and most leading men in this Province," as Sir William Johnson described those in the forefront of opposition against a more general vacating act. Lieutenant-Governor DeLancey to Lords of Trade, 22 July 1754, Sir William Johnson to Lords of Trade, 10 Sept. 1756, *DRCNY*, 6:850, 7:129; Smith, *History of New-York*, 2:205.

114. Katz, "Politics of Law," 273–274. For a glimpse of other elements of the DeLancey legislative settlement, see *NY Laws*, 3:1153–1154 [Militia Act]; Lieutenant-Governor James DeLancey to Lords of Trade, 3 Jan., 22 Apr., 21 May, 8 Oct., 15 Dec. 1754, and 31 Jan., 18 Mar. 1755, *DRCNY*, 6:820–821, 834, 838, 908–909, 929, 937, 940–941.

115. Governor Hardy to Lords of Trade, 2 Dec. 1756, *DRCNY*, 7:202–203.

116. See chapter 5, pp. 167–169.

117. For the continuing strength of the assembly, see, e.g., Governor Moore to Lords of Trade, and id. to the earl of Shelburne, 14 Jan., 21 Feb. 1767, *DRCNY*, 8:891, 906.

118. *CR*, 2:35.

119. Under the 1683 Frame of Government, the council's election of sheriffs and coroners was not to take place until after Penn's death.

120. For a copy of the Charter of Privileges, see *CR*, 2:56–60.

121. *Pa. Votes*, 1:393–401; *The Statutes-at-Large of Pennsylvania from 1682–1801*, James T. Mitchell and Henry Flanders, eds., 15 vols. (Harrisburg, Pa., 1896–1911), 2:148–159 (hereinafter cited as *Pa. Statutes*).

122. Roy N. Lokken, *David Lloyd, Colonial Lawmaker* (Seattle, 1959), 103–107; Winfred T. Root, *The Relations of Pennsylvania with the British Government, 1696–1765* (Philadelphia, 1912), 159–162.

123. *CR,* 2:59.

124. Lokken, *David Lloyd,* 18–123.

125. Quoted in Sister Joan de Lourdes Leonard, "The Organization and Procedure of the Pennsylvania Assembly, 1682–1776," *PMHB* 72 (1948): 238; see also pp. 236–238; *Pa. Votes,* 1:403–406, 416.

126. Sister Joan, "Organization and Procedure," 225–238; *Pa. Votes,* 2:467, 503, 782–783, 3:1095–1096; *Pa. Statutes,* 2:137–140, 212–221, 272–275. When the assembly began printing its minutes in 1718, it gained control of the government printer. *Pa. Votes,* 3:1258, 1291.

127. See chapter 7.

128. Lokken, *David Lloyd,* 139–140; *Pa Votes,* 1:415, 417–418, 467, 571–572, 2:802.

129. Lokken, *David Lloyd,* 98–101, 109–115, 179; Nash, *Quakers and Politics,* 215–217, 227–229; *Pa. Votes,* 1:433.

130. Lokken, *David Lloyd,* 113.

131. Ibid., 143.

132. Fifty-three of the 105 acts. *Pa. Statutes,* 3:449–456.

133. *CR,* 2:312.

134. Ibid., 310–311.

135. Ibid., 302–304; Lokken, *David Lloyd,* 167–168.

136. *Pa. Statutes,* 2:500–506; Lokken, *David Lloyd,* 177–181.

137. Lokken, *David Lloyd,* 85.

138. *Penn-Logan Corresp.,* 1:223n, 2:4–5.

139. Nash, *Quakers and Politics,* 191.

140. Lokken, *David Lloyd,* 135–136.

141. *Penn-Logan Corresp.,* 1:247–248.

142. *CR,* 2:35.

143. Ibid.

144. Ibid. My emphasis.

145. Lokken, *David Lloyd,* 136–144.

146. Nash, *Quakers and Politics,* 216.

147. "Overplus" land was that included within an original survey or patent in excess of the amount actually purchased.

148. Nash, *Quakers and Politics,* 254–255.

149. *Pa. Votes,* 1:433; Lokken, *David Lloyd,* 147.

150. *CR,* 2:293.

151. *PWP,* 4:221, 262–265.

152. Ibid., 295–304.

153. Ibid., 369.

154. Ibid., 373–384, 399.

155. Ibid., 394; Lokken, *David Lloyd,* 116; Nash, *Quakers and Politics,* 268.

156. Lokken, *David Lloyd,* 86–87.

157. *Penn-Logan Corresp.,* 1:18.

158. Turner to Penn, Dreer Coll., as quoted in Nash, *Quakers and Politics,* 143; *PWP,* 4:342; *Penn-Logan Corresp.,* 2:337.

159. *PWP,* 4:304–306.

160. Nash, *Quakers and Politics*, 258–259.

161. Issac Norris, Sr., to Thomas Lloyd, Jr., 29 Dec. 1699, Norris Letter Book (1699–1701), as quoted in Nash, *Quakers and Politics*, 213.

162. Frederick B. Tolles, *James Logan and the Culture of Provincial America* (Boston, 1957), 60–75.

163. Lokken, *David Lloyd*, 180–186; Nash, *Quakers and Politics*, 269–273.

164. Nash, *Quakers and Politics*, 182–224, 295–299.

165. *Penn-Logan Corresp.*, 1:65.

166. Deborah M. Gough, "Pluralism, Politics, and Power Struggles: The Church of England in Colonial Philadelphia, 1695–1789" (Ph.D. diss., University of Pennsylvania, 1978), 25–72; Nash, *Quakers and Politics*, 182–198, 206–207, 248–250.

167. Lokken, *David Lloyd*, 80–83.

168. Nash, *Quakers and Politics*, 295–299.

169. Lokken, *David Lloyd*, 84–85.

170. Ibid., 220–221; *Pa. Votes*, 1:433–434.

171. Lokken, *David Lloyd*, 122; *Pa. Votes*, 1:434.

172. See, e.g., *CR*, 2:575.

173. Lokken, *David Lloyd*, 194; Charles P. Keith, *Chronicles of Pennsylvania from the English Revolution to the Peace of Aix-la-Chapelle, 1688–1748* (Philadelphia, 1917), 575–576, 686.

174. Lokken, *David Lloyd*, 57.

175. *CR*, 2:231–232.

176. Ibid., 518, 559–560, 594.

177. Court clerks remained proprietary appointees; public house licensing stayed with the governor; JP's were appointed and removed at executive discretion.

178. *Pa. Statutes*, 2:301–333, 3:14–21, 33–37, 65–83, 298–308, 4:84–85, 229–230.

179. Ibid., 2:355–357, 425–427, 3:39–40, 58–60, 427–431.

180. Ibid., 2:349–385, 400–409, 3:53–57.

181. Ibid., 3:175–191, 295–297, 4:10–26.

182. Ibid., 2:414–421.

183. Ibid., 4:131–134. Between 1704, when the three Lower Counties withdrew from the union, and 1729, the Pennsylvania Assembly consisted of eight representatives from each of Bucks, Philadelphia, and Chester counties and two representatives from Philadelphia City. With its creation in 1729, Lancaster County gained four seats in the house.

184. Ibid., 5:728–29; Thomas Penn to James Hamilton, 18 Oct. 1760, Penn-Hamilton Corresp., HSP.

185. *Pa. Statutes*, 2:109–113.

186. Ibid., 280–291.

187. *CR*, 2:412, 433–434, 438, 442, 453.

188. *Pa Statutes*, 2:373–385, 3:83–95, 112–117, 121, 4:159; *Pa. Votes*, 2:798–801, 806, 975, 1038, 1043, 1099, 1109, 1290–1291.

189. *Pa. Votes*, 3:1042–43, 1172.

190. Mary M. Schweitzer, *Custom and Contract: Household, Government, and the Economy in Colonial Pennsylvania* (New York, 1987), 115–168.

191. Alan Tully, "Quaker Party and Proprietary Policies: The Dynamics of Politics in Pre-Revolutionary Pennsylvania, 1730–1776," in *Power and Status: Officeholding in Colonial America*, Bruce C. Daniels, ed. (Middletown, Conn., 1986),

85; James H. Hutson, *Pennsylvania Politics, 1746–1770: The Movement for Royal Government and Its Consequences* (Princeton, 1972), 6–12; id., "Benjamin Franklin and Pennsylvania Politics, 1751–1755: A Reappraisal," *PMHB* 93 (1969): 322.

192. Sister Joan, "Organization and Procedure," 230.

193. Katz, "Politics of Law," 266–270; Alan Tully, *William Penn's Legacy: Politics and Social Structure in Provincial Pennsylvania, 1726–1755* (Baltimore, 1977), 18–19, 34.

194. George Thomas to Board of Trade, 20 Oct. 1740, *Pa. Statutes*, 4:475; Tully, *William Penn's Legacy,* 128–129.

195. Keith, *Chronicles,* 733; Mabel P. Wolff, *The Colonial Agency of Pennsylvania, 1712–1757* (Philadelphia, 1933), 77–116; *Pa. Statutes*, 5:111–128.

196. Tully, *William Penn's Legacy,* 23–32.

197. Richard Peters to Proprietors, 29 Apr. 1749, Penn Misc. Papers, Penn v. Baltimore, 1740–1756, HSP.

198. Governor Thomas to Ferdinand John Paris, 14 May 1741, Penn Papers, Official Correspondence (hereinafter cited as PPOC), HSP.

199. Tully, *William Penn's Legacy,* 8–15, 19–20.

200. Tully, "Quaker Party and Proprietary Policies," 94–95.

201. Governor Thomas to John Penn, 5 Nov. 1739, PPOC, HSP.

202. Tully, *William Penn's Legacy,* 37–43.

203. Richard Peters to Thomas Penn, 30 Jan. 1751, PPOC, HSP.

204. Richard Peters to Thomas Penn, 4 Feb. 1751, James Hamilton to Thomas Penn, 22 Feb. 1751, PPOC, HSP. See also Edward Shippen to Dr. Richard Shackleton, 27 Mar. 1754, Edward Shippen to William Shippen, 29 Mar. 1754, Edward Shippen Letter Books, American Philosophical Society (hereinafter cited as APS).

205. Thomas Penn to James Hamilton, 31 July 1749, Penn-Hamilton Corresp., HSP.

206. James Hamilton to Thomas Penn, 24 Sept. 1750, PPOC, HSP.

207. James Hamilton to Thomas Penn, 18 Mar. 1752, PPOC, HSP.

208. Tully, *William Penn's Legacy,* 131–133.

209. *Pa. Votes,* 2:1620–1671.

210. See, e.g., Root, *Relations of Pennsylvania,* 193–195.

211. The most complete description of Penn's policies is Hutson, "Benjamin Franklin and Pennsylvania Politics," 303–371.

212. Hutson, *Pennsylvania Politics,* 10n.

213. Tully, "Quaker Party and Proprietary Policies," 98.

214. Ibid., 99.

215. *CR,* 7:401.

216. *Pa. Votes,* 5:4340.

217. Hutson, *Pennsylvania Politics,* 114–117.

218. Isaac Norris, Jr., to Robert Charles, 7 Oct. 1754, Isaac Norris Letter Book, 1719–1756 (hereinafter cited as INLB), HSP.

219. *Pa. Votes,* 6:4499; *Pennsylvania Gazette,* 18 Dec. 1755.

220. Nicholas B. Wainwright, "Governor William Denny in Pennsylvania," *PMHB* 81 (1957): 170–198. Although see the editors' reservations in Leonard W. Labaree et al., eds., *The Papers of Benjamin Franklin,* 30 vols. to date (New Haven, 1959–), 8:327n, 419n, 420n (hereinafter cited as *PBF*); *Pa. Statutes*, 5:396–466.

221. Benjamin H. Newcomb, *Franklin and Galloway: A Political Partnership* (New Haven, 1972), 60–63.

222. *Pa. Statutes*, 5:697–737; Hutson, *Pennsylvania Politics,* 59–61.

223. John Watts to Robert Monckton, 11 Sept. 1760, *Aspinwall Papers,* 2 vols. (Massachusetts Historical Society, *Collections,* 4th ser., vols. 9–10 [Boston, 1870–71]), 2:320 (hereinafter cited as *Aspinwall Papers*).

224. See chapter 5.

225. Early Pennsylvania Quakers had always harbored ambivalent attitudes toward the Crown. On the one hand, while in England, they had often looked to the Crown for protection from persecution; on the other, they maintained that "the King has nothing more to do here [in Pennsylvania] than to receive a bear skin or two yearly" (Robert Suder to the governor, 20 Nov. 1698, *Historical Collections Relating to the American Colonial Church,* William S. Perry, ed., 5 vols. [Hartford, Conn., 1971] 2:11). The political power their progeny came to wield in Pennsylvania and their preoccupation with an intransigent Thomas Penn gradually dimmed their collective memory of the arbitrary ways of English royalty and distracted them from recent unsettling experiences neighboring royal colonies had suffered at the hands of the British.

226. Lynford Lardner to Richard Penn, 7 Mar. 1758, Lynford Lardner Papers, HSP; *Pa. Statutes,* 5:320–330; Thomas Penn to James Hamilton, 24 May 1760, Bancroft Transcripts, New York Public Library (hereinafter cited as NYPL); Thomas Penn to James Hamilton, 15 Nov. 1760, 25 Apr. 1762, Penn-Hamilton Corresp., HSP.

227. But note various characteristics of the Quaker regime, described in subsequent chapters, that created some important, long-term political weaknesses irrespective of the institutional strength of the assembly.

228. Cf. Greene, *Quest for Power.*

229. See, e.g., Peter R. Livingston to Oliver Wendell, 2 Sept. 1765, Livingston Papers, MCNY; John Morton to Joseph Pennock, Sr., 23 June 1764, Misc. MSS, Chester County Historical Society; Israel Pemberton, Jr., to David Barclay, 6 Nov. 1764, Pemberton Papers, HSP.

230. Greene, "Political Mimesis"; Bailyn, *Origins of American Politics.* But note how the assemblies' early achievement of considerable political power reduced the salience of both the seventeenth-century English opposition and radical Whig paradigms for New York and Pennsylvania during the second and third quarters of the eighteenth century. For further elaboration, see chapters 6, 7, and 10.

231. Alison G. Olson, "Eighteenth-Century Colonial Legislatures and Their Constituents," *JAH* 79 (1992): 550, 552.

232. Alison G. Olson, "The 'Rise' of Three Colonial Legislatures in the Eighteenth Century: Virginia, Massachusetts and Pennsylvania," MS version of "Eighteenth-Century Colonial Legislatures," p. 38.

233. Ibid.

234. *NY Votes,* 1:792; Lewis Evans, "A Brief Account of Pennsylvania . . . " (MS), HSP.

235. *NY Votes,* 1:792.

236. Sister Joan, "Organization and Procedure," 219.

237. Labaree, *Royal Government,* 223.

238. Elmer B. Russell, *The Review of American Colonial Legislation by the King-in-Council* (New York, 1915), 208.

239. Root, *Relations of Pennsylvania,* 134–148.

240. *New-York Weekly Journal,* 8 Aug. 1737.

241. George Clarke to Mr. Walpole, 24 Nov. 1725, *DRCNY,* 5:769. See more generally chapter 8.

242. See chapter 6.

243. Tully, *William Penn's Legacy,* 110; Clair W. Keller, "The Pennsylvania County Commission System, 1712–1740," *PMHB* 93 (1969): 381–382; Rosemary S. Warden, "The Revolution in Political Leadership in Chester County, Pennsylvania, 1765–1785" (Ph.D. diss., Syracuse University, 1979), 42–43. There was, of course, some initial enthusiasm for election as an officer in the voluntary militias of 1747–48 and 1756. *PBF,* 3:180–188, 308–309; 8:passim.

244. See, e.g., proprietary negotiations with John Kinsey. Richard Peters to Proprietors, 14 Mar., 23 Apr., 4 June 1743, Richard Peters Letter Books (hereinafter cited as RPLB), HSP. Once appointed as attorney-general and then chief justice, however, Kinsey pretty much went his own way. On Kinsey, see Tully, *William Penn's Legacy,* 97–98, and Edwin B. Bronner, "The Disgrace of John Kinsey, Quaker Politician, 1739–1750," *PMHB* 75 (1951): 400–415.

245. Mary Patterson Clarke, *Parliamentary Privilege in the American Colonies* (New Haven, 1943), 15, 17–21, 35–36, 43, 55, 58–59; David W. Jordan, *Foundations of Representative Government in Maryland, 1632–1715* (Cambridge, 1987), passim; Olson, "Eighteenth-Century Colonial Legislatures," 546–547.

246. Clarke, *Parliamentary Privilege,* 58–59.

247. Patricia U. Bonomi, *A Factious People: Politics and Society in Colonial New York* (New York, 1971), 267–275.

248. Lokken, *David Lloyd,* 234. The term "general Inquisitor" was also used. *CR,* 2:375, 377.

249. Clarke, *Parliamentary Privilege,* 57.

Three / The Pursuit of Popular Rights

1. John Phillip Reid, *Constitutional History of the American Revolution: The Authority of Rights* (Madison, Wis., 1986), 5.

2. Morgan, *Inventing the People.*

3. *NY Votes,* 1:186; Governor Hunter to Lords of Trade, 12 Sept. 1711, *DRCNY,* 5:255–256; Isaac Norris, Sr., *The Speech Delivered from the Bench . . .* (Philadelphia, 1727), Evans # 2937. Note the opinion of Richard West, counsel to the Board of Trade: "Let an Englishman go where he will, he carries as much of law and liberty with him, as the nature of things will bear." *Opinions of Emminent Lawyers on Various Points of English Jurisprudence,* collected by George Chalmers, 2 vols. (London, 1814), 1:195.

4. *New-York Weekly Journal,* 30 May 1737; *Pa. Votes,* 1:406.

5. *Pa. Votes,* 2:1631.

6. "Speech of Vincent Matthews . . . October 21, 1735," *Colden Papers,* 8:227.

7. *New-York Weekly Journal,* 13 Feb. 1736.

8. *NY Votes,* 1:188. As Pennsylvanians put it, the "Rights and freedoms of England, (the best and Largest in Europe) shall be in force here." *CR,* 2:344.

9. Reid, *Constitutional History,* 50, 135; Morgan, *Inventing the People,* 52. As Cadwallader Colden expressed the sentiment, there was an *"inalienable Righ[t] of the People to Defend themselves against their Destroyers."* "History of Governor William Cosby's Administration and of Lieutenant-Governor George Clarke's Administration through 1737," *Colden Papers,* 9:343.

10. For representation, see *New-York Weekly Journal,* 30 May 1737; for redress of grievances, see *Pa. Votes,* 6:4838, 4855; for freedom to petition, see *New-York Weekly Post-Boy,* 17 Feb. 1746; for no taxation without representation, see Horace Wemyss Smith, *Life and Correspondence of Rev. William Smith, D.D.,* 2 vols. (Philadelphia,

1879–1880), 1:190; for trial by jury, see *American Weekly Mercury,* 9 Aug. 1733; for habeas corpus, see Milton Cantor, "The Writ of Habeas Corpus: Early American Origins and Development," in *Freedom and Reform: Essays in Honor of H. S. Commager,* H. M. Hyman and Leonard W. Levy, eds. (New York, 1967), 55–77; for due process, see *NY Votes,* 1:566. On the right to security of property, see also Sons of Liberty to ? 14 Feb. 1766, New York Misc. MSS, Box 8, NYHS; on the right against excessive bail, Katz, "Politics of Law," 243n; on the "natif wright of voteing," *Journal NYLC,* 1:169; on the right to an independent judiciary, *Pa. Votes,* 6:4540; on the right of "Writing and Preaching," Horace Wemyss Smith, *Life of . . . William Smith,* 1:184; and on the right to trial in the venue of the alleged crime, *DHNY,* 1:719.

11. *CR,* 6:221; *Pa. Votes,* 5:3803. In James H. Hutson's words "the eighteenth century was a period . . . in which the public's penchant for asserting its rights outran its ability to analyze them and to reach a consensus about their scope and meaning." Hutson, "The Bill of Rights and the American Revolutionary Experience," in *A Culture of Rights: The Bill of Rights in Philosophy, Politics, and Law—1791 and 1991,* Michael J. Lacey and Knud Haakonssen, eds. (Cambridge, 1991), 63. Also of relevance in this collection is Knud Haakonssen, "From Natural Law to the Rights of Man: A European Perspective on American Debates," 19–61.

12. See chapters 1, 2, and 7.

13. Lewis Morris, Jr., to Lords of Trade, 19 July 1729, *DRCNY,* 5:887.

14. Lewis Morris, Sr., to Lords of Trade, 27 Aug. 1733, "Articles of Complaint against Governor Cosby by Rip Van Dam, Esq.," 17 Dec. 1733, *DRCNY,* 5:953, 978.

15. James Alexander, *A Brief Narrative of the Case and Trial of John Peter Zenger, Printer of the New York Weekly Journal,* Stanley Nider Katz, ed. (Cambridge, Mass., 1963), 3–4.

16. On Morris's New York career, see Sheridan, *Lewis Morris,* 91–180.

17. Governor Cosby to the duke of Newcastle, 3 May 1733, *DRCNY,* 5:949. From 1702 to 1738 New York and New Jersey shared royal governors.

18. "Reasons of Governor Cosby for removing Chief Justice Morris," 19 June 1734, *DRCNY,* 6:11.

19. Sheridan, *Lewis Morris,* 150–152.

20. Smith, *History of New-York,* 2:26.

21. Katz, *Newcastle's New York,* 23–24.

22. Lewis Morris, Esq., to Lords of Trade, 27 Aug. 1733, *DRCNY,* 5:951–955.

23. Katz, *Newcastle's New York,* 101–107.

24. Sheridan, *Lewis Morris,* 155–157.

25. Ibid., 157.

26. Katz, *Newcastle's New York,* 92–95.

27. Smith, *History of New-York,* 1:166, 169; Joseph H. Smith, "Adolphe Philipse and the Chancery Court Resolves of 1727," in *Court and Law in Early New York: Selected Essays,* Leo Hershkowitz and Milton M. Klein, eds. (Port Washington, N.Y., 1978), 30–45, 129–134; Norton, *Fur Trade,* 35–147; and chapter 6, pp. 233–234.

28. For the dispute over the equivalent lands, see Fox, *Land Speculation,* 16–27; Cadwallader Colden, "History of Governor William Cosby's Administration . . . ," *Colden Papers,* 9:305–312; Joseph H. Smith and Leo Hershkowitz, "Courts of Equity in the Province of New York: The Cosby Controversy, 1732–1736," *American Journal of Legal History* 16 (1972): 41–46.

29. For a list of investors, see "Leger of Accounts concerning Equivalent Lands begun 1732" (MS), NYHS.

30. Cadwallader Colden, "History of Governor William Cosby's Administration . . . ," *Colden Papers,* 9:308.

31. Ibid., 305; *New-York Weekly Journal,* 27 Oct. 1735; Vincent Buranelli, "Governor Cosby's Hatchet-Man," *NY Hist.* 54 (1956): 26–39.

32. Cadwallader Colden, "History of Governor William Cosby's Administration . . . ," *Colden Papers,* 9:305. Although Colden was one of those with shares, his relationship with Alexander, William Smith, Jr., and the Morrises was equivocal during much of this time. Wayne Bodle, "'To Join with Some Countryman': Cadwallader Colden and the Politics of Survival in Cosby's New York" (unpublished paper). The equivalent-lands suit died along with Cosby in 1736. Smith and Hershkowitz, "Courts of Equity," 46.

33. Cadwallader Colden, "History of Governor William Cosby's Administration . . . ," *Colden Papers,* 9:305, 306.

34. *NY Votes,* 1:682.

35. Ibid., 687. As speaker, Philipse appointed the committee.

36. James Alexander to Ferdinand John Paris, 19 Mar. 1733, Rutherford Coll., roll 1, NYHS.

37. "Articles of Complaint against Governor Cosby by Rip Van Dam, Esq.," 17 Dec. 1733, *DRCNY,* 5:975–978; "Speech of Vincent Matthews . . . on October 21, 1735," *Colden Papers,* 8:226–240.

38. Alexander, *Brief Narrative,* Katz, ed., 110.

39. Lewis Morris, Jr., to Cadwallader Colden, 17 Jan. 1734, *Colden Papers,* 2:101.

40. Alexander, *Brief Narrative,* Katz, ed., 117–138; "Articles of Complaint against Governor Cosby by Rip Van Dam, Esq.," *DRCNY,* 5:975–978; "Speech of Vincent Matthews . . . October 21, 1735," *Colden Papers,* 8:226–240.

41. David S. Shields, *Oracles of Empire: Poetry, Politics, and Commerce in British America, 1690–1750* (Chicago, 1990), 154–172.

42. Cadwallader Colden, "History of Governor William Cosby's Administration . . . ," *Colden Papers,* 9:319.

43. Leonard W. Levy, *Emergence of a Free Press* (New York, 1985), 29, 32, 48.

44. The following two paragraphs are based on Levy, *Emergence of a Free Press,* and Alexander, *Brief Narrative,* Katz, ed., 1–35.

45. Alexander, *Brief Narrative,* Katz, ed., 17–19.

46. Katz, *Newcastle's New York,* 166, 207–212.

47. Cadwallader Colden, "History of Governor William Cosby's Administration . . . ," *Colden Papers,* 9:344.

48. Ibid., 343–344; Alexander, *Brief Narrative,* Katz, ed., 17–18, 146–147.

49. Cadwallader Colden, "History of Governor William Cosby's Administration . . . ," *Colden Papers,* 9:323.

50. Alexander, *Brief Narrative,* Katz, ed., 56. DeLancey clearly anticipated no need for a packed jury. He expected to decide the law on the issue, and the only matter to be left to the jury would be the question of whether or not Zenger had published the offensive material. And that was easily demonstrated.

51. Ibid., 53. The suspension lasted for two years, a circumstance that caused some lasting bitterness on the part of Smith and his son William, Jr.

52. Ibid., 19–21, 52–56.

53. Smith, *History of New-York,* 2:19–20.

54. Alexander, *Brief Narrative,* Katz, ed., 61.

55. Ibid., 61–101.

56. Ibid., 78.

57. For a different view of the turning point of the trial, see Ellen M. James, "Decoding the Zenger Trial: Andrew Hamilton's 'Fraudful Dexterity' with Language," in *The Law in America, 1607–1861,* William Pencak and Wythe W. Holt, Jr., eds. (New York, 1989), 1–27.

58. Alexander, *Brief Narrative,* Katz, ed., 91–94.

59. Ibid., 86, 67.

60. Ibid., 84.

61. Ibid., 87.

62. Ibid., 99.

63. Ibid., 101.

64. Leonard W. Levy, "Did the Zenger Case Really Matter?" *WMQ,* 3d ser., 17 (1960): 35–50; id., *Emergence of a Free Press,* 124–134; Morris D. Forkosch, "Zenger versus Croswell and the Rule of Law," in *Law in America,* Pencak and Holt, eds., 28–72; and, for the older view, Alexander, *Brief Narrative,* Katz, ed., 1.

65. Alexander, *Brief Narrative,* Katz, ed., 1.

66. Stephen Botein, "'Meer Mechanics' and an Open Press: The Business and Political Strategies of Colonial American Printers," *Perspectives in American History* 9 (1975): 127–228.

67. Id., *"Mr. Zenger's Malice and Falshood:" Six Issues of the New York Weekly Journal, 1733–34* (Worcester, Mass., 1985), 6.

68. Levy, *Emergence of a Free Press,* 89–143. The other notion of freedom of the press that had some currency was that printers should publish various opinions on controversial issues. But colonial printers "deliberately" did not open their pages "wide enough to allow a full range of controversial matter into the public forum." Botein, "'Meer Mechanics,'" 191, as quoted in Levy, *Emergence of a Free Press,* 86. According to Levy, the colonial press was "dull and docile" compared to that of London. Ibid., 87.

69. Ibid., 112, 117–118.

70. "The reformation of the law of libel and the associated unshackling of the press came about, when it did, as if Peter Zenger had never existed." Alexander, *Brief Narrative,* Katz, ed., 1–2. See also Forkosch, "Zenger versus Croswell," and Levy, *Emergence of a Free Press,* 173–349.

71. Levy, *Emergence of a Free Press,* 63–64; Botein, "'Meer Mechanics.'"

72. See also Alexander, *Brief Narrative,* Katz, ed., 33–35. In *A Distant Heritage: The Growth of Free Speech in Early America* (New York, 1993), Larry D. Eldridge explores the seventeenth-century colonial basis for this popular prejudice in behalf of the freedom to criticize government.

73. *PWP,* 2:143.

74. *CR,* 2:57.

75. For a full-length treatment of the subject, see J. William Frost, *A Perfect Freedom: Religious Liberty in Pennsylvania* (Cambridge, 1990).

76. *CR,* 2:57.

77. Ibid., 7:404.

78. Fischer, *Albion's Seed,* 459; Schwartz, *"Mixed Multitude,"* 152–153.

79. "An Early Description of Pennsylvania: A Letter of Christopher Sower . . . ," R. W. Kelsey, ed. and trans., *PMHB* 45 (1921): 249.

80. Lawrence H. Leder, *Liberty and Authority: Early American Political Ideology, 1689–1763* (Chicago, 1968), 69; *Pennsylvania Journal, or Weekly Advertiser,* 21 Mar. 1744; *Pennsylvania Gazette,* 19 Jan. 1748.

81. Frost, *Perfect Freedom,* 14.

82. Schwartz, *"Mixed Multitude,"* 12–35.

83. Preface to the Frame of Government of 1682, *Pa. Votes,* 1:xlvii. For elaboration on this point, see Frost, *Perfect Freedom,* 10–28.

84. For discussions of the early peace testimony, see Schwartz, *"Mixed Multitude,"* 46–49; Frost, *Perfect Freedom,* 29–32; Hermann Wellenreuther, "The Political Dilemma of the Quakers in Pennsylvania, 1681–1748," *PMHB* 94 (1970): 135–172; Alan Tully, "Politics and Peace Testimony in Mid-Eighteenth-Century Pennsylvania," *Canadian Review of American Studies* 13 (1982): 159–177.

85. *CR,* 2:79.

86. Samuel Chew, *The Speech of Samuel Chew, Esq.,* . . . (Philadelphia, 1742), Evans # 4930.

87. *PWP,* 4:335.

88. *PBF,* 3:180–204.

89. Tully, "Politics and Peace Testimony," 176 n. 19; Chew, *Speech*; Samuel Chew, *The Speech of Samuel Chew, Esq.,* . . . (Philadelphia, 1741), Evans # 4708; William Currie, *A Treatise on the Lawfulness of Defensive War* . . . (Philadelphia, 1948), Evans # 6120; Benjamin Gilbert, *Truth Vindicated, and the Doctrinnes of Darkness Manifested* . . . (Philadelphia, 1748), Evans # 6148. The same refrains continued with the outbreak of war in 1755. For example, *Pa. Votes,* 5:4115, 4152; Gilbert Tennent, *The Happiness of Rewarding the Enemies of Our Religion* . . . (Philadelphia, 1756), Evans # 7798.

90. *PBF,* 4:475–476.

91. Ibid., 120, 234, 477–486, 5:158–160; Alan Tully, "Englishmen and Germans: National-Group Contact in Colonial Pennsylvania," *Pa. Hist.* 45 (1978): 237–256.

92. William Sturgeon to the archbishop of Canterbury, 29 Nov. 1758, in *Historical Collections,* Perry, ed., 2:269.

93. Grace Galloway Poetry Book, Galloway Collection, Library of Congress, as quoted in Bruce R. Lively, "The Speaker and His House: The Impact of Joseph Galloway upon the Pennsylvania Assembly, 1755–1776" (Ph.D. diss., University of Southern California, 1975), 111.

94. William Smith, *A Brief State of the Province of Pennsylvania* (London, 1755), 9.

95. Ibid., 19.

96. Ibid., 25, 15, 13.

97. Ibid., 35, 36–37.

98. Ibid., 40, 29.

99. Ibid., 20.

100. Ibid., 35, 37.

101. Ibid., 42.

102. Ibid., 40.

103. *PBF,* 5:18–21, 158–160.

104. Smith, *Brief State,* 40–42.

105. William Smith, *A Brief View of the Conduct of Pennsylvania for the Year 1755* (London, 1756).

106. Henton Brown to James Pemberton, 11 July 1755, Pemberton Papers, HSP.

107. Report of the Board of Trade on the Pennsylvania Petition, Colonial Office, 5/1295, fols. 197–211, as quoted in Wolff, *Colonial Agency,* 180.

108. Wolff, *Colonial Agency,* 178n.

109. Alison G. Olson, "The Lobbying of London Quakers for Pennsylvania Friends," *PMHB* 117 (1993): 131–152; id., *Making the Empire Work,* 94–125, 134–173; Marietta, *Reformation,* 142–144, 158–161.

110. For background on the dissenting deputies, see N. C. Hunt, *Two Early*

Political Associations: The Quakers and the Dissenting Deputies in the Age of Sir Robert Walpole (Oxford, 1961), and Alison G. Olson, "The Eighteenth-Century Empire: The London Dissenters' Lobbies and the American Colonies," *Journal of American Studies* 26 (1992): 41–58.

111. Ibid., 160; Wolff, *Colonial Agency,* 180–181, 187.

112. Penn Papers, acts of Parliament, orders in council, etc., as quoted in Wolff, *Colonial Agency,* 180.

113. Ferdinand John Paris to William Allen, 14 Feb. 1756, PPOC, HSP.

114. Wolff, *Colonial Agency,* 188–189; Marietta, *Reformation,* 161.

115. John Fothergill to Israel Pemberton, 3 Apr. 1756, Pemberton Papers, Etting Collection, as quoted in Marietta, *Reformation,* 161.

116. Marietta, *Reformation,* 164–165.

117. William Smith to Thomas Penn, 1 May 1755, PPOC, HSP.

118. Wolff, *Colonial Agency,* 172; Israel Pemberton to John Fothergill, 19 May 1755, *PBF,* 6:53.

119. *Pa. Votes,* 5:4137.

120. Israel Pemberton to John Fothergill, 19 May 1755, *PBF,* 6:55.

121. *Pa. Votes,* 5:4116–4117; Don R. Byrnes, "The Pre-Revolutionary Career of Provost William Smith, 1751–1780" (Ph.D. diss., Tulane University, 1969), 70.

122. Israel Pemberton to John Fothergill, 19 May 1755, *PBF,* 6:53. Franklin was one of the last holdouts. Benjamin Franklin to Richard Jackson, 7 Oct. 1755, *PBF,* 6:216–217.

123. *Pennsylvania Journal,* 25 Mar. 1756.

124. Benjamin Franklin to Peter Collinson, 27 Aug. 1755, *PBF,* 6:170; William Smith, *The Rev. Mr. Smith Vindicated . . .* (Philadelphia, 1756), Evans # 7793.

125. Wolff, *Colonial Agency,* 176, 176n, 195.

126. *Pa. Votes,* 5:4273.

127. Ibid., 4274.

128. Compare *PBF,* 6:468–469 with 456–457.

129. Horace Wemyss Smith, *Life of . . . William Smith,* 1:184.

130. Richard Bauman, *For the Reputation of Truth: Politics, Religion and Conflict among Pennsylvania Quakers, 1750–1800* (Baltimore, 1971), 27–28.

131. Israel Pemberton, Jr., to Zaccheus Collins, 2 Dec. 1755, Pemberton Papers, HSP.

132. Fischer, *Albion's Seed,* 587–589.

133. Ibid., 585.

134. Linda Colley, "Eighteenth-Century English Radicalism before Wilkes," Royal Historical Society, *Transactions,* 5th ser., 31 (1981): 17–18.

135. Frost, *Keithian Controversy.*

136. *The Trials of Peter Boss, George Keith, . . .* (London, 1693), in ibid., 77.

137. Ibid., 79.

138. Levy, *Emergence of A Free Press,* 16–61. On Rhode Island's limited influence, see Thomas J. Curry, *The First Freedoms: Church and State in America to the Passage of the First Amendment* (New York, 1986), 20–21, 91.

139. A. R. Meyers, *Parliaments and Estates in Europe to 1789* (London, 1975); Dietrich Gerhard, "Assemblies of Estates and the Corporate Order," in *Liber Memorialis Georges De Lagarde* (Louvain, 1970), 283–308; R. R. Palmer, *The Age of the Democratic Revolution: A Political History of Europe and America 1760–1800.* 2 vols. (Princeton, 1959–1965), 1:27–52; Jack P. Greene, *Peripheries and Center: Constitutional Development in the Extended Polities of the British Empire and the United*

States, 1607–1788 (Athens, Ga., 1986), 83–85; Robert W. Tucker and David C. Hendrickson, *The Fall of the First British Empire* (Baltimore, 1982), 162, 187–188.

140. Reid, *Constitutional History;* Lois G. Schwoerer, *The Declaration of Rights, 1689* (Baltimore, 1981).

141. For the rights of property vs. property in rights distinction, see Reid, *Constitutional History,* 96–113.

142. On the importance of corporations, see Judith M. Diamondstone, "The Philadelphia Corporation, 1701–1776" (Ph.D. diss., University of Pennsylvania, 1969); Hendrik Hartog, *Public Property and Private Power: The Corporation of the City of New York in American Law, 1730–1870* (Chapel Hill, N.C., 1983); Merwick, *Possessing Albany,* passim.; Alice P. Kenney, *The Gansvoorts of Albany: Dutch Patricians in the Upper Hudson Valley* (Syracuse, N.Y., 1969), passim. On the group consciousness of artisans, see Olton, "Philadelphia Artisans and the American Revolution" (Ph.D. diss., University of California, Berkeley, 1967), 1–99; Graham R. Hodges, *New York City Cartmen, 1667–1850* (New York, 1986). But cf. the much stronger evidence for England in Robert W. Malcolmson, "Workers' Combinations in Eighteenth-Century England," in *The Origins of Anglo-American Radicalism,* Margaret Jacob and James Jacob, eds. (London, 1984), 149–161. Acting as corporate bodies (no matter how informally constituted), local communities would occasionally plead the issue of rights as a grievance before the assembly. For example, when some residents of southeastern Long Island advanced their right to take their produce to New York City in their own boats rather than on the city ferry, they petitioned the assembly as the freeholders of Brookland. When the hearing took place, the trustees of Brookland attended the presentation of the aggrieved party's case. The rights of the Brookland freeholders were town rights as well as individual rights. *NY Votes,* 2:117–119.

143. E.g., *NY Votes,* 1:188. See also Reid, *Constitutional History,* 97–113.

144. Appleby, *Economic Thought.*

145. Alan Macfarlane, *Origins of English Individualism: The Family, Property, and Social Transition* (Oxford, 1978); id., *The Culture of Capitalism* (Oxford, 1987).

146. Greene, *Pursuits of Happiness;* McCusker and Menard, *Economy of British America;* J. R. Crowley, *This Sheba, Self: The Conceptualization of Economic Life in Eighteenth-Century America* (Baltimore, 1974).

147. The New York assemblyman Vincent Matthews made that point clear when he claimed in 1734 that the liberty of a provincial representative was "the Great Guard & Security of all the Peoples Liberty in this Province" ("Speech of Vincent Matthews . . . October 21, 1735," *Colden Papers,* 8:227).

148. *New-York Weekly Journal,* 17 May 1735.

149. Levy, *Emergence of a Free Press,* 16–61.

150. Ibid., 18.

151. Ibid., 47.

152. Ibid., 75–81, 83; Bonomi, *Factious People,* 267–275.

153. Perhaps heeding Thomas Penn's advice that proprietary supporters should compose their differences with Quakers on "the best terms we can." Thomas Penn to William Smith, 6 Oct. 1756, Penn Papers, letter book 5, as quoted in Wolff, *Colonial Agency,* 191.

154. *New-York Weekly Post-Boy,* 22 June 1747; *Pa. Votes,* 5:4099, 4173. Moore's father had been a strong Quaker opponent as well. See Nash, *Quakers and Politics,* 206, 250. For Smith's election activities, see chapter 4.

155. *Pa. Votes,* 6:4419, 4428, 4434, 4435, 4437, 4459, 4482, 4521, 4546, 4556.

156. For a treatment of the assembly's court functions, see Clarke, *Parliamentary Privilege*, 14–60.

157. *Pa. Votes*, 6:4557, 4611, 4619–4620, 4625, 4633, 4645; *CR*, 7:764–765.

158. *CR*, 7:766, 767. Governor Denny eventually convened a council hearing in response to Moore's appeal and absolved him of magisterial wrongdoing. Ibid., 8:161–162.

159. For the most complete treatment of the Moore/Smith affair, see William R. Riddell, "Libel on the Assembly: A Prerevolutionary Episode," *PMHB* 52 (1928): 176–192. Also see Ralph L. Ketcham, "Benjamin Franklin and William Smith: New Light on an Old Philadelphia Quarrel," ibid., 88 (1964): 142–163, and Peter C. Hoffer, "Law and Liberty: In the Matter of Provost William Smith of Philadelphia," *WMQ*, 3d ser., 38 (1981): 681–701.

160. *Pa. Votes*, 6:4681–4682.

161. Ibid., 4692.

162. Ibid., 4703–4704.

163. Ibid., 4707.

164. Ibid., 4715.

165. Byrnes, "William Smith," 113–114, 115–116. Freed on a writ of habeas corpus after the adjournment of the assembly, but rearrested and threatened with further incarceration under the new 1758 assembly, Smith eventually sailed to England in late 1758 to expedite his slow-moving appeal. Ibid., 116–121.

166. On the character of the renewed Quaker Party, see chapter 4.

167. Isaac Norris, Jr., to Robert Charles, 18 May 1755, INLB, 1719–1756.

168. For some examples of appeals to natural law, see the *New-York Evening-Post*, 7 Dec. 1747; *New-York Weekly Journal*, 7 July 1735; *Pennsylvania Gazette*, 21 Mar. 1738, 14 Jan. 1748; Alexander, *Brief Narrative*, Katz, ed., 84; *Pa. Votes*, 5:3945, 4115, 4152, 6:4539, 4807; Chew, *Speech*; Currie, *Treatise*; Gilbert, *Truth Vindicated*.

169. Edward Shippen, Jr., to Edward Shippen, 28 Jan. 1758, Balch Papers, Shippen, as quoted in Byrnes, "William Smith," 110.

Four / The Organization of Popular Politics

1. See Chapter 1, pp. 25–26.

2. Roeber, "'The Origin of Whatever Is Not English,'" 226. On the other hand, they did maintain control of municipal government in New York City, and, of course, of local governments in Albany, Schenectady, and elsewhere. For New York City, see Howe, "Accommodation and Retreat."

3. Roeber, "'The Origin of Whatever Is Not English,'" 226–234. See Adrian Howe, "Accommodation and Retreat," 192–370, for an extended argument that after the early 1700s the Dutch backed away from any political activism that might encourage Dutch/English political confrontations, and the suggestion that the Morris/Alexander appeals to some elements of the Dutch vote in the 1730s were cloaked in the rhetoric of class conflict. There are one or two allusions in the context of the political competition of the 1730s to a Morris/Alexander attempt to mobilize the "Dutch mob," and it is certainly possible that a major portion of the disproportionately large lower-class Dutch population enlisted in the campaign against Governor Cosby's friends (*New-York Weekly Journal*, 15 Mar. 1736, 6 Oct. 1735; Howe, "Accommodation and Retreat," 320–353). However, the Morris/Alexander political appeal to the working poor, coupled with the prominence of Dutch leaders like Rip Van Dam and Cornelius Van Horne in their ranks, was enough to explain that. In

retrospect, the single most significant characteristic of Dutch political behavior during the Cosby/Morris political wars was the relative balance between the two sides. The New Yorkers who backed Lewis Morris, Sr., during the Van Dam case consisted of roughly equal proportions of Dutch and British, along with a small French minority. Howe, "Accommodation and Retreat," 192–370; Nash, *Urban Crucible,* 458 n. 56.

4. Balmer, "Schism on Long Island"; id., *Perfect Babel of Confusion,* 54, 72–98; William Livingston to Rev. David Thompson, 28 Oct. 1754, William Livingston Letter Book, William Livingston Papers, Massachusetts Historical Society, microfilm, YUL.

5. Balmer, *Perfect Babel of Confusion,* 64–71, 99–140.

6. Ibid., 127–133.

7. Alexander J. Wall, "The Controversy in the Dutch Church in New York Concerning Preaching in English, 1754–1768," *NYHSQ* 12 (1928): 39–58. Note the context of anglicization in which A. G. Roeber locates this rift in his "'The Origin of Whatever Is Not English,'" 220–237.

8. Milton M. Klein, "The American Whig: William Livingston of New York" (Ph.D. diss., Columbia University, 1954), 327–437; William Livingston to Noah Welles, 15 Dec. 1753, Livingston-Welles Correspondence, Johnson Family Papers (hereinafter cited as LWC-JFP), YUL; Samuel Miller, D.D., *Memoir of the Rev. John Rodgers, D.D.* (New York, 1813), 147–166.

9. See chapter 8, pp. 331–332.

10. Gough, "Pluralism, Politics, and Power Struggles," 25–72.

11. Lemon, *Best Poor Man's Country,* 13–14; Marianne S. Wokeck, "The Flow and the Composition of German Immigrants to Philadelphia, 1727–1775," *PMHB* 105 (1981): 249–278; id., "German and Irish Immigration to Colonial Philadelphia," American Philosophical Society, *Proceedings* 133 (1989): 128–143; id., "Harnessing the Lure of the 'Best Poor Man's Country': The Dynamics of German-Speaking Immigration to British North America, 1683–1783," in *"To Make America": European Emigration in the Early Modern Period,* Ida Altman and James Horn, eds. (Berkeley, 1991), 204–243; id., "'A Tide of Alien Tongues': The Flow and Ebb of German Immigration to Pennsylvania, 1683–1776" (Ph.D. diss., Temple University, 1983); Farley Grubb, "German Immigration to Pennsylvania, 1709–1820," *Journal of Interdisciplinary History* 20 (1990): 417–436; Roeber, "'The Origin of Whatever Is Not English,'" 237–244; R. J. Dickson, *Ulster Emigration to Colonial America, 1718–1775* (London, 1966); Audrey Lockhart, *Some Aspects of Emigration from Ireland to the North American Colonies between 1660 and 1775* (New York, 1976).

12. Ibid., 77–83.

13. Tully, "Englishmen and Germans."

14. For differences between Presbyterians and Quakers, see chapters 3 and 5. For divisions among Presbyterians, see Leonard J. Trinterud, *The Forming of an American Tradition: A Re-examination of Colonial Presbyterianism* (Philadelphia, 1949), Elizabeth I. Nybakken, "New Light on the Old Side: Irish Influence on Colonial Presbyterianism," *JAH* 68 (1982): 813–832, and Marilyn J. Westerkamp, *Triumph of the Laity: Scots-Irish Piety and the Great Awakening, 1625–1760* (New York, 1988); among Anglicans, Gough, "Pluralism, Politics, and Power Struggles"; among German Lutherans, Leonard R. Riforgiato, *Missionary of Moderation: Henry Melchior Muhlenberg and the Lutheran Church in English America* (Lewisberg, Pa., 1980); and among Quakers, Bauman, *For the Reputation of Truth,* and Marrietta, *Reformation.*

15. Bonomi, *Factious People*, 140–143. The most informative short treatment of DeLancey is Bradshaw, "George Clinton," 24–52.

16. See chapter 2, p. 63.

17. Nicholas Varga, "New York Government and Politics during the Mid-Eighteenth Century" (Ph.D. diss., Fordham University, 1960), 61–67, 73n; Bradshaw, "George Clinton," 75–84.

18. *NY Votes*, 1:751, 815, 825, 2:5; Varga, "New York Government," 91–92; Ziebarth, "Role of New York in King George's War," 86–116. Note, however, the prominence at times of Lewis Morris, Jr., between 1743 and 1745. Varga, "New York Government," 282–285. There was considerable legislative fluidity between 1739 and 1745.

19. *NY Votes*, 1:763, 772–773, 781, 784, 787; Bradshaw, "George Clinton," 88.

20. *NY Votes*, 1:753, 765, 2:19, 41.

21. Governor Clinton to Lords of Trade, 22 June 1747, *DRCNY*, 6:354.

22. Bradshaw, "George Clinton," 93–94, 97–101. Cadwallader Colden's opinion was that during the summer of 1746 "the Speaker of the Assembly . . . was not then let into the Secrets of the [DeLancey's] Cabal" (Cadwallader Colden to Dr. John Mitchell, 6 July 1749, *Colden Papers*, 9:26–27).

23. The best treatment of Clinton's break with DeLancey is Bradshaw, "George Clinton," 66–239. She makes a strong case that Clinton's lack of understanding of traditional wartime policies in New York, and his determination to wage war on a scale that would overshadow Massachusetts Governor William Shirley's accomplishments, led to the breech.

24. See, e.g., Katz, *Newcastle's New York*, 165–176.

25. For DeLancey's British connections, see Bradshaw, "George Clinton," 33–36, and Stanley Nider Katz, "Between Scylla and Charybdis: James DeLancey and Anglo-American Politics in Early Eighteenth-Century New York," in *Anglo-American Political Relations, 1675–1775*, Alison G. Olson and Richard M. Brown, eds. (New Brunswick, N.J., 1970), 92–108.

26. Robert Livingston, Jr., to Abraham Yates, 10 Feb. 1759, Yates Papers, NYPL.

27. *An Answer to a Pamphlet Entitled A Letter to the Freemen and Freeholders* . . . (New York, 1752), Evans # 6809.

28. David Jones to Daniel Horsmanden, 31 July 1764, Henry Van Schaack Papers, box 1, NYSL.

29. "Draft relating to the Proposals," Oct. 1750, *Colden Papers*, 4:233–236; Nicholas Varga, "Robert Charles: New York Agent, 1748–1770," *WMQ*, 3d ser., 18 (1961): 211–235. In July 1755, Jones relinquished his sole control of agent affairs to a committee composed of the New York members of assembly. *NY Votes*, 2:452.

30. Varga, "New York Government," 144; Cadwallader Colden to Governor George Clinton, 29 Jan. 1748, Clinton to Colden, 4 Feb. 1752, *Colden Papers*, 4:9, 222, 310; Robert J. Dinkin, *Voting in Provincial America: A Study of Elections in the Thirteen Colonies, 1689–1776* (Westport, Conn., 1977), 154.

31. Jones courted both Quakers and Presbyterians in Queens County. See *NY Votes*, 1:822, 2:28, 41. For Quaker support of the coalition in Westchester and Dutchess counties, see Henry Beekman to Henry Livingston, 10 Feb. 1750, Beekman Papers, box 1, NYHS. See also Varga, "New York Government," 388, 406.

32. William Smith, Jr., *Historical Memoirs of William Smith*, William H. W. Sabine, ed., 2 vols. (New York, 1956–1958), 1:147.

33. Beverly McAnear, "Politics in Provincial New York, 1689–1761" (Ph.D. diss.,

Stanford University, 1935), 673, 696; Howe, "Accommodation and Retreat," 390–394; Varga, "New York Government," 181; Cadwallader Colden to Governor George Clinton, 4 Feb. 1752, *Colden Papers*, 4:309.

34. Governor Clinton to R. H. Morris, 17 Jan. 1752, Robert Hunter Morris Papers, as quoted in Bonomi, *Factious People*, 164.

35. The Montreal trade consisted of the exchange of British-manufactured Indian-trade goods for furs. On the importance of privateering, see James G. Lydon, *Pirates, Privateers, and Profits* (Upper Saddle River, N.J, 1970), and *NY Laws*, 3:446–448. For concerns about the strength of Fort George, see *NY Laws*, 3:339–346, 403–414, 528–538, 543–546. For the relative uninvolvement of New York merchants in the Montreal trade after 1720, see Norton, *Fur Trade*, 148–151, and David A. Armour, *The Merchants of Albany, New York, 1686–1760* (New York, 1986), 72–155. Also see Armour, pp. 156–227, on the importance of agricultural and lumber products in the upriver economy. For emphasis on unloading the cost of northern defense on the fur trade and on local residents, see *NY Laws*, 3:352–371, 442–443, 563–568. On downriver militia units' reluctance to serve on the frontier, see Governor George Clinton to Cadwallader Colden, 2 Jan. 1747, *Colden Papers*, 4: 1.

36. Philip Livingston to Jacob Wendell, 14 Jan. 1746, Livingston Papers, MCNY.

37. Philip Livingston to Jacob Wendell, 2 June, 14 Jan. 1746, ibid. Henry Beekman revealed something of the same disgust when an Ulster County representative voted "with 2 Long Islandrs against a new fort" at Saratoga. "Sure we must be very Safe if our outmost frontier whants no Defance." Beekman to Gilbert Livingston, 3 June 1746, Beekman Papers, box 1, NYHS.

38. The Indian commissioners who had run New York's native affairs throughout the late seventeenth and early eighteenth centuries were in marked decline during the 1730s and 1740s. Albany lost its fur trading monopoly in the 1720s, and the commissioners in turn lost influence to Schenectady and Oswego traders, to Sir William Johnson among the eastern Six Nations tribes, and to John Henry Lydius among the north Hudson River Indians. Simultaneously, relations among the commissioners themselves became acrimonious. The secretary of the board, Philip Livingston, alienated large numbers of his fellows; no strong personality emerged from the ranks of the commissioners to take his place; and animosities between Schenectady and Albany, and among different regions of the Mohawk and Hudson valleys in both Albany County and Livingston Manor, increased under the pressure of wartime danger. As the fur trade became less important to Albany, economic interests tugged local leaders in various directions; some cooperated (occasionally with old antagonists from Schenectady) to exploit the Oswego trade; some became far more preoccupied with trading in agricultural goods and lumber than in fur; and some became deeply involved in land speculation and the encouragement of agricultural settlement. See Norton, *Fur Trade*; Armour, *Merchants of Albany*; Stephen E. Sale, "Colonial Albany: Outpost of Empire" (Ph.D. diss., University of Southern California, 1973); Bradshaw, "George Clinton"; James Alexander to Cadwallader Colden, 5 Dec. 1751, *Colden Papers*, 4:303.

39. That is, through March, 1745. See Bradshaw, "George Clinton," 74–95, and Varga, "New York Government," 64–78. Clinton wanted a successful and profitable administration and initially was prepared to sacrifice a good deal to achieve that goal. For Clinton's concern for place and income, see Varga, "New York Government," 56–60.

472 / Notes to pp. 131–133

472 / Notes to pp. 131–133

40. For Massachusetts's aggressiveness, see John A. Schutz, *William Shirley, King's Governor of Massachusetts* (Chapel Hill, N.C., 1961), 80–103; Pencak, *War, Politics, and Revolution,* 119–123, 133–137.

41. Cadwallader Colden to ——, 7 Aug. 1745, *Colden Papers,* 3:137.

42. *NY Votes,* 2:62.

43. Bradshaw, "George Clinton," 88–89; Varga, "New York Government," 82–83.

44. The following paragraph is based on Bradshaw, "George Clinton," and Varga, "New York Government."

45. Henry Lloyd II to Henry Lloyd, 7 May 1745, Lloyd Family Papers, as quoted in Bradshaw, "George Clinton," 86–87.

46. James Alexander reported to Cadwallader Colden that the drafting of a parliamentary currency bill making royal instructions to governors "obligatory" brought New Yorkers together despite their differences. "Never was there so nearly an union in any place as there was in this agt these clauses" (13 Jan. 1745, *Colden Papers,* 3:101).

47. McAnear, "Politics," 592.

48. Philip Livingston to Jacob Wendell, 14 June 1746, Livingston Papers, MCNY.

49. Paul Richards to Jacob Wendell, 21 June 1746, Paul Richards Misc. MSS, NYHS.

50. According to Cadwallader Colden, DeLancey pushed a plan to attack both "Croun Point" and Oswego in the fall of 1747. "Copy of the Chief Justice Plan," 29 July 1747, *Colden Papers,* 3:408–409. See also Bradshaw, "George Clinton," 103, 114, 129–130, 172, 198.

51. Bradshaw, "George Clinton," 102.

52. The best detailed treatment of Clinton's initiatives is ibid., 97–239.

53. *NY Votes,* 2:184.

54. When the British cancelled the 1746 expedition against Canada, the assembly became even more careful, and from Clinton's point of view, recalcitrant. Remembering the Crown's failure to carry out similar plans late in Queen Anne's War, many New Yorkers concluded that the British were just as unreliable as they had been a generation earlier. And when Clinton insisted on keeping the provincial troops together during the 1746–1747 winter in anticipation of a new plan of attack, legislators visibly shuddered, recalling the high cost of the aborted Canada expedition and knowing that they were responsible for the continued provisioning of the current roster of provincial troops. As a result, the provincial politicians lost much of the enthusiasm for offensive action that they had shared a year earlier. They would not finance any kind of offensive without specific British orders, or without the New England colonies' sharing the cost; they made renewed efforts to push the cost of Indian diplomacy off on the Crown; and they refused either to help Clinton find money with which to pay the troops or to cede to the governor any new administrative power. For an extended treatment of these themes, see Bradshaw, "George Clinton."

55. Lewis Morris, Jr., made the point most clearly by comparing Governor Cosby's position in the 1730s to Clinton's current dilemma. Whereas "Cosby had some people of the province to assist him," Clinton had only Colden. Lewis Morris, Jr., to Ephemia Norris, 20 Sept. 1747, Morris Papers, NYHS.

56. *NY Votes,* 2:95–97, 108, 109; Varga, "New York Government," 285–287, 287n.

57. It is arguable that an important political division existed between a number of "expansionists" and "non-expansionists" (or some similarly named groups) in the 1720s, whose differences revolved around the desirability of closing off or keeping open the Montreal trade, and in either actively opposing the French in the Great Lakes region or continuing an accommodative relationship with them. Changes in economic structure and political concerns, however, made such divisions of little relevance in the politics of the 1730s. And attempts to apply such a scheme to the 1740s both ignore the major political division of the decade and lack sensitivity to the plurality of contemporary interests. While one may always find a few articulate individuals more concerned about expansion than others, to treat this difference as the linchpin of New York politics clearly distorts the character of New York factionalism. For an early attempt to combine the expansionist thesis with some recognition of the complexities of change over time, see Norton, *Fur Trade*. For an ardent, one-dimensional embrace of this thesis, see Egnal, *Mighty Empire*, 51–67.

58. Henry Beekman to Gilbert Livingston, 14 Jan. 1746, Beekman Papers, box 1, NYHS.

59. Henry Beekman to Henry Livingston 12 Nov. 1747, in "A Packet of Old Letters," Dutchess County Historical Society, *Yearbook*, 1921, p. 32.

60. In fairness to Clinton, it should be pointed out that it took talent as well as political insensitivity for a New York governor to bring such opprobrium on himself. The governor was successful in conducting his own Indian diplomacy in the late months of the war. He recognized the importance of integrated British/intercolonial military activity if the colonies were to wage war rather than simply defend themselves against New France, and he tried to promote those ends. Moreover, he understood some of the ways in which British political and familial connections could be used to advantage in New York politics. But Clinton lacked the kind of political deftness necessary to implement his goals. His narcissistic predilection for self-justification, when combined with a "damn the torpedoes . . . " attitude in many military and prerogative matters, spelled political disaster. He had no understanding of how, or why, his policies and peccadilloes set off alarm bells among provincial politicians; nor did he care to find out. Insensitive to the texture of New York's peculiar political culture, and unconcerned about how his behavior threatened various provincial interests, Clinton had an important hand in making the political coalition that he eventually faced.

61. Bradshaw, "George Clinton," 258, 262, 265–323; Howe, "Accommodation and Retreat," 373–395.

62. Varga, "New York Government," 129–188.

63. See p. 154.

64. As quoted in Jurgen Herbst, *From Crisis to Crisis: American College Government, 1636–1819* (Cambridge, Mass., 1982), 85. The Anglican response to the Presbyterians' preemptive strike in New Jersey was to press the provincial legislature there to deny the college any form of public support.

65. David C. Humphrey, *From King's College to Columbia, 1746–1800* (New York, 1976), 18–35.

66. John W. Pratt, *Religion, Politics, and Diversity: The Church-State Theme in New York History* (Ithaca, N.Y., 1967), 26–78; Balmer, "Schism on Long Island," 95–113; Jean P. Jordan, "The Anglican Establishment in Colonial New York, 1693–1783" (Ph.D. diss., Columbia University, 1971). The Society for the Propagation of the Gospel was a zealous English missionary organization founded in 1701 and dedicated to supplying the colonies with subsidized Anglican priests. See John

Calam, *Parsons and Pedagogues: The S.P.G. Adventure in American Education* (New York, 1971).

67. Pratt, *Religion, Politics, and Diversity,* 45.

68. Prior to 1700, Jamaica had been one of those towns that had long agreed to support a Presbyterian church and minister, and when the 1693 Ministry Act passed, Presbyterians simply used the elected vestryboard to continue their town policies. Viewing this as defiance of the law, Governor Cornbury dispossessed the Presbyterians of their church, installed an Anglican priest, and forced the vestryboard to raise taxes for his support. The Anglican placements in the other two parishes, one in Westchester and one in Queens, were peaceful. Ibid., 53–54; Jordan, "Anglican Establishment," 112–125, 132–154.

69. "Instructions for Colonel Henry Sloughter, Governor of New York," 13 Mar. 1689, *DRCNY,* 3:689. See also "Articles of Capitulation on the Reduction of New Netherland," *DRCNY,* 2:251.

70. Pratt, *Religion, Politics, and Diversity,* 9–11, 13–14, 32–33. The desire of both Dutch- and English-speaking Calvinists to continue what establishment practices they could (consistent with Anglican policies) is best illustrated by a 1699 law "to Enable ye Respective Townes . . . to build & repair their meeting houses & other public buildings," under which town trustees, or their equivalent, were permitted to raise local taxes, not only for jails and meetinghouses, but also for churches. In practice, under this law, Reformed Protestant communities built and repaired churches and raised taxes or equivalent subscriptions for the support of a minister. It is unclear how far into the eighteenth century this practice continued, or how extensive it was. *NY Laws,* 1:427–428; Randall H. Balmer, "Dutch Religion in an English World: Political Upheaval and Ethnic Conflict in the Middle Colonies" (Ph.D. diss., Princeton University, 1985), 1–28; Nelson R. Burr, "The Episcopal Church and the Dutch in Colonial New York and New Jersey," *Historical Magazine of the Protestant Episcopal Church* 19 (1950): 94 (hereinafter cited as *HMPEC*); Pratt, *Religion, Politics, and Diversity,* 60–61.

71. *NY Laws,* 3:842–844; Humphrey, *King's College to Columbia,* 31–35.

72. Samuel Johnson to George Berkeley, 10 Sept. 1750 as quoted in Humphrey, *King's College to Columbia,* 19.

73. William Livingston to Noah Welles, Feb. 1753, LWC-JFP, YUL.

74. *The Independent Reflector* was modeled after the English periodicals *The Independent Whig, The Tatler,* and *The Spectator.* On the planning of the paper, see Klein, "William Livingston," 307–313.

75. See Klein, "William Livingston," 446–449 for the other occasional contributors.

76. The essays are available in *The Independent Reflector,* Milton M. Klein, ed. (Cambridge, Mass., 1963).

77. Ibid., 171. The six essays ran through 26 April 1753. See ibid., 171–214.

78. Ibid., 182.

79. Ibid., 175, 178.

80. Ibid., 182.

81. Ibid., 214, 181.

82. Ibid., 213.

83. *New-York Mercury,* 30 Apr. 1753; Donald F. M. Gerardi, "The King's College Controversy, 1753–1756, and the Ideological Roots of Toryism in New York," *Perspectives in American History* 11 (1977–1978): 164–65.

84. *New-York Mercury,* 9 July, 11 June, and 18 June 1753.

85. Ibid., 23 July 1753.

86. William Livingston, *A Preface to the "Independent Reflector"* (New York, 1753), Evans # 7041.

87. On 25 November, 1754, Livingston and his associates began a new essay series entitled the "Watchtower," which ran for fifty-two weeks. For a description of the participants, the topics they covered, and the Anglican response, see Klein, "William Livingston," 418–424, 748–751.

88. William Livingston to Noah Welles, 7 Dec. 1754, LWC-JFP, YUL; Humphrey, *King's College to Columbia,* 49.

89. In July and December, 1753, the legislators had authorized a new college lottery and voted a seven-year, £500 per annum subsidy for college operating expenses out of the provincial excise. *NY Laws,* 3:908–910, 930–939.

90. Subsequent to Sir Danvers Osborne's suicide in October 1753, Whitehall appointed Sir Charles Hardy to succeed him as governor. Hardy arrived in New York to take up his duties in early September 1755.

91. William Smith, Jr., to Aaron Burr, 23 Sept. 1754, William Smith Papers, box 1, lot 190, NYPL.

92. James DeLancey's prolonged disqualification of William Smith, Sr., from practicing before the New York Supreme Court during the early stages of the Zenger trial, just at the time when Smith was trying to establish himself in the upper echelons of New York City's competitive legal world, was a serious financial setback. The feud continued into the 1740s when Smith was the only New York lawyer willing to try to prosecute DeLancey's younger brother, the tavern-crawling Oliver, for his brawling assaults. It was no accident that when James DeLancey died in 1760, William Smith, Jr., who had since grown prosperous, bought and made over DeLancey's New York City mansion. L. F. S. Upton, *The Loyal Whig: William Smith of New York and Quebec* (Toronto, 1969), 16–50.

93. William Smith Papers, box 1, lot 189, NYPL. Quotation from "Draft Acc't."

94. William Smith Papers, box 1, lot 189, NYPL.

95. *NY Votes,* 2:421, 422.

96. "Draft Acc't," William Smith Papers, box 1, lot 189 # 12, NYPL. Nicoll was one of two Anglican swing voters on college support questions.

97. Ibid.

98. Humphrey, *King's College to Columbia,* 59–63; Balmer, *Perfect Babel of Confusion,* 127–133.

99. William Livingston to Rev. Aaron Burr, 29 May 1754, William Livingston Letter Book, William Livingston Papers, microfilm, YUL; Wall, "Controversy in the Dutch Church," 39–43.

100. Humphrey, *King's College to Columbia,* 63–66.

101. For the votes on which this analysis rests, see *NY Votes,* 2:396, 419, 421–22, and 447.

102. Smith, *History of New-York,* 2:208; Elizabeth H. Lang, "Colonial Colleges and Politics: Yale, King's College, and the College of Philadelphia, 1740–1764" (Ph.D. diss., Cornell University, 1976), 205–207, 223–231.

103. Smith, *History of New-York,* 2:168.

104. *New-York Gazette, or, the Weekly Post-Boy,* 21 July 1755; *New-York Mercury,* 15 Sept. 1755.

105. *New-York Mercury,* 15 Nov. 1756; Samuel Johnson to William Samuel Johnson, 8 Nov. 1756, in *Samuel Johnson, President of King's College: His Career and Writings,* Herbert and Carol Schneider, eds., 4 vols. (New York, 1929), 1:268. The

Presbyterians had as little luck in two other by-elections. In Richmond, the Anglican Benjamin Seaman replaced the deceased Anglican swing voter John LeCount, and in Ulster a good friend of the county Anglicans, Vincent Matthews, took the seat of the King's College advocate Samuel Gale.

106. *New-York Gazette, or, the Weekly Post-Boy,* 29 Jan. 1759.

107. *NY Votes,* 2:329, 584.

108. Of the other five, two had died, one was replaced by a family member, and two were appointed to the council.

109. *NY Votes,* 2:396, 419, 421–22, 447; William Smith Papers, box 1, lot 189, NYPL.

110. William Livingston to Noah Welles, 15 Dec. 1753, LWC-JFP, YUL; "Draft Acc't," William Smith Papers, box 1, lot 189 # 12, NYPL; Klein, "William Livingston," 397, 397n.

111. Chauncey Graham to William Smith, Jr., 11 July 1755, William Smith Papers, box 1, lot 189 # 6, NYPL.

112. *Independent Reflector,* Klein, ed., 179. For William Livingston's view of the differences among the Dutch, which he recognized as being of their own making, and not as dependent on the *conferentie/coetus* split as many historians have emphasized, see William Livingston to Rev. Mr. John Light [Bright?], 12 Jan. 1756, William Livingston Letter Book, William Livingston Papers, microfilm, YUL. The more ornate liturgy of the continental Reformed churches and a distinctive confession of faith set them apart from the Presbyterians and may have predisposed them more toward Anglicanism. Balmer, *Perfect Babel of Confusion,* 104–107; Schwartz, *"Mixed Multitude,"* 149.

113. Howe, "Accommodation and Retreat," 408–414; New York *Mercury,* 23 Dec. 1754, 14 Apr. 1755, supplement, 28 July 1755, 29 Sept. 1755.

114. *New-York Mercury,* 23 Dec. 1754.

115. See the *Independent Reflector* and "Watchtower" essays, passim.

116. Thomas Cornell and William Walton.

117. William Livingston to Noah Welles, 24 Jan. 1746, LWC-JFP, YUL.

118. *NY Votes,* 2:435–36, 441.

119. Ibid., 460, 468, 474, 485, 513, 515, 519, 537, 542, 558, 572, 574, 575, 578.

120. Shirley served as second-in-command of the British and colonial forces during the summer of 1755 and subsequent to General James Braddock's death was commander-in-chief until relieved of duty in July 1756. Schutz, *William Shirley,* 187–224; McAnear, "Politics," 865, 867–870.

121. "A Review of the Military Operations," Massachusetts Historical Society, *Collections,* 1st ser., 10 vols. (Boston, 1792–1809, repr. New York, 1968), 7:67–163. On Shirley's fortunes and the supply contracts, see Schutz, *William Shirley,* 187–247, and Bonomi, *Factious People,* 175–76.

122. Egnal, *Mighty Empire,* 61–66.

123. *CR,* 6:48; *PBF,* 5:357; Bonomi, *Factious People,* 175. On the Albany Plan, see *PBF,* 5:272–278, 335–338, 344–353, 357–364, 374–392, 397–417.

124. Cadwallader Colden to Governor Charles Hardy, [11 May 1756?], Governor Charles Hardy to Cadwallader Colden, 3 Dec. 1756, Alexander Colden to Cadwallader Colden, 15 Oct. 1757, Cadwallader Colden to Lord Loudoun, 11 and 21 Oct. 1757, Cadwallader Colden to Lieutenant Governor DeLancey, [November, 1757?], *Colden Papers,* 5:75–76, 98–99, 107, 199, 201, 205–206, 209–211; James DeLancey to Cadwallader Colden, 4 Nov. 1757, Colden Papers, box 11, NYHS; Bonomi,

Factious People, 174; Smith, *History of New-York*, 2:168; McAnear, "Politics," 870–871; William Corry to William Johnson, 25 Aug. 1757, New York Colonial Manuscripts, vol. 85 (hereinafter cited as NY Col. MSS), New York State Archives (hereinafter cited as NYSA).

125. McAnear, "Politics," 763.

126. Bonomi, *Factious People*, 176; McAnear, "Politics," 898.

127. Notably those of 1726, 1737, and 1768.

128. *New-York Mercury*, 30 July 1753; William Livingston to Robert Livingston, Jr., 24 [?] Feb. 1754, Livingston-Redmond Papers, Franklin Delano Roosevelt Library, Hyde Park (hereinafter cited as Livingston-Redmond), microfilm copy, NYHS, reel 5; Jordan, "Anglican Establishment," 146–148; Jean B. Peyer, "Jamaica, Long Island 1656–1776: A Study of the Roots of American Urbanism" (Ph.D. diss., City University of New York, 1974), 234–247.

129. Benjamin Hinckman to William Smith, Jr., 12 July 1754, box 1, lot 189, # 8, William Smith Papers, NYPL.

130. *New-York Mercury*, 23 June 1755.

131. See chapter 8, pp. 322–323.

132. See n. 118 above and Cadwallader Colden to Governor Charles Hardy, [Summer 1756?], Alexander Colden to Cadwallader Colden, 16 Feb. 1757, *Colden Papers*, 5:107, 220; McAnear, "Politics," 879, 902–903; Petition from Orange County, New York Colony Box, NYPL; "James Robertson, Dep. Quartermaster-General, to Lt.-Gov. James DeLancey," 29 Jan. 1759, NY Col. MSS, vol. 86., NYSA.

133. Tully, *William Penn's Legacy*, 23–24. When word arrived in Philadelphia immediately before the election that war had broken out, Allen and his friends felt themselves to be "tied down" by their earlier public statements that they would not stand for election. William Allen to John Penn, 27 Mar. 1741, PPOC, HSP.

134. *Pa. Votes*, 3:2657.

135. William Allen to John Penn, 17 Nov. 1739, PPOC, HSP.

136. Samuel Blunston to Thomas Penn, 9 Apr. 1735, Cadwallader Coll., Box 2, Thomas Penn Letters, HSP.

137. Tully, *William Penn's Legacy*, 3–22.

138. *Pa. Votes* 3:2465, 2467–69, 2474–75, 2481, 2482–83.

139. Alan Tully, "Ethnicity, Religion, and Politics in Early America," *PMHB* 107 (1983): 491–536; Schwartz, *"Mixed Multitude,"* 74, 76–77, 163–164. For the political impact of Scotch-Irish and German immigration during the late 1710s and the 1720s, see Schwartz, *"Mixed Multitude,"* 85–99.

140. Tully, "Quaker Party and Proprietary Policies," 95; id., *William Penn's Legacy*, 24–32.

141. In this respect, Quaker Party supporters were not wrong. With the exception of the disqualification of Friends from office, Penn was in agreement with Governor Thomas's sentiments.

142. Ryerson, "Quaker Elite," 112; Tully, *William Penn's Legacy*, 170–173.

143. Ryerson, "Quaker Elite," 109–119.

144. Ibid., 123.

145. Tully, *William Penn's Legacy*, 38–40; id., "Quaker Party and Proprietary Policies," 81.

146. *Pa. Votes*, 4:2988.

147. Richard Hockley to Thomas Penn, 1 Nov. 1742, PPOC; Isaac Norris, Jr., to Richard Partridge, 18 May 1745, INLB, 1735–1755, HSP; Tully, *William Penn's*

Legacy, 32–38, 226; Norman S. Cohen, "The Philadelphia Election Riot of 1742," *PMHB* 92 (1968): 306–319; William T. Parsons, "The Bloody Election of 1742," *Pa. Hist.* 36 (1969): 290–306.

148. Minutes, Philadelphia Yearly Meeting (1747–79), 55, Friends Historical Library, Swarthmore College (hereinafter cited as FHL).

149. On the participation of Quaker women in public affairs, see chapter 8, pp. 350–352. For the controversy, see Tully, *William Penn's Legacy,* 22–38.

150. Richard Peters to Thomas Penn, 3 June 1743, 3 Oct. 1744, RPLB, 13 July 1750, PPOC, n.d., p. 107, PPOC, vol. 6; James Hamilton to Thomas Penn, 13 Oct. 1750, PPOC, HSP; Tully, *William Penn's Legacy,* 38–40; Tully, "Quaker Party and Proprietary Policies," 81, 289 n. 13.

151. Tully, "Ethnicity," 498–501.

152. William Allen to Proprietors, 27 Mar. 1741, PPOC, HSP.

153. Richard Peters to Proprietors, 17 Nov. 1742, RPLB, HSP.

154. As quoted in Horace Wemyss Smith, *Life of . . . William Smith,* 1:69.

155. William Allen to John Penn, 27 Mar. 1741, PPOC, HSP.

156. Governor George Thomas to Board of Trade, 20 Oct. 1740, *Pa. Statutes,* 4:470–471. See also chapter 7, pp. 294–295.

157. Schwartz, *"Mixed Multitude,"* 160–163. See also A. G. Roeber, *Palatines, Liberty, and Property: German Lutherans in Colonial British America* (Baltimore, 1993), 176–190.

158. Marietta, *Reformation,* 147–158.

159. Ibid., 152–154, 175–176. As James Pemberton admitted, "There is indeed a majority amongst us who show little regard to the Principles of their profession" (Pemberton to Jonah Thompson, 25 April 1756, Thompson MSS, transcript, FHL).

160. Hutson, "Benjamin Franklin"; id., *Pennsylvania Politics.*

161. Hutson, *Pennsylvania Politics; PBF,* 6:266–269, 296n.

162. Marietta, *Reformation,* 139–141. By May 1755, Isaac Norris, Jr., was reporting that "weaknesses & scruples within Doors" were causing him and other defense-minded Quakers some difficulties (Norris to Robert Charles, 24 May 1755, INLB, 1719–1756, HSP).

163. Marietta, *Reformation,* 152–176; *CR,* 6:563; Robert S. Hohwald, "The Structure of Pennsylvania Politics, 1739–1766" (Ph.D. diss., Princeton University, 1978), 197–198.

164. *PBF,* 6:282n.

165. Isaac Norris, Jr., to Robert Charles, 18 May 1756, INLB, 1719–1756, HSP.

166. Hutson, "Benjamin Franklin."

167. For Norris's supposition that secret proprietary instructions lay behind the deadlock, see Isaac Norris, Jr., to Robert Charles, 18 and 24 May 1756, INLB, 1719–1756, HSP.

168. As Provost William Smith made clear in his *Brief State* and *Brief View.*

169. *PBF,* 6:170.

170. *Pa. Votes,* 6:4391. "The cloaking our parsimony under Disguises of Religious Scruples," complained Isaac Norris, Jr., "has been ye General Misrepresentation of us everywhere" (Norris to Robert Charles, 24 May 1755, INLB, 1719–1756, HSP).

171. Horace Wemyss Smith, *Life of . . . William Smith,* 1:119; Marietta, *Reformation,* 159–160; Byrnes, "William Smith," 70; Woolf, *Colonial Agency,* 156–158, 166–168, 176–188.

172. Franklin's accomplishments and reputation through 1756 are best followed in *PBF*, vols. 1–6.
173. *PBF*, 6:86.
174. Hutson, "Benjamin Franklin."
175. *PBF*, 6:3–4.
176. Whitfield J. Bell, Jr., and Leonard W. Labaree, "Franklin and the Wagon Affair," American Philosophical Society, *Proceedings*, 101 (1957): 551–558.
177. *PBF*, 6:295–306.
178. J. Bennett Nolan, *General Benjamin Franklin: The Military Career of a Philosopher* (Philadelphia, 1936).
179. *PBF*, 6:170–171.
180. Ibid., 502–515.
181. Ibid., 415–420; *Pennsylvania Journal*, 4 March 1756.
182. *Pennsylvania Journal*, 15 Apr., and 20 May 1756.
183. Thomas H. Montgomery, *A History of the University of Pennsylvania from Its Foundation to A.D. 1770* (Philadelphia, 1900), 272.
184. *PBF*, vols 7 and 8:passim.
185. *Pa. Votes*, 5:4246.
186. *PBF*, 7:13.
187. Ibid., 6:456–457n; Richard Peters to Thomas Penn, 29 April 1756, PPOC, HSP; Lively, "Speaker and His House," 74–76.
188. *Pa. Votes*, 5:4245–4249; Lively, "Speaker and His House," 74.
189. William S. Hanna, *Benjamin Franklin and Pennsylvania Politics* (Stanford, 1964), 114; Lively, "Speaker and His House," 74–77.
190. Horace Wemyss Smith, *Life of . . . William Smith*, 1:132–133, 147, 150; *Pa. Votes*, 6:4450–4457, 4543; *Pennsylvania Journal*, 10 June 1756; Smith, *Brief View*, 58.
191. Horace Wemyss Smith, *Life of . . . William Smith*, 1:150.
192. The establishment of the College of Philadelphia was basically a non-issue for Friends. They had no need of a college-educated clergy and they felt that their own emphasis on practical educational skills would best foster the values that promoted coherence within their Society. Beyond that, Pennsylvania's guarantee of religious liberty gave the right to other denominations to establish what educational institutions they wished.
193. On the trustees, faculty, and curriculum of the College of Philadelphia, see Ann D. Gordon, "The College of Philadelphia, 1749–1779: Impact of an Institution" (Ph.D. diss., University of Wisconsin-Madison, 1975) and William L. Turner, "The College, Academy, and Charitable School of Philadelphia: The Development of a Colonial Institution of Learning, 1740–1779" (Ph.D. diss., University of Pennsylvania, 1952).
194. On Alison, see Elizabeth A. Ingersoll, "Francis Alison: American Philosophe, 1705–1799" (Ph.D. diss., University of Delaware, 1974).
195. Samuel Edwin Weber, *The Charity School Movement in Colonial Pennsylvania* (Philadelphia, 1905); Horace Wemyss Smith, *Life of . . . William Smith*, 1:146. The early history of the Philadelphia Academy and its continuing relationship to the College of Philadelphia may be traced in Montgomery, *University of Pennsylvania*, and *PBF*, vols. 3–5.
196. For the term "Franklinists," see Richard Peters to Thomas Penn, 1 June 1756, PPOC, HSP.

197. Richard Peters to Thomas Penn, 16 and 22 Sept. 1756, PPOC, William Logan to John Smith, 1 Oct. 1756, Correspondence of John Smith (hereinafter cited as CJS), HSP.

198. Lively, "Speaker and His House," 74–77, 93–94, 112–115.

199. Allen and Turner to John Barclay, 28 Dec. 1754, as quoted in Wolff, *Colonial Agency*, 161.

200. Isaac Norris, Jr., to Robert Charles, 16 June 1756, INLB, 1756–1766.

201. Ibid.

202. Albert F. Gegenheimer, *Provost William Smith and His Group* (Philadelphia, 1940); Ingersoll, "Alison."

203. Ingersoll, "Alison," 109–110. Smith contributed to Alison's unease and to the disaffection of Old Light Presbyterians with their Anglican partners by stressing the Anglican nature of the college at the same time as he emphasized its non-denominational character. Ingersoll, "Alison," 491–492; Gordon, "College of Philadelphia," 96–98, Horace Wemyss Smith, *Life of . . . William Smith*, 1:143.

204. Despite William Allen's example, Old Light Presbyterians were as likely to be Quaker as Proprietary supporters. Witness George Bryan and Charles Thompson. See Joseph S. Foster, "George Bryan and the Politics of Revolution" (Ph.D. diss., Temple University, 1989), 63–77, and Boyd S. Schlenther, *Charles Thomson: A Patriot's Pursuit* (Newark, Del., 1990), 3–53. Note that Foster dates Bryan's defection from the Quaker Party to 1758.

205. Thomas Secker to Thomas Moore, 1 Mar. 1759, Lambeth MSS, Hawks Transcripts, as quoted in Byrnes, "William Smith," 124; *Pennsylvania Journal*, 20 May, 10 and 17 June 1756; Gough, "Pluralism, Politics, and Power Struggles," 124–179, 193–199, 203–207, 286. Roberdeau's personal religious odyssey was a confusing one. From being a high-profile Anglican at midcentury, he became an active Presbyterian in the late 1760s. Lively, "Speaker and His House," 70–71; Gough, "Pluralism, Politics and Power Struggles," 259n.

206. Richard Peters to Thomas Penn, 29 Apr. 1756, PPOC, HSP.

207. There was bad blood between Smith and the New Light champion, whom Smith referred to as "Hell-fire T[enne]nt." When both were in England in 1754, Smith took great satisfaction in embarrassing Tennent by producing an old sermon the latter had preached during the heyday of his evangelicalism, which maligned Presbyterian practices and beliefs akin to those of the British Presbyterians from whom Tennent was currently trying to raise money on behalf of the College of New Jersey. Two years later, when Smith became involved in the Roberdeau controversy, who should join Roberdeau's Anglican defenders but Gilbert Tennent and his church elders. Horace Wemyss Smith, *Life of . . . William Smith*, 1:103; *PBF*, 5:210n, 211; *Pennsylvania Journal*, 17 June 1756. For the competition between the Philadelphia Academy and the College of New Jersey, see Bruce R. Lively, "William Smith, the College and Academy of Philadelphia and Pennsylvania Politics, 1753–58," *HMPEC* 8 (1969): 243–250. For relations between New Lights and Old Lights, see Trinterud, *American Tradition*, and Ingersoll, "Alison." For some sense of what Tennent preached during the early stages of the French and Indian War, see *Happiness of Rewarding the Enemies of Our Religion*, and *The Good Man's Character and Reward Represented . . .* (Philadelphia, 1756), Evans # 7797.

208. Weber, *Charity School Movement*, 53–54; Horace Wemyss Smith, *Life of . . . William Smith*, 1:68–69; Tully, "Englishmen and Germans"; Schwartz, *"Mixed Multitude,"* 185–193.

209. Richard Peters to Thomas Penn, 2 Oct. 1756, *PMHB* 31 (1907): 246–247.

210. *Pennsylvania Journal,* 14 Oct. 1756.

211. Tully, "Quaker Party and Proprietary Policies," 79–80; Ryerson, "Quaker Elite," 112. Responding to promises made by British Friends to British politicians that in exchange for *not* disqualifying Pennsylvania Quakers from holding office in their province, Pennsylvania Quakers would avoid constituting a majority in the assembly, and, perhaps, to private scruples of their own, four Quakers who had just been elected in the October general election resigned immediately. That brought the number of Friends down well below a majority. *Pa. Votes,* 6:4385; John Fothergill to Israel Pemberton, Jr., 18 Mar. 1756, Etting Coll., Pemberton Papers; Henton Brown to James Pemberton, 11 Mar. 1756, John Hunt to John Pemberton, 23 Mar. 1756, Pemberton Papers, HSP; Christopher Wilson and John Hunt to Friends, 4 Nov. 1756, Misc. MSS, transcript, FHL; Marietta, *Reformation,* 160–165; Wolff, *Colonial Agency,* 176–190.

212. Richard Peters to Thomas Penn, 30 Oct. 1756, PPOC, HSP.

213. Lively, "Speaker and His House," 69–73, 76–79, 130–131.

214. Richard Peters to Thomas Penn, 30 Oct. 1756, PPOC, HSP. For what I term the ideology of civil Quakerism, see chapter 7.

215. Lynford Lardner to Richard Peters, 7 Mar. 1758, Lardner Papers, HSP.

216. Richard Peters to Thomas Penn, 30 Oct. 1756, PPOC, HSP.

217. Isaac Norris, Jr., spoke for this group of Friends as early as October 1754 when he testified as follows: "I am satisfied the Laws of Nature and perhaps the Christian system leaves us a right to defend ourselves as well against the enemies who are within the reach of our Laws as those who owe no subjection to them" (Norris to Robert Charles, 7 Oct. 1754, INLB, 1719–1756, HSP). To justify their position, Friends like Norris—erroneously—cited the "Precedent" of the 1711 assembly's vote of money "to the Crown," and the fact that British Quakers paid taxes that financed military activities (Norris to John Fothergill, 25 May 1755, INLB, 1719–1756, HSP; see also Norris to Richard Partridge, 16 Nov. 1755, INLB, 1735–1755, Logan Coll., HSP). For British Friends' reinforcement of this logic, see Jonah Thompson to John Smith, 26 Apr. 1756, CJS, HSP. On the misleading nature of the analogy, see Marietta, *Reformation,* 154; Tully, "Politics and Peace Testimony."

218. Although roughly a quarter of the new assembly's members were Anglicans, and another quarter other non-Quakers, "almost all" were chosen by the influence of Quakers (*Pennsylvania Journal,* 14 Oct 1756). Isaac Norris, Jr., stressed the continuity of the assemblies when he pointed out that "the present Assembly do not seem to please a small party among us any better than those they have formerly railed at" (Norris to Richard Partridge, 1 July 1757, INLB, 1756–1766, HSP).

219. The Assembly Party also tried to cut the financial ground out from under the College of Philadelphia. Quaker politicians discouraged people from participating in the lotteries that financed the college, and in 1759 the assembly passed a law making such lotteries illegal. Later, Franklin lent a hand in England by discouraging potential British contributors from donating money to the institution. Note the similarity of these tactics to those of the Livingston/Smith faction in the latter's fight against King's College. Gordon, "College of Philadelphia," 95; *Pennsylvania Journal,* 30 Nov. 1758, 25 Jan. 1759; David Dove, *The Lottery. A Dialogue between Mr. Thomas Trueman and Mr. Humphrey Dupe* (Philadelphia, 1758), Evans # 8114; *Pa. Statutes,* 5:445–448; Gegenheimer, *Provost William Smith,* 150–154.

220. *PBF,* 7:34–35.

221. C. Hale Sipe, *The Indian Wars of Pennsylvania* (Harrisburg, Pa., 1929), 203–386.

222. John Armstrong to James Burd, 28 Jan. 1757, Shippen Papers, HSP.

223. Dunbar, *Paxton Papers*, 294; see also 188, and Hutson, *Pennsylvania Politics*, 25–26.

224. *Pa. Votes*, 5:4113.

225. Tully, "Quaker Party and Proprietary Policies," 87–88; Theodore Thayer, "The Friendly Association," *PMHB* 67 (1943): 356–376; id., *Israel Pemberton, King of the Quakers* (Philadelphia, 1943); Newcomb, *Franklin and Galloway*, 37–70.

226. Richard Peters to Thomas Penn, 2 Oct. 1756, PPOC, HSP.

227. Ryerson, "Quaker Elite," 112; Lively, "Speaker and His House," 130–196.

228. Tully, "Quaker Party and Proprietary Policies," 78–79, 80, 290 n. 19.

229. For the later tensions, see Hutson, *Pennsylvania Politics*, 156; Hohwald, "Structure," 272–274. For the earlier period, see Tully, *William Penn's Legacy*, 32–43.

230. George Bryan, Diary, as quoted in Lively, "Speaker and His House," 140.

Five / The Electorate and Popular Politics

1. *NY Laws*, 1:405.

2. Dinkin, *Voting in Provincial America*, 156, 158–160; Archdeacon, *Conquest and Change*, 123–146; Bonomi, *Factious People*, 114–115, 132–133, 136, 246–257; Nash, *Quakers and Politics*, 308, 332–334; Tully, *William Penn's Legacy*, 28–34; Newcomb, *Franklin and Galloway*, 32–36; 122–124, 144; Nash, *Urban Crucible*, 88–92, 99–100, 144–146, 229–231, 264–271, 288–291, 365–366.

3. *NY Votes*, 2:599–601.

4. Philip Livingston II was the brother of William Livingston and of Robert Livingston, Jr., the third lord of Livingston manor. For a detailed comment on the 1761 New York City and County election, see chapter 8, pp. 317–318.

5. Bonomi underplays the extent of voting agreement between the Livingstons in the legislature, but their cohesiveness as a legislative voting bloc, however we measure it, was far less important in establishing the Livingston reputation than the growing eminence of Robert R. and Philip Livingston, and the combined clout of the three New York lawyers, William Livingston, William Smith, Jr., and John Morin Scott. Bonomi, *Factious People*, 232.

6. Thomas Jones, *History of New York during the Revolutionary War . . .* , 2 vols. (New York, 1879), 1:5; Smith, *Memoirs*, 1:24, 48, 49; William Smith, Jr., to Philip Schuyler, 18 Jan. 1768, Schuyler Papers, NYPL.

7. The first of these controversies began with the termination of Lieutenant-Governor James DeLancey's commission as chief justice on his death, and broadened shortly thereafter when George II's demise voided the remaining supreme court commissions. All of these commissions had been for good behavior. The second began in the summer of 1763, when an undistinguished New Yorker, Waddel Cunningham, assaulted and badly injured another obscure city resident, Thomas Forsey. Found guilty and fined in a criminal case, Cunningham was also assessed £1,500 damages in a civil suit. Unwilling to accept such a large judgment, Cunningham wanted to appeal the supreme court decision to the governor-in-council. Hitherto, such appeals had only been allowed by grant of a writ of error claiming a mistake in application of the law or irregularities in legal procedures. Cunningham, however, wanted a review of the facts as well; in other words, he wanted to challenge the decision of a jury by appealing to an executive tribunal. For a detailed treatment of these two controversies, see Milton Klein, "Prelude to Revolution in New York:

Jury Trials and Judicial Tenure," *WMQ*, 3d ser., 17 (1960): 439–462.

8. Cadwallader Colden to Governor William Shirley, 25 July 1749, *Colden Papers*, 4:124–125.

9. For an example of Colden's assertions, see "State of the Province of New York," 6 Dec. 1765, *The Cadwallader Colden Letter Books*, 2 vols. (hereinafter cited as *CCLB*), *Colls.* NYHS, vols. 9–10 (New York, 1877–1878), 2:70–71.

10. Smith, *Memoirs*, 1:89.

11. Robert R. Livingston to Robert Monckton, 23 Feb. 1765, Livingston Family Papers, NYPL.

12. John Watts to Robert Monckton, n.d., *Aspinwall Papers*, 2:549.

13. Smith, *Memoirs*, 1:27–28.

14. In their view, Governor Cosby's dismissal of Lewis Morris, Sr., prior to the Zenger trial proved the danger of a dependent judiciary.

15. Klein, "William Livingston," 511–515.

16. *New-York Gazette, or, the Weekly Post-Boy*, 18 July 1765; John Watts to Robert Monckton, 6 Nov. 1764, *Aspinwall Papers*, 2:537.

17. Kim, *Landlord and Tenant*, 363–365.

18. John Watts to Robert Monckton, 22 Feb. 1766, *Aspinwall Papers*, 2:590.

19. John Watts to Robert Monckton, 10 Dec. 1764, 8 Nov. 1765, ibid., 545, 562.

20. John Watts to Robert Monckton, 24 Sept. 1765, Chalmers Coll., 3, NYPL. For discussion of the events of the Stamp Act crisis generally, see Edmund S. and Helen M. Morgan, *The Stamp Act Crisis: Prologue to Revolution* (Chapel Hill, N.C., 1953; rev. ed., New York, 1963) and P. D. G. Thomas, *British Politics and the Stamp Act Crisis: The First Phase of the American Revolution, 1763–1767* (Oxford, 1975); Merrill Jensen, *The Founding of a Nation: A History of the American Revolution, 1763–1776* (New York, 1968), 98–182.

21. "Representation of the Lords of Trade on Appeals from the New-York Courts," 24 Sept. 1765, Governor Moore to Lords of Trade, 22 Feb. 1766, "Report of the Attorney and Solicitor General on Appeals in New-York," 2 Nov. 1765, *DRCNY*, 7:762–764, 814–816.

22. Smith, *Memoirs*, 1:30; William Livingston to Eleazar Wheelock, 22 Mar. 1764, Wheelock Papers, as cited in Bernhard Knollenberg, *Origin of the American Revolution, 1759–1766*, rev. ed. (New York, 1965), 190–191.

23. Pauline Maier, *From Resistance to Revolution: Colonial Radicals and the Development of American Opposition to Britain, 1765–1776* (New York, 1972), 51–76; Countryman, *People in Revolution*, 37; Jesse Lemisch, "Jack Tar in the Streets: Merchant Seamen in the Politics of Revolutionary America," *WMQ*, 3d ser., 25 (1968): 383–384, 393, 396; Robert R. Livingston to Robert Monckton, 8 Nov. 1765, *Aspinwall Papers*, 2:560.

24. Robert R. Livingston to Robert Monckton, 8 Nov. 1765, *Aspinwall Papers*, 2:561–562.

25. *New-York Gazette, or, the Weekly Post-Boy*, 6 June 1765; Philanthropos, *To the Freeholders and Freemen of the City and County of New York* (New York, 1768), Evans # 11040.

26. Klein, "William Livingston," 531.

27. *New-York Gazette, or, the Weekly Post-Boy*, 31 Oct. 1765.

28. *New-York Journal*, 21 June 1770; G. D. Scull, ed., *The Montresor Journals*, *Colls.* NYHS, 14 (1882), 362, 367–68.

29. Smith, *Memoirs*, 1:30.

30. *New-York Mercury*, 2 Dec. 1765. Another witness to the late November meet-

ing reported the intentions of the original convenors as follows: "let us totally disallow the Force of that Act . . . and unanimously proceed in the course of our *internal* business as if no such Act had ever Pas'd." *Considerations upon the Rights of the Colonists to the Privileges of British Subjects* . . . (New York, 1766), Evans # 10273; *New-York Gazette, or, the Weekly Post-Boy,* 28 Nov. 1765.

31. Goldsbrow Banyar to George Clarke, Jr., 21 Dec. 1765, Goldsbrow Banyar Papers, box 1, NYHS; *New-York Mercury,* 23 Dec. 1765; *New-York Journal,* 10 May 1770.

32. *New-York Gazette, or, the Weekly Post-Boy,* 4 April 1765.

33. For detailed coverage of the land riots, see Kim, *Landlord and Tenant,* 281–415; Irving Mark, *Agrarian Conflicts in Colonial New York, 1711–1775* (New York, 1940); Staughton Lynd, "Who Should Rule at Home? Dutchess County, New York, in the American Revolution," *WMQ,* 3d ser., 18 (1961): 330–359; Countryman, *People in Revolution,* 6–71. For further treatment of the riots, see chapter 9, pp. 382–384.

34. Klein, "William Livingston," 571–572.

35. Bonomi, *Factious People,* 227.

36. Ibid., 233.

37. *Dictionary of American Biography,* 3, pt. 1:213–214.

38. John Watts to Robert Monckton, 23 Jan. 1768, Chalmers Coll., vol. 2, NYPL. For more detail on the 1761 election in New York City and County, see chapter 8, pp. 000–00.

39. Robert J. Christen, "King Sears: Politician and Patriot in a Decade of Revolution" (Ph.D. diss., Columbia University, 1968), 59–61, 98–99.

40. Smith, *Memoirs,* 1:32–33.

41. Becker, *History of Political Parties,* 44n.

42. John Watts to Robert Monckton, 23 Jan. 1768, *Aspinwall Papers,* 2:600. In 1766, Governor Moore demanded that the assembly comply with the British Mutiny Act, which in his view required that the colonies provide billets and various articles of maintenance, the most controversial of which was a daily liquor allowance, for British troops stationed in North America. Viewing this demand as another version of unauthorized taxation, the assembly refused to acknowledge the act, but did vote money for the military expenses—a backhanded acquiescence offering enough in the way of compliance that if he so chose, Governor Moore "might make a meal of what he had got them to do" (Smith, *Memoirs,* 1:33). The British, who were still smarting from their retreat over the Stamp Act, and who had their anger renewed by the New York merchants' temerity in petitioning against a new regulatory Revenue Act in 1766, passed the New York Restraining Act, which lifted the New York Assembly's legislative powers as of 1 Oct. 1767 unless it recognized the Mutiny Act. The assemblymen got out of this predicament by voting enough money for troop maintenance to provide all of the articles listed in the Mutiny Act, a compromise the British accepted.

The well-known second attempt to tax the colonies commenced simultaneously with this testing of New York. Beginning in November 1767, the Townsend Duties were to be levied on all glass, lead, painters' colors, tea, and paper that the North American merchants imported. The proceeds from these duties were to be used for the support of judicial and civil government in the colonies in order to make bench and governors less dependent on the assemblies. In Boston, some residents responded by trying to establish a non-importation agreement. In Philadelphia, John Dickinson began to mobilize public opinion against the new duties by publishing his influential *Letters from an American Farmer*. But in New York, quiescence reigned. See Jack P. Greene, "Social Context and the Causal Pattern of the American Revolution: A Preliminary Consideration of New-York, Virginia and Massachusetts," in *La Revolution americaine et l'Europe* (Paris, 1978), 25–63; Nicholas Varga, "The New York Restraining Act: Its Passage and Some Effects, 1766–68," *NY Hist.* 37 (1956): 233–258; Becker, *History of Political Parties,* 53–94. More generally, see P. D. G. Thomas, *The Townsend Duties Crisis: The Second Phase of the American Revolution, 1767–1773* (Oxford, 1987), and Jensen, *Founding of a Nation,* 183–372.

43. A sixth candidate, Amos Dodge, was a house carpenter by trade and former constable of New York City. "His rejection, even by his fellow mechanics was overwhelming" (Roger J. Champagne, "Liberty Boys and Mechanics of New York City, 1764–1774," *Labor History* 8 [1967]: 130).

44. James Duane to Abraham Ten Broeck, 6 Feb. 1768, Ten Broeck Coll., Albany Institute of History and Art.

45. Bayard had been an influential member of the assembly. He was, however, quite old, had not managed to retain his reputation among the public during the Stamp Act crisis, and finished a poor fifth in the election. Leonard Lispenard had not been a particularly effective representative and did not seek reelection. The remaining incumbent, John Cruger, was highly respected but decided to retire.

46. *From Parker's New-York Gazette, Feb. 15, 1768. On the Cry "No Lawyer in the Assembly."* . . . (New York, 1768), Evans # 10908.

47. *To the Freeholders and Freemen of the City and County of New-York: The Following Remarks on a Piece with 17 Queries* . . . (New York, 1768), Evans # 11088; Philanthropos, *To the Freeholders and Freemen* . . . , Evans # 11040.

48. *A Portrait. Behold! The Barrator with Haughty Stride!* . . . (New York, 1768), Evans # 11048. See also *To the Freemen and Freeholders* . . . (New York, 1768), Evans # 11089; *A Word of Advice* . . . (New York, 1768), Evans # 11125; *The Voter's New Catechism* (New York, 1768), Evans # 11108.

49. *A Card. Mr. Axe and Mr. Hammer Being Solicited* . . . (New York, 1768), Evans # 10849.

50. *A Political Creed for the Day* (New York, 1768), Evans # 11047. For De-Lancey's preeminence on the New York/Philadelphia horseracing and cockfighting circuit, see "Extracts from the Diary of Jacob Hiltzheimer, 1768–1798," *PMHB* 16 (1892): 94–95.

51. *From Parker's New-York Gazette* . . . *"No Lawyer in the Assembly."* The fact that Livingston, Smith, Jr., and Scott could cite their roles in punishing the tenant rioters of 1766 as evidence of laudable service to the community without drawing any rejoinder reveals something of both the local orientation and the oligarchic temper of public debate in New York's provincial politics.

52. Thomas Bradbury Chandler, *An Appeal to the Public, in Behalf of the Church of England in America* (New York, 1767), Evans # 10578; William Livingston to Noah Welles, 2 Feb. 1768, LWC-JFP, YUL.

53. *New-York Gazette, or, the Weekly Post-Boy,* 14 Mar. 1769.

54. *To the Worthy freeholders and Freemen* . . . (New York, 1768), Evans # 11091; *For the Information of the Public* . . . (New York, 1768), Evans # 10898; *From Parker's New-York Gazette* . . . *"No Lawyer in the Assembly."* Klein, "William Livingston," 580, 605.

55. When the religious issue did touch a raw nerve, the DeLancey men fought back with rapier and bludgeon. "Blunder ye *false Tongue* Son of a Bitch . . . Who

Killed the King? not St. Paul's Steeple." "I believe some People would make the religious Rights of their Neighbors, the bone of Dissension, while they themselves are stealing the Flesh." Ditto, *City-hall, High Noon, 10th March, 1768. A Kick for a Bite* . . . (New York, 1768), Evans # 10883; *A Better Creed than the Last* (New York, 1768), Evans # 10832.

56. The election results were Livingston 1,325, DeLancey 1,207, Walton 1,174, Jauncey 1,051, Scott 873, Bayard 587, and Dodge 255. *A Copy of the Poll List of the Election for Representatives for the City and County of New York . . . 1768* (New York, 1880). The totals are my own.

57. Klein, "William Livingston," 583.

58. Bonomi, *Factious People,* 239–240.

59. Lieutenant-Governor Colden to the earl of Hillsborough, 25 Apr. 1768, *DRCNY,* 8:61.

60. And there is no direct evidence that it did, although it is possible to infer such an outcome from the correspondence of William Smith, Jr., with one or two Dutchess County Presbyterian ministers.

61. Klein, "William Livingston," 622–624.

62. *New-York Gazette, or, the Weekly Post-Boy,* 16 May 1768; The chief author of the "Centinel" essays was Francis Alison, with assistance from George Bryan and John Dickinson. See *The Centinel: Warnings of Revolution,* Elizabeth I. Nybakken, ed. (Newark, Del., 1980), and Edmund S. Morgan, *The Gentle Puritan: A Life of Ezra Stiles, 1727–1795* (Chapel Hill, N.C., 1962), 240–249.

63. There were other personal motivating factors that made Livingston eager to pick up his pen and determined him, once he began writing, to wage a protracted war. He was angered by another British refusal to incorporate New York's Brick Presbyterian Church, and evidence existed that the bishop of London himself had lobbied against such a grant. Carl Bridenbaugh, *Mitre and Sceptre: Transatlantic Faiths, Ideas, Personalities, and Politics, 1689–1775* (New York, 1962), 261; Arthur L. Cross, *The Anglican Episcopate and the American Colonies* (New York, 1902), 181. The election results of 1768 also galled the "American Whig" and determined him to push the religious issue until it made a difference in provincial politics.

64. *New-York Gazette, or, the Weekly Post-Boy,* 22 Aug. 1768; Klein, "William Livingston," 589.

65. The "church posse" was composed "chiefly" of those Anglican priests who had "been bred in America & among the dissenters" (*Extracts from the Itineraries and Other Miscellanies of Ezra Stiles, D.D., LL.D. 1755–1794, with a Selection from his Correspondence,* Franklin B. Dexter, ed. [New Haven, 1916], 447, 598).

66. As quoted in Klein, "William Livingston," 631–632. On the bishopric controversy, generally, see Donald F. M. Gerardi, "The Episcopate Controversy Reconsidered: Religious Vocation and Anglican Perceptions of Authority in Mid-Eighteenth-Century America," *Perspectives in American History,* n.s., 3 (1987):81–114.

67. For an example of reported tensions among New Yorkers, see Thomas Ellison, Jr., to Thomas Ellison, Sr., 29 Oct. 1768, Ellison Papers, NYHS. Generally, see Becker, *History of Political Parties,* 53–94.

68. Jensen, *Founding of a Nation,* 250–299.

69. Governor Moore to the earl of Hillsborough, 4 Jan. 1769, *DRCNY,* 8:143.

70. Christen, "King Sears," 105–106; Smith, *Memoirs,* 1:46–47; *New-York Journal,* 1 Dec. 1768.

71. For different views of the legislative maneuvering, see Roger J. Champagne, "The Sons of Liberty and the Aristocracy in New York Politics, 1765–1790" (Ph.D.

diss., University of Wisconsin-Madison, 1960), 175–184; Leopold S. Launitz-Schurer, Jr., *Loyal Whigs and Revolutionaries: The Making of the Revolution in New York, 1765–1776* (New York, 1980), 57–63; Don R. Gerlach, *Philip Schuyler and the American Revolution in New York* (Lincoln, Nebr., 1964), 161–170.

72. Governor Moore to the earl of Hillsborough, 20 Jan. 1769, *DRCNY,* 8:147.

73. Peter R. Livingston to Oliver Wendell, 19 Jan. 1769, Livingston Papers, MCNY.

74. James Duane to Robert Livingston, Jr., 14 June 1769, Livingston-Redmond, reel 6, microfilm, NYHS. See also John Stevens to Lord Sterling, 28 Jan. 1769, William Alexander Papers, NYPL. The day after the assembly's dissolution, a large number of New Yorkers met and agreed that they should support the four incumbents. Immediately thereafter, Captain James DeLancey and his two close associates, Walton and Jauncey, requested Philip Livingston to be their "Chief and Head." By this time, Livingston had the largest following in the city, and despite his increased popularity "Captain DeLancey was not of importance enough (tho' a Gent. of Some Weight)" to challenge him (James Duane to Robert Livingston, Jr., 14 June 1769, Livingston-Redmond, reel 6, microfilm, NYHS). But a group of Presbyterians and a faction of the Dutch Reformed populace that had promoted the introduction of English-language services in their church (among the leaders of whom was William Livingston), were not satisfied with the old ticket. In order to try to strengthen their hand in the assembly, they wrote to DeLancey and Walton asking that these two men stand with two nominees of their choice on a joint Anglican/dissenter ticket. One of their candidates would have been the Dutch Reformed church attender Philip Livingston, the other John Morin Scott. What they were really asking, then, was for DeLancey and Walton to dump Jauncey for a different Presbyterian—one who, in their view, had not sold out to Anglicanism, as Jauncey had done by associating so closely with Episcopalians and remaining indifferent to the bishopric issue. When DeLancey and Walton refused to do so by eleven o'clock, January 4, arguing that they could not bind other Anglicans to support such a ticket, the dissenter-led faction called a public meeting of its own at two o'clock the same day, and nominated a four-person ticket consisting of Philip Livingston, Peter Van Brugh Livingston, Theodorus Van Wyke, and John Morin Scott.

Apparently, Philip Livingston had originally responded negatively to the De-Lancey, Walton, and Jauncey offer because he did not want to be party to another acrimonious election. He would rather refuse to stand. Apparently, too, he initially gave the same answer to his brother William and his gang. But the only hope of avoiding a contested election—and Philip was far too politically prescient not to realize this—was for him to have accepted inclusion on an incumbents' ticket. Once he refused the initial overture, and once the dissenting groups nominated a slate of candidates, with or without Philip Livingston, there would be a bruising battle. When the members of the DeLancey ticket heard that Philip Livingston had been nominated by a rival group, they responded by drafting John Cruger, a former mayor and assemblyman. Immediately thereafter, Philip Livingston changed his mind and accepted nomination on the non-Episcopalian ticket. It is impossible to know at what point Philip Livingston decided to be party to his brother William's scheme, but to some of his old friends, Philip had clearly been guilty of duplicity. Claiming to stand above dissension, he had acted to encourage it. Philip was "said to have played a double Game" in joining "the Presbyterian party; because whether he meant to do it or not his Conduct had that Colour" (John Jay to Robert R. Livingston, [?] 1769, Robert R. Livingston Coll.; James Duane to Robert Livingston,

Jr., 14 June 1769, Livingston-Redmond, reel 6, microfilm, NYHS). The sources for my construction of these events are William Smith, Jr., to Robert R. Livingston, 5 Jan. 1769, Robert R. Livingston Coll., and James Duane to Robert Livingston, Jr., 14 June 1769, Livingston-Redmond, reel 6, microfilm, NYHS; *As a Scandalous Paper has Appeared* . . . (New York, 1769), Evans # 11163; John Cruger et al., *To the Freeholders and Freemen* . . . (New York, 1769), Evans # 11229; James DeLancey et al., *To the Freeholders and Freemen* . . . (New York, 1769), Evans # 11234; *The Conclusion of the Answers . . . No. III* . . . (New York, 1769), Evans # 11262; George Harison et al., *City of New-York, ss. January 6th, 1769* . . . (New York, 1769), Evans # 11284; Honestus, *An Anecdote of a Certain Candidate* . . . (New York, 1769), Evans # 11293; Philip Livingston, *To the Freeholders and Freemen* . . . (New York, 1769), Evans # 11311; Philip Livingston et al., *To the Freeholders and Freemen* . . . (New York, 1769), Evans # 11312; *New-York, January 4, 1769* . . . (New York, 1769), Evans # 11375.

75. Peter R. Livingston to Philip Schuyler, 16 Jan. 1769, Schuyler Papers, NYPL.

76. *Reasons for the Present Glorious Combination of the Dissenters* . . . (New York, 1769), Evans # 11436.

77. John Wetherhead to Sir William Johnson, 9 Jan. 1769, in *The Papers of Sir William Johnson,* James Sullivan et al., eds., 14 vols. (Albany, 1921–1965), 6:574–576.

78. *The Examiner, No. III* . . . (New York, 1769), Evans # 11254.

79. Cruger et al., *To the Freeholders and Freemen* . . . ; id., *Whereas a Paper, signed Philo Patriae* . . . (New York, 1769), Evans # 11230. This distribution of religious representation replicated that of the four 1768 city representatives.

80. *The Querist . . . No. I* . . . (New York, 1769), Evans # 11431. Livingston and his friends again demonstrated the narrow side of their peculiar provincialism by their failure to recognize that although the term "dissenters" had positive connotations to themselves, it was anathema to some German Lutherans. To these, being a dissenter meant both to be derivative in the sense of not being an "Original Religion" and to be vulnerable because of being not quite legitimate. Those Lutherans most closely attuned to a statist tradition still looked favorably on the apparent benefits of religious establishments. Roeber, *Palatines, Liberty, and Property,* 24, 108, 292, and passim.

81. *The Querist . . . No. II* . . . (New York, 1769), Evans # 11432.

82. The Freeholder, *Conclusion to the Answers . . . No. III* . . . . These last two charges refer to the influence of Presbyterians in fomenting a split between English-service advocates and Dutch-service traditionalists in the Dutch Reformed church, and the fact that the Presbyterians went over the heads of City Dutch Reformed dominies by appealing directly to the *classis* of Amsterdam to further their ends. Wall, "Controversy in the Dutch Church."

83. *Observations on the Reasons, Lately Published* . . . (New York, 1769), Evans # 11394.

84. Ibid.

85. Cruger et al., *To the Freeholders and Freemen.* . . .

86. *New-York Mercury,* 20 Feb. 1769. See also n. 74 for further evidence of how Philip Livingston's reputation suffered during the campaign.

87. *An Answer to the Foolish Reason* . . . (New York, 1769), Evans # 11160; *As a Scandalous Paper has Appeared.*

88. *Querist . . . No. I; A Card. Jack Hatchway, and Tom Bowling* . . . (New York, 1769), Evans # 11199.

89. *The Freeholders and the Freemen of the City of New-York* . . . (New York, 1769), Evans # 11264; Gezelena Rousby, *To the Freeholders and Freemen* . . . (New York, 1769), Evans # 11447; id., *New York, January 20, 1769* . . . (New York, 1769), Evans #11448; *A Contrast* . . . (New York, 1769), Evans # 11223; James Jauncey, *Mr. Jauncey Heartily Thanks His Worthy Friends* . . . (New York, 1769), Evans # 11302.

90. *The English Independent* . . . (New York, 1769), Evans # 11249.

91. John Jay to Robert R. Livingston, [?] 1769, Bancroft Coll., Transcripts, Livingston Papers, # 264, NYPL. Others referred to the contest as one between churchmen and "non-Episcopalians," or between "Church" and "Discenters." Gerard Bancker to Lord Sterling, 9 Jan. 1769, William Alexander Papers, NYPL; Peter R. Livingston to Oliver Wendell, 19 Jan. 1769, Livingston Papers, MCNY.

92. John Stevens to Lord Sterling, 28 Jan. 1769, William Alexander Papers, NYPL.

93. Gerlach, *Philip Schuyler,* 174–183; Peter R. Livingston to Philip Schuyler, 16 and 23 Jan. 1769, Schuyler Papers, NYPL.

94. Peter R. Livingston to Philip Schuyler, 6 Feb. 1769; Robert R. Livingston to Philip Schuyler, 28 Jan. 1769, Schuyler Papers, NYPL.

95. Although Lewis Morris III was expelled from the assembly in April 1769 for nonresidence (Bonomi, *Factious People,* 311).

96. Peter R. Livingston to Philip Schuyler, 6 Feb. 1769; Robert R. Livingston to Philip Schuyler, 28 Jan. 1769, Schuyler Papers, NYPL; Peter Van Schaack to Henry Van Schaack, 27 Jan. 1769, Francis L. Hawks Papers, NYHS.

97. There was none as well in the 1768 election.

98. Gerlach, *Philip Schuyler,* 178–180.

99. Which is not to say that religious issues were of no relevance. That in the short time Lewis Morris III sat in the assembly before his expulsion in favor of DeLancey, he introduced a bill exempting all Protestants in the four establishment counties from taxes to support ministers of congregations to which they did not belong, and that the Westchester County assemblyman John Thomas, an Anglican minister's son, brought in a later bill to exempt all Protestants from compulsory religious taxation, seems to indicate that both legislators felt the need to play to their dissenting constituents. (Both may have been practicing sharp-minded, cynical politics, for they surely knew that the Anglicans in New York's council would refuse such legislation.) Perhaps the religious issue gained some immediacy when Frederick Philipse petitioned the assembly to allow mandatory taxation on his Westchester Manor to support a minister for the Anglican church the Philipse family had built (Jordan, "Anglican Establishment," 348, 409, 472). Even though Philipse claimed that all his tenants save three supported the petition, the assembly refused to act on his request. The Freeholder, *A Continuation of the Answers, to the Reasons, Freeholder, No. II* . . . (New York, 1769), Evans # 11261.

100. Chauncey Graham to William Smith, Jr., 11 July 1755, William Smith Papers, box 1, lot 189 # 6, NYPL. Note that Jordan ("Anglican Establishment," 411) identifies one of Livingston's opponents, Leonard Van Kleeke, as an Anglican. It seems quite likely that by 1765, the self-consciously religious Robert R. Livingston had become a covert supporter of colonial episcopacy. See the draft of an essay on the need for bishops (approximately 1766) in the Robert R. Livingston Coll., reel 1, NYHS.

101. *An Address to the Freeholders of Dutchess County* . . . (New York, 1769), Evans # 11135; *A Letter from a Gentleman in New-York, to his Friend in Dutchess*

County . . . (New York, 1769), Evans # 11309; John Jay to Robert R. Livingston, [?] Jan. 1769, Robert R. Livingston Coll., reel 1; Robert R. Livingston to Robert Livingston, Jr., 21 Feb. 1768, Livingston-Redmond, reel 6, microfilm, NYHS; Robert R. Livingston to Philip Schuyler, 28 Jan. 1769, Schuyler Papers, NYPL.

102. DeLancey headed the poll with 936 votes. Philip Livingston received 666 votes, the highest of the losing candidates. *A Copy of the Poll List of the Election for Representatives for the City and County of New-York . . . 1769* (New York, 1880).

103. Countryman, *People in Revolution,* 91, 93–94.

104. The former on grounds of nonresidency, and the latter with a highly specific place-bill argument that supreme court judges should no longer be allowed to sit in the provincial assembly. Bonomi, *Factious People,* 259–260; Champagne, "Sons of Liberty," 176–183, 190–194.

105. James Duane to Robert Livingston, Jr., 17 May 1769, Livingston-Redmond, reel 6, microfilm, NYHS.

106. Peter R. Livingston to Robert Livingston, Jr., 20 April 1770, ibid.

107. Klein, "William Livingston," 632–634; Herbert L. Osgood, "The Society of Dissenters founded at New York in 1769," *AHR* 6 (1901):498–507. But notice the counterproductive side of this organization mentioned in n. 80.

108. Osgood, "Society of Dissenters," 499.

109. See pp. 202–209 for further comment on the ethnoreligious dimensions of politics.

110. Alexander McDougall, *To the Betrayed Inhabitants of the City and Colony of New York* (New York, 1769), Evans # 11319. On McDougall, see Roger J. Champagne, *Alexander McDougall and the American Revolution in New York* (Schenectady, N.Y., 1975).

111. Gerlach, *Philip Schuyler,* 191, 197–198; Launitz-Schurer, *Loyal Whigs and Revolutionaries,* 72–96; Champagne, "Sons of Liberty," 190–194, 201–248; James S. Olson, "The New York Assembly, the Politics of Religion, and the Origins of the American Revolution, 1768–1771," *HMPEC* 43 (1974): 21–28.

112. Olson, "New York Assembly."

113. Howard H. Peckham, *Pontiac and the Indian Uprising* (Chicago, 1961), 15–16, 96–107. For contemporary speculation on the causes of the French and Indian War, see *PBF,* 10:303–304.

114. *PBF,* 10:293–294.

115. Sipe, *Indian Wars of Pennsylvania,* 450–469.

116. Dunbar, *Paxton Papers,* 17–22.

117. Ibid., 18–19; Hutson, *Pennsylvania Politics,* 10, 73–77.

118. Dunbar, *Paxton Papers,* 20–21; Hutson, *Pennsylvania Politics,* 79.

119. My account of the Paxton Boys episode is based on Brooke Hindle, "The March of the Paxton Boys," *WMQ,* 3d ser., 3 (1946): 461–486; Herbutis M. Cummings, "The Paxton Killings," *Journal of Presbyterian History* 44 (1966): 219–243; James E. Crowley, "The Paxton Disturbances and Ideas of Order in Pennsylvania Politics," *Pa. Hist.* 37 (1970): 317–339; Peter A. Butzin, "Politics, Presbyterians and the Paxton Riots, 1763–1764," *Journal of Presbyterian History* 51 (1973), 71–84; Dunbar, *Paxton Papers,* and Hutson, *Pennsylvania Politics,* 84–86.

120. The negotiating committee included Franklin and a number of other civic leaders.

121. Richard Peters to General Robert Monckton, 19 Jan. 1764, Chalmers Papers, vol. 2, Philadelphia, 1760–1789, NYPL. See also anonymous to governor [?], 31 Dec. 1763, *PA,* 1st ser., 4:156.

122. William Logan to John Smith, 21 Jan. 1764, CJS; John Harris to James Burd, 1 Mar. 1764, Shippen Papers, HSP.

123. Rev. John Elder to Col. Shippen, 7 Feb. 1764, in *Notes and Queries, Historical, Biographical, and Genealogical relating Chiefly to Interior Pennsylvania*, William H. Egle, ed., 3d ser., 3 vols. (1895–1896), 1:164–165.

124. *The Journals of Henry Melchior Muhlenberg*, Theodore G. Tappert and John W. Doberstein, eds. and trans., 3 vols. (Philadelphia, 1942–1958), 2:18–22. Apparently there was also considerable sympathy for the rioters even in the Quaker-dominated eastern counties. According to William Logan "3/4 of all the county . . . [take] the rioters parts." Even an "Indian half-breed" was not safe in Marlborough Township in Chester County. William Logan to John Smith, 28 Jan. 1764, CJS, HSP. See also Sir William Johnson to Governor Penn, 7 June 1765, PA, 1st ser., 4:227.

125. Dunbar, *Paxton Papers*, 104.

126. Ibid., 101. Theodore Thayer, *Israel Pemberton, King of the Quakers* (Philadelphia, 1943).

127. Dunbar, *Paxton Papers*, 104.

128. Ibid.

129. Ibid., 79–82.

130. Ibid., 57.

131. Ibid., 60–61.

132. Taking their cue from Franklin, the Presbyterian writers graphically described the atrocities Indian savagery had visited on the frontier inhabitants in the 1750s and again during the preceding year (ibid., 185–187). They argued that the Quakers' "thirst for Domination" had kept them in government too long during the French and Indian War, and had brought them oozing back into office in the early 1760s (ibid., 188). Quaker pacifism was at the root of Friends' lack of concern for western defense, yet rather than admit this and disqualify themselves from the legislature at the first echo of a war whoop, they used any subterfuge at hand to stay in the seats of power (ibid., 187–188, 211–212, 214, 270). At the same time, Quakers were guilty of coddling those very Indians whom backcountry residents knew to be in league with the waring tribes (ibid., 190–193, 200, 272, 274). The Paxton Boys had every right, then, to extirpate those Indian "traytors" and to come peaceably, as they did, to Philadelphia to air the grievances they suffered under Quaker legislative leadership (ibid., 293, 210). Those who wrote against the Paxton Boys saw a different situation. Rather than dwelling on the atrocities Indian warfare had brought to the frontier, they emphasized the barbarous nature of the Conestoga massacres (ibid., 56–61). In perpetrating their crime and marching on Philadelphia, the frontiersmen had ignored the law of nations, flouted the standards of civility, and, within their own province, counseled rebellion. They "flew in the face" of government by taking the law into their own hands and by attempting to intimidate the assembly (ibid., 203, 234, 235, 253). What they had in mind, clearly, was a Presbyterian takeover of the Quaker colony (ibid., 255).

133. Ibid., 239.

134. Ibid., 238, 90.

135. Ibid., 134–136.

136. Trinterud, *American Tradition*, 144–165; James McLachlan, *Princetonians, 1748–1768: A Biographical Dictionary* (Princeton, 1976); Dickson, *Ulster Emigration to Colonial America;* John Elder to Col. Shippen, 7 Feb. 1764, in Egle, *Notes and Queries,* 3d ser., 1:164–165; John Armstrong to Thomas Penn, 5 Nov. 1759, PPOC, HSP.

137. James Pemberton to Richard Partridge, 23 Oct. 1755, Pemberton Papers, HSP.

138. Bauman, *Reputation of Truth*, 14. For an example of this kind of thinking, see John Churchman, *An Account of the Gospel Labours and Christian Experiences of . . . John Churchman* (Philadelphia, 1842) 200–201.

139. The last sustained answers individual Quakers wrote to meet Presbyterian criticism of pacifism appeared in the defense crisis of 1747–1748. Thereafter, one of the Quaker meetings might author a short collective defense of their position, but that was all. Dunbar, *Paxton Papers*, 131–138.

140. Dunbar, *Paxton Papers*, 133–138.

141. Ibid., 138.

142. Ibid., 208, 211.

143. James Pemberton to John Fothergill, 7 May 1764, Pemberton Papers, Pemberton-Fothergill, vol. 34, HSP.

144. Dunbar, *Paxton Papers*, 274.

145. Ibid., 211–212. See also Mühlenberg, *Journals*, 2:20.

146. Ibid., 175.

147. Ibid., 133–138.

148. Dunbar, *Paxton Papers*, 246.

149. Ibid., 246–250.

150. Isaac Hunt, *A Letter From a Gentleman in Transilvania . . .* (Philadelphia, 1764), Evans # 9701; Dunbar, *Paxton Papers*, 248, 250.

151. Dunbar, *Paxton Papers*, 250.

152. Ibid., 309.

153. Ibid., 121.

154. Ibid., 305.

155. Ibid., 89.

156. Ibid., 253.

157. Samuel Auchmuty to Richard Peters, 2 Apr. 1772, Peters Papers, HSP.

158. Benjamin Franklin, a founder of the college, Provost William Smith, the former Grammar School teacher David J. Dove, the tutor Isaac Hunt, and the mathematics professor Hugh Williamson were all major contributors to the Paxton riot literature. Franklin and Smith's mutual hostility was, by this time, of long duration, and it is not surprising to see them on opposite sides of the controversy. David J. Dove was an irascible individual who would turn his acid pen on whoever happened to be his most recent bête noire—in 1764, the Quakers. (Joseph Jackson, "A Philadelphia Schoolmaster of the Eighteenth Century," *PMHB* 35 [1911]: 315–332.) The two college teachers, Hunt and Williamson, reveal more about the tensions in the college than the others. The Anglican Hunt felt that the Presbyterians had virtually taken over the college in the early 1760s. At that time, Provost William Smith was the only Anglican professor, and Alison-taught Presbyterians tended to fill the positions of tutor. (Archbishop of Canterbury to Jacob Duche, 16 Sept. 1763, in *Historical Collections*, Perry, ed., 2:389–391; Dunbar, *Paxton Papers*, 310; Gough, "Pluralism, Politics, and Power Struggles," 420–422.) Hunt felt that the college was threatened by the same kind of aggressive Presbyterian quest for dominance that the Paxton Boys seemed to represent in society at large. The Presbyterian Hugh Williamson saw things much differently. Despite Presbyterian and Baptist presence on the faculty, the Board of Trustees was dominated by Anglicans, and Williamson perceived Provost William Smith as a dangerous influence, whose personal agenda was to promote Anglicanism within the college. (Gough, "Pluralism, Politics, and

Power Struggles," 411–412.) The fact that some of Alison's Presbyterian students were "enticed" by "Episcopal acquaintances" and an acquired "taste for high life" to forsake their church for episcopal orders, seemed to prove the case. Alison to Stiles, 30 Oct. 1766, in Dexter, *Itineraries . . . of Ezra Stiles,* Dexter, ed., 428. Presbyterians needed to strike out against the encroaching power of Anglicanism in order to protect themselves.

159. Robert H. Morris to John Armstrong, [?] Sept. 1756, Gratz Coll., box 18, case 15, HSP; Ingersoll, "Alison," 109–111.

160. Contemporaries understood the Paxton Boys' demands for equality in a variety of ways. See , e.g., James Pemberton to John Fothergill, 7 May 1764, Pemberton Papers, Pemberton-Fothergill, vol. 34, HSP; Dunbar, *Paxton Papers,* 105; William Allen to Benjamin Chew, 13 Apr. 1764, "William Allen–Benjamin Chew Correspondence, 1763–1764," *PMHB* 90 (1966): 222–223; Francis Alison to Ezra Stiles, 15 Apr. 1764, Alison-Stiles Correspondence, transcripts, Presbyterian Historical Society (hereinafter cited as PHS).

161. Dunbar, *Paxton Papers,* 105. Protest against underrepresentation had already begun in 1763, prior to the Paxton affair, *Pa. Votes,* 6:5419–5420.

162. Dunbar, *Paxton Papers,* 342.

163. Tully, "Englishmen and Germans."

164. *An Address to the Rev. Dr. Alison, the Rev. Mr. Ewing, and others . . .* (Philadelphia, 1765), 19–20, Evans # 9892.

165. *To the Freeholders and other Electors for the City and County of Philadelphia, and Counties of Chester and Bucks* (Philadelphia, 1764), Evans # 9854.

166. Dunbar, *Paxton Papers,* 226–227, 237.

167. It was precisely on these grounds that Cumberland County petitioners challenged the assembly. *Pa. Votes,* 7:5582.

168. Dunbar, *Paxton Papers,* 304–305.

169. Taxes to redeem the currency that the 1759 act authorized were not to be levied until 1764, and in the case of that authorized by the 1760 act, not until 1767.

170. These are printed in Hutson, *Pennsylvania Politics,* 60–61.

171. For thorough treatment of this prolonged episode of proprietary/assembly conflict, see Hutson, "Benjamin Franklin," and *Pennsylvania Politics.*

172. Thomas Penn's nephew John became governor in November 1763.

173. Hutson, *Pennsylvania Politics,* 60.

174. Actually, the decision to interpret the Privy Council stipulation in this literal fashion was not Thomas Penn's at all but that of Attorney-General Benjamin Chew. Penn repudiated Chew when he learned of the proceedings in Pennsylvania, but by that time it was too late to avoid the consequences. Hutson, *Pennsylvania Politics,* 114–115.

175. *PBF,* 11:123–133.

176. Franklin had gone to London in 1757 as the assembly's commissioner to try to persuade Thomas Penn to relax his instructions that demanded joint executive/legislative appropriation of all revenues, and to reconcile himself to the considerable political powers that the Pennsylvania Assembly had accrued. Penn made a fool of Franklin in the subsequent negotiations, prying from the Pennsylvania agent a written list of demands, which the proprietor then used to elicit opinions from legal counsel to the Privy Council, buttressing Penn's position. Although Franklin stayed in Great Britain until 1762, and gained some satisfaction when the Privy Council upheld the right of the Pennsylvania government to tax proprietary property, he returned to Philadelphia filled with loathing for that "low Jockey" Thomas

Penn (*PBF*, 7:362). When that judgment seemed substantiated by the events of early 1764, Franklin was ready to take radical action. While he had been in Great Britain, Franklin had played with the idea of petitioning for royal government as a way of wreaking vengeance on Thomas Penn, and, ever the opportunist, he exaggerated the opinions of a handful of minor Whitehall hangers-on (that the Crown was both eager to assume proprietary charters, and that in any such change, existing provincial rights would be secure) into a strong promise of help and protection. Royalization of the colonies seemed to dovetail with the centralizing tendencies evident in the British imperium subsequent to the French collapse in North America. That was something Franklin's Philadelphia friends could conclude on their own, but they were also eager to defer to Franklin's judgment on such matters, for the former printer's credibility jumped dramatically the moment he succeeded in gaining the governorship of New Jersey for his illegitimate son, William. Anyone with that kind of clout had to know the minds of important British ministers. Hutson, *Pennsylvania Politics*, 41–59, 145–146. For Franklin's relationship with his son William, see Sheila Skemp, *William Franklin: Son of a Patriot, Servant of a King* (Oxford, 1990).

177. During this period, the letters of Galloway, Hughes, Pemberton, and a few others bristle with invective against the Presbyterians. Literal acceptance of their occasional ramblings can lead to the proposition that a strong "Presbyterian Party" was the focal point of provincial politics in the 1760s and 1770s. For this interpretation, see Hutson, *Pennsylvania Politics*, 211–243.

178. *PBF*, 11:134–144.

179. Dunbar, *Paxton Papers*, 339–351, 367, 386; *PBF*, 11:153–173; *An Address to the Freeholders and Inhabitants of the Province of Pennsylvania* . . . (Philadelphia, 1764), Evans # 9561.

180. John Dickinson, *A Speech, Delivered in the House of Assembly* . . . (Philadelphia, 1764), Evans # 9641; Joseph Galloway, *The Speech of Joseph Galloway, Esq.* . . . (Philadelphia, 1764), Evans # 9671.

181. Galloway, *Speech*, 29.

182. John Dickinson, *A Reply to a Piece Called the Speech of Joseph Galloway* . . . (Philadelphia, 1764), 17, Evans # 9640.

183. Dickinson, *Speech*, 3.

184. Ibid. From Provost William Smith's "Preface."

185. Dunbar, *Paxton Papers*, 341.

186. Ibid., 348.

187. Ibid., 341.

188. Ibid., 351.

189. Hutson, *Pennsylvania Politics*, 111. Whatever support the proprietary men had extended to the frontiersmen was both recent and opportunistic in nature. See John Elder to Richard Peters, 30 July 1757, Gratz Coll., American Clergy, HSP; *The Scribbler: Being a Letter from a Gentleman in Town to his Friend in the Country* . . . (Philadelphia, 1764), 15, Evans # 9831; and Tully, "Quaker Party and Proprietary Policies," 99–100.

190. Hutson, *Pennsylvania Politics*, 126–127.

191. Ibid., 127.

192. Ibid., 147.

193. *Observations on a Late Epitaph* . . . (Philadelphia, 1764), Evans # 9772.

194. Dunbar, *Paxton Papers*, 311–312.

195. William Logan to John Smith, 28 Jan. 1764, CJS, HSP; Mühlenberg, *Journals*, 2:19.

196. Hutson, *Pennsylvania Politics,* 129.

197. Ibid., 164, 168.

198. Ibid., 173–174.

199. Joseph Galloway, *Historical and Political Reflections of the Rise and Progress of the American Rebellion* (London, 1980), 49–53.

200. Hutson, *Pennsylvania Politics,* 165–166. The vice-admiralty judge Edward Shippen, Jr., also played a role in party organization (*PBF,* 11:526). Members of the Shippen family profited immensely from the naturalization fees Germans paid in the Proprietary Party's drive to increase the number of eligible voters (see Edward Burd to Sarah Burd, 5 Oct. 1765, *Burd Papers,* Walker, ed., 9).

201. Gough, "Pluralism, Politics, and Power Struggles," 460, 462–464, 480–481. Distrust of Smith's church ambitions went back to midcentury (*Pennsylvania Journal,* 25 Mar. 1756). It was one of the ironies of Smith's life that he was trapped on the wrong side of a policy he would dearly have liked to support.

202. One of the projects Alison had poured great energy into was the Presbyterian Ministers' Fund, an insurance cooperative for the clergy and their dependents. In late 1763, Alison found out that Smith had persistently tried to sabotage the efforts of the fund's money raiser, Charles Beattie, when both were appealing for support in Great Britain (Ingersoll, "Alison," 278–282). Alison papered over his differences with Smith in the short run, but he had virtually decided that he could no longer work with the provost and had begun exploring options at the College of New Jersey and the New Ark Academy. Despite his support for Presbyterian politicians in the current disputes, Alison deplored the fighting between his co-religionists and Quakers. He feared that contention between them would work to the advantage of what he perceived as an increasingly aggressive Anglicanism. He shared the fear of his fellow Presbyterian Hugh Williamson that the reorganization of the British empire in the wake of the French and Indian War meant "stamp-offices, customs, excises and duties," and possibly "tythes in the bargain" (Dunbar, *Paxton Papers,* 350). As Alison lamented to the Rhode Island Congregationalist Ezra Stiles, "the mice and Frogs may fight, till Kite devours both" (15 Apr. 1764, Alison-Stiles Corresp., transcripts, PHS).

203. Isaac Hunt, *The Birth, Parentage, and Education of Praise-God Barebone* . . . (Philadelphia, 1766), Evans # 10339; *PBF,* 11:296.

204. John Penn to Thomas Penn, 12 Sept. 1766, PPOC, HSP.

205. Isaac Hunt, *Advertisement* . . . *Proposals, for Printing by Subscription* . . . (Philadelphia, 1766), Evans # 10338.

206. William Logan to John Smith, 25 Mar. and 28 Sept. 1764, CJS, HSP.

207. *PBF,* 11:381–384.

208. Ibid., 389.

209. *The Scribbler,* Evans # 9576.

210. In Bucks and Chester counties, only a sprinkling of Quakers signed the petitions for a change of government and both Scotch-Irish and German churchmen were sturdily opposed. Rural Anglicans apparently maintained an equivocal position, their ministers "sign[ing] . . . neither [Quaker nor Proprietary party petitions]; encourag[ing] . . . neither; but . . . [keeping] close to the duties of . . . [their] missions" (Hugh Neill to the secretary, SPG, 18 Oct. 1764, in *Historical Collections,* Perry, ed., 2:365).

211. William Allen to Thomas Penn, 21 Oct. 1764, PPOC, HSP. See also Hutson, *Pennsylvania Politics,* 170, 178–179.

212. If Allen is to be taken literally, his comment meant that country assembly-

men and other rural Quaker Party leaders recognized how strongly public opinion ran against the petition for royal government and turned a somersault on the issue, accusing their rivals of advocating the change! They could do so because they had more credibility and for decades had possessed a near monopoly on political news outside Philadelphia. Once back in the assembly, Quaker Party leaders could work to play down the quest for royal government, unless it was certain of succeeding with Pennsylvania's rights intact. A second, and more likely, meaning of Allen's statement was that if the Proprietary Party won, government as Pennsylvanians had known it would be changed—for the governor's men had very different ideas about the proper distribution of executive and legislative power and the accountability of the proprietary than did members of the Quaker Party (Lively, "Speaker and His House," 232n). If this was the meaning of his letter, what Allen pinpointed was an effort by the Quaker Party to capitalize on its historic role as champion of popular rights. Pennsylvanians voted the Assembly Party record despite their disagreement with the petition for royal government, perhaps fearing the Proprietary Party as a worse alternative, and thinking that they could trust the Old Party to proceed with Franklin's scheme only if traditional rights were guaranteed.

213. Quaker Party stalwarts saw the issue as who would be the best "friend[s] to Liberty and the [provincial] Constitution" (John Morton to Joseph Pennock, Sr., 23 June 1764, Misc. MS, Chester County Historical Society). For the values and policies associated with Quaker power, see chapter 7.

214. *PBF,* 11:390–394. Although once the House convened, one of the six, Henry Pawling, consistently supported the Quaker Party.

215. Ibid., 397.

216. Tully, "Englishmen and Germans."

217. Roeber, *Palatines, Liberty, and Property,* 178, 194–195.

218. Ibid., 285–286; Newcomb, *Franklin and Galloway,* 95.

219. *PBF,* 11:294–295.

220. See chapter 7.

221. *PBF,* 11:397, 402n.

222. Ibid., 408–412, 424.

223. Ibid., 409, 439–441.

224. Ibid., 486–516, 12:44, 83; Evans # 9892, 10014–10022, 10033, 10143.

225. Hutson, *Pennsylvania Politics,* 180–190.

226. *PBF,* 11:168–169.

227. Ibid., 12:47–60.

228. Ibid., 106–107.

229. Ibid., 207–208.

230. Ibid., 234–235.

231. Hutson, *Pennsylvania Politics,* 192–194.

232. *PBF,* 11:431–432.

233. Hutson, *Pennsylvania Politics,* 196–201.

234. Gough, "Pluralism, Politics, and Power Struggles," 417–419.

235. *PBF,* 11:527–528, 12:241.

236. Ibid., 11:528.

237. Lively, "Speaker and His House," 251.

238. *PBF,* 12:258.

239. Ibid., 258; James Biddle, *To the Freeholders and Electors of the Province of Pennsylvania* (Philadelphia, 1765), Evans # 9915.

240. *PBF,* 12: 374.

241. *To the Freeholders and Other Electors of Assembly-Men, For Pennsylvania* (Philadelphia, 1765), Evans # 10184.

242. Newcomb, *Franklin and Galloway,* 122; Edward Shippen, Sr., to James Burd, 11 Dec. 1765, Burd-Shippen Papers, APS. Quite likely Quaker Party leaders scented some of the ambivalence of German Lutheran leaders such as Mühlenberg, who were strong for the proprietary charter but counseled acceptance of the Stamp Act (Roeber, *Palatines, Liberty, and Property,* 292).

243. *The Counter Medley* . . . (Philadelphia, 1765), Evans # 9943; *The Lamentation, of Pennsylvania* (Philadelphia, 1765), Evans # 10031; *The Whiteoak Anthum* . . . (Philadelphia, 1765), Evans # 10211.

244. Newcomb, *Franklin and Galloway,* 122.

245. *PBF,* 12:290.

246. Sons of Liberty in Philadelphia to Brethren, 15 Feb. 1766, John Lamb Papers, reel 1, NYHS.

247. *PBF,* 12:263–266, 269–270.

248. Newcomb, *Franklin and Galloway,* 144–145; *PBF,* 12:356–357, 392n; Dinkin, *Voting in Provincial America,* 146.

249. Ryerson, "Quaker Elite," 123–124, 131–132.

250. John Penn to Thomas Penn, 12 Nov. 1766, William Allen to Thomas Penn, 8 Oct. 1767, PPOC, HSP. See also Samuel Purviance to Ezra Stiles, 1 Nov. 1766, in *Itineraries . . . of Ezra Stiles,* Dexter. ed., 556–557.

251. Francis Alison to Ezra Stiles, 4 June 1768, Alison-Stiles Corresp., transcripts, PHS.

252. Richard R. Ryerson, *The Revolution Is Now Begun: The Radical Committees of Philadelphia, 1765–1776* (Philadelphia, 1978), 25–38; Hutson, *Pennsylvania Politics,* 230–243.

253. Peter Van Schaack to Henry Van Schaack, 27 Jan. 1769, Francis L. Hawks Papers, NYHS.

254. Scott accounted for 33 percent of these, and Jauncey for only 16 percent. An additional 30.5 percent of the Presbyterians' votes went to the Dutch Reformed candidate Philip Livingston. The evidence for this and related generalizations about voting behavior in the 1761, 1768, and 1769 elections is in Tully, "Religion and Voting Behavior in Late Colonial New York" (MS).

255. Two-fifths of the split tickets sacrificed the Dutch Reformed candidate Theodorus Van Wyke for the nominal Presbyterian James Jauncey.

256. Tully, "Ethnicity," 516.

257. Hugh Neill to secretary, SPG, 17 Oct. 1763, in *Historical Collections,* Perry, ed., 2:354–355; Westerkamp, *Triumph of the Laity,* 165–213. While the main divisions were between Old and New Lights, acrimony also distinguished the relationships of both Old and New Lights with Covenanters and Seceders. See, e.g., Ingersoll, "Alison," 249–252. For the sharp disagreements among Philadelphia Presbyterians, see Foster, "George Bryan," 37–53.

258. Tully, "Ethnicity," 516–518, 526, 528, 531.

259. Howe, "Accommodation and Retreat."

260. On the extensive influence of sectarians among other Germans, see Schwartz, *"Mixed Multitude,"* 143–144. For Saur's importance and linkage with the traditions established by his father, see Roeber, *Palatines, Liberty, and Property,* 195–198, 284–287. For the confusing and more restricted impact of Henry Miller's *Der Wöchentliche Philadelphische Staatsbote,* see ibid., 188, 204, 284–285, 290.

261. Peter Van Schaack to Henry Van Schaack, 27 Jan. 1769, Francis L. Hawks Papers, NYHS.

262. *PBF,* 11:397; Samuel Purviance, Jr., to James Burd, 20 Sept. 1765, Shippen Papers, HSP.

263. Unfortunately the destruction of Trinity Church membership records precludes any possibility of exploring the provincial voting record of New York City and County Anglicans.

264. Firth H. Fabend, *A Dutch Family in the Middle Colonies, 1660–1800* (New Brunswick, N.J., 1991), 178–189. See also chapter 4, pp. 139–140.

265. Of the identifiable voting members of the English-language faction, 97.2 percent and 87.7 percent supported Philip Livingston and John Morin Scott respectively.

266. Of the identifiable voting members of the Dutch-language faction, 27.5 percent and 20.0 percent supported Livingston and Scott respectively. Amos Dodge, a house builder, drew only a smattering of votes and occupied seventh place on both factions' lists.

267. Robert P. Swierenga, "Ethnoreligious Political Behavior in the Mid-Nineteenth Century: Voting, Values, Cultures," in *Religion and American Politics: From the Colonial Period to the 1980s,* Mark A. Noll, ed. (New York, 1990), 146–171, is a good, up-to-date summary of much of the important literature developing the argument for ethnoreligious politics, and also citing some of the worthwhile pieces critical of that approach. On the concept of negative-reference groups in ethnocultural politics, see 149–150. See also Ronald P. Formisano, "The Invention of the Ethnocultural Interpretation," *AHR* 99 (1994): 453–477; McCormick, *Party Period and Public Policy,* 29–63, 89–140; and Robert Kelley, *The Cultural Pattern in American Politics: The First Century* (New York, 1979), 48–80. Wayne L. Bockelman and Owen S. Ireland, "The Internal Revolution in Pennsylvania: An Ethnic-Religious Interpretation," *Pa. Hist.* 41 (1974): 125–159, and Tully, "Ethnicity," are also of relevance.

268. Cornelius Van Horne to [John] White, 3 June 1743, Cornelius Van Horne, Personal Misc., NYHS; Balmer, *Perfect Babel of Confusion,* 104–107; Schwartz, *"Mixed Multitude,"* 149.

269. As quoted in Martha J. Lamb, *History of the City of New York: Its Origin, Rise, and Progress,* 2 vols. (New York, 1877), 1:703–704.

270. It is important to note in this context that New York Presbyterians were by no means united. James Jauncey's close connections with Anglicans, and those of the Scots Seceders with Captain James DeLancey's brother-in-law, John Watts, suggest that divisions among Presbyterians added another ethnoreligious dimension to New York politics that brought supposed Presbyterian and Anglican enemies together in opposition to a coalition of some Presbyterians and Dutch Reformed.

271. Of the 409 white males on our extant list of Dutch Reformed church members, 43.3 percent did *not* record a vote in the division between English and Dutch factions over the church consistory. In the 1768 election, 38.7 percent of the identifiable Dutch Reformed church member voters had *not* participated in the division over the church consistory.

272. That figure rises to 34 percent if we accept the Presbyterian James Jauncey as the least objectionable additional candidate for each side and count votes for the three Anglicans plus Jauncey, or the threesome of Livingston, Scott, and Jauncey, as evidence of a high degree of ethnoreligious consciousness.

273. The distribution of votes cast in the 1768 election by identifiable Dutch

Reformed church members *not* directly involved in the English-Dutch language consistory dispute was as follows: Philip Livingston, 73.9 percent; William Walton, 64.1 percent; Captain James DeLancey, 59.8 percent; John Morin Scott, 55.4 percent; William Bayard, 50.0 percent; James Jauncey, 43.5 percent; Amos Dodge, 3.3 percent.

274. Champagne, "Liberty Boys and Mechanics," 115–135; Nash, *Urban Crucible*, 367; Graham R. Hodges, "The Cartmen of New York City, 1667–1801" (Ph.D. diss., New York University, 1982), 92–97. Despite contemporary comment emphasizing ethnoreligious ties. See, e.g., Peter Van Schaack to Henry Van Schaack, 27 Jan. 1769, Francis L. Hawks Papers, NYHS; I. N. Phelps Stokes, *The Iconography of Manhattan Island*, 6 vols. (New York, 1915–1928), 4:791.

275. It seems likely that the Dutch-language faction of the Collegiate Church was predominantly lower- and lower-middle-class. See, e.g., William Livingston to Rev. David Thompson, 12 Jan. 1756, Livingston Papers, microfilm, YUL. For some slender evidence of religious-based cohesion among lower-middle-class and lower-class Philadelphians, see Steven Rosswurm, *Arms, Country and Class: The Philadelphia Militia and the "Lower Sort" during the American Revolution* (New Brunswick, N.J., 1987), 68. For the relative weakness of community ties among many poorer city artisans, which was as likely in New York as in Philadelphia, see Billy G. Smith, *The "Lower Sort": Philadelphia's Laboring People, 1750–1800* (Ithaca, N.Y., 1990).

276. Dinkin, *Voting in Provincial America*, 156.

277. Some additional reasons for the drop in participation include a strict scrutiny of potential voters' qualifications, resistance to intimidation, distaste for the unfamiliar two-ticket format, and less than favorable weather. For the first two of these, see Gerard Bancker to Lord Sterling, 9 Jan. 1769, William Alexander Papers, NYPL; Nash, *Urban Crucible*, 366–368.

278. See chapter 6 for the structuring of midcentury politics around popular and provincial Whig traditions.

279. On community, see chapter 3, 117; chapter 9, 379–80.

280. Richard Charton [?] to James Duane, 12 February 1768, Duane Papers, NYHS.

281. Tully, "Ethnicity."

282. Mühlenberg, *Journals*, 2:273. In the preceding year Mühlenberg had emphasized the political solidarity of the voting members of "our Lutheran congregation." Ibid., 122.

283. Nor is Mühlenberg's testimony a very helpful guide in unraveling either the ethnic complexities among German-speaking Pennsylvanians or the tensions that accompanied the processes of Pennsylvania German ethnicization. In fact, Pennsylvania Germans were an incredibly diverse collection, and even the Lutherans were fundamentally divided by competing expressions of religious pietism. Of most immediate relevance to the provincial politics of the mid 1760s was the infighting that tore apart Mühlenberg's Philadelphia congregation and led to a schism in St. Michael's of Germantown earlier in the decade. These divisions along with others among Pennsylvania's German-speaking citizens may have gained expression in provincial politics, but that is impossible to tell without poll lists. For fissures among the Lutherans, see Roeber, *Palatines, Liberty, and Property*. On the Germantown schism, see Stephanie G. Wolf, *Urban Village: Population, Community, and Family Structure in Germantown, Pennsylvania, 1683–1800* (Princeton, 1976) 225–226.

284. Roeber, *Palatines, Liberty, and Property*, 191–192.

285. Newcomb, *Franklin and Galloway,* 145.

286. For an extended discussion of civil Quakerism, see chapter 7.

Six / *Factional Identity and Political Coherence in New York*

1. Patricia Bonomi has made that argument the basis of her influential general interpretation of colonial New York, *Factious People.*

2. H. T. Dickinson, *Liberty and Property: Political Ideology in Eighteenth-Century Britain* (London, 1977), 144.

3. On mixed government and the balanced constitution, see Dickinson, *Liberty and Property,* 142–149 and Bailyn, *Ideological Origins,* 70–73.

4. *The Examiner, No. II* . . . (New York, 1769), Evans # 11253.

5. "Colden's Observation on the Balance of Power in Government" [1744–1745?], *Colden Papers,* 9:251. See also F. S., *The Sentiments of a Principal Freeholder* . . . (New York, 1736), Evans #4074.

6. Robert R. Livingston, *The Address of Mr. Justice Livingston* . . . (New York, 1769), Evans # 11313.

7. *New-York Weekly Journal,* 16 Sept. 1735.

8. Livingston, *Address.* See also William Smith Papers, box 2, lot 204 # 3, NYPL; *New-York Evening Post,* 7 Dec. 1747; *NY Votes,* 1:705, 709.

9. Robert R. Livingston to Robert Monckton, 26 Jan. 1765, *Aspinwall Papers,* 2:556.

10. Smith, *History of New-York,* 1:272.

11. Henry Holland to Jacob Glenn, 3 Feb. 1761, Henry Holland Misc. MSS, NYHS.

12. Murrin, "English Rights as Ethnic Aggression."

13. Smith, *History of New-York,* 1:266n.

14. William Livingston made the clearest effort to confront the issue. See *New-York Mercury,* 17 Feb. 1755.

15. *Opinions of Emminent Lawyers,* 1:195; *New-York Mercury,* 30 July 1753; Greene, *Peripheries and Center,* 23–24.

16. See chapters 1 and 2.

17. Joseph Murray, *Mr. Murray's Opinion Relating to the Events of Justice in the Colony of New York* . . . (New York, 1734), Evans # 3799; William Smith, Sr., *Mr. Smith's Opinion Humbly Offered to the General Assembly of the Colony of New York* . . . (New York, 1734), Evans # 3834.

18. Smith, *History of New-York,* 1:267n. And it appears that there was very uneven and inconsistent application of English statutes. See Herbert Alan Johnson, "The Advent of Common Law in Colonial New York," in *Law and Authority in Colonial America,* George Athan Billias, ed. (Barre, Mass., 1964), 74–87, and id., "English Statutes in Colonial New York," *NY Hist.* 57 (1977): 277–296. See also Greene, *Peripheries and Center,* 25–28.

19. Cadwallader Colden to Archibald Kennedy, 4 Apr. 1745, *Colden Papers,* 8:311.

20. *New-York Weekly Journal,* 5 Sept. 1737. See also Robert R. Livingston to Robert Livingston, Jr., 12 Apr. 1766, Robert R. Livingston Coll., reel 1, NYHS; Murray, *Mr. Murray's Opinion,* Evans # 3799.

21. *New-York Gazette, revived in the Weekly Post-Boy,* 27 Jan. 1752.

22. Ibid., 17 Mar. 1756.

23. Pocock, *Machiavellian Moment,* 446–461, 464; Dickinson, *Liberty and*

Property, 91–192; W. A. Speck, *Stability and Strife: England, 1714–1760* (London, 1977), 155.

24. Historians who have picked up on the distinction and used it as an organizing principle of New York politics during the second and third decades of the eighteenth century include Bonomi, *Factious People,* 82–102, and Sheridan, *Lewis Morris,* 97, 99–146. For a further-reaching treatment of New York in these terms, see McAnear, "Politics."

25. Hunter, *To All Whom These Presents May Concern;* Sheridan, *Lewis Morris,* 108–109.

26. *NY Laws,* 1:785–788, 801–804, 815–826, 847–857, 938–991.

27. By the mid 1720s the principal figure in this group was Adolphe Philipse. Stephen DeLancey was also of importance.

28. *NY Laws,* 1:254–272.

29. Ibid., 2:53–56, 109–115, 121–125, 137–148, 173–186, 254–272, 273–280, 426–446, 498–500, 530–535. On Morris's inconsistencies on taxation, see also John R. Strassburger, "The Origins and Establishment of the Morris Family in the Society and Politics of New York and New Jersey, 1630–1746" (Ph.D. diss., Princeton University, 1976), 353–354.

30. *NY Laws,* 2:426–446, 688–696, 876–884, 885–892; Governor Montgomerie to Lords of Trade, 21 Dec. 1730, *DRCNY,* 5:906. Rumor had it that the Philipse faction had originally dropped the tonnage duty in the 1720s, not because of any principled mercantile stand against it, but because the collector of the tax was the father-in-law of their political enemy Governor Burnet. New York *Weekly Journal,* 5 Sept. 1737.

31. *NY Laws,* 1:1047–1061.

32. Sheridan, *Lewis Morris,* 99–146.

33. Kim, *Landlord and Tenant,* 147n, 161; Virginia D. Harrington, *The New York Merchant on the Eve of the Revolution* (New York, 1935), 11–15; Cynthia A. Kierner, *Traders and Gentlefolk: The Livingstons of New York, 1675–1790* (Ithaca, N.Y., 1992).

34. "George Clarke to Mr. Walpole," 24 Nov. 1725, as quoted in Kim, *Landlord and Tenant,* 147n.

35. "Mr. [Cadwallader] Colden to Secretary Popple," 4 Dec. 1726, *DRCNY,* 5:806.

36. Bonomi, *Factious People,* 82–85.

37. This calculation is based on the value of land taxes listed in *NY Laws,* vol. 1, during the appropriate years. These were to be collected through 1718 but, in fact, arrearages were so great that collection went on through the 1720s. *NY Laws,* 1:730–732, 751–752, 757–760, 2:41–44, 45–48, 93–94, 420–421, 502–503.

38. "We have experimented in the elections," Governor Hunter advised the Lords of Trade, 14 Mar. 1713, *DRCNY,* 5:356–358.

39. Hunter, *To All Whom These Presents May Concern;* Sheridan, *Lewis Morris,* 107–109.

40. Governor Hunter to Lords of Trade, 3 Nov. 1718, *DRCNY,* 5:520.

41. Hunter, *To All Whom These Presents May Concern;* Sheridan, *Lewis Morris,* 107–109; "Lewis Morris, Esq., to the Secretary of State," 9 Feb. 1708, *DRCNY,* 5:37.

42. Mulford, *Speech;* Governor Hunter to Lords of Trade, 2 Oct. 1716, *DRCNY,* 5:480.

43. Governor Hunter to Secretary Popple, 3 Dec. 1717, *DRCNY,* 5:494.

44. Strassburger, "Morris Family," 281n; *NY Votes,* 1:411; Bonomi, *Factious People,* 85.

45. *The Interest of the Country in Laying Duties* . . . (New York, 1730), Evans # 3289; *The Interest of the Country in Laying No Duties* (New York, 1730), Evans # 3290; *The Two Interests Reconciled* (New York, 1730), Evans # 3363.

46. Governor Montgomerie to Lords of Trade, 30 Nov. 1728, *DRCNY,* 5:872.

47. Aside from its imposition of import duties on wine and spirits.

48. *NY Laws,* 2:426–446.

49. Ibid., 843–847, 867–868.

50. See chapter 8, p. 344.

51. For the court/country dichotomy, see pp. 224–233.

52. *Independent Reflector,* Klein, ed., 61–68.

53. For a detailed description of the election, see *New-York Weekly Journal,* 5 Nov. 1733.

54. Ibid., 23 May 1737.

55. For conflict over colonywide quotas, see, e.g., *NY Votes,* 2:95–97, 109–110. For conflict within counties, see ibid., 2:338; *NY Laws,* 5:110–112; *NY Votes,* 2:338.

56. *NY Laws,* 1:473–474, 3:996–998.

57. John Sidney, *Reply to the Speech of Governor Cosby* (New York, 1734), Evans # 3841.

58. As surveyor-general, Colden well knew that any inventory of unimproved land for tax purposes would assist him in his efforts to collect quitrents, and one of Colden's consistent goals was to bring in enough quitrent revenue to incline the king to grant him a salary from this fund. Colden also hated enough large landowners to spice his quests for land taxes with a nice dash of venom. Although there is no indication that Colden himself wrote the essay in the *New-York Gazette* (11 November 1751) that called for the taxing of unimproved land, it was most likely the work of one of a small number of Colden's associates who supported Governor Clinton in the late 1740s and early 1750s. For a different view of the origins of this piece, see "Mr. Robert R. Livingston's Reasons against a Land Tax," Beverly McAnear, ed., *Journal of Political Economy* 48 (1940): 63n.

59. Robert A. Becker, *Revolution, Reform, and the Politics of American Taxation, 1763–1783* (Baton Rouge, 1980), 64–65. For Colden's interest in taxing land during the mid 1760s, see "Cadwallader Colden to the Rt Honble Lords Commissioners for Trade & Plantations," *CCLB,* 1:361–364.

60. The most noted defender of the large landowners' claim to continued tax exemption was Robert R. Livingston ("Robert R. Livingston's Reasons against a Land Tax," McAnear, ed.) Residents of Suffolk, Queens, and Richmond counties expressed a concern for equitable taxation but it is not at all clear that the perceived inequities included the exemption of unimproved land from taxation. While it is possible to infer that, and Ulster County residents did begin to tax unimproved land in 1762, it is also arguable from the same evidence that the custom of excluding unimproved land was so well established that it needed no statutory mention. It was the rule in neighboring Orange County not to tax unimproved land. *NY Laws,* 3:325, 959–962 4:677–680, 680–682, 721–724, 826–828, 5:110–112.

61. Harrington, *New York Merchants,* 11–15; John Watts to James Napier, 1 June 1765, *JWLB,* 355; Becker, *Politics of American Taxation,* 64.

62. *Examiner, No. II.*

63. See chapter 5, pp. 173–174.

64. Edward Collins to Daniel Horsmanden, 21 [Oct. ?] 1745, Horsmanden Papers, NYHS.

65. See chapter 5, pp. 177–179.

66. Kierner, *Traders and Gentlefolk,* 10–110.

67. See, e.g., "Robert R. Livingston's Reasons against a Land Tax," McAnear, ed.

68. Kierner, *Traders and Gentlefolk,* 121–127. See also Kierner's Ph.D. dissertation, on which her book is based, "Traders and Gentlefolk: The Livingstons of Colonial New York, 1675–1790" (University of Virginia, 1986), 296–297, 335–339.

69. Kierner, "Traders and Gentlefolk," 340–342; "Robert R. Livingston's Reasons against a Land Tax," McAnear, ed.

70. Although note Robert R. Livingston's effort to smear the New York City mercantile community by referring to it as the "monied" interest ("Robert R. Livingston's Reasons against a Land Tax," McAnear, ed., 82).

71. Use of the terms "court" and "country" has become ubiquitous. My understanding of the concepts, upon which the following discussion is based, has been informed by J. G. A. Pocock, "Machiavelli, Harrington, and English Political Ideologies in the Eighteenth Century," *WMQ,* 3d ser., 22 (1965): 547–583; id., *Machiavellian Moment; Perez Zagorin, The Court and the Country: The Beginnings of the English Revolution* (New York, 1970); Caroline Robbins, *The Eighteenth-Century Commonwealthman: Studies in the Transmission, Development, and Circumstances of English Liberal Thought from the Restoration of Charles II until the War with the Thirteen Colonies* (Cambridge, Mass., 1959); Dickinson, *Liberty and Property;* Bailyn, *Origins of American Politics;* Wood, *Creation of the American Republic;* Murrin, "The Great Inversion"; P. G. M. Dickson, *The Financial Revolution in England* (London, 1967); Reed Browning, *Political and Constitutional Ideas of the Court Whigs* (Baton Rouge, 1982).

72. See chapters 1 and 2; Greene, "Political Mimesis."

73. Greene, "Political Mimesis"; Bailyn, *Origins of American Politics,* 70–91.

74. In New York, governors tried, with little success, to have some influence over the disposition of the officerships of the four independent companies.

75. Katz, *Newcastle's New York,* 63–90; *Brief Narrative,* id., ed., 6.

76. Sydney, *Reply to the Speech,* Evans # 3841.

77. *New-York Weekly Journal,* 23 May 1737.

78. The *New-York Weekly Journal* began publication in November 1733.

79. Sheridan, *Lewis Morris,* 133–135; *New-York Gazette,* 14 Oct. 1734.

80. *New-York Gazette,* 18 Mar. 1734.

81. Ibid., 11 Mar., 9 Dec. 1734.

82. James Alexander to Cadwallader Colden, 18 June 1729, *Colden Papers,* 1:285–286.

83. Katz, *Newcastle's New York,* 92–95.

84. James Alexander to Cadwallader Colden, 5 May 1728, *Colden Papers,* 1:259.

85. *New-York Weekly Journal,* 10 June 1734.

86. Ibid.; *NY Votes,* 1:571–572; Governor Montgomerie to Lords of Trade, 30 Nov. 1728, *DRCNY,* 5:874; James Alexander to Patrick Graeme, 17 Oct. 1728, Alexander Papers, box 2, NYHS.

87. *NY Laws,* 2:16–32; "George Clarke to Mr. Walpole," 24 Nov. 1725, *DRCNY,* 5:769. On local perception of the salt tax, see *New-York Weekly Journal,* 28 Jan. 1740.

88. But it is very important to keep in mind that Adolphe Philipse was elected in

a by-election shortly after the general election, and once back in the assembly, he commanded substantial support as well.

89. Sheridan, *Lewis Morris*, 181–201.

90. "History of Governor William Cosby's Administration," *Colden Papers*, 9:352. On the "court" inclinations of the 1737–39 assembly, see Varga, "New York Government," 280.

91. Ibid., 353–354.

92. *New-York Weekly Journal*, 2 Feb. 1736, 27 June 1737.

93. Ibid., 5 Sept., 18 July 1737.

94. Ibid., 8 Aug. 1737.

95. Ibid., 11 July 1737.

96. Ibid., 8 Aug. 1737.

97. *NY Laws*, 2:951–952, 980–981, 1015–1047, 1047–1061.

98. Governor Hunter to Lords of Trade, 7 May 1711, *DRCNY*, 5:230; Sheridan, *Lewis Morris*, 139–140.

99. James Alexander to Cadwallader Colden, 5 May 1728, *Colden Papers*, 1:259.

100. "History of Governor William Cosby's Administration," *Colden Papers*, 9:352.

101. Philip Livingston to Jacob Wendell, 17 Oct. 1737, Livingston Papers, MCNY.

102. *New-York Gazette*, 13 Sept. 1736.

103. *New-York Weekly Journal*, 28 Oct. 1734.

104. McAnear, "Politics," 688–690.

105. William Livingston, *A Letter to the Freemen and Freeholders of the City of New-York* . . . (New York, 1750), Evans # 6865.

106. Philanthropos, *A Few Observations on the Conduct of the General Assembly of New-York* . . . (New York, 1768), Evans # 11039.

107. Governor Burnet inherited Hunter's friends and watched his predecessor's coalition fall apart.

108. Bonomi, *Factious People*, 158–171.

109. The designations "popular" and "provincial" are arbitrary ones. I call the Philipse and DeLancey/Jones factions popular Whigs because they were able to dominate electoral office during the mid eighteenth century, and that required a preponderance of popular appeal. The Morris/Alexander and Livingston/Smith factions of the same period were provincial in their self-conscious adoption of what they took to be the most attractive aspects of early eighteenth-century English polemics and tried, by articulating them in combination with their parochial interests, to put them to their own particular use.

110. Burnet also dismissed the senior councillor Peter Schuyler, who was one of Philipse's confidants. Cadwallader Colden to Alexander Colden, n.d., *Colden Papers*, 5:311–312.

111. See p. 228.

112. Philipse took the lead against the chancery court, at least in part because he saw an opportunity to exploit the "general clamour" that occurred when a number of Burnet's judgments for quitrents "fell heavy on several Patentees." Governor Burnet to Lords of Trade, 21 Dec. 1727, *DRCNY*, 5:848. Philipse's opponents attributed his action solely to "pique" at an adverse decision Burnet had brought down in a case affecting Philipse. Smith, *History of New-York*, 1:185; Cadwallader Colden to Alexander Colden, n.d., *Colden Papers*, 5:317–318; *To the Honourable Adolph Philipse, Esq.* (New York, 1728), Evans # 3112.

113. *NY Votes,* 1:572.
114. D. A. Story, *The DeLanceys: A Romance of a Great Family* (London, 1931), 13–16; Kim, *Landlord and Tenant,* 420.
115. Jordan, "Anglican Establishment," 131.
116. Samuel Mulford, "An Information," *DHNY,* 3:230.
117. Smith, *History of New-York,* 1:180–181.
118. Ibid., 181. DeLancey also associated himself with the cry for frequent elections in the 1720s. See Nicholas Varga, "Election Procedures in Colonial New York," *NY Hist.* 41 (1960): 256.
119. See chapter 3 and pp. 227–229 above.
120. *NY Votes,* 1:525; Governor Montgomerie to Lords of Trade, 30 Nov. 1728, *DRCNY,* 5:874; *NY Laws,* 2:426–446.
121. For an explication of the Catonic perspective, see Browning, *Court Whigs,* 1–10, 18–20, 228.
122. *New-York Weekly Journal,* 5 Sept. 1737.
123. See chapter 3.
124. Smith, *History of New-York,* 2:56–57, 140.
125. Governor Shirley to Governor Clinton, 13 Aug. 1748, "The Present State of the Province of New-York," 12 Dec. 1746, Governor Clinton to Lords of Trade, 15 Nov. 1748, *DRCNY,* 6:432–437, 462, 466. See also chapter 2.
126. See chapter 4, pp. 126–133.
127. *DRCNY,* 6:571–574; Varga, "New York Government," 371–373.
128. Smith, *History of New-York,* 2:210.
129. *NY Laws,* 4:199–202, 301–304.
130. Ibid. 3:1007–1008.
131. Smith, *History of New-York,* 2, 168; Klein, "William Livingston," 207; Lieutenant-Governor DeLancey to Lords of Trade, 15 Dec. 1754, *DRCNY,* 6:929. Complaints against informations went back at least to 1727. See, e.g., *NY Votes,* 1:566.
132. A justice's fees might be five shillings or less, while provincial court fees could run from thirty shillings to £10. *New-York Gazette, or, the Weekly Post-Boy,* 15 Feb. 1755; Philanthropos, *A Few Observations.*
133. New York Col. MSS, vol. 86, p. 129, NYSA.
134. *NY Laws,* 3:1011–1016, 4:296–301, 372–377; Smith, *History of New-York,* 2:168, 177, 242; Lieutenant-Governor DeLancey to Lords of Trade, 15 Dec. 1754, 5 Jan. 1758, *DRCNY,* 6:929, 7: 342.
135. *New-York Weekly Journal,* 1 Apr. 1734.
136. Ibid., 3 Dec. 1733, 26 Aug., 20 May 1734.
137. Bailyn, *Origins of American Politics;* id., *Ideological Origins of the American Revolution,* 55–93.
138. *Brief Narrative,* Katz, ed., 110.
139. *New-York Weekly Journal,* 3 June 1734.
140. Ibid., 23 May 1737. See also chapter 2 and p. 227 above.
141. *New-York Weekly Journal,* 27 June, 18 July, and 8 Aug. 1737.
142. See chapter 4.
143. *Independent Reflector,* Klein, ed., 35.
144. See chapter 4.
145. Sheridan, *Lewis Morris,* 25–34; Strassburger, "Morris Family," 112–149.
146. *New-York Weekly Journal,* 23 May 1737.
147. *New-York Evening Post,* 23 Nov. 1747; *NY Votes,* 2:173, 192–193.

148. See, e.g., *NY Votes,* 1:566, 571–572, 2:261–262, 265–268, 269; *New-York Evening Post,* 28 Dec. 1747, 11 Jan. 1748.

149. For description of these paradigms, see Greene, "Political Mimesis," and Bailyn, *Origins of American Politics.*

150. *New-York Evening Post,* 7 Dec. 1747.

151. See the *New-York Weekly Journal* and *Independent Reflector,* Klein, ed., passim.

152. Smith, *History of New-York,* 2:247; *Review of the Military Operations,* Massachusetts Historical Society, *Collections,* 1st ser., 7:79; Governor Clinton to the duke of Bedford, 28 June 1749, 12 June 1750, *DRCNY,* 6:513–514, 571; Sheridan, *Lewis Morris,* 118.

153. Smith, *History of New-York,* 2:244–245. And note Oliver DeLancey's sensitivity to community opinion despite his better-known reputation for high-handed acquisitiveness and violence. "It will take some time to call in the Money [over]due [from Cortlandt Manor debts] unless I take such harsh Measures as would bring on Me some Disesteem in the Country I am always to live in." Oliver DeLancey to Susannah Warren, 1 Feb. 1755, Gage Papers, as quoted in Kim, *Landlord and Tenant,* 115.

154. *New-York Gazette, revived in the Weekly Post-Boy,* 29 July 1751. See also Cadwallader Colden to James Alexander, 30 June 1728, Rutherford Coll., roll 1, NYHS.

155. Livingston Rutherford, *Family Records and Events* (New York, 1894), 105; Hunter, *To All Whom These Presents May Concern;* Strassburger, "Morris Family," 281.

156. The best illustration of this is *JWLB.*

157. James DeLancey to Robert Monckton, 28 July 1760, *Aspinwall Papers,* 1:239; Smith, *History of New-York,* 2:246.

158. *New-York Evening Post,* 22 Jan. 1750.

159. Steven Rosswurm has nicely pointed out the confluence of upper-class/lower-class colonial lifestyles (*Arms, Country, and Class,* 34–39). But it seems clear that, just as middle-class attitudes clearly percolated down into the lower classes, both upper-class and lower-class patterns of male sociability frequently ran strong through many of those who by any standard of economic well-being were of middling rank.

160. "History of Governor William Cosby's Administration," *Colden Papers,* 9:299.

161. McAnear, "Politics," 727.

162. *New-York Gazette, or, the Weekly Post-Boy,* 15 Apr. 1756.

163. *New-York Mercury,* 3 Mar. 1755; Klein, "William Livingston," 110–119, 144–149.

164. Smith, *Memoirs,* 1:91.

165. *New-York Gazette,* 10 Oct. 1737.

166. Jones, *History of New York,* 1:4.

167. Philanthropos, *To the Freeholders and Freemen.* . . .

168. Klein, "William Livingston," 116–119.

169. James Alexander to Cadwallader Colden, 5 May 1728, *Colden Papers,* 1:259; James Alexander to Cadwallader Colden, [draft, 1728?], Rutherford Coll., roll 1, p. 83, NYHS. For the sexual implications of these names, see Winthrop D. Jordan, *White over Black: American Attitudes towards the Negro, 1550–1812* (Chapel Hill, N.C., 1968), 29–30.

170. Governor Clinton to Robert Hunter Morris, 21 Jan. 1752, as quoted in Howe, "Accommodation and Retreat," 394.

171. *Review of the Military Operations,* 79, 85.

172. See, e.g., *NY Votes,* 2:131; "Cadwallader Colden to the Right Honorable H. S. Conway, Esq.," 9 Nov. 1765, *CCLB,* 2:62.

173. *New-York Evening-Post,* 25 Jan. 1748.

174. *New-York Weekly Journal,* 23 May 1737.

175. See, e.g., Chauncey Graham to William Smith, Jr., 11 July 1755, William Smith Papers, box 1, lot 189, #6; *New-York Mercury,* 28 July 1755, supplement; *New-York Weekly Post-Boy,* 8 Sept. 1746; *Better Creed than the Last.* Occasionally, individuals used "jargon" as a synonym for "cant." See, e.g., *New-York Gazette, revived in the Weekly Post-Boy,* 24 Feb. 1752.

176. William Livingston to Noah Welles, 2 Feb. 1768, LWC-JFP, YUL.

177. William Livingston to Robert Livingston, Jr., 24 [?] Feb. 1754, Livingston-Redmond, reel 5, microfilm, NYHS.

178. McAnear, *Income of the Colonial Governors.*

179. Henry Beekman to Gilbert Livingston, 14 Dec. 1736, 11 Aug. 1744, Beekman Papers, box 1, NYHS.

180. McAnear, "Politics," 688–690; Varga, "New York Government," 368.

181. James Duane to Abraham Ten Broeck, [?] Mar., 9 May 1768, Ten Broeck Papers, Albany Institute of History and Art; box 32, folder 2, Van Rensselaer Manor Papers, NYSL; David Colden to William Livingston, 27 Apr. 1762, *Colden Papers,* 6:155–156.

182. Nash, *Urban Crucible,* passim.

183. John Watts to General Monckton, 30 Mar. 1765, *JWLB,* 340.

184. For a similar argument, see Linda Colley, *In Defiance of Oligarchy: The Tory Party, 1714–1760* (Cambridge, 1982), 3–24.

185. Tully, "Religion and Voting Behavior."

186. Robbins, *Eighteenth-Century Commonwealthman.* See also the republican literature cited in the Introduction.

187. *New-York Weekly Journal,* 11 July 1737.

188. Josiah Quinby, *A Short History of a Long Journey . . .* (New York, 1740), Evans # 4589.

189. *New-York Evening Post,* 26 Sept. 1748.

190. *New-York Gazette,* 18 Mar. 1734; James Duane to Robert Livingston, Jr., 14 June 1769, Livingston-Redmond, reel 6, microfilm, NYHS.

191. For some comment on the meanings of virtue, see Greene, *Imperatives, Behaviors & Identities,* 208–235, and Wood, *Radicalism of the American Revolution,* 104–109, 215–217.

192. For further development of this argument, see chapter 10.

193. See chapter 9.

194. Marc Egnal and Joseph A. Ernst, "An Economic Interpretation of the American Revolution," *WMQ,* 3d ser., 29 (1972): 3–32; Egnal, *A Mighty Empire,* 126–149; Thomas Ellison, Jr., to Thomas Ellison, Sr., 29 Oct. 1768, Ellison Papers, NYHS; John Watts to General Monckton, 24 Nov. 1763, *JWLB,* 202.

195. Smith, *Memoirs,* 1:32–33.

196. Ibid.

197. Ibid., 33.

198. Klein, "William Livingston," 531, 534, 537–568.

199. Ibid., 531, 553, 565, 571; Philanthropos, *A Few Observations;* Launitz-

Schurer, Jr., *Loyal Whigs and Revolutionaries,* 18; *Review of the Military Operations,* 80.

200. Philanthropos, *A Few Observations.*

201. Smith, *Memoirs,* 1:25, 89; *Review of the Military Operations,* 80.

202. Philanthropos, *To the Freeholders and Freemen. . . .*

203. *New-York Weekly Mercury,* 20 Feb. 1769.

204. Robert R. Livingston to General Monckton, 8 Nov. 1765, *Aspinwall Papers,* 2:559–567.

205. It is unlikely that William Smith, Jr., would have recommended them had they been averse to such an appointment. Smith, *Memoirs,* 1:44, 45.

206. Lieutenant-Governor Colden to Lords of Trade, 8 July 1763, *DRCNY,* 7:528; Robert R. Livingston to General Monckton, 4 Dec. 1769, Livingston Family Papers, NYPL.

207. Philanthropos, *A Few Observations;* id., *To the Freeholders and Freemen . . . ,* Evans # 11040; *To the Freeholders and Freemen . . . ,* Evans # 11088.

208. Philanthropos, *A Few Observations;* id., *To the Freeholders and Freemen . . . ,* Evans # 11040; Gerlach, *Philip Schuyler,* 158.

209. *New-York Mercury,* 13 Jan. 1766; Cruger et al., *To the Freeholders and Freemen . . . ;* Bonomi, *Factious People,* 314, 316.

210. Notably on the adoption of the ballot. Champagne, "Sons of Liberty," 222–225.

211. Ibid., 264–265.

212. Ibid., 231–240.

213. Bonomi, *Factious People,* 267–276; Gerlach, *Philip Schuyler,* 183–191.

214. Ibid.

215. "Resolutions in Favour of Sitting Judges of the Supreme Court of New York in the House," Robert R. Livingston Coll., reel 1, NYHS.

216. *Political Creed for the Day;* Peter Van Schaack to Henry Van Schaack, 27 Jan. 1769, Francis L. Hawks Papers, NYHS.

217. *Diary and Autobiography of John Adams,* Lyman H. Butterfield, ed., 4 vols. (Cambridge, Mass., 1961), 2:107; John Stevens to Lord Sterling, 28 Jan. 1769, William Alexander Papers, NYPL; Lydon, *Pirates, Privateers, and Profits,* 272–273, 278; Stuyvesant Fish, *The New York Privateers, 1756–1763* (New York, 1945), 12.

218. Joseph F. X. McCarthy, "The Cruger Family in the Eighteenth Century" (Ph.D. diss., Fordham University, 1959); Smith, *Memoirs,* 1.

219. See, e.g., James Duane to Robert Livingston, Jr., 14 June 1769, Livingston-Redmond, reel 6, microfilm, NYHS; *Examiner, No. II.*

220. *Examiner, No. II.*

221. *From Parker's New York Gazette . . . "No Lawyer in the Assembly."*

222. For charges of Livingston, Smith, and friends' arrogance in this matter, see The Freeholder, *Answers to the Reasons, Lately Published . . .* (New York, 1769), Evans # 11260.

223. See chapters 5 and 10.

224. James Duane to Robert Livingston, Jr., 14 June 1769, Livingston-Redmond, reel 6, microfilm, NYHS.

225. See, e.g., Peter R. Livingston to Philip Schuyler, 6 Feb. 1769, Schuyler Papers, NYPL; Bonomi, *Factious People,* 230–232.

226. Smith, *History of New-York,* 2:237.

227. For a short summary of the political interaction between various Livingstons and other politically active groups during the 1730s, 1740s, and early 1750s, see Kierner, *Traders and Gentlefolk,* 166–173.

228. Peter R. Livingston to Jacob Wendell, Jr., 19 Jan. 1769, Livingston Papers, MCNY.

229. A few examples are Goldsbrow Banyar to George Clarke, Jr., 23 Nov. 1754, Goldsbrow Banyar Papers, box 1; John Livingston to Robert Livingston, Jr., 23 Aug. 1750, Livingston-Redmond, reel 5, microfilm, NYHS; *New-York Weekly Journal,* 1 Dec. 1735; Smith, *Memoirs,* 1:59.

230. Edward Collins to Daniel Horsmanden, 21 [Oct?] 1745, Horsmanden Papers, NYHS; Kierner, *Traders and Gentlefolk,* passim.

231. Olson, "New York Assembly"; Launitz-Schurer, Jr., *Loyal Whigs and Revolutionaries,* 97–199; Janice Potter, *The Liberty We Seek: Loyalist Ideology in Colonial New York and Massachusetts* (Cambridge, Mass., 1983); Bernard Mason, *The Road to Independence: The Revolutionary Movement in New York, 1773–1777* (Lexington, Ky., 1966).

Seven / Understanding Quaker Pennsylvania

1. *PWP,* 3:499.

2. See chapters 1, pp. 35–38 , and 2, pp. 74–75. For summaries of popular grievances against Penn, see *PWP,* 4:295–304, 373–384.

3. Lokken, *David Lloyd,* 160–161, 187.

4. See pp. 267–274.

5. The following discussion of the 1710s and 1720s is based on Thomas Wendel, "The Life and Writings of Sir William Keith, Lieutenant-Governor of Pennsylvania and the Three Lower Counties, 1717–1726" (Ph.D. diss., University of Washington, 1964); id., "The Keith-Lloyd Alliance: Factional and Coalition Politics in Colonial Pennsylvania," *PMHB* 92 (1968): 289–305; Nash, *Quakers and Politics;* Lokken, *David Lloyd;* Tolles, *James Logan;* and Tully, *William Penn's Legacy.*

6. For James Logan's contribution to this reaction and the new relationship between Logan and Lloyd, see Lokken, *David Lloyd,* 225. Tully, "Englishmen and Germans," 238–239.

7. Nash, *Quakers and Politics,* 318–335.

8. Ibid., 328.

9. Tully, *William Penn's Legacy,* 3–43; id., "Quaker Party and Proprietary Policies," 75, 105; Hutson, *Pennsylvania Politics;* Edward O. Smith, "Thomas Penn, Chief Proprietor of Pennsylvania: A Study of His Public Governmental Activities from 1763 to 1775" (Ph.D. diss., Lehigh University, 1966).

10. See pp. 284, 298.

11. Tully, *William Penn's Legacy,* 15–19.

12. See chapter 3.

13. Thomas Penn to John and Richard Penn, 14 Jan. 1735, Penn Papers, Unbound MSS, HSP.

14. Tully, *William Penn's Legacy,* 18–19.

15. Ibid., 3–15; id., "Quaker Party and Proprietary Policies," 92–95.

16. Ibid.

17. Tully, *William Penn's Legacy* 9–10, 15.

18. Thomas Penn to John and Richard Penn, 16 Aug. 1738, Penn Papers, Small Letter Book, HSP.

19. Thomas Penn to John Penn, 4 Dec. 1739, Penn Papers, Small Letter Book, HSP.

20. Minutes of Donegal Presbytery, 1b (1736–1740): 255, PHS.

21. Richard Peters to Thomas Penn, 8 Oct. 1741, RPLB, HSP; Tully, *William Penn's Legacy,* 23–28; id., "Quaker Party and Proprietary Policies," 95–96.

22. Tully, *William Penn's Legacy,* 23–24.

23. William Allen to John Penn, 17 Nov. 1739, PPOC, HSP.

24. Ibid.

25. Tully, *William Penn's Legacy,* 24–32.

26. *Pa. Votes,* 4:2996, 2981.

27. James Alexander to Governor Hunter, 3 Feb. 1730, Rutherford Coll., roll 1, NYHS.

28. Isaac Norris, Jr., to Richard Partridge, 18 May 1745, INLB, 1735–1755, HSP.

29. Thomas Penn to James Hamilton, 31 July 1749, Penn-Hamilton Corresp., HSP; Tully, "Quaker Party and Proprietary Policies," 96–97.

30. *PBF,* 11:11.

31. Richard Peters to Thomas Penn, 3 Feb. 1753, PPOC, HSP; Tully, "Quaker Party and Proprietary Policies," 98–99.

32. *Pa. Votes,* 6:4391.

33. Richard Peters to Thomas Penn, 2 Oct. 1756, RPLB, HSP.

34. Horace Wemyss Smith, *Life of . . . William Smith,* 1:204; William Allen to Ferdinand John Paris, 18 Mar. 1758, PPOC; Edward Shippen, Sr., to James Burd, 22 May 1757, Shippen Papers, HSP.

35. *PWP,* 2:212.

36. Ibid., 4:335.

37. *Penn-Logan Corresp.,* 1:147.

38. Ibid. 205.

39. *PWP,* 4:374.

40. Levy, *Quakers and the American Family,* 58–60, 123–152.

41. *Penn-Logan Corresp.,* 1:205.

42. *PWP,* 4:363, 377, 575.

43. *Penn-Logan Corresp.,* 1:205.

44. See chapters 1 and 2.

45. Frederick B. Tolles, *Meeting House and Counting House: The Quaker Merchants of Colonial Philadelphia* (Chapel Hill, N.C., 1948); Marietta, *Reformation*; Levy, *Quakers and the American Family;* Lemon, *Best Poor Man's Country,* passim.

46. *PWP,* 2:502; Richard T. Vann, "Quakerism: Made in America?" in *The World of William Penn,* Richard S. Dunn and Mary Maples Dunn, eds. (Philadelphia, 1986), 157–170.

47. Logan thought, however, that because Friends predominated in the countryside, Quakers and non-Quakers were about equal in number in Philadelphia City and County taken together. *Penn-Logan Corresp.,* 1:102.

48. *PWP,* 3:510.

49. Nash, *Quakers and Politics,* 298–301.

50. Lokken, *David Lloyd,* 226–233.

51. Chapter 4; Tully, "Ethnicity," 497–501.

52. Fischer, *Albion's Seed,* 567–568; James T. Lemon and Gary B. Nash, "The Distribution of Wealth in Eighteenth-Century America: A Century of Change in Chester County, Pennsylvania, 1693–1802," *Journal of Social History* 2 (1968): 1–24.

53. Levy, *Quakers and the American Family,* passim; Marietta, *Reformation,* 46–72.

54. *Pa. Votes,* 5:4102.

55. Shepherd, *History of Proprietary Government,* 525.

56. *Penn-Logan Corresp.,* 1:205.

57. James Logan to Governor Thomas, 1 Oct. 1741, James Logan Letter Book, 1731–32, 1741–42, HSP.

58. Marrietta, *Reformation,* 31–168; Wellenreuther, "Political Dilemma."

59. On the evolution of Quaker benevolence, see Marietta, *Reformation,* and Sydney V. James, *A People among Peoples: Quaker Benevolence in Eighteenth-Century America* (Cambridge, Mass., 1963).

60. John Churchman to Israel Pemberton, Jr., 14 Dec. 1756, Pemberton Papers, HSP.

61. John Smith to Jonah Thompson, 26 June 1756, CJS. See also James Pemberton to John Fothergill, [?] Nov. 1756, Pemberton Papers, Pemberton-Fothergill, vol. 34, HSP.

62. Israel Pemberton, Jr., to John Fothergill, 6 Apr. 1758, Pemberton Papers, Pemberton-Fothergill, vol. 34, HSP.

63. James Pemberton to Jonah Thompson, 25 Apr. 1756, Thompson MSS, transcript, FHL.

64. Isaac Norris, Jr., to John Fothergill, INLB, 1719–1756, HSP.

65. *Answer to an Invidious Pamphlet, intitled, A Brief State . . .* (London, 1755), 64–66.

66. Alan Tully, "One Quaker's View: William Fishbourn's Remarks on the Settlement of Pennsylvania," *Quaker History* 66 (1977): 51–58.

67. See, e.g., *Pa. Votes,* 4:2753.

68. Ibid., 2:1666.

69. David Lloyd, *A Defence of the Legislative Constitution of the Province of Pennsylvania . . .* (Philadelphia, 1728), Evans # 3050.

70. *Pennsylvania Gazette,* 5 June 1735; Joseph Galloway, *A True and Impartial State of the Province of Pennsylvania . . .* (Philadelphia, 1759), Evans # 8349.

71. *Pa. Votes,* 2:1701.

72. Ibid., 5:4336. See also Isaac Norris, Jr., to Robert Charles, 7 Oct. 1754, INLB, 1719–1756, HSP.

73. Lokken, *David Lloyd,* 90.

74. John Churchman, *Account of the Gospel Labours,* 96–98.

75. Tully, *William Penn's Legacy,* 95; *Pennsylvania Gazette,* 27 Sept. 1750.

76. Charles P. Keith, *Provincial Councillors of Pennsylvania* (Philadelphia, 1883), 228.

77. Ryerson, "Quaker Elite," 109–110.

78. Ibid., 106–135.

79. *CR,* 2:281.

80. *PWP,* 2:211–228.

81. *CR,* 2:312. See also 1:35–36.

82. *PWP,* 3:317.

83. My emphasis.

84. *CR,* 2:281–282. See also the *Pennsylvania Journal,* 10 Oct. 1754; *To the Honourable Patrick Gordon, Esq. . . .* (Philadelphia, 1728), Evans # 3089; Galloway, *Speech,* 17.

85. *PWP,* 3:335; *CR,* 2:340. See also *CR,* 2:35.

86. *CR,* 1:19.

87. Ibid., 2:333. See also, e.g., *Pa. Votes,* 2:1626, and the *Pennsylvania Gazette,* 8 May 1747.

88. *CR,* 2:358–359. See also ibid., 344, for insistence that the "Rights and free-

doms of England, (the best and Largest in Europe) shall be in force here."

89. Ibid., 2:174; *Remarks on the Late Proceedings of Some Members of Assembly at Philadelphia* . . . (Philadelphia, 1728), Evans # 3098.

90. *Pa. Votes*, 5:4041–4050, 4123–4129.

91. *CR*, 2:311.

92. Ibid., 375.

93. *The Proceedings of Some Members of Assembly at Philadelphia* . . . (Philadelphia, 1728), Evans # 3096.

94. *CR*, 2:378.

95. Lewis Evans, "Brief Account of Pennsylvania" (MS), HSP.

96. *CR*, 2; 175.

97. Ibid., 196.

98. *Penn-Logan Corresp.*, 1:267–268.

99. *Pa. Votes*, 2:1632, 1635.

100. Ibid., 1622.

101. Ibid., 1627.

102. Tolles, *James Logan*, 134–141.

103. *To the Freeholders, to Prevent Mistakes* . . . (Philadelphia, 1727), Evans # 2970.

104. Evans, "Brief Account of Pennsylvania" (MS), HSP.

105. *A Dialogue between Mr. Robert Rich and Roger Plowman* (Philadelphia, 1725), Evans # 2624.

106. Sir William Keith, *A Letter from Sir William Keith* . . . (Philadelphia, 1725), Evans # 2646.

107. *Pa. Votes*, 2:1621; *Pennsylvania Gazette*, 24 Dec. 1735.

108. Tully, "Quaker Party and Proprietary Policies," 96–102.

109. *Pa. Votes*, 2:1626; *CR*, 6:704–705.

110. *Penn-Logan Corresp.*, 1:268; *CR*, 2:146–147.

111. The Crown retained a veto, of course, but royal priorities were frequently different from proprietary ones.

112. *CR*, 3:36.

113. Lokken, *David Lloyd*, 166–176.

114. For the prolonged conflict between the assembly and various governors over taxation at midcentury, see Hutson, *Pennsylvania Politics*.

115. *Pa. Votes*, 5:4018.

116. Galloway, *Speech*, 40–41.

117. *Pa. Votes*, 5:3898. See also 3944–3947.

118. Richard Peters to John Penn, 10 Apr. 1739, RPLB, HSP.

119. *Pennsylvania Gazette*, 24 Dec. 1735.

120. Ibid.; *CR*, 2:453.

121. *To the Freeholders, to Prevent Mistakes*. . . .

122. Hutson, *Pennsylvania Politics*, 6–70.

123. *The Conspiracy of the Cataline* . . . (Philadelphia, 1727), Evans # 2858.

124. Galloway, *Speech*, 27.

125. Isaac Norris, Sr., *Friendly Advice to the Inhabitants of Pennsylvania* (Philadelphia, 1710, repr. 1728), Evans # 3078.

126. Lokken, *David Lloyd*, 57; *CR*, 2:231–232, 518, 559–560, 594.

127. Tully, *William Penn's Legacy*, 14–15.

128. Galloway, *Speech*, vii. In England, the colonial agent Richard Jackson concurred: "The Subject's Money is never so well disposed of as in the Maintenance of

Order and Tranquillity and the Purchase of good Laws" (*Historical Review of the Constitution and Government of Pennsylvania* [London, 1759], 73).

129. Evarts B. Greene, *The Provincial Governor in the English Colonies of North America* (New York, 1898), 9.

130. *CR*, 2:317.

131. Ibid., 333.

132. Ibid.

133. See, e.g., *CR*, 2:338, 6:540–546; *Brief Narrative*, Katz, ed., 86; *Pa. Votes*, 5:3944.

134. *Pennsylvania Gazette*, as quoted in Anna Janney DeArmond, *Andrew Bradford, Colonial Journalist* (Newark, Del., 1949), 102.

135. *Pa. Votes*, 4:3198.

136. *Pennsylvania Gazette*, 16 June 1748.

137. *CR*, 2:378; *Pa. Votes*, 6:4694–4696, 4699, 4708, 4710, 4817.

138. *The Christian's Duty to Render to Caesar the things that are Caesar's . . .* (Philadelphia, 1756), Evans #7635; *Advice and Information to the Freeholders & Freemen of the Province of Pennsylvania . . .* (Philadelphia, 1727), Evans #2831.

139. *The Christian's Duty.* Occasionally, the proprietary interest was labeled a separate estate. See, e.g., *Pa. Votes*, 5:4124.

140. *Remarks upon the Advice of the Freeholders, etc. . . .* (Philadelphia, 1727), Evans #2951.

141. Lloyd, *Defence of the Legislative Constitution.*

142. *PWP*, 4:394, 677.

143. Proprietaries to Jeremiah Langhorne, 28 Feb. 1730, Penn Papers, Thomas Penn Letter Book, 1, HSP.

144. *CR*, 2:384, 432; *The Christian's Duty.*

145. *Pennsylvania Gazette*, 30 Mar. 1738.

146. *Some Necessary Precautions, Worthy to be Considered by all English Subjects . . .* (Philadelphia, 1727)), Evans # 2964.

147. Evans, "Brief Account of Pennsylvania" (MS), HSP.

148. *Pa. Votes*, 6:4644.

149. Ibid. 5:4017, 4027. For a riposte to charges of republicanism, see *CR*, 2:340.

150. *Pennsylvania Gazette*, 30 Mar. 1738.

151. James Logan, *The Charge Deliver'd from the Bench to the Grand Jury . . .* (Philadelphia, 1723), Evans #2441.

152. Smith, *Brief State*, 12–15.

153. *Penn-Logan Corresp.*, 2:9; *CR*, 6:49. Andrew Bradford was another noteworthy dissenter. See, e.g., *The Remainder of the Observations Promised in the Mercury . . .* (Philadelphia, 1735), Evans # 3956.

154. *Pennsylvania Gazette*, 30 Mar. 1738.

155. Isaac Norris, Jr., to Robert Charles, 29 April 1755, INLB, 1719–1756, HSP.

156. *Pa. Votes*, 5:4124.

157. *CR*, 4:532–533; *Pa. Votes*, 4:2728; John Locke, *The Second Treatise of Government*, J. W. Gough, ed. (3d ed., Oxford, 1966), 73–75.

158. For the minor place this meaning of balance had in English Whig thought, see Dickinson, *Liberty and Property*, 142. For examples of local, generalized expressions of this idea, see *Pa. Votes*, 6:4638, and *To the Free-Holders of the Province of Pennsylvania* (Philadelphia, 1742), Evans # 5075.

159. Thomas Penn to Richard Peters, 10 June 1754, Penn Papers, Thomas Penn Letter Book, 3, HSP; *Pa. Votes,* 3:3709.

160. Isaac Norris, Jr., to Robert Charles, 7 Oct. 1754, INLB, 1719–1756, HSP.

161. Isaac Norris, Jr., to Robert Charles, 7 Oct. 1754, 28 April 1755, ibid.

162. *Pennsylvania Gazette,* 30 Mar. 1738. I attribute this piece to Hamilton for the following reasons: (1) there are internal consistencies and language similarities between this essay and prose that we know he authored; (2) it seems more than a coincidence that this piece appeared in the *Gazette* a week before Franklin published material praising Hamilton for his international renown earned in the Zenger trial; (3) I do not believe there was any other Philadelphian who could have summed up so well the popular view of the Pennsylvania constitution, developed under the intellectual tutelage of David Lloyd, and combined it so effectively with the kind of rationality and irreverence that distinguishes the piece.

163. *A Letter from a Gentleman in Philadelphia to his Friend in Bucks* (Philadelphia, 1728), Evans # 3048; *Pa. Votes,* 5:4027.

164. *Pennsylvania Gazette,* 24 Dec. 1735, 30 Mar. 1738.

165. Ibid., 24 Dec. 1735.

166. Ibid.

167. Ibid., 30 Mar. 1738.

168. *Pa. Votes,* 5:3945, 3992, 4333; Burton Alva Konkle, *The Life of Andrew Hamilton, 1676–1741: "The Day-Star of the American Revolution"* (Philadelphia, 1941), 131–135.

169. *Pennsylvania Gazette,* 24 Dec. 1735; *Pa. Votes,* 5:4027.

170. *CR,* 7:448.

171. Isaac Norris, Jr., to Robert Charles, 24 May 1755, INLB, HSP.

172. Horace Wemyss Smith, *Life of . . . William Smith,* 1:220.

173. Thomas Graeme to Thomas Penn, 18 Mar. 1752, PPOC, HSP.

174. See pp. 305–309 and chapter 5, p. 190. See also C. H. Lincoln, "Representation in the Pennsylvania Assembly prior to the Revolution," and Theodore Thayer, "The Quaker Party of Pennsylvania, 1755–1765," *PMHB* 23 (1899): 23–34, and 71 (1947): 19–43.

175. Tully, "Quaker Party and Proprietary Policies," 84–86.

176. John Penn to Thomas Penn, 19 Oct. 1764, PPOC, HSP; *Pa. Votes,* 5:3942–3943, 3986, 4028, 6:5123–5124; *CR,* 8:473.

177. Tench Francis to Thomas Penn, 21 Feb. 1745, James Hamilton to Thomas Penn, 7 July 1753, PPOC; Thomas Penn to Richard Peters, 7 June 1745, Penn-Papers, Saunders-Coates, HSP.

178. See Kramnick, *Republicanism and Bourgeois Radicalism,* 29–30, for a good concise discussion of political ideology and a useful definition of it as a set of "ideas and values . . . put in the service of politicized interests involved in a struggle to effect the distribution of power and the outcomes of public policy."

179. Bauman, *For the Reputation of Truth;* Marietta, *Reformation.*

180. Richard Peters to Thomas Penn, 2 Oct. 1756, PPOC, HSP.

181. John Watts to Robert Monckton, 30 May 1774, *Aspinwall Papers,* 2:711.

182. *A Dialogue Shewing, What's Therein to be Found* (Philadelphia, 1725), Evans # 2652.

183. *Pa. Votes,* 3:2506.

184. Ibid., 2507.

185. Ibid., 2506–2507; Dickinson, *Speech,* 15–16; William Livingston, "History

of the American Revolution . . . to Nov. 8, 1775," John Jay Papers, reel 1, NYHS; *Pennsylvania Gazette,* 24 Dec. 1735.

186. Smith, *Brief State.*

187. Fischer, *Albion's Seed,* 585, 594.

188. *PWP,* 2:143.

189. *CR,* 2:57.

190. Ingersoll, "Alison," 134.

191. Christopher Saur I to Wittgenstein Friends, 1 Aug. 1725, in *The Brethren in Colonial America,* Donald F. Durnbaugh, ed. (Elgin, Ill., 1967), 35, as quoted in Schwartz, *"Mixed Multitude,"* 84.

192. My emphasis.

193. Richard Locke to secretary, 11 Apr. 1747, Society for the Propagation of the Gospel in Foreign Parts, Letters, ser. B, 25 vols. (microfilm, University of British Columbia Library), vol. 15 (hereinafter cited as SPG, Letters, B); *Pennsylvania Gazette,* 14 Aug. 1732.

194. David Seibt to his brother, 20 Dec. 1734, in *The Journals and Papers of David Schultze,* Andrew S. Berky, ed. and trans., 2 vols. (Pennsburg, Pa., 1952) 1:53, as quoted in Schwartz, *"Mixed Multitude,"* 118.

195. Frost, *Perfect Freedom,* 23–25; Gough, "Pluralism, Politics, and Power Struggles," 25–123.

196. Frost, *Perfect Freedom,* 13–16.

197. Tully, "Politics and Peace Testimony," 159–177.

198. David Seibt to his brother, 20 Dec. 1734, *David Schultze Papers,* 1:53, and [F. Hall], *The Importance of the British Plantations in America to this Kingdom . . .* (London, 1731), preface, 89, as quoted in Schwartz, *"Mixed Multitude,"* 118.

199. *To the Honourable Patrick Gordon, Esq.* See also Joseph Fox, Joseph Richardson, John Ross, and John Hughes to Richard Jackson, 1 Nov. 1764, R. R. Logan, Dickinson Papers, HSP.

200. "The Address of the People Called Quakers," 27 Oct. 1775, as quoted in Rosswurm, *Arms, Country and Class,* 58. See also *CR,* 6:404.

201. *Dialogue Shewing, What's Therein,* 39.

202. Mary M. Schweitzer, *Custom and Contract: Household, Government, and the Economy in Colonial Pennsylvania* (New York, 1987), 15–167. On the importance of the loan office in financing new land patents, see Thomas Penn to Richard Peters, 22 Mar. 1755, Peters Papers, Letters of Thomas Penn to Richard Peters, 1752–1772, HSP.

203. Roughly 1723–1756. After 1756, the loan office mortgages were phased out because of the huge emissions of paper currency, funded on the promise of future tax collections, to finance the French and Indian War. Schweitzer, *Custom and Contract,* 130.

204. Ibid., 125–129.

205. The 1729 printing added £30,000 to the £45,000 issued in 1723. Ibid., 129.

206. Ibid., 129–130; Tully, *William Penn's Legacy,* 128–131.

207. Tully, "Quaker Party and Proprietary Policies," 84–85.

208. *Pa. Votes,* 3:2197.

209. Ibid., 5:3900, 4021.

210. Ibid., 3:2117–2119, 2120, 4:3520, 5:3712, 3713, 3718, 3834, 3986, 4021, 4035; John Smith's Diary, 24 Sept. 1750, MS, HSP.

211. Lemon, *Best Poor Man's Country.*

212. *Dialogue Shewing, What's Therein*, 39.

213. *CR*, 7:767.

214. James Logan, *The Antidote* . . . (Philadelphia, 1725), Evans # 2650.

215. Fischer, *Albion's Seed*, 585.

216. William White to James Wilson, 27 Nov. 1768, Gratz Collection, Protestant Episcopal Ministers, HSP.

217. William Livingston, "A History of the American Revolution," John Jay Papers, reel 1, NYHS.

218. *CR* 7:139.

219. James Pemberton to Jonah Thompson, 25 Apr. 1756, Thompson MSS, transcript, FHL; Tully, "Quaker Party and Proprietary Policies," 80–81.

220. Governor Samuel Ogle to Patrick Gordon, 24 Feb. 1734, Dreer Collection, Governors of the Colonies; Thomas Penn to Samuel Blunston, 5 Feb. 1737, Penn Papers, unbound MSS; "Memorial of Messers Jennings and Dulany . . . ," Board of Trade Journals, transcripts, vol. 13, S90, HSP; Tully, *William Penn's Legacy*, 7–10.

221. Isaac Norris, Jr., to Robert Charles, 20 June 1755, INLB, 1719–1756, HSP. For the provincial eminence of James Wright, see Edward Shippen, Sr., to Joseph Shippen, 14 Feb. 1757, Shippen Papers, HSP.

222. Minshall, Pope, and Blackburn were all prominent community leaders. Tully, "Quaker Party and Proprietary Policies," 86–87.

223. George Stevenson to Richard Peters, 30 Apr. 1758, in *PA*, 1st ser., 3:384–385.

224. Lewis Weiss to Timothy Horsefield, 1 Aug. 1763, Northampton County Papers, Misc. MSS, Bethlehem and Vicinity, 1741–1849, HSP.

225. *Pa. Votes*, 1:xxxvi–xxxvii.

226. For Governor Thomas's description of the short life cycle of voluntary militias, see Thomas to John Penn, 27 Oct. 1741, PPOC, HSP.

227. *PBF*, 3:180–212.

228. *Pa. Statutes*, 5:197–201.

229. Robert Dinwiddie, *Official Records . . . 1751–58*, R. D. Brock, ed., 2 vols., Virginia Historical Society, *Collections*, n.s., 3–4 (Richmond, Va., 1883–84), 2:313 as quoted in Greene, *Provincial Governor*, 102.

230. *Pa. Votes*, 6:4640–4642; *Pa. Statutes*, 5:219–221, 266–268, 281–283, 335–337, 424–427, 6:51–53, 93, 297–301, 321–325, 367–371.

231. *CR*, 7:405.

232. *PWP*, 4:378.

233. Richard Peters to Proprietors, 4 Nov. 1756, Peters Papers, Letters to Proprietors, HSP.

234. Richard Peters to Proprietors, 17 Oct. 1742, Peters Papers, RPLB, HSP; Schweitzer, *Custom and Contract*, 199; Roeber, *Palatines, Liberty, and Property*, 178.

235. Thomas Cookson to Conrad Weiser, 12 Sept. 1741, Correspondence of Conrad Weiser, vol. 1, 1741–1756, HSP.

236. "Answer to Conrad Weiser's Published Letter to the Germans," 29 Sept. 1741, PPOC, HSP. See also Governor Thomas to Board of Trade, 20 Oct. 1740, *Pa. Statutes*, 4:468–477.

237. *Pa. Votes*, 5:3947.

238. Ibid., 3998.

239. Ibid., 4177.

240. Ibid., 3991. Germans were not a majority but had become the largest of a number of minorities. Lemon, *Best Poor Man's Country*, 14.

241. Isaac Norris, Jr., to Robert Charles, 29 Apr. 1755, INLB, 1719–1756, HSP.

242. Governor Denny to the proprietors, 30 June 1757, *PA,* 1st ser., 3:194.

243. Roeber, "'The Origin of Whatever Is Not English,'" 276–277.

244. George Stevenson to Richard Peters, 8 May 1758, *PA,* 1st ser., 3:391–392.

245. John Elder to Governor Penn, 15 Nov. 1763, ibid. 4:135–136; *Pa. Votes,* 6:4642; Smith, *Brief State.*

246. Tully, "Ethnicity," 501.

247. Schweitzer, *Custom and Contract,* 194.

248. Hutson, *Pennsylvania Politics,* 6–70.

249. Tully, *William Penn's Legacy,* 14–15.

250. For the popularity of that initiative, see Richard Peters to General Monckton, 29 Aug. 1760, Chalmers Collection, Philadelphia (1760), NYPL. For Thomas Penn's belated acknowledgment of the equity of such a demand, see Thomas Penn to James Hamilton, 15 Nov. 1760, Penn-Hamilton Correspondence, HSP.

251. Tully, *William Penn's Legacy,* 18–19.

252. *Pa. Votes,* 6:4699.

253. This paragraph is based largely on my reading of Roeber, *Palatines, Liberty, and Property.* See esp. his ch. 6. Because of his focus on liberty and property in the context of the republican historians' view of colonial and Revolutionary political culture, Roeber has not fully appreciated how closely Pennsylvania German ideas were interwoven with mainstream Pennsylvania political discourse.

254. *Penn-Logan Corresp.,* 1:327.

255. Tully, "Quaker Party and Proprietary Policies," 81.

256. Galloway, *Speech,* 28.

257. Robert Jenney to secretary, 18 Oct. 1748, SPG Letters, B, 16, microfilm, UBC Library; Fischer, *Albion's Seed,* 563. See Fischer on the practice of shaking hands and the Maryland traveler Dr. Alexander Hamilton's observations on the practice in Philadelphia. *Albion's Seed,* 574–575, and Hamilton's *Itinerarium,* 21. Note also Hamilton's general impressions of Philadelphia: "I never was in a place so populous where the *gout* for publick gay diversions prevailed so little" (*Itinerarium,* 25).

258. Edmund Peckover Journal, Quaker Collection, Haverford College Library. Marietta, *Reformation,* 62–64; Robert Jenney to secretary, 26 Oct. 1749; Thomas Thompson to secretary, 25 Apr. 1752, SPG Letters, B 17 and 20, microfilm, UBC Library; Richard Backhose to secretary, 12 Mar. 1728; Thomas Barton to secretary, 28 June 1763, in *Historical Collections,* Perry, ed., 2:161, 347.

259. Fischer, *Albion's Seed,* 424.

260. *Pa. Votes,* 3:2443. The practice of disabling continued on in New York, so far as we know, through the mid eighteenth century. See *NY Votes,* 1:702, 750, 2:2, 64, 222, 276.

261. Lynford Lardner to Richard Penn, 19 June 1759, Lynford Lardner Papers, HSP.

262. Richard Peters to John Penn, 5 June 1742, RPLB, HSP.

263. *Pa. Votes,* 5:4157.

264. Tully, "Quaker Party and Proprietary Policies," 87 and "Ethnicity," 508–509. I am indebted to Marianne Wokeck for sharing her knowledge of Pennsylvania's German communities with me.

265. Hutson, *Pennsylvania Politics;* Newcomb, *Franklin and Galloway,* 71–135.

266. See chapter 6, pp. 224–227.

267. Ibid.; Dickinson, *Liberty and Property.*

268. See pp. 274–285.

269. Frost, *Perfect Freedom*, 10–59; Wellenreuther, "Political Dilemma"; Tully, "Politics and Peace Testimony."

270. Edward Shippen, Jr., to [?], 2 Feb. 1768, Shippen Papers, John Penn to Thomas Penn, 30 Mar. 1768, PPOC, HSP.

271. Central to the country tradition was an "obsession with corruption," defined as an absence of virtue. Gordon S. Wood, "Rhetoric and Reality in the American Revolution," *WMQ*, 3d ser., 23 (1966): 26, 29, 31. For a useful discussion of corruption, see Wood, *Creation of the American Republic*, 28–36.

272. Levy, *Quakers and the American Family*, 123–152.

273. See, e.g., *Paxton Papers*, Dunbar, ed.

274. For examples of the standard country metaphors on the dangers of power, see Isaac Norris, Jr., to Robert Charles, 4 Apr. 1757, INLB, 1756–1766, and John Wright, *The Speech of John Wright, Esq. . . .* (Philadelphia, 1741), Evans # 4872.

275. Greene, "Political Mimesis."

276. For the ubiquity of these discourses, see Isaac Kramnick, "The 'Great National Discussion': The Discourse of Politics in 1787," *WMQ*, 3d ser., 45 (1988): 3–32.

277. For this tradition, see Browning, *Court Whigs*.

278. John Trenchard and Thomas Gordon, *Cato's Letters; or, Essays on Liberty, Civil and Religious, and on Other Important Subjects*, 4 vols. (3d ed., London, 1733; repr., New York, 1969), 1:72. For remarks about the Pennsylvania aversion to cant in a different context, see Hamilton, *Itinerarium*, 22.

279. See, e.g., *Penn-Logan Corresp.*, 1:323; *PBF*, 12:290; James Pemberton to John Smith, 5 Oct. 1765, William Logan to John Smith, 1 Oct. 1756, CJS, HSP. Note its absence from German discourse as well. Roeber, *Palatines, Liberty, and Property*, 4.

280. William Smith, *The Reverend William Smith Vindicated . . .* (Philadelphia, 1756), Evans # 7793; Lively, "Speaker and His House," 252; Thomas Penn to James Hamilton, 9 Jan. 1760, Penn-Hamilton Correspondence, HSP.

281. See William Smith, *Brief State*, id., *Brief View*, his writings in Horace Wemyss Smith, *Life of . . . William Smith*, and his "Watchman" articles in the *Pennsylvania Journal*, 23 Feb., 16 and 30 Mar., 27 Apr., 11 May, and 3 and 17 Aug. 1758. For a very different view of Smith and the significance of his writings, see Bailyn, *Origins of American Politics*, 140–145. The literature of the 1720s and 1760s is readily available in the Evans Collection.

282. *Penn-Logan Corresp.*, 2:226.

283. See, e.g., Benjamin Hinchman to William Smith, Jr., 12 July 1754, Smith Papers, box 1, lot 189 # 8, NYPL.

284. Newcomb, *Franklin and Galloway*, 105–298; Ryerson, *Revolution Has Now Begun*, 26–33; Milton Flower, *John Dickinson, Conservative Revolutionary* (Charlottesville, Va. 1983), 76–99; Hutson, *Pennsylvania Politics*, 92–253; Schlenther, *Charles Thomson*, 7–94, 96.

285. Flower, *Dickinson*, 93–96; Schlenther, *Charles Thomson*, 96.

286. Charles S. Olton, *Artisans for Independence: Philadelphia Mechanics and the American Revolution* (Syracuse, N.Y., 1975), 33–54.

287. Lively, "Speaker and His House," 235–443.

288. For Pennsylvania's reputation as a society with more liberty than the English, see *Considerations upon the Rights of the Colonists . . .* (New York, 1766), Evans # 10273; William Livingston, "History of the American Revolution to Nov. 8, 1775," John Jay Papers, microfilm, NYHS; Dickinson, *Speech*.

289. I except Benjamin Franklin because he was only in Pennsylvania for two years (Nov. 1762– Nov. 1764) between June 1757 and the outbreak of the Revolution.

290. Dickinson, *Speech.*

291. Galloway, *A True and Impartial State of the Province of Pennsylvania . . .*, 9.

292. "Answer to Conrad Weiser's Published Letter to the Germans," 29 Sept. 1741, PPOC, HSP.

293. Isaac Norris, Jr., to Robert Charles, 5 Oct. 1755, INLB, 1719–1756, HSP.

294. Dunbar, *Paxton Papers,* 226–227, 237.

295. Tully, "Quaker Party and Proprietary Policies," 89; William Allen to Thomas Penn, 25 Feb. 1768, PPOC, HSP.

296. Marietta, *Reformation.*

297. Abel James to Thomas Wharton, 16 Oct. 1773, Thomas Wharton, Sr., Coll., as quoted in Ryerson, *Revolution Has Now Begun.*

298. Hutson, *Pennsylvania Politics,* 236–243.

299. Ibid., 216–240; Tully, "Quaker Party and Proprietary Policies," 103; and chapter 5.

300. William Smith to Thomas Penn, [?] 1755, PPOC, HSP; *CR,* 8:472–477, 479.

301. Tully, "Englishmen and Germans," 245–256.

302. John Elder to Richard Peters, 30 July 1757, Gratz Coll., American Clergy, HSP.

303. Edward Shippen, Sr. to James Burd, 25 Jan. 1764, Shippen Papers, HSP; Richard Peters to Robert Monckton, 19 Jan. 1764, Chalmers Papers, Philadelphia, vol. 2, NYPL; Tully, "Quaker Party and Proprietary Policies," 102–103; id., "Ethnicity," 528, 528n.

304. The earliest use of the term "Presbyterian Party" I have found is in John Drinker and Stephen Collins to Israel Pemberton, Jr., 25 Sept. 1766, Pemberton Papers, HSP.

305. For a different view, see Hutson, *Pennsylvania Politics,* 211–253, who, I think, takes the charges of a few leading Quaker Party veterans too much at face value. For evidence suggesting a more complicated view of Philadelphia politics, see ibid., 211n. It is arguable, of course, that the term "Presbyterian Party" is more appropriately used of the out-of-doors Philadelphia politics of protest, but to do so discounts Ryerson's evidence that the "patriots" came from a broad religious spectrum. Ryerson, *Revolution Has Now Begun,* 1–147.

306. See chapter 5.

307. William Allen to Thomas Penn, 12 Oct. 1768, PPOC, HSP; *PBF,* 14:257.

308. Ingersoll, "Alison," 91, 113, 247, 273–276; Dunbar, *Paxton Papers,* 255.

309. Foster, "George Bryan," 34–62.

310. "The Circular Letter and Articles of 'some Gentlemen of the Presbyterian Denomination' . . . ," as quoted in Joseph Galloway, *Historical and Political Reflections,* 50.

311. *Itineraries . . . of Ezra Stiles,* Dexter, ed., 556–557.

312. That is, in Chester and Lancaster counties. See Rosemary S. Warden, "The Revolution in Political Leadership in Chester County, Pennsylvania, 1765–1785" (Ph.D. diss., Syracuse University, 1979), 1–48.

313. Presbyterians did make one effort to establish a broad political network in 1764, but, although momentarily promising, it quickly fell apart. Foster, "George Bryan," 96–97.

314. For early debate on the question of underrepresentation, see Lincoln, "Rep-

resentation in the Pennsylvania Assembly," and Thayer, "Quaker Party." More recent writers have not advanced the argument any further.

315. There was no consensus among contemporaries on what equitable representation entailed. See chapter 5, n. 160.

316. See Lincoln, "Representation in the Pennsylvania Assembly," and Thayer, "Quaker Party."

317. There are a number of other plausible counterfactual hypotheses. For example, even a slight augmentation of western representation might have driven eastern elitists in the Proprietary Party to embrace their Assembly Party foes with even greater ardor in order to shore up the old popular order that the Quaker Party represented. That would have strengthened the Old Party in and around Philadelphia but would probably have widened the chasm between the majority eastern party and a minority western one.

Eight / *Some Comparative Dimensions of Political Structure and Behavior*

1. James A. Henretta, *"Salutary Neglect"*: *Colonial Administration under the Duke of Newcastle* (Princeton, 1972); Katz, *Newcastle's New York*.

2. See, e.g., Leder, *Robert Livingston*; Sheridan, *Lewis Morris*; Olson, *Anglo-American Politics*; Henretta, *"Salutary Neglect,"* 155–162.

3. See chapter 3.

4. Katz, *Newcastle's New York*, 91–134. Morris left for England in November 1734.

5. At that time the lieutenant-governor's commission was vacant.

6. Katz, *Newcastle's New York*, 134–138.

7. See chapter 4.

8. Bailyn, *Origins of American Politics*; Henretta, *"Salutary Neglect,"* 242–243.

9. Jonathan Belcher to Lord Hardwicke, 25 Nov. 1749, as quoted in Henretta, *"Salutary Neglect,"* 303.

10. *Two Early Political Associations*, 1–112.

11. Olson, "Lobbying of London Quakers," 143–145.

12. Ibid., 145–149; Wolff, *Colonial Agency*, 79–203; Marietta, *Reformation*, 142–144, 158–168; Labaree, *Royal Government*, 47; Henretta, *"Salutary Neglect,"* 212.

13. Richard Peters to John Penn, 30 Aug. 1740, RPLB, HSP. The Quakers began to lose their clout in the late 1750s. Olson, "Lobbying of London Quakers," 149–151. See also id., *Making the Empire Work*.

14. McAnear, *Income of the Colonial Governors*.

15. See chapter 2.

16. Ibid.

17. The exceptions in Pennsylvania were James Hamilton and Robert Hunter Morris. In New York there were none, but the office of lieutenant-governor was most frequently held by a colonial.

18. Labaree, *Royal Government*, 134. During the late seventeenth century, the size of the council fluctuated somewhat (Sloughter, 12; Fletcher, 15; and Bellomont, 13) but beginning with Cornbury it stabilized at 12. Spencer, *Phases of Royal Government*, 47.

19. Peter Warren to George Clinton, 22 Aug. 1742, Clinton Papers, as quoted in Varga, "New York Government," 21.

20. Ibid.; Labaree, *Royal Government*, 92–93n. "A Seat is Realy not Lucrative,"

observed John Cruger, "but merely honourary & Expensive." John Cruger to Edmund Burke, 3 Feb. 1773, as quoted in McCarthy, "Cruger Family," 18.

21. Jessica Kross, "'Patronage Most Ardently Sought': The New York Council, 1665–1775," in *Status and Power,* Daniels, ed., 210–214.

22. Ibid. 219–221.

23. John Watts to Robert Monckton, 23 Jan. 1768, Chalmers Coll., vol. 2, NYPL.

24. John Kinsey argued that in the absence of a governor, the president of the council and his board were simply administrative caretakers; they were "no Part of the Legislature, nor are intrusted with any Share in the making of Laws" (*Pa. Votes,* 4:3198). The "Assembly" "always treated [them] with Contempt" because of the legislators' conviction that the councillors' one consistent goal was the subversion of the Pennsylvania constitution. Governor Thomas to John Penn, 14 July 1741, PPOC, HSP.

25. See, e.g., Governor Thomas to John Penn, 14 July 1741; Richard Penn to Thomas Penn, 15 June 1764; John Penn to Thomas Penn, 16 June 1764, PPOC, HSP.

26. For example, the three creole councillors who were appointed before they were thirty years old all had fathers who were powerful assemblymen. Kross, "New York Council," 218.

27. The argument that New York experienced conciliar government during the late 1740s is one that Stanley Katz developed in *Newcastle's New York,* 164–244, largely on the basis of Clinton's evolving efforts to justify himself in the documents in *DRCNY.* For its refutation, see the evidence in Bradshaw, "Clinton," and Varga, "New York Government," 232–234. On the nature of DeLancey's power, see chapter 4, pp. 126–134.

28. John Murrin has wryly observed that Pennsylvania was the "only" colony in which the assembly could, in effect, absorb the council. Murrin, "Political Development," 438–439. See also Nash, *Quakers and Politics,* 310–311.

29. The third was the exceptional (in terms of the impact of imperial policies) election of 1768. See chapter 5, pp. 173–175. Robert Dinkin assigns turnout figures (voters relative to adult white males) of 56.1 percent in 1761 and 55.4 percent in 1737 (53.6 percent in 1768). *Voting in Provincial America,* 144–145, 156. These figures replicate those produced by Milton M. Klein, "Democracy and Politics in Colonial New York," *NY Hist.* 40 (1959): 221–246. Adrian Howe produces revised figures to argue that the highest participation rate occurred in the 1737 by-election. "Accommodation and Retreat," 356n.

30. *Weyman's New-York Gazette,* 2 Feb. 1761.

31. It is arguable that the divisions between Leislerians and anti-Leislerians polarized society more at the turn of the century, but the two factions did not sustain themselves in electoral terms beyond a decade or so.

32. For some of the complexities lying behind voter participation, see pp. 324–327 and chapter 9, pp. 370–381.

33. Queens County also had a high turnout of 56.2 percent in the case of a re-run election in 1761. The little we do know about the circumstances of political affairs in Queens indicates that the context of provincial political debate was of some importance. David Jones and Thomas Cornell were important popular Whigs, and opposition to them owed something to provincial Whig criticism.

34. The voter turnout in Philadelphia County was 42.2 percent in 1764 and 46.1 percent in 1765; in Philadelphia City, the figures were 42.2 percent and 61.8 percent. The 1765 vote represented 45.8 percent and 47.7 percent respectively in Bucks and Lancaster counties. Dinkin, *Voting in Provincial America,* 159.

35. Voter participation in Philadelphia County was 37.6 percent in 1740 and 34.2 percent in 1742. In Lancaster County, in which the high points were 1741 and 1742, turnout rose from 36.9 percent in the former year to 44.8 percent in the latter. Ibid., 158.

36. Occasionally, there were additional marginal candidates.

37. Cadwallader Colden to Lieutenant-Governor George Clarke, [Aug. 1741], *Colden Papers*, 8:275. Even in the much-noticed general election of 1737, in which the Morris/Alexander faction managed to defeat Adolphe Philipse and elect James Alexander, Alexander either headed a partial ticket or accepted some very questionable characters as running mates. John Walters was a business partner of Paul Richards and Anthony Rutgers, both close associates of the Philipses and DeLanceys. Simon Johnson was a well-known friend of the DeLanceys and an enemy of Philip Livingston II.

38. *Pa. Votes*, 3:2162–2163.

39. Lokken, *David Lloyd*, 226–228.

40. Dinkin, *Voting in Provincial America*, 154.

41. *New-York Gazette, revived in the Weekly Post-Boy*, 3 Sept. 1750.

42. Dinkin, *Voting in Provincial America*, 153; *New-York Gazette*, 30 Mar. 1739.

43. For the manor contests, see Kim, *Landlord and Tenant*, 120.

44. *Pa. Votes*, 4:3225.

45. *Hazard's Register* 5 (1830): 21.

46. John Smith, Diary, 1 Oct. 1750, HSP.

47. *Advice to the Free-Holders and Electors of Pennsylvania* (Philadelphia, 1735), Evans # 3863.

48. Compiled from membership lists in *NY Votes*.

49. See, e.g., Cadwallader Colden to Governor George Clinton, [Dec. 1749], *Colden Papers*, 7:346–347.

50. "Speech of Vincent Matthews . . . ," *Colden Papers*, 8:226–240. For an example of county leaders taking a stand against provincial authorities, see "Dutchess County Freeholders to John Chambers," 12 Apr. 1743, John Chambers Papers, box 1, NYSL.

51. George Thomas to Ferdinand John Paris, 14 May 1741, PPOC, HSP.

52. "Answer to Conrad Weiser's Published Letter to the Germans," 29 Sept. 1741, PPOC, HSP. For the significance of the electoral duties of the sheriff, see pp. 327–328.

53. C. G. to Friend Humphrey, 20 Sept. 1743, *PMHB* 22 (1898), 386.

54. James Logan to Governor Thomas, 1 Oct. 1741, James Logan Letter Book, 1731–32, 1741–42, HSP; *A Dialogue Shewing, What's Therein to be Found*. Again in 1750, only about 1,800 Philadelphia County and City residents voted for assemblyman, while approximately 2,000 voted for sheriff and coroner. John Smith, Diary, 1 Oct. 1750, HSP. The governor actually chose *one* of the top two finishers in each category to serve as sheriff and coroner. It was important for the voters to have two popular candidates running for each office so that the governor's choice would mean little.

55. *Advice to the Free-Holders and Electors of Pennsylvania*.

56. Lewis Morris, Jr., to James Alexander, n.d., Rutherford Coll., roll 1, p. 105; *Brief Narrative*, Katz, ed., 81; Robert R. Livingston to Philip Schuyler, 28 Jan. 1769, Schuyler Papers, NYPL; John Smith, Diary, 3 Oct. 1749, Richard Peters to Thomas Penn, 5 June 1742, RPLB, HSP.

57. John Morton to Joseph Pennock, Sr., 23 June 1764, Chester County Historical Society.

58. See, e.g., Robert R. Livingston to Philip Schuyler, 28 Jan. 1769, Schuyler Papers, Robert Livingston to Abraham Yates, 11 Jan. 1759, Yates Papers, NYPL.

59. Robert Livingston, Jr., to Abraham Yates, 6 Aug. 1759, Yates Papers, NYPL.

60. Arent Stevens to William Johnson, 30 Jan. 1752, *Johnson Papers*, 1:362.

61. John Smith, Diary, 1 Oct. 1750, HSP; Dinkin, *Voting in Provincial America*, 102. Of James Wright, Charles Norris wrote, "its true that J. W. does not seek it, [a seat in the assembly] but we do return him besides the sense we have of his own merit, in gratitude to the memory of his father" (to Susanna Wright, 16 Apr. 1761, Norris MSS, Misc., HSP).

62. Henry Beekman to Henry Livingston, 10 Feb. 1750, Beekman Papers, box 1, John Jay to Robert R. Livingston, [?] Jan. 1769, Robert R. Livingston Coll., roll 1, NYHS.

63. Philanthropos, *To the Freeholders and Freemen*. . . .

64. William Parsons to Richard Peters, Northampton County Misc. MSS, HSP.

65. Richard Hockley to Thomas Penn, 1 Oct. 1754, Penn Papers, Corresp. of the Penn Family, Richard Peters to Thomas Penn, 2 Oct. 1756, PPOC, HSP; Cadwallader Colden to Governor George Clinton, 19 Feb. 1749, *Colden Papers*, 4:102.

66. Gary B. Nash, "The Transformation of Urban Politics, 1700–1765," *JAH* 60 (1973): 617n.

67. Richard Peters to Proprietors, 17 Nov. 1742, RPLB, HSP; chapter 7.

68. Henry Beekman to Gilbert Livingston, 24 Nov. 1747, Beekman Papers, box 1, NYHS.

69. *Some Necessary Precautions, Worthy to be Considered by all English Subjects*. . . .

70. Timothy Telltruth, *To Morris Morris* . . . (Philadelphia, 1728), Evans # 3111. For a discussion of intimidation and clientage, see chapter 9, pp. 375–377.

71. Peter Van Schaack to Henry Van Schaack, 27 Jan. 1769, Francis L. Hawks Coll., NYHS.

72. Cohen, "Philadelphia Election Riot"; *Pa. Votes*, 4:3357, 3398.

73. Lynford Lardner to Richard Penn, 20 Nov. 1742, Lynford Lardner Letter Book, HSP.

74. Dinkin, *Voting in Provincial America*, 116–117; Lively, "Speaker and His House," 217; Newcomb, *Franklin and Galloway*, 122. In New York, candidates occasionally offered to serve without pay, a form of bribery that was outlawed in Pennsylvania. Kim, *Landlord and Tennant*, 121–122.

75. Dinkin, *Voting in Provincial America*, 102, 106.

76. *From Parker's New-York Gazette* . . . *"No Lawyer in the Assembly"; The Election, a Medly* . . . (Philadelphia, 1764), Evans # 9650.

77. See, e.g., George Clinton to James Alexander, 7 Oct. 1752, *Colden Papers*, 4:344–345.

78. Nicolas Varga, "Election Procedures in Colonial New York," *NY Hist.* 41 (1960): 249–277; Dinkin, *Voting in Provincial America*, passim.

79. William Corry to Sir William Johnson, 25 Aug, 1757, NY Col. MSS, vol. 85, NYSA.

80. Sister Joan de Lourdes Leonard, "Elections in Colonial Pennsylvania," *WMQ*, 3d ser., 11 (1954): 385–401.

81. John Dickinson to Mother, 7 Oct. 1765, R. R. Logan Coll., Dickinson Papers, HSP.

82. John Watts to Robert Monckton, 23 Jan. 1768, Chalmers Coll., vol. 2, NYPL.

83. Abraham Ten Broeck to James Duane, 22 Feb. 1768, Duane Papers, NYHS.

84. John Cannon, *Parliamentary Reform, 1640–1832* (Cambridge, 1973), 276–289; J. H. Plumb, *The Growth of Political Stability in England, 1675–1725* (London, 1967). Linda Colley has restored some needed perspective to the debate over the political stability of eighteenth-century England by suggesting that the late seventeenth- and very early eighteenth-century period was more stable, and the years of Whig ascendancy less so, than Plumb and others have argued. Colley, *In Defiance of Oligarchy,* 3–24.

85. John G. Kolp, "The Flame of Burgessing: Elections and the Political Communities of Colonial Virginia, 1728–1775" (Ph.D. diss., University of Iowa, 1988), 95. Given the poor records we have for many counties, it is impossible to offer an accurate count of uncontested elections in New York and Pennsylvania. My guess would be that regional variations were more significant than change over time. New York City and County, Albany, Schenectady, Queens, Ulster, and Orange were the centers of New York partisan politics, with significant spillover into Westchester, occasionally into Richmond, and near the end of the colonial period into Dutchess. At the other end of the spectrum were Kings and Suffolk counties. For obvious reasons, the manors of Livingston, Rensselaerswyck, and Cortlandt were special cases. In Pennsylvania, not only are the records weak, but any tentative count of uncontested elections would be terribly misleading. Uncontested elections between parties were high at times *precisely because* Pennsylvania had a powerful partisan political culture. Yet there were simultaneously a considerable number of poorly reported intraparty contests at elections because of the number of officers (assemblymen, sheriffs, coroners, commissioners, and assessors) that provincials voted for on the first of October.

86. Jack P. Greene, "Legislative Turnover in British America, 1696 to 1775: A Quantitative Analysis," *WMQ,* 3d ser., 38 (1981): 456. Note that Greene's periodization of turnover rates in New York (pp. 446–447) obscures the important patterns that emerge from an election-by-election calculation of those rates. (See p. 322.) Also note the willingness of Pennsylvanians to change their representatives (according to Greene's figures) fairly frequently as long as they did not feel much of a threat from non-Quakers. Once Friends' minority status seemed to imperil their political hegemony, they began to close ranks. My guess is that length of service would be a better measure of stability in Pennsylvania's political leadership during the early eighteenth century than turnover, but the necessary work is just now being done to establish this prior to 1729 (Craig W. Horle, Marianne S. Wokeck et al., *Lawmaking and Legislators in Pennsylvania: A Biographical Dictionary,* vol. 1 [Philadelphia, 1991], *1682–1709;* later volumes to follow). For post-1729 figures and the importance of long service in Pennsylvania's political culture, see Ryerson, "Quaker Elite."

87. And three of these occurred within one five-year period when Governor Clinton was isolated by the DeLancey/Jones coalition.

88. It is possible to argue for the late seventeenth and early eighteenth century as the period in which turnout was the highest. But the statistics are so fragmentary and, in cases in which we do have some rough counts, the evidence of large-scale corruption so overwhelming, that such a case would be suspect.

89. The strongest proponent of this view is Gary Nash in his "Transformation of Urban Politics." Also see his *Urban Crucible* and Patricia Bonomi's *Factious People.*

Nash estimates that New York's population grew from approximately 5,110 in 1708 to about 21,310 in 1771, and Philadelphia's from approximately 2,465 in 1709 to about 21,880 in 1772. *Urban Crucible,* 407–408. For the most recent attempt to estimate Philadelphia's population—an estimate that projects figures of 4,263 in 1709 and 30,384 in 1772—and citation of other literature on the subject, see P. M. G. Harris, "The Demographic Development of Colonial Philadelphia in Comparative Perspective," American Philosophical Society *Proceedings* 133 (1989): 262–304.

90. Dinkin, *Voting in Provincial America,* 156.

91. Ibid., 158–159.

92. For a similar argument in a far less inclusive political system, see Frank O'Gorman, *Voters, Patrons, and Parties: The Unreformed Electoral System of Hanoverian England, 1734–1832* (Oxford, 1989), 384–393.

93. Howe, "Accommodation and Retreat"; Tully, "Religion and Voting Behavior."

94. Tully, "Religion and Voting Behavior."

95. "Dirck Ten Broeck & Philip Schuyler to Messers Jan Wempel, Arendt Braedt, Johs Mynderse & Jacob Glenn," 25 Feb. 1728, Schuyler Papers, NYSL. For a different view of Albany politics, see Kenney, "Dutch Patricians in Colonial Albany," and id., "Patricians and Plebeians in Colonial Albany."

96. For an example of continuing German influence in the management of Quaker Party politics, see John Smith, Diary, 24 Sept. 1750, HSP.

97. On local government and the legitimacy it gained, see, e.g., Jessica Kross, *The Evolution of an American Town: Newtown, New York, 1642–1775* (Philadelphia, 1983); Wright, "Local Government"; Peyer, "Jamaica, Long Island"; McLaughlin, "Dutch Rural New York"; Patricia U. Bonomi, "Local Government in Colonial New York: A Base for Republicanism," in *Aspects of Early New York Society and Politics,* Judd and Polishook, eds., 29–50; Clair W. Keller, "Pennsylvania Government, 1701–1740: A Study of the Operation of Colonial Government (Ph.D. diss., University of Washington, 1967); id. "The Pennsylvania County Commission System, 1712–1740," *PMHB* 93 (1969): 372–382; Lemon, *Best Poor Man's Country,* 98–149; William M. Offutt, "Law and Social Cohesion in a Plural Society: The Delaware Valley, 1680–1710" (Ph.D. diss., Johns Hopkins University, 1987), 396–461; Tully, *William Penn's Legacy,* 103–121.

98. Bonomi, *Factious People,* 28. "With eastern Long Island and Albany each located about 150 miles—a three to five days' journey—from the capital of the colony at New York City, it is not surprising that sectional particularism should have developed" (ibid. 26).

99. Wright, "Local Government," 8.

100. Bonomi, "Local Government." For the European tradition of city and community particularism, see Voorhees, "'In Behalf of the True Protestants Religion,'" 52–53.

101. Merwick, *Possessing Albany;* Kim, *Landlord and Tenant;* Hartog, *Public Property and Private Power.*

102. Bonomi, *Factious People,* 34–36.

103. Kim, *Landlord and Tenant,* 93–103.

104. Bonomi, *Factious People,* 36n.

105. Kross, *Newtown;* Peyer, "Jamaica, Long Island"; McLaughlin, "Dutch Rural New York"; Bonomi, "Local Government."

106. Bonomi, *Factious People,* 33. Westchester and Schenectady were granted

special borough and township status respectively. In addition to Rensselaerswyck Manor, which had assembly representation in 1691, the governor granted seats to Livingston Manor in 1716 and to Cortlandt Manor in 1734.

107. Lemon, *Best Poor Man's Country,* 99–102.

108. Ibid., 54–55.

109. Wolf, *Urban Village,* 176; Lokken, *David Lloyd,* 44.

110. Judith Diamondstone, "Philadelphia's Municipal Corporation," *PMHB* 90 (1966): 183–201; Tully, *William Penn's Legacy,* 107.

111. Lemon, *Best Poor Man's Country,* 124, 126. Lancaster was the closest to an exception. Jerome J. Wood, *Conestoga Crossroads: Lancaster, Pennsylvania, 1730–1790* (Harrisburg, Pa. 1979).

112. Keller, "County Commission System."

113. Tully, *William Penn's Legacy,* 103–104.

114. Lewis Morris, Jr., to Lords of Trade, 19 July 1729, *DRCNY,* 5:887; NY Col. MSS, vol. 85, p. 103, NYSA.

115. "Mr. George Clarke to Mr. Walpole," 24 Nov. 1725, *DRCNY,* 5:769.

116. Cadwallader Colden to Governor George Clinton, 9 May 1748, Clinton to Colden, 7 Sept. 1748, *Colden Papers,* 4:62, 75–76; David S. McKeith, "The Inadequacy of Men and Measures in English Imperial History: Sir William Johnson and the New York Politicians" (Ph.D. diss., Syracuse University, 1971), 171–174.

117. Sir William Johnson to Cadwallader Colden, 18 June 1761, 7 Feb. 1762, *Colden Papers,* 6:43, 116–117; McKeith, "Johnson and the New York Politicians," 171–174; Henry Beekman to Henry Livingston, 26 July 1751, Beekman Papers, box 1, NYHS.

118. *NY Laws,* 1:660–661; Philip L. White, *The Beekmans of New York in Politics and Commerce, 1647–1877* (New York, 1956), 187. Note the disrepute the militia had fallen into by midcentury. Lieutenant-Governor DeLancey to Lords of Trade, 3 Jan. 1754, *DRCNY,* 6:820; Cadwallader Colden to Archibald Kennedy, 7 Aug. 1755, *Colden Papers,* 5:21. The result was that the assembly would not renew the militia law for several years. *NY Laws,* 3:1153–1154.

119. Cadwallader Colden to Archibald Kennedy, 7 Aug. 1755, *Colden Papers,* 5:21. Individuals had no interest in accepting commissions for sparsely settled regions. NY Col. MSS, vol. 61, p. 3, NYSA.

120. Lewis Morris, Jr., "Draft Essay on the Magistracy" (n.d.), Morris Papers, NYHS. See also "On County Justices," 1775, Robert R. Livingston Coll. reel 1, NYHS.

121. Henry Beekman to Henry Livingston, 19 Dec. 1743, Beekman Papers, box 1, NYHS. Sir William Johnson's list of nominees for his area of influence in Albany County in 1769 numbered 78. Johnson to Goldsbrow Banyar, 29 Jan. 1769, Goldsbrow Banyar Papers, box 3, NYHS.

122. Justices, Berks, 1769, Misc. County Papers, Philadelphia, Berks, and Montgomery, HSP. The population figures for Dutchess and Berks counties are derived from Greene and Harrington, *American Population,* 98, 99, 117.

123. Tully, *William Penn's Legacy,* 111.

124. NY Col. MSS, vol. 85, p. 103, NYSA.

125. Ibid., vol. 86, p. 13.

126. Tully, "Quaker Party and Proprietary Policies," 84–85. On the loan office operations, see Schweitzer, *Custom and Contract,* 115–168.

127. *NY Laws,* 2:1019.

128. Thomas Penn to James Hamilton, 31 July 1749, Thomas Penn Letter Book, 2; William Peters to Thomas Penn, 4 June 1768, PPOC, HSP.

129. Turbutt Francis et al. to John Penn, 25 Mar. 1771, *PA*, 1st. ser. 4:409–410.

130. Samuel Finley to Richard Peters, 15 Nov. 1755, Roberts Coll., Haverford College Library.

131. James Hamilton to Thomas Penn, 29 Apr. 1749, 12 Mar. 1750, James Hamilton Letter Book, 1749–1783, Andrew and James Hamilton Papers; Thomas Penn to William Peters, 10 Aug. 1764, Thomas Penn Letter Book, 8, HSP.

132. Samuel Finley to Richard Peters, 15 Nov. 1755, Roberts Coll., Haverford College Library. The result was that magistrates frequently shared the popular prejudices of county opinion. See, e.g., *Pa. Votes*, 6:5030–5031.

133. Edward Shippen, Sr., to Edward Shippen, Jr., 18 Mar., 6 Apr. 1754, Edward Shippen Letter Books, APS; Tully, *William Penn's Legacy*, 109.

134. For the considerable attention a representative might pay to this problem, see Henry Beekman's correspondence in Beekman Papers, box 1, NYHS.

135. Smith, *History of New-York*, 1:309.

136. *NY Laws*, 3:74, 270, 777.

137. Ibid., 54, 262, 327, 350, 418.

138. Ibid., 667.

139. Ibid., 1029.

140. Ibid., 225. For a similar point relating to the manors, see Kim, *Landlord and Tenant*, 127.

141. My count is from *NY Laws* and *Pa. Statutes*.

142. Sir Lewis Namier and John Brooke, *The History of Parliament: The House of Commons, 1754–1790*, 3 vols. (London, 1964).

143. See, e.g., *NY Votes*, 2:95–97, 109–110.

144. Ibid., 338; *NY Laws*, 3:996–998, 5:110–112.

145. *Pa. Statutes*, 4:15.

146. Ibid., 122, 296–299.

147. Ibid., 382–339.

148. That method, of course, provided its own inequities.

149. And if we take the sixty years between 1713 and 1773 in order to exclude the rather busier early years (just as the 1691–1701 decade in New York saw an uncharacteristically heavy volume of laws passed), the average number of Pennsylvania acts passed per year drops to a little under eight. For other comparisons, see Murrin, "Political Development," 440.

150. 1698, 1707, 1738, and 1749.

151. 1701–1706, 1706–1709, 1710, 1713–1715, 1715–1717, 1719–1721, 1727–1728, 1732–1734, 1736–1738, 1739–1743, 1747–1749, 1752–1755.

152. *Pa. Statutes*, 2:3–141. For the pre-1701 record, see *Charter to William Penn and Laws of the Province of Pennsylvania, Passed between the Years 1682 and 1700 . . .* (Harrisburg, Pa., 1879).

153. Levy, *Quakers and the American Family;* Fischer, *Albion's Seed*, 585.

154. Murrin, "Political Development," 39; Hohwald, "Pennsylvania Politics." On Quakers and limited government, see Fischer, *Albion's Seed*, 594.

155. There was no frame of government in effect from June 1700 to October 1701.

156. They did between 1719 and 1721.

157. See chapter 7.

158. It should not be surprising that voluntarism flourished in Pennsylvania. Witness Franklin's Voluntary Association and the practice of citizen diplomacy through the Friendly Association.

159. See chapter 6.

160. *New-York Weekly Post-Boy,* 17 Mar. 1746. See also chapter 6, p. 215.

161. Kim, *Landlord and Tenant,* 3–86.

162. See, e.g., Robert R. Livingston to Robert Livingston (of Clermont), 12 Apr. 1766, Robert R. Livingston Coll., reel 1, NYHS; Robert Livingston, Jr., to Abraham Yates, 10 Feb.1759, Yates Papers, NYPL; Kierner, *Traders and Gentlefolk,* 115–116.

163. The claim of "ancient" property rights on behalf of New York residents in the eighteenth century is strained at best. It accepts the landlord rationale on its own terms. See Kim, *Landlord and Tenant,* 295 and passim.

164. *NY Laws,* 3:882; Kim, *Landlord and Tenant,* 122; George Clinton to Cadwallader Colden, 6 Jan. 1752, *Colden Papers,* 4:306.

165. William Hicks to [?], 10 May 1767, Peter Dubois Misc. MSS, NYHS; Robert Hunter Morris to John Armstrong, [?] Sept. 1756, Gratz Coll., box 18, case 15, HSP.

166. One might add Richmond and Kings simply because of their size.

167. On the place of patrons, see O'Gorman, *Voters, Patrons, and Parties,* passim.

168. Jack P. Greene, *Pursuits of Happiness,* 186–187.

169. John C. Guzzardo, "Sir William Johnson's Official Family: Patron and Clients in an Anglo-American Empire" (Ph.D. diss., Syracuse University, 1975).

170. "To the Voters at Canajoharie," July, 1750, *Johnson Papers,* 1:294.

171. William Corry to William Johnson, 31 Dec. 1751, *Johnson Papers,* 1:358. My emphasis.

172. Robert Livingston, Jr., to Abraham Yates, 31 Jan. 1755, Yates Papers, NYPL.

173. Henry Beekman to Gilbert Livingston, 1 May 1744, Henry Beekman to Henry Livingston, 8 Dec. 1744, 26 July 1751, [?] Dec. 1751, Beekman Papers, box 1, NYHS.

174. Henry Beekman to Henry Livingston, 7 Feb. 1752, ibid.

175. Henry Beekman to Henry Livingston, 3 Mar. 1753, in "A Packet of Old Letters," 39; Henry Beekman to Henry Livingston, 9 May 1744, Beekman Papers, box 1, NYHS.

176. Henry Beekman to Henry Livingston, 23 Jan. 1752, in "A Packet of Old Letters," 35.

177. Mark A. Kishlansky, *Parliamentary Selection: Social and Political Choice in Early Modern England* (Cambridge, 1986), 193.

178. Ibid., 15–16, 16n.

179. Ibid., 182; *New-York Gazette, revived in the Weekly Post-Boy,* 3 Sept. 1750; Stokes, *Iconography,* 4:790.

180. Dinkin, *Voting in Provincial America,* passim; Kim, *Landlord and Tenant,* 121–122; O'Gorman, *Voters, Patrons, and Parties,* passim.

181. Robert Livingston, Jr., to Abraham Yates, 6 Aug. 1759, NYPL.

182. Bibibus, *A Tooth-Full of Advice* . . . (New York, 1768), Evans # 10833.

183. "To the Voters of Canajoharie," July, 1750, *Johnson Papers,* 1:294.

184. "Controverted Election (Richmond) before the House of Assembly" (1761), Duane Papers, NYHS.

185. *New-York Weekly Journal,* 5 Nov. 1733.

186. Peter Van Schaack to Henry Van Schaack, 27 Jan. 1769, Francis L. Hawks Papers, NYHS; Stokes, *Iconography,* 4:791. For the English parallel, see O'Gorman, *Voters, Patrons, and Parties,* 256.

187. For a similar emphasis on the functional character of election rituals in late eighteenth-century England, see Frank O'Gorman, "Campaign Rituals and Ceremonies: The Social Meaning of Elections in England, 1780–1860," *Past and Present* 135 (1992), 79–115. Three major differences between the English and colonial practices stand out: (1) relatively little social inversion took place during colonial campaigns; (2) there is little evidence of "traditional" social practices imported from the premodern Old World seeking expression in the colonial campaigns; (3) the colonial campaign rituals centered more directly on partisanship than did their English counterparts. These differences seem to suggest a shorter evolutionary distance existed between colonial political practices and party politics than existed in England during the period O'Gorman treats.

188. Hamilton, *Itinerarium,* 228–229.

189. Robert Livingston, Jr., to Abraham Yates, 8 Feb. 1761, Yates Papers, NYPL.

190. See Sir Lewis Namier, *England in the Age of the the American Revolution,* 2d ed. (London, 1961); id., *The Structure of British Politics at the Accession of George III,* 2d ed. (London, 1957); Colley, *In Defiance of Oligarchy;* O'Gorman, *Voters, Patrons, and Parties.*

191. On political relations in the manors, see Kim, *Landlord and Tenant,* 87–128. The contrast between manor politics and large county politics is most explicitly expressed in the dealings of Robert Livingston, Jr., within his manor as opposed to his participation in the larger context of Albany County politics.

192. Kishlansky, *Parliamentary Selection,* 182; Richard Hockley to Thomas Penn, 1 Nov. 1742, PPOC, HSP.

193. William Allen to John Penn, 27 Mar. 1741, PPOC, HSP.

194. William T. Parsons, "Isaac Norris II, The Speaker" (Ph.D. diss., University of Pennsylvania, 1955); Flower, *Dickinson;* Schweitzer, *Custom and Contract,* 106–109; Tolles, *Meeting House and Counting House,* 109–143.

195. Telltruth, *To Morris Morris;* Philip Livingston to Jacob Wendell, 26 Feb. 1747, Livingston Papers, MCNY.

196. Schweitzer, *Custom and Contract,* 97–106, 110–113; Lucy Simler, "Tenancy in Colonial Pennsylvania: The Case of Chester County," *WMQ,* 3d ser., 43 (1986): 542–569.

197. I know of only two instances in which a landlord's political stripe was alleged to influence tenants' votes. *PBF,* 4:410–411; John Watson, Jr., to Israel Pemberton, Jr., 9 Aug. 1757, Etting Coll., Misc. Mss, HSP.

198. *Pa. Votes,* 4:2966; *Pa. Statutes,* 5:159. The only allegation of bribery I have found occurred in 1773 when Lebanon Valley residents were pushing for separation from Lancaster County. James Burd to Edward Burd, 11 Sept. 1773, Balch Papers, Shippen, HSP.

199. Even in the case of closely contested elections. See, e.g., Isaac Norris, Jr., to Robert Charles, 7 Oct. 1754, INLB, 1719–1756; William Logan to John Smith, [?] Oct. 1764 [misdated 1765], CJS, HSP.

200. Isaac Norris, Sr., to Jonathan Scarth 21 Oct. 1726, Isaac Norris Letter Book, 1716–1730; James Logan to John Penn, 17 Oct. 1726, Patrick Gordon to John Penn, 18 and 22 Oct. 1726, PPOC, HSP.

201. Paul Verrit, *To My Friends in Pennsylvania* (Philadelphia, 1738), Evans # 4316. For evidence of strong Quaker support to bring in the ballot in New York,

see Peter R. Livingston to Robert Livingston, Jr., 25 Dec. 1769, Livingston-Redmond, reel 6, microfilm, NYHS.

202. Contemporary Pennsylvanians believed the intent of the ballot was to make voting a private decision. Evans, "Brief Account of Pennsylvania" (MS), HSP.

203. John Smith, Diary, 1 Oct. 1747, 2 Oct. 1749, 1 Oct. 1750, HSP; Richard Hockley to Thomas Penn, 1 Nov. 1742, "Letters from the Letter Book of Richard Hockley," *PMHB* 28 (1904): 41; Charles Petitt to Joseph Reed, 23 Nov. 1764, Joseph Reed Papers, reel 1, NYHS.

204. William Parsons to Richard Peters, 2 Oct. 1754, Northampton County Misc. MSS, HSP.

205. Isaac Hunt, *The Substance of an Exercise, Had this Morning in Scurrility-Hall. No. VII* (Philadelphia, 1765), Evans # 10015.

206. *A Dialogue Shewing, What's Therein to be Found.*

207. Ibid.

208. On the two violent election-day confrontations in colonial Pennsylvania, see *Pa. Votes*, 4:3357, 3398, and Cohen, "Philadelphia Election Riot."

209. For other considerations relevant to this judgment, see Fischer, *Albion's Seed*, 419–603.

210. *PWP*, 3:472.

211. See chapter 7.

212. James Logan to Henry Goldney, 7 Mar. 1725, as quoted in Konkle, *Life of Andrew Hamilton*, 38. Also see p. 24.

213. *American Weekly Mercury*, 18 Oct. 1733, as quoted in DeArmond, *Andrew Bradford*, 112.

214. James Hamilton to Thomas Penn, 22 Feb. 1750, PPOC, HSP.

215. John Smith, Diary, 14 June 1749; William Peters to Thomas Penn, 4 June 1764; William Allen to Thomas Penn, 8 Oct. 1767, PPOC; James Hamilton to Thomas Penn, 29 Apr. 1749, James Hamilton Letter Book, 1749–1783, Andrew and James Hamilton Papers; Joseph Shippen, Jr., to Edward Shippen, Sr., 22 June 1770, Shippen Papers, HSP.

216. *Penn-Logan Corresp.*, 2:33.

217. *Pennsylvania Gazette*, 8 Dec. 1737. Compare this to the "radical" *New-York Weekly Journal*: "the Reason why men enter into Society, is the Preservation of their Property" (9 Aug. 1736); assembly representatives should have "a Considerable Interest in the Property of the Colony" (23 May 1737); "Property & Liberty are . . . [so] interwoven" that the weakening of one adversely affects the other (16 June 1735). See also *An Unanswerable Answer to the Cavils and Objections . . .* (New York, 1739), Evans # 4440, in which a Morris/Alexander writer asserted that the council was an important part of the legislature "as most . . . [councillors] have Estates in the Province equal to any of the Representatives of the People."

218. Douglas Hay, "Property, Authority, and the Criminal Law," in *Albion's Fatal Tree: Crime and Society in Eighteenth-Century England*, Douglas Hay et al., eds. (London, 1975), 17–64.

219. Ibid., 27, 29; Offutt, "Law and Social Cohesion," 450.

220. Hay, "Property, Authority," 33; Offutt, "Law and Social Cohesion," 450.

221. Hay, "Property, Authority," 27, 31, 47; Offutt, "Law and Social Cohesion," 450.

222. Offutt, "Law and Social Cohesion," 451.

223. See, e.g., Konkle, *Life of Andrew Hamilton*, 27–28.

224. Benjamin Hinchman to William Smith, Jr., 12 July 1754, William Smith Papers, box 1, lot 189, # 8, NYPL.

225. Richard Hockley to Thomas Penn, 4 Aug. 1754, Penn Family Correspondence, as quoted in Wolff, *Colonial Agency,* 157.

226. William Smith to Thomas Penn, 27 Nov. 1755, PPOC; Richard Peters to Thomas Penn, 23 Nov. 1743, RPLB, HSP; *CR,* 4:533. That, too, was the implication of Henry Mühlenberg's charge that the Pennsylvania Assembly was a "Cromwellian Parliament" (quoted in Roeber, *Palatines, Liberty and Property,* 261).

227. See chapter 7.

228. *Pennsylvania Journal,* 27 May 1756; George Stevenson to Richard Peters, 15 May 1758, *PA,* 1st ser., 3:359–360. See also Levy, *Quakers and the American Family.*

229. Goodfriend, *Before the Melting Pot;* Levy, *Quakers and the American Family;* Roeber, *Palatines, Liberty, and Property.*

230. David E. Narrett, *Inheritance and Family Life in Colonial New York City* (Ithaca, N.Y., 1992); but note some circumscription of Dutch women's rights by 1750. Id., "Men's Wills and Women's Property Rights in Colonial New York," in *Women in the Age of the American Revolution,* Ronald Hoffman and Peter J. Albert, eds. (Charlottesville, Va., 1989), 100–102, 133; McLaughlin, "Dutch Rural New York," passim. Linda Briggs Biemer, *Women and Property in Colonial New York: The Transition from Dutch to English Law, 1643–1727* (Ann Arbor, Mich., 1983); Joan R. Gundersen and Gwen Victor Gampel, "Married Women's Legal Status in Eighteenth-Century New York and Virginia," *WMQ,* 3d ser., 38 (1982), 114–134. On the restrictions and limitations on Quaker widows in Pennsylvania, see Levy, *Quakers and the American Family,* 197–205; Marylynn Salmon, *Women and the Law of Property in Early America* (Chapel Hill, N.C., 1986), 163–167. But note the contradictory evidence and the argument that the omission of their widows as executors may have been motivated by husbands' desire "to limit the widow's burden" rather than serving as evidence of male assumptions about female incompetence. Lisa Wilson, *Life after Death: Widows in Pennsylvania, 1750–1850* (Philadelphia, 1992), 50–51. Important, too, is Wilson's larger argument demonstrating a broader engagement of women in business affairs in heavily Quakerized communities. Of relevance, too, are Joan M. Jensen, *Loosening the Bonds: Mid-Atlantic Farm Women, 1750–1850* (New Haven, 1986), and Carole Shammas, "Early American Women and Control over Capital," in *Women in the Age of the American Revolution,* Hoffman and Albert, eds., 134–154.

231. Mary Maples Dunn, "Women of Light," in *Women of America: A History,* Carol Ruth Berkin and Mary Beth Norton, eds. (Boston, 1979), 114–133; Isabel Ross, *Margaret Fell: Mother of Quakerism* (London, 1949); Helen G. Crosfield, *Margaret Fox of Swarthmoor Hall* (London, 1913). For William Penn's consciousness of this tradition, see Frost, *Perfect Freedom,* 15.

232. Jean R. Soderlund, "Women's Authority in Pennsylvania and New Jersey Quaker Meetings, 1680–1760," *WMQ,* 3d ser., 44 (1987): 745.

233. For the argument in favor of the Quakers as the originators and paragons of the "cult of domesticity," see Levy, *Quakers and the American Family.*

234. Soderlund, "Women's Authority," 724.

235. Levy, *Quakers and the American Family,* 195.

236. *New-York Weekly Post-Boy,* 19 Jan. 1747; George Stevenson to Richard Peters, 15 May 1758, *PA,* 1st ser., 3:359–360.

237. Levy, *Quakers and the American Family;* Marietta, *Reformation,* 58–62, 73–74, 135–136.

238. Morgan, *Inventing the People,* 174–208; O'Gorman, "Campaign Rituals and Ceremonies," 111.

239. John Smith to Elizabeth Hudson, 10 Oct. 1750, CJS; Charles Norris to

Susanna Wright, [Oct. 1757], 2 and 16 Apr. 1761, Norris MSS, Misc.; Richard Peters to Proprietors, 17 Nov. 1742, RPLB, HSP.

240. Richard Peters to Proprietors, 17 Nov. 1742, RPLB, HSP. For a brief statement on the personal context relevant to Hoskins's political influence, see Levy, *Quakers and the American Family,* 216–218.

241. Ibid.

242. Catherine Phillips, *Memoirs of the Life of Catherine Phillips* (Philadelphia, 1778), 141–142.

243. Churchman, *Account of the Gospel Labours,* 68–73.

244. Murray, *Mr. Murray's Opinion;* Smith, *Mr. Smith's Opinion.*

Nine / Oligarchical Politics

1. The best example of this interpretation is Nash, *Urban Crucible.* For variations on this theme, see Ronald Schultz, "The Small-Producer Tradition and Artisan Radicalism in Philadelphia, 1720–1810," *Past and Present* 127 (1990): 84–116; id., *The Republic of Labor: Philadelphia Artisans and the Politics of Class, 1720–1830* (New York, 1993); Alfred F. Young, "English Plebeian Culture and Eighteenth-Century American Radicalism," in *Origins of Anglo-American Radicalism,* Jacob and Jacob, eds., 185–212; Countryman, *People in Revolution,* 1–98; Dirk Hoerder, *Crowd Action in Revolutionary Massachusetts* (Cambridge, Mass., 1979); Philip S. Foner, *Labor and the American Revolution* (Westport, Conn., 1976); Edward Countryman, "'Out of the Bounds of the Law': Northern Land Rioters in the Eighteenth Century," in *The American Revolution: Explorations in the History of American Radicalism,* ed. Alfred F. Young, (De Kalb, Ill., 1976), 37–70; Staughton Lynd, "The Mechanics in New York Politics, 1774–1785," in id., *Class Conflict, Slavery, and the United States Constitution* (Indianapolis, 1967), 79–108; Jesse Lemisch, "Jack Tar in the Streets: Merchant Seamen in the Politics of Revolutionary America," *WMQ,* 3d. ser., 25 (1968): 371–407; Egnal and Ernst, "Economic Interpretation," 3–32. These interpretations, of course, go back to Becker's *Political Parties* and Lincoln's *Revolutionary Movement.* They also slide sideways to E. P. Thompson's writings on eighteenth-century England. See, in particular, Thompson's "The Moral Economy of the English Crowd in the Eighteenth Century," *Past and Present* 50 (1971): 76–137; "Patrician Society, Plebeian Culture," *Journal of Social History* 7 (1974): 382–405; and "Eighteenth-Century English Society: Class Struggle without Class," *Social History* 3 (1978): 133–165. But note Thompson's subsequent emphasis on the particular type, or "political culture," of the crowd he examined in his "Moral Economy" article and his ambivalence toward academics who have extended the notion of a moral economy to very different historical circumstances. Those who have done so without due rigor, he seems to disown; those who have expanded the concept in imaginative yet disciplined fashion, he seems to laud. E. P. Thompson, *Customs in Common* (London, 1991), 259–351. See esp. pp. 336–351.

2. Nash, *Urban Crucible,* 140–156.

3. Timothy Wheelwright, *Two Letters on Election of Aldermen* (New York, 1734), Evans # 3853.

4. *A Dialogue between Mr. Robert Rich and Roger Plowman.* See also Lokken, *David Lloyd,* 221, and Jotham, *To My Respected Friend. I.*[saac] *N.*[orris] (Philadelphia, 1727), Evans # 2889.

5. *New-York Weekly Journal,* 23 May 1737.

6. Schweitzer, *Custom and Contract,* 125–126, 175–191.

7. That is so whether class is defined according to: (1) some arbitrary classification of wealth distribution; (2) some broad occupational categorization; (3) some apparent, if intermittently shared, group experience based on conflict with, or some sense of differentiation from, other socioeconomic groups; or (4) contemporary usage. On contemporary usage of the term *class,* see P. J. Corfield, "Class by Name and Number in Eighteenth-Century Britain," *History* 72 (1987): 38–61. See also Thompson, "Eighteenth-Century English Society," and Kulikoff, *Agrarian Origins of American Capitalism.*

8. For 1764 through 1770, see pp. 381–389.

9. McAnear, "Politics," 520–524; Egnal and Ernst, "Economic Interpretation," 14; Nash, *Quakers and Politics,* 252–254.

10. Egnal and Ernst, "Economic Interpretation"; Marc Egnal, "The Pennsylvania Economy, 1748–1763: An Analysis of Short-Term Fluctuations in the Context of Long-Run Changes in the Atlantic Trading Community" (Ph.D. diss., University of Wisconsin-Madison, 1974). There is controversy over the timing, nature, and extent of colonial economic crises, but none of these affect my focus on high turnover in elections. See Doerflinger, *Vigorous Spirit of Enterprise,* 171–180.

11. See chapter 8, p. 322.

12. Ibid.

13. Wellenreuther, "Quest for Harmony," 545; Lokken, *David Lloyd,* 166–187.

14. See chapter 7.

15. *To the Freeholders & Freemen. A Further Information* (Philadelphia, 1727), Evans # 2969. See also Morris Morris, *Reasons for His Conduct . . .* (Philadelphia, 1728), Evans # 3069.

16. *New-York Weekly Journal,* 23 May 1737.

17. Klein, "William Livingston," 76, 85, 89–90.

18. Bruce M. Wilkenfeld, "The New York City Common Council, 1689–1800" (M.A. thesis, Columbia University, 1970), 36–42.

19. Gary B. Nash, "Artisans and Politics in Eighteenth-Century Philadelphia," in *Origins of Anglo-American Radicalism,* Jacob and Jacob, eds., 163.

20. Nash, *Urban Crucible,* 148; id., "Artisans and Politics," 162.

21. Nash, "Artisans and Politics," 162. By the time he wrote his post–*Urban Crucible* article reviewing the part artisans played in colonial Philadelphia politics, Nash seems to have departed considerably from his still-influential earlier pronouncements.

22. They comprised 38 percent of the voters in 1774 and 62 percent in 1780. O'Gorman, *Voters, Patrons, and Parties,* 56.

23. Smith, *"Lower Sort."* On colonial artisans, see Carl Bridenbaugh, *The Colonial Craftsman* (New York, 1950); Charles S. Olton, "Philadelphia Artisans and the American Revolution" (Ph.D. diss., University of California, Berkeley, 1967), 1–131. Thomas J. Schlereth, "Artisans and Craftsmen: A Historical Perspective," in *The Craftsman in Early America,* Ian M. G. Quimby, ed. (New York, 1984), 34–61; R. W. Moss, Jr., "Master Builder: A History of the Colonial Philadelphia Building Trades" (Ph.D. diss., University of Delaware, 1972); Sharon Salinger, "Artisans, Journeymen, and the Transformation of Labor in Eighteenth-Century Philadelphia," *WMQ,* 3d ser., 40 (1983): 62–84.

24. Pauline Maier, "Popular Uprisings and Civil Authority in Eighteenth-Century America," *WMQ,* 3d ser., 27 (1970): 3–35; Gordon S. Wood, "A Note on Mobs in the American Revolution," ibid., 23 (1966): 635–642; John Lax and William Pencak, "The Knowles Riot and the Crisis of the 1740s in Massachusetts,"

Perspectives in American History 10 (1976): 161–214; Sung Bok Kim, "The Impact of Class Relations and Warfare in the American Revolution; The New York Experience," *JAH* 69 (1982): 326–346; James H. Hutson, "An Investigation of the Inarticulate: Philadelphia's White Oaks," *WMQ*, 3d ser., 28 (1971): 3–25, and Hutson's reply to Jesse Lemisch and John Alexander in ibid., 29 (1972): 136–142.

25. Thompson, "Eighteenth-Century English Society," 156–158. See also id., "Moral Economy."

26. Young, "English Plebeian Culture."

27. Paul A. Gilje, *The Road to Mobocracy: Popular Disorder in New York City, 1763–1834* (Chapel Hill, N.C., 1987), 16–35; Lemisch, "Jack Tar," 383; Smith, *History of New-York,* 2:149.

28. Steven J. Rosswurm, "'That They Were Grown Unruly': The Crowd and Lower Classes in Philadelphia, 1765–1780" (M.A. thesis, Northern Illinois University, 1974); *CR,* 4:284; John Smith, Diary, 21 Aug. 1749; James Logan to John, Thomas, and Richard Penn, 30 Apr. 1729; Lynford Lardner to Thomas Penn, 16 June 1748, PPOC, HSP.

29. See Suzanne Desan, "Crowds, Community, and Ritual in the Work of E. P. Thompson and Natalie Davis," in *The New Cultural History,* Lynn Hunt, ed. (Berkeley, 1989), 47–71. See also Tim Harris, *London Crowds in the Reign of Charles II: Propaganda and Politics from the Restoration to the Exclusion Crisis* (Cambridge, 1987), 8–13, and James Titus, *The Old Dominion at War: Society, Politics, and Warfare in Late Colonial Virginia* (Columbia, S.C., 1991), 64.

30. Kim, *Landlord and Tenant,* 281–345.

31. Charles D. Dutrizac, "Local Identity and Authority in a Disputed Hinterland: The Pennsylvania-Maryland Border in the 1730s," *PMHB* 115 (1991): 35–62; id., "Empire, Province, Frontier: Perspectives on the Pennsylvania-Maryland Boundary Dispute, 1681–1738" (Ph.D. diss., University of Western Ontario, 1986).

32. *Pa. Votes,* 4:3357, 3398. *A Modest Apology for the Eight Members* (Philadelphia, 1728), Evans # 3065.

33. *Pa. Votes,* 4:2961.

34. Tully, *William Penn's Legacy,* 32–43.

35. Scott, " Slave Insurrection."

36. Thomas J. Davis, *A Rumor of Revolt: "The Great Negro Plot" in Colonial New York* (New York, 1985).

37. Gilje, *Mobocracy,* 15–16.

38. *Pa. Votes,* 4:2961, 2966; Gilje, *Mobocracy,* 5–35.

39. Gilje, *Mobocracy,* 22–23.

40. Thomas P. Slaughter, "Crowds in Eighteenth-Century America: Reflections and New Directions," *PMHB* 115 (1991): 31.

41. In the Philadelphia election of 1742, approximately 300 voters allegedly struck William Allen's name off the ballot after the riot, but the discredited candidate would likely have been defeated in any case. Richard Hockley to Thomas Penn, 1 Nov. 1742, "Letters," 41.

42. President Clarke to the duke of Newcastle, 7 Oct. 1736, *DRCNY,* 6:76; *NY Laws,* 1:575.

43. Kim, *Landlord and Tenant,* 281–415; Douglas Greenberg, *Crime and Law Enforcement in the Colony of New York, 1691–1776* (Ithaca, N.Y., 1976), 121–124.

44. See, e.g., Greenberg, *Crime and Law Enforcement;* Offutt, "Law and Social Cohesion"; David T. Konig, *Law and Society in Puritan Massachusetts: Essex County, 1629–1692* (Chapel Hill, N.C., 1979); William E. Nelson, *Dispute and Conflict Reso-*

lution in Plymouth County, Massachusetts, 1725–1825 (Chapel Hill, N.C., 1981); David H. Flaherty, "Crime and Social Control in Provincial Massachusetts," *Historical Journal* 24 (1981): 339–360; Linda Kealey, Patterns of Punishment: Massachusetts in the Eighteenth Century," *American Journal of Legal History* 30 (1986): 163–186; Peter Charles Hoffer, "Honor and the Roots of American Litigiousness," ibid., 33 (1989): 295–319; Bruce Mann, *Neighbors and Strangers, Law and Community in Early Connecticut* (Chapel Hill, N.C., 1987).

45. Greenberg, *Crime and Law Enforcement,* 71.
46. Ibid., 64–67, 140–141, 146–148.
47. See chapter 8, pp. 333–334.
48. Offutt, "Law and Social Cohesion," 458–460.
49. Smith, *Memoirs,* 1:22.
50. Greenberg, *Crime and Law Enforcement,* 154–187.
51. On civil actions and arbitration, see Deborah A. Rosen, "The Supreme Court of Judicature of Colonial New York: Civil Practice in Transition, 1691–1760," *Law and History Review* 5 (1987): 213–247; John R. Aitken, "New Netherland's Arbitration in the Seventeenth Century," *Arbitration Journal* 29 (1974): 145–160; Eben Moglen, "Commercial Arbitration in the Eighteenth Century: Searching for the Transformation of American Law," *Yale Law Journal* 93 (1983): 135–152. See also A. G. Roeber's brief comments in "'The Origin of Whatever Is Not English,'" 230, 235.
52. William Smith, Jr., to Philip Schuyler, 30 May 1768, Schuyler Family Papers, NYSL.
53. Offutt, "Law and Social Cohesion."
54. Ibid.; Tully, *William Penn's Legacy,* 190–191.
55. Marietta, *Reformation,* 3–72; "Records of the Session, 1740–1793, New Londonderry Congregation, Faggs Manor, Pennsylvania," PHS.
56. Offutt, "Law and Social Cohesion."
57. *American Weekly Mercury,* 30 July 1741.
58. Minutes of the Presbytery of Philadelphia, 1758–1781, 95, PHS. For comments on both the Germans' willingness to use and efforts to avoid courts, see Roeber, *Palatines, Liberty, and Property,* 152, 197–201, and passim.
59. *Pa. Votes,* 6:5002; Richard Peters to Proprietors, 3 June 1742, RPLB, HSP; Edward Shippen, Sr., to Edward Shippen, Jr., 6 Apr. 1754, Edward Shippen Letter Book, APS.
60. Schwartz, *"Mixed Multitude,"* 99.
61. *PBF,* 11:467–468.
62. See chapter 8, pp. 333–334.
63. William Peters to Thomas Penn, 4 June 1764, PPOC, HSP.
64. John Penn to Thomas Penn, 1 Sept. 1764, PPOC, HSP.
65. The *Oxford English Dictionary* defines an oligarchy as "government in the hands of a few."
66. Greene, "Legislative Turnover," 461.
67. *Historical Statistics of the United States, Colonial Times to 1957,* 2:1168.
68. Ibid.
69. For the comparative size of the legislatures, see Greene, "Legislative Turnover," 461.
70. Ryerson, "Quaker Elite," 111.
71. Bonomi, *Factious People,* 302–308; Tully, *William Penn's Legacy,* 181–182.

72. James Duane to John Dickinson, 12 Nov. 1770, R. R. Logan Coll., Dickinson Papers, HSP; Ryerson, "Quaker Elite," 106.

73. *PBF*, 11:93; Ryerson, "Quaker Elite," 134; James Duane to John Dickinson, 12 Nov. 1770, R. R. Logan Coll., Dickinson Papers, HSP.

74. Divisions were fitful at best in New York, and virtually nonexistent in Pennsylvania. *The Christian's Duty . . . ; Pa. Votes*, 6:4810.

75. Abraham Ten Broeck to James Duane, 22 Feb. 1768, Duane Papers, NYHS; James Pemberton to Samuel Fothergill, [?] Nov. 1756, Pemberton Papers, Pemberton-Fothergill, vol. 34. See also Smith, "Draft Acco't," William Smith Papers, box 1, lot 189 # 12, NYPL.

76. Governor Thomas to John Penn, 27 Oct. 1741, PPOC. See also Richard Peters to Thomas Penn, 1 June 1753, PPOC, HSP.

77. David Van Der Heyden to Sir William Johnson, 3 Feb. 1761, *Johnson Papers,* 3:325.

78. With the exception of 1699 and 1769.

79. Archibald Kennedy to Cadwallader Colden, 15 Apr. 1751, *Colden Papers,* 4:264.

80. Bonomi, *Factious People,* 307–308.

81. Henry Beekman to Gilbert Livingston, 15 May 1745, Beekman Papers, box 1, NYHS.

82. David Van Der Heyden to Sir William Johnson, 3 Feb. 1761, *Johnson Papers,* 3:325.

83. Abraham Yates to Robert Livingston, Jr., 16 Feb. 1761, Yates Papers, NYPL.

84. Sir William Johnson to Philip Schuyler, 29 Feb. 1768, *Johnson Papers,* 6:127.

85. *New-York Gazette,* 27 Feb. 1739. For a different view, see Carl Becker, "Nominations in Colonial New York," *AHR* 6 (1901):260–275. See my comments on the 1769 election, chapter 5, pp. 177–180 and n. 74, pp. 487–488.

86. Wellenreuther, "Quest for Harmony," 545; Israel Pemberton to John Fothergill, 17 Nov. 1755, Pemberton Papers, Pemberton-Fothergill, vol. 34, HSP; Edward Shippen, Jr., to Joseph Shippen, Sr., [Sept. 1756], in *Letters and Papers Relating Chiefly to the Provincial History of Pennsylvania,* Thomas Balch, ed. (Philadelphia, 1855), 64.

87. *Penn-Logan Corresp.,* 1: 108. Something of the differing characters of the three old counties is discernable in Levy, *Quakers and the American Family,* and Marietta, *Reformation.*

88. *To the Freeholders; Remarks on the Late Proceedings.*

89. *A Dialogue Shewing, What's Therein to be Found.*

90. William Allen to John Penn, 17 Nov. 1739, PPOC; John Smith, Diary, 24, 27, and 28, Sept. 1750, HSP.

91. John Taylor to William Moore, 20 Sept. 1738, Taylor Papers, Correspondence, 1723–1750, HSP.

92. C. G. to Friend Humphrey, 20 Sept. 1743, *PMHB* 22 (1898): 386–387.

93. R. G. to Friend John Taylor, 1 Sept. 1743, ibid., 387–388.

94. On the Quaker Party's efforts to include Philadelphia County Germans, see John Smith, Diary, 24 Sept. 1750, HSP.

95. Charles Norris to Susanna Wright, 2 and 16 Apr. 1761, Norris MSS, Misc., HSP.

96. James Logan to Governor Thomas, 1 Oct. 1741, James Logan Letter Book, 1731–1732, 1741–1742, HSP.

97. C. G. to Friend Humphrey, 20 Sept. 1743, *PMHB* 22 (1898): 386–387.

98. *PWP*, 2:509; *Pennsylvania Journal*, May 1756, as quoted in Lang, "Colonial Colleges and Politics," 251. See also Warden, "Revolution in Political Leadership," 1–48.

99. Sir William Johnson to Philip Schuyler, 29 Feb. 1768, *Johnson Papers*, 6:127.

100. *Pennsylvania Gazette*, 27 Sept. 1770.

101. New York defined freeholders as those with an estate worth £40 or more. Tenants with lifetime leasehold could vote, and a resident of New York City or Albany could qualify by paying a fee to become a freeman. Pennsylvania required a 50-acre freehold in the counties and ownership of a tenement or a £50 personal estate in Philadelphia. Chilton Williamson, *American Sufferage: From Property to Democracy, 1760–1860* (Princeton, 1960), 12–14, 27–28, 33–34.

102. W. A. Speck, *Stability and Strife: England, 1714–1760* (London, 1977), 16.

103. J. G. A. Pocock, "The Classical Theory of Deference," *AHR* 81 (1976): 516–523. Quotations from 516, 518, and 519.

104. Greenberg, *Crime and Law Enforcement,* 154–187; C. G. to Friend Humphrey, 20 Sept. 1743, *PMHB* 22 (1898): 386.

105. Court and Road Records MSS, Kings County, as quoted in Greenberg, *Crime and Law Enforcement,* 181.

106. Sir William Johnson to Cadwallader Colden, 10 Aug. 1763, *Colden Papers,* 6:233; Philip Livingston to Jacob Wendell, 14 June 1746, Livingston Papers, MCNY. For the prevalence of egalitarian elements in Dutch communities, see McLaughlin, "Dutch Rural New York," 74–75 and passim.

107. For the importance of gentlemanly behavior among the main Livingston family branches, see William Livingston to Noah Welles, 18 Feb. 1749, LWC-JFP, YUL.

108. Chauncey Graham to William Smith, Jr., 11 July 1755, William Smith Papers, box 1, lot 189 # 6, NYPL.

109. Joseph Shippen to James Burd, 24 July 1763, Shippen Papers, HSP.

110. See chapter 7.

111. *CR* 2:314–319.

112. Charles Norris to Susanna Wright, n.d. [1757 or 1758], Norris MSS, Misc., HSP.

113. Richard Peters to Joseph Shippen, n.d., [1757 or 1758], Misc. MSS, Richard Peters, NYHS. See also the offhand way in which non-Quaker Pennsylvanians referred to high-status clothes as "Dudds" and the disapproval of those who, on assuming office, would "give . . . [themselves] some aires." Fischer, *Albion's Seed,* 146; Asher Clayton to provincial commissioners, 26 Nov. 1763, *PA,* 1st ser., 4:142.

114. "History of Governor William Cosby's Administration . . . ," *Colden Papers,* 9:286.

115. Governor George Clinton to Robert Hunter Morris, 21 Jan. 1752, R. H. Morris Papers, as quoted in Howe, "Accommodation and Retreat," 394. A year and a half earlier, Clinton had complained to Morris that the chief justice had his "two Bullies, Peter and Oliver, to frighten those that his artfull Condesention & Dissimulation could not persuade to vote their conscience" (29 Aug. 1750, Morris Papers, as quoted in Leo Hershkowitz and Isidore S. Meyer, eds., *The Lee Max Friedman Collection of American Jewish Colonial Correspondence: Letters of the Franks Family, 1733–1748* [Waltham, Mass., 1968], 118).

116. Peter R. Livingston to Philip Schuyler, 16 Jan. 1769, Schuyler Papers, NYPL.

117. "Petition to Society from Newburgh," 1752, SPG Letters, B, vol. 20, p. 86,

microfilm, UBC Library; Kim, *Landlord and Tenant*, 118–119n; Henry Beekman to Gilbert Livingston, 14 Dec. 1736, 11 Aug. 1744, Beekman Papers, box 1, NYHS; Smith, *History of New-York*, 2:138, 146; Robert Livingston, Jr., to Abraham Yates, 8 Feb. 1761, Yates Papers, NYPL.

118. Stephen Brobeck, "Changes in the Composition and Structure of Philadelphia Elite Groups, 1756–1790" (Ph.D. diss., University of Pennsylvania, 1972), 76–181.

119. R. G. to Friend John Taylor, 1 Sept. 1743, *PMHB* 22 (1898): 387.

120. At the present time, we simply do not have enough in the way of detailed, regional, socioeconomic studies and biographical data on the large numbers of colonials who participated in the power structures of provincial, county, and township government to make possible any kind of sensitive analysis of the interplay of the personal, social, economic, and political forces underlying the New York and Pennsylvania oligarchies. For the beginning of such a data bank on provincial legislators in Pennsylvania, see Horle, Wokeck et al., *Lawmaking and Legislators*. For some of the kind of information we need on local figures, see Warden, "Revolution in Political Leadership."

121. Smith, *History of New-York*, as quoted in Bailyn, *Origins of American Politics*, 85; *Pennsylvania Gazette*, 27 Sept. 1770; Pocock, "Deference," 519. See also Governor Moore's comment to Lord Hillsborough, that "the greatest part of the Assembly is composed of plain well-meaning Men, whose notions from their Education are extremely confined" (4 Jan. 1769, *DRCNY*, 8:143). Cadwallader Colden was more dismissive of many New York assemblymen in the 1720s, calling them "Dutch boors, grossly ignorant and rude" (letter to Alexander Colden, 15 Oct. 1759, in Smith, *History of New-York*, 1:308). On the Chester County assemblymen of Pennsylvania in the late colonial years, see Warden, "Revolution in Political Leadership," 1–3, 36–38.

122. Lewis Morris, Sr., "The Mock Monarchy, or, the Kingdom of the Apes: A Poem," as quoted in Shields, *Oracles of Empire*, 157.

123. Charles Norris to James Wright, 31 Aug. 1753, Norris MSS, Misc.; Lynford Lardner to Richard Penn, 19 June 1759, Lynford Lardner Papers, HSP.

124. Edward Shils, "Deference," in *Social Stratification*, J. A. Jackson, ed. (Cambridge, Mass., 1968), 123.

125. Ibid.

126. Joy B. and Robert R. Gilsdorf, "Elites and Electorates: Some Plain Truths for Historians of Colonial America," in *Saints and Revolutionaries: Essays on Early American History*, David D. Hall, John M. Murrin, and Thad W. Tate, eds. (New York, 1984), 227. For a critique of deference coupled with an attempt to stay much more within the mainstream republican framework, see Richard R. Beeman, "Deference, Republicanism, and the Emergence of Popular Politics in Eighteenth-Century America," *WMQ*, 3d ser., 49 (1992): 401–430. For evidence of how tenuous any deferential interpretation of politics may be even in that quintessentially deferential eighteenth-century colony, Virginia, see Titus, *The Old Dominion at War*, 33–36, 60, 64, 77, 107–109, 117–120, 140–141, 144–148.

127. Henry Beekman to Henry Livingston, 10 Feb. 1750, Misc. MSS, Henry Beekman, NYHS.

128. See, e.g., Stephen Innes, *Labor in a New Land: Economy and Society in Seventeenth-Century Springfield* (Princeton, 1983), 38–43.

129. Nash, *Urban Crucible*, 362–372.

130. See, e.g., Kim, *Landlord and Tenant*, 120n.

131. Lieutenant-Governor Colden to the earl of Hillsborough, 25 Apr. 1768, *DRCNY*, 8:61.

132. Peter R. Livingston to Philip Schuyler, 27 Feb. 1769, Schuyler Papers, NYPL.

133. Innes, *Labor in a New Land*, 36–43.

134. Staughton Lynd, "Who Should Rule at Home? Dutchess County, New York, in the American Revolution," in id., *Class Conflict, Slavery, and the United States Constitution*, 27–28. Kim, "Landlord and Tenant," 179–180.

135. Kierner, *Traders and Gentlefolk*, 109–110; Kim, *Landlord and Tenant*, 213–214.

136. Henry Beekman to Henry Livingston, 10 Feb. 1750, Beekman Papers, box 1, NYHS.

137. Hermann Wellenreuther, "A View of the Socio-Economic Structures of England and the British Colonies on the Eve of the American Revolution," in *New Wine in Old Skins*, Erich Angermann, Marie-Luise Frings, and Hermann Wellenreuther, eds. (Stuttgart, 1976), 20.

138. Thompson, "Patrician Society, Plebeian Culture," 387–390.

139. Colley, *In Defiance of Oligarchy*, 129–133, 154, and passim.

140. One oft-noted exception was apparently Philipsburgh Manor, where the Anglican Church served as a shrine to the landlord. Far more numerous are the examples of suspicion and hostility between various churches and large landlords.

141. Greene, *Pursuits of Happiness*, 195–196.

142. Bibibus, *A Tooth-Full of Advice. . . .*

143. Colley, *In Defiance of Oligarchy*, 148.

144. Nash, *Urban Crucible*, 362–372.

145. *New-York Gazette, revived in the Weekly Post-Boy*, 27 Jan. 1752; Klein, "William Livingston," 235; Harrington, *New York Merchants*, 13.

146. See, e.g., William Corry to William Johnson, 31 Dec. 1751, *Johnson Papers*, 1:358–359.

147. James Alexander to Cadwallader Colden, 15 Feb. 1744, *Colden Papers*, 3:48. For the relatively small number of merchants voting in the 1768 and 1769 elections, see Charles F. Collins, "The Artisans' Battle against Political Subordination in Colonial New York," *UCLA Historical Journal* 2 (1981): 38, 42. Although, to my knowledge, we have no accurate count of New York merchants, Thomas M. Doerflinger's *A Vigorous Spirit of Enterprise: Merchants and Economic Development in Revolutionary Philadelphia* (Chapel Hill, N.C., 1986), 17, gives us some idea about how large such a group would be. For the relatively high number of the politically uncommitted among some of New York's elite social and occupational groups, see Jacquetta M. Haley, "Voluntary Organizations in Pre-Revolutionary New York, 1750–1775" (State University of New York, Binghamton, 1976), 113–138. Philadelphia also had its powerful moderates who stayed out of the political brawl of the mid 1760s. See Charles Petitt to Joseph Reed, Sept. 21 1764, Joseph Reed Papers, reel 1, NYHS.

148. That is very clear in the case of New York City cartmen, an occupational group of some coherence, within which we might expect to see unquestionable evidence of patronal politics. In fact, what quantitative data do exist are more easily reconciled with the political *inefficacy* of patron/client relations than the reverse. Hodges, "Cartmen of New York City," 84–97.

149. See chapter 5, pp. 177–180.

150. For evidence of economic coercion in the Quaker Party's drive to secure signatures for its royal government campaign, see Dunbar, *Paxton Papers*, 369.

For the apolitical nature of many merchants, see Doerflinger, *Vigorous Spirit of Enterprise*, 182–183.

151. I owe the phrase "intimate citizenship" to the poet Donald Hall, *Here at Eagle Pond* (New York, 1990), 116.

152. See chapter 2.

153. *NY Votes*, 2:131; Cadwallader Colden to H. S. Conway, 9 Nov. 1765, *CCLB*, 2:62; Isaac Norris, [Sr.], *Friendly Advice to the Inhabitants of Pennsylvania* (Philadelphia, 1710, repr. 1728), Evans 1483 and 3078; William Allen to John Penn, 27 Mar. 1741, PPOC, HSP.

154. Henry Beekman to Henry Livingston, 7 Jan. 1745, Beekman Papers, box 1, NYHS. See chapters 2 and 7 on Pennsylvania's aversion to general provincial taxes.

155. Greene, "Social Context and the Causal Pattern of the American Revolution," 27–28, 40.

156. *Brief Narrative*, Katz, ed., 22; chapters 2 and 7 above.

157. Robert Livingston, Jr., to Abraham Yates, 10 Feb. 1759, Yates Papers, NYHS; Dutchess County Freeholders to John Chambers, 12 Apr. 1743, John Chambers Papers, box 1, NYSL.

158. See the Beekman Papers, box 1, NYHS.

159. David W. Jordan, "'God's Candle' within Government: Quakers and Politics in Early Maryland," *WMQ*, 3d ser., 39 (1982): 628–654.

160. See, e.g., *Pa. Votes*, 4:2718; "Message from the Pennsylvania Assembly to the Governor," 12 Sept. 1760, Chalmers Coll., Philadelphia, NYPL; William Logan to John Smith, 25 Mar. 1764, CJS, HSP.

161. "They have reposed a great trust in me, and [to] betray it would be hateful to both God and Man," David Cooper went on to say (Diary, quoted in Wellenreuther, "Quest for Harmony," 574; see also 553–556). Cooper was one of those New Jersey Quaker assemblymen who shared many attitudes with their counterparts in Pennsylvania. For similar musings, see John Smith's Diary, Oct. 1750, HSP, on the responsibilities that election brought.

162. *Pa. Votes*, 6:4644.

163. A leader like Isaac Norris, Jr., could foster what might be called reverse deference—that is, an exaggerated rhetorical respect for his constituents. But he could do so because his position was unassailable.

164. Edward Shippen to Joseph Shippen, 2 Oct. 1770, Shippen Papers, HSP; *New-York Gazette*, 23 Jan. 1738; *Pa. Votes*, 4:3078, 6:4641–4642; *An Answer to a Pamphlet Entitled A Letter to the Freemen and Freeholders.* . . . Samuel Johnson defined "capacity" as "the force or power of the mind" (*A Dictionary of the English Language*, 7th ed. [London, 1783]).

165. *New-York Gazette*, 23 Jan. 1738; *An Answer to a Pamphlet Entitled A Letter to the Freemen and Freeholders.* . . .

166. Jack P. Greene, "Independence, Improvement, and Authority: Toward a Framework for Understanding the Histories of the Southern Backcountry during the Era of the American Revolution," in *An Uncivil War: The Southern Backcountry during the American Revolution*, Ronald Hoffman, Thad W. Tate, and Peter J. Albert, eds. (Charlottesville, Va., 1985), 28–30.

167. For a similar view in the context of eighteenth-century Europe and Britain, see Margaret C. Jacob, "The Enlightenment Redefined: The Formation of Modern Civil Society," *Social Research* 58 (1991): 475–495. The literature examining the many facets of voluntary sociability in New York and Pennsylvania is vast and rapidly growing.

168. *The Christian's Duty*. . . .
169. Morris, *Reasons for His Conduct* . . . ; *Pa. Votes*, 6:4810.
170. Lloyd, *Defence of the Legislative Constitution*. . . .
171. Benjamin Hinchman to William Smith, Jr., 6 Aug. 1754, William Smith Papers, box 1, lot 189 # 9, NYPL; *PBF*, 6:246.
172. *Pennsylvania Gazette*, 12 Apr. 1739; *New-York Weekly Journal*, 10 Dec. 1733, 7 Jan. 1734.
173. John Watts to Robert Monckton, 1 June 1765, *Aspinwall Papers*, 2:573.
174. Robert R. Livingston to Robert Monckton, 8 Nov. 1765, ibid., 559–567.
175. Henry Beekman to Henry Livingston, 28 Dec. 1743, Beekman Papers, box 1, NYHS; Kim, *Landlord and Tenant*, 349–350.
176. Kim, *Landlord and Tenant*, 346–415.
177. Isaac Vrooman to James Duane, 6 Jan. 1766, Duane Papers, NYHS.
178. As quoted in Kim, *Landlord and Tenant*, 388.
179. *Montressor's Journals*, 365; Kim, *Landlord and Tenant*, 388–389.
180. Kim, *Landlord and Tenant*, 396n.
181. Kierner, *Traders and Gentlefolk*, 98–104.
182. The New Jersey land riots involved the same sorts of complexities. See Thomas L. Purvis, "Origins and Patterns of Agrarian Unrest in New Jersey, 1735 to 1754," *WMQ*, 3d ser., 39 (1982): 600–627.
183. Kim, *Landlord and Tenant*, 415, 292.
184. Ibid., 298.
185. Thompson, "Moral Economy."
186. "Land Cases in Colonial New York, 1765–1767: The King v. William Pendergast," Irving Mark and Oscar Handlin, eds., *New York University Law Quarterly Review* 19 (1942): 175.
187. For these characteristics, see Kierner, *Traders and Gentlefolk*.
188. See, e.g., Alan Taylor, *Liberty Men and Great Proprietors: The Revolutionary Settlement on the Maine Frontier, 1760–1820* (Chapel Hill, N.C., 1990); Purvis, "Agrarian Unrest in New Jersey." Even in peripheral areas, the real conflict took place, not between squatters and absentee proprietors, but among members of the local community. In Pennsylvania, agrarian unrest followed proprietary efforts to lease, rather than sell, some manor tracts. Politically, such sentiments gained expression in the antiproprietary cast of Quaker Party policies. Agrarian radicals were thus most frequently not dissidents at all, but supporters of the Quaker Party. In developed areas, tenantry was less frequently perceived as a problem than as a perfectly acceptable feature of a complex, interdependent society. So, too, was the development of a "cottager" class in the eastern rural areas. See Simler, "Tenancy in Colonial Pennsylvania"; id., "The Landless Worker: An Index of Economic and Social Change in Chester County, Pennsylvania, 1750–1820," *PMHB* 114 (1990): 163–200; Paul G. E. Clemens and Lucy Simler, "Rural Labor and the Farm Household in Chester County, Pennsylvania, 1750–1820," in *Work and Labor in Early America*, Stephen Innes, ed. (Chapel Hill, N.C., 1988), 106–143.
189. See chapter 5.
190. Richard Peters to Robert Monckton, 19 Jan. 1764, Chalmers Papers, vol. 2, Philadelphia, NYPL.
191. Kim, *Landlord and Tenant*, 393–396, 400–409.
192. Bonomi, *Factious People*, 276; Christen, "King Sears," 148.
193. Smith, *Memoirs*, 1:46.
194. When that action failed because of the death of a witness, the assembly

recommited MacDougall on charges of contempt. He was finally released from jail in April 1770. Roger J. Champagne, *Alexander McDougall and the American Revolution*, 13–39.

195. James Duane to Robert Livingston, Jr., 17 May 1770, Livingston-Redmond, reel 6, microfilm, NYHS.

196. John Watts to Robert Monckton, 23 Jan. 1768, *Aspinwall Papers*, 2:600; Greene, "Social Context and the Causal Pattern of the American Revolution," 40, 59–63.

197. *PBF*, 12:192.

198. Ryerson, "Quaker Elite," 117, 123, 128, 131–134.

199. Isaac Norris, Jr., to John Dickinson, 24 Oct. 1764, INLB, 1756–1766, HSP.

200. Arthur J. Mekeel, *The Relation of the Quakers to the American Revolution* (Washington, D.C., 1979), 45–46.

201. *Pa. Votes*, 8:6683–6684.

202. Pauline Maier, *From Resistance to Revolution;* Countryman, *People in Revolution,* 5–98.

203. Gary B. Nash, "Urban Wealth and Poverty in Prerevolutionary America," *Journal of Interdisciplinary History* 4 (1976): 545–584; Egnal and Ernst, "Economic Interpretation."

204. Dinkin, *Voting in Provincial America,* 156, 159.

205. John Harris to James Burd, 1 Mar. 1764, Shippen Papers, HSP; "Resolutions in Favour of Sitting Judges of the Supreme Court in the House," Robert R. Livingston Coll., reel 1; Robert Livingston, Jr., to James Duane, 17 Feb. 1772, Duane Papers, NYHS.

Ten / The Legitimation of Partisan Politics

1. Alan Tully, "Constituent-Representative Relationships in Early America: The Case of Pre-Revolutionary Pennsylvania," *Canadian Journal of History* 11 (1976): 139–154.

2. For an example of contemporary classification of social groups, see "Mr. Colden's Account of the State of the Province of New York," 6 Dec. 1765, *DRCNY,* 7:795.

3. Olton, "Philadelphia Artisans," 1–131; Smith, *"Lower Sort";* Sharon Salinger, *"To serve well and faithfully": Labor and Indentured Servants in Pennsylvania, 1682–1800* (Cambridge, 1987).

4. Dunbar, *Paxton Papers,* 331; Francis Alison to John Dickinson, 4 Jan. 1772, R. R. Logan Coll., Dickinson Papers, HSP.

5. Sally F. Griffiths, "'Order, Discipline, and a Few Cannon': Benjamin Franklin, the Association, and the Rhetoric and Practice of Boosterism," *PMHB* 116 (1992): 131–156; Wayne A. Huss, "Pennsylvania Freemasonry: An Intellectual and Social Analysis, 1727–1826" (Ph.D. diss., Temple University, 1985); Steven C. Bullock, "The Ancient and Honorable Society: Freemasonry in America, 1730–1830" (Ph.D. diss., Brown University, 1986); id., "The Revolutionary Transformation of American Freemasonry, 1752–1792," *WMQ,* 3d ser., 47 (1990): 347–369; Moss, "Master Builders"; Olton, "Philadelphia Artisans," 1–131; Hodges, *New York City Cartmen;* Daniel R. Gilbert, "Patterns of Organization and Membership in Colonial Philadelphia Club Life, 1725–1755" (Ph.D. diss., University of Pennsylvania, 1952); Carl and Jessica Bridenbaugh, *Rebels and Gentlemen: Philadelphia in the Age of Franklin* (New York, 1962).

6. Francis Alison, *Peace and Union Recommended* . . . (Philadelphia, 1758), Evans # 8070.

7. NY Col. MSS, vol. 85, p. 73, NYSA.

8. The writings of New York and Pennsylvania social historians over the past two decades have demonstrated this repeatedly.

9. For examples, see Wall, "Controversy in the Dutch Church"; *Pa. Votes,* 5:3871–3872, 3882–3884; Cadwallader Colden to James Alexander, 21 May 1737, Rutherford Coll., roll 1, NYHS.

10. James Alexander to Peter V. B. Livingston, 11 Feb. 1756, as quoted in Lamb, *History of the City of New York,* 1:658n.

11. Bonomi, *Factious People;* "Petition to Society from Newburgh, 1752," SPG Letters, B, vol. 20, p. 86; Richard Peters to William Smith, 28 May 1763, *PMHB* 10 (1886), 352.

12. *PBF,* 9:90.

13. Sydney, *Reply to the Speech*; James Duane to Robert Livingston, Jr., 14 June 1769, Livingston-Redmond, reel 6, microfilm, NYHS.

14. *New-York Weekly Journal,* 13 Oct. 1735.

15. This was also a reflection of an anticorporate attitude toward colonial settlement emanating from Whitehall in the wake of the Dominion of New England fiasco, and on the organization of the Board of Trade.

16. William Allen to Thomas Penn, 24 Oct. 1741, PPOC, HSP.

17. J. A. W. Gunn, *Beyond Liberty and Property: The Process of Self-recognition in Eighteenth-Century Political Thought* (Kingston, Ont., 1983), 47; Henry Beekman associated corporatism more with French tyranny than with English liberty. Beekman to Henry Livingston, 7 Dec. 1748, "A Packet of Old Letters," 33–34.

18. See, e.g., Cadwallader Colden to James Alexander, 21 May 1737, Rutherford Coll., roll 1, NYHS. Tully, "Religion and Voting Behavior."

19. See chapter 5.

20. Both New York and Pennsylvania are rife with examples of crosscutting political alliances. For a general treatment of religion and politics, see Patricia U. Bonomi, *Under the Cope of Heaven: Religion, Society, and Politics in Colonial America* (New York, 1986).

21. Thompson, "Patrician Society, Plebeian Culture."

22. Ibid.

23. Peter R. Livingston to Robert Livingston, Jr., 15 June 1769, Livingston-Redmond, reel 6, microfilm, NYHS; Lemon, *Best Poor Man's Country;* Jones, *Wealth of a Nation.*

24. "Robert R. Livingston's Reasons against a Land Tax," McAnear, ed., 73, 74n; Wheelwright, *Two Letters on Election of Aldermen;* Richard Peters to Proprietors, 25 Mar. 1748, PPOC, HSP; *The Two Interests Reconciled.*

25. James Pemberton to John Fothergill, 11 Oct. 1764, Pemberton Papers, Pemberton-Fothergill, vol. 34, HSP; *New-York Gazette, revived in the Weekly Post-Boy,* 28 Jan. 1748, supplement.

26. Lewis Morris, Sr., "The Mock Monarchy," as quoted in Shields, *Oracles of Empire,* 156.

27. For the notion of "simplified" settler societies, see R. Cole Harris, "The Simplification of Europe Overseas," *Annals of the Association of American Geographers* 67 (1977): 469–483.

28. See Introduction, nn. 5 and 6.

29. Quinby, *Short History of a Long Journey.* . . .

30. Galloway, *Speech*, 27.

31. The term *liberalism* did not emerge as a clear concept until the very late eighteenth and early nineteenth centuries (*Oxford English Dictionary*, s.v.).

32. *American Weekly Mercury*, 18 Sept. 1729; Joyce Appleby, "The Social Origins of American Revolutionary Ideology," *JAH* 64 (1978): 935–958.

33. *NY Votes*, 1:272.

34. Tully, *William Penn's Legacy*, 124.

35. Bernard Friedman, "The Shaping of the Radical Consciousness in Provincial New York," *JAH* 56 (1970): 781–801.

36. Galloway, *A True and Impartial State of the Province of Pennsylvania . . .*, 21–23. See also *A Letter to the People of Pennsylvania . . .* (Philadelphia, 1760), Evans # 8636. For purposes of debate, during the campaign for royal government, Galloway took the tactful and more orthodox Whig position that the Crown had no private interest. See his *Speech*, Evans # 9671.

37. "Thomas Cockerill to Mr. Popple," 2 July 1709, *DRCNY*, 5:81; *Independent Reflector*, Klein, ed., 143–146, 287; William Livingston to Noah Welles, 8 Aug. 1757, LWC-JFP, YUL.

38. Evans, "Brief Account of Pennsylvania" (MS), HSP.

39. *New-York Weekly Journal*, 27 June 1737.

40. Corfield, "Class by Name and Number," 45–46.

41. *New-York Mercury*, 23 July 1753.

42. For succinct summaries of these attitudes, see Wood, *Creation of the American Republic*, 58–59, and Isaac Kramnick, *Bolingbroke and His Circle: The Politics of Nostalgia in the Age of Walpole* (Cambridge, Mass., 1968), 153.

43. Jack P. Greene, "An Uneasy Connection: An Analysis of the Preconditions of the American Revolution," in *Essays on the American Revolution*, Stephen G. Kurtz and James H. Hutson, eds. (Chapel Hill, N.C., 1973), 35–41. See also chapters 2 and 3.

44. By "informal language" I mean the language of private correspondence, and informal speech as opposed to the crafted prose of pieces designed for publication or formal public oration. For a useful discussion of the ornamental character of formal discourse, see Harry S. Stout, "Religion, Communications, and the Ideological Origins of the American Revolution," *WMQ*, 3d ser., 34 (1977): 530–533.

45. Kramnick, *Bolingbroke and His Circle*, 153–155; Thomas L. Pangle, *The Spirit of Modern Republicanism: The Moral Vision of the American Founders and the Philosophy of Locke* (Chicago, 1988), 30–33.

46. Colley, *In Defiance of Oligarchy*.

47. Peter R. Livingston to Oliver Wendell, 19 Jan. 1769, Livingston Papers, MCNY; Henry Beekman to Gilbert Livingston, 15 May 1745, Beekman Papers, box 1, NYHS; James Alexander to Cadwallader Colden, 14 Apr. 1729, *Colden Papers*, 1:279; Abraham Yates to Robert Livingston, Jr., 16 Feb. 1761, NYPL; Henry Cruger, Jr., to Henry Cruger, Sr., 3 May 1775, as quoted in McCarthy, "Cruger Family," 206–208; John Smith, Diary, 2 Oct. 1747; John Smith to Elizabeth Hudson, 10 Oct. 1750, CJS; John Penn to Thomas Penn, 12 Sept. 1766, PPOC; Samuel Purviance, Jr., to James Burd, 20 Sept. 1765, Shippen Papers, HSP; *Pa. Votes*, 4:2964, 2976, 3005–3006; Samuel Wharton to William Franklin, 29 Sept. 1765, as quoted in Newcomb, *Franklin and Galloway*, 106.

48. What I mean by "legitimate" is that party activities were considered to be "normal" or "regular" (*Oxford English Dictionary*, s.v.). My assumption here is that public figures would not willingly describe themselves in odious terms. My inference

from their language and behavior is that the pursuit of party goals was acceptable behavior with no noticeable social cost; rather, party activities proffered the possibility of considerable gain in public prominence.

49. Robert R. Livingston to Robert Livingston, Jr., 21 Feb. 1768, Livingston-Redmond, reel 6, microfilm, NYHS; Robert Livingston, Jr., to Abraham Yates, 11 Jan. 1759, Yates Papers; Robert R. Livingston to Philip Schuyler, 28 Jan. 1769, Schuyler Papers, NYPL.

50. Governor Clinton to Lords of Trade, 30 July 1750, *DRCNY,* 6:578; Henry Beekman to Henry Livingston, 26 Nov. 1747, in "A Packet of Old Letters," 33.

51. *NY Votes,* 1:712.

52. Livingston, *Letter to the Freemen.*

53. Ronald P. Formisano, "Deferential-Participant Politics: The Early Republic's Political Culture, 1789–1840," *American Political Science Review* 68 (1974): 475.

54. Samuel Auchmuty to Sir William Johnson, 20 Jan. 1769, Gratz Coll., American Clergy, HSP.

55. Peter R. Livingston to Philip Schuyler, 16 Jan. 1769, Schuyler Papers, NYPL. For evidence of information exchange but little cross-county cooperation, see James Duane to Abraham Ten Broeck, Mar. 1768, Ten Broeck Papers, Albany Institute of History and Art; Peter Van Schaack to Henry Van Schaack, 27 Jan. 1769, Francis L. Hawks Papers, NYHS. See also John Watts's inability to remember the slate of candidates for New York City and County from the last election. John Watts to Robert Monckton, 23 Jan. 1768, Chalmers Coll., vol 2, NYPL.

56. With the notable exception of the 1768–1769 New York City elections.

57. Stefan Bielinski, *Abrahm Yates, Jr., and the New Political Order in Revolutionary New York* (Albany, 1975), 3–5.

58. Robert Livingston to Abraham Yates, 8 June, 6 Aug. 1759, 17 July 1760, 8 and 16 Feb. 1761; Abraham Yates to Robert Livingston, 16 Feb. 1761, Yates Papers, NYPL.

59. Henry Beekman to Henry Livingston, 18 Sept. 1750, Beekman Papers, box 1, NYHS.

60. Robert Livingston, Jr., to James Duane, 31 Jan. 1763, 14 Aug. 1767, 13 May 1769, James Duane Papers, NYHS; Peter R. Livingston to Philip Schuyler, 23 Jan., 6 Feb., 13 Mar., 17 Aug., 11 Sept. 1769, Schuyler Papers, NYPL. For an assertion of geographical interests before party, see Robert Livingston, Jr., to Abraham Yates, 10 Feb. 1759, Yates Papers, NYPL. For differences arising from the religious issue, see George Dangerfield, *Chancellor Robert R. Livingston of New York, 1746–1813* (New York, 1960), 23. On the lack of cohesion on the other side of the political fence, see John Watts to Robert Monckton, 30 June 1764, *JWLB,* Peter Van Schaack to Henry Van Schaack, 27 Jan. 1769, Francis L. Hawks Coll., NYHS., and Watt's and Walton's voting record on the college issue in the 1750s.

61. See chapter 6, pp. 224–227.

62. Rev. Silas Leonard to William Smith, Jr., 23 Aug. 1754, William Smith Papers, box 1, lot 189 # 7.

63. Philip Livingston to Jacob Wendell, 17 Oct. 1737, Livingston Papers, MCNY.

64. The proportion of controverted elections as a percentage of the total number of elections in New York between 1701 and 1769 was 8.7 percent. For Pennsylvania, see p. 410. This figure is far closer to the Virginia figure of 8 percent than to the much higher English one (see n. 65). Kolp, "Flame of Burgessing," 89.

65. O'Gorman, *Voters, Patrons, and Parties,* 164–168. The proportion of election petitions to the number of English constituencies in the eighteenth century

ranges from a high of 41 percent in 1722 to a low of 16 percent in 1790. For a count of English constituencies, see Cannon, *Parliamentary Reform,* 278–289.

66. For example, there were three petitions each in 1701, 1726, 1737, 1761, and 1768.

67. *NY Votes,* 2:599; Abraham Yates to Robert Livingston, Jr., 16 Feb. 1761, Yates Papers, NYPL.

68. *The Idea of a Patriot King* (London, 1749; repr. Indianapolis, 1965), 46.

69. *Independent Reflector,* Klein, ed., 143–148, 219. See also James Duane to Robert Livingston, Jr., 19 Feb. 1770, Livingston-Redmond, reel 6, microfilm, NYHS.

70. Sir William Johnson to Goldsbrow Banyar, 29 Jan. 1769, Goldsbrow Banyar Coll., box 3, NYHS; McKeith, "Sir William Johnson and the New York Politicians," 207n.

71. "Robert R. Livingston's Reasons against a Land Tax," McAnear, ed., 82.

72. *New-York Weekly Journal,* 4 Feb. 1734.

73. Lieutenant-Governor Colden to the earl of Hillsborough, 7 July 1770, *DRCNY,* 8:217.

74. *New-York Weekly Journal,* 27 Jan. 1734. See also *Independent Reflector,* Klein, ed., 143–148, 215–220.

75. *New-York Gazette,* 15 Apr. 1734.

76. Ibid., 10 June 1734; Robert Livingston, Jr., to Abraham Yates, 8 Dec. 1761, Yates Papers, NYPL; Livingston, *Letter to the Freemen,* Evans # 6865.

77. *New-York Mercury,* 2 Dec. 1754; *To the Worthy Freeholders and Freemen . . .* (New York, 1768), Evans # 11091; *New-York Gazette,* 25 Mar. 1734; Rev. Silas Leonard to William Smith, Jr., 23 Aug. 1754, William Smith Papers, box 1, lot 189 #7, NYPL.

78. *New-York Gazette,* 9 Dec. 1734, 19 Sept. 1737; *An Answer to a Pamphlet,* Evans # 6809.

79. The *New-York Weekly Journal* is a classic example of such activity.

80. *The Examiner, No. II . . .* ; Livingston, *Address of Mr. Justice Livingston. . . .*

81. Peter Van Schaack to Henry Van Schaack, 27 Jan. 1769, Francis L. Hawkes Coll., NYHS.

82. *Independent Reflector,* Klein, ed., 148.

83. Ibid., 195.

84. *New-York Gazette,* 18 Mar. 1734.

85. *New-York Gazette, revived in the Weekly Post-Boy,* 9 Jan. 1749.

86. *To the Freeholders and Freemen of the City and County of New-York: The Following Remarks on a Piece with 17 Queries . . . ; The Occasionalist . . .* (New York, 1768), Evans # 11017.

87. J. G. A. Pocock, "The Concept of a Language and the *métier d'historien:* Some Considerations on Practice," in *The Languages of Political Theory in Early-Modern Europe,* Anthony Pagden, ed. (Cambridge, 1987), 25.

88. W. S. Lewis et al., eds., *Horace Walpole's Correspondence with Sir Horace Mann,* The Yale Edition of Horace Walpole's Correspondence, vols. 17–27 (New Haven, 1954–1971), 17:336–337.

89. *PWP,* 3:357; Richard Peters to William Smith, 18 Dec. 1762, Smith Papers; William Allen to Thomas Penn, 12 Nov. 1766, PPOC, HSP; Abel James to Henry Drinker, 5 July 1770, as quoted in Mekeel, *Relation of the Quakers to the American Revolution,* 59.

90. See, e.g., *Advice and Information to the Freeholders & Freemen of the Province of Pennsylvania*. . . .

91. James Logan, *To Robert Jordan, and Others* . . . (Philadelphia, 1741), Evans # 4740.

92. Levy, *Quakers and the American Family,* passim.

93. *Pennsylvania Gazette,* 1 Apr. 1736, as quoted in DeArmond, *Andrew Bradford,* 101. On the conflation of "the people," "representatives," and "Quakers," see Wellenreuther, "Quest For Harmony," 553–554, 554n.

94. *CR,* 2:432.

95. Ibid.

96. *Pa. Votes,* 5:4157, 6:4644.

97. For some suggestive comments on these associations, see Wellenreuther, "Quest For Harmony."

98. *Pa. Votes,* 4:2802. See also Wellenreuther, "Quest For Harmony," 553–554.

99. Thomas Penn to William Peters, 10 Aug. 1764, Thomas Penn Letter Book, HSP.

100. *Pa. Votes,* 4:4287–4288; Samuel Purviance, Jr., to James Burd, 20 Sept. 1765, Shippen Papers; Isaac Norris, Jr., to Robert Charles, 29 Apr. 1755, INLB, 1719–1756, HSP; Samuel Finley to Richard Peters, 15 Nov. 1755, Roberts Coll., Haverford College Library.

101. Dunbar, *Paxton Papers,* 325.

102. See, e.g., Richard Hockley to Thomas Penn, 5 May 1743, Penn MSS, Additional Misc. Letters, HSP.

103. William Allen to Thomas Penn, 26 Oct. 1755, PPOC, HSP. For a further example of Allen's emphasis on the factional episodes in Pennsylvania politics, see William Allen to David Barclay and Sons, 20 Nov. 1764, *Burd Papers,* Walker, ed.

104. Wellenreuther, "Quest For Harmony."

105. Levy, *Quakers and the American Family.*

106. Tully, *William Penn's Legacy,* 158.

107. Isaac Norris, Jr., to Robert Charles, 29 Apr. 1755, INLB, 1719–1756, HSP.

108. Isaac Norris, Jr., to Robert Charles, 7 Oct. 1754, ibid.; William Logan to John Smith, [?] Oct. 1764, CJS, HSP.

109. For a thorough canvass of definitions of American parties, see John F. Hoadley, *The Origins of American Political Parties, 1789–1803* (Lexington, Ky., 1986), 15–17.

110. See chapter 7.

111. See chapters 4 and 7.

112. See chapters 5 and 8.

113. In fact, I have found *no* case in which they used the first person possessive with "party" at all. Occasionally they used the third person, singular possessive to indicate an individual's allegiance to a larger party entity.

114. Governor Denny to Proprietors, 30 June 1757, *PA,* 1st ser., 3:194; Isaac Norris, Jr., to Robert Charles, 26 Oct. 1741, INLB, 1719–1756; John Smith to Elizabeth Hudson, 10 Oct. 1750, CJS, HSP.

115. *Pa. Votes,* 3:2163, 4:3222–3225, 3279–3280, 6:4423, 4429, 4438, 4441–4445, 4447, 4452–4453, 4455, 4617, 4635; "Examination of Witness in Alleged Northampton County Election Fraud of 1756," Etting Coll., Provincial Council, HSP.

116. William Logan to John Smith, [?] Oct. 1764, CJS, HSP; *PBF,* 11:390–394.

117. Richard Peters to Proprietors, 25 Nov. 1748, 8 Dec. 1749, RPLB; Lynford

Lardner to Richard Penn, 20 Nov. 1742, Lynford Lardner Letter Book, HSP; *A Letter from a Gentleman of Philadelphia to a Freeholder in the County of Northampton* (Philadelphia, 1757), Evans # 7929; *CR*, 3:277–278.

118. Formisano, "Deferential-Participant Politics," 475.

119. John Watts to Robert Monckton, 23 July 1763, *JWLB*, 159.

120. *Pa. Votes*, 4:2996.

121. Ibid., 4:2996. See also Richard Peters to Proprietors, 17 Nov. 1742, RPLB, HSP.

122. Fischer, *Albion's Seed*, 547.

123. Ibid., 544–552.

124. Tully, "Quaker Party and Proprietary Policies," 101.

125. Isaac Norris to Robert Charles, 5 Oct. 1755, INLB, 1719–1756, HSP.

126. See, e.g., Thomas Cookson to Conrad Weiser, 12 Sept. 1741, as quoted in Paul A. W. Wallace, *Conrad Weiser, Friend of Colonist and Mohawk* (Philadelphia, 1945, repr. New York, 1971), 112; James Pemberton to Jonah Thompson, 25 Apr. 1756, Jonah Thompson MSS, transcript, FHL.

127. Charles Pettit to Joseph Reed, 2 May 1764, Joseph Reed Papers, roll 1, NYHS.

128. Roeber, *Palatines, Liberty, and Property*, 289.

129. Samuel J. Attlee to Col. James Burd, 30 June 1770, Burd-Shippen Papers, APS; James Burd to Samuel Purviance, Jr., 17 Sept. 1764, Shippen Papers, HSP.

130. Jasper Yeates to James Burd, 28 Mar. 1772, Shippen Papers, HSP.

131. Ibid.

132. Jasper Yeates to James Burd, 28 Mar. 1772, ibid.

133. Samuel Purviance, Jr., to James Burd, 10 Sept. 1764; William Attlee to James Burd, 26 Sept. 1768, Shippen Papers; James Burd to Edward Burd, 11 Sept. 1773, Balch Papers–Shippen, HSP.

134. Jasper Yeates to James Burd, 17 Sept. 1769, Shippen Papers, HSP.

135. Samuel J. Attlee to Col. James Burd, 30 June 1770, Burd-Shippen Papers, APS.

136. Jasper Yeates to James Burd, 17 Sept. 1769, Shippen Papers, HSP.

137. Ibid.

138. John Morris to John Dickinson, 3 Oct. 1770, R. R. Logan Coll., Dickinson Papers, HSP. "Ticket," of course, was ubiquitous, dating back to the late seventeenth-century innovation of vote by ballot.

139. Pocock, "Concept of a Language," 25. For the comparatively late development of this process in Massachusetts, see Ronald P. Formisano, *The Transformation of Political Culture: Massachusetts Parties, 1790s–1840s* (New York, 1983).

140. Archibald S. Foord, *His Majesty's Opposition, 1714–1830* (Oxford, 1964).

141. Livingston, *Letter to the Freemen*.

142. William Livingston to Noah Welles, 7 Dec. 1754, 19 Jan. 1756, JFP-LWC, YUL.

143. See the correspondence of Isaac Norris, Jr., with Robert Charles in INLB, 1719–1756, HSP.

144. *Letter from a Gentleman of Philadelphia to a Freeholder in the County of Northampton*.

145. *Pa. Votes*, 4:2959–3014.

146. Stout, "Religion, Communications, and the Ideological Origins of the American Revolution," 530–533.

147. Bailyn, *Origins of American Politics*, 125–135.

148. Ibid. 130–131. For a much more abrupt dismissal of the possibility of such developments in colonial America, see Wood, *Radicalism of the American Revolution*.

Conclusion

1. See Brobeck, "Changes in the Composition and Structure of Philadelphia Elite Groups," 1–181. To my knowledge there is no comparable study of New York.
2. For this tradition, see Greene, "Political Mimesis."
3. For this tradition, see Bailyn, *Origins of American Politics*.
4. Benjamin Franklin, *The Interest of Great Britain Considered* (London, 1760), in *PBF*, 9:90.
5. In comparison with the New England literature, particularly election sermons, there is very little exploration or even mention of the ruler/ruled dyad in the New York and Pennsylvania sources. The few references to it that exist are almost all from the pen of first-generation Quaker settlers, Anglican ministers, or New Englanders who had migrated to New York. See, e.g., Morris, *Reasons for His Conduct . . .* ; Wright, *Speech of John Wright. . .* ; Archibald Cummings, *The Character of a Righteous Ruler* (Philadelphia, 1736), Evans # 4009; Rev. Silas Leonard to William Smith, Jr., 23 Aug. 1754, William Smith Papers, box 1, lot 189, # 7, NYPL. Overlapping of the magisterial and legislative function was symbolized by the provincial office of assistants. See Timothy H. Breen, *The Character of the Good Ruler: Puritan Political Ideas in New England, 1630–1730* (New Haven, 1970), passim. For a different expression of the same tendency, see Brooke, *Heart of the Commonwealth,* 36, 36n; John Murrin, "Review Essay," *History and Theory* 11 (1972): 268–270.
6. Harry S. Stout, *The New England Soul: Preaching and Religious Culture in Colonial New England* (New York, 1986), 20.
7. Fischer, *Albion's Seed,* 41–42, 74, 103–104, 177–180. See also Clarke, *Parliamentary Privilege,* 195. For comparison with New York, see Kierner, "Traders and Gentlefolk," 135–138, 149, 151.
8. Elizabeth Mancke, "Public Communalism and Private Corporatism in Colonial New England" (paper presented to the Organization of American Historians, Louisville, Ky., 14 April 1991), 3.
9. Ibid., 11. It is significant that Mancke's observations are based on a comparative study that took her outside the confines of New England. See her "Two Patterns of New England Transformation: Machias, Maine and Liverpool, Nova Scotia" (Ph.D. diss., Johns Hopkins University, 1990). Also important in this context are the corporate-based similarities of the New England towns. From the perspective of someone outside the area, these are striking, despite the minute differences among them that a plethora of local studies have detailed.
10. Standard modern accounts argue variously that Massachusetts's popular political behavior and language is reflected in court/country terms (Breen, *Character of the Good Ruler;* Pencak, *War, Politics, and Revolution;* and Murrin, "Political Development," 440); in a seventeenth-century English opposition/country sequence; within a monarchical culture (Bushman, *King and People*); and in a classical republican/liberal tension (Brooke, *Heart of the Commonwealth*). Although based on Connecticut, one of the most influential statements of the communal-to-individualism theme is Richard Bushman, *From Puritan to Yankee: Character and the Social Order in Connecticut, 1690–1765* (Cambridge, Mass., 1967). On the repetitiousness of that approach and the consequent limitations of it, see Thomas H. Bender, *Community*

and Social Change in America (New Brunswick, N.J., 1978). New England was no monolith, of course, and it is certainly conceivable that there were important, if subtle, differences between Connecticut's political culture and that of Massachusetts, particularly in the light of the very different impact of the Great Awakening in the two colonies and of the intense political partisanship that revivalism inspired in the former. Rhode Island was again a different world from the two orthodox colonies. See Sydney James, *Colonial Rhode Island: A History* (New York, 1975).

11. Edmund S. Morgan, *American Slavery–American Freedom* (New York, 1975); William H. Seiler, "The Anglican Church: A Basic Institution of Local Government in Colonial Virginia," in *Town and County: Essays on the Structure of Local Government in the American Colonies,* Bruce C. Daniels, ed. (Middletown, Conn., 1978), 134–159; A. G. Roeber, "Authority, Law, and Custom: The Rituals of Court Day in Tidewater Virginia, 1720–1750," *WMQ,* 3d ser., 37 (1980): 29–52; Robert M. Weir, *"The Last of American Freemen": Studies in the Political Culture of the Colonial and Revolutionary South* (Macon, Ga., 1986), 159–211; Timothy H. Breen, *Tobacco Culture: The Mentality of the Great Tidewater Planters on the Eve of Revolution* (Princeton, 1985); Alison G. Olson, "The Virginia Merchants of London: A Study in Eighteenth-Century Interest-Group Politics," *WMQ,* 3d ser., 40 (1983): 363–388.

12. Greene, *Quest For Power.*

13. Robert M. Weir, "'The Harmony We Were Famoes For': An Interpretation of Pre-Revolutionary South Carolina Politics," *WMQ,* 3d ser., 26 (1969): 473–501; id., *"The Last of American Freemen,"* xiii.

14. Jack P. Greene, "Virtus et Libertas: Political Culture, Social Change, and the Origins of the American Revolution in Virginia, 1763–1766," in *The Southern Experience in the American Revolution,* Jeffery J. Crow and Larry E. Tise, eds. (Chapel Hill, N.C., 1978), 55–108; id., "Political Mimesis," 355–356. If nothing else, the Robinson affair illustrates again how New York and Pennsylvania were relatively free of country-inspired preoccupation with corruption. To my knowledge, every treasurer of New York and every acting trustee of the Pennsylvania loan office raided the public funds for unauthorized use. But none of these scandals, although well known and always with political dimensions, ever blew up into a major issue.

15. Charles A. Barker, *The Background of the Revolution in Maryland* (New Haven, 1940); Robert J. Brugger, *Maryland: A Middle Temperament* (Baltimore, 1988), 84–112.

16. Kramnick, "'Great National Discussion'"; James T. Kloppenberg, "The Virtues of Liberalism: Christianity, Republicanism, and Ethics in Early American Political Discourse," *JAH* 74 (1987): 9–33; Rodgers, "Republicanism." Some interesting attempts to push beyond the boundaries of established discursive traditions include Timothy H. Breen, "Narrative of Commercial Life: Consumption, Ideology, and Community on the Eve of the American Revolution," *WMQ,* 3d ser., 50 (1993): 471–501; James R. Stoner, Jr., *Common Law and Liberal Theory: Coke, Hobbes, and the Origins of American Constitutionalism* (Lawrence, Kans., 1992); Cathy Matson and Peter S. Onuf, *A Union of Interests: Political and Economic Thought in Revolutionary America* (Lawrence, Kans., 1990); id., "Republicanism and Federalism in the Constitutional Debate," in *Republican Synthesis Revisited,* Klein, Brown, and Hench, eds., 119–141; Alan Taylor, "'The Art of Hook & Snivey': Political Culture in Upstate New York during the 1790s," *JAH* 79 (1993): 1371–1396. Other, older literature, of course, continues to be of relevance. See, e.g., Edmund S. Morgan, "The Puritan Ethic and the American Revolution," *WMQ,* 3d ser., 24 (1967): 3–43;

Ralph Lerner, "Commerce and Character: The Anglo-American as a New Model Man," *WMQ*, 3d ser., 36 (1979): 3–26; and Ruth Bloch, *Visionary Republic: Millenial Themes in American Thought, 1756–1800* (New York, 1985).

17. The clearest example of such conflation occurs in Lance Banning, "Republican Interpretation," where he suggests that we should understand "articulate Americans" from "the beginning of the Revolution" until the 1990s as "liberal republicans" (p. 100). See also Bailyn, *Ideological Origins of the American Revolution*, 25 anniv. enlarged ed., vi; Mark E. Kann, *On the Man Question: Gender and Civic Virtue in America* (Philadelphia, 1991); Richard C. Sinopoli, *The Foundations of American Citizenship: Liberalism, the Constitution, and Civic Virtue* (New York, 1992). For a broader, but still limited, view of late eighteenth-/early nineteenth-century American public discourse, see Kloppenberg, "Virtues of Liberalism." For an instructive appeal for careful historical consideration of the relationship between various discursive traditions, see James Tully, review of *The Unvarnished Doctrinne: Locke, Liberalism, and the American Revolution*, by Steven M. Dworetz (Durham, N.C., 1990), *Eighteenth-Century Studies* 26 (1992): 170–175.

18. It will also facilitate the scholarly process now underway of defining the shape and varieties of American liberalism and of exploring what that term meant and did not mean in this aspiring, increasingly nationalistic, and self-consciously republican society. For a recent attempt to deal with the Civil War in the context of liberal ideologies, see J. David Greenstone, *The Lincoln Persuasion: Remaking American Liberalism* (Princeton, 1993). Of relevance in the Revolutionary period is John E. Crowley, *The Privileges of Independence: Neomercantilism and the American Revolution* (Baltimore, 1993).

19. For the results of the Revolutionary release of ethnocultural forces in Pennsylvania, see Owen S. Ireland, "The Crux of Politics: Religion and Party in Pennsylvania, 1778–1789," *WMQ*, 3d ser., 42 (1985): 453–475.

20. Thomas Hun to Abraham Hun, 4 Mar. 1786, Hun Family Papers, Albany Institute of History and Art.

21. Countryman, *People in Revolution*, 278.

22. John Hubley to George Bryan, [?] 1782, Bryan Papers; Benjamin Rush to John Dickinson, 14 Apr. 1786, R. R. Logan Coll., Dickinson Papers, HSP.

23. David Redick to William Irvine, 2 Oct. 1788, Irvine Papers, HSP.

24. Wood, *Radicalism of the American Revolution*, 256. Yet for all his emphasis on interests as the crucial development in the onset of democracy, and for all his reliance on the mid-Atlantic perspective in arguing for the prominence of interests, Wood pays little attention to the colonial matrix from which that sprang. His featuring of a traditional patriarchal society as an underpinning of classical republicanism precludes that. Ibid., 11–92, 243–270.

25. Ibid., 256–258.

26. For the party systems approach and the identification of the First Party System, see *The American Party Systems*, William N. Chambers and Walter Dean Burnham, eds. (New York, 1967), and Paul Kleppner et al., *The Evolution of American Electoral Systems* (Westport, Conn., 1981).

27. Joel H. Silbey, *The American Political Nation, 1838–1893* (Stanford, 1991), 7; id., "Beyond Realignment and Realignment Theory: American Political Eras, 1789–1989," in *The End of Realignment? Interpreting American Electoral Eras*, Byron E. Shafer, ed. (Madison, Wis., 1991), 3–23; Wood, *Radicalism of the American Revolution*, 298. Of considerable relevance, too, is Formisano, *The Transformation of Political Culture*.

28. Silbey, *American Political Nation.*

29. Formisano, *Transformation of Political Culture;* Richard Hofstadter, *The Idea of a Party System: The Rise of Legitimate Opposition in the United States, 1780–1840* (Berkeley, 1969); Michael Wallace, "Changing Concepts of Party in the United States: New York, 1815–1828," *AHR* 74 (1968–69): 453–491.

30. Wood, *Radicalism of the American Revolution,* 211.

31. William Bingham to [?], 28 Sept. 1785, Gratz Coll., "Members of Old Congress," HSP.

32. *Aurora General Advertiser,* 20 Sept. 1797.

33. Letters to the Trojan Whig Society, NYSA. For an interesting effort to deal with the texture of politics in this milieu, see Taylor, "'Art of Hook & Snivey.'" For political scientists' efforts to deal with some of the complexities of political behavior in this era, see Walter Dean Burnham, "Critical Realignment: Dead or Alive?" in *The End of Realignment,* Shafer, ed., 101–139; John F. Hoadley, *The Origins of American Political Parties, 1789–1803* (Lexington, Ky., 1986); Richard P. McCormick, *The Presidential Game: The Origins of American Presidential Politics* (New York, 1982), 16–163.

34. See, e.g., William N. Chambers, *Political Parties in a New Nation* (New York, 1963).

35. Formisano, "Deferential-Participant Politics," 473–487; Richard P. McCormick, *The Second American Party System: Party Formation in the Jacksonian Era* (Chapel Hill, N.C., 1966).

36. Donald B. Cole, *Martin Van Buren and the American Political System* (Princeton, 1984).

37. Such development was uneven, however, and can easily be overstated. See, e.g., Countryman, *People in Revolution,* 252–279, 310–311. See also Alfred F. Young, *The Democratic Republicans of New York: The Origins, 1763–1797* (Chapel Hill, N.C., 1967) and Taylor, "'Art of Hook & Snivey.'"

38. Douglas M. Arnold, "Political Ideology and the Internal Revolution in Pennsylvania, 1776–1790" (Ph.D. diss., Princeton University, 1976). For further treatment of party politics in Pennsylvania, see Robert L. Brunhouse, *The Counter-Revolution in Pennsylvania, 1776–1790* (Harrisburg, Pa., 1942); Harry M. Tinkcom, *The Republicans and Federalists in Pennsylvania, 1790–1891* (Harrisburg, Pa., 1950); Sanford W. Higginbotham, *The Keystone in the Democratic Arch: Pennsylvania Politics, 1800–1816* (Harrisburg, Pa., 1952); Roland M. Baumann, "The Democratic-Republicans of Philadelphia: The Origins, 1776–1797" (Ph.D. diss., Pennsylvania State University, 1970).

39. For a similar point of view, see John Zvesper, *Political Philosophy and Rhetoric: A Study of the Origins of American Party Politics* (Cambridge, Mass., 1977), 6–7.

40. For their success even in the nineteenth-century glory days of democracy and high voter turnout, see Robert H. Weibe, *The Opening of American Society: From the Adoption of the Constitution to the Eve of Disunion* (New York, 1984).

Index

Library of Congress Cataloging-in-Publication Data

Tully, Alan.
Forming American politics : ideals, interests, and institutions
in colonial New York and Pennsylvania / Alan Tully.
p.   cm.
Includes bibliographical references and index.
ISBN 0-8018-4831-8 (alk. paper)
1. Political culture—New York (State)—History.   2. New
York (State)—Politics and government—to 1775.   3. Political
culture—Pennsylvania—History.   4. Pennsylvania—Politics
and government—To 1775.   I. Title.
JK99.N69T85   1994
306.2'09747'10903—dc20   94-7517